BASLE AND FRANCE
IN THE
SIXTEENTH CENTURY

PETER G. BIETENHOLZ

BASLE AND FRANCE
IN THE
SIXTEENTH CENTURY

The Basle Humanists and Printers
in Their Contacts with Francophone Culture

LIBRAIRIE DROZ

UNIVERSITY OF TORONTO PRESS

First published in North America and the British Commonwealth by
University of Toronto Press, Toronto and Buffalo, 1971
ISBN 0-8020-1754-1

Publié avec l'aide du Fonds national suisse de la recherche scientifique

" Lo sol sen va " soggiunse, " e vien la sera :
Non v'arrestate, ma studiate il passo,
Mentre che l'occidente non s'annera."

Purg. 27.61-63.

E quale, annunziatrice degli albóri,
L'aura di maggio muovesi ed olezza,
Tutta impregnata dall'erba e da' fiori...

Purg. 24.145-147.

To Doris

ACKNOWLEDGMENTS

Generous financial support towards the completion of this study was granted by the Fonds national suisse de la recherche scientifique and by the Canada Council. The author also wishes to thank the Board of Governors of the University of Saskatchewan, the Principal of the Saskatoon Campus and the Head of the History Department for their kind approval of two requests for leave of absence. Monsieur Alain Dufour read the entire manuscript and made a number of very helpful suggestions. He agreed to publish the book although he must better than many others be aware of its shortcomings. Some chapters were also read by Dr. Hilda Neatby who found the time to do so at the expense of her own distinguished work in Canadian history. Mrs. Margaret MacVean typed the manuscript and Mrs. Mildred Mair proof-read it, both trying to improve the author's imperfect English as best they could.

This study could never have been completed without the courtesy and assistance of the librarians and the staff of several libraries. In particular the author is indebted to Dr. C. Vischer, Dr. M. Burckhardt, Dr. M. Steinmann of the Universitätsbibliothek, Basle, and to Madame J. Veyrin-Forrer of the Bibliothèque Nationale, all of whom helped the author either by granting him special privileges or by offering their knowledgeable advice.

A particular debt of gratitude is owed to The Harvard University Center for Italian Renaissance Studies, Villa I Tatti, Florence, and to its director, Professor M. P. Gilmore, for it is in the Villino Corbignano that this last page of the book was written on the day of the vendemmia, 1969. May the wine of I Tatti turn well.

CONTENTS

ABBREVIATIONS

ABR = Aktensammlung zur Geschichte der Basler Reformation in den Jahren 1519 bis Anfang 1534, ed. E. Dürr and P. Roth, Basle 1921-1950.

ADB = Allgemeine Deutsche Biographie, ed. Königliche Bayrische Akademie der Wissenschaften, Leipzig 1875-1912.

Allen = *Opus epistolarum Des. Erasmi Roterodami*, ed. P. S. Allen et al., Oxford 1906 ff.

Arcana = Arcana seculi decimi sexti: Huberti Langueti epistolae secretae, ed. J. P. Ludovicus, Halle 1691.

Armstrong, *Estienne* = E. Armstrong, *Robert Estienne, Royal Printer*, Cambridge 1954.

Autour de Servet et de Castellion = Autour de Michel Servet et de Sébastien Castellion, ed. B. Becker, Haarlem 1953.

Bainton, *Joris* = R. H. Bainton, *David Joris* (Archiv für Reformationsgeschichte, Ergänzungsband 6), Leipzig 1937.

Bainton, *Studies* = R. H. Bainton, *Studies on the Reformation*, London 1964.

Basilea = P. de La Ramée (Ramus), *Basilea*, ed. with a German transl. by H. Fleig, Basle 1944.

Baudrier = J. and H. Baudrier, *Bibliographie lyonnaise*, Lyons 1895-1921, with *Tables*, ed. G. Tricou, Geneva 1950, and *Complément à la table des imprimeurs*, ed. H. Joly, Lyons 1963.

Benzing = J. Benzing, *Die Buchdrucker des 16. und 17. Jahrhunderts im deutschen Sprachgebiet*, Wiesbaden 1963.

BHR = Bibliothèque d'humanisme et renaissance, Paris-Geneva 1941 ff.

Bibl. Erasmiana = Bibliotheca Erasmiana: Répertoire des œuvres d'Erasme and *Bibliographie des œuvres d'Erasme*, ed. F. Vander Haeghen, etc., Ghent 1893, 1897-1915.

Bietenholz, *Erasmus und der Basler Buchhandel in Frankreich* = P. G. Bietenholz, Erasmus und der Basler Buchhandel in Frankreich, *Scrinium Erasmianum*, Leyden, 1969, I, 293-323.

Bietenholz, *Ital. Humanismus* = P. [G.] Bietenholz, *Der italienische Humanismus und die Blütezeit des Buchdrucks in Basel*, Basle 1959.

Bietenholz, *History and Biography* = P. G. Bietenholz, *History and Biography in the Work of Erasmus of Rotterdam*, Geneva 1966.

Biographie nat. Belgique = Biographie nationale, publiée par l'Académie royale des sciences, des lettres et des beaux-arts de Belgique, Brussels 1866 ff.

BM = The British Museum, London.

BMC = British Museum General Catalogue of Printed Books, photolithographic edition to 1955, London 1965-1966.

BMC *15th c.* = *Catalogue of Books Printed in the XVth Century now in the British Museum*, London 1908 ff.

BMC ST Germany = *Short-Title Catalogue of Books Printed in German-Speaking Countries... from 1450 to 1600 now in the British Museum*, London 1962.

BN = Bibliothèque Nationale, Paris.

BNC = *Catalogue Général des livres imprimés de la Bibliothèque Nationale, Auteurs*, Paris 1897 ff.

Bohatec = J. Bohatec, *Budé und Calvin*, Graz 1950.

Bourrilly, *Langey* = V.-L. Bourrilly, *Guillaume du Bellay, seigneur de Langey, 1491-1543*, Paris 1904.

Bouvier = A. Bouvier, *Henri Bullinger, Réformateur et conseiller œcuménique, d'après sa correspondance avec les réformés et les humanistes de langue française*, Zurich 1940.

Bremme = H. J. Bremme, *Buchdrucker und Buchhändler zur Zeit der Glaubenskämpfe: Studien zur Genfer Druckergeschichte 1565-1580*, Geneva 1969.

B.Rh.B. = *Der Briefwechsel des Beatus Rhenanus*, ed. A. Horawitz and K. Hartfelder, Leipzig 1886; photo reprint: Nieuwkoop 1966.

BSHPF = *Bulletin de la Société de l'histoire du Protestantisme français*, Paris 1853 ff.

Budé, *Opera* = G. Budé, *Opera omnia*, Basle 1557; photo reprint: Farnborough 1966.

Buisson, *Castellion* = F. Buisson, *Sébastien Castellion, sa vie et son œuvre*, Paris 1892; photo reprint: Nieuwkoop 1964.

Burckhardt, *Amerbach* = T. Burckhardt-Biedermann, *Bonifacius Amerbach und die Reformation*, Basle 1894.

Burckhardt, *Herold* = A. Burckhardt, *Johannes Basilius Herold, Kaiser und Reich im protestantischen Schrifttum des Basler Buchdrucks um die Mitte des 16. Jahrhunderts*, Basle 1967.

Burckhardt, *Joris* = P. Burckhardt, David Joris und seine Gemeinde in Basel, *BZGA* 48 (1949), 5-106.

Busson = H. Busson, *Le rationalisme dans la littérature française de la Renaissance*, 2nd ed., Paris 1953.

BZGA = *Basler Zeitschrift für Geschichte und Altertumskunde*, Basle 1902 ff.

Calvini opera = *Ioannis Calvini opera quae supersunt omnia*, ed. G. Baum, E. Cunitz, and E. Reuss, Brunswick 1863 ff. *(Corpus Reformatorum)*; photo reprint: Frankfurt and New York 1964.

Cantimori, *Ital. Haeretiker* = D. Cantimori, *Italienische Haeretiker der Spätrenaissance*, transl. W. Kaegi, Basle 1949.

Chaix, *Recherches* = P. Chaix, *Recherches sur l'imprimerie à Genève de 1550 à 1564*, Geneva 1954.

Correspondance de Bèze = *Correspondance de Théodore de Bèze*, ed. H. Aubert, H. Meylan, A. Dufour et al., Geneva 1960 ff.

Correspondance de B. Vulcanius = *Correspondance de Bonaventura Vulcanius pendant son séjour à Cologne, Genève et Bâle (1573-1577)*, ed. H. de Vries de Heekelingen, The Hague 1923.

Dareste = R. Dareste, François Hotman, sa vie et sa correspondance, *Revue historique* 2 (1877), 1-59, 367-435.

Davis, *Holbein's Pictures of Death* = N. Z. Davis, Holbein's *Pictures of Death* and the Reformation at Lyons, *Studies in the Renaissance* 3 (1956), 97-130.

DBF = *Dictionnaire de Biographie française*, ed. J. Balteau, etc., Paris 1929 ff.

Delaruelle, *G. Budé* = L. Delaruelle, *Etudes sur l'humanisme français: Guillaume Budé*, Paris 1907.

Delaruelle, *Répertoire* = L. Delaruelle, *Répertoire analytique et chronologique de la correspondance de Guillaume Budé*, Toulouse and Paris 1907.

Delaruelle, *Une amitié d'humanistes* = L. Delaruelle, Une amitié d'humanistes : Etude sur les relations de Budé et d'Erasme d'après leur correspondance, *Le Musée Belge* 9 (1905), 321-351.

DGK = *Deutscher Gesamtkatalog* (early vols. : Gesamtkatalog der Preussischen Bibliotheken), ed. Preussische Staatsbibliothek, Berlin 1931-1939.

Douglas, *Sadoleto* = R. M. Douglas, *Jacopo Sadoleto, 1477-1547*, Cambridge, Mass. 1959.

Droz, *Etudiants français* = E. Droz, Les étudiants français de Bâle, *BHR* 20 (1958), 108-142.

Droz, *Hendrik van Schor* = E. Droz, Hendrik van Schor et autres traducteurs de David Joris, *Studia bibliographica in honorem Herman de la Fontaine Verwey*, ed. S. van der Woude, Amsterdam 1968, 90-118.

Droz, *Veuve Berton* : E. Droz, *La Veuve Berton et Jean Portau, 1573-1589* (L'Imprimerie à La Rochelle, 3), Geneva 1960.

Duquesne = J. Duquesne, François Bauduin et la Réforme, *Bulletin de l'Académie Delphinale*, 5th series, 9 (1914-1917), 55-108.

Erasmus, *LB* = *Des. Erasmi Roterodami opera omnia*, ed. J. Leclerc, Leyden 1703-1706.

Evennett, *Lorraine* = H. O. Evennett, *The Cardinal of Lorraine and the Council of Trent*, Cambridge 1930.

Febvre, *Cousin* = L. Febvre, Un secrétaire d'Erasme : Gilbert Cousin et la Réforme en Franche-Comté, *BSHPF* 56 (1907), 97-158.

Febvre-Martin = L. Febvre and H.-J. Martin, *L'Apparition du livre*, Paris 1958.

France prot. = E. and E. Haag, *La France protestante*, Paris 1846 ff.

France prot.[2] = *La France protestante*, 2nd ed. by H. Bordier, Paris 1877 ff.

François, *F. de Tournon* = M. François, *Le Cardinal François de Tournon*, Paris 1951.

Geisendorf = P.-F. Geisendorf, *Théodore de Bèze*, Geneva 1949.

GKW = *Gesamtkatalog der Wiegendrucke*, Leipzig 1925-1938.

Grimm, *Buchführer* = H. Grimm, Die Buchführer des deutschen Kulturbereichs und ihre Niederlassungsorte in der Zeitspanne 1490 bis um 1550, *Archiv für Geschichte des Buchwesens* 7 (1965-1966), 1153-1772.

Guggisberg = H. R. Guggisberg, *Sebastian Castellio im Urteil seiner Nachwelt vom Späthumanismus bis zur Aufklärung*, Basle 1956.

Haebler = K. Haebler, *Die deutschen Buchdrucker des 15. Jahrhunderts im Auslande*, Munich 1924.

Harrisse = H. Harrisse, *Les premiers incunables bâlois et leurs dérivés...*, 2nd ed., Paris 1902.

Hartmann = *Die Amerbachkorrespondenz*, ed. A. Hartmann and B. R. Jenny, Basle 1942 ff.

Hase, *Die Koberger* = O. von Hase, *Die Koberger*, 3rd ed., Amsterdam 1967.

HBLS = *Historisch-biographisches Lexikon der Schweiz*, Neuchâtel 1921-1934 (Simultaneously published in a French version : *Dictionnaire historique et biographique de la Suisse*.

Heitz-Bernoulli = P. Heitz and C. C. Bernoulli, *Basler Büchermarken bis zum Anfang des 17. Jahrhunderts*, Strasbourg 1895.

Herminjard = *Correspondance des Réformateurs dans les pays de langue française*, ed. A.-L. Herminjard, Geneva-Paris 1866 ff.; photo reprint: Nieuwkoop 1965.

Herzog = *Realencyklopädie für protestantische Theologie und Kirche*, founded by J. J. Herzog, 3rd ed., Leipzig 1896-1909.

Hirsch = *Biographisches Lexikon hervorragender Aerzte aller Zeiten und Völker*, ed. A. Hirsch, etc., 2nd ed., Berlin-Vienna 1929-1935.

Hotomanorum epistolae = F. et J. Hotomanorum... et clarorum virorum ad eos epistolae, Amsterdam 1700.

Imbart, *Origines* = P. Imbart de la Tour, *Les Origines de la Réforme*, Paris 1905-1935.

Jöcher = C. G. Jöcher, *Allgemeines Gelehrten-Lexicon*, Leipzig 1750-1751; photo reprint: Hildesheim 1960.

Johnson, *Basle Ornaments* = A. F. Johnson, Basle Ornaments on Paris Books, 1519-36, *The Library* 8 (1927-1928), 355-360.

Kingdon, *Geneva and the Coming* = R. M. Kingdon, *Geneva and the Coming of the Wars of Religion in France, 1555-1563*, Geneva 1956.

Kingdon, *Geneva and the Consolidation* = R. M. Kingdon, *Geneva and the Consolidation of the French Protestant Movement, 1564-1572*, Geneva and Madison 1967.

Koegler, *Wechselbeziehungen* = H. Koegler, Wechselbeziehungen zwischen dem Basler und Pariser Buchschmuck in der ersten Hälfte des XVI. Jahrhunderts, *Festschrift zur Eröffnung des Kunstmuseums*, Basle 1936, 159-230.

Lecler, *Tolérance* = J. Lecler, *Histoire de la tolérance au siècle de la Réforme*, Paris 1955.

J. Lefebvre = J. Lefebvre, Imprimeurs lyonnais et imprimeurs bâlois à la fin du XVe siècle, *Actes du Ve Congrès national de la Société française de littérature comparée*, Annales de l'Université de Lyon (Lettres), 3rd series, No. 39, Paris 1965, 23-29.

Lefranc, *Collège de France* = A. Lefranc, *Histoire du Collège de France*, Paris 1893.

Mann = M. Mann [Phillips], *Erasme et les débuts de la réforme française*, Paris 1934.

Matrikel = Die Matrikel der Universität Basel, ed. H. G. Wackernagel et al., Basle 1951 ff.

Mesnard, *Essor* = P. Mesnard, *L'Essor de la philosophie politique au XVIe siècle*, Paris 1936.

Michaud = *Biographie universelle*, ed. L.-G. Michaud, 2nd ed., Paris 1854 ff.

Naef, *Conjuration d'Amboise* = H. Naef, La Conjuration d'Amboise et Genève, *Mém. et Doc. Société d'Hist. et d'Archéol. de Genève* 32 (1922), 324-722.

NDB = Neue Deutsche Biographie, ed. Bayerische Akademie der Wissenschaften, Berlin 1953 ff.

Ong, *Ramus* = W. J. Ong, *Ramus, Method and the Decay of Dialogue*, Cambridge, Mass. 1958.

Ong, *Inventory* = W. J. Ong, *Ramus and Talon Inventory*, Cambridge, Mass., 1958.

Panzer = G. W. Panzer, *Annales typographici ab artis inventae origine ad annum 1536*, Nuremberg 1793-1803.

Piccard = G. Piccard, Papiererzeugung und Buchdruck in Basel bis zum Beginn des 16. Jahrhunderts, *Archiv für Geschichte des Buchwesens* 8 (1966-1967), 25-322.

T. Platter = T. Platter, *Lebensbeschreibung*, ed. A. Hartmann, Basle 1944.

Propagande religieuse = Aspects de la propagande religieuse, by diverse authors, preface by H. Meylan, Geneva 1957.

Rechnungsbuch = *Rechnungsbuch der Froben und Episcopius, Buchdrucker und Buchhändler zu Basel, 1557-1564*, ed. R. Wackernagel, Basle 1881.

Renaudet, *Humanisme et Renaissance* = A. Renaudet, *Humanisme et Renaissance*, Geneva 1958.

Renaudet, *Préréforme* = A. Renaudet, *Préréforme et humanisme à Paris pendant les premières guerres d'Italie* 2nd. ed., Paris 1953.

Renouard, "ms." = P. Renouard, "Bibliographie parisienne" (manuscript notes), Bibliothèque Nationale, Usuels Réserve (Bureau) J. 27 (9).

Rott = E. Rott, *Histoire de la représentation diplomatique de la France auprès des Cantons Suisses*, Berne 1900-1935.

Schneeli-Heitz = *Initialen von Hans Holbein*, ed. G. Schneeli and P. Heitz, Strasbourg 1900.

Staehelin, *Polanus* = E. Staehelin, *Amandus Polanus von Polansdorf*, Basle 1955.

Stehlin = K. Stehlin, Regesten zur Geschichte des Buchdrucks (... bis 1520, aus den Basler Archiven), *Archiv für Geschichte des deutschen Buchhandels* 11, 12, and 14 (Leipzig 1888, 1889 and 1891).

Steinmann = M. Steinmann, *Johannes Oporinus*, Basle 1966.

UBB = Universitätsbibliothek Basel.

Viénot, *Montbéliard* = J. Viénot, *Histoire de la Réforme dans le pays de Montbéliard*, Montbéliard 1900.

Vivanti = C. Vivanti, *Lotta politica e pace religiosa in Francia fra Cinque e Seicento*, Turin 1963.

Wackernagel, "Aktensammlung" = Staatsarchiv Basel-Stadt, Aq. 148 : R. Wackernagel, "Aktensammlung zur Geschichte der Basler Buchdrucker, Buchhändler und Buchbinder."

Wackernagel = R. Wackernagel, *Geschichte der Stadt Basel*, Basle 1907-1924, with a *Register der Personen- und Ortsnamen*, ed. J. K. Lindau, Basle 1954.

Waddington = C. Waddington, *Ramus (Pierre de la Ramée), sa vie, ses écrits et ses opinions*, Paris 1855.

Wernle, *Calvin und Basel* = P. Wernle, *Calvin und Basel bis zum Tode des Myconius, 1535-1552*, Basle 1909.

In the footnotes numbers printed in bold face (e.g. **No. 637**) refer to the bibliographical section of this volume.

INTRODUCTION

Students of sixteenth century Basle can resort to a general history of that town and to a considerable number of monographs devoted to its church, its university and schools, its economy, trade and book industry. On the other hand, the bibliography on France and French-speaking people in the sixteenth century is wide-ranging and many-faceted. The present study does not fall entirely into either category. To the degree in which the facts it presents are unknown it may supplement some existing studies, but none will be duplicated and none will be rendered obsolete.

The basic aim of this book is rather more general than its title may suggest or its contents can document. On the one hand the French language together with the general culture based on it may serve to set apart a vast reading public, no doubt the largest of its kind existing in the sixteenth century. These Francophones were politically divided, their loyalties being due to the French crown, the kings of Navarre and of Spain, the dukes of Savoy, the city fathers of Geneva and Berne, the authorities in Germany, England, and wherever else French-speaking refugees found shelter. As the Francophones were divided politically they also split in matters of faith: Catholics, Calvinists, a few Lutherans vied with each other and with radicals, *politiques* or their forerunners, and the odd sceptic. The social disparities between educated Francophones were such that they could rank anywhere from the grand seigniorial families of France, richly endowed with secular power and ecclesiastical preferment, to the poorest refugees and outspoken profligates living upon the pity of others. On the other hand there was Basle, a medium-sized town not very far from, but definitely outside, the boundaries of the French language. Its citizens were politically powerless, even inside the small Swiss confederacy, and noteworthy for the remarkably homogeneous character of their life and thought. Mildly opposing tendencies veering towards the Zwinglian or the Lutheran orthodoxies, or heterodoxy; tendencies favouring the humanities or the sciences with or without a touch of alchemy or occultism coexisted in the general abhorrence of violent clashes. The citizens differed in wealth and in the respect they commanded, but none possessed the power of a Calvin or the wide prestige of a Bullinger or a Bucer. The presence of Erasmus brought fame to Basle, but Erasmus died in 1536.

It is here that the focal problem of this study arises, since a proportion of the French reading public, scattered through various regions and social strata, were in contact with the city of Basle. Beneath the individual and circumstantial layers of their connections with Basle, did these Francophones respond to common motives and common expectations? Did the name of Basle stand for certain basic and specific values? Did her intellectual and spiritual inheritance exert an influence that justified the expectations of approaching Francophones? Can the 'culture' of Erasmian Basle be characterized as a corporate effort on the part of its local keepers and its foreign sympathizers, contributors, and beneficiaries? Does its influence form a recognizable factor in the composite tissue of the sixteenth century French mind?

Historians have not to my knowledge succeeded very well in defining their notion of a culture, or in devising methods for the description and analysis of cultures. In both respects anthropologists may have done better than historians, only the meshes of their nets are too wide to catch the subtle nuances exposed in the above questions. The approach historians choose most commonly when trying to analyse a cultural environment is the investigation of the thought of outstanding representatives of their times. This approach is valuable, and this study will pay tribute to it when trying to relate such men as Lefèvre d'Etaples, Postel, or Ramus to the intellectual climate of Basle. More recently, however, historians have tended to emphasize that the thought of great men may give us some indication of the depth of a culture, but hardly of its breadth, and that therefore historical research must aim for another dimension. The history of the university, for example, must for the most part do without a Thomas Aquinas or a Descartes, and yet we do want to know what successive generations within a specific cultural circle taught and learned. On the other hand, were we to assemble the rudimentary documentation preserved in the sources on the greatest possible number of lesser figures, we might find ourselves, as at cocktail parties, socializing with too many people whom we can never get to know.

Ever since Marcel Bataillon's magisterial *Erasme et l'Espagne* students of cultural history have learned to isolate the strand of a specific influence upon their chosen area and to show its changing impact over a number of years. This method is at once precise and broad enough to bring a number of major and lesser figures into a natural relationship, and it indicates what inspiration a cultural circle received from outside. It therefore tends to emphasize that cultural phenomena are best examined by way of comparison between different cultural circles. The present study is guided by the same basic idea although its approach was further determined by the fact that it had to encompass a series of reciprocal influences which often emanated from groups of people, rather than single individuals; in the case of French-speaking people even from large and heterogeneous groups.

The proposed topic could not be tackled merely by investigating the Francophone expatriate community at Basle, graced as it was from time to time by the presence of a distinguished visitor or troubled by heterodox agitation. It is clear that the Huguenot refugees and other expatriates deserve our attention, yet only thanks to the wide appeal of Basle printing do their destinies occasionally stand out from the framework of local history. A similar impression of domestic confinement pervades the records of Basle's diplomatic correspondence. On rare occasions only did the town council divert its attention from the routine handling of small scale neighbourhood problems and rise to the level of truly international contacts with the French government and others of comparable status. The real depth of Franco-Bâlois relations is not revealed unless the Francophone participation in Basle's printing industry is considered. Throughout the sixteenth century the printing industry was a major, although not a crucial, factor in Basle's economy. What is more, it acquired its own clientèle among the intellectuals of all Europe and offered the city's only contribution of truly European significance. In an age as cosmopolitan and universal-minded as the sixteenth century it reflected the fascinating entanglement of the most diverse issues.   This was the time when political agents composed rhetorical treatises and even masterpieces of historical scholarship, when distinguished lawyers devoted themselves to alchemy, when paganizing poets turned into grave ministers of the Word and exiled physicians became the chief instruments of theological turmoil, the time when even modest merchants were to some extent theologians.   Indeed, what could bring us closer face to face with the true character of the sixteenth century than the study of its printed books, since they reveal not only the thoughts of individuals but also the broad reception they were given or denied ?

It is the merit of Rudolf Wackernagel and Werner Kaegi to have recognized the full significance of printing for the history of sixteenth century Basle.   Both rightly insisted upon an approach that emphasized the wide cultural significance, rather than particular technical data, of the books printed at Basle.   Kaegi also directed to this field the researches of some of his doctoral students and so inspired a number of studies which should sooner or later engender analogous inquiries into the book production of neighbouring Strasbourg and many other printing centres. The present study is hugely indebted to the entire work of Kaegi's school, particularly so because the progress of their researches caused it to depart in one point from the school's common emphasis.

Naturally, Wackernagel and Kaegi endeavoured to establish an unmistakable identity for the circle of Basle humanists.   The common outlook of the circle was to be investigated in their own writings, and also in the works they recommended for publication and prefaced.   It was to be revealed in the relations they maintained, together with the printers or sometimes in their name and for their benefit with scholars and patrons abroad.   It cannot be doubted that there exists a nucleus of such a Bâlois cultural identity.   However, as research into Basle printing and the unedited humanist correspondence progresses, it becomes increasingly clear that after the death of Erasmus very few of the Basle humanists had a clear vision of purpose, let alone a mission, that was specifically Bâlois in its orientation.   Nor were the printers, on the whole, guided by profound considerations at the level of personal conviction when selecting their texts for publication.   In our case, the survey of copy originating from French language territory reveals conclusively the gradual lowering of aims and slackening of enterprise in Basle's printing industry. As a result one should definitely not visualize the Basle humanists as a self-conscious *sodalitas* gathered around their own set of beliefs and ideals.   If the titles indicated in the bibliographical section of this study, and the publishing programmes of the Basle presses in general, are likely to suggest a marked sense of coherence, this uniform tendency probably originated less in Basle than among the Francophone, and other foreign, co-operators and their peculiar impression of what Basle stood for.   In many cases it may even be correct to say that the less the intellectual and spiritual climate in which an associate lived resembled the Rhenish air, the loftier became the dream and the livelier the ideals of the Erasmian Basle.   Intellectuals of sixteenth century France, then, were primarily influenced by a humanistic programme that may be termed Erasmian and Bâlois.   The proliferation of this programme, however, through their books published at Basle, lay essentially in their own hands and formed an integral part of the Francophone cultural effort.

It is, however, obvious that the Basle publishers reprinted many books by French authors without the knowledge of the latter or the encouragement of other Francophones.   The interest in the authors of ancient Gaul or the French Middle Ages, for instance, derived largely from the Rhenish humanists themselves.   In general, the aims of this study require a careful distinction as to whether an author or his friends persuaded a Basle printer to publish a specific work, or whether the printer and his advisers picked a text and published it with or without the co-operation of its author.

To obtain a balanced approach to the depth and breadth of this cultural exchange, this study has been divided into two parts. The first, presented in this volume, is devoted to people known to have been engaged in Franco-Bâlois relations. It wishes to explore not only the extent of these relations but also their nature. Any attempt to list all Francophones who passed through Basle and *vice versa*, all Bâlois in France, not to speak of every evidence of correspondence without personal acquaintance, would have defeated this aim. But an attempt has been made to assemble the relevant biographical information in some detail, especially with regard to little known circles and individuals that deserve a new look from the viewpoint of this investigation. A bibliographical section completes the first part. It is chiefly intended to facilitate the researches of others in the same way that it formed the basis for the analytical sections of this study. It includes the books of Francophone lawyers, physicians, and scientists, and other material which this author has not been able to analyse, either because of his lack of competence or from the necessity for compression. It also covers a somewhat wider period than the preceding chapters, which concentrate on the sixteenth century alone.

The scope of the introductory and biographical section precluded a broad exposition of the ideas exhibited in Basle books. Moreover, the authors of the past and some living ones could not find place in the biographical section since they had no visible contacts with their publishers in Basle. The second volume, to be published at a future date, has been set aside for an analysis of books. Since it should also serve to illustrate the themes that have a peculiarly Bâlois touch to them, emphasis will have to fall on relevancy in the light of this study rather than general importance. The second part will be supplemented by a number of *pièces justificatives* which because of their length could not find place in the footnotes.

PART ONE

FRANCE AND PRINTING IN BASLE

CHAPTER ONE

BASLE PRINTERS
AND BOOK MERCHANTS IN FRANCE

As the new art of printing fanned out from Mainz, its carriers ascending the Rhine valley reached Basle, where the first books were printed in 1471, if not earlier.[1] However, for many enterprising craftsmen Basle was only the threshold to further migration undertaken in the exploitation of their new skill. Restlessness caused by the need for substantial operating capital—a need that was unusual for the time and not easily met—and a frank disregard for the conventional rules of craft and labour accompanied the new trade wherever it went. In the public records of Basle the references to printing begin significantly with a labour dispute which induced the printing workers to strike against their employers. In 1471 the city court arbitrated a settlement that would seem to have authorized any dissatisfied party to terminate employment without notice.[2]

In Lyons, by contrast, in spite of the unruly character of many printing workers, no strikes were recorded until about seventy years later,[3] and yet Lyons was the usual destination of printers who went south from Basle. Since the High Middle Ages, and long before the opening of the Saint Gotthard pass brought additional trade to the knee of the Rhine, riverbound merchandise from Flanders and the Rhineland had been unloaded in Basle, from where it continued its journey via Burgundy or Geneva towards Lyons and the Mediterranean.[4] The same route, of course, was followed in the reverse direction,[5] and from the fifteenth century the noted fairs of Lyons and Frankfurt emerged as its focal points. It seems that the printers themselves had travelled along this route even before their products were carried on it in conspicuous numbers. Guillaume Leroy, the first printer to be set up in

---

[1] Wackernagel 2.2.606f.; Piccard 195f., 315ff.

[2] Stehlin No. 4; Harrisse 5f., 65f.; Wackernagel 2.2.605; Piccard 191f.

[3] P. Chauvet, *Les ouvriers du livre en France des origines à la Révolution de 1789*, Paris 1959, 15ff.

[4] Wackernagel 2.1.483, 504. For Basle books shipped to Picardie (Calais and Boulogne), Flanders, and England between 1486 and 1497 see Stehlin No. 474, 666, 1194, 1230, 1239.

[5] The traces of Lyonnais and other Frenchmen in Basle's typography prior to the 1510s are very scarce (cf. below p. 81): Hanns Brenndler, who seems to be a German book merchant domiciled in Lyons appears in the Basle records as witness in a court case (1490), see Stehlin No. 762.

Lyons, was a native of Liège who was educated in Cologne and had touched Basle on his way south. He used a type face cut in Germany.[6] Other immigrants from Germany used founts brought from Basle or modelled upon the types used by Bernhard Richel and Johann Amerbach.[7]

Some printers passed through Lyons on their way to new abodes in Southern France. Johann Schilling, or Solidus, had operated a press in Basle before he printed in Vienne around 1478 and probably had work executed for him at Lyons.[8] The Vienne press also used type faces of Bâlois origin. It was continued by Eberhard Fromolt, a native Bâlois who had been Schilling's assistant and was like him enrolled at the University of Basle. Fromolt's fellow citizen, Heinrich Turner, worked in Toulouse from 1475 until his death in 1477, using a fount he had taken with him from Basle. His wife and son were still living in his native city, and the Basle Council wrote on their behalf to Toulouse to claim Turner's estate.[9]

Others who like Turner descended the Rhone valley in search of the capital that was needed to establish a permanent press found it difficult to achieve their project, but instead helped to promote the growing trade in books printed at Basle. Peter Mettlinger, of Augsburg, a priest turned printer, sold Amerbach's books at the Lyons fair and in Paris. Between 1487 and 1492 he tried his luck as a printer in Besançon, Dole and Dijon, always using typographical material obtained from Amerbach.[10] Paul Hürus of Constance, who spent much of his life as a printer in Spain, asked Amerbach to send him books to Geneva where he was to pick them up on his way to the Lyons spring fair of 1483. He wanted to touch the merchandise only after completing a pilgrimage which he had vowed to make when struck by the plague.[11]

Best known among the emigrating Basle printers is Michael Wenssler. Born in Strasbourg, he was one of Basle's leading typographers in the 1470s and 1480s before his business went into decline. After his escape from Basle, his debts and his family, he printed in Cluny and Mâcon before settling down in Lyons (1494-98) where he produced more of the legal works of very large size that had been his speciality in the Basle days.[12]

The route from Basle to the Rhone was chosen most frequently because of the Lyons fairs, and the secondary markets in Southern France, Italy and Spain opened up by the fairs, but the earliest known connections lead from the Rhine to Paris. However, Basle's initial role in the establishment of printing at Paris was of short duration. In 1470 three printers were recruited from the upper Rhine region to set up Paris' first press in the Sorbonne. From 1473 two of them, U. Gering of Constance and M. Friburger of Colmar, plied their trade in the rue Saint-Jacques.[13]

[6] Febvre-Martin 112, 178; H. B[audrier], *Une visite à la Bibliothèque de l'Université de Bâle par un bibliophile lyonnais*, Lyons 1880, 6f.

[7] Harrisse 51; Haebler 203; [Herta] W[escher], Aus der Frühzeit des Basler Buchdrucks, Sonntagsbeilage der *National-Zeitung*, Basle, 17, 24, and 31 January, 1943 (with special emphasis on the contacts with France, but not always reliable). Johann Trechsel may have learned his trade at Basle before settling at Lyons in 1487: J. Lefebvre 24.

[8] Harrisse 38-50; Haebler 241ff.; *Matrikel* 1.13, 27.

[9] Harrisse 30-37; Stehlin No. 1132; Haebler 233ff.

[10] Hartmann 1.5f.; Haebler 245f.

[11] Hartmann 1.9ff.

[12] Heitz-Bernoulli xiiif.; Haebler 228f.

[13] Cf. Febvre-Martin 269 and below p. 168.

There they were joined by a second pair of German printers.   One of them, Johannes Stoll, was probably indentical with a bearer of this name registered at Basle University in 1465.[14]

* * *

In the earliest stage the financial power of international merchants such as Anton Koberger of Nuremberg was needed to bring the Basle book to the key international markets including Lyons and Paris.[15]   However, after the 1480s much of the book trade between Basle and France was gradually taken over by a commercial agency which developed its operations on the basis of special affiliation with the Basle printers, and in turn was drawn by them ever more closely into the orbit of Basle's own financial and intellectual life.   In the process Basle's typography attained its unmistakable identity.   No proper estimate of the volume of the French trade can be given, but it would be hard to overrate its significance for the developing book industry in Basle, and it can safely be said that the activities of this group established for the Basle book an unmatched reputation in France that afterwards was to hold out successfully even against the competition of the Aldine firm or the Estiennes.

This commercial group was characterized by the homely touch of kinship and compatriotism.   Not surprisingly, much the same ties asserted themselves elsewhere in the fledgling typographical industry as it expanded from its original location on the middle Rhine.   Communications were slow, operations stretched far, and competition was often ruthless.   Consequently relatives were naturally drawn together, and so were men who had known and trusted each other from childhood and might later strengthen their association by means of marriage.   Only towards the middle of the sixteenth century the Frankfurt fairs, in particular, offered the needed clearing facilities and reasonable guarantees for the proper settlement of outstanding credits. As a result, Basle's participation in the international book trade ceased to feature the widely strung family business, yet it was the latter which established Basle's reputation in France.

No fewer than three natives of Bottwar in Württemberg played a role in the early history of printing in Basle.   Niklaus Kessler,[16] who was to be admitted to Basle's citizenship and to establish a very successful press, had already graduated from Basle University when another enterprising lad from Bottwar registered there in 1473-74: Johann Schabler, more commonly called Wattenschnee.[17]

Since Wattenschnee did more than anyone else to introduce the Basle book to the French market, a careful examination of the scarce testimony we have of his

---

[14] Haebler 179f.; *Matrikel* 1.28.

[15] Hase, *Die Koberger* 272ff.   In his correspondence with J. Amerbach, Koberger's Paris agent, Johannes Blumenstock alias Heydelberg, showed such a familiarity with Basle that Hase concluded he must have been living there for some time; cf. Hartmann 1, passim, and below p. 31.   Of a more transitional nature was the book trade of Gottfried Hittorp and Ludwig Hornken.   During the 1510s Hornken traded and lived both in Paris and Cologne, but had occasionally books produced for him by some Basle presses : Heitz-Bernoulli xxiv; Haebler 193; Grimm, *Buchführer* 1532f., 1637f.

[16] Heitz-Bernoulli xvi; Grimm, *Buchführer* 1355f.

[17] *Matrikel* 1.124; Wackernagel 3.202f.; Hartmann 1.127; Allen 5.567; Haebler 217ff.; Grimm, *Buchführer* 1389f.; Febvre-Martin 451ff.; Baudrier 10.449ff.

character is in order. Some references from the pen of his contemporary Albert Burer can hardly be termed impartial.[18] Accusations of his selfishness and stinginess may reveal no more than the tough and successful businessman Wattenschnee must have been. Burer's further insinuation of duplicity is rendered improbable by Wattenschnee's continued dealings with Johann Amerbach and Johann Froben. Amerbach, in particular, whose character is known from many letters, was not the man to countenance anybody who lacked fairness or tact. Unsentimental and short-spoken as Wattenschnee may well have been, he was not heartless. His only known letter, written in German and mailed from Lyons after the death of his daughter, offers condolence to his son-in-law, Bruno Amerbach:

Salutatione premissa. Dear domine Brunone [sic]. I sorrow as you sorrow, etc. However for my part you may look forward to nothing but good friendship, as if my daughter—God have mercy on her—were still alive. Let people chatter and chant: wicked tongues shall bring no discord between you and me. You will always find me willing to serve you and I hope the same of you. Do not grieve. Since a thing cannot be brought back, leave it in the hand of God. May he comfort you. Herewith, be remembered to God...[19]

Wattenschnee was enrolled in the University of Basle in 1473-74. We do not know when and why he proceeded to Lyons, but it is not unlikely that when he went he had already begun his career in the book trade. In 1483 we find him in Lyons associated with Mathis Huss.[20] Mathis was the heir and operator of the press that belonged to Martin Huss, another native of Bottwar and in all likelihood another trainee of the Basle printers who had set up business at Lyons in 1477. As early as

---

[18] *B.Rh.B.* 170ff.: In 1519 Rhenanus had temporarily withdrawn to Sélestat and was quarrelling with Wattenschnee and his associate, Johann Froben, about the balance of an interest in their enterprises, probably earned bis his services or resulting from a bequest by Lachner, as over against some cash advance and the cost of lodging for three years during which he had lived in Froben's house *zum Sessel*. Albert Burer, Rhenanus' *famulus*, presented his case in Basle. From the beginning Burer reserved the worst suspicions for Wattenschnee without, however, drawing a neat distinction between him and his associates. Reporting to Rhenanus, he wrote: " Felicem illum iudicarim, domine, et plus quam fortunatum, cui cum huiusmodi hominibus nihil esset, quod ageret. Socer Brunonis, homo ipso germine Germanus, sed iam aliquot annos in Gallia idque Lugduni cum Gallis atque adeo inter ipsos Gallos diu noctuque huc atque illuc, sursum ac deorsum agens volutansque, qui putas illum hoc temporis intervallo non aliquid astutiae Gallicanae contraxisse, immo condidicisse ? " (172f.) " Quod Bruno apud socerum rem perperam egit, doleo ... " (174). " Brunonem super hac re semel monui, posthac saepius moniturus ; videbo, num tandem ab ingratis illis canibus verius quam hominibus aliquid etiam ipsis invitis queat extundi " (179). Only after his sudden death, Bruno Amerbach was fully cleared by Burer. Indeed, the latter now alleged that an inheritance dispute between Wattenschnee and his son-in-law might have helped to bring about the sudden death of Bruno (182). Rhenanus seems to have accepted a final offer and not long afterwards was again co-operating with Froben's firm. In return for his services Burer himself now tried to obtain a study loan from Rhenanus. But all he received was the friendly advice to look for a job, preferably a tutorship. He thanked Rhenanus for this fine advice which, he said ironically, was as welcome as the requested money would have been (187-195).

[19] Hartmann 2.159f.; cf. 2.187: Bruno probably accepted Wattenschnee's invitation to visit him at Lyons. They must have reached an agreement on the inheritance, for they travelled together back to Basle and nothing further is heard about the matter.

[20] Haebler 203ff., 217.

1478 we find him using plates that two years earlier had illustrated a Basle edition.[21] In 1494 Mathis Huss lent some of his equipment [22] to Michael Wenssler, who had shortly before left Basle, leaving behind his tools along with his debts. When Wattenschnee joined his business Huss may have been exchanging books with some Basle printers for sale in the shops which most printers operated in connection with their presses. In 1483 an agent acting for Richel's estate had books which belonged to Huss and Wattenschnee judicially seized in the Basle *Kaufhaus*.[23] They were to serve as security for some outstanding debt, probably for books which Richel had sent to Lyons.

In 1488 Huss and Wattenschnee defaulted on some tax payment in Lyons, and in 1490 Wattenschnee did so again.[24] His difficulties may have been tactical rather than real; at any rate they were temporary. There can be no doubt that both the volume and the significance of Wattenschnee's transactions were growing. He may not himself have been a printer, and even publishing remained a side-line in his business, the bulk of which was the importation and distribution of Basle books.

By 1494 Wattenschnee must have been well respected in Basle, for he obtained both citizenship and membership in the Saffron Guild. But although he was constantly travelling, Lyons seems to have remained the headquarters of his business until about 1504. At that time he went to Paris,[25] and the book shop he opened in the rue Saint-Jacques may soon have surpassed in importance the one he still kept in Lyons. In Paris he adopted the Basle coat of arms (*écu de Bâle*, *scutum Basiliense*) as the ensign of his shop.[26] The same name consequently appeared above the Lyons shop, and in the imprint of books published by his firm and even in the leather binding of the books it sold.[27]

Although he continued his travelling, in the years that follow most references to Wattenschnee record his presence in Paris.[28] Since 1515 he had found in Conrad Resch a permanent associate in the management of the *Ecu* at Paris, and as a result his visits to Basle and Lyons may have become more frequent and extended. At the same time his connection with the most important Basle press, that of Amerbach and Froben, appears greatly intensified. Johann Froben,[29] who in 1502 had become Johann Amerbach's partner, may have been a distant relative of Wattenschnee, although the references which suggest such kinship are late, inconclusive, and surprisingly rare.[30] Alternatively, if this interpretation is not accepted, they

---

[21] These woodcuts first appeared in the Cologne ed. of the *Speculum humanae salvationis* (1474) and were subsequently used in the *Spiegel menschlicher Behaltnis* (Basle, B. Richel, 1476) and in Huss's *Mirouer de la Redemption* (1478). Cf. Febvre-Martin 132 ; A. Pfister, *Das deutsche Speculum humanae salvationis*, Basle 1937.

[22] Haebler 228.

[23] Stehlin No. 312, 325. The *Kaufhaus* was a warehouse where merchandise could be stored without, or prior to, the payment of import duty.

[24] Haebler 217.

[25] Baudrier 10.450.

[26] The earliest clear reference to the ensign is, to my knowledge, that of Conrad Pellican in May 1516: see below p. 181.

[27] *BSHPF* 69 (1920), 125.

[28] Hartmann 1, passim.

[29] Cf. Allen 2.250n ; Heitz-Bernoulli xx ; *NDB* ; Benzing 30.

[30] The evidence assembled by Allen (3.17 ; 5.193 ; 5.567) remains inconclusive, even though Hartmann 3.240 and *B.Rh.B.* 173ff. can be interpreted the same way. If Allen's

might still reflect the fact that Wattenschnee was closer to Froben than he ever was to Johann Amerbach. When the latter died in 1513, Froben became head of the firm while Amerbach's educated sons helped with all types of work demanding an erudition which Froben did not possess. Froben's father-in-law, Wolfgang Lachner, who had been in the book trade all his life, organized the distribution of the firm's output and had great influence in the selection of copy. The death of Lachner in 1518 caused grave financial problems for Froben's business. One may conjecture that Wattenschnee invested money in the firm at this time, although nothing suggests a permanent and regular partnership.[31] In the same year the friendly ties between the Froben firm and Wattenschnee were strengthened by the marriage of the latter's daughter Anna to Bruno Amerbach. The couple lived at Basle, but when Wattenschnee himself took up permanent residence there, probably in 1521, there was, alas, no lively family to comfort the ageing man. Both Anna and Bruno had died of the plague in 1519. In 1521 or 1522 Wattenschnee also bought Lachner's house *zum roten Ring* on the *Fischmarkt* and thus became the owner of Basle's most important book shop, which his predecessor had managed separately from his participation in Froben's publishing firm.[32]

Wattenschnee's motives for his return to Basle may have been largely personal and can only be guessed at. Trade between France and the Swiss cantons was definitely favoured by the treaty of 1521 between the two countries.[33] Moreover, by this time Paris and Lyons could hardly be called dangerous places for any one privately attracted by the Lutheran Reformation. But Wattenschnee was no doubt a clear-sighted man. ⁀The condemnation of Luther's teachings by the Sorbonne (15 April, 1521) coincided with extraordinary business opportunities in Basle where the proliferation of *Lutheriana* and other Evangelical literature was tacitly tolerated, and where book trading procedures with the neighbourly French kingdom were well established and had been favoured of late by the political alliance.

Until his death in 1540 Wattenschnee kept his book store, which during this time became the fashionable foyer of the Basle humanists,[34] and continued to export books to France. Of his religious sympathies there can be no doubt. His shop, along with that of Cratander, was denounced in 1524 by Erasmus as a place where anonymous Protestant publications of the more radical[35] kind were sold. In the following year he had Lefèvre's French *New Testament* printed in Basle.[36]

---

suggestion is correct that the *affinis mea charissima* in whose honour Froben reprinted Erasmus' *Encomium matrimonii* was Wattenschnee's daughter who then married Bruno Amerbach, the *affinis Frobenii* mentioned in Allen 5.193 might well be Benoît Vaugris, a close relative to Wattenschnee's wife (see below p. 31f.). The clear but completely isolated reference to Conrad Resch as *Frobenio affinis* by Capito, who was in a position to know the matter, (Allen 4.211) would also make sense, since Resch's mother was Wattenschnee's sister.

[31] Cf. above p. 28, n. 18 and many indications in Hartmann; the most suggestive one (1.420) mentions a common *famulus* of Wattenschnee and Lachner at Lyons (1511). He may have been Vaugris or Parmentier or Resch.

[32] On Lachner see Grimm, *Buchführer* 1366-1372 where Lachner's importance, however, seems overstated. Lachner and J. Froben too travelled occasionally to Paris or Lyons: Hartmann 1. 220, 288f., 329.

[33] See below p. 105.

[34] Cf. e.g. Hartmann 4.11.

[35] See below p. 34f.

[36] **No. 687.**

From the little we know of Wattenschnee's activities, it seems clear that they did not conform to the usual patterns of book trading operations. His beginnings were inconspicuous, and we may be assured that he never attained the discreet but substantial wealth of his associate and successor, Resch, much less the towering position of international publishing and book trading magnates, like Koberger or Buyer, who chose their printers in various centres, as well as the texts to be published, and had entire editions printed to their own specifications.[37]   Only in rare and special cases does Wattenschnee seem to have financed a whole edition; [38] yet on the other hand he was certainly not a mere agent for Amerbach and Froben, or any other printer.   His specific business was to select and buy such books in Basle, and no doubt other printing centres, as he knew he could sell in France.

Without Wattenschnee the name of Basle might have a different sound in French ears to this very day.   If Koberger gradually moved from placing orders for whole editions with Basle printers to production in his own presses, Wattenschnee rather moved in the opposite direction.   From individual cases where Basle founts and illustrations were reemployed in France he recognized their appeal to the French public.   He realized that Basle's geographical position, her low export duties and cheap paper coincided with the high-brow appeal and Evangelical tendencies of the Basle book to create promising markets in France.   With their ensign *A l'écu de Bâle* his shops projected an image that might arouse the envy of advertising experts steeped in modern psychology.

* * *

Once Wattenschnee was established in his shop and comfortable home [39] on the *Fischmarkt* in Basle, his further participation in the affairs of the *Ecus de Bâle* in Lyons and Paris becomes a matter of conjecture.   It rather looks as if the two agencies each continued under independent management, although joint operations on an *ad hoc* basis must have been frequent.   The new principals were all former collaborators of Wattenschnee and also were—or became—members of his family. In a more modest frame, kinship here played again the role one knows perhaps best from the Giunta family.[40]

Wattenschnee's wife, Claudia Vaugris, was a close relative of Jean Vaugris [41] who worked for Wattenschnee in Lyons and Paris.   In 1524 Jean Vaugris received the citizenship in Basle; his wife was Gertrud Wingarter, whose father [42] was Wattenschnee's cousin and likewise employed in his book trade.   Vaugris, a native

---

[37] Cf. Febvre-Martin 175ff.

[38] See below, Index. A Greek *New Testament* was printed for him by J. Bebel (1524 and again 1531) and by T. Platter (1538); cf. T. Platter 123. For his participation in monumental Paris eds. of the Canon Law between 1504 and, at least, 1522 cf. Febvre-Martin 451.

[39] His wife employed four servant girls: Wackernagel 3.92*.

[40] Febvre-Martin 184ff.

[41] For Vaugris see Hartmann 2.247; Grimm, *Buchführer* 1390f. Cf. also his letters in Hartmann 2 and Herminjard 1.

[42] On Andreas Wingarter (Weingartner, etc.) see below p. 35 and p. 107. Cf. Wackernagel, " Aktensammlung "; he is not mentioned in Grimm, *Buchführer*, since apparently he did little business in German language territory.

of Charly near Lyons, emerges from the sources as a modest and very busy man, constantly *en route*, with a genuine attachment to the Reformation and a staggering spelling problem. The humble tone of his letters to the young scholar Bonifacius Amerbach is as typical of him as the trouble he took to obtain a German text by Luther for a friend at Lyons who could obviously not manage Latin.[43]

After 1523 Wattenschnee's name is no longer mentioned in connection with the *Ecu* in Lyons,[44] but in the hands of Jean Vaugris and his partner, Michel Parmentier,[45] the firm continued its close co-operation with the Basle printers. After Vaugris's early death in 1527 Parmentier alone took charge. He was a native of Lyons and had first entered the business as Wattenschnee's employee, but was now to rise to a degree of prominence which Vaugris never enjoyed. Although a number of books were printed for him in Lyons and the character of the *Ecu* was now Lyonnais rather than Bâlois, Parmentier faithfully preserved the traditional relations with the Rhine town. His personal presence in Basle is not documented, but in 1526 he too acquired citizenship along with membership in the Saffron guild, and in 1542 a house belonging to him was sold by his agent.[46]

In spite of his publications Parmentier remained essentially a book seller. He expanded the business of the *Ecu* and around 1536 maintained his own agencies in Avignon and Toulouse [47] which both promoted and facilitated contacts between Basle and Southern France. This expansion was carried even further by enterprising members of the Vaugris family, which seemed forever devoted to the promotion of the Basle book as well as inspired by the successful image of the *Ecu de Bâle*. Jean's brother Benoît, described as a *Buchführer*, appears in the judicial records of Basle for having seriously wounded another man. To secure his release from prison Wattenschnee went bail for him and even Erasmus was induced to write in his favour to the City Council. Benoît paid taxes at Lyons from 1518 to 1523. In 1523 he opened a book store in Constance and continued to move books between Basle and Venice.[48] In Venice, finally, a third Vaugris brother, Vincent, better known as Valgrisio, established a highly successful book shop and publishing house, *Al segno d'Erasmo (officina Erasmiana)*. Vincent too was repeatedly in Basle. After the death of Jean, he took an active part in the liquidation of his brother's affairs.[49] His son Giorgio renewed the old family links with Basle when he studied there in 1557-58.[50]

---

[43] Hartmann 2.268f., Vaugris to Bonifacius Amerbach, Lyons 23 November 1520: " ... Ich bit euch, das, wenn ir den deutsch Luter verdenn haben lesenn, so schickenn wider vff gen Lyonn, denn es ist ein gut gesel, der sy gernn vot haben lesen..."

[44] Cf. the passages in Hartmann 2.287, 389, 420, 446, 461 (1521-1523) which refer to the Lyons *Ecu* as Wattenschnee's *officina* and to Parmentier as his *Diener* or *institor* with the reference to the *Ecu* in Herminjard 1.443 (1526) which concerns Parmentier rather than Wattenschnee.

[45] See Baudrier 10.387ff.; J. Plattard, A l'écu de Bâle, *Revue du Seizième Siècle*, 13 (1926), 282-285.

[46] Wackernagel, " Aktensammlung "; it was likely the same house on which Vaugris, his wife, and Parmentier as joint owners took out a mortgage in 1526 *(ibid.)*.

[47] Febvre-Martin 451; Baudrier 10.383-387.

[48] Wackernagel, " Aktensammlung "; Wackernagel 3.92*; Grimm, *Buchführer* 1345f.; Hartmann 3.130f., 222f.; Allen 5.346f., 587; 8.78; 9.179; Baudrier 10. 457ff.

[49] Baudrier 10.459; Davis, *Holbein's Pictures of Death* 129. Cf. below p. 35.

[50] *Matrikel* 2.110; G. Busino, Italiani all'Università di Basilea dal 1460 al 1601, *BHR* 20 (1958), 525f.

The *Ecu de Bâle* in Paris also developed an autonomous identity under the direction of Conrad Resch.[51] A native of Kirchheim on the Neckar, near Bottwar, Resch had early connections with the Basle book industry. His mother was Wattenschnee's sister and in 1508-09 he was in Paris and Lyons as the representative of Wolfgang Lachner.[52] His residence in Paris is documented from 1515. Three years later he was naturalized and in 1523 he appears as a *libraire juré en l'Université de Paris*.[53] In 1526 he sold the *Ecu* to Chrétien Wechel, an immigrant from Brabant and his former employee.[54] Resch now joined Wattenschnee in Basle where he too in 1522 had obtained citizenship and membership in the Saffron guild. He acted repeatedly as a collecting agent for Paris book merchants. References to his services in transferring sums of money into and out of France are so numerous that international financing may have ranked as prominently as the book trade proper among the sources of his considerable income. Little is known about Resch's personality. Inscrutability, however, well suited a man so frequently involved in dealings that required as much discretion and shrewdness as capital. He was probably well educated; in Basle he enjoyed a considerable reputation and he moved freely among elevated circles of the French capital. The candid Thomas Platter remembered him with warm sympathy[55] and the uncompromising Sebastian Franck was apparently his guest.[56] Having studied in France, Servetus addressed himself naturally to Resch when he arrived at Basle in search of a publisher for his *De Trinitatis erroribus*. Unable to find one in Basle, Resch sent Servetus' manuscript to Haguenau where it was published.[57] After Wattenschnee's death he brought the book store on the *Fischmarkt* to the height of its reputation. His widow[58] may have carried on the business after his own death, which was not before 1552. When she died in 1569 there was considerable wealth to be disposed of. The executor of her will, the Francophone Basle publisher Thomas Guarinus, received a gold-plated bowl which

[51] Hartmann 2.44; 6.312ff.; Grimm, *Buchführer* 1391-1393. It is not clear what financial interests Wattenschnee still had in the *Ecu* of Paris nor, indeed, what association there was between them after Resch's move to Basle, but while in Paris Resch made no doubt his own decisions. In December, 1529 Bonifacius Amerbach refers to Resch as the associate of Parmentier: Hartmann 3.471.

[52] Stehlin No. 1835; Koegler, *Wechselbeziehungen* 184f.; Hartmann 2.44; Wackernagel 3.203.

[53] P. Renouard, *Documents sur les imprimeurs... à Paris, 1450-1600*, Paris 1901, 235; C. Jourdain, *Index chronologicus chartarum pertinentium ad historiam universitatis Parisiensis*, Paris 1862, 329.

[54] E. Armstrong, The Origins of Chrétien Wechel re-examined, *BHR* 23 (1961), 341-345; Febvre-Martin 454f.

[55] T. Platter 123: " Die lieben alten herren (als herr Cuonrat Rösch sälig und Cratander) gesachen woll, das ich mich in gross gelt schuld wolt steken.... Sprach herr Cuonrad: " Thoman, hiet dich und nim war, das du dich am meisten vor den kleinen schuldneren [hietest]... ; dan die kleinen hündlin machend eim gar ein böss geschrei, das man eim den kum mer gloubet; den grossen hund kan man vill bass geschweigen'."

[56] A letter by Franck to Eberhard von Rümlang in Berne ends as follows: " 22 May in Basel. Bey Conradt Reschen Bibliopolae insigni et diviti auf dem Vischmarckt. Anno MDXXXIX." It is not impossible that Franck wanted no more than indicate his mail delivery address, but his words are very specific indeed: *Handschriftenproben des 16. Jahrhunderts nach Strassburger Originalen*, ed. J. Ficker and O. Winckelmann, Strasbourg 1906, 2.76.

[57] This information was given by Servetus during his trial: *Calvini opera* 8.767f.

[58] Katharina Klein. She was not identical with another Katharina Klein who lodged Calvin and Ramus in her house: see below p. 154.

the French ambassador, A. Morelet du Museau, had presented to her. Other legacies went to her numerous kindred in France, which included members of such well known book trade families as the Bades and de Roignys.[59]

In Paris Conrad Resch had no press of his own, but through the presses of Josse Bade, his godson Pierre Vidoue, and others he published a number of significant titles.[60] Under his successor Wechel the *Ecu de Bâle* in Paris became primarily the trade name of an independent publishing house. As such it had a long history before it. Books were still being published at its address in the earlier decades of the seventeenth century.[61] The emblem also gave rise to imitations. In 1557 a Bâlois student, Felix Platter, found in Poitiers a book shop with the Basle coat of arms as its sign, and learned that a compatriot of his, Bernhard Brand, had boarded there a decade earlier while attending the local university.[62] The *scutum Basiliense* also appears in the imprint of books published in Bourges and in Antwerp.[63] In the 1560s Nicolas Chesneau was publishing and selling anti-Calvinist and anti-Lutheran treatises under the ensign of the *Ecu de Froben* in Paris.[64]

* * *

Under the direction of Wattenschnee, Vaugris, Resch, and—although less obviously—Parmentier, both *Ecus* became increasingly involved in the religious agitation of the Reformation period. No doubt Froben's *Erasmica* and other *Basiliensia* which advocated the educational and erudite programme of Christian humanism were faithfully distributed by the *Ecus*, but a brisk business was also done with printers in Basle and other cities on the upper Rhine who owed their copy— and their prosperity—to Lutheran rather than Erasmian inspiration. Up to the 1530s Geneva's book output and its remarkable clandestine distribution in France were to some degree anticipated by the book merchants operating out of Basle and the two *Ecus*. Protected as they were in part by their Basle citizenship, their activities were not in themselves secret or illegal, but clearly shady enough to arouse the apprehensions of the defenders of the old faith and such authorities as might back them.

In October 1524, Erasmus himself in a letter to the town council of Basle associated Wattenschnee with Cratander and Bebel when denouncing the production

---

[59] Hartmann 6.313; Wackernagel, "Aktensammlung."

[60] **No. 3001ff.**

[61] E.g. J. Papire Masson, *Renati Choppini... vita*, Paris, apud Michaelem Sonnium ... via Iacobea sub scuto Basiliensi, 1606. Cf. P. Renouard, *Répertoire des Imprimeurs Parisiens*, Paris 1965, 401, 448.

[62] *Thomas und Felix Platter*, ed. H. Boos, Leipzig 1878, 283; Hartmann 6.299 shows that the *Ecu* of Poitiers existed already in 1544. For Brand see below p. 173.

[63] E.g. A. Contius, *Tractatus de pactis futurae successionis*, Bourges, apud Petrum Bouchierium, sub scuto Basiliensi, 1570. Bouchier worked until 1579: L.-C. Sylvestre, *Marques typographiques*, Paris 1867, No. 410; Hartmann 6.299. For Antwerp. e.g. B. Georgievits, *De Turcarum vita* et caeremoniis, Antwerp, apud Georgium Boutinum, sub scuto Basiliensi, 1544.

[64] E.g. G. Lindanus, *Les contrarietez... en la doctrine de Jean Calvin et de Luther et autres nouveaux evangelistes*, Paris, chez Nicolas Chesneau ... à l'enseigne de l'escu de Froben & du chesne verd, 1561; the same address with the year 1564 in: René Benoist, *Epistre à Jean Calvin* and *Septiceps Lutherus*. Cf. P. Renouard, *Répertoire, op. cit.* 80.

and distribution of anonymous pamphlets in French. These insulted himself along with the Pope, Erasmus alleged, and their author was Farel, a *homo seditiosus*. According to Erasmus' informants they were displayed in Lyons as well as in Constance.[65] Both towns, one notes, figured prominently in the commercial network of the Vaugris brothers.

In 1524-25 Resch was unable to secure the privilege when he wished to reprint in Paris Froben's edition of Erasmus' *Paraphrasis in Evangelium Lucae* and in view of the Sorbonne's firm opposition, brought about by Noël Béda,[66] he abandoned the project. This was after the battle of Pavia, when the French king was in Spanish hands, and when Berquin and Lefèvre d'Étaples, who both frequented the *Ecu de Bâle* in the rue Saint-Jacques,[67] were respectively arrested and exiled. However, it may be typical of Resch that a year later he was again close to trouble, this time for having bought the largest single lot of Béda's *Annotationes* against Lefèvre and Erasmus, printed by Josse Bade. By that time Francis I was back in his kingdom and on Erasmus' plea he tried to suppress the book.[68] Such a *volte-face* was certainly characteristic of the entire religious situation in France and may have influenced Resch's decision to shift the basis of his operations from Paris to Basle.

Jean Vaugris had already been instrumental in bringing about Wattenschnee's Basle edition of Lefèvre's *Nouveau Testament*.[69] Suffering from syphilis, he died in August 1527 at Nettancourt in Lorraine on his way to Paris. His estate included a large stock of books left in Paris on the premises *A la Licorne* which belonged to the Kerver family, for some time business partners of Wattenschnee.[70] Many of these books were purchased on credit from their publishers, so that Froben, Cratander, Valentin Curio and Wattenschnee together with Vaugris' family faced the threat of a severe loss when the entire stock was confiscated by the chapter of Saint-Benoît-le-Bétourné. Difficult negotiations followed in which A. Wingarter, Jean Vaugris' father-in-law, was joined by Vincent Vaugris. The Basle council gave them a letter to the king[71] in which it did not attempt to deny that Jean Vaugris' assortment included *Lutheriana*. Among them were, presumably, plenty of copies of Wattenschnee's recent edition of Lefèvre's *Nouveau Testament*. Finally the king authorized Vaugris' heirs to sell the books in Paris, on condition however that all suspect titles be set apart and re-exported. However, on its way back to Basle the barrel filled with the books rejected in Paris was confiscated by the abbot of Beaulieu near Bar-le-Duc. Once again the Basle Council intervened to safeguard the interests of Vaugris' heirs, this time appealing to the Duke of Lorraine.[72]

---

[65] Allen 5.567 ; cf. below p. 92f.

[66] Allen 6.66, 98.

[67] Allen 6.317 ; Herminjard 1.225, 228.

[68] Allen 6.360ff. ; P. Renouard, *Documents sur les imprimeurs, op. cit.* 6.

[69] **No. 687.** Cf. Herminjard 1.280 and below p. 92f.

[70] Febvre-Martin 453.

[71] *ABR* 2.719.

[72] *ABR* 3.133f. ; the document presents some curiosities. Jean Vaugris and Conrad Resch, his cousin, who acts as a guardian, are both not given their family names, but instead called ' Wattenschnee '. This, one remembers, was not Johann Schabler's real name but a surname. As such it could naturally be applied to Schabler's relatives and business partners. Benoît Vaugris too is once called " Hans Wattinschnes bruoder " (Hartmann 3.222). But while the application of the surname ' Wattenschnee ' to the Vaugris and to Resch might indicate how closely the public associated these men, the document seems otherwise to imply that Jean Vaugris traded for his own account

Even the *Placards* affair of 1534 could not seriously disrupt the operations of the Basle book merchants and their self-confident exploitation of the special relationship between the Swiss cantons and the crown of France continued. In 1537 and again in 1543 we find Conrad Resch in some form of partnership with Jean Frellon, his former employee, who now together with his brother ran a press and book store in Lyons and persistently favoured works of doubtful orthodoxy.[73] In the spring of 1538 the Basle council wrote an cheeky letter to the Paris police authorities on behalf of Resch and Frellon, their citizens.[74] It refused to check the merchandise of the two men, who would zealously observe the royal decree which forbade the import of books *Lutheranae farinae*. Admitting that their activities prior to the decree might have aroused some suspicion, the council nevertheless admonished the Paris officials to listen in future to the reasonable excuses of Resch and Frellon rather than to the allegations of calumniators. Rather blandly the council concluded with the usual formula, offering to requite the good services of the Paris authorities on the first occasion, and advised them to appoint their own book censors, as if censorship had been unknown in Paris.

There is a neat contrast between the elusive and cautious moves of the Basle book merchants in France and the boldly illegal operations of their counterparts in Geneva, who often risked their necks in clandestine trade, although expectation of a handsome profit may have motivated the Genevans as much as sincere religious conviction animated the Bâlois. And yet one senses the difference in attitude when Resch, again supported by the Basle Council, could take legal action to safeguard his interest in the estate of two Geneva book pedlars, Nicolas Besque and Guillaume du Boys, who owed him sixty crowns, when word reached him that they had been caught in France and executed.[75]

* * *

when he died. The place of death is wrongly stated to be Paris. In spite of this the hypothesis that there was a Johann Wattenschnee junior who died in Paris the year after Jean Vaugris' death can safely be discarded. Vaugris' name presented a problem, especially to German writers; sometimes he was called ' Walch ' (cf. Hartmann 2.247).

[73] Jean (II) Frellon appears in 1533 as Resch's *serviteur* in Basle, but in the same year he seems to have set up his own business in Lyons. 1536 he is in Paris, presumably for the winter fair, and is said to do much business with Resch. 1543 he passed through Basle and B. Amerbach referred to him as Resch's *Gemeinder*: Hartmann 4.220, 467f.; 5.381f.; cf. Baudrier 5.155ff. Febvre-Martin 455f.; Davis, *Holbein's Pictures of Death* 119ff. The Frellons—as the Wechels at Paris—continued to publish Erasmus editions through the years when not so many other French printers would: cf. Erasmus, *De pueris*, ed. J.-C. Margolin, Geneva 1966, 174ff., 210ff.

[74] Staatsarchiv Basel-Stadt, Missiven B. 2.164recto. Jean Frellon had probably purchased a letter of citizenship and chosen to pay an extra tax *(Schirmgeld)* which freed him from the obligation to take up residence and to participate in the watch. Precisely such a letter was issued in 1560 to two residents of Lyons, Jean and Guillaume Darud, who maintained business connections with Basle: *Urkundenbuch der Stadt Basel*, ed. R. Wackernagel, R. Thommen, etc., Basle 1890ff., 10.454-456. For the Darud brothers cf. *Thomas und Felix Platter, op. cit.* 324; R. Gascon in *Actes du Vᵉ Congrès national de la Société française de littérature comparée*, Annales de l'Université de Lyon (Lettres), 3rd series, No. 39, Paris 1965, 83, 85. For book censorship in Paris cf. Febvre-Martin 458ff.

[75] Staatsarchiv Basel-Stadt, Missiven B. 3.115r-v (June 1541). Cf. ibid. A. 31.507: in 1544 books belonging to Resch and Oporinus were seized in Besançon on their way from Lyons to Basle. The motive is left in the dark.

Far from exhibiting a Calvinist sense of mission, Resch's enterprises mirror the flexible and complex atmosphere of Basle, a town where conflicting views and interests coexisted, where quarrels and clashes were abhorred, where an Erasmus could feel at home while a Farel was expelled. If Resch did not manifest the same strength of Protestant conviction as Calvin's friend, Laurent de Normandie,[76] whom he resembled in the volume and success of his book trade, he must not, on the other hand, be seen as either a faithful Erasmian intellectual or simply a money-grubber. His own publications rather indicate that he was essentially a businessman whose interests were often—though not always—convergent with those of a Froben, a Lachner, a Wattenschnee in Basle. Beyond that he followed the basic approach of Basle's book industry at large when carefully matching his co-operation with opposing camps.

In 1519 when the writings of Erasmus already figured prominently in the programme of the Froben firm, although the great humanist had not yet returned to live in Basle under Froben's roof, Resch began in Paris his own publication of *Erasmica*, producing among others a reprint of the unauthorized *editio princeps* of the *Colloquies*, arranged by Beatus Rhenanus and, some years later, the *Epistola... de interdicto esu carnium*. Both, incidentally, were among Erasmus' most controversial writings. The publication of the first exasperated the author himself; the second was a principal target for the attacks of the Sorbonist Noël Béda.[77] Erasmus no doubt was more pleased with Resch's editions of his *Paraphrases*, but Resch published in the same years J. Latomus' dialogue against Erasmus, *De trium linguarum ratione*, as well as J. Lopez Zúñiga's *Annotationes... contra D. Erasmum*.

At the same time Erasmus was involved in a controversy with Edward Lee, who was finding fault with his *Novum Testamentum*. Editions of the *Novum Testamentum* were to follow each other at short intervals and occupied the attention of the author as much as the presses of Froben and Cratander.[78] Undoubtedly they were also for sale in the *Ecu de Bâle* in Paris. Thus the controversy over them was of major importance and Resch's part in it was remarkable. In the summer of 1519 he published a reply to Lee that seems indebted to the inspiration and possibly even the pen of Erasmus.[79] However, early in 1520 Resch also produced the belated first edition of Lee's *Annotationes* against Erasmus and took them personally to Basle, where Froben and Erasmus' friends rushed in to defend their injured master.[80] The controversy obviously caused much excitement, and Resch probably found buyers aplenty for the polemical statements of both sides. But whether he calculated that the controversy would have the effect of an incentive on the larger and far more important market for the *Novum Testamentum* is not so clear. He might have considered that Lee's treatise would do some damage there. When he published it none the less, Resch pursued a course of action which Erasmus himself was to follow when shortly afterwards he published the critical portions of Lee's *Annotationes* and his own replies, supressing, however, the merely polemical parts. This edition by Froben was visible proof of a peace to which the antagonists had consented under the pressure of mutual friends.[81]

---

[76] Cf. H.-L. Schlaepfer, Laurent de Normandie, *Propagande religieuse* 176-230.

[77] **No. 3003, 3023**; cf. Allen 3.464n., 496n.; 5.46n.; 6.97f., 104, 164, 242. Cf. below p. 177.

[78] Allen 4.58n.

[79] **No. 3008**; cf. Allen 4.171f.; 8.14n.

[80] **No. 3011**; Allen 4.108ff., 210f.

[81] Allen 4.259.

Resch reacted the same way to the bitter animosity between Erasmus and Béda, and also when he matched an anonymous defense of Luther [82] with anti-Lutheran treatises by Johann Eck and even John Fisher, who had shortly before antagonized many Paris humanists with his opposition to Lefèvre d'Etaples. From among the circle of these Paris humanists and academics Resch honoured Nicolas Bérauld and Gervasius Wain, Erasmus' especial friends, with two of his editions; but he also published Germain de Brie's *Antimorus*, the publication of which Erasmus sincerely regretted and which he had striven to prevent.[83]

The policies of Michel Parmentier in Lyons were hardly different from those of Conrad Resch in Paris. Year after year the *Ecu de Bâle* in Lyons faithfully distributed Froben's new *Erasmiana*.[84] Yet, when Parmentier informed Bonifacius Amerbach, then studying in Avignon, of the books he had stocked for the fall and winter of 1523, he also listed treatises against Erasmus by Hutten and Luther, together with others against Luther by Fisher, Cochlaeus, and Johannes Fabri. Amerbach promptly ordered and received some of them, together with Erasmus' *Paraphrases* on John and Luke. He also passed the first list on to Alciato in Milan.[85]

Thus the two *Ecus* in Lyons and Paris must not be represented as intelligence centres of a Protestant conspiracy. Their broad selection of controversial books does not suggest merely a compromise between conviction and camouflage. The French authorities were neither negligent nor stupid in not seriously trying to suppress the book trade between the *Ecus* and their suppliers in Basle and elsewhere. Nor should the commerce of the *Ecus* be associated too closely with the widespread admiration of intellectual and ecclesiastical circles in France for Erasmus of Rotterdam, at least not during its formative period up to 1522. It is true that Froben published many editions of Erasmus' writings, especially some large and voluminous ones,[86] but he did not by any means enjoy a monopoly, and the first editions of Erasmus' smaller treatises were not normally given to, or accepted by, Basle presses. Erasmus still lived in Louvain, and the legend of his deep and affectionate friendship with Johann Froben had not yet developed, nor did his letters during this period contribute towards its emergence.

For the investigation in which we are engaged it is, in fact, essential to realize that in the crucial years around 1520, when the *Ecus* had put up their signs with the Basle escutcheon and so identified the Basle book assortment in a way visible to the public at large, Basle was not yet in any obvious sense the 'Erasmian' Basle. When Erasmus' own letters of this period refer to the Froben press and its scholarly staff it is often with a blunt note of distrust and dissatisfaction. His treatment of Johann Froben himself was at times rough, if not rude.[87] When in 1522 he decided to go back to Basle one obvious reason was his determination to prevent henceforward what seemed to him undesirable and mismanaged publications of his own

---

[82] **No. 3014**; cf. Moore 56f. : this pamphlet played a part in the trial of L. Berquin.

[83] **No. 3005**; cf. below p. 195.

[84] Hartmann 2.258, 268f., 286, 399f., 426f., 462 ; 3.208, 235, etc.

[85] Hartmann 2.440-450.

[86] *Novum Testamentum* 1516, 1518 (2 eds.), 1519, 1521 (2 eds.), 1522 (2 eds.) ; *Adagia* 1517, 1517-18, 1518, 1520; *St. Cyprian* 1520, 1521 : *Bibl. Erasmiana*.

[87] Cf. Allen 3.53, 160ff., 421ff. Note the contemptuous instruction on top of his last preserved letter to Johann Froben : " Lege hanc epistolam cum Beato aut aliquo qui sciat Latine. "

works by the press of Froben.[88]   Even after settling down in Basle he endeavoured
to preserve the good will of some great Italian and French presses, occasionally
in ways that were directly detrimental to the man in whose house he lived.[89]   The
crisis in finance and policy which overcame Froben's business following Lachner's
death in 1518 coincided with Erasmus' momentary intention to return to Basle,
an intention conceivably caused by concern.[90]   He deplored the *regnum muliebre*
of Lachner's daughter and heiress, and brutally complained about the stupidity of
Froben, her husband.[91]   Yet 1519 was the year in which Wattenschnee's involvement in Froben's affairs is clearly visible in our scarce sources.[92]   In 1519-20 finally,
Conrad Resch in Paris published Latomus' and Lee's attacks upon Erasmus.   Thus
the co-operation between the Froben press and the *Ecu* merchants can hardly be
assumed to have taken shape under the auspices of Erasmus.

The record of such difficulties does not point to a full-fledged crisis in the relations
of Erasmus with his Basle printers, and it should not distract attention from the
warm recommendations by Erasmus of Froben's press in earlier years [93] as well as
later ones.   It should, however, indicate that the image of the Basle book as propagated by the *Ecus*, and Erasmus' fame in France, are nevertheless separate issues.
If we glance at the evidence of the growing reputation of Froben's products in Paris,
it seems to show that Erasmus' recommendations merely reinforced the attention
aroused by the typographical presentation of the Basle books and by their promotion through the merchants associated with the *Ecu*.

On his first visit to Germany, in August of 1514, Erasmus had come to stay
with Froben.   In October a messenger (perhaps a book merchant) who came from
Basle and was returning there called on Lefèvre d'Etaples to greet him in the name
of Erasmus. Lefèvre gave him a short note for Erasmus, expressing his satisfaction in
knowing the friend *in Germania inter typographos*.[94]   To Lefèvre Germany was thus
still generically the land of printing; he seems not to have been impressed by the
names of Basle and Froben.   Soon afterwards, however, Froben must have become
to the Parisian Evangelicals a representative *par excellence* of German typography.

---

[88] Cf. Allen 3.464ff. ; 4.498ff., 558, 564f., 604 and Allen's notes : 3.157, 445 ; 4.498.
Erasmus' anger about the publication of the *Farrago nova epistolarum* did not cool down
for quite a while : Allen 5.55, 64.   Once arrived in Basle, he soon made efforts to secure
an invitation to Paris : Allen 5.136 ff., 217.

[89] Already in April 1518 he wrote to Josse Bade : " Utinam, mi Badi, fuisset tibi
copia formularum Graecanicarum. Nunc capitis periculo Basileam adire cogor : neque
enim edi potest Novum Testamentum nisi coram adsim." At the same time, however,
he asked for Bade's help in preventing a reprint of Froben's *Jerome* by the press of
Jean Petit (Allen 3.286).   This latter threat was one of the many worries which beset
Froben at the time (Allen 3.256f., 422).   On Erasmus' negotiations with Francesco
Asolano about an enlarged edition of the *Adagia* (1523-25) see Allen 5.252f. (" ... Nec
cum Frobenio nec cum ullo typographorum foedus habeo... ") and Allen 6.133f.   On
Chevallon's ed. of *Jerome*, with Erasmus' co-operation see Allen's n., 5.492f. and Allen
10.83, 123f., 144ff.   A comparison between the Aldus and Froben eds. of the Greek
Galenus, somewhat unfavourable to the Basle printer, is found in Erasmus' preface for
another publication undertaken by Froben : Allen 6.249.

[90] Cf. Allen 3.240, 250n., 256f.

[91] Allen 3.423 : " ... Frobenio nihil fingi potest stupidius."

[92] Cf. above p. 28, n. 18.

[93] Cf. for recommendations to Leo X and Budé : Allen 2.88, 228f. ; for Martin Dorp's
high opinion : Allen 3.350.

[94] Allen 2.38.

Nine books from the library of Antoine Papillon have been traced in the *Bibliothèque de l'Université de Paris*; four of them were printed in Basle between 1517 and 1523 when the *Ecu de Bâle* was flourishing; three were *Frobeniana*.[95] Bérauld introduced himself to Erasmus by expressing his eager interest in the master's newest publications but also in the typographical excellence of Froben's books.[96] Another admirer of Erasmus in Paris, Germain de Brie, showed himself dissatisfied with the faulty manner in which Josse Bade had produced a translation of his, and wished that Froben might reprint it at once, offering to purchase fifty copies and to pay for them generously.[97]

Beyond the circle of Erasmus' friends admiration for the Basle book must have been widespread, even before Erasmus returned to live permanently in the city. In February 1519 Froben wrote to Luther, proudly reporting that six hundred copies of a work by him had been sent to France alone. Froben added that even Sorbonists read and approved it, and the statement was far from incredible.[98] If the Paris book merchants and their customers thus turned sympathetic eyes on the contents of the Basle book, the attention they gave to its typographical presentation was more than sympathetic. The relations between Basle and Paris in the field of book decoration have been termed quite exceptional. Already before 1512 each printing centre was imitating some of the other's woodcut material.[99]

It has been noted that a remarkable number of books turned out by such highly reputable Paris printers as R. Estienne, G. Tory, and S. de Colines are rather reminiscent of the products of Froben and his rivals in Basle, especially in the use of title borders, decorated initials and illustrations. In 1519-20 a number of books which may conveniently be grouped together were published in Paris with or without mentioning the printer's name. They all display one of three title borders, all of which were designed by Urs Graf. Some of the books state explicitly that they were comissioned by Conrad Resch, the master of the *Ecu de Bâle*. In the other cases this may be inferred, for the plates appear to have been Resch's property and could not have been used without his consent.[100]

Next to Graf, or even before him, the distinctive look of the Basle book was due to the title borders, initials and illustrations of Hans Holbein the Younger. In 1521 a curious printer's device, designed by Holbein and cut at Basle, was first inserted in a Paris book. It reappeared repeatedly until 1526, always in books published by some Paris printer in conjunction with Conrad Resch.[101] Soon Holbein worked for other Paris customers too, but even more significantly for their rivals at Lyons, and in 1524 he may have visited the Rhone city.[102] A series of his designs illustrating the stories of the Old Testament was cut into wood by the Basle engraver

---

[95] N. Weiss in *BSHPF* 71 (1922), 61f.; Allen 6.150. The four Basle eds.: M. Riccio, *De regibus Francorum*, Froben 1517 (**No. 892**); L. Valla, *De libero arbitrio*, Cratander 1518; Suetonius, ed. Erasmus, Froben 1518, and *Auctores historiae ecclesiasticae*, Froben 1523. Erasmus wrote: " Periit Papilio, non sine gravi suspitione veneni ": Allen 6.362.

[96] Allen 3.505.

[97] Allen 6.378; cf. Hartmann 3.536 for a similar wish expressed by Sadoleto.

[98] Moore 46.

[99] Koegler, *Wechselbeziehungen* 159ff.

[100] Johnson, *Basle Ornaments*, passim.

[101] Koegler, *Wechselbeziehungen* 188ff.

[102] Davis, *Holbein's Pictures of Death* 107 and passim for what follows. P. Ganz, *Handzeichnungen H. Holbeins des Jüngeren*, Basle 1943, 16.

40

Hans Lützelburger and first appeared in 1538-45 in two Lyons productions printed for the Trechsel brothers, sons of Johann Trechsel, who had perhaps learned his trade at Basle. Holbein's name was expressly mentioned in a laudatory epigram by Nicolas Bourbon which was added to the second production, a Latin Bible. It was also included in Bourbon's new edition of *Nugae* (Gryphius, Lyons 1538) and together with this collection was issued two years later from Basle.[103]

The Trechsel brothers also acquired Holbein's famous Dance of Death woodcuts, which were engraved by the same Lützelburger, and published them, also in 1538, suitably captioned with French rhymes commissioned for the purpose. Holbein's name was not mentioned in this first edition of *Les simulachres*, which avoided any conspicuous departure from Catholic orthodoxy. Four years later the cuts reappeared in a frankly Protestant context, now published by Resch's sometime associate Jean Frellon and his brother, who in 1543 also re-employed the Old Testament woodcuts. What happened to the woodcut stocks of either series after Lützelburger died in Basle in 1526 remains most uncertain. One does, however, notice that Wattenschnee was listed in the estate papers as one of Lützelburger's creditors, and that Vincent Vaugris came to Basle in 1526 to liquidate the affairs of his brother Jean who had died in that same year. In 1545 Vincent published an Italian edition in Venice with the Dance of Death cuts, much to the displeasure of Jean Frellon, who complained about Vaugris in his own Italian *Simolachri* of 1549.[104]

In the same year of 1526 Holbein himself moved to England. It was thus only during the later, English, phase of his life that his masterly cycles of book illustrations were launched from Lyons. But in Basle too his alphabets of decorated initials and his title frames lived on for decades to come, and undoubtedly contributed to the popularity of the Basle book in France. *Vice versa*, the Basle typography from an early date was profoundly influenced by French taste and techniques in book decoration. As a result the Basle book acquired an appearance quite different from prevailing formats in Germany, and no doubt more pleasing to the French public.[105] From the beginning of the 1520s, if not earlier, a metal engraver from Lorraine, Jacques Lefevre (Faber), was working at Basle and occasionally travelling to Lyons. Lefevre had learned his trade at Paris. In Basle metal engraving was a novelty; Froben especially proved eager to adopt the new fashion in preference to the traditional woodcut. The artists whose designs were engraved by Lefevre included Graf and Holbein.[106] From the end of the 1520s decorations appeared in Basle books which have been recognized as the original work of a Paris artist.[107]

* *
*

The benefits accruing to the Basle presses from their special relationship with the *Ecus* in Paris and Lyons were not limited to an advantageous position on the French markets. The *Ecus* also played an outstanding role in establishing and maintaining contacts between the Basle printers and scholars on the one hand and

---

[103] A.B. Chamberlain, *Hans Holbein the Younger*, London 1913, I.211 ; **No. 183.**

[104] Davis, *Holbein's Pictures of Death* 119ff., 129 and passim.

[105] Koegler, *Wechselbeziehungen* 160, 223.

[106] *Ibid.* 173ff. ; cf. below p. 81, n. 49.

[107] *Ibid.* 204ff.

French authors and patrons on the other. All travelling book merchants in the sixteenth century doubled as letter carriers. The larger operators were often willing to accept money in one town and to make payments in another. Many also helped their printer customers by searching for manuscripts, and they kept a watch abroad for interesting copy to reprint. The merchants associated with the *Ecus* served the public in all these capacities,[108] and the frequency and regularity of their connections with the upper Rhine made their services highly reliable.

Michel Parmentier in Lyons forwarded letters not only between Bonifacius Amerbach and Alciato and his other friends in Avignon, but also between Amerbach, Erasmus and Sadoleto and his circle in Carpentras.[109] Rabelais' letter to Erasmus and possibly other contacts with Basle were probably negotiated through Parmentier, since four years later when Rabelais was in Rome with the Cardinal Du Bellay he availed himself of Parmentier's services to forward letters and books to Geoffroi d'Estissac once they had reached Lyons in the diplomatic coffer.[110] The first edition of the *Tiers Livre* was printed by Chrétien Wechel at the *Ecu de Bâle* in Paris and by a partner.[111] In the same way Lazare de Baïf when he was French ambassador to the *Serenissima* used the Lyons *Ecu* as a clearing house for the letters and books he sent to Sadoleto in Carpentras. Baïf, Sadoleto and many of their friends had close relations with Basle where some of their writings were published.[112]

The less smoothly contacts between the Bâlois and their French correspondents ran, the more outspoken the sources. In 1529 Erasmus and Bonifacius Amerbach accused Wattenschnee and Resch of withholding the only copy of Budé's recent *Commentarii linguae Graecae* actually available in Basle and, what was more, of ensuring that no other copies would arrive from Paris. Bonifacius soon learned that the work was being reprinted for Resch in Bebel's workshop as a result of an agreement between Resch and Bade, the original publisher. Failing to get Bebel's copy, Bonifacius obtained by stealth the single sheets as they came from the press.[113] Fortunately Erasmus' suspicion that Budé's *Comentarii* might contain unfriendly references to him proved unfounded. Budé angrily contradicted Bonifacius' contention of his complicity.[114]

Far more serious was the dispute about Alciato's treatise *De verborum significatione*. From Avignon the author promised it to Bonifacius Amerbach for publication by Cratander's press. Accordingly he sent it to Parmentier in Lyons, who was to forward it to Basle.[115] Of what happened next Alciato later gave a number of somewhat contradictory accounts which in turn accused Parmentier and pleaded

---

[108] Numerous cases in point may be found in the subsequent chapters to which the following may be added : in 1518 Resch sent a *compendium* of Hebrew grammar arranged by Agostino Giustiniani to Basle. However, Froben was not interested and the work appeared as the first Hebrew book printed in Paris (Allen 3.278n.). When Calvin was a poor refugee in Strasbourg, Du Tillet asked him to reconsider his defection from the Catholic church and offered to send money via Resch (*Calvini opera* 10.2.245).

[109] Cf. e.g. Hartmann 3.377.

[110] J. Plattard, A l'écu de Bâle, *Revue du Seizième Siècle* 13 (1926), 282-285 ; Rabelais' letters from Rome can be found in many eds. of his works.

[111] Cf. P.-P. Plan, *Bibliographie rabelaisienne*, Paris 1904, 123ff.

[112] J. Plattard as referred to above in n. 110 ; cf. below pp. 197ff., 228ff.

[113] Hartmann 3.449-456.

[114] Hartmann 4.11f.

[115] Hartmann 3.377ff.

his own ignorance and even Parmentier's innocence.[116]   Parmentier himself finally admitted having given the manuscript—or a copy of it—to Gryphius in Lyons, by whose press it was published in the spring of 1530.   Cratander learned the truth by chance, while undergoing a cujac potion cure which entailed a thirty day confinement to his chamber.   He wrote off a furious note to Bonifacius Amerbach, bitterly denouncing the *Gallorum versutia*.   Together with Parmentier he accused Resch of having financed Gryphius' edition.   For good measure he also listed Heinrich Bebel among the foul Gauls though the latter, a native of Strasbourg, had little to qualify him for such a distinction except perhaps his nickname *Welsch-hans*, and occasional business relations with the Wattenschnee group.[117]   Bonifacius severed all relations with Parmentier and for more than a year used other channels to correspond with his friends in Avignon.   However, because he either did not find the alternative mail route satisfactory, or he finally accepted Parmentier's excuses,[118] which were in fact rather less far-fetched than those of Alciato, Amerbach finally renewed his frequent contacts with the *Ecu de Bâle* in Lyons and was never again given reason for complaint.   The Basle library still preserves a copy of Gryphius' ill-gotten first edition with Parmentier's autograph dedication to Bonifacius Amerbach.

The two incidents must be considered in the light of the hardly restricted practice of reprinting.   The events themselves are far less astonishing than the reactions of Amerbach and his friends.   While Erasmus was living in Basle he was intimately associated with the Frobens, yet felt free to disregard the interests of his friends in ways [119] similar and perhaps worse than those practised by Resch, Parmentier and Alciato.   The noticeable outrage of Amerbach and Cratander, at least, gives some idea of how close and trusting the co-operation of the *Ecu* merchants with the Froben and other Basle presses generally was.   A measure of loyalty was expected and generally obtained in their relations, which entitles one to say that the latter were as unusual as were, thanks to them, the fortunes of the Basle book in France.

---

[116] Hartmann 3.412, 421f., 439f., 441f., 475, 484
[117] Hartmann 3.468f.
[118] Hartmann 3.489f.
[119] Cf. above p. 39, n. 89.

CHAPTER TWO

THE VOLUME AND DECLINE OF
BASLE'S BOOK TRADE WITH FRANCE

The productions of the Basle presses were held in high esteem throughout the Francophone territories and thus had an assured market there. How large was this market? Indirectly, the frequent evidence of collaboration between French authors and Basle publishers, and the respectable number of entries in the bibliographical section of this study give an idea of its size. But one would obviously like to know what role the French markets played in comparison with the sales of Basle books elsewhere. One would also like to know how the number of books listed in the bibliography compared with the total output of the Basle presses, if and how the ratio changed over the decades, and how the total book production of Basle compared with that of other publishing centres. Due to the scarcity of statistical data at present available the answers, alas, must remain somewhat hypothetical. Since 1564 a collective catalogue of books for sale, or more than one, appeared for each of the semi-annual Frankfurt fairs, and since 1594 similar catalogues exist for the Leipzig fairs. A statistical analysis of these catalogues was prepared by Gustav Schwetschke in 1850.[1] His figures certainly do not represent the total number of Basle books marketed at Frankfurt, nor were all Basle books sent to the fairs. However, the same is obviously true of other publishing centres. Considering the high cost of transportation, it seems logical to expect that the completeness of a book assortment marketed at Frankfurt varied in proportion to the distance separating Frankfurt from the respective places of publication. However, other factors too must be considered, in particular perhaps the language factor. In clear contrast to the proportional decline of Latin books on the French market [2] and the adjustments thus necessitated for French publishers, the Frankfurt fairs continued to be dominated by the Latin book, while the relatively restricted trade in vernacular books left little room for modern languages other than German. On the whole these marketing conditions should have benefited Basle in comparison to Lyons or Venice, for instance, but a closer look is necessary. A number of relevant figures, copied from Schwetschke, are presented in the table on p. 46-47. How do the figures of this table compare with the total book production of a publishing centre in a given year? An example for comparison is made available by H. J. Bremme's graph of the total production of Geneva over the years 1550-1600.[3]

---

[1] *Codex nundinarius..., Mess-Jahrbücher des deutschen Buchhandels von... 1564 bis... 1765*, ed. G. Schwetschke, Halle 1850.

[2] See below p. 219.

[3] Bremme 92.

The trends shown in this graph are, in a general way, supported by the Frankfurt figures; for instance both indicate a crisis in the years 1571-72 which according to the Frankfurt figures extended to the Lyons book industry as well as to that of Geneva, and a near-record production at Geneva in 1592-94. However, the ratio between the total production of Geneva and the assortment listed at Frankfurt varies considerably. The Frankfurt figures never reach more than 55% and never less than 25% of the total production, on the average about one third. No comparable figures are available for the total production of Basle, but working from the indications in the *Druckerkatalog* a vague guess is possible. One might have expected the proportion of Basle books available at Frankfurt to be much higher than that of Genevan books. Surprisingly no more than one to two thirds of all new Basle editions seem to have been listed in the fair catalogues. Unlike the Genevan book industry, which in spite of strong annual fluctuations showed on the average a small advance in its production between 1550 and 1600, the output of Basle dropped considerably over the same period. The high production level reached during the later years of Erasmus' life was initially retained and probably further improved during the 1540s and 1550s, thanks mostly to Oporinus. His yearly production must have reached 50 to 60 new editions in the mid 1550s, and thus surpassed the number of new books published in the whole city of Geneva.[4] The total output of new editions by all Basle presses must have continued at a level somewhat better than 100 a year, at least until the early 1560s. In later 1560s when the Basle book had definitely passed its prime, it still supplied an average of 7% of all titles offered in the Frankfurt fair catalogues. While the total number of books listed in the catalogues rose persistently and had trebled before it slumped at the time of the Thirty Years' War, the Basle figure dropped to 6% during the 1570s and to 4% during the 1580s; thereafter it was never more than 2%.[5] These figures do not, of course, reflect the quality and size of the books, nor the number of copies in each impression. The more prestigious Basle presses specialized in Collected Works and other large folio editions, and on the whole seem to have been able to sell them in respectable quantities despite the high price of each copy. Between 1561 and 1564 the firm of Froben and Episcopius, for example, published on the average rather less than ten editions annually, but among them were a Galen in four giant folio volumes, a Bartolus in five folio volumes, C. S. Curione's *Thesaurus linguae Latinae* in three, and Plato's *Opera* in folio. What is more, the partners managed to make a reasonable profit from such expensive products. In the case of this firm it is possible to supplement the statistical information gained from the fair catalogues with the financial statements contained on odd pages of their accounts book which have been preserved. In analysing the accounts of a single firm one may not hope to find a basis for reliable conclusions of a general nature, yet in the absence of other information this one example may be worth looking at.

---

[4] In his 25 years of publishing Oporinus produced close to 1000 different editions (Steinmann 60); Geneva produced 636 known editions between 1565 and 1580 (Bremme 91). Much depends, of course, on the number of copies in each impression. Oporinus printed normally with 6 presses, the Froben and Episcopius firm perhaps with the same number. Robert Estienne, when arriving in Geneva in 1559, printed with 4-5 presses. By 1563 the total number of presses for Geneva seems to have been 30-40, i.e. at least as many as the Bâlois may have used at the same time. It seems to follow that the Genevans printed less editions than the Bâlois, but on the average more copies of each: cf. *Rechnungsbuch* 97; Armstrong, *Estienne* 46f.; Bremme 92f.

[5] Bietenholz, *Ital. Humanismus*, 16n.

Year	Total	Languages				Places of Origin								
						Basle			Frankfurt a. M.			Strasbourg		
		Latin	Germ.	French	Italian	Total	Latin	French	Total	Latin	French	Total	Latin	French
1565	550	378	171	—	1	24	20	—	41	8	—	19	16	—
1566	224	163	61	—	—	19	19	—	21	11	—	9	7	—
1567	294	217	77	—	—	22	19	—	20	12	—	16	13	—
1568	494	331	156	5	2	44	40	—	34	20	—	27	19	—
1569	477	331	134	2	10	36	35	—	35	15	—	9	5	—
1570	475	290	163	5	15	36	32	—	33	17	—	24	14	—
1571	533	343	170	10[?]	10	32	28	—	39	18	—	15	7	—
1572	547	364	158	16	7	37	30	—	37	16	—	14	6	—
1573	465	300	134	10	21	28	24	—	36	20	—	15	7	—
1574	471	321	123	14	11	26	15	1	40	28	—	20	12	—
1577	553	368	139	35	11	38	32	—	56	41	—	18	7	1
1580	493	355	126	9	3	32	30	—	65	41	—	23	13	—
1581	415	265	138	10	2	18	14	—	46	23	—	14	11	—
1585	722	497	205	8	12	16	14	—	64	43	—	19	14	—
1586	665	459	188	10	8	23	21	—	63	41	—	35	23	—
1590	875	545	297	15	14	41	27	—	83	60	2	35	23	1
1591	930	605	280	22	21	29	18	2	107	82	—	38	30	—
1592	452	259	166	11	15	7	5	—	44	28	—	13	9	—
1593	898	575	305	14	2	26	20	—	117	62	—	45	38	—
1594	659	427	215	15	2	6	4	—	80	57	2	29	20	—
1599	827	519	246	39	19	22	11	1	97	68	—	28	18	—
1600	1059	700	292	25	40	18	11	2	148	118	—	30	26	—
1605	1374	801	481	29	48	24	11	—	161	111	1	38	22	—
1610	1511	961	464	54	26	24	11	—	203	151	1	41	27	—
1615	1541	892	547	66	23	33	23	—	156	106	1	27	17	1
1620	1377	908	413	28	24	34	32	—	186	125	—	32	20	1
1630	1346	832	461	30	17	21	16	—	106	72	—	73	47	—
1640	730	416	276	33	5	20	9	—	62	29	—	15	9	—
1650	948	613	305	25	4	5	4	—	128	77	—	49	43	—

| | Places of Origin | | | | | | | | | | | | | | |
| Antwerp | | Geneva | | | Lyons | | | Paris | | | Venice | | | Sine loco | |
Latin	French	Total	Latin	French	Total	Latin	French	Total	Latin	French	Total	Latin	French	Total	French
41	—	6	6	—	10	10	—	37	37	—	78	78	—	6	—
20	—	8	6	—	15	15	—	10	10	—	24	24	—	12	—
15	—	5	5	—	11	11	—	17	17	—	51	51	—	12	—
51	4	7	7	—	9	9	—	11	10	1	45	43	—	21	—
31	2	10	9	1	10	10	—	5	5	—	88	80	—	15	—
25	—	8	8	—	22	21	1	24	22	2	40	29	—	17	1
26	1	5	5	—	7	6	1	23	12	10	69	64	—	25	—
33	3	5	5	—	9	7	2	25	17	8	76	68	—	24	—
24	1	17	17	—	16	15	1	19	12	7	64	49	—	32	1
35	—	8	8	—	20	19	1	24	21	3	43	35	—	46	6
30	2	21	15	6	30	21	8	27	24	3	18	12	—	30	6
29	5	18	17	1	3	3	—	29	28	1	23	22	—	13	—
23	1	19	15	4	17	16	1	12	12	—	8	7	—	14	2
33	3	22	21	1	29	29	—	32	30	2	42	38	—	28	—
31	2	18	15	3	33	33	—	14	13	1	34	31	—	29	—
28	2	15	15	—	15	14	—	2	2	—	31	23	—	65	3
33	3	25	18	6	39	33	4	1	1	—	36	23	—	70	1
14	2	17	15	2	23	19	2	2	1	1	26	18	—	32	2
37	1	22	17	5	51	46	5	2	2	—	36	36	—	14	—
25	6	27	23	4	11	11	0	2	1	1	23	23	—	8	—
36	1	19	8	11	23	22	1	27	20	7	29	22	—	9	—
42	5	25	19	6	19	18	1	27	17	10	92	63	—	5	—
51	15	28	26	2	11	10	1	29	26	2	82	46	—	2	—
49	1	48	28	19	19	10	8	47	30	17	46	33	—	1	—
67	4	28	16	12	30	23	7	47	25	22	48	31	—	—	—
67	1	20	19	1	24	19	5	53	39	13	70	49	—	—	—
91	3	13	9	4	17	17	—	43	28	15	28	14	—	2	—
15	—	41	20	18	—	—	—	1	—	1	—	—	—	—	—
60	—	15	13	2	1	—	1	1	—	1	—	—	—	5	—

		fl.	s.	d.
Half year ending spring 1562	Receipts	3884	18	7
	Expenses	3407	21	2
	Profit	476	22	5
Half year ending autumn 1562	Receipts	3759	6	—
	Expenses	3387	19	11
	Profit	371	11	1
Half year ending spring 1563	Receipts	3318	—	2
	Expenses	2889	—	5
	Profit	428	24	9 [6]

Within twelve months the firm's revenue had thus declined by nearly 15%. However, fluctuations of that order were certainly not unusual in the book trade, and personal circumstances undoubtedly contributed to mark this particular decline as part of a general trend. Hieronymus Froben and Nicolaus Episcopius, the firm's senior partners, died in March 1563 and 1564 respectively. At this point the original company dissolved. Nicolaus Episcopius the younger survived his father by only twenty months.[7] But another factor may also have contributed to the decline in sales from 1562 to 1563. Did this decline reflect the outbreak of the second war of religion in France? In fact, did the entire period of civil strife and disorder in France over the next three decades contribute significantly to the gradual decrease of Basle publishing, especially in the Latin language? At first glance the evidence offered by the Froben and Episcopius accounts book seems quite convincing.

Accounts at Frankfurt were generally settled at the fair after the one at which the books had changed hands. In the spring of 1562 a number of book merchants from French-speaking territories contributed the following to the total receipts of fl. 3884 18 s. 7d. from the sales at the preceding fair, plus some new cash sales:

		fl.	s.	d.
Geneva	Nicolas Barbier	22	10	—
	Thomas Courteau	38	—	—
	idem	15	—	—
	Jacques Guichet	90	—	—
	Richard Neudin	13	—	—
Lyons	Clément Baudin	24	—	—
Paris	Jacques Dupuys	185	—	—
	Jean Foucher	65	—	—
	idem	20	—	—
	Sébastien Nivelle	100	1	—
	André Wechel	151	3	—
Dole	Pierre Morot (Moret)	28	12	6
	Total	752	1	6 [8]

---

[6] *Rechnungsbuch* 96.

[7] *Ibid.* 81, 87, 89.

[8] *Ibid.* 26-29; for the Genevan merchants cf. Bremme and Chaix, *Recherches*; for Baudin cf. Baudrier 5.2off.; for the Parisians cf. P. Renouard, *Répertoire des Imprimeurs Parisiens*, Paris 1965, passim.

Thus merchants from French-speaking towns accounted for almost 20% of the firm's total revenue, not to mention Francophone traders operating abroad who paid the firm another *fl.* 166 1s.[9] The importance of Francophone customers, and by implication French markets, is confirmed in the list of fresh sales made during the same accounting period and to be settled at the following Frankfurt fair. Outstanding debts reached a total of *fl.* 5320 and involved the following Francophones:

		fl.	*s.*
Geneva	Thomas Courteau	146	—
	Jacques Guichet	17	7
	Richard Neudin	12	14
Lyons	Clément Baudin	16	2
Paris	Jacques Dupuys	224	—
	Sébastien Nivelle	51	—
	Jean de Roigny	151	—
	André Wechel	147	—
Dole	Pierre Morot	38	8
Montbéliard	Hieremias Meder	15	—
	Total	818	6 [10]

This figure again exceeds 15% of the total sales. In addition, purchases made by French merchants abroad totalled *fl.* 312 17s.[11] Many of these names appear on the other pages still extant of the accounts book, but the value of sales to Francophones nowhere reached the same level.

	Outstanding debts			Customers from French-speaking towns			Francophone merchants abroad		
	fl.	*s.*	*d.*	*fl.*	*s.*	*d.*	*fl.*	*s.*	*d.*
Half year ending autumn 1557 *(incomplete)*	2314	15	—	135	16	—	56	14	— [12]
	Receipts								
Half year ... spring 59 *(incomplete)*	1019	11	6	37	5	—	—	—	— [13]
	Outstanding debts								
Half year ... autumn 59 *(incomplete)*	1440	14	—	149	14	—	100	—	— [14]

---

[9] Giorgio Valgrisio (Vaugris) of Venice *fl.* 28 and *fl.* 7; Michael Schirat (Chirard; cf. Benzing) then at Frankfurt *fl.* 11 1s.; Thomas Guarinus of Basle *fl.* 120. Guarinus, in particular, must have bought many Froben books to sell them at Lyons and elsewhere in France.

[10] *Rechnungsbuch* 34-37.

[11] Thomas Guarinus *fl.* 306; Michael Schirat *fl.* 1 17s.; Pierre Estiard of Strasbourg (cf. Febvre-Martin 466) *fl.* 5.

[12] *Rechnungsbuch* 2-5: N. Barbier *fl.* 6; J. Guichet *fl.* 1 12s.; J. Dupuys *fl.* 6 11s.; J. Foucher *fl.* 3 10s.; and only the Lyonnais with larger sums: C. Baudin *fl.* 31 8s. and Guillaume Rouillé (cf. Febvre-Martin 467) *fl.* 87. The figures are incomplete, but it is possible that the Edict of Compiègne, 24 July, 1557 and the war with Spain still dragging on may have discouraged French buyers.

[13] *Rechnungsbuch* 12f.: J. Foucher *fl.* 17 5s.; C. Baudin *fl.* 20.

[14] *Ibid.* 14-16: J. Guichet *fl.* 19 3s.; J. Dupuys *fl.* 34 12s.; J. Foucher *fl.* 36 and *fl.* 19 15s.; Oudin Petit, also of Paris, *fl.* 35; C. Baudin *fl.* 1 5s.; J. Derbilly (cf. below p. 79) and P. Estiard *fl.* 4 4s.; T. Guarinus *fl.* 100.

	Receipts			Customers from French-speaking towns			Francophone merchants abroad		
	fl.	*s.*	*d.*	*fl.*	*s.*	*d.*	*fl.*	*s.*	*d.*
Half year ... autumn 1562	3759	6	—	189	1	4	130	5	— [15]
Outstanding debts	4240	5	—	462	9	—	107	15	— [16]
Receipts									
Half year ... spring 1563	3318	—	2	208	11	8	173	20	— [17]

The figures for the earlier years are all incomplete, but even the complete ones for the autumn of 1562 and the spring of 1563 suggest average sales to French-speaking markets amounting to between 5% and 10% rather than the 20% reached in the spring of 1562. However, in the clearly documented decline of revenue from French markets from 20% in the spring of 1562 to 5% in the autumn (but 11% new sales) and 6% in the spring of 1563, the religious war in France may have played its part. One notes that the firm could not recover the loss suffered in French markets through increased sales elsewhere. The loss of total revenue is in proportion to the loss of French customers. The figures leave no doubt about the potential value of the French market for the Basle book trade, especially if one considers that the Froben and Episcopius firm after the great Budé edition of 1556-57 for some time published no new titles which would seem as immediately attractive to the French public as some of the products of Oporinus, H. Petri and Guarinus.[18] It is quite possible that, apart from all ideological implications,[19] the decision to launch a French translation of Erasmus' *Paraphrases* was taken in the light of the promising sales figures of spring 1562, and that it was designed to establish the firm more solidly on the Francophone markets where its rivals at Basle had been supplanting it. If so, the outbreak of the religious war must have been a rude blow for the firm.

That the years around 1560 had a crucial importance for Basle's book trade with France is further confirmed by the unprecedented number of royal privileges then granted to Basle publishers, and by the number of important personal contacts with French scholars, most of them pointing to Paris. In this case cultural ideals and commercial interest worked for one another. The fact that the success of Basle publishing was intimately connected with the Paris book trade is underlined not only by the important purchases of Paris merchants, above all Jacques Dupuys, documented in the accounts of the Froben firm, but also by the measure in which, according to Schwetschke's figures, the Basle book industry shared the misfortunes of Paris publishers during the disastrous years from 1591 to 1594 when the French

---

[15] *Rechnungsbuch* 44-47: J. Guichet *fl.* 16; J. Dupuys *fl.* 57 10s.; C. Baudin *fl.* 50 12s. and *fl.* 35 4s. 4d.; P. Morot " per Ioannem Dron " *fl.* 30; T. Guarinus *fl.* 120; M. Schirat *fl.* 1 5s.; P. Estiard *fl.* 9.

[16] *Rechnungsbuch* 52-55: T. Courteau *fl.* 3 9s.; J. Guichet *fl.* 53; J. Dupuys *fl.* 165 and *fl.* 48; C. Baudin *fl.* 160; P. Morot *fl.* 43; T. Guarinus *fl.* 84; M. Schirat *fl.* 5 15s.; Joannes Duwalt Frankfortensis (= Jean Duval) *fl.* 18.

[17] *Rechnungsbuch* 62-65: J. Guichet *fl.* 20; J. Dupuys *fl.* 83 6s. 8d.; C. Baudin *fl.* 34 10s.; J. Dron (for P. Morot) *fl.* 52 20s.; " Servais Charlemayng den zyns " *fl.* 18; T. Guarinus *fl.* 100 and *fl.* 46 and *fl.* 4 5s.; M. Schirat *fl.* 5; P. Estiard *fl.* 11; " Gallus quidem studiosus " (at Basle) *fl.* 7 15s.; " Franciscus de Insola " (?, not counted) *fl.* 5.

[18] Cf. e.g. **No. 90, 93, 244f., 441f., 765f., 792, 861, 1023.** Cf. also **No. 12.**

[19] See below p. 205.

capital was victimized by the last stand of the Catholic League against Henry IV.[20] *
While leaving Basle's representation in the Frankfurt catalogues at an unprecedented
low, the same years seem to have benefited Geneva and Lyons, whose entries in the
catalogues reached new peaks. *Vice versa*, the crisis in the book industry of Geneva
and Lyons in 1571 and 1572 did not visibly affect Basle. In the accounts of the
Froben and Episcopius firm too Lyons merchants apparently played a secondary
role; however, such an isolated observation may be misleading. Thomas Guarinus
was still travelling back and forth between Basle and Lyons, and Genevan merchants
too occasionally bought large quantities of Froben books which were certainly not
absorbed by their local market. One also notes that Barthélemy Vincent does not
appear among the Frankfurt customers of the Froben and Episcopius firm; yet the
co-operation between Oporinus and this great Lyons publisher continued over many
years, and must have produced agreements and transactions of considerable
importance.[21] *

An idea of the extent of the collaboration of Francophone authors and scholars
in the book production of Basle may be gained from the following graph which is
based on the bibliography included in this volume and indicates the total count of
publications for each decade.

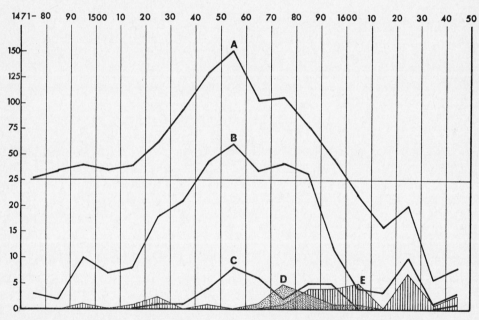

		Total number, 1470-1650
A	Number of books included in the bibliography, below, pp. 253-336 (Collective volumes are counted once only, although some may be listed more than once in the bibliography; cf. below, p. 251.)	1011
B	Number of " O "-books, i.e. original editions containing substantial contributions by Francophones	306
C	Number of publications in French	33
D	Number of translations from French into Latin	11
E	Number of translations from French into German	31

* For the notes 20 and 21 see on the next page.

No comparable figures are available for the total book output of Basle, but it seems reasonably certain that the curve indicating the number of books included in the bibliography follows the general pattern of Basle's total production, and that to the end of the sixteenth century the curve represents about 10%, or perhaps slightly more, of the total production. For the sake of comparison, the number of books produced with the collaboration of Francophones, or covering subjects relating to France, may be set against the number of books written, entirely or in part, by Italians:

	1541-60	1561-80	1581-1600
Francophone	279	220	117
Italian (approximately) [22]	170	135	43

The comparison shows that towards the end of the century the decline in the reproduction of Italian authors was even more marked than in the case of Francophones.

The above graph also gives some indications of the extent to which the French language played a role in the Basle book output. The general swing from Latin to the vernacular languages, to which Basle publishing adjusted itself very reluctantly and slowly, is reflected in the very modest increase of translations from French into German, although this figure, more than any other, might be raised dramatically if it were possible to assign to Basle a number of anonymous books and treatises in German, and to identify the sources of numerous news letters. The figures for books published in French and translations from French into Latin are equally modest, and here it is unlikely that further research will produce substantial changes. Both categories obviously involved the printers in an economic venture which was only feasible during the peak years. There is no evidence that printing in French was particularly affected by the censorship laws or significantly encouraged by the patronage of political agencies.[23]

Finally the above graph also attempts to present the number of original editions containing substantial contributions by Francophones. It cannot be expected that on this count the record of Francophones would be particularly impressive. A German or Swiss author would approach the Basle presses more readily than would a French one; on the other hand a Basle press would have to expect more trouble from reprinting a recent publication from Strasbourg or Frankfurt than one from Lyons or Paris. Throughout the sixteenth century relations between publishing firms at Basle and French printing centres do not seem to have suffered much from

---

[20] Already in 1577 B. Vulcanius had the impression that the Basle printing industry was in deep trouble (*Correspondance de B. Vulcanius* 243ff.). Statistical evidence does not indicate a special crisis at this time; yet Vulcanius knew the book trade too well to be altogether mistaken, even though his remarks may reflect his disappointment over the negative reception of some of his personal publishing proposals. His statements certainly serve to underline the general decline of the industry.

[21] Cf. Steinmann 59 and passim.

[22] Cf. Bietenholz, *Ital. Humanismus* 16n.

[23] The books listed in the Bibliography were also analysed statistically according to subjects, but the results do not warrant reproduction. At no point does there appear an unexpected emphasis. Using a rough classification, the following totals may be given for the period 1471-1650:

Philosophy and Education	176	History and Cosmography	114
Religion	279	Law	87
Philology	160	Medicine	71
Poetry	38	Science	36

the widely employed practice of unauthorized reprinting.   If there is some evidence of individual clashes,[24] there is more of friendly co-operation.[25]   Even though rival editions from Basle and Paris or Lyons must have competed repeatedly at the great fairs, each centre also had its safe markets, protected from its rivals by the high cost of transportation and other factors.   Typically, complaints filed with the Basle authorities about unauthorized reprints mostly seem to date from the early seventeenth century rather than the sixteenth, and to involve competitors at short range, in Strasbourg and above all in Geneva.[26]   From the figures on which the above graph of Francophone co-operation is based it may however be learned that among the contributions by Francophones those which were original remained at a stable 35% between 1541 and 1600, thus being appreciably higher than in preceding and subsequent decades.

	1471-1540	1541-1600	1601-1650
Total	323	616	72
Original	69	216	21

This fact is highly significant, for it reflects not only the great attention of French authors to the Basle presses long before the wars of religion caused the greatest flow of French refugees into the Rhine town, but also the peculiar policy of Basle publishers during the most successful decades of their industry.   Gone were the happy freebooters of the type of Andreas Cratander ; and perhaps only Thomas Guarinus, who had learned his business at Lyons, still exposed himself methodically to the trouble of finding suitable copy among the recent editions of other publishing centres. The great Basle publishers of this period, on the whole, refrained from such practices, in part no doubt because their international reputation required adherence to a superior code of conduct, but also from a certain lack of initiative. They never broke with the great traditions founded by Erasmus.   In the wake of his Complete Works editions of the Christian fathers they produced similar folio volumes offering the collected writings of the Greek philosophers, of the classic authors of Renaissance humanism and humanistic jurisprudence, and of yet others.   They also accepted willingly many, perhaps too many, of the fresh manuscripts offered to them by hopeful contemporary authors.   In doing so, however, they would have had to learn that few of these writers could expect successes even faintly comparable with those of the new works Erasmus had been entrusting to Froben year after year.   While it is understandable that Basle publishers wished to honour a tradition on which their special reputation was based, it is nevertheless obvious that their lack of flexibility and their failure to adjust to new circumstances contributed heavily to the decline of their business towards the end of the sixteenth century.

To realize the full significance of this point it must be considered that German-speaking collaborators almost certainly raised the level of original publications to an even higher percentage than the 35% indicated for the Francophones alone.   It should further be considered that while thus reducing the risk of conflicts with rival

---

[24] Cf. above pp. 39, n. 89, 42f.

[25] To the evidence stated in the preceding chapter the following example of co-operation may be added : in 1570 a royal privilege was issued to Jacques Dupuys and Thomas Guarinus jointly, protecting their new Latin editions of Plutarch's *Moralia*. It was printed in Guarinus' editions of this text of 1570, 1572 and 1573. In addition, the 1570 edition also contained an imperial privilege granted to the translator, G. Xylander

[26] Staatsarchiv Basel-Stadt, Handel und Gewerbe JJJ .3.

presses, the Basle publishers accepted an unusually heavy financial responsibility, for the expense incurred in producing a book from manuscript is appreciably higher than the cost of reprinting. No wonder that the Basle presses were anxious to protect their production with privileges. In the first place it was the protection of the emperor which they tried to secure through individual or categorical privileges.[27] However, French royal privileges too were obvious assets, especially for editions which were likely to attract French readers, such as the books by Francophone authors published at Basle. From about 1550 individual royal privileges were often granted either to the Basle publisher or, less frequently, to the French author himself.[28] In many cases the French text of the privilege was reproduced in extenso on the back of the title page. In 1559 fifteen Basle publishing firms were blacklisted by the Council of Trent.[29] Perhaps as a result of this royal privileges were especially sought after around 1560. However they became less numerous after 1565, evidently not because of the papal verdict since some were still granted to the blacklisted presses, but because of political events and the gradual decline of French markets for the Basle book. Never again would Basle publishers enjoy such excellent connections with the royal administration as they did in the days of Michel de L'Hospital.[30]

---

[27] Cf. Burckhardt, *Herold* 48ff.

[28] Cf. the preceding n. 25 to which the following examples may be added: In 1561 a royal privilege was granted for the ed. of Concenatius (**No. 320**) to "...nostre bien ayme Nicolas L'Evesque le Jeune, marchant libraire et bourgeois de la Ville de Basle, l'un des cantons de nos chiers, bien aymez alliez, confederez et bons comperes, les Suisses." Likewise all eds. of S. Münster's *Cosmography* in French translation (**No. 762ff.**) exhibited the text of a royal privilege, dated from Paris, 20 January, 1552. In 1554 and 1558 N. Episcopius published two large eds. of Philo Iudaeus, protected by an imperial as well as a royal privilege. The text of the former was inserted in the first ed., that of the latter in the second. An elaborate royal privilege is also inserted in the Gregory of Nyssa ed. of N. (II) Episcopius, 1562. P. Perna often referred to privileges on his titlepages, probably not always with justification. However, his ed. of Gregory of Tours in 1568 (**No. 480**) " cum gratia et privilegio Caes. Maiestatis ad annos sex ", although an obvious reprint of Guillaume Morel's Paris ed., need not necessarily have interfered with the royal privilege granted to Morel, since French privileges were not valid outside the realm. Still in 1580 T. Guarinus secured a royal privilege in addition to the imperial for his *Opera* of Alciato (**No. 14**), and in 1587 L. Osten did likewise for the *Praelectiones* of Gaultier-Chabot (**No. 455**). **No. 401** appeared in 1552 with a royal privilege granted to the author, Charles Du Moulin, although this ed. was not essentially different from two immediately preceding eds., published at Paris and Lyons also under royal privilege. Du Moulin co-operated with the Basle printer. Likewise the text of a royal privilege is inserted in F. Hotman's *Iurisconsultus* of 1559 (**No. 558**). It is issued in favour of the author and does not even mention the publisher.

[29] Cf. Steinmann 97f.

[30] See below pp. 204ff.

PART TWO

FRANCOPHONE EXPATRIATES AT BASLE

CHAPTER ONE

VISITORS TO TOWN AND UNIVERSITY

Throughout the sixteenth and early seventeenth centuries Frenchmen were drawn to Basle for several reasons. The university, founded in 1460, enjoyed from the middle of the sixteenth century a measure of European reputation which was lost only gradually in the course of the seventeenth. It is significant that the university's golden age coincided with the presence of great numbers of confessional exiles from many corners of the continent. More than any other single factor, the printing industry had prepared the way for both these developments. Before it lost momentum towards the end of the sixteenth century it attracted French-speaking book merchants, famous authors, and lesser figures hoping or even desperate to break into print. It also employed dozens of Francophones in the various professions associated with the production of books.

The more distinguished the arriving Frenchmen were, however, the more likely they were to remain but passing visitors. As early as 1504 Cardinal Raymond Perault, a papal legate to Germany, commissioned some publications in Basle which were suitable for distribution along his way.[1] Once the Froben press had succeeded in retaining Erasmus, his presence accounted for the arrival of eager youths and eminent callers whom neither the university nor the presses might of themselves have lured into town. Among them was Pierre Lamy, the friend of Rabelais and Budé, who died at Basle in 1525 and was buried in the Franciscan churchyard, although without the ' seraphic ' cowl he had worn and shed together with Rabelais. Lamy had met Erasmus before ; when he now reached Basle in the company of the wealthy Polish noble, Jan Lasky, Erasmus was confirmed in his liking for him.[2] In 1527 another enquiring French youth lived for some months in Erasmus' house. The rich and pompous Pierre Duchâtel, who was to become an influential bishop attached to the court of France and a protector of Dolet and Ramus, visited Erasmus again at Freiburg before setting out on travels that took him to Rome, Cairo, and Constantinople.[3] Other boarders or *famuli* of Erasmus were more or less closely

---

[1] Cf. R. Wackernagel, Mitteilungen über Raymundus Peraudi und die kirchlichen Zustände seiner Zeit in Basel, *BZGA* 2(1903), 171-273. I have no evidence that Perault's *Admonitio paterna ... de dignitate sacerdotali* was also printed in Basle : UBB : D.B.IV. 12 (3) and E.W.II.34 (2).

[2] Allen 9.184 ; Hartmann 5.3 ; Herminjard 1.225.

[3] Allen 8.275 ; 11.47f. and passim. Lefranc (*Hist. du Collège de France* 92ff.) relates his efforts to learn Hebrew in Basle and identifies him with the pompously groomed youth in Thomas Platter's Hebrew course who failed to recognize the master because of his shabby garb until he was enlightened by Oporinus ; cf. T. Platter 82.

connected with France. Karel Utenhove, a native of Ghent, arrived in 1528 with an introduction from Berquin.[4] Gilbert Cousin, Erasmus' secretary from 1529 to 1535, brought about a momentous exchange between the Basle typographers and many leading circles of Franche-Comté.

By that time, however, it was for religious reasons that most newly arriving Francophones had temporarily or permanently left their homes. Members of the French aristocracy and others who could support themselves without encroaching upon the business of the local population were always welcome. Basle still lay at the cross-roads of the continent. Few distinguished travellers missed the town and many would stop for several months or even a year or two. In 1525 the Sieur de Chastelard, Anémond de Coct, died in Switzerland, having lived in Basle for the last twelve months of his life. He associated with Pierre Toussain and all other Francophones, and he borrowed money from his compatriot Guillaume Farel pending the arrival of funds from his family.[5] Antoine du Blet, a rich Lyons merchant of noble descent, visited Basle in 1524 and from there sent liberal gifts of books to Lefèvre d'Etaples.[6] He shared with Coct the friendship of Farel, an unconcealed scorn for Erasmus,[7] and most of all a personal devotion to promoting French markets for the Protestant Basle book, a devotion which ended only with the premature death of both.

When Erasmus returned to Basle in 1535 he noticed that the recent religious strife culminating in the *Placards* affair had driven many French nobles to seek refuge there ; he also learned that the Edict of Coucy had attempted to recall them by a number of concessions.[8] The most remarkable individual in this group, and the one best known to Erasmus, was Antoine Morelet du Museau (Maurus Musaeus). He arrived shortly before the *Placards* affair, and was to reside in Basle until 1537. In 1523 a Claude Morelet had written from Dijon, close to the family's estates, introducing himself to Erasmus.[9] In the same year Guillaume Budé thanked Erasmus for the good reception he had afforded to a son of Jean Morelet du Museau, a French treasurer.[10] The Morelets were related by marriage to the Briçonnets, and the young man who visited Erasmus was probably the same who a year later received at Paris an encouraging letter from Oecolampadius—the friend of the Meaux circle—in which the addressee was styled a royal secretary and commended for his zeal for the Gospel.[11] Oecolampadius' letter most likely concerned that same Antoine, who later lived in Basle as a religious exile. Antoine Morelet put Simon Grynaeus in touch with his former teacher Nicolas Bérauld,[12] and at the suggestion of Grynaeus he exchanged letters with Martin Bucer. He expressed doubts about the sincerity of the diplomacy of Francis I and Guillaume Du Bellay, Sieur de Langey towards the German and Swiss Protestants, he also voiced concern

---

[4] Allen 7.541. To the end of his long life he preserved his friendship for Jean Bauhin and the children of Castellio : Allen 8. 42 ; Buisson, *Castellion* 2.277.

[5] Herminjard 1.203, 343 and passim ; N. Weiss in *BSHPF* 70 (1921), 197-205.

[6] Herminjard 1.207 and passim.

[7] Allen 5.570 ; Herminjard 1.281.

[8] Allen 11.215f. ; cf. G. Berthoud, Les "ajournés" du 25 janvier 1535, *BHR* 25 (1963), 307-324.

[9] Allen 5.270f.

[10] Allen 5.296f. ; cf. Herminjard 4.76f.

[11] Herminjard 1.248ff.

[12] See below p. 195f.

about Melanchthon's compliance with their wishes.[13] In 1536 he mediated from Basle between Calvin and Bucer[14] and in 1537 the Basle town council wrote to Francis I to thank him for having Morelet recalled from his exile and restored to his offices.[15] It seems most unlikely that Morelet at this time was one of Langey's agents in Basle posing as an Evangelical refugee. He did, however, come back to Switzerland, and between 1543 and his death at Basle in 1552 he served repeatedly both as the king's ordinary ambassador and special envoy. He clearly had a personal affection for Basle and resided there as often as possible, both while on mission and on leave.[16] In this period several Basle books were dedicated to him by Castellio and others,[17] but he also remained a friend of Calvin and Bullinger.[18] Morelet's case was not the only one in which the city council tried to clear the homeward path of a distinguished exile. In 1538 the city fathers solicited the protection of Marguerite de Navarre for the returning Antoine de Castenet of Toulouse whom they described as a steadfast Protestant.[19]

It was not only when returning home, however, that French noblemen might expose themselves to danger. Another émigré in Basle, the poor Sieur de Rochefort was killed by kidnappers in 1537 while riding with some friends outside the city walls. The affair involved the city government in long negotiations and difficult decisions until the main culprit could be brought to justice.[20] Most unpleasant, though not fatal, was a similar incident in 1543 of which Jacques Reignauld, Sieur d'Alleins, was the victim. Reignauld and Bonifacius Amerbach knew each other indirectly from the latter's days in Avignon. This wealthy noble was now searching for a convenient residence « aux lieus où Jésu-christ règne,» and consulted Amerbach about Basle citizenship. On his way back from Strasbourg he was kidnapped in nearby Habsburg land and put up for ransom. As in the case of Rochefort the Habsburg authorities proved far from co-operative. The governments of Strasbourg and Basle finally secured his release, but he complained bitterly that such lawlessness should be possible in a peaceful region. Although apparently Reignauld did not falter in his intention to settle in Protestant lands, he must have dropped Basle from his choice.[21]

Among noble visitors to Basle in the later 1540s[22] Jacques de Bourgogne, Seigneur de Falais, was the most distinguished and the most interesting. This

---

[13] Herminjard 3.194ff., 198ff.

[14] Herminjard 4.117f.; Wernle, *Calvin und Basel* 4f. and passim.

[15] Herminjard 4.268f. The Basle council made Morelet a citizen and wrote several letters on his behalf: Staatsarchiv Basel-Stadt, Missiven B. 1.299f., B.2.10 and passim; Hartmann 6.287f.

[16] Rott 1.565 and passim.

[17] **No. 280, 394, 890**; cf. Buisson, *Castellion* 1.116, 282; 2.84, 409. That the refugee and the later ambassador were one and the same person is often confirmed: e.g. Herminjard 4.77.

[18] *Calvini opera* 14.251, 326, 387; Bouvier 203ff.; cf. Herminjard 7.27, 113f.

[19] Staatsarchiv Basel-Stadt, Missiven B.2.178r-v; *Matrikel* 2.17.

[20] Staatsarchiv Basel-Stadt, Missiven B.2.115ff.; [C.] Buxtorf-Falkeisen, *Basler Stadt- und Landgeschichten aus dem sechszehnten Jahrhundert* 2 (Basle 1865), 48-53; *Calvini opera* 20.363f.

[21] Herminjard 9.3ff., 8ff., 36ff., 150; Hartmann 5.457f. For a similar incident eleven years later see below p., 76 n. 17.

[22] See *Matrikel* passim, e.g. 2.57: Nicolas de La Melinière (Laminière) and his company; cf. *Calvini opera* 13.48. *Matrikel* 2.58 and Droz, *Etudiants français*: Matthieu de Bombelles, probably the son of a French special envoy then negotiating in Switzerland.

descendant of a natural son of Charles the Good of Burgundy had acquired Erasmian leanings from Jan Lasky during his studies at Louvain. From the court of Charles V he later withdrew to Protestant Strasbourg until the war of the Schmalkaldic league sent him on to Basle. Here he gracefully accepted citizenship in February 1547, but he also met Calvin. Impressed by him, he moved on to an estate in the neighbourhood of Geneva, where he settled in the summer of 1548. During the year he spent at Basle Valérand Poullain, a Belgian minister attached to Falais, was sent back to the Netherlands on his master's business. He returned with three ladies, among them a young relative of Falais. Upon arrival, however, the escort turned suitor, much to the displeasure of Falais. The town's marriage court had to decide whether or not the young lady had given Poullain a promise of marriage. The judgment, on the whole, disappointed his expectations.[23]

The climax of Basle's role as a centre for Huguenot refugees came after the massacre of Saint Bartholomew. Arriving from Berne in the last days of October 1572, the two sons of Coligny took residence at Basle together with their cousin, Guy-Paul de Châtillon, count of Laval, his mother, Andelot's widow, Anne, countess of Salm, and other members of that illustrious family. During the year of their stay at Basle the town council actively shared in diplomatic efforts to improve the lot of Coligny's widow, who was kept under arrest by the Duke of Savoy.[24] In 1573 Henri de Condé arrived, the son of Louis de Bourbon, who had succeeded his father as chief of the Huguenot army. Condé and his numerous following were still at Basle when after the assembly of the estates of Languedoc in January 1575 Protestant delegates from Southern France met with him and representatives of the exile churches prior to negotiations with the newly crowned Henry III. Condé's stay at Basle thus figures in the history of the first alliance between *politiques* and Huguenots which led the latter to the short-lived triumph of the peace of Beaulieu; all the more so as from Basle Condé also managed to obtain a loan from Berne and to recruit a number of Swiss mercenaries.[25] Among many other noblemen and refugees attracted to Basle during these climactic years one finds Paul Choart,[26] Sieur de Buzanval, and the dubious figure of the Vidame de Chartres.[27] The Francophones at Basle now had their own ministers and church services. A reflection of Basle's newly gained respectability in Calvinist eyes may be found in Innocent Gentillet's famous *Anti-Machiavel*, first published at Geneva in 1576. Its second part describes a conversation in which the author allegedly shared while travelling from Paris to Basle. That trip might almost have a symbolical significance, for it is this second

---

[23] Wernle, *Calvin und Basel* 56ff.; *Biographie nat. Belgique*; Herminjard 9.72f. and passim; Hartmann 6.468ff., 579ff., 610f.; *Calvini opera* 12.514ff. and passim. Later both protagonists, Falais as well as Poullain, fell out with Calvin and their presence at Basle may have contributed to the later disagreements. Falais later solicited Basle's support for Bolsec, his physician, when the latter was on trial in Geneva: Wernle, *Calvin und Basel* 89. For Poullain cf. K. Bauer, *Valérand Poullain*, Elberfeld 1927.

[24] A. Pascal, *L'ammiraglia di Coligny*, Turin 1962, 206ff., 256ff.; *BSHPF* 4 (1856), 467-469; 17 (1868), 583-590; 24 (1875), 289ff. Also for what follows: L. A. Burckhardt, Die französischen Religionsflüchtlinge in Basel, *Beiträge zur vaterländischen Geschichte* 7 (Basle 1860), 301-333.

[25] Cf. below p. 113, n. 52 and Rott 2.215ff., 345f.; *Arcana* [2.]80. For Condé's approaches to Bullinger cf. Bouvier 308f. and passim.

[26] Droz, *Etudiants français* and *Matrikel* 2.216; cf. *ibid.* 208 for Richard Dinoth and his distinguished party.

[27] *Correspondance de B. Vulcanius* 103f., 107.

60

part which introduces the concept of religious toleration in a work that otherwise reflects the typical thoughts of French Calvinists after the massacre of Saint Bartholomew.[28] Yet as will shortly be seen Basle, and especially her university, were soon again to harbour many opponents of the Calvinist leaders in Geneva, some of them outspoken admirers of Machiavelli.[29]

As long as Erasmus lived at Basle the university carried on somewhat in the great man's shadow. After his death it exerted more attraction of its own, but faster than did the book industry it also developed a measure of resistance to foreigners, and before the end of the century it had basically adopted what was to be its permanent function in the town's history. In offering careers to the academic-minded of their sons, it provided the local bourgeoisie with its own intellectual centre of gravity. In the process, its international reputation of the sixteenth century flattened to a regional one in the seventeenth. It is true that Francophones, like other foreigners, were welcome as students, and that poor refugees could count on the remission of enrolment fees and often on a subsidy from the Erasmus bequest.[30] But down to the end of the French religious wars name entries in the rector's roll reveal primarily the composition of the upper echelons of Basle's Francophone community.[31] Only after 1585 did the proportion of those who studied seriously towards a degree increase.[32] Both in the sixteenth century and later there was little enthusiasm generally for the inclusion of Francophones in the teaching body. By contrast it was considered very proper that local scholars should receive their degrees from French universities prior to joining the ranks of Basle professors. L. Ber's Sorbonne doctorate, the juridical one which Bonifacius Amerbach received at Avignon, Felix Platter's medical degree from Montpellier, are just a few cases among the more noted ones. French-speaking professors, however, were less numerous than Italians in the first century of the university's existence, although the ratio was clearly reversed among the students.

It is true that in the legal profession, where prestige ran high and salaries were commensurate, Basle failed at times to retain, or to secure, the desired services of a highly reputed French professor. Claude Chansonnette, who taught civil law from 1518 to 1524, finally left Basle although the position of town clerk and consultant had been added to his university appointment.[33] The famous Charles Du Moulin was offered a chair when he visited Basle in 1552 as the guest of Antoine Morelet du Museau. He declined, and may have regretted it later. In Basle he concentrated on the revision of his *Commentarius ad edictum Henrici secundi contra parvas et abusus curiae Romanae.*[34] In the two years following its first publication this treatise

---

[28] I. Gentillet, *Discours sur les moyens de bien gouverner et maintenir en bonne paix un royaume ou autre principauté ... contre Nicholas Machiavel Florentin.* Of the many editions to my knowledge only a German translation was published at Basle in 1646 : **No. 459.**

[29] Cf. below p. 117.

[30] Cf. E. de Beaulieu and S. Castellio : below p. 97f. and p. 125. For others see *Hartmann* 5.87f., 416, 418; 6.437f.

[31] See below p. 89, n. 4.

[32] See **No. 2001ff.** For the history of the university in general see E. Bonjour, *Die Universität Basel, 1460-1960,* Basle 1960.

[33] *Hartmann* 2.289 and passim. For Chansonnette see also *Matrikel* 1.334; G. Kisch, *Erasmus und die Jurisprudenz seiner Zeit,* Basle 1960, 90ff. and passim. Cf. below p. 243.

[34] **No. 401.** The ed. was intended for sale outside France. The additions on the whole are Latin translations added to the introduction and documents which earlier

had gained him international fame, although it now necessitated his temporary removal from Paris. When Du Moulin left Basle his contact with Bonifacius Amerbach continued through a series of letters. Though the first disagreements between him and the Calvinist leaders in Geneva and Lausanne occurred soon afterwards, his resounding attacks on the Calvinist view of justification belong to a later phase of his life. In spite of his still easy relations with Calvin, however, Du Moulin while refreshing his secular-nationalistic and Gallican ideals at Basle may have been prepared by them for his subsequent ambiguous relation to Lutheranism and for his outspoken Erastianism.[35] The only other text by him to be published at Basle is noteworthy in this context. In 1566 the ultra-Lutheran Flacius Illyricus appended to a polemical work of his own an address which Du Moulin had given earlier at Tübingen. While basically rejecting the historical and legal bases for papal power, it also reiterated Du Moulin's high opinion of the legitimate rights of secular princes. The choice of this text by Flacius was hardly accidental. Only a year earlier Du Moulin had published his *Collatio et unio quatuor Evangelistarum* at Paris. Condemned at a Huguenot national synod in Paris and publicly burned in Geneva, this work had reinforced his position as a leader of the anti-Calvinist French Protestant movement.

If Du Moulin had declined the chair offered to him, it happened more frequently however that the Bâlois felt unable to accommodate French-speaking candidates for academic positions. This happened to several jurists,[36] among them the Franche-Comtois Pierre Lorriot, a professor at Bourges who wrote in 1539 to the Basle council to offer his services. It was a long and painstaking letter that envisaged a reform of Roman Law as the author's contribution to purified religion. No doubt Lorriot would have breathed more freely in a Protestant land, even though his letter seems also motivated by his desire to get a higher salary. On behalf of the city council Bonifacius Amerbach drafted a polite reply, regretting that there was no vacancy.[37]

That the theological faculty would not hire any members from outside the German nation could perhaps be expected. More surprising is the reluctance to appoint Italian and Gallic professors to the faculty of arts, where the salaries were low and a mastery of Ciceronian Latin was in high demand. As it was, Sébastien Castellio and Samuel Mareschal, professor of music,[38] remained the only Francophone immigrants who were given even modest positions. Although only one of its members in the sixteenth century was of Francophone descent, the medical faculty presents a somewhat different picture. Most Basle professors of medicine between the early sixteenth and early seventeenth centuries had undergone some medical training in French universities. Many had ties with French colleagues and showed

---

editions had printed in French only; cf. *Calvini opera* 14.387ff. and Du Moulin's letter to C.S. Curione on the subject of the Basle ed.: UBB ms. G.I.66, fol. 101f. UBB possesses some more letters to Curione and mostly to Bonifacius Amerbach. The correspondence also shows that **No. 401** was printed by Parcus to the orders of the publisher, M. Isengrin. Cf. *France prot.*[2]

[35] Kingdon, *Geneva and the Consolidation* 138ff., also for what follows.

[36] So Philippe de La Garde, Sieur de Francheville, a Toulouse professor escaped from the Saint Bartholomew's massacre. He had to go on to Strasbourg where he taught Law: *Matrikel* 2. 215. For the case of François Hotman see below p. 118.

[37] Hartmann 5.237ff., 248f.

[38] *Matrikel* 2.246. This native of Tournai was also the director of the university choir and the organist of the cathedral.

considerable interest in French students who sought instruction from them in rather larger numbers than was normally the case with other faculties. However, the special significance attached to the group of Francophone medical students and doctors who visited Basle lay rather more in the field of religion than in that of medicine. One family, the Bauhins, played an appreciable role in both.

Jean Bauhin, the elder (1511-1582), a native of Amiens, arrived at Basle in 1541. After an initial spell of proof reading he soon was a popular general practitioner although, like other surgeons, he seems to have lacked a medical degree. To a stay at Paris he probably owed, apart from his wife and his training, his first acquaintance with the Protestant faith and its repression by the authorities. Nothing is known about the beginning of his contacts with Anabaptists, but after his escape from Paris he lived in Antwerp at the same time as David Joris who was later to be his patient at Basle.[39] Joris, the famous Anabaptist leader, worn by the exigencies of clandestine field work and incessant persecution, found finally a shelter in Basle. He lived there incognito and in quiet comfort, surrounded by a small clan of family and other faithful. Bauhin's connection with this sect were more or less severed late in 1553, four years before the death of the old arch heretic. An immediate cause for Bauhin's withdrawal may be seen in the warning example provided by the burning of Servetus in Geneva, but the underlying process of alienation probably resulted from a slow change of heart which can be documented with some statements made by his opponents. Unswerving members of the Anabaptist sect called him a dialectician and criticized his independent judgment of the teachings of their master. In the unsparing polemics of Farel, on the other hand, Bauhin appears primarily as a Castellionist. It seems that he had come under the intellectual influence of Castellio and there encountered religious and moral views which were clearly superior to those of Joris. When the Basle authorities belatedly discovered the identity of Joris and his followers, Bauhin was arrested but regained his freedom almost at once. His name is not mentioned in the records of the subsequent trial.[40]

His independence in religious matters is beyond doubt, but his only direct confrontation with orthodox Calvinism occurred during a visit to Lyons, and not at Basle.[41] Curiously he was not registered in the university roll before 1557. In 1575 he was recognized as a consultant by the medical faculty and in 1580 he presided over an academic disputation as the dean of the medical profession.[42] Bauhin's elder son, also named Jean (1541-1613), was born in Basle and briefly served there as a professor of rhetoric before he moved to Montbéliard and an honourable appointment as court physician. He inherited his father's unorthodox mind and his father's friends often became his own.[43] Not so his younger brother, Gaspard Bauhin. Gaspard steered his considerable talents clear of all controversial issues, an achievement that his fellow citizens rewarded with quick advancement and high honours. As ambitious as he was gifted, he made the most of incessantly launching and re-arranging his publications. Initially professor of Greek, in 1589 he succeeded to a

---

[39] Burckhardt, *Joris* 37ff.; cf. W. S. Mitchell, Jean Bauhin the Elder (1511-1582), *The Medical Bookman and Historian* 2 (London 1948), 202-206; *France prot.*[2] (also for his sons).

[40] Burckhardt, *Joris* 41f., 53, 75 and passim; Droz, *Hendrik van Schor* 114.

[41] See below p. 223f.

[42] *Matrikel* 2.107 and **No. 2020**.

[43] *Matrikel* 2.89; F. Hasler, Johannes Bauhin d. J. (1541-1613), *Gesnerus* 20 (1963), 1-21. Many ms. letters by him are in UBB. Cf. below p. 246f.

newly established chair of anatomy and botany. In botany he earned himself a lasting reputation; in anatomy, however, he reverted to the Galenic tradition and thus delayed the impact of the methods of Vesalius, which were advocated by his colleague Felix Platter, whom he succeeded in 1614 as professor of practical medicine and as town physician. He was four times rector of the university. He had studied in Italy and France, and he knew how to flatter well-situated students and colleagues from Geneva and France,[44] but his name is not mentioned in connection with emigrant circles or the French church. Among his publications the successive versions of an anatomical text book proved most successful. Steadily growing in volume, these finally exceeded the capacity of Basle's book industry, ailing after the turn of the century, so he took the work to Frankfurt where it continued to appear as the well-known *Theatrum anatomicum* in the lavishly illustrated editions of the De Bry family.[45] There was less demand for his significant botanical works.[46] Occasionally his pharmacological studies took a more speculative turn, again not uncommon in Basle at this time. In his treatise on the bezoar stone [47] he applied to the sphere of the marvellous the same methodical gathering of information that distinguished his botanical studies. Yet when he looked back upon the material he had collected, he shrank from the rational conclusions which he ought to have drawn from the many contradictions. In the same way he proved himself a good Bâlois when choosing the dignity of man as his theme for an academic address.[48] Although he treated his topic more from a medical view-point, Bauhin's theme recalls the continuing respect in Basle for the tradition stemming from G. Pico della Mirandola.

Not all of his French students, however, shared Gaspard Bauhin's comfortable talent for accommodation. Some held views rather similar to those of Jean Bauhin the father. No documentation is available at present for his specific role in keeping alive the tradition of his friend Castellio, and in passing it on to subsequent sympathizers in the medical profession. However, his very presence at Basle must have presented an element of continuity as medical men came and went who were all in one way or another critical of Geneva. Numerous sources remain to be investigated before this fascinating story can be adequately understood, but from the outset it is remarkable how some professional approaches to the science of medicine interacted with politico-religious views and how Geneva provided a target for both.

Among the town's medical community, G. Bauhin's Galenism, F. Platter's Vesalianism, T. Zwinger's Aristotelianism, and G. Gratarolo's Paracelsism indicate

---

[44] In **No. 99** Gaspard Bauhin lists a number of colleagues and students who witnessed his anatomical dissections of years preceding. Among them are Esaïe Colladon (**No. 2042f.**; *Matrikel* 2.350), son of the Geneva theologian; Antoine Boucard, a Protestant student from Lorraine (*Matrikel* 2.359; **No. 2031ff.**), and the royal physician Jean Albosius (cf. below p. 72) who even contributed some verse in honour of Bauhin. For Gaspard Bauhin see *Matrikel* 2.212f.; *NDB*; W. Kolb, *Geschichte des anatomischen Unterrichtes an der Universität Basel*, 1460-1900, Basle 1951, 30ff. and passim.

[45] The series of major anatomical works runs from **No. 100** to **No. 94-96** and **No. 99** and finally to *Theatrum anatomicum*, Frankfurt 1605. *BMC* lists: "*Vivae imagines...*, [Basle], 1620*": This is merely a part of the Frankfurt *Theatrum*, 1621, and there is no reason to think that it originated in Basle. Bauhin also produced an anatomical text book of lesser size and expense, the *Institutiones*: **No. 103-104** and later Frankfurt 1616.

[46] **No. 106-107, 97-98.**

[47] **No. 101**; cf. especially "*Conclusio*" 278f.

[48] **No. 2017.** Cf. Bietenholz, *Ital. Humanismus* 121ff.

no more than preferences, sufficiently subdued to avoid the occurrence of clashes. Among the French-speaking visitors, however, partisan approaches to medical questions tended to coincide with religious commitment. In this group of physicians one encounters both Castellio's spiritualism and his rationalism, the latter spilling over from metaphysics to physics. Both tendencies combined to clash with a curious alliance between orthodox Calvinism and alchemy. · Usually the conflicts exploded at some distance from the city of Basle, but Basle and her printing industry provided a kind of neutral ground where controversial views could be traded freely. Viewed numerically, the forces opposing Geneva were indeed a minority, but they were articulate as well as original and therefore deserve to be introduced before their enemies.

It is appropriate to turn first to Claude Aubery. His presence at Basle in the very years when the refugees from the massacre of Saint Bartholomew arrived and the French church was established is indeed indicative of the situation that was to develop over the next thirty years. A native of Champagne, Aubery graduated from the medical faculty in 1574 after having been in Basle for several years.[49] From 1576 onwards he taught at the Lausanne academy, but his links with Basle continued, chiefly through his correspondence with Theodor Zwinger and others. With Zwinger Aubery shared a solid grounding in Aristotelian logic. In Lausanne he emerged as the champion of an anti-Ramist faction in defense of Aristotle. His letters to Zwinger, accordingly, for the most part refer to the translating and editing of Greek philosophical and medical texts. However, on 23 August, 1587, Aubery sent his friend [50]—and also Basilius Amerbach and J. J. Grynaeus—a gift that was to cause turmoil in Lausanne, Berne, Geneva, and eventually in Basle. It was his newly printed *Orationes apodicticae de fide catholica apostolica Romana*, a theological essay based on *Romans* and, according to its author, devoted to anti-popish propaganda. What Aubery did not tell Zwinger was that it also featured an anti-Calvinist doctrine of justification closely reminiscent of Castellio's. The book had been condemned by the Geneva ministers even before it was published. Now Grynaeus and his colleagues at Basle found it equally unacceptable. Still, they contributed actively to a temporary settlement of the issue before the authorities of Berne, who permitted Aubery and his friends at Lausanne an honourable retreat. Nevertheless, the book was out. Despite Beza's efforts to prevent its distribution it aroused interest and controversy among French Protestants throughout Europe. By 1590 the conflict had focused on Basle where Aubery's friend Antoine Lescaille was disseminating somewhat the same views. The ensuing scandal will be discussed in another context.[51] At the height of it Aubery appeared again in Basle. By 1593 he was made to resign his position at Lausanne. He moved to Dijon and there died a Catholic in 1596. At the peak of the crisis Beza's letters to J. J. Grynaeus express genuine alarm. It seemed to him that the Basle ministers persistently underrated the gravity of the situation. In reality he may himself have gone too far in suspecting a general plot of « Arians » and « Servetians » reaching from Switzerland to the French churches in Strasbourg and elsewhere in Germany and even to the Polish

---

[49] *Matrikel* 2.223 ; for the following see H. Meylan, Claude Aubery : L'affaire des " Orationes ", in Université de Lausanne, Faculté de Théologie, *Recueil des travaux publiés à l'occasion du quatrième centenaire...*, Lausanne 1937, 9-87 ; H. Meylan, *La Haute Ecole de Lausanne*, Lausanne 1937, 28-33.

[50] UBB ms. Fr. Gr. II.8, No. 18 ; cf. No. 14-23 ; G. II. 1, fol. 116f. (to J. J. Grynaeus), etc.

[51] See below pp. 99ff.

Antitrinitarians.[52]   What alarmed him in particular were the connections with the court of Henry IV.   Already on 5 January, 1591 he noted that the king had learned about Aubery's potential usefulness in reconciling Calvinists and Catholics [53] and still in October 1596, after the conversion of the king and many of his close adivsors,[54] he warned of some perplexing contacts between these circles and Antoine Lescaille.[55]

Still another medical excursion into theology took place while Aubery studied at Basle.   Once again, and more outspokenly than in the case of Aubery, it was caused by concern for the religious reconciliation and based upon the Erasmian concept of the truly Catholic church of the patristic age.   In the winter of 1572-73 Theodor Zwinger, who was then the university rector, received a visit from a rather eccentric Francophone doctor, Josse de Harchies (Harchius), a native of Mons who practised his profession in Liège and later in Strasbourg and Saarbrücken.[56]   Zwinger not only won the lasting confidence of his visitor, he also assisted him with the business that had brought him—like so many others—to Basle, namely the publication of his books.   They included a pharmacological treatise which Perna could produce without qualms, but also a treatise on religious concord which in all likelihood issued from the same press.[57]   If in this case the printer preferred to withhold his name, at least Basle was indicated as the place of publication.   The topic as such was irreproachable in the Erasmian town, and the author's preface added respectability by characterizing his short essay as a New Year's gift to the Strasbourg city fathers.   He assured them how much a good physician stood in need of philosophy and theology, even though this view was branded as heresy by the papists. He also did not spare his praise for Strasbourg and her famous men.

Harchies brought still a third manuscript to Basle and showed it to Zwinger. It too was printed soon afterwards under the title of *De Eucharistiae mysterio, dignitate et usu*.   The only impression I have seen displays type faces, woodcut initials, and a fleuron which were all used by Perna, although it purports to be the work of an otherwise unknown David Cephalaeus at Worms.[58]   This work was to arouse considerable controversy.   As late as 1580 Beza deemed it worthy of a rejoin-

---

[52] Especially in his letters to J. J. Grynaeus: UBB ms. Ki. Ar. 18*b*, fol. 113-235. At the same time he continued to express his alarm at the writings of another Basle doctor now dead, Thomas Erastus: *ibid*. fol. 155, 175.

[53] *Ibid*. fol. 174: "... ut ad Galliae usque regis aures perlatum esset non deesse insignem quendam philosophum et medicum, qui multa certius ac melius in praecipuis religionis capitibus doceri et aliquam concordiam inter nos et Catholicos conciliari posse irrefragabilibus argumentis demonstret, adeo quidem ut audeat etiam iste, praetextens regii medici nomen, magnifica quaedam apud nonullos iactare.   Sed quid rex ipse ore suo cuidam responderit ista pollicenti, bene novi et confido facile fore adversus ista remedium."

[54] Cf. e.g. Beza's outburst against Jean de Sponde when he revisited Geneva: *ibid*. fol. 218.

[55] *Ibid*. fol. 233: " Lescalius ille cum duobus apostatis insignibus Caÿero et Duperrone multa molitur ea qua solet insania, quae procul dubio in illorum caput redundabunt."

[56] Cf. Jöcher and *Biographie nat. Belgique*; for the text of Harchies' letters to Zwinger see vol. 2 of this study.

[57] **No. 512** and **No. 510**, which shows type faces and initials identical with those used in other impressions by Perna.

[58] **No. 511.** David Cephalaeus is not mentioned in Benzing or in F. W. E. Roth, *Die Buchdruckereien zu Worms* ..., Worms 1892, or by A. Schmidt in *Zentralblatt für Bibliothekswesen* 10 (1893), 222-227.   The recent *Catalogue of Books Printed on the Continent...* *in Cambridge Libraries* lists a copy with Perna's own imprint.

der.[59] Zanchi too condemned Harchies' views on the Eucharist.[60] By contrast, the pro-Lutheran Strasbourg professor and friend of Harchies, Hubert Giphanius, associated it with the controversial *Diallacticon*, now attributed to John Ponet.[61] Harchies certainly did not wish to be a Lutheran any more than a Calvinist. The friendly relations he established at Basle—no doubt upon the recommendation of his Strasbourg friends—with Sulzer's brother-in-law and colleague, U. Koch, were later exposed to severe strain. In the summer of 1576 he sent Zwinger another manuscript, a summary of his views on the Eucharist. It was followed by a short letter in which he invited the Basle professor to go over the text before passing it on to his other friend, the printer Perna. Zwinger reacted cautiously. He must have written back to Harchies, raising objections not only on his own behalf but also in the name of Koch, the theologian. Now Harchies answered with a very long letter full of the spiritualist's fiery sense of commitment. He rejected *in globo* all excisions that Zwinger had suggested to him, and invited Zwinger's theological advisers, both Calvinist and Lutheran, to state their objections in appendices to be published along with his treatise. For good measure he also enclosed a French text on the topic of the Eucharist, hoping that Perna could publish both in time for the next Frankfurt fair. It might have been expected that Zwinger and Perna at this point would shy away from the project, but their respect for their candid old friend —and possibly the steps taken by another friend of his who seemed willing to subsidise the edition—carried the day. At least the Latin text appeared, presumably in the same year.[62] Again the anonymous edition is indistinguishable from other productions by Perna.

Harchies' views have not to my knowledge received much attention so far. They will be examined carefully in the second volume of this study ; here it should merely be mentioned that he seems to have developed them independently while brooding over the church fathers. Yet if he should not be associated too closely with Aubery, it is nevertheless clear that both considered the Calvinist doctrine of justification as the major obstacle in the way of church unity. If Harchies rejected the Calvinist understanding of the Eucharist, he did no more than Bonifacius Amerbach had been doing quietly all his life and Sulzer was still doing at the helm of his officially Zwinglian congregation. In fact, their agreement on this negative point was more obvious than any positive convictions they might have shared.

The very year when Harchies' second book on the Eucharist was published at Basle, Beza and his friends were gnashing their teeth at yet another product of her

---

[59] *De coena Domini adversus Iodoci Harchii Montensis dogmata . . . responsio*, Geneva 1580 ; cf. Geisendorf 350.

[60] G. Zanchi, *Opera*, [Geneva] 1613, 8 [part 2], 135.

[61] UBB ms. Fr. Gr. II.27, No. 110 : letter to T. Zwinger, s.l., 22 December, s.a. : " De Harchio gratiam tibi habeo, qui eum tam humaniter et ipse acceperis et scholae vestrae universae commendaris. Ipse certe cum aliorum tum tuam praecipue cum se liberalitatem saepe praedicat. De libro tibi assentior eum valde modeste in hoc negotio versari, si quorundam paene furiosas scriptiones cum eo comparemus. Editus est olim in hac urbe liber hoc indice : *Diallacticon*, viri cuiusdam eruditi de coena Domini ec., non expresso tamen autoris et typographi nomine. Quem librum si videris, eandem fere sententiam reperies. Confirmat tamen Harchius eum librum se antea nunquam vidisse." For the *Diallacticon* cf. *BMC* 144.540 ; Giphanius probably refers to the French transl. of the *Diallacticon* by Etienne de Malescot, 1566.

[62] **No. 513.** Another manuscript " *De confessione* " was sent to Basle according to Harchies' last letter to Zwinger. UBB ms. Fr. Gr. II. 24, No. 15, finally, contains a short text by Harchies : " Descriptio coenae Dominicae catholica."

presses.   Giovanni Antonio Fenotti's *Alexipharmacum* [63] did not meddle with theological issues, but its provocative nature was, nonetheless, perfectly clear.   On what seemed purely medical grounds it attacked the authoritarian character of the Genevan regime, and it did so with a liberal dose of personal invective.   Born in Cremona and subsequently a member of the Italian community at Lyons, Fenotti had settled at Geneva in 1570.   Before long he quarrelled with a highly respected fellow doctor, Joseph Du Chesne, who advocated iatrochemical practices without being necessarily a " Paracelsist " in the strict sense of Fenotti's charges.   He was close to Beza and even closer to François Hotman, that fervent amateur alchemist. When Fenotti was forced to leave Geneva, the Basle printing industry made itself the instrument of his revenge.   Fenotti moved to Basle and there found a printer for his manuscript.   The character of his attacks upon the Genevans is perhaps best illustrated in a letter appended to the *Alexipharmacum*.   It was addressed to Du Chesne and allegedly written by one Magister Antitus de Cressonieres, who proves himself a worthy medical variation of those ' Obscure Men ' who on the eve of the Reformation had provided all Germany with a good laugh at the expense of her scholastic theologians.

Geneva's reaction was predictable.   Bonaventura Vulcanius, who had recently moved from Geneva to Basle, had a hard time explaining to Beza the presence of some epigrams of his in Fenotti's volume,[64] even though Beza's name, unlike Hotman's, had not been mentioned openly.   It is quite obvious that not only the opponents of Genevan Calvinism but also some Basle professors of medicine watched Fenotti's performance gloatingly from the wings.   Six years later Fenotti wrote a friendly letter to the Basle *antistes*, J. J. Grynaeus.   It spoke of past dangers—presumably incurred during a visit to his Italian homeland—and added greetings to such " *fideles medicos et amicos* " as Theodor Zwinger, the addressee's kinsman Simon Grynaeus and Thomas Erastus, who had already received praise in the opening pages of the *Alexipharmacum*.[65]

The salute to Erastus is especially relevant, for this Swiss physician found fault with Geneva in matters far more crucial than Fenotti's dislike of alchemy, which he shared.   He opposed nothing less than the basic ecclesio-political concept of Calvin and Beza.   As a prelude to discussing his presence in Basle, we must mention an intriguing entry in the university roll for 1576-77.   No one so far seems to have paid attention to one Claudius Villerius whom the roll identifies vaguely as a *Gallus*. He arrived in the company of two noble students, sons of Jean de La Fin who served Condé as councillor and officer.   Villerius, the preceptor of the two young men, used a name remarkably similar to the one with which Jean Morély, Sieur de Villiers, had earlier signed some of his letters : Claudius Villierius.[66]   Since the publication

<hr>

[63] *Alexipharmacum sive antidotus apologetica ad virulentias Iosephi cuiusdam Quercetani Armeniaci evomitas in libellum Iacobi Auberti de ortu et causis metallorum contra chymistas* ..., Basle s.a. (**No. 436**).   Jacques Aubert too was compelled to leave Geneva. Although a book of his was printed here in 1579, I could not trace any personal links between him and Basle.   For Du Chesne cf. below p. 71.   The *Alexipharmacum* contained a preface by the Lyons physician J. A. Sarasin.

[64] *Correspondance de B. Vulcanius* 87ff., 191ff. and passim.

[65] UBB ms. G.II.4, No. 448, from Chiavenna, 15 July, 1582.   Fenotti also urged that his " Disputatio cum Jesuitis " be published, apparently without success.   For Simon (II) Grynaeus see *Matrikel* 2.72.

[66] *Matrikel* 2.241 with a reference to the trio's presence at Zurich in 1574 ; Kingdon, *Geneva and the Consolidation* 43 and passim for the following ; for Morély also Naef, *Conjuration d'Amboise* 437ff. and passim.

of his *Traicté de la discipline et police chrestienne* (Lyons, 1562) Morély had been widely branded by Calvinist church leaders from within the ranks of the movement ; somewhat mistakenly so, since his pleas for democratic procedure in dealing with cases of heresy and breaches of discipline, in particular for a greater voice for local congregations in such matters, were hardly meant to launch a frontal attack on the Calvinist hierarchy. The book was immediately condemned by the ministry, but Morély found protection in high quarters of the Huguenot nobility and even acted for some time as tutor of the future Henry IV. For a decade his views caused a noticeable current in the life of the French church and only the tragedy of Saint Bartholomew proved sufficiently menacing to restore unity. While Ramus, Morély's most eloquent supporter at the time, was killed in the massacre, Morély himself dropped out of sight and nothing certain is known about his remaining years.[67] That he should have turned up in Zurich and Basle as the tutor of two noble youths is quite conceivable in view of his professional qualifications as well as the friendly response that Ramus had received in these places.[68]

Whatever the identity of Claudius Villerius, there can be no doubt as to the subsequent presence at Basle of Thomas Erastus. When he returned to Basle in 1580 he had won an international reputation for his attacks upon the consistory, as set up in Geneva and elsewhere. The similarity between his views and those of Morély was quite noticeable, even though Erastus sought to limit the rights of the presbytery in favour of secular governments, rather than of the congregation as did Morély.[69] In Heidelberg Erastus had won the friendship of an Italian colleague, Simone Simoni of Lucca, who was occasionally collaborating with the Basle printer Pietro Perna. Earlier, however, he had gone through a short term of medical teaching at Geneva's academy. When this ended in an atmosphere of mutual disappointment Simoni departed, forever resentful of Beza's tyranny, as he saw it, and eager to lend his prestige and his eloquence to promulgating the views of Erastus.[70] Dogma, however, had no part in this conflict. The firm opposition of both friends to Lutherans and Ubiquitarians in the Tübingen controversy on the Eucharist should have gratified Beza. Erastus, at any rate, died a strict Zwinglian. Both men were also highly respected doctors and served at times as personal physicians to princes. Erastus was, moreover, sternly critical of contemporary Paracelsians, and his medical works, published at Basle, contained attacks that were

---

[67] Kingdon, *Geneva and the Consolidation* 130f.

[68] Two letters make the mystery about Villerius even more intriguing : UBB ms. Fr. Gr. II.26, No. 506, in which the writer reports to [Theodor] Zwinger on 27 November, 1576 : " Gasparum salvum et incolumem Lausannae reliqui in hospitio Leonis, ita sane ut eodem die quo discessurus eram cum meis commigraturus esset ad quendam hospitem a D. Auberio designatum... T [uus] A. Villerius." Indeed, was it Morély who took on his departure from Basle Zwinger's young relative with him to Lausanne and there made the acquaintance of Claude Aubery, the Castellionist? Aubery, in turn, reported to Zwinger on 30 November, [1576] : that he had found accomodation for " Gasparum Cocum affinem tuum." He added : " Nobilum illorum Gallorum praeceptor comitem se praestitit adolescenti et commodum et fidelem. Is me rogavit, tibi significarem, ut vel hoc officio testatam habeas suam observantiam " : UBB ms. Fr. Gr. II.4, No. 9.

[69] Kingdon, *Geneva and the Consolidation* 123f. For Erastus see *NDB* and R. Wesel-Roth, *Thomas Erastus*, Lahr 1954.

[70] For Simoni see : *ibid.* 66 ; Bietenholz, *Ital. Humanismus* 134f., 151f. ; Cantimori, *Ital. Haeretiker* 256 ; Geisendorf 262f., 381ff. ; C. Bourgeaud, *Histoire de l'Université de Genève*, Geneva 1900ff., 1.94ff. ; L. Gautier, *La Médecine à Genève*, *Mém. et Doc. Société d'Hist. et d'Archéol. de Genève* 30 (1906), 30ff. C. Cantù, *Gli eretici d'Italia*, Turin 1865, 2.473.

at the same time more fundamental and less personal than those of Fenotti. Simoni, finally, found himself again in opposition to official Geneva when he favoured the Ramist method.

Erastus died at Basle in 1583. Even in the year of his death he presided over the disputation of a medical student, who came from Beaumont-de-Lomagne (Tarn-et-Garonne). From the printed theses one would not conclude that the candidate, Robert Augier, held exceptional views, but that he should have chosen to discuss physiological theses on the faculties of the soul shows at least that his mind was not absorbed by clinical problems.[71] In the following year Augier received his M.D. and before the year was out he was established as the town physician at Payerne in the Vaud. There he circulated a verse paraphrase of the Apocalypse which smacked suspiciously of Joachite millennarianism and of Anabaptism. Beza rushed to the support of the local minister and discovered in the Payerne doctor yet another Antitrinitarian. In 1585 Augier lost his position. He later turned up in England. So also did another medical graduate of Basle, the Genevan Théodore Colladon, whose doctoral theses were published in 1590, the year all Basle was talking about Antoine Lescaille, the friend and disciple of Claude Aubery. And it was to none other than Aubery, his " *praeceptor colendissimus* " that Colladon dedicated his *Theses medicae de tussi*.[72] Meanwhile the battle against Paracelsians was resumed by a native of Champagne, the Protestant physician Georges Bertin. In 1586 the newly erupted war had driven him first to Montbéliard where he met and liked the younger Jean Bauhin, and subsequently to Basle where he published two medical works. He seems to have died a few years later at Metz.[73]

Among the Basle professors of medicine none may have better known this unconventional group of physicians than did Theodor Zwinger. Who, after all, was this Zwinger, the teacher of Claude Aubery, the confidant of Harchies, the friend of Castellio, Postel and of Fenotti ? He was also the teacher of Erastus who still feared and venerated him at the climax of his own career and who asked him to supply information for his writings against Paracelsus.[74] Yet the same Zwinger also participated in the alchemist adventures of a Jean de Sponde.[75] A full-scale study of the Basle professor of medicine would be necessary to answer the question. Here we must be content to accept him as a typical representative of post-Erasmian Basle : friendly to refugees and flattered by the esteem of noted scholars abroad, deliberate—perhaps even courageous—in his non-committal attitude to the ideological and professional controversies of the day, but for the same reason failing to make a historical impact. In some ways he seems to prefigure the comfortable bourgeoisie of a subsequent age. His rich library, his personal ease and culture, even his sense of humour at the expense of the stern Genevans, are well illustrated in a short note which the musician Pascal de Lestocart wrote to him on one of his

---

[71] No. **2006** ; *Matrikel* 2.315 ; H. Meylan, *Silhouettes du 16e siècle*, Lausanne 1943, 163-188 ; Droz, *Etudiants français*.

[72] No. **2045** ; *Matrikel* 2.382. A number of letters to Jacob Zwinger are in UBB ms. Fr. Gr. II. 4, No. 33-34 ; II.8, No. 409-416, etc.

[73] No. **150** and **151** : *Medicina libris viginti methodice absoluta in qua Graecorum et Araborum consensus, legitima veteris medicinae adversus Paracelsistas defensio, vera animadversionum Argenterii in Hippocratem et Galenum confutatio ... continentur;* the ref. to Jean Bauhin in the preface ; cf. Jöcher and *Matrikel* 2.349. A few months later a Jean Bertin was matriculated : *Matrikel* 2.352 and No. **2026**.

[74] UBB ms. Fr. Gr. II.4, No. 91-95.

[75] See below p. 83f.

70

visits to Basle from Geneva. Lestocart apologized because a private concert, it would seem at Zwinger's house, had to be postponed, and asked for music from his library which he wished to copy "*pour faire danser Monsieur de Beze quant nous serons a Geneve.*" [76]

The list of Zwinger's Francophone friends and colleagues is not exhausted by the above references to those who shared, if little else, a critical attitude towards Geneva. At least the name of Guillaume Arragos should be added to it. This Protestant doctor, who could claim the title of personal physician to three kings of France and one German emperor, lived from 1570, with interruptions, in Basle, partly in the house of Theodor Zwinger's son Jacob. Like his host, he was obsessed with alchemy, and when he died in 1610, almost a centenarian, he left his library and his instruments to Jacob. [77] His extensive correspondence still awaits scrutiny. [78] It does not seem that he was directly involved in theological confrontations, but the fact that he was trusted by Antoine Lescaille, and greeted by Claude Aubery and the Italo-Hungarian A. Dudith, might cast some slight doubt on his Calvinist loyalties. [79]

Neither the Zwingers personally, nor the medical faculty or the town at large should, however, be seen as parties to an anti-Calvinist plot. As proof of this other physicians may be cited, above all perhaps that Joseph Du Chesne, Sieur de la Violette, so unkindly attacked in Fenotti's *Alexipharmacum.* In 1573 he received a doctoral degree in a private ceremony at the home of Theodor Zwinger. Apart from advocating alchemy, he gained a reputation as an author, a royal physician, and a member of Geneva's Council of Two hundred. He later wrote to Jacob Zwinger, including him in the friendship with his father, and even commented with dignity on the publication of the *Alexipharmacum.* [80] Guillaume Baucinet, a Basle M. D. in 1584, returned subsequently to his native Orléans and he also supported Du Chesne and other defenders of alchemy in a new feud with the medical faculty of Paris. He too corresponded occasionally with Jacob Zwinger. [81] Already in 1535 Eustache du Quesnoy had received at Basle a medical doctorate. He later became a personal friend of Calvin, whom he informed from Frankfurt about the bustle of local Castellionists. He was, nonetheless a sincere advocate of

---

[76] UBB ms. Fr.Gr. II.5*a*, No. 89, dated: " De Basle en vostre pouvre [!] maison," 22 June 1583. For Lestocart see E. Droz, Jean de Sponde et Pascal de L'Estocart, *BHR* 13 (1951), 312-326.

[77] *Matrikel* 2.248 ; Staehelin, *Polanus* 98.

[78] UBB possesses the mss. of more than fifty letters to both Zwingers and many others.

[79] Cf. below p. 103. UBB ms. Fr. Gr. II.4, No. 114f., Dudith to J.J. Grynaeus from Bratislava, 26 February, 1581 and 26 May, 1583, expressing profound admiration for Erastus and adding sincere greetings to Arragos. *Ibid.* No. 2 and 7, Aubery to T. Zwinger, [1576].

[80] *Matrikel* 2.218 ; Droz, *Etudiants français* ; *Correspondance de B. Vulcanius* 88f. The two letters to T. and J. Zwinger, s.l., s.a. : UBB ms. Fr. Gr. II.28², No. 273 and II.26, No. 3. Cf. also Jacques Gohory's Paracelsian compendium (**No. 476**) which Perna reprinted in 1568 as a result of his endeavour to publish all *Paracelsica* he could get. In this case, however, a difficulty arose. The author's attitude towards Paracelsianism was somewhat ambiguous, and he was downright critical of the Basle Paracelsists A. von Bodenstein and G. Dorn. The least that could be done was to add in the appendix a new introduction and another text in defense of the two. Erasmus' letter to Paracelsus opens the volume.

[81] *Matrikel* 2.261 ; *BNC* ; L. Thorndike, *A History of Magic and Experimental Science*, London-New York 1923ff., 6.248. UBB ms. Fr. Gr. II.23¹, No. 52-53.

reconciliation and had friendly contacts with Melanchthon and, especially, Languet.[82] Like Du Quesnoy, other medical students at Basle published some of their works in the local presses, for instance Blaise Hollier,[83] who was later in Geneva, and Pascal Le Coq.[84] Jacques Pasquier (Pascharius), a native of Lorraine, was another student and friend of Theodor Zwinger, who had already composed and published verse while studying at Basle at the same time as Claude Aubery. His graduation ceremony was graced by the presence of Condé and his entourage of high nobility, and commemorated in a broadsheet by a fellow student.[85] In 1589 Zwinger again published five epigrams by him, styling him a " *regius medicus.*" [86] In fact he had written to Zwinger in 1580, reporting his return to France and the " *aulica incommoda commoda et invita vita.*" At the same occasion he sent greetings to the famous alchemist Leonhard Thurneisser and to François Hotman who were then living at Basle.[87] Jean Albosius (d'Ailleboust), finally was already famous when his name appeared in the university roll for 1587-88. He maintained friendly contacts with Gaspard Bauhin and the Basle printers. He also attended the ailing François Hotman.[88]

Once the French church was properly organized, the essential respectability of town and university in Calvinist eyes was emphasized by the presence of such students as Beza's nephew,[89] a son of Simon Goulart,[90] and many others who prepared themselves for the ministry among French-speaking congregations. Illustrious travellers from France continued to include in their journeys at least a passing visit to Basle ; so did Michel de Montaigne,[91] Jacques-Auguste de Thou [92] and a natural

---

[82] *Matrikel* 2.9 ; H. Meylan in *Revue historique vaudoise* 56 (1948), 219-225 ; *Calvini opera* 16.214 ; 17. 218f., 341f., 366f. ; 18.288ff. ; 19.257ff. ; cf. Buisson, *Castellion* 2.121f.

[83] *Matrikel* 2.76 ; Droz, *Etudiants français* ; **No. 538ff.** Letters to Bonifacius Amerbach and Theodor Zwinger show how Hollier was helped by them with the publication of his books. He also appealed to Amerbach for money from the Erasmus fund : UBB ms. G.II.19, fol. 64-65 ; Fr. Gr. II.4, No. 133.

[84] *Matrikel* 2.363 ; Droz, *Etudiants français* ; **No. 682**, which offers short information on the medical men of all times, listed in alphabetical order. It also expresses his admiration for Theodor Zwinger. Le Coq wrote a number of lively and entertaining letters to Jacob Zwinger and other Bâlois : UBB ms. Fr. Gr. I.12, fol. 156-169, etc.

[85] **No. 2091.** Cf. *Matrikel* 2.223 and Droz, *Etudiants français*.

[86] N. Reusner, *Icones sive imagines vivae*, Basle 1589, appendix. Following the epigrams, the author's name is given as " Ioan. Pascharius ", but I think that Droz has correctly identified him with Jacques Pasquier. For his contacts in printing circles see below p. 86.

[87] UBB ms. Fr. Gr. II.19², fol. 278, dated Sammaria [?], 30 March, 1589. The preceding letter, *ibid.*, was written by Pasquier to Zwinger from Freiburg, 5 May, 1575.

[88] *Matrikel* 2.354 ; Droz, *Etudiants français* ; **No. 908.** There are some commendatory verses by Albosius in two of G. Bauhin's publications : **No. 99** and **100.** Cf. *Hotomanorum epistolae* 247f.

[89] *Matrikel* 2.375 (1589-1590). In 1581-1582 one notices two sons of the Genevan pastor Antoine de Chandieu : *Matrikel* 2.306.

[90] *Matrikel* 2.499 (1600-1601).

[91] See : Journal d'un voyage en Italie, *Œuvres complètes*, Bibliothèque de la Pléiade, Paris 1962, 1108, 1128f. Montaigne and his party arrived on 29 September, 1580 and left on 1 October. After describing the botanical and anatomical collection of Felix Platter, Montaigne continues : " Nous y vismes force gens de sçavoir, come Grineus, et celui qui a faict le *Theatrum* [Theodor Zwinger], et ledit medecin (Platerus), et François Hottoman. Ces deux derniers vindrent soupper avec messieurs, lendemein qu'ils furent arrivés. M. de Montaigne jugea qu'ils estoint mal d'accord de leur religion par les responses qu'il

son of Théodore Agrippa d'Aubigné, the famous Nathan.[93]   Numerous other noteworthy or curious visitors would deserve mentioning,[94] but a limit must be set to
the listing of mere individuals.   Those who can be placed in a specific context of
historical significance, at least in the framework of this study, will be found in
subsequent chapters.

---

en receut : les uns se disans zingluiens, les autres calvinistes, et les autres martinistes ;
et si fut averty que plusieurs couvoint encore la religion romene dans le cœur..."

[92] Cf. below p. 211f.

[93] *Matrikel* 3.282f. (1625-1626).

[94] See Droz, *Etudiants français*, for instance s.v. Abel Béranger, Jacques Bongars,
Adam Falaiseau, Pierre Pineton de Chambrun.   Bongars borrowed books from Jacob
Zwinger, while visiting Basle, and continued to correspond with him : UBB ms. Fr. Gr. I.
15, No. 43f., etc.

CHAPTER TWO

THE FRANCOPHONES
IN THE PRINTING INDUSTRY

"*A Basle, de l'imprimerie de François Forest*" runs a typical fictitious imprint. From the third decade of the sixteenth century such *fausses adresses* were used to make the public and the authorities believe that a certain book had been produced in Basle rather than by the true publisher elsewhere.[1] Since they were considered plausible the French-speaking public evidently knew not only that French books were being published in Basle, but also that some of the local presses were operated by Francophones. It was natural that these immigrant printers should maintain close ties with many transients and members of the French colony in Basle, and that a comparatively large number of their productions should be written by French authors, perhaps even published in the French language. If measured against the total output of all Basle presses, their share may be no more than about ten per cent, but their activities gain a special relevance within the context of this study.

Although Wattenschnee and the other merchants associated with the *Ecus de Bâle* had some books printed for them in Basle, they never ran their own press. The first Frenchman to do so, Jacobus Parcus, emerges from the few available scraps of information as a highly intriguing character. Born apparently in 1504, Parcus worked in Lyons prior to moving to Basle. He called himself a *Celta* and French was his native tongue,[2] but one wonders whether he may not have descended from one of the German immigrants to Lyons who were especially numerous in the printing industry. A Jacques Quadier surnamed Estauge is recorded in 1546 as a coeval friend of the older Jean de Tournes. In all likelihood this man was identical with the Basle printer Parcus, for it is to the latter that Gilbert Cousin referred, calling him "Jaques Quadier."[3] His activities in Basle and Lyons seem to have overlapped, since Jacques Quadier (or Cadier) was taxed at Lyons in 1558 and published

---

[1] No. 4001ff.

[2] But he seems to have been fluent in German as well. Of **No. 788** he states in his preface to "Monsieur le Protonotoire Iehan Perain": "*L'Instrument* ... que i 'ay mis en nostre langue celtique" and further: "... ses *Canons* en Latin lesquels translatasme en allemant y a un an et ores en nostre vulgaire comme tu voys." In fact Parcus published in 1553 an *Auszlegung desz Instruments*, but the name of the translator is given as Marcus Wallpach.

[3] In a letter to T. Zwinger, s.d.: UBB ms. Fr. Gr. II.27, No. 22. A similar ref. is noted in Wackernagel, "Aktensammlung."

books in 1546, 1556, and 1561.[4] Nevertheless, in 1537 Jacobus Parcus became a citizen of Basle where, a year later, his son of the same name was christened.[5] In Basle he used his Latin name, Parcus, in the imprint of his Latin productions. For his publications in German he preferred the name Kündig, a dialectal translation of Parcus, and in his French ones the name Estauge. As he was apparently dividing his attention between his modest operations in Basle and Lyons, it is not surprising that he had many friends halfway between in the Franche-Comté. Among them was the inevitable Gilbert Cousin, and others who shared Cousin's taste for bad verse and the exposure of monastic vice. Not overawed by their poetic talent, Parcus published his own French verse together with that of his friends.[6]

For the most part he printed to the orders of Oporinus and other large scale publishers. However, when he produced smaller books and pamphlets at his own expense, he proudly used a couple of printer's marks, one exhibiting astrological symbolism, the other surrounded by Greek and Hebrew inscriptions.[7] For the Italian emigrant Francesco Stancaro, who was perhaps himself of Jewish stock, Parcus published some small treatises of Hebrew grammar, using Hebrew type where necessary.[8] In another vein he twice reprinted the ninth century poem in praise of baldness by Hucbaldus of Saint-Amand. The earlier edition was preceded by a bizarre preface, attesting to the printer's humanistic education no less than to his sense of humour and—conceivably—his own baldness.[9] There is no clear evidence of his religious leanings except that his devotion to Monsieur de Falais and Charles Du Moulin would not endear him to Calvin and his friends [10] while his frequent

---

[4] A. Cartier, Les *Dixains Catholiques* et Jaques Estauge imprimeur à Bâle, *Mélanges offerts à M. Emile Picot*, Paris 1913, 1.307-313 ; Baudrier 1.368 ; cf. 1.145 ; 11.452f.

[5] At Saint Martin's, 13 August 1538 (Heitz-Bernoulli xxxi). He probably is the "filius eiusdem nominis" mentioned by Jacobus senior in 1557. Nothing, however, suggests that he succeeded to his father's business. Rather the press was operated by his widow in conjunction with her second husband, Balthasar Franck, from 1564 to 1569. In the latter year Franck's estate was sold by the auctioneer. It is therefore most unlikely that **No. 4017** should be the only known impression by Jacobus Parcus junior. The name Parcus-Kündig was not uncommon ; in particular more than one *Johannes* Parcus is known from the sources. One, at least, must be a relative of our Jacobus Parcus : "Hansen Estange, zu teutsch Kündigs, von Lyon, des Truckers" (Staatsarchiv Basel-Stadt, Abscheidbuch, 1526-1542, 183 recto. Another Johannes Parcus, son of Johannes and later a well known minister in the Basle territory, does not seem to be a relation of the printer (cf. *Matrikel* 2.187 and K. Gauss, *Basilea Reformata*, Basle 1930, 120). A kinsman of this Johannes was presumably the Jacobus Parcus (Hans Jacob Kündig) mentioned in *Matrikel* 2.193.

[6] See especially **No. 619** : F. Julyot, *Elegies de la belle fille* (1557), with various epigrams and other verses by Parcus-Estauge himself, one of them indicating that he printed Julyot's collection, also a woodcut used by Parcus in some of his other Basle productions.

[7] Reproduced in Heitz-Bernoulli 98f.

[8] Bietenholz, *Ital. Humanismus* 28f., 56.

[9] **No. 575** : dedicated to a G. Simon Sylvius [Dubois] whom Parcus calls his συμπατῆρα. Part of it runs : "Ecloga ista solis viris, imo igneis, conducit, non spadonibus, mulieribus, aut animalibus, si demas struthiocamelum, corvum aquaticum et equum. Imo Calvus Orator laminis quibusdam plumbeis Venerea cohibebat, neque ob id Venus calva dicta, sed Gallorum impetus Romanas depilavit. Κύτος calva est, unde calvaria. Item calveta loca pro glabris dicuntur, calveta vinea pro rara."

[10] Cf. *Calvini opera* 12.553 : Apparently Parcus tried to mediate in the dispute between Monsieur de Falais and Valérand Poullain. The *Dixains catholiques* (**No. 4019**) contain

collaboration with Oporinus aroused the suspicion of Beza.[11] Among his authors
were the Ubiquitarian Brenz, Castellio's friend Martin Borrhaus and the abstruse
spiritualist and prophet Giovanni Leone Nardi.[12] Parcus may have owed it to the
modest scale of his operations if, unlike Oporinus, he remained untroubled by
censorship and criticism. In 1557 he worthily celebrated his twenty years of Basle
citizenship by buying himself a copy of one of the earliest incunables printed in the
city. On the title page he recorded the details of the purchase, showing his pride
in the beginning of the art in which he himself had reached a respectable position.[13]
Yet a few months later Parcus and his son were temporarily jailed together with
the Castellionist Léger Grymoult.[14]

The success of Parcus was modest enough if compared with that of Thomas
Guarinus (Guérin, 1529-1592). He may have left Tournai, his native city, for
religious reasons. In 1553 he settled in Lyons, and closely collaborating with some
members of the local colony of Italian Protestants,[15] soon made a name for himself
in the book business. His contacts with the Italian Reformation continued after
he had moved to Basle.[16] During a transitional period he seems to have operated
his business from both Lyons and Basle.[17] He became a Basle citizen in 1557 and
married the daughter of the printer Michael Isengrin, who died in the same year.
Guarinus first entered his mother-in-law's business, but from 1561 he printed under
his own name.

Year after year he produced beautiful and important editions, many of them in
folio. In the volume of works printed in the French language and in the number
of his contacts with French authors, no other Basle publisher could compare with
him. Apart from his original editions he is remarkable for his courage and dis-
crimination in undertaking unauthorized reprints at a time when most Basle printers
were content to publish such copy as was offered them. A good example is his

---

predominantly anonymous verse which cannot be attributed to Parcus. However, the
opening *dixain* addressed to Madame de Falais seems to be his. It also seems that this
lady had died four years earlier and that **No. 4019** therefore is the reprint of an earlier
edition. In **No. 619** there are verses by Parcus-Estauge addressed to Du Moulin, whose
Commentarius contra parva datas he reprinted in 1552 (**No. 401**).

[11] *Correspondance de Bèze* 1.133f.

[12] Cf. UBB, Druckerkatalog, and *BMC ST Germany* s.v. Kuendig. For Nardi cf.
Bietenholz, *Ital. Humanismus* 34f. and Cantimori, *Ital. Haeretiker* 157ff.

[13] UBB, Inc. 601 (Justinian, *Institutiones imperiales*). Parcus adds to the title:
" impressae 1478 in Augusto, absolutae per Michaelem Wenssler tunc habitans [sic] in
aedibus dictae [sic] zum Lupfft " and states : " Emptae hodie sabbati 18. Septembris 1557
per me, qui Jacobus Parcus Celta, legitimus et senex vocor : tam propter filium eiusdem
nominis quam ob id, quod nunc ultra 53. annum vixi. Qui vendidit mihi est Georgius
Erny Basiliensis et librorum compactor." Four more pages are covered with his ms.
notes about Roman history from the Trojan war to the end of the Western Empire.

[14] See below p. 113f.

[15] Heitz-Bernoulli xxxvif. ; Baudrier 5.24 ; 10.362ff.

[16] Bietenholz, *Ital. Humanismus* 20.

[17] In 1553 Guarinus traded from Lyons with Basle as well as Montpellier ; in 1557,
after his move to Basle he still owned a book depository in Lyons : *Thomas und Felix
Platter*, ed. H. Boos, Leipzig 1878, 200, 324. In 1554 the French ambassador, Basse-
fontaine, complained to Ferdinand, the Roman King, on behalf of Guarinus and other
merchants who had been robbed in Alsace : *Correspondance de Bèze* 1.126. There is an
ed. of Beza's *Poemata* (**No. 161**), c. 1580, which Guarinus apparently printed in Basle,
but sold at Lyons.

beautiful re-edition of Amyot's translation of Plutarch in 1574. His interest in Plutarch, as well as the resources of his typography, are further demonstrated by his huge Latin editions of that author. The first one (1570) was published in conjunction with Jacques Dupuys, a *libraire juré* of Paris. Dupuys secured a royal privilege for Guarinus' production, while the Bâlois obtained another from the emperor.[18] He also produced a number of Bibles in all sizes. In 1569 he issued his famous Spanish Bible, but preferred to substitute the name of one of his employees for his own.[19] Five years earlier he copied from a Lyons edition the Latin Bible as arranged by Vatable and Pagnini.[20] The artist Tobias Stimmer designed for him a series of Biblical illustrations which were first issued separately in conjunction with Jobin, but shortly afterwards appeared in Guarinus' beautiful Vulgate of 1578.[21] On other occasions he launched a cheap reprint of Erasmus' New Testament (1570) and even a Hebrew Pentateuch (1583). Only Castellio's Bibles—indeed any texts by the controversial humanist—were conspicuously missing in his production. His dedication to a brand of humanism acceptable both in Geneva and Paris was further emphasized by the employment which he offered to Bonaventura Vulcanius [22] and by the verses the younger Karel Utenhove wrote in his praise.[23] Regrettably, no private letters of Guarinus seem to have survived, so that his personality remains largely unknown. He must, however, have been a forceful man, gifted with sure business instinct and outstanding esthetic taste. He insisted on neat work and carefully balanced his fine type faces with the right number of initials and other unobtrusive decoration. He showed boldness in freely copying the work of others, but he preferred conventional topics that were known to sell well. On the whole he produced the most beautiful books to emerge from Basle in the second half of the sixteenth century.

In 1579 Thomas Guarinus presented to the Saffron guild two applicants who had just become citizens of Basle and planned to set up their own press. It was fitting that they should be introduced by a former resident of Lyons, for both were born near the Rhone. The more important of the two, Jacques Foillet (1554-1619), had come to Lyons from the neighbourhood. He may have learned his trade there ; he was a journeyman printer in 1576, but in the same year he went to Geneva.[24] In 1578 Foillet was in Basle working for Pietro Perna. He now met his future partner, Jean Exertier, who was born near Geneva and was then employed in the Basle press of Leonhard Osten. In 1580 Foillet and Exertier bought a house together, no doubt the domicile of their jointly operated press.

Foillet must have been close to Perna, his former employer. From Perna, who died in 1582, or from his estate, he may have bought some of his typographical equipment. Most of his productions seem indistinguishable from those of Conrad Waldkirch who took over Perna's press. Like Waldkirch he also continued to publish controversial authors who had figured prominently in Perna's list, such as

---

[18] See above p. 52, 25.

[19] On Cassiodor de Reina and his Bible cf. *Matrikel* 2.171f. ; Steinmann 82ff.

[20] Cf. **No. 1023** with the Bibles produced by Jean de Tournes at Lyons, e.g. in 1556 and 1569.

[21] Heitz-Bernoulli xxxvii.

[22] *Correspondance de B. Vulcanius* 235, 249, 309, 333 and passim.

[23] In **No. 200**.

[24] L. Nardin, *Jacques Foillet*, Paris 1906, 12ff. and passim for what follows. For Exertier see also Bremme 160.

Machiavelli and Paracelsus. Like Waldkirch he worked for the prominent and idealistic, if elusive, Strasbourg publisher Lazarus Zetzner. His friendship with the unorthodox Jean Bauhin junior fits well into the pattern of Perna's radical heritage. Frédéric Castellio, the undistinguished son of the great Sébastien, translated for Foillet La Primaudaye's *Academy* into German.[25]

Neither Foillet nor Exertier remained in Basle for very long. Foillet lived from 1586 until his death in 1619 mostly in Montbéliard where he was the official printer to the court. Exertier returned to Basle in 1592 to direct a press which probably belonged to Foillet and him jointly. It produced some books, but mostly dissertations under the imprint of one or the other partner.[26] In 1599 Foillet acquired another house in Basle and kept it until 1608, the year after the death of Exertier. Supported even by his duke, he stubbornly battled the Basle authorities who were trying to cancel his citizenship, which entailed exemption from customs dues. He seems to have prevailed, for in 1598 his son was enrolled in the university as a *civis Basiliensis*, while the father proudly used the same epithet in the imprint of some of his books as late as 1613.[27]

Foillet's personality remains in the dark. It is clear, however, that he lent his efforts to a fascinating intellectual tradition strongly reminiscent of Pietro Perna, Lazarus Zetzner, and their friends, a tradition proudly displaying such political writers as Bodin, Francesco Patrizi, Jean de Serres and, above all, Machiavelli. Foillet also printed works by such reformers as Luther and Osiander, but the respect paid to the Lutheran orthodoxy of Württemberg and Montbéliard was handsomely balanced by his taste for the works of Rabelais, the occultist G. B. della Porta and Paracelsus.

Even though our scanty sources yield but sketchy profiles there is reason to stress the independent-mindedness of Parcus, Guarinus, and Foillet. None of them could match the originality and determination of their fellow immigrant Pietro Perna, but together with Perna they managed to generate a fresh breeze amid the increasingly torpid atmosphere which filled the workshops of their local competitors especially after the death of Oporinus.

Foillet had come and gone but to the end of his life remained involved with the Basle printing industry. The passing visits of Jean Aubry and Claude de Marne, by contrast, produced no comparable after-effects. They were the sons-in-law and heirs of André Wechel, the son of Conrad Resch's successor at the Paris *Ecu de Bâle*. André Wechel transferred his press to Frankfurt in the year after the massacre of Saint Batholomew and there died in 1581. Following a conflict with the Lutheran ministers of Frankfurt his successors strengthened the firm's earlier contacts with Basle.[28] Formerly they commissioned a few books to be printed for them in the

---

[25] Montbéliard 1594 ; L. Nardin, *op. cit.* 195.

[26] Their press in Basle worked until 1607, probably with interruptions ; cf. UBB, Druckerkatalog and the bibliography collected by L. Nardin, *op. vit.* 185ff.

[27] *Ibid.* 38ff., 124f. ; *Matrikel* 2.460.

[28] Cf. Benzing 42, 120, 176f. ; *ADB* s.v. Wechel ; Wackernagel, " Aktensammlung ". In keeping with their upright Calvinism the heirs of Wechel maintained contacts with the Basle theologian A. Polanus of Polansdorf whose most comprehensive work they published at Hanau in 1609 : cf. Staehelin, *Polanus* 21, 102 and UBB ms. Fr. Gr. II. 12, No. 9 (S. Goulart to A. Polanus, Saint-Gervais, 31 August, 1600) : " De compatris tui Dn. Aubrii negotiis egi cum Choueto nostro et, multis ultro citroque habitis sermonibus, tandem obtinui, ut cum ipsis conquerentibus, nempe DD. Aubrio et Marnaeo, Francofurti coram agat, donec amicorum opera, si fieri potest (ut spero) tota lis componatur."

local presses, [29] but in 1596 they bought a house and became members of the Saffron guild. Aubry, who settled in the city, knew how to impress the Bâlois. He boasted the possession of the prestigious *Grecs du Roi*, the Greek type originally used by Robert Estienne, the king's printer in Greek.[30] The Basle plant however remained a weak offshoot of the flourishing Frankfurt business. At the most a handful of books were issued at Basle with the imprint of Aubry and de Marne.[31] In 1599 they sold their house. Claude de Marne's son Jean matriculated at Basle in 1600,[32] but by 1601 the partners had founded a more promising branch amid the Walloon refugee community at Hanau. The Lyons book merchant and publisher Jean Mareschal, who preferred elusive international operations, and his Genevan colleagues Jacques Derbilly, Nicolas Barbier, and Thomas Courteau, may frequently have passed through Basle.[33] If the occasion arose, they had one of their publications printed by a local press. Such arrangements were no doubt much more frequent than the imprints of books would lead us to think.

If the activities of even publishers and master printers are often inadequately documented as imprints might or might not appear in their publications, what is one to say about the journeymen and correctors whose names never show in the books they actually produced? The sources permit only a rough idea of the proportion of Francophones among the staff of the Basle presses. From the little we know, however, it can be inferred that in the second half of the sixteenth century French printing workers must have been numerous. In view of their presence one is inclined to credit the Basle printing industry with a fair proportion of the countless anonymous tracts and pamphlets in French and their German translations which appeared between 1530 and the end of the century and which for the most part still await convincing attribution to specific publishers.

If in 1539 only sixteen or so foreign journeymen—and those probably not all Francophones—joined some fifty citizens in a complaint about their masters,[34] both the total number of journeymen and the proportion of Francophones must

---

[29] E.g. in 1593 C. Waldkirch printed for them an *Ars aurifera* (UBB).

[30] Dr. M. Steinmann has kindly drawn my attention to the existence of Aubry's letter in the Staatsarchiv Basel-Stadt. In a first attempt I have failed to trace it, but I hope to publish it in vol. 2 of this study. Cf. Armstrong 31.

[31] Cf. below, Index. It is, however, possible that some of their books published at Frankfurt, or parts of them, may have been printed at Basle. Benzing claims that between 1603 and 1614 the firm's publications with the imprint of Frankfurt were really printed at Hanau.

[32] *Matrikel* 2.495; Droz, *Etudiants français*.

[33] For Mareschal see Baudrier 6.357; 11.432 (placing too much emphasis on his ties with Basle). *BMC ST Germany* shows that Mareschal did much business with Heidelberg. He must have passed through Basle on his trips between Rhone and Neckar. For the Genevans cf. Chaix, *Recherches*, and Bremme, passim. Derbilly applied in 1559 in Geneva for a permit to publish Baduel's French transl. of Bucer's *De regno Christi*, perhaps only days after Oporinus had launched the original ed. in Latin : E. Droz in *BHR* 17 (1955), 347. Cf. also *Papistische Ordnung der Communion*, ed. M. Schalling, s.l. 1558. The UBB copy has a ms. entry by a 16th or 17th century hand : " Gedruckt zu Basel bey Jacob König durch Jacob Derbilleÿ." From Schalling's correspondence with Calvin (*Calvini opera* 16. 408, 428ff., 598, 651) we learn that Schalling gave this confutation of a Bavarian *Communionis ritus Catholicus* to Derbilly for publication against payment in Zurich. The pamphlet may be printed in Basle, after all, but it is clear that Derbilly did not reside, let alone operate a press, in Basle. Cf. **No. 226**.

[34] Steinmann 39.

have gone up over the next twenty years. Once again the account book of the Froben and Episcopius press yields some precious information. From September 1557 to May 1558 the firm listed among their employees in the house *zum Lufft* the journeyman printer Simon Chatellion,[35] who was working on the same job as Ogier Barthol,[36] the compositors Johannes Parcus [37] and his son, and in the house *zum Sessel* the corrector Léger Grymoult and the journeymen printers Joann Isorne,[38] Dionysius de la Fosse and Joann Dufoys. Other names on the same wage list do not rule out the possibility of Francophone extraction.[39] Simon Chatellion was conceivably a distant relation of Sébastien Castellio, for other members of that same family were connected in a similarly modest way with the printing industries of Lyons, Geneva and Basle.[40] Léger Grymoult was a known supporter of Castellio. In 1551-52 he matriculated at the University of Basle and a year later he was involved in the preparation of Castellio's French Bible.[41]

For the accounting period from September 1559 to May 1560 the firm continued to employ Grymoult and Parcus but had added another Francophone corrector Jean Le Petit (Parvus), who subsequently matriculated at the university in 1564-65.[42] In addition there were two new journeymen, Jacobus Marcorellus, stemming no doubt from an Italian family whose connection with the book trade reached from Aix-en-Provence and Lyons to Geneva,[43] and a Savoyard, Johannes Sabaudus. While several of these mentioned so far continued to serve the firm, two new French names appear in the accounts for the half year period from spring to autumn 1562, Robert Gyrart, a journeyman printer, and Moyses Wyller Gallus, a compositor. In the following half year one finds the corrector Pierre Lambelly (Lambellerus) from Estavayer, who is also listed in the university roll for 1564-65.[44]

Out of a total 1053 *l.* which the firm paid out in regular wages between September 1557 and March 1558 the Francophones, not counting any doubtful cases, received together 214 *l.* For the winter half year 1559-60 their share was 270 *l.* out of a total of 1108 *l.* and from March to September 1562 they earned 173 *l.* out of a total of 1326 *l.* Taking into account that every total includes a large unspecified amount of " press wages " and that there were most probably other Francophones among the journeymen who could not be identified, it is safe to assume that throughout this period the firm recruited at least twenty per cent of its labour force from French-speaking territories.

---

[35] *Rechnungsbuch* 8 and passim.

[36] *Matrikel* 2.104 and below p. 246.

[37] Also called Toutin and Estauge ; cf. above p. 75 n. 5 and *Rechnungsbuch* 109f. Wackernagel, " Aktensammlung ", lists references to him between 1541 and 1565.

[38] Subsequently his name is given as " Jehann Iseret Gallus ". Could he be identical with the Jean Ysoret mentioned in Baudrier 1.446 ? For the Isoré family in Geneva cf. Bremme 181.

[39] " Carolus Colsonet " ; " Jacob Ryellin " (later on given as " Rellin ", " Ressin ", " Russin "), perhaps a member of the Roussin family repeatedly mentioned by Baudrier ; cf. Chaix, *Recherches* 221 ; Bremme 223. See also below p. 114.

[40] Buisson, *Castellion* 2.108f., 224f., and passim.

[41] *Matrikel* 2.74 ; cf. below p. 127.

[42] *Matrikel* 2.156 and Droz, *Etudiants français*.

[43] Cf. Baudrier 10.181, 375ff. and passim ; Chaix, *Recherches* 204 ; Bremme 202ff.

[44] *Matrikel* 2.155.

The Froben and Episcopius firm may be considered as old stock Bâlois, although N. Episcopius senior who was an Alsatian by birth had worked in Saint-Didier for some time.[45]   It can accordingly be expected that Guarinus, who had closer contacts with the French emigrant community and published a high percentage of French authors, also employed a greater proportion of Francophone staff.   It must also be noted that the university roll lists relatively few Frenchmen for the years in question.   When the Francophone colony of Basle was at its peak—in the early fifties and after the Saint-Bartholomew massacre—the number of those looking for jobs in the printing industry was conceivably higher.

More Frenchmen were working in the Basle presses before and after the short period illuminated for us by the account book of the Froben and Episcopius firm, but for those who remained labourers and were largely outside the circles of letter-writing intellectuals, our information is exceedingly scarce.   As so often, the sources remain largely silent unless the Bâlois had some unpleasant experience to record. So it happened with Celse-Hugues Descousu, who in 1511 escaped to Lyons with books and money stolen from Johann Amerbach, his employer.[46]   A native of Normandy, Thomas Lenu, is mentioned in Basle between 1536 and 1539.   He worked as a sales clerk in the book shop of Conrad Resch.   On his behalf Resch was involved in a lawsuit with the Basle bookbinders, since Lenu did some binding of his own.[47]   In 1541 the printer Claude Lampellin from Besançon was knifed to death by his colleague Paulin Curention from Turin.[48]   In 1563 a P. Chapuis, " *imprimeur, demourant à Basle*," a distant relation of Castellio, sent two copies of the latter's *Conseil à la France désolée* to Geneva.[49]

In 1578-79 the name of the Genevan Pierre Chevalier (Cheallerius, Ceralerius) was entered in the university roll.   With the assistance of Bonaventura Vulcanius who knew him from his stay in Geneva, this specialist was called in to read the proofs of Ambrosius Froben's edition of the Hebrew Talmud.   When the job was done he left with a testimonial of good conduct from the authorities of Basle, eventually to become Professor of Hebrew in Geneva.[50]   Grymoult and Chevalier clearly were scholars whose duties lay not wholly inside the mechanical routine of the printing process.   Yet their place was in the press, and they did not enjoy the status of fully independent advisers as had Heynlin, Erasmus, or even Beatus Rhenanus who retained his scholarly freedom although he may at times have received some regular remuneration.   Michel Bentin's position, by contrast, resembles that of Grymoult and Chevalier.   During the years he spent in Basle he depended on the presses for

---

[45] Cf. Allen 6.346 and 8.247 where Erasmus calls him a " Gallus ".

[46] Hartmann 1.415ff., 419ff.

[47] Wackernagel, " Aktensammlung ".   *Ibid.*: a book binder Frantz Parin admitted to the Saffron guild in 1526.

[48] *Ibid.*

[49] Buisson, *Castellion* 2.225f.; cf. *Matrikel* 2.222: an " Abrahamus Schappuisius Genevensis "studying medicine at Basle (1573).   Some further bits of miscellaneous information may be added to this survey.   Jacques Cler of Montbéliard worked in 1577 for L. Osten.   In 1581 a Pierre Charretier from Lyons was employed by Foillet and presented to the Saffron Guild (L. Nardin, *op. cit.* 22f., 32).   Jacques Lefèvre (Faber), a metal engraver from Lorraine, worked in the early 1520s—and perhaps earlier—for J. Froben.   Jacques and a Pierre, perhaps his brother, also carried messages between Basle and Lyons: see above p. 41 and Wackernagel 3.279; Allen 5.567; Herminjard 1.249, 309, 382n.; *Rhenanus Briefwechsel* 84 (with erroneous date).

[50] *Matrikel* 2.259; *Correspondance de B. Vulcanius* 263, 438f., 475ff.; *HBLS*.

a living and there is no indication that he had much influence in the crucial decisions on what should be printed. Nevertheless he enjoyed the highest respect of his employers and the friendship of men more privileged than himself.

A native of Flanders, Bentin first worked and lived in Froben's house *zum Sessel*. His presence there is mentioned between 1520 and 1522. In 1524 we find him temporarily in Flanders.[51] On his return to Basle he married and became closely attached to the group of French émigrés around Farel. Through the latter and Lefèvre d'Etaples he tried to obtain a position among the retainers of Briçonnet, the bishop of Meaux.[52] This failing, he was associated with his distinguished friend, Anémond de Coct, in an ambitious plan for the establishment of an independent press devoted to Protestant publishing in French.[53] The plan proved impracticable and Bentin continued to hire himself to several printers for the purpose of seeing specific editions through the press. Like other emigrants he kept to Farel even after the latter had been expelled by the Basle authorities. His more than careless remarks in this matter may have been the reason for Erasmus' lasting resentment.[54] In August 1525 Bentin went to Lyons in what seems to have been another effort to enter the service of a prelate. He attached himself temporarily to the exiled Archbishop of Salerno, Federigo Fregoso, while waiting and hoping, that Michel d'Arande would soon be in a position to surround himself with an episcopal retinue. At the same time, however, he wrote to Oecolampadius in search of a living in Basle.[55] Although he had probably hoped for something better, he was soon back working for the presses of Valentin Curio and Cratander until, late in 1527, the plague swept him away together with his entire family. His employers and some humanists remembered him with praise and gratitude.[56]

In the presses of Basle the humble Bentin had found, if not fulfilment, at least relief from the squalid tanner's craft at which he had earlier worked. By contrast, Jean de Sponde relied on the printers less for his daily living than for publicizing the first-fruits of his talents, as a suitable fanfare for a humanistic career. Jean de Sponde sprang from an influential Basque family. His father served the crown of France in the county of Soule, but was at the same time secretary to Queen Jeanne d'Albret and her son, the future Henry IV. Arriving from Geneva, Jean was

---

[51] Hartmann 2.257f., 334, 348f., 366 ; Allen 5.423.

[52] Herminjard 1.224f.

[53] Herminjard 1.282, A. de Coct to Farel (2 Sept., 1524) : " Frater communis Michael Bentinus ad te scribit. Caeterum literis signatis illi in mentem aliud venit consilium, quod si probas non improbo. Vult enim non a tot hominum nutu pendere, quodque tale sit negocium in quo ipse multum praestare possit. Cogitabat tipographiam adoriri, me in vertendis Gallice libris comite. Ego, ut verum fatear, animo ad eam rem ita sum propenso, ut quod maxime velim id etiam me posse confidam. Opto enim Galliam evangelicis voluminibus abundare, siquidem illa sunt quae de Iesu testimonium perhibent. Praeterea, quum Vaugris Lugdunum ibit, scribam ad fratres, ut pecuniae aliquid ad me mittant."

[54] Allen 5.423, 436, 507 ; 6.24f. ; 7.93.

[55] Herminjard 1.398ff. Three months earlier Pierre Toussain traced the movements of Cardinal Jean de Lorraine to Lyons and speculated on his possible sympathies for the " Word of God ".

[56] Allen 7.342 ; Hartmann 4.455 : as late as 1536 Sixtus Birk placed Bentin in most distinguished company when he wrote that Basle could take pride in offering a last repose to such men as Oecolampadius, the Amerbachs and Frobens, and Bentin. Sincere appreciation of Bentin is also expressed in Cratander's and Isengrin's prefaces to **No. 127** and **128**.

enrolled in the university during the spring of 1581.[57] Four years later he left Basle with several publications to his credit, eventually to become the king's *lieutenant-général* in La Rochelle, Henri IV's fellow convert, and a noted author of religious verse and prose as well as propaganda for the *politiques*. While residing in Basle he maintained friendly contacts with the Genevan circle of Simon Goulart and more than once was visited by his friend, the musician Pascal de Lestocart.[58] What attracted Sponde to the Rhine, apart from his ambition to break into print, was perhaps a hope for Ramist and Paracelsian instruction,[59] and also the presence there of Theodor Zwinger, a moderate adherent of both schools, who was highly popular with French students.

Guarinus too received the young Béarnais with kindness and published some notes by him in his 1581 edition of Turnèbe's *Adversaria*.[60] In the following year when Zwinger as part of his comprehensive Aristotelian corpus re-edited the *Politics*, Sponde was permitted to append to it his Latin translation of the Pythagorean fragments. In 1583 he saw a cheap bilingual class-room edition of Aristotle's *Organum* through the press. In its preface he spoke of Ramus' contempt for Aristotle's dialectic as the only fault of that great man. Also in the same year he published his *pièce de résistance*, a voluminous edition of Homer. If the Latin translation as well as the Greek text was taken from earlier editions, at least the full, if rather commonplace, commentary was by Sponde himself. We have no information on Sponde's remaining year in Basle. It is, however, clear that he was excluded from the French church, most likely because of Castellionist aberrations, less probably also because of his immoral conduct.[61] The grapes even of literary fame may have tasted rather sour, and the inventive young man turned to his interest in Paracelsian ideas and technology tinged with occultism. He boasted freely that he had produced artificial gold before and he succeeded in getting no less a man than the professor Theodor Zwinger involved in his business, presumably in the first place with money. However, Theodor's son Jacob, who was Sponde's fellow student, was later a passionate alchemist, and it seems by no means impossible that father and son also helped with the actual distilling. On one occasion Sponde invoked the assistance of Theodor Zwinger in an attempt to persuade the printer Eusebius Episcopius to acquire a share in the expected profits of the group.[62] Soon,

---

[57] *Matrikel* 2.291 ; Droz, *Etudiants français* ; J. de Sponde, *Poésies*, Geneva 1949, 25ff. (biographical introduction by F. Ruchon).

[58] *Matrikel* 2.301 ; cf. above p. 70f.

[59] Cf. A. Boase's biographical introduction to his ed. of J. de Sponde, *Méditations*, Paris 1954, xxiii, xxviii and passim. As a parallel Boase mentions the famous Jacobus Arminius who left Geneva for Basle in 1582 to continue his studies there. Arminius too was interested in Ramism. Cf. *Matrikel* 2.313.

[60] **No. 1016.** Dated from Basle, 26 November, 1580, Sponde's preface "Thomaso Guarino typographo, amico suo " : " Cum primum hanc urbem appulissem, Guarine, non cessasti beneficiis tuis me cumulare."

[61] Boase, *op. cit.* xxxviif.

[62] Among the many messages, mostly short and undated, which Sponde sent to Zwinger see in particular UBB ms. Fr. Gr. II. 28², No. 349-352, e.g. No. 351, Sponde to [Theodor] Zwinger, s.l., s.a. : " Conveni hesterna die Episcopium, cum quo de Aristotele nostro verba feci. Is respondit se crastina die a concione te alloquuturum. Id ut faciat, tu, quaeso, occasionem, si tantum a rebus tuis tibi est otii, capta atque etiam, si placet, interpella — δοκεῖ γὰρ ὀκνηρότερος — in istis praecipue negotiis. Vide quid ei proponam : lucrum illud ex nostra χρυσοτέχνη velim illi impertiri, hoc est, si me centum

however, he had to concentrate his efforts on appeasing Zwinger's own fears which were no doubt well founded.[63] Another Basle citizen may also have been a partner in this business, Nikolaus Wasserhun, perhaps a distant relative of the Zwingers, who seems to have wandered through Europe as a courier, but also as an inventor and a charlatan.[64] Already in his commentaries on Homer Sponde had praised the Paracelsian expertise of his friend and fellow Basque, Paul de La Treille (Trellius) ;[65] in 1585 Sponde was in Paris, together with La Treille and Wasserhun, boasting of inventions which ranged from the *perpetuum mobile* to hydraulic devices, and obtaining letters patent for the improvement of the water supply system of the French capital.[66]

Among the Frenchmen attracted to Basle by its printing industry were also men of means and established reputation. In 1568 four sons of Pierre Pithou, a barrister in Troyes, registered together at the university. The family was Protestant —at least at heart—and the young men may have been sent away at the approach of the second war of religion. The best known of the four, Pierre, was in spite of his youth already a distinguished lawyer. An outstanding career lay before him which after a narrow escape on the night of Saint Bartholomew eventually led to his conversion.[67] At the peak of his fame as a great lawyer and *politique* he maintained epistolary exchanges which included Basilius Amerbach and Josias Simler in Zurich [68] among the more illustrious correspondents.

Costly antiquarian hobbies seem to have been a tradition in the Pithou family. Pierre was the owner of a famous library. The two years or so he spent in Basle were devoted to the enlargement of his collections, a learned correspondence about ancient and medieval legal traditions and related matters, and miscellaneous publications. In the preface to his edition of the *Historia miscella* (1569) he revealed to his friend Basilius Amerbach the depth of his gloom at the current situation in France and the uncertain fate of his library. But he also spoke of the comfort he was finding among the books of Amerbach and in the study of the German *autores antiquissimi* until such time as God would permit his return to a pacified homeland

---

coronatis iuverit et alios centum aut quantum voluerit pro se impendere volet, quicquid emolumenti inde orietur ad eum redeat. Est autem ex decem marcis argenti plusquam decem coronatorum (omnibus expensis detractis) singulis hebdomadis, ut iam monui, neque demuto sententiam quia res illa mihi est exploratissima..."

[63] *Ibid.* No. 352, Sponde to [Theodor] Zwinger, s.l., s.a. : "... Si non fidis plane chymico, fide Christiano et studioso pietatis... "

[64] *Matrikel* 2.190. UBB has a number of letters and short, undated messages by him, many of them to Jacob Zwinger, e.g. : UBB ms. Fr. Gr. I. 15, No. 480-482 ; Fr. Gr. II.28 ², No. 369-370.

[65] Boase, *op. cit.* xxxvf., xxxviiiff. ; *Matrikel* 2.250. UBB has six letters on the subject of iatrochemy which La Treille addressed to Theodor Zwinger from Montbéliard, 1578 : UBB ms. Fr. Gr. II. 28¹, No. 165-170.

[66] F. Ruchon, Jean de Sponde, ingénieur, *BHR* 14 (1952), 277-282.

[67] *Matrikel* 2.181f. ; Droz, *Etudiants français*. Jean Pithou, a half brother of Pierre, matriculated in 1595-1596. For all Pithous cf. *France prot.*, for Pierre cf. also L. de Rosanbo, Pierre Pithou, *Revue du Seizième Siècle* 15 (1928), 279-305 ; 16 (1929), 301-330.

[68] There are numerous ms. letters exchanged between Pierre and François Pithou and Basilius Amerbach in UBB, also one from Pierre to Theodor Zwinger. The unpublished letters to and from J. Simler are in the BN and in Zurich.

and his investigation of the French legal tradition.   With a touch of condescension he also praised the willingness of Pietro Perna to print the works which he suggested. Turning to his reasons for editing the *Historia miscella* he modestly pointed out that all copies of the earlier editions had vanished from the market, and that a manuscript in the possession of the Amerbachs enabled him to supply a few critical additions and corrections.   Sadness and scholarly composure also inform the preface of his edition of Otto of Freising addressed to his former teacher Cujas [69] and his correspondence with J. Simler.

Pierre's brother François Pithou was still—or again—in Basle by 1576.   In that year he published an edition of Justinian's *Novellae* with the help of a manuscript from his brother's library.   A year earlier Simler had edited some smaller antiquarian texts [70] from the same source for Guarinus, who also published some fragments of early legal texts with Pierre's notes.   Since Guarinus apologized for acting without Pierre's knowledge, this manuscript too may have remained in Basle, presumably in the hands of his brother.[71]

To Bentin the Basle printing meant subsistence, to Sponde it offered the beginning of a career and a reputation, to Pierre it was a sort of mental hygiene.   These three cases present just a few of the many ways in which French visitors and refugees came to co-operate with the Basle presses.   In the case of such authors as Castellio, Postel, Baudouin, and Ramus this co-operation became so substantial and lasting in its effects that it requires a separate treatment.   Other visitors came to Basle merely to publish a book there.   Vesalius, for one, arrived in the wake of a line of mules which had carried the precious woodcut blocks across the Alps so that *De Humani corporis fabrica* might be published by his friend Oporinus.[72]   Turning to Frenchmen, the lasting monument to Calvin's short stay in Basle was the first edition of the *Institutio Christianae religionis*.   There were other Francophones like him who reached the Rhine with a manuscript for printing and little else in their baggage.   There are books which present the only record of the months or years their emigrant authors spent at Basle, perhaps in loneliness and misery.   Who was the Champenois Nicolas Gallot ?   All we know is that he could not pay his registration fee when enrolling at the university in 1558.   In 1560 he edited for Oporinus a scholastic edition of Demosthenes' *Olynthiac Orations*, the text accompanied by a

---

[69] From the preface to Cujas : " Itaque cum inter hos vere Gallicos tumultus communisque patriae miserias unum in me illud valde angat, quod neque ubi sis neque quo in statu res tuae versentur scire possum.   Hos tandem conquisitores dimittere visum est, publicos quidem illos et versicoloria veste amictos, adde etiam, si placet, ne quid Petronianorum solemnium desit, fumosam magis quam lucidam facem quassantes, non tamen a praetore petitos, ut apud comicum, sed ultro nescio qua nuper sorte oblatos.   Nam cum in hoc infelici ocio rebus non iam prolatis, sed potius dimissis, pene dixi depositis, graviores illas cogitationes posteriorum temporum historiis saepe obruere, saltem fallere, tentarem, quarum hodie bona pars non usque adeo obvia est, coepi typographo auctor esse, ut omnes omnino qui quidem alicunde recuperari possent Germanicae historiae supra nostram patrumque memoriam Latinos scriptores duobus voluminibus concluderet, ex quibus recentiorum fides repeti posset.   Id cum ille lubens recepisset... "

[70] **No. 858.**

[71] **Na. 855** : *Mosaycarum et Romanarum legum collatio ex integris Papiniani, Pauli, Ulpiani, Gaii, Modestini aliorumque veterum iuris auctorum libris ante tempora Iustiniani Imp. desumpta.   Eiusdem Imp. Iustiniani Novellae constitutiones III. Iuliani antecessoris CP. dictatum de consilariis.   Eiusdem Iuliani collectio de contutoribus.   Ex bibliotheca P. Pithoei IC. cuius etiam notae emendatoriae adiectae sunt,* Basle, T. Guarinus, 1579.

[72] Steinmann 35ff. ; G.A. Lindeboom, *A. Vesalius*, Harlem 1964, 75f.

Latin translation.   In his fine preface he knew how to present the remote Macedonian war in the light of actuality.   Venetian or Polish ambassadors, he suggested, might rehearse the arguments which Demosthenes had put into the mouths of the Olynthian envoys to Athens.   So might the spokesmen of Metz, Strasbourg, and Geneva when imploring Swiss help against their powerful Catholic neighbours.   The ancient Athenians of course would not listen, and today their country lay prostrate in the grip of Turkish masters... Without insisting on the obvious parallel, Gallot has expressed the gloom and concern of many a poor refugee.[73]

Unlike Gallot, Louis Des Masures was a well-known figure.   He had served as a secretary to Cardinal Jean de Lorraine and addressed his verse freely to the members of that house and to the Chancellor de l'Hospital, as well as Cardinal Jean Du Bellay.   But when Des Masures—he was now the Huguenot pastor of Sainte-Marie-aux-Mines—arrived in Basle shortly after the massacre of Saint Bartholomew, next to the son who accompanied him, his manuscripts must have been his most treasured possession.   Even when matriculating he insisted that the words " *scriptor Borboniados* " be entered in the roll as a statement of his intent to publish his epic there.   However, he did apparently not succeed in doing so.[74]

In Basle Des Masures very likely met a scholarly antiquarian from Besançon, Jean Jacques Boissard.   Boissard too arrived, matriculated, and published a collection of poems.[75]   Both found a common friend in the Lorrain Jacques Pasquier (Pascharius) who knew his way around in the local presses, was always on hand with miscellaneous epigrams, and in 1575 graduated from the university's medical faculty.[76]   The bizarre Jacques Peletier, finally, had recently acquired a medical doctorate when he arrived late in 1563 to publish at once some medical and mathematical treatises.   Apart from these he left no record of his presence, and must soon have left to continue his unstable life, in the course of which places changed as frequently as friends and interests.[77]

Just as the sons of Basle printing families were being sent to France, some young visitors bear names familiar in the history of French printing, and their presence in Basle reflects the business contacts which their fathers maintained there. In 1540 Conrad Bade, son of the late Josse and godson of Conrad Resch, matriculated and took lodgings with Simon Grynaeus, who accommodated him together with Sébastien Castellio and others.   In the following year he took the promising French youth along with him to the Diet of Worms.   After Grynaeus' unexpected death from the plague a few months later, Conrad Bade's glowing admiration for his former host induced Beza to write an epitaph.[78]   Even more significant was the stay of Barthélemy Vincent, son of and a worthy successor to the important Lyons publisher Antoine Vincent.   After the father had lent substantial sums to Oporinus,

---

[73] *Matrikel* 2.112 and Droz *Etudiants français* ; **No. 450.**

[74] *Matrikel* 2.216 ; *Biographie nat. Belgique; France prot.*[2]

[75] *Matrikel* 2.220.   In Boissard's *Poemata* (**No. 170**) one notes verses in honour of Boissard by J. Pasquier, P. Choart de Buzanval and others, as well as Boissard's epigrams in praise of his friends.   Pasquier suggests that his own epigrams were included at the request of Guarinus, among them one in praise of Ramus.

[76] See above p. 72.

[77] *Matrikel* 2.150 and Droz, *Etudiants français*. Cf.N.Z. Davis, Peletier and Beza Part Company, *Studies in the Renaissance* 2 (1964), 188-222.

[78] *Matrikel* 2.25 and E. Droz in *BHR* 24 (1962), 394-396.   Bade later wrote a comedy in which Castellio is portrayed selling himself to the Devil.   It was promptly performed in Geneva : see Buisson, *Castellion* 2.253ff.

Barthélemy was received into the printer's house when he arrived and matriculated at Basle in 1561.[79] This business relationship was prepared for by the association of Antoine with the Frellon brothers, formerly business partners of Wattenschnee and Resch, and it continued after Barthélemy's departure from Basle. In 1586 Jean-Antoine Huguetan, Barthélemy Vincent's son-in-law, was registered at the university. He too would in his day be a pillar of the Lyons book trade.[80] Finally, Henri (II) Estienne would seem to have visited Basle in 1578, where he was honoured by a reception at the university.[81]

[79] *Matrikel* 2.131 and Steinmann 59, 113.

[80] *Matrikel* 2.340; Droz, *Etudiants français*; Baudrier 11. 353ff.

[81] Armstrong, *Estienne* 32; Droz in *Etudiants français* suggests that Estienne Prévosteau of Chartres (*Matrikel* 2.218) may be identical with the later son-in-law and successor of Guillaume Morel, a Royal printer in Paris.

CHAPTER THREE

RELIGIOUS REFUGEES
AND THE FRENCH CHURCH

The majority of the Francophones who came to sixteenth century Basle had given up a home in Catholic territory. There is no way of telling their approximate numbers. While men of status or intellectual ambition would often have their names registered in the university roll, we must assume that merchants and artisans usually did not. Many who came from France would merely cross the Rhine on Basle's bridge. Others would follow them, after a short stay, to take up residence in Germany or Poland. Of the students and distinguished visitors registered at the university most would sooner or later return to their native countries even though many were, and some remained, Protestants. Some Francophones, however, stayed in Basle. They, or at least their children, were admitted to citizenship and gradually, not always painlessly, assimilated. The Battier family provides a typical example. A wealthy merchant from Saint-Symphorien near Lyons, Jacques Battier, had emigrated to Geneva. Two of his sons came to Basle. Jean Battier was made a citizen in 1569; his brother Jacques, who had first settled in Montbéliard, was naturalized in 1573. Neither matriculated in the university, but both married daughters of another Francophone immigrant, the physician Jean Bauhin. While their brother-in-law Gaspard Bauhin quickly climbed the rungs to local prominence and international prestige—he was a professor of medicine, rector of the university, and a well-known author—the Battiers discreetly prospered in business life. Only when a solid foundation was laid for their wealth and future comfort over many generations did the family begin to join the intelligentsia. Jacques Battier's grandson Simon, born in 1629 of a mother who was also of Francophone descent, studied in Geneva and Italy before rising to the lucrative university chair of civil law.[1] There are exceptions to the rule, but in most cases a quick admission to the ranks of citizenship, as granted to the Battiers, depended on financial ease, as it still does in Switzerland. By contrast, Sébastien Castellio was never made a citizen, although after much hardship he was finally employed in the lower echelons of the university faculty. Of his several sons only one is recorded beyond the point of university matriculation. Frédéric Castellio became a staid Bâlois, pastor of a rural parish and later a modest professor of rhetoric in the university. He managed to free

---

[1] *HBLS* and *Matrikel* 3.424 and passim for other members of the family. The older Jacques Battier was an elder in the French church at Basle and a staunch supporter of Couet at the time of the Lescaille affair.

himself from his father's shadow.   Untroubled by controversy, he lived quietly and died without a message for posterity.[2]

Especially in the first half of the seventeenth century, when the French church had overcome internal rifts and friction with the city pastorate, the number of successful immigrant families of the Battier type multiplied.   Among those destined to dominate locally in the nineteenth century and beyond, the Passavant family arrived in 1594, the Sarasins in 1628, the Legrands in 1640, and the Raillards in 1641.[3] Besides these how many others, whose destiny was less remarkable, may have arrived ?   Suggestively enough, the city council resolved in 1648 that no further " Welsche " (i.e., people of Romance tongue) should be admitted to citizenship. A similar decree, however, had been passed in 1546 and there is no indication that the city fathers respected their own legislation of the seventeenth century any more consistently than they had done in the sixteenth.

At least the fluctuations in the size of Basle's Francophone community may be reflected by the number of entries in the university roll although, of course, registrations were less exclusively motivated by religious exile than were applications for citizenship.   Matriculation figures were influenced by developments outside the politico-religious order such as the outbreak of plague at Basle in 1564-65.   They do, however, suggest that the numbers of Francophones in town were generally larger during the 1550s than during the 1560s.   One further notices peaks in 1568-73, 1578-82, and 1585-87.[4]   The first peak, as well as a low in 1570-71 are accounted

---

[2] Buisson, *Castellion* 2.281ff.; *Matrikel* 2.280 and passim for other members of the family.   Cf. **No. 2040**.

[3] L.A. Burckhardt, Die französischen Religionsflüchtlinge in Basel, *Beiträge zur vaterländischen Geschichte* 7 (Basle 1860), 301-333 ; *HBLS*.

[4] Both the total enrolment and the percentage of French-speaking students fluctuates considerably.   Moreover, not all students were registered in the roll.   Prior to the Basle Reformation enrolment figures were too low and erratic for any pattern to emerge. Hereafter the following trends may be noted.

I. During the 1530s and 1540s the total annual registration was low (11-53) and the number of Francophones not considerable except in 1537-1538, 1542-1544, and 1548-1549.

II. During the 1550s the level of 1548-1549 was sustained and the Francophone percentage normally 10-20%.   However, odd lows occurred in 1550-1551 and 1554-1556.

III. Up to 1567-1568 the percentage of Francophone students was twice between 13% and 14%, but often well below 10%.   Then followed the short explosion.

IV. During the 1570s the total annual enrolment rose to an average of about 100. The proportion of Francophones continued at a level of better than 10%, rising up to the absolute peak in 1578-1582.

V. Between 1583 and 1595 total enrolment figures remained around 100 while fluctuations eased.   The Francophone percentage, however, was erratic with peaks of close to 20% in 1585-1587 and 1592-1593.

IV. Between 1595 and 1606 the total enrolment average rose to 125 and the Francophone percentage stabilized at about 10%.   However, among the French-speaking students for the first time the Swiss exceeded the others.   After 1606 the total was falling off and the enrolment of non-Swiss Francophones remained negligible.

The following examples may be suggestive :

	Total enrolment	1. Francophones	2.
1537-1538	45	4	13
1542-1543	69	2	10
1543-1544	33	0	8
1548-1549	76	3	8

Continuation of this note on page 90.)

for by military operations in France, the peace of Saint-Germain (August 1570), and the massacre of Saint Bartholomew. After the massacre and while the princes of the blood were residing at Basle the French colony was permitted to hold services, with the sermon being preached in French. The foundation of the Catholic League and the activation of religious strife in France correspond with the second peak. The third followed the death of the anti-Calvinist Basle *antistes* Simon Sulzer. Under his successor J. J. Grynaeus, the French church was finally permitted to celebrate its own communion service (1586). It was also given a temporary assembly hall (1588) and subsequently a permanent centre in the former Dominican church (1614).[5]

Only the seventeenth century, however, brought an increased measure of stability to the French congregation. To the end of the sixteenth century emotions remained tense and opinions frequently clashed. Although painful, many of these episodes illustrate the true Reformation atmosphere of dynamic commitment which had not yet given way to the quiet, respectable exercise of one's faith. Whereas the various impulses and tensions of the sixteenth century are richly documented in Basle book production, the ailing typographical industry of the subsequent period offers but a thin and erratic record of the great confessional debates of the early seventeenth century and of their modest echoes in town.

In the person of François Lambert the Bâlois encountered for the first time that fermenting spirit of southern France which attracted Dolet and Rabelais as well as Servetus and Cornelius Agrippa. In the summer of 1522 the hot-tempered Franciscan had set out from his Avignon convent and travelled to Geneva, where he met his old friend Agrippa. From there he proceeded to Lausanne and Switzerland.

	Total enrolment	1. Francophones	2.
1550-1551	34	1	1
1554-1555	71	1	4
1555-1556	59	2	1
1560-1561	75	8	2
1562-1563	109	7	6
1564-1565	42	2	2
1566-1567	65	3	6
1567-1568	73	2	1
1568-1569	175	5	30
1569-1570	93	9	9
1570-1571	68	3	1
1571-1572	102	4	15
1572-1573	89	1	19
1578-1579	134	9	29
1581-1582	155	12	24
1582-1583	68	0	2
1585-1586	121	2	17
1592-1593	88	5	11
1593-1594	84	1	4
1599-1600	157	9	4
1604-1605	141	10	3
1609-1610	134	9	3

1. Francophones from regions presently located in Switzerland or belonging to Switzerland or Geneva at that time.

2. Other Francophones.

In the case of bilingual regions a French family name was equated with Francophone status; doubtful cases were excluded.

[5] L. A. Burckhardt, *op. cit.* 324f. and A. Bernus in *BSHPF* 39 (1890), 515ff. and 41 (1892), 401.

Although he preached the Gospel wherever he went, he still wore his cowl and even elicited a letter of recommendation from the Prince-Bishop of Lausanne. A similar letter from B. Haller, the Berne reformer, introduced him to Zwingli in Zurich. Though he did not think that Lambert's ideas were highly original, Haller admitted that a French friar was the last person from whom he would have expected to hear them. From Zurich Lambert went to Basle, furnished with letters of Agrippa to Chansonnette and Capito.[6] Claiming to be a relative of Jean Montaigne, the Avignon friend of Bonifacius Amerbach, he hoped to meet Erasmus but was probably refused this honour.[7] Resuming his migration, he finally came to play a prominent role in the reformation of Hesse and died as a professor at Marburg. All along his way he published pamphlets and treatises, and it is not impossible that he may have done so at Basle.[8] But his unbridled language won him few friends. The circle of Meaux disapproved of his publications,[9] and in the end he antagonized even Luther. In his correspondence with Jean Montaigne, Bonifacius Amerbach did not conceal his disgust of Lambert's " nugae " and twice refused to supply the friend with copies.[10]

Amerbach's displeasure at Lambert's coarse language was no doubt heightened by the public scandal caused by Guillaume Farel two years after Lambert's visit. This second encounter between Erasmian Basle and an apostle of the French Reformation ended disastrously. Over the next twenty years Basle still played a noticeable role in promoting Protestantism à la française, but was prevented from playing a capital one as she might well have done without Farel. The young Paris master of arts had been a colleague of Lefèvre and Roussel in the Cardinal Lemoine College before joining Briçonnet's circle at Meaux. His views became too radical for Meaux, and after being rudely turned away from his native Gap where he had attempted to preach he finally appeared in Basle, perhaps as early as July 1523.[11] His friends in Paris and Meaux no doubt reflected his own feelings when they rejoiced to know him safe in that haven, that royal ("βασιλική") town where the King of Kings permitted men to profess, and live, the Gospel, and where distinguished scholars abounded.[12] For the benefit of Lefèvre, Briçonnet and Roussel, Farel would list the Evangelical publications available in Basle and speedily despatch all the titles they desired.[13] In February 1524 he proceeded to a public disputation which was

[6] Herminjard 1.101ff. G. Müller (*Franz Lambert von Avignon und die Reformation in Hessen*, Marburg 1958, 7ff.) prefers to think that Lambert did not fully embrace the Reformation before he met Luther in Wittenberg and there defrocked himself and got married. On Lambert see also : R.L. Winters, *Francis Lambert of Avignon*, Philadelphia 1938, and N. Weiss in *BSHPF* 75 (1926), 477-486.

[7] Hartmann 2.433.

[8] Cf. Herminjard 1.112ff., 138ff. I have not found copies of *Causae exaecationis,* Basle 1523, mentioned by Panzer, or of *Exegeseos in ... Apocalypsim lib. VIII*, Basle 1539, mentioned in *France prot.* and T. Dufour, *Notice bibliographique sur le catéchisme ... de Calvin*, Geneva 1878, cclxii.

[9] Herminjard 1.312f.

[10] Hartmann 3.93, 115, 526.

[11] N. Weiss, Guillaume Farel — Ses premiers travaux, *BSHPF* 68 (1919), 179-214 ; cf. Herminjard 1.240ff. For the following cf. : *Guillaume Farel, 1489-1565*, Neuchâtel-Paris 1930, 116ff.

[12] Herminjard 1.178f., 242 : J. Canaye to Farel : " ... te velut ad salutis portum et asylum confugisse Basileam, inquam, vere βασιλικήν, quod Rex regum in ea Evangelium suum legesque aethernas vigere, legi, promulgari velit."

[13] Herminjard 1.183f., 206f., 222ff., 234.

authorized by the town council, but boycotted by church and university officials. The printed broadsheet of his theses opened on a quasi-Erasmian note, insisting that Christ had set " *absolutam ... vivendi regulam*," but soon drifted to more radical expressions of Protestantism. The latter were representative of the views of Oecolampadius and his unpolished supporters in the guilds, many of whom must have listened to the German *ad hoc* translation provided at the proceedings. Among others a friend of Erasmus, Ludwig Ber, had worked energetically to prevent the disputation, and Farel's lasting aversion to Erasmus—and in the end even the shadow of Erasmus—may be dated from this hour.[14]

As a result of the disputation Farel engaged in a free lecture course on Evangelical doctrine and eventually preached to the French community. As he was never one to mince words, his references to Erasmus and his party were soon to cause vexation to Erasmus' *famulus* Hilarius Bertulphus who was also a friend of Farel.[15] The issue came to a head when Erasmus stopped the fiery Frenchman on the street and requested an explanation as to why Farel had likened him to Balaam, the prophet who accepted pay to curse the people of God. Farel replied bluntly and Erasmus denounced him in a letter to the city council.[16] His subsequent expulsion from Basle, however, was not entirely the result of intrigue on the part of Erasmus. In particular his inflammatory approach to fellow Francophones must have offended the deeply rooted sense of moderation and the patriotic feelings of many Bâlois. He succeeded in alarming not only Oecolampadius, but also Lefèvre at Paris, and his subsequent preaching in Montbéliard caused open tumults.[17]

Farel's eager interest in Basle book production is amply documented in his letters and by his book shipments to friends in France. Froben's corrector, Michel Bentin, was his friend.[18] It seems very likely that some of his pamphlets were published in Basle either during his stay or shortly after his involuntary departure,[19] but no copies have come to light in recent times. Farel's visit to Basle helped to strengthen the ties between his friends and sympathizers in France and the Gospel-minded book merchants of the *Ecu* group. Jean Vaugris looked after an impression of Farel's exposition of the Lord's prayer. He arranged for two hundred copies to be sent to Farel, who had meanwhile gone to Montbéliard, together with fifty copies of another work described as *Epistolae*.[20] Vaugris also considered publishing Luther's *New Testament* in French. This project was finally dropped in favour of a reprint of Lefèvre d'Etaples' translation. The French Evangelicals even maintained ambitious plans for establishing their own presses. When Farel was still at Basle Gérard Roussel wrote from Meaux to request type faces identical with or

---

[14] Herminjard 1. 193ff., 202f. N. Weiss, Guillaume Farel — la dispute de Bâle, le conflit avec Erasme, *BSHPF* 69 (1920), 115-145.

[15] Herminjard 1.211ff.

[16] Allen 5.566ff., 569ff.; cf. 1.31; Herminjard 1.358ff.

[17] Herminjard 1.223, 253ff., 265ff.; cf. Erasmus, *LB* 10.1617f.

[18] See above p. 82.

[19] Herminjard 1.223, 246ff., 252; Allen 5.548f., 567; E. Droz in *BHR* 20 (1958), 164. The first two editions of *Summaire et briefve declaration*, " Turin 1525 " and " Venice 1529 " are no longer attributed to a Basle printer but to Pierre de Vingle, see E. Droz, Pierre de Vingle, l'imprimeur de Farel, *Propagande religieuse* 56ff. It is, however, suggestive of Basle's reputation that in 1530 the *Parlement* of Dole believed to know that the second edition was published in Basle : see L. Febvre in *BSHPF* 60 (1911), 184f.

[20] Herminjard 1. 279-281.

similar to the ones used by Froben.[21]   Bentin and the French nobleman Anémond de Coct hoped to set up in Basle their own press for French *Evangelica* and discussed their project with Farel.[22]

Originally the book industry may have helped to attract Farel to Basle.   However, his presence there, together with that of Pierre Toussain, A. de Coct, and the well-to-do Lyons merchant A. du Blet,[23] undoubtedly accelerated the transformation of many French admirers of Erasmus into avid readers of *Lutheriana*.   Yet in the direct confrontation between Farel and Erasmus, Basle had opted for the humanist. No love was lost in future between Farel and the Rhenish city.   Once he had left the town, even Wattenschnee and Vaugris refused to publish his writings.[24]   After the *Placards* affair the well-informed Erasmus circle suspected that it had been engineered by Farel.[25]   A final incident occurred on 20 September, 1557, more than twenty years after the death of Erasmus, when Farel and Beza stopped in the inn *zum Wilden Mann* on their way to Germany where they were to plead the cause of the French Protestants and to discuss theology with Melanchthon.   Before a numerous audience Farel reverted to his old habit of traducing Erasmus.   Beza followed suit by suggesting that he had been an Arian.   The incident produced a dignified reply in writing, signed by Bonifacius Amerbach, Hieronymus Froben and Nicolaus Episcopius [26] : the Basle circle was committed.

Back in 1524 Farel's wrangles in Basle had created wounds that were not easy to heal.   A severe dearth in 1530-31 [27] further diminished the charitable disposition of the Bâlois towards refugees.   The effects were described in an eloquent and provocative manner by Pierre Toussain, who was at the time probably the most interesting figure in the Basle émigré community.   He had studied there as early as 1514-15.[28]   The Bâlois had seen more of him in 1524-25.   Throughout this period he managed to retain a degree of familiarity with Farel and Oecolampadius as well as with Erasmus by supplying each with suitably offensive information about the others.[29]   It was an improbable role, but he succeeded so well with it that in the end nobody bore him ill-will.   After he had left Basle he continued his ambiguous path by deploring the hesitations of the Meaux group in his letters to Oecolampadius, just as he had deplored those of the Basle reformer in his correspondence with Farel.[30]   Erasmus, who had earlier recommended him to Budé and Cardinal Jean de Lorraine,[31] now learned about his close contacts with Berquin [32] in Paris.   Between 1531 and 1533 Toussain again spent much of his time at Basle.   It was now that he launched his scathing attack on the hypocrisy and lack of charity which the Bâlois

---

[21] Herminjard 1.237. The plan does not seem to have materialized. Three months later Roussel wished to publish his commentary on *Romans* in Basle : *ibid.* 1.292f.

[22] See above p. 82, n. 53.

[23] See above p. 58.

[24] Herminjard 1.281, 385. ; cf. 2.325f.

[25] Hartmann 4.316f.

[26] *Correspondance de Bèze* 2.114. Farel also passed through Basle in 1526 : Herminjard 1.451ff.

[27] P. Ochs, *Geschichte der Stadt und Landschaft Basel* 6 (Basle 1821), 17, 26f., 39.

[28] *Matrikel* 1.323 ; cf. Herzog.

[29] Herminjard 1.284ff., 299, 376f. ; Allen 5.570.

[30] Herminjard 1.444ff. ; cf. 376f.

[31] Allen 6.52ff., 179f. ; Herminjard 1.365, 464.

[32] Allen 7.472.

showed towards French emigrants.[33] One has to bear in mind that Toussain's observations followed in the wake of a dearth and that they were addressed to Farel, a man even more biased against the Bâlois than was Toussain at the time. Yet the fact remains that a number of Francophones, especially intellectuals,[34] obviously did not find the shelter and livelihood here for which they had been hoping. Toussain finally found his life task as the reformer of the County of Montbéliard. Even though he never overcame his disposition to intrigue, he gradually transformed this territory with its German rulers and French subjects into a minor outlet for some of the Erasmian and Castellionist traditions of Basle.[35]

Meanwhile the *Placards* affair of 1534 brought a fresh number of French emigrants to Basle, among them noblemen who, according to Erasmus, returned to their homes as soon as the Edict of Coucy revived their confidence in the future.[36] However, relations between Basle and the French Evangelicals of Paris and Meaux had not recovered from the strain caused by Farel's visit. A decade earlier Lefèvre d'Etaples had followed Farel to Strasbourg rather than spend his exile at Basle. Now, again, few prominent figures of the French reform came to Basle. One who did was Pierre Caroli, who registered proudly in the university as *doctor theologicus Sorbonicus*.[37] A quarrel with Farel had driven him away from Geneva: reason enough for the Bâlois to listen to him more sympathetically than he deserved. Before long he left for Montbéliard and there again burst into wild accusations against Calvin, Viret and the government of Berne, as well as Farel. Three successive changes of confession soon exposed him to general contempt wherever he went ; but initially his stories had impressed the Bâlois ministers. Incredibly, the *antistes* Myconius went so far as to warn the Bernese of the Servetian Arianism which Farel and Calvin were spreading in Geneva.[38]

Caroli was still in Basle[39] when another refugee arrived from Paris. By publishing the first edition of the *Institutes* in Basle Jean Calvin may be said to have laid there the foundations of his lasting fame ; yet one cannot help contrasting the attentions lavished on Caroli with the state of near-anonymity in which Calvin spent the year of 1535 among the Bâlois. It cannot be stated precisely either when he arrived or departed, and when the *Institutes* appeared in March 1536, after he had left town, the surprised reaction of a local minister showed that Calvin's name was still meaningless to him.[40] In justice to Calvin the inauspicious beginnings of his

[33] Herminjard 3.3ff. : " ... Brefz, je treuve moin icy [à Bâle] de foy et de charité, je ne dis point entre les populaires (que j'entends estre du tout refroidiz et alliénéz de la Parolle, voyant les meurs de leurs pasteurs), mais entre les prélatz, que je ne trouvay jamais entre paillars et ruffians. Et n'ay encore icy trouvé ung seul qui m'aye présenté ung petit disné ou consolé d'une seulle parolle, combien que, tesmoing Dieu, n'y suis venus pour leur disner, ne pour les charger ; mais sy fait y grand bien, quant on abandonne le sien pour cuyder vivre avecque eulx selont Dieu, et que on y treuve du moyn quelque amour et consolation, ce que on trouveroit entre les gentilz et payens ; mais de tout, rien. ... Bruslez ces présentes, affin que personne n'en faice mal son prouffit."

[34] Cf. e.g. Hartmann 6.437f.

[35] Cf. below pp. 244ff.

[36] Cf. above p. 58 n. 8.

[37] *Matrikel* 2.10 ; cf. *France prot.*

[38] Wernle, *Calvin und Basel* 4, 14f., 24ff. ; Herminjard 4.241f. and passim.

[39] Herminjard 3.374n.

[40] Wernle, *Calvin und Basel* 3, 6 ; **No. 227.**

relations with Basle must be emphasized. If the growing polarity between Basle and Geneva is to occupy so much space in the pages of this study, the reason is not so much that Calvin's disposition was unfriendly as that the Bâlois tended to ignore his true stature, while attracting his personal opponents. The best that may be said for the Bâlois is that their Erasmian preoccupation with human nature, and the resulting tolerance and concern for the individual, left them inadequately prepared for the exigency, rigours and logical power of Calvin's theology.[41] The same tolerance, however, later helped to avoid an official rupture between the churches of Basle and Geneva. Although a good deal of anti-Calvinist agitation was concentrated in Basle, the government and the city in general never gained the reputation of being a kind of anti-Geneva. Correspondence between the Bâlois ministers and Geneva continued in the days of Calvin as well as later in the days of Beza, and it remained for the most part polite, if not friendly. On several subsequent occasions Calvin, by now no longer an unknown refugee, was warmly welcomed when he passed through Basle.

Back in 1535, however, Caroli was not the only Frenchman in town to outshine Calvin. The year was filled with high-level diplomatic activity instigated by Guillaume Du Bellay, Sieur de Langey, and we shall see that the Basle authorities as well as the printers took an active part in it. Langey himself stopped in Basle a few months after Calvin had left. Throughout the time of Calvin's presence, however, some of Langey's men were in Basle, among them the wealthy and highly respected Jean Morel, who knew everyone of prominence in the community, including Erasmus who had then returned from Freiburg to die in Basle.[42] Such prestigious contacts were denied to the young Calvin and probably he would not have cared for them. He had come to think and write quietly. Nevertheless, among the final touches to the *Institutes* which were added in Basle there was the famous epistle dedicatory to Francis I, and its direct, impassioned approach should be seen against the background of Langey's diplomatic mission. Throughout his stay at Basle, Calvin's fears as well as his hopes for the progress of French Protestantism remained focused on Paris and the French Court. The earlier flight to Basle of his Paris friend, Nicolas Cop, must to some degree have been instrumental in making Calvin choose the same way. Cop was the son of a native Bâlois who had become a personal physician to Francis I. It was after delivering his famous address in favour of the new Gospel, a speech inspired by Calvin, that Cop had been compelled to leave the realm.[43] In the summer of 1536 Calvin returned briefly to Paris after he had visited the Duchess of Ferrara, Renée de France.

A direct result of that visit were the two letters to French Evangelicals to be published in Basle a year later in spite of the last minute intervention of the Strasbourg reformers, who disapproved of Calvin's severity with the Nicodemists.[44] The Basle publishers by now had recognized Calvin's potential, but his co-operation

---

[41] A case in point is the role played by the Basle ministers during the trial of Bolsec in Geneva: Wernle, *Calvin und Basel* 86ff.

[42] See below p. 108f.

[43] J. Rott, Documents strasbourgeois concernant Calvin, *Revue d'histoire et de philosophie religieuses* 44 (1964), 290-335, esp. 290ff.

[44] **No. 228**; Wernle, *Calvin und Basel* 8, 12, 28; *Calvini opera* 11.26f. A letter from Leo Jud seems to indicate that one of the *Epistolae duae* appeared at Basle anonymously in German translation whereas a similar translation of the other one was rejected by the printers. No copy of this impression seems to be known today.

ended essentially with the Latin translation of his first Geneva catechism in 1538.[45] The second, enlarged version of the *Institutes* may largely represent the work he did during his second stay in Basle after the unhappy removal from Geneva in the summer of 1538, but Robert Winter idled away his chance to publish the book, and Calvin thereafter preferred the Strasbourg press of W. Rihel.[46] Oporinus wrote him repeatedly soliciting more copy,[47] but only much later and more or less by accident did he re-appear among the Basle authors.[48]

At the time of his second visit Calvin's theological fame was safely established, but even now, the university made no move to secure his services. The project of a French church in Basle had been mentioned in 1535 and now came up once again, but was never seriously considered.[49] It remained for Strasbourg to call on Calvin for the sake both of its theological school and its Francophone congregation. Strasbourg, unlike Basle, offered him access to the crucial political events and religious debates of the day. It also offered him a practical model for the church of Geneva.[50]

While the French church in Strasbourg thus attracted those Francophones who, guided by Calvin's *Institutes*, desired to join the sort of congregational life based on its principles, Basle acquired in the 1540s and 1550s the dubious and not quite justified reputation of a centre that merely tolerated upright followers of Calvin, but especially welcomed those Francophones who had learned to defy him. The very absence of a properly organized French church had earlier facilitated the political activities of Langey and his staff of agents. Now it encouraged Castellio to settle there amid the circle of his Italian friends and sympathizers. It also assisted the physician Jean Bauhin to retain his respectability in spite of his friendship with the Anabaptist David Joris and of the stubborn Castellionism which he exhibited abroad.[51] With the exception of Castellio, Bauhin, and some members of the printing profession, few Francophones are known to have settled at Basle in this period. Among the French-speaking visitors who arrived in the later 1540s or during the 1550s there are those who came especially to meet Castellio or, at any rate, had been deeply influenced by his character and his views when they left. Such was the Sieur de Falais[52] who proceeded to Geneva, such the brothers Des Gouttes who returned to Lyons, Thomas La Farge who later lived in that same town, Jean Vertunien de Lavau who returned to Poitiers,[53] François Perrucel de La Rivière who continued to correspond with Castellio as he went on to become a

---

[45] **No. 225.**

[46] Wernle, *Calvin und Basel* 21ff.

[47] *Ibid.* 12f., 42f., 53; Steinmann 14f.; *Calvini opera* 10^2. 90f.; 11.464ff; 12.238.

[48] For *Admonitio paterna* (**No. 229**) see *Calvini opera* 12.56, 81 which confirm that the impression was made in Basle and that Calvin was not pleased with its quality; cf. Wernle, *Calvin und Basel* 48. For *Francisci Spierae ... historia* (**No. 482f.**) see *ibid.* 73f.; Bietenholz, *Ital.Humanismus* 24.

[49] Wernle, *Calvin und Basel* 19.

[50] Wernle, *Calvin und Basel* 22; H. Strohl, La théorie et la pratique des quatre ministères à Strasbourg avant l'arrivée de Calvin, *BSHPF* 84 (1935), 123-144 and: Bucer et Calvin, *BSHPF* 87 (1938), 254-360.

[51] See above p. 63.

[52] Cf. above p. 59f. and below p. 127.

[53] *Matrikel* 2. 87; Buisson, *Castellion* 2.248f., 443.; Droz, *Etudiants français*.

French pastor in London and later in Frankfurt,[54] and others.[55] Sooner or later most of them would openly clash with the leaders of Geneva.   In the same period other Francophone visitors to Basle were equally prone to arouse the suspicion of Calvin.   Postel was a Catholic.   Baudouin, Charles Du Moulin,[56] and even Hubert Languet [57] were markedly tolerant, if not equivocal, in their approaches to other confessions.   All were content to live over long periods among Catholics or Lutherans ; on one or another occasion all were severely criticized by Calvin and Beza.   No wonder that so faithful a Calvinist as François Hotman pointedly expressed his vexation when he visited Basle in 1555.   Calvinism, he felt, was no more popular here than in Paris.[58]

An extreme, yet not untypical, illustration of Basle's curious role in the religious emigration is presented by Eustorg de Beaulieu.   When he died there in 1552, in spite of his musical talent a desolate eccentric, 150 gold crowns came to light in a box full of filthy boots.[59]   He probably knew Castellio from their common years at Lyons where both nourished poetical ambitions.[60]   With some very bad, if licentious, French verse to his credit Beaulieu finally went to Geneva and Lausanne, where he studied for the ministry without attaining a correct use of Latin.   Through the favours of a Bernese patrician he was, nevertheless, settled in a Vaudois parsonage until his private conduct made him intolerable.   Eventually he moved to Basle where he had already published an edifying treatise in French verse.[61]   He registered in the university and persuaded a printer to publish his *Espinglier des filles*.[62]   The first edition was a poor job.   Numerous errors suggest that the compositor knew little French, but Beaulieu's text hardly deserved a greater effort.   This short selection of moral precepts for young girls, clumsily paraphrased from Vives and others, seems now shallow and boring.   Yet Beaulieu should have been able to write from experience.   His dismissal from the ministry was due to an affair with a girl of fifteen whom he continued to mistreat after he had finally agreed to marry her.

In 1549 Farel had written to Oporinus, warning him of Beaulieu's past.[63]   Yet Beaulieu managed to persuade Bonifacius Amerbach to support him with grants from

---

[54] He came to Basle in 1550; cf. *France prot.* and Buisson, *Castellion* 2.247, 423f., 427, 454ff. ; *Correspondance de Bèze* 4.36, 39 and passim.

[55] E.g. Guillaume Aubert who was at Basle in 1555 (*Matrikel* 2.92). His death three years later was reported to Castellio by Jean L'Archier (Buisson, *Castellion* 2.442).

[56] See above p. 61f.

[57] See below p. 119f.

[58] *Calvini opera* 15.803f., Hotman to Bullinger : " ... Castalionis ita sunt studiosi et amantes plerique, ut hoc quasi Atlante coelum fulciri religio et pietas existimetur. ... Calvinus autem nihilo melius hic audit quam Lutetiae. Quod si quis aut deierantem aut lascivientem coarguat, Calvinista contumeliae causa nominatur" (29 September, 1555).

[59] M. A. Pegg in his bibliographical introduction to E. de Beaulieu, *Les divers rapportz*, Geneva 1964, 28ff. and passim ; cf. also H. Harwitt, *E. de Beaulieu, a Disciple of Marot*, New York 1918 (reprint 1966). On Beaulieu as a composer : P. Pidoux, *Le Psautier huguenot du XVIe siècle*, Basle 1962, 2.188 and passim.

[60] Buisson, *Castellion* 1.28.

[61] **No. 110**, stated to be in part extracted from a book *Chrestienne resiouyance*. In Allen 5.28 an ed., Basle 1546, is mentioned, but I have not seen a copy.

[62] *Matrikel* 2.55 and **No. 111f.** ; cf H. P. Clive, The Calvinist Attitude to Music, *BHR* 19 (1957), 300ff.

[63] *Calvini opera* 13.426.

the Erasmus bequest.   To this end he once composed an ingenious letter,[64] describing how Erasmus appeared to him one night when his nagging poverty would not let him sleep. Erasmus recalled Beaulieu's earlier interest in his paraphrase of Saint Luke and ordered him to apply for another subsidy from the bequest.   Amerbach sympathized and helped him as he helped Curione and Castellio during the same years.   No wonder that Calvin, Viret and Farel accused them of complicity in Beaulieu's attempts to have a paraphrase of Saint Paul in French verse accepted by Oporinus.   According to Beza's information Beaulieu's text opened with a sharp attack upon his enemies.[65]   As the book was never published it remains doubtful to what degree Beaulieu succeeded in passing at Basle for a victim of Calvinist persecution.

In the second half of the century the French émigré community at Basle gradually came to look more respectable in the eyes both of native citizens and of Calvinist leaders in Geneva and elsewhere.   Guests like Hotman, Ramus and the Pithou brothers enhanced its prestige, and when after the Saint Bartholomew's massacre the princes of the blood arrived, it looked brilliant by any standards.   The splendour was short-lived, as the princes and their numerous party left before long, but the organizational foundations laid in 1572 survived.   There was now a French church with its own ministers.   The first of these, Daniel Toussain the older, had grown up in Montbéliard and studied at Basle, but unlike his father he enjoyed a record of unblemished Calvinist orthodoxy.   On a December Sunday, 1572, he was the speaker at a brilliant academic ceremony.   After referring to the recent persecutions in France he conveyed to the hospitable town the thanks of his fellow refugees, especially the Coligny sons.[66]   Toussain was soon called away to more demanding duties in the Palatinate.   In the spring of 1573 his place was taken by another refugee, Jean Tenant, who also acted as a Hebrew instructor in the university.[67]   His successor, Matthieu Virel, quarrelled publicly with the *antistes* Sulzer and other local pastors with Lutheran leanings, but the city council did not act on their suggestion to close down the French church after the peace of Beaulieu and the resulting exodus of émigrés.[68]   Virel's successor, Jean Desfos [69] ministered to a growing congregation and died in 1588, the year in which the French church won official status.   There were now two ministers, Léonard Constant who had been registered in the university roll for 1585 [70] and died in the Basle plague of 1609-10, and Jacques Couet du Vivier

---

[64] UBB ms. G.II.15[1], fol. 100-103 ; cf. A. Hartmann, Bonifacius Amerbach als Verwalter der Erasmusstiftung, *Basler Jahrbuch*, Basle 1957, 7-28. Beaulieu's epitaph for Erasmus, still composed at Lyons, is as poor as his other verse (*Les divers rapportz*, *op. cit.*, 376).

[65] *Calvini opera* 13.411, 426 ; Wernle, *Calvin und Basel* 80f.

[66] *Matrikel* 2.94 and A. Bernus, Trois pasteurs échappés aux massacres de la Saint-Barthélemy, *BSHPF* 41 (1892), 393-408, also for what follows.

[67] *Matrikel* 2.215 and Droz, *Etudiants français*.

[68] *Matrikel* 2.246 : "Matheus Virellus Massiliensis, principis Condei minister " ; *France prot.* ; *Correspondance de B. Vulcanius* 237ff., 419f., 451. Virel published in Basle a calendar manual : **No. 1038**.

[69] *Matrikel* 2.274 : "dominus Johannes Fossius, Aquitanus, pastor ecclesiae Gallicae in hac urbe."

[70] *Matrikel* 2.333 ; Droz, *Etudiants français; France prot.*[2] Constant had first visited Basle in 1576. He corresponded with J. J. Grynaeus and T. Zwinger. Especially to the latter he addressed a number of letters from Geneva where he seems to have remained for most of 1586-1587 : see UBB ms., in particular, Fr. Gr. II. 8, fol. 422-430.

from Paris, who succeeded Desfos in 1588.[71]   Couet deserves our attention. Although he died at Basle in 1608, he frequently visited Paris and Metz during the last decade of his life. Catherine, Duchess of Bar, the Protestant sister of Henry IV, did not succeed in retaining him permanently, but to strengthen her conviction he confronted a Jesuit doctor in a disputation in 1599 before the court of Nancy, and published in Basle an account of this event. Couet also took an active and benevolent interest in the Francophone students at Basle,[72] but above all he steadfastly presented the dogmas of Genevan Calvinism in the face of stormy manifestations of heterodoxy which continued to rock the boat of the French church.

As early as the spring of 1577 Couet, then a minister at Avallon, had paid a passing visit to Basle and spent an evening in debate with another guest of the same inn, Fausto Sozzini. The memorable result of this chance encounter was Sozzini's manifesto of his Antitrinitarian doctrine, *De Jesu Christo servatore.* While Sozzini was working on this treatise he salvaged, and subsequently published, part of the Castellio manuscripts.[73] The year in which Couet debated with Sozzini was also that of Sulzer's efforts to close the French church. Orthodox Calvinism at Basle was thus engaged in a two-pronged battle, against Lutheran tendencies on the one hand and Antitrinitarian on the other. Both had at least certain points in common, such as their strong objection to the Calvinist doctrine of predestination. F. Hotman, who had once so bitterly denounced Castellio's own circle, was again on hand to attack with equal zest both the *antistes* Sulzer and the professor and editor of Machiavelli, N. Stupanus, exponent of the Castellionist and Erastian circle of Italian émigrés.[74] Also in 1576-77 the university roll recorded the presence at Basle of a « Claudius Villerius Gallus » perhaps identical with Jean Morély. As far as France was concerned Morély had lost his battle against the rigid Presbyterianism of Beza by 1572, but as we have seen it continued in Germany and frequently spilled over into Basle's university circles.[75]

It was during Couet's ministry that these smouldering conflicts merged and jointly erupted in one *cause célèbre* that nearly split the French congregation, produced a flood of polemical pamphlets and books, kept the entire town breathless, and involved the council in a frantic correspondence with governments from Geneva to the Rhineland. Couet's upright orthodoxy first compelled the opponents to give battle. His strategy dominated the ensuing operations and led to a victory that confirmed and perpetuated the *rapprochement* between the French church and the civic and ecclesiastical authorities. His main opponent, and the central figure in the conflict, was Antoine Lescaille. Born in Bar-le-Duc, this former monk reached Basle in 1573 among the many refugees who arrived in the wake of the Saint Bartholomew's massacre. He built a respectable business as passement weaver and merchant.[76] He became a citizen and was elected elder of his church while his sons were approaching university age. Couet had chosen his man well. For all

---

[71] *Matrikel* 2.431 ; Couet's son was registered the year thereafter : 2.446. Cf. Droz, *Etudiants français; France prot.*[2] A number of ms. letters by J. Couet and by his son, especially to Jacob Zwinger, are in UBB : ms. Fr. Gr. II. 23[1], No. 117-120, etc.

[72] Several of them acknowledged his assistance when publishing their theses, so Louis Allard, Jacques Corne, Frédéric Stapedius, and Paul Toussain.

[73] See below p. 134f. and Buisson, *Castellion* 2.316f.

[74] See below p. 117.

[75] See above p. 68f. and Kingdon, *Geneva and the Consolidation* 122ff.

[76] Cf. H. Vuilleumier, *Histoire de l'Eglise réformée du Pays de Vaud sous le régime bernois*, Lausanne 1927-1933, 2.141ff. ; Geisendorf 386ff.

his stubborn spiritualism, Lescaille possessed neither much education nor a logical intelligence, nor had he a truly speculative disposition. It does not appear that he ever referred to Morély or Erastus, but at the gatherings in his church he must have met Claude Aubery when the latter studied in Basle for his medical degree.[77] From him Lescaille acquired a superficial and somewhat simplified grasp of various arguments which questioned the doctrinal authority and especially the disciplinary competence of the presbytery. For a man like Lescaille it would be surprising if he had not known the famous preface to Castellio's French Bible which contained a summary of his doctrine of justification, that doctrine which Castellio himself elaborated in one of the treatises posthumously edited by Sozzini and which Aubery also reiterated.[78] It was around this issue that the conflict between Lescaille and Couet hinged. Lescaille's repeated denials that he was indebted to Aubery were undoubtedly designed to protect his friend. Yet it is true that Lescaille added an emphasis of his own to Castellio's and Aubery's views on justification. As a man who toiled with his hands, Lescaille was profoundly critical of intellectuals.[79] The sting of Calvinism against which he reacted with violent protest was its blatant disregard of good works. In his own view sanctification, which formed an integral part of justification, came very close to being equated with good works in the sense of manual labour. In his youth the simplicity of his convent—perhaps a Franciscan house—may have prepared him for this view, as in the end it would facilitate his retreat into Catholicism after he had been repudiated by all Protestant churches. Except for its naïve formulation this same stand might have associated Jean Lescaille with Jean Hotman de Villiers [80] and others who kept a watchful eye on the political stage and hoped to achieve a reconciliation with the Catholics at the price of easing radical Calvinist positions in favour of Lutheran compromises.

The various stages of the quarrel can be reconstructed from the rich crop of pamphlets published by both sides, especially a miscellaneous collection bound together in the volume D. 22014 of the *Bibliothèque Nationale*.[81] In the summer

---

[77] See above p. 65.

[78] Cf. Buisson, *Castellion* 2.204f., 215f. and passim. For the popularity of the 1572 bilingual ed. of Castellio's *New Testament* among the Francophone colony of Basle cf. *Correspondance de B. Vulcanius* 127f.

[79] See especially the *Anti-Inquisitor* (below n. 81) where ch. 13 in entitled : " Homines literati semper restitisse veritati."

[80] He was at Basle in 1592-1593 ; see below pp. 212ff.

[81] The contents are as follows :

(1) *Declaration et confession de foy d'Antoine Lescaille*... Contains five short pieces, among them a letter " A Monsieur mon compere, Monsieur Castiglion. "

(*) *Lettres d'Antoine Lescaille a M. Theodore de Beze* ; dated 2 January, 1592.

(2) *Advis a Antoine Lescaille, marchant habitant de Basle sur certain escrit publié par luy touchant le merite des œuvres* ; dated 10 March, 1592.

(3) *Lettres de Frere Iean des Antomeures a l'autheur sans nom de la lettre d'avis...* (= proceding No.) ; dated 1 May, 1592.

(4) *L'Anti-Inquisiteur*, 1592. Appended are two letters, one to Constant, the other to Battier.

(5) *Responsio ... ad calumnias et invectivas publicatas contra Antonium Lescalleum per M. Theodorum Bezam in libro eius qui Apologia pro iustificatione etc. ab eo inscriptus est* ; impressa Germaniae, 1592.

(6) *La doctrine ancienne du premier, deuxieme, troisieme et dernier iugement ...*, par ALPDDGGH, 1592 (pp. 26ff. : Lescaille's account of the Basle affair down to the autumn of 1591).

(**) *Protestation d'Antoine Lescaille contre la nouvelle inquisition couetesque*, 21 November, 1591.

(Continuation of this note on next page.)

of 1590 the minister Léonard Constant explained in a sermon that the Evangelists were referring only to the reprobate when they said that God would judge everybody according to his works, or so at least Lescaille understood the sermon. On 23 October Lescaille called on Constant with a written statement of his own view of the matter. There followed discussions in private and at various levels of the congregation. On 4 November Lescaille stepped down as an elder and on the same day Constant and Couet consulted the Basle *antistes* J. J. Grynaeus. For some time the latter tried to mediate. However, when it became clear to Lescaille that Grynaeus sided with the French ministers, he first appealed to the master of his guild and finally, on 20-21 April, 1591, to the burgomaster and the council, in an attempt to

(7) *Lettres envoyees aux tresmagnifiques Seigneurs de Bernn. Avec la Response categorique a la condamnation ... d'Antoine de Lescaille*; De l'imprimerie de Theophile Guotman, anno DXCIII [sic]. Dated from Hegenheim, 13 June, 1593.

(8) *Demande aux Ministres, successeurs de M. I. Calvin*, dated from Spires, 15 January, 1593.

(9) *Anti-Inquisitor*, 1593 (*BNC* attributes this piece erroneously to S. Castellio).

(10) *Descouverte et refutation des mensonges et calomnies impudemment imposees a M. Auberi ... en deux livres imprimez a Geneve par Iacob Stoer, 1593, dont les tiltres sensuivent: Responses chrestiennes aux doctrines ... d'Antoine Lescaille, par Iaques Couet ...; et une Remonstrance chrestienne ed Leonard Constant, aussi ministre, audit Lescaille*, A Thurin, par Philippes de Garignan, 1593.

(11) *Epistola Antonii Lescallei ad omnes pastores ecclesiarum confessionis Augustanae, Saxonicae ...*, T. Gutman, 1593.

(12) *Lettres envoyees au Roy Tres-chrestien avec la response ... d'Antoine de Lescaille au volume de M. Iaques Couet ...*, T. Gutmann, 1593.

(13) *Response d'Antoine de Lescaille a M. Leonard Constant*; dated from Hegenheim, 10 June, 1593.

(14) *Response d'Antoine de Lescaille a une lettre imprimee, a luy adressee par Iaques Bastier* (appended to Couet's book); dated from Hegenheim, 1 June, 1593.

(15) *Lettres envoyees a tous les tres illustres princes, reverendissimes prelats, officiers de la Couronne et principaux seigneurs catholiques de toute la Sainte Eglise Gallicane par Antoine de Lescaille, serviteur de ce Dieu qui a eslu les choses folles de ce monde pour confondre les sages*, T. Gutmann, 1593.

(16) *Response briefve aux mesdisances ... contre Maistre Claude Aubery ... par Nicolas D'Aubenerd* (in Couet's book), De l'imprimerie de Iacob Schandoz, 1593.

(17) *Brieve declaration et veritable de Messeigneurs ... de la ville de Basle* (= **No. 697**).

(18) *Dialogus de statu turbulento ecclesiae huius seculi* (= **No. 378**; see below p. 214.).

This collection poses a typographical problem. There can be little doubt that (17) was printed at Basle together with the German text of which it is a translation. Yet another five pieces could be the products of the same press, e.g. that of Foillet or that of Waldkirch. While thus the possibility that some of Lescaille's pamphlets were printed at Basle cannot be dismissed altogether, it seems more likely that this group originated in some small Alsatian press, using the same standard material: (1, 4, 6, 9). Most of the other pieces probably belong to another (Alsatian?) printer who often uses the pseudonym of Theophil Gutmann: (2, 7, 10, 11, 12. 13, 14, 15, 16). It may, finally, be added that Martin Böckler at Freiburg i. Br. printed for Lescaille a *Antithesis verae antiquae Christianae religionis et novae Antichristianae, cum declaratione quatuor praecipuorum errorum confessionis Calvinisticae et oppositis refutationibus ecclesiae Catholicae*, 1597. The text makes it rather unlikely that Lescaille should ever have reverted to a Catholicism of any profundity.

Among the very numerous mss. in UBB, referring to the Lescaille affair only the following may be mentioned: Ki.Ar. 22[b], fol. 199f., a supplication to the Basle ministers composed in the name of Lescaille's wife an dated 16 November, 1593. *Ibid.* fol. 193f., two theological statements by Lescaille, probably submitted with his wife's supplication. Ki.Ar. 23[b], fol. 221-227: the copy of an apologia by Claude Aubery for his book *De fide catholica*, addressed to J. J. Grynaeus. *Ibid.* fol. 59f.: a letter (in German) by Lescaille to the Basle government, dated from Strasbourg, 8 April, 1595.

ward off the threatened excommunication by his church. On 31 July Lescaille was in Geneva to plead his case with Beza.[82] It seems that the latter persuaded him to make a public submission before his church in Basle. Lescaille did so on 29 August, but the short statement he read failed to satisfy the ministers and to quell the trouble. After attending the Frankfurt autumn fair, Lescaille apparently did not return to Basle.

By this time Claude Aubery had become deeply involved in the Lescaille affair. When Lescaille first presented his views in writing to Constant, the Calvinist ministers thought they recognized in Aubery the author of the statement submitted. Both Aubery and Lescaille denied the charge, although the latter admitted that the writing was « un enfant dividu et par consequent peut avoir plusieurs peres.» [83] Next Aubery appeared in Basle on his way to the Frankfurt autumn fair of 1590. New suspicions and accusations were the result. If Lescaille is to be believed, Couet finally followed Aubery to the fair in an attempt to stop him from distributing his book De fide catholica.[84] A year later, after the autumn fair of 1591, Lescaille accused Beza of having contrived the virtual suppression of Aubery's book so that noblemen and scholars from Germany, Flanders and Poland looked in vain for a copy.[85] Renewed denunciation in the wake of the Lescaille affair invalidated Aubery's former excuses, and in 1593 he had to resign his position in Lausanne.

Lescaille's family remained in Basle. His son Nicolas entered the university in 1591, and an Adam who was perhaps Nicolas's brother, did so in 1592.[86] The father, Antoine Lescaille, meanwhile lived on and off in the Alsatian vicinity of Basle, spending much money and energy on publicity. He published open letters to Beza and to prominent members of the refugee church in Basle, such as Jacques Battier and Giovan Francesco Castiglione.[87] These were followed by appeals to the governments of Basle's confederates and allies, including the Most Christian King. There were also open letters to the pastors of the Augsburg confession and the « seigneurs catholiques de toute la Sainte Eglise Gallicane,» and there were wild apologies such as L'Anti-Inquisiteur. Among the usual fulminations against his enemies like « trompettes de Satan », « race de Caïn », « pharisiens aveugles », this treatise occasionally offers a deep insight into the common concerns of all radical Protestants. To quote one :

O combien de catholiques ont esté plus gens de bien la premiere annee qu'ils sont devenus evangeliques que la seconde, et plus gens de bien la seconde que la troisieme, et plus gens de bien la troisieme que la quatrieme : tant qu'en fin ayans desraciné de leurs cœurs ceste ancienne doctrine, ascavoir que Dieu rendra au dernier iour à chacun selon les œuvres, ils sont par ce moyen allez tous les iours en empirant, tant que la mort eternelle s'en est ensuivie.[88]

---

[82] Lescaille's own indications are confirmed by Beza's letter to J.J. Grynaeus of 3 August, 1591 : UBB ms. Ki.Ar. 18b, fol. 183. In his extensive correspondence with the Basle ministers Beza was continually pressing for a hard line against Lescaille.

[83] BN : D. 22014 (*).

[84] BN : D. 22014 (10).

[85] BN : D. 22014(*).

[86] Matrikel 2.391, 402.

[87] He must, at least for some time, have been sympathetic to Lescaille and tried to mediate between him, Couet and Grynaeus, as, fifteen years earlier, he had acted as a go-between for Couet and Sozzini : BN : D. 22014 (1) and Buisson, Castellion 2.284n., 317. Cf. Matrikel 2.215, 416, 488.

[88] BN : D. 22014 (4).

In the autumn of 1595 the affair Lescaille came to a head as far as Basle was concerned. Antoine must have returned to the city, since in September he was in prison together with his son Nicolas as a result of yet another religious dispute. Adam Lescaille was jailed at the same time; curiously, however, on the charge of being a public nuisance in the *Zunftstube zum Himmel*, where he drank wine out of his shoe. The family must now have left the city. In 1596 Adam Lescaille was studying at Leipzig [89], and the Huguenot national synod at Saumur condemned Antoine, then said to be residing at Altkirch. The widespread concern caused by Lescaille indicates that he was not without friends. At Basle such highly respected men as G. F. Castiglione already referred to, Denis Godefroy of Paris and the French doctor Guillaume Arragos [90] showed varying degrees of sympathy for his stand. Writing to J. J. Grynaeus from Heidelberg, Daniel Toussain dismissed Lescaille as a madman, but blamed those who put weapons in his hands.[91] He may well have been right, although it may have been his enemies like Couet who pushed him forward rather than his friends. As late as 1599 Couet was still preoccupied with the defence of predestination.[92]

It seems that the Lescaille affair was the last major upheaval to trouble the quiet life of the French congregation among their fellow Protestants at Basle. The printing industry continued to bear witness to the presence of French immigrants and their connections with Francophones abroad. The authors accepted, however, were all good Calvinists or Zwinglians and, with negligible exceptions, they refrained from polemics even against the Lutherans and concentrated instead on pastoral edification and spiritual fortification against the popish wolf. The existence of Basle's Francophones after the heat of the Lescaille affair had cooled down is well reflected in the scanty records left by another passement weaver and merchant. Typically we do not know much about the quiet life at Basle of Martin Du Voisin except that he had immigrated and been made a citizen, whereas his wife had been executed at Bruges in 1597. In 1608 while travelling on business he spent a night at a Catholic town near Lucerne. At his inn he had a disagreement with a woman, a Catholic pilgrim. His arguments about pilgrimages and the sinlessness of the Virgin were reported to the authorities. He was executed, despite the pleas of the Basle government, which despatched a special courier to save him. Du Voisin's friends in Basle may at least have drawn comfort from the special sermon which the widely respected *antistes* J. J. Grynaeus preached in honour of the martyr.[93]

[89] *Matrikel* 2.402; an Antonius Lescailleus, baptized at Basle in 1587, however, matriculated at Basle in 1603-1604: *Matrikel* 3. 35.

[90] Arragos' attempt at mediation is revealed in a short statement preserved among the papers of J.J. Grynaeus: UBB ms. Ki.Ar. 22b, fol. 205. Godefroy moved from Basle to Strasbourg and may have done so in order to protest against the way the Lescaille affair was handled by the French ministers: cf. below p. 213; also *France prot.*[2] s.v. L. Constant. By contrast, Pierre Le Noble of Troyes supported Couet: BN: D. 22014 (6 and **); *Matrikel* 2.387.

[91] UBB ms. G.II.12,[1] fol. 263, D. Toussain to J.J. Grynaeus, s.l., 22 January [1595?]: "Infelix ille Lescallius certas theses nobis inscripsit et misit: verum hominem palam insanum contemnemus sicut a Maguntino et aliis principibus, ad quos eum non puduit anno superiore nugas suas mittere eosque palam compellare, contemtus fuit. Sed destandi sunt illi qui homini amenti tela subministrant, et dolendum est ecclesiam Gallicam ... talibus carcinomatibus laborare ... "

[92] No. 331. In the same year Frédéric Castellio published a German translation of Couet's earlier treatise on the Eucharist: No. 329.

[93] No. 416. More biographical information on Du Voisin is given in an enlarged re-edition of Grynaeus' sermon, Amberg, J. Schönfeld, 1609.

In spite of the continuous assimilation of Francophones, however, the French church continued its existence and still carries on today. Once its independent status had reluctantly been granted by the authorities, its perserverance and its faithful observation of the Huguenot virtues was bound to impress the Bâlois. It set an example and undoubtedly helped to bring about Basle's increasingly strict adherence to the camp of Calvinist orthodoxy in the seventeenth century.[94]

---

[94] M. Geiger, *Die Basler Kirche und Theologie im Zeitalter der Hochorthodoxie*, Zollikon-Zurich 1952, passim.

CHAPTER FOUR

FRENCH DIPLOMATS AND POLITICAL AGENTS

In the early 1530s Guillaume Du Bellay, Sieur de Langey, himself seems to have picked Basle as a relay station for the French political service. From that date to the close of the religious wars the city continued to be visited by agents representing the French Crown, Huguenots and on occasions even Catholic Spain. Although Basle never attained the importance of a diplomatic nerve-centre such as Strasbourg, there were several reasons to make Langey's choice a sensible one. Basle lay beyond the fringe of the Habsburg territories along the French border, yet was within easy reach of the frontier of the realm and permitted ready access to the Empire. She was also conveniently close to the permanent French embassy in the Swiss cantons established at Soleure since 1522. She enjoyed a reputation for independence and ' Erasmian ' restraint which permitted her to maintain generally good relations with the reformed towns and Lutheran princes no less than with the house of Habsburg. Her efficient and comparatively unrestricted printers, finally, were willing to serve any customer as long as he would pay.

Langey's choice of Basle thus was a clever one, all the more so that from the outset it was far from obvious. Initially Basle's German nationalism and faith in the Empire was as strong as her distrust of the French. As late as November 1519 she was the site of successful negotiations between the Swiss cantons and the imperial ambassadors aptly supported by Cardinal Schiner.[1] By contrast French diplomats throughout the second decade of the sixteenth century apparently had no business there. In 1520-21, however, a liberal supply of French gold restored the friendship between France and all cantons except Zurich,[2] while rumours reached Bonifacius Amerbach that French agents had tried to kidnap Schinner *en route* from Zurich to Freiburg im Breisgau.[3] No matter how faithfully humanists like Amerbach might perpetuate their affection for the Empire and their aversion to France, the Basle government endorsed the Franco-Swiss military convention in May, 1521,[4] and in

---

[1] Wackernagel 3.304 ; Hartmann 2.214 ; Piccard 104ff.

[2] Rott 1.237ff.

[3] Hartmann 2.255.

[4] A typical statement of Amerbach's reaction to the deal may be found in a letter to Alciato (Hartmann 2.309) : " Concurritur undique tam ab hiis, qui sacramento in imperii verba adacti sunt, quam ab aliis ad Galliarum regem. Helvetii foedus cum Gallo pepigere ea sub conditione, ne quid contra imperium moliatur. Videres apud nos tot ferme stipendiarios quot homines. Mirum hercule, unde Gallo tanta pecuniarum vis. Nihil non promittit, plurima elargitur ; inaurabit nos, quod pollicetur. Sed quid promittere ledit ? Vel si fiet, vereor, ne auro (quod aiunt) Tolosano. " The enemies of the French alliance managed to bring about the fall and ruin of Hans Gallician, one of the

1522 the future Cardinal of Tournon visited Erasmus at Basle while on a diplomatic mission.[5]

The continued retention of Swiss regiments in French pay gave the cantons henceforward a degree of political influence with the crown. In 1531 Francis I heeded the pleas of Berne for the liberation of the preacher Antoine Saunier.[6] A succession of similar steps and even special embassies to Paris followed in years to come. Their success varied, but in 1557 Henry II decided that he had better comply, at least in part, with Swiss representations on behalf of the Huguenots arrested during a religious service in the rue Saint-Jacques.[7] In this way and in others, the crown had to cope with a fair share of Swiss unpleasantness as long as it relied on their mercenaries. The Swiss in turn were frequently annoyed with French delays in delivering the promised moneys. In 1525 a special French ambassador to the cantons was detained in Berne to enforce the settlement of arrears in the regular pensions as well as to exact some disputed fringe payments. The victim, Jean Morelet du Museau, a former royal secretary and a friend of Budé, finally obtained his freedom in the following year, but he had to leave his son Antoine behind as a hostage.[8] Coming in the wake of Pavia, the incident reveals a most uncharitable disposition in the face of the French calamities. In Basle too chauvinism and greed were running high.[9] It was in these circumstances that Langey was despatched to Rome by way of Switzerland to attempt first to ease the rigidity of the Swiss. However, he brought no money and consequently had to depart without success. The mission to Rome also ended in the disaster of the Sack, with grave danger to his life.[10]

In the 1530s when Langey showed renewed interest in Switzerland, and actually arrived in Basle, his activities bore little relation to those of the ordinary French ambassador at Soleure. While the latter was again facing a crisis over Swiss financial demands and the Basle council in 1536 even temporarily stopped recruitment for France,[11] Langey represented what seemed a noble cause and met with genuine good will on the part of Basle. Led by Langey's brother, Cardinal Jean Du Bellay, the family was then at the peak of its influence. It set the pace for French diplomacy as well as for cultural aspirations. Basle was chosen to serve both.[12] Between 1532 and 1536 Langey was mostly in Germany, where he master-minded and co-ordinated various French efforts to secure a better understanding among Protestant lands. He hoped to weld all German and Swiss Protestants into a large, French-dominated system of forces opposing the emperor for diverse reasons. When Langey first crossed the Rhine the Swiss cantons had just concluded a peace (the second *Landfrieden*, 1531-32) which for more than a century was to prevent them

---

prominent friends of France who was accused of fraud with pension money, but his exit had little or no political consequences: Piccard 109ff.

[5] Allen 5.217.

[6] Herminjard 2.329f.; G. Berthoud, L'arrestation d'Antoine Saunier, *BSHPF* 82 (1933), 321-325.

[7] *Calvini opera* 16.643f., 694, 736 and passim; *Correspondance de Bèze* 2.8 and passim; Kingdon, *Geneva and the Coming* 62. Cf. in this context Wernle, *Calvin und Basel* 32, 50ff.; *BSHPF* 17 (1868), 162ff., 546.

[8] Rott 1.274.

[9] Wackernagel 3.405ff.

[10] Bourrilly, *Langey* 21f. and passim for what follows; Rott 1.318, 322.

[11] Staatsarchiv Basel-Stadt, Missiven B.2.27 verso.

[12] Cf. below p. 203.

from relapsing into religious civil war. Since this settlement had been greatly helped by the tactful mediation of French diplomats,[13] Langey could expect the Protestant cantons to support his mission willingly.

When he set out for Germany in March 1532 at least one of the men selected to go with him had personal contacts in Basle and could count on a friendly welcome from the Frobens and Amerbachs. This man, Gervasius Wain, a native of Memmingen, must have been a surprising figure even in an age when scholarly learning and political intelligence work formed a popular combination. A Sorbonne doctor and a former rector of the university, Wain had visited Basle in 1528 to greet his old teacher Ber and to render homage to Erasmus [14]. While there is no immediate record of Wain's renewed presence in Basle, there is evidence that the city received serious consideration when Langey himself was facing the Swiss Diet in May 1534. No doubt he was asked to give some explanation for his king's recent conference with the pope in Marseille, where he himself had been present. According to his set of instructions he was prepared to say that Francis I's contacts with the pope offered the best hope for the speedy realization of a council in ways acceptable to the Germans and Swiss. According to Langey, Clement VII had been urged to summon it to a place " *à eulx agréable et de bien seur accès, just à Constance, Basle, Genève ou ailleurs.*" The instructions emphasized that Francis had dissuaded the pope from accepting the emperor's proposals for a Council in Italy. There, amid the Spanish armies, Charles V was said to have planned a sort of Catholic war council to work out strategy for the total suppression of Lutherans and Zwinglians alike.[15]

These instructions provided a suitable basis for Langey's further steps. As he had done with the leading Lutherans, he now invited the Swiss theologians to prepare for council and concord. In briefs addressed to the king they should list the points on which they were willing to make concessions, or, alternatively, would have to insist on modifications of Catholic dogma. Unlike the Lutherans, the Swiss theologians were sceptical and complied with Langey's wishes only after much hesitation. But the Bâlois Myconius, who seems to have met Langey personally, at least was convinced of his sincerity. Myconius also noted the softening of French domestic policies which occurred at about the same time and culminated in the humiliation of Noël Béda, to be followed by his confinement in Mount Saint-Michel.[16]

While Langey still waited for the Swiss briefs to follow those already submitted by the Germans, the chances for the success of his mission were further thwarted by the *Placards* affair, which caused a new wave of religious persecution in France. Among the refugees arriving from Paris was the Bâlois book merchant Andreas Wingarter, whose wife was still detained in jail.[17] In the same winter of 1534-35 more fuel was added to Swiss indignation as Francis openly entertained the Turkish ambassadors in his capital. But Langey was far from giving up. In the king's name he issued a manifesto to the estates of the Empire, printed copies of which were distributed among the cantons. Bullinger at once assumed that Langey himself was the author of this able presentation.[18] After the granting of a royal amnesty

---

[13] Rott 1.316.

[14] See below p. 178.

[15] Bourrilly, *Langey* 174ff., and : François I et les Protestants, *BSHPF* 49 (1900), 337-365, 477-495 ; Rott 1.284, 318.

[16] Herminjard 3.146f., 181-186.

[17] Herminjard 3.240.

[18] Herminjard 3.249-254 ; Bouvier 197ff.

in July 1535 Langey felt confident enough to have the king invite Melanchthon to Paris. Thus he tried to capitalize on the friendly and moderate tenor of the briefs which Melanchthon and Bucer had submitted prior to the *Placards* affair. Meanwhile the Swiss theologians too had turned in their statements, but they offered little ground for satisfaction. Even Myconius's answer was far from encouraging. The Basle *antistes* praised the desire for concord, but presented the question of papal authority as the crucial, insoluble problem in the way of agreement.[19]

But Langey carried on. After having visited southern Germany in the spring of 1536 he came to Basle and settled down for some months, assessing the situation, directing the movements of his aides, and supplying them with printed propaganda. Although in a letter to Francis I he had to admit the failure of his recent mission in Germany,[20] he continued to present the French viewpoint on the most recent international developments. In particular he edited the *Exemplaria*, a short collection of letters issued in the name of Francis, the royal sons, and himself, which offered in essence a reply to the emperor's menacing speech at Rome in April 1536. Not surprisingly his arguments were most impressive when vindicating the French claims to Milan, for it was now, after the death of the last Sforza duke, that Charles V resolved to drop all pretence of trying to achieve a negotiated settlement of the disputed succession. Turning to the Turkish alliance, Langey's letter collection protested that the French king had no money to befriend the Sultan. Sarcastically it added that the king was willing to send a crusading army into northern Italy if he were called upon to do so. This letter collection was published promptly at Basle and also translated into German.[21]

When Langey returned to France an aide was ordered to stay behind at Basle. The noble-minded, gentlemanlike, impeccably educated Jean Morel of Embrun will also be encountered later on in this study, for he remained a warm and influential friend of the Basle humanist circle.[22] Morel had come to Basle not later than 1533-34, when his name appears in the university roll.[23] In 1537 he had to leave for a visit to his native Embrun (Hautes-Alpes), where he was immediately suspected of heresy. Langey himself had to intervene on his behalf, declaring that his agent's interest in *Lutheriana* was purely professional.[24] By that time the Basle agency must have been firmly established, for Langey did not wish to leave it unattended during the

---

[19] Bourrilly, *François et les Protestants, op. cit.* 338ff.; cf. R. Hari in *Propagande religieuse* 141. Only the Lutheran briefs suited Langey's purpose and he submitted them to the Sorbonne. In 1607 they were published by Jean Hotman de Villiers (cf. below p. 215). Bullinger and Myconius knew the replies of Melanchthon and Bucer; their dislike of them was shared among the Huguenots of Paris: Herminjard 3.340.

[20] Bourrilly, *Langey* 223ff.

[21] **No. 393.** The initials make the attribution to Basle virtually certain and to Oporinus and his associates probable (cf. Schneeli-Heitz, tables 25, 41 and 87). The *Exemplaria* were reprinted with further additions by R. Estienne in 1537 and subsequently distributed among Swiss and German merchants at the Lyons fair (Bourrilly, *Langey* 250 and Armstrong, *Estienne* 141ff.). I cannot decide whether a partial German translation was printed in Basle: BM, 1193 h 40 (1). On the other hand, there can be no doubt that the press of Froben and Episcopius produced a pamphlet which may have caused Langey to publish his reply from Basle: *Exemplum protestationis qua Caesarea maiestas usa est apud Rom. pont.*, 1536. For the origins and contents of the *Exemplaria* see Bourrilly, *Langey* 214ff.

[22] See below p. 206.

[23] *Matrikel* 2.5 and Droz, *Etudiants français* and *BHR* 21 (1959), 564-568.

[24] Bourrilly, *Langey* 249f., 255 n., 322.

absence of Morel. He therefore ordered Barnabé de Voré, Sieur de la Fosse, to replace the latter. Voré had been working in Germany for some time; in Basle he met again another Frenchman, who may have arrived there some months earlier, the megalomaniac and profligate "philosopher" Guillaume Bigot. Voré's son— we may assume—matriculated at the university after Barnabé's arrival [25] and Bigot may have served the young man as a tutor. Indeed it seems that he had formerly done so in Germany.[26] That Bigot himself would have been employed as an agent seems improbable in view of his character. Whereas Morel and Voré possessed the spy's virtue of self-effacement, Bigot is frequently mentioned in contemporary letters and usually with contempt. He might have deserved pity. His emphatic account of past misfortunes, which he freely offered to the world on repeated occasions, reveals a sick, unbalanced mind.[27]

The association of Bigot with Langey's men emphasizes the one aspect of their mission which is of overriding importance in this study. If Langey's projects were to succeed in Switzerland as well as in Germany, it was vital to reach the theologians along with the princes and magistrates. It was equally important to court the humanists and through them public opinion, and finally to cultivate the universities and the presses. The Du Bellays always combined their political ends with the promotion of culture. Where expediency ended and personal taste took over is now hard to say, but Langey's staff certainly achieved a degree of familiarity with everything that seemed typically Bâlois.

While its members operated in and out of Basle, the ailing Erasmus returned in 1535 to die in Froben's house. Already in 1533 Morel had introduced himself to the Bâlois with letters of recommendation which Cardinal Sadoleto had addressed to Froben and Erasmus.[28] It seems that he later claimed—without foundation— to have been Erasmus' *famulus* and to have closed the great man's eyes.[29] Bigot too composed a tetrastich in honour of Erasmus which was hesitatingly included in a collection of epitaphs published by H. Froben and B. Amerbach in 1536.[30] This collection was appended to Erasmus' own catalogues of his writings and further supplemented by a letter which Germain de Brie addressed to Langey on the occasion of Erasmus' death.[31] From his days at Tübingen Bigot also knew Simon Grynaeus and after his arrival in Basle he laboured without success to please the distinguished

---

[25] René de Voré: *Matrikel* 2.15 and Droz, *Etudiants français*.

[26] Bourrilly, *Langey* 322f.; on Bigot see also M.-J. Gaufrès, *Claude Baduel et la réforme des études au 16e siècle*, Paris 1880, 31f., 82ff.; and: La Jeunesse de G. Bigot, *BSHPF* 28 (1879) 2-18, 97-114.

[27] Jöcher's short biography offers a classical abstract: "ein Gelehrter Medicus und Philosophus von Laval in der Landschaft Maine, wurde 1502 mit zwey Zähnen gebohren, daher ihn niemand säugen wolte. Kriegte zu Tübingen, darauf zu Nimes eine Profession und machte sich überall viel Feinde. Seine Frau courtesierte mit einem Musico, Petro Fontano, welcher deswegen seiner Mannheit beraubet wurde. Bigots Feinde warffen darüber der Frau einen Criminal-Process an den Hals, wegen dessen ihr Mann, als er sich derselben annahm, in das Gefängniss geworfen und erst nach langer Zeit in elendem Zustand losgelassen wurde. Er war in den meisten Wissenschaften ein αὐτοδίδακτος …"

[28] Hartmann 4.243; cf. 5.42f. (calling Morel a "iuvenis in utraque lingua haud infeliciter versatus"); Allen 10.306.

[29] H. Chamard, *Joachim Du Bellay*, Lille 1900, 390f. and still A. Buisson, *M. de L'Hospital* 24f.; also Droz (see above n. 23).

[30] Hartmann 4.450. The collection also included two pieces by Jean Morel.

[31] See below p. 195.

Greek scholar and reformer. Morel too was so close to Grynaeus that when the latter died in 1541 Oporinus wrote to Morel imparting the sad news and referring to Grynaeus as their common preceptor.[32] The same Oporinus corresponded with Bigot, while Claude Baduel, another member of Langey's team, later translated Bucer's *De regno Christi* into French as soon as it was out of Oporinus' press.[33]

Langey himself was careful to establish a record of friendship with the Basle scholars and printers. In 1538 Hieronymus Gemusaeus gratefully dedicated to him the first volume of the immense Basle edition of Galen in Greek.[34] In the same year Bonifacius Amerbach wrote to him to solicit his help in seeking a royal privilege for Erasmus' *Opera omnia*, then in press.[35] Also in 1538 Thomas Platter reprinted Sadoleto's educational treatise with its dedicatory epistle to Langey.[36] This was the year in which Platter had started to print on his own account; for the two preceding years he had published in association with Winter, Oporinus, and Lasius. While this short-lived partnership lasted, the associates were continually looking for prosperous customers, and Langey and his men seem to have obliged them. Langey's own *Exemplaria* of 1536, although published anonymously, most likely issued from this press. Jean Morel contributed a long epistle dedicatory to its 1537 edition of François Dubois' *Lucubrationes* on the orations of Cicero. Dated from Basle and addressed to Antoine Morelet du Museau, this preface shows that Morel was not at a loss when an intelligent and elegant disquisition on the humanistic *ars bene dicendi* seemed appropriate.[37]

---

[32] BN, *Mscr. lat.* 8588, 10 : the address : Taurini, apud D. Gul. Bellaium Langaeum. Cf. Steinmann 134. The letter ends with greetings to Langey.

[33] Bigot's reply to a letter by Oporinus in **No. 164**. For Baduel cf. above p. 79, n. 33. He may have passed through Basle in 1535 : Gaufrès, *Baduel, op. cit.* 31f.

[34] This joint production of the presses of Cratander, Herwagen and Bebel was protected by a royal privilege, conceivably secured with the assistance of Langey.

[35] Hartmann 5.124 ; no such privilege was granted for this edition.

[36] See below p. 229.

[37] **No. 394.** A part of it may be quoted : " Verum enimvero, quid in terris augustius, quid humanae mentis praestantia dignius, quid rerum denique Conditori adeoque hominibus ipsis gratiosum magis vel conspici usquam vel excogitari posse dicemus multitudine ea et societate hominum sic inter se coniunctorum, Deo ut primum Optimo Maximo suus honos et cultus summa religione et fide servetur ? Disciplinae deinde pulcherrimae artesque omnes bonae omniaque virtutum genera, cum pertractentur illic, summo in honore habeantur ? Ac quemadmodum virtute praeditis honesta praemia hic non desinit, ita et de flagitiosis commeritae poenae citra omnem exceptionem desumantur ? Huic cedo reipublicae quid ob futurum mali vel boni unquam defuturum arbitrabimur ad summam vitae recte et honeste transigendae tum quietem tum felicitatem ? Haec igitur recte culti numinis, haec literarum, inquam, sunt maxima praemia, fructus proventusque beatissimi : ut nimirum sive publice sive privatim bene tamen et honeste ubique vivant !

Verum pars illa altera, Maure patrone optime, quam in pietatis cultu sitam esse vides, cum pauca haec apud te de literis iam loqui ingrederer, necessario sese nostro sermoni obtulisse videtur eam cum iisdem literis complecterer, partim quod prima natura et dignitate sit et tibi nihil probari intelligam, in quo ea primas semper non obtineat ; partim quod, illa neglecta longiusve amandata, quid boni aut laudabilis ipsae literae haberent haud facile discernerem ; partim vero quod sic inter se coniunctae videbantur, ut quas Deus semper voluisset esse quam coniunctissimas, idque adeo ut has pietati perpetuo famulari iusserit èt pietatem hominibus non nisi per illas consueverit tradere.

... Istis tu quidem animi dotibus, ut verum quod est ingenue dicam, non mihi soli sed omnibus, apud quos hactenus diversari tibi contigit, sic te amabilem colendumque exhibuisti, ut nomini etiam Gallico apud exteros — quod in paucis equidem vidi — non

It was Bigot, however, who offered Oporinus and his partners the most generous supply of copy—and the least acceptable one. Soon after his arrival from Tübingen he published his *Catoptron* with them, a tearful confession of his earlier trespasses combined with hidden attacks on those who had trespassed against him, the whole most clumsily versified for the moral benefit of youthful readers. The little book was dedicated to Simon Grynaeus and Johannes Fichard. During his stay in Basle Bigot must have been working on a kind of sequel to the *Catoptron*. In the form of a dream the laboured verses tell of his unhappy experiences in Tübingen, where Bigot had rendered himself unbearable by criticizing Melanchthon for his deviation from Aristotle. He was also composing a philosophical treatise " *contra neotericos* " which was probably inspired by the same controversy.[38] Neither of the two works proved publishable at Basle, but the *Somnium* was printed in 1537 at Paris, and contained a dedication to Langey which was still dated from Basle.[39] The work also indulged in attacks upon Charles V. Since its publication, unfortunately, coincided with the meeting of king and emperor at Aigues-Mortes it may have caused some embarrassment even to Langey. The Bâlois, however, found yet another reason to dislike Bigot. Myconius accused him afterward of false Evangelical pretences during his stay at Basle.[40] In fact he owed it to the intervention of the Cardinals Jean Du Bellay and Odet de Coligny that he was finally permitted to return to France. In spite of such ecclesiastical support it rather seems that his exile from the realm, like his subsequent quarrels with Claude Baduel, and indeed all the tragedies in his life, were the result of personal conduct rather than of his convictions.

On the whole Langey's mission to Germany ended in failure. The protagonist himself accepted a new responsibility and in 1538 went as the French governor to Turin. Morel followed in his wake, while in Paris some strong reaction to the Du Bellay policies developed. In the years to come, political and military collaboration with the German Protestants was gradually achieved, and proved feasible without a religious understanding. However, in spite of his removal from the scene Langey's personal commitment to the spirit of his earlier mission continued, and it was to be revived by other French statesmen after him. In Basle too his influence continued to be felt, although less directly, even after the above-mentioned publication of 1538. Lazare de Baïf was an old friend of Langey, and it was hardly a mere coincidence that important reprints of his works were published in 1537 while Morel was still in Basle. They were produced by the firm of Oporinus and his partners together

---

levi profecto ornamento esse dicaris. Vale. Datum Basileae ad 14. Calend. Mart. M. D. XXXVII." One notes how within the framework of eloquence several points are made with diplomatic precaution as well as precision : unequivocal praise of religious consensus ; a tribute to the interrelatedness of piety and *bonae literae* which must have pleased the Bâlois ; respect for Morelet's religious choice (but Morel carefully avoids a commitment of his own) ; full marks, finally, for, Morelet's exemplary conduct in Basle in contrast to that of other émigrés such as perhaps Bigot.

[38] This information was given in the letter to Oporinus which was published in the *Catoptron*. It also explains the orgin of a collection of epigrams appended to this work. Oporinus, we learn, had written to Bigot for more copy since the *Catoptron* text left several empty pages on the end of the last fascicle. Panzer mentions *Carmina* by Bigot, published by Winter in 1536. This must be the *Catoptron*, I think. Winter, Platter and Lasius were all partners in one press.

[39] *Gulielmi Bigotii Lavallensis Somnium, ad Gulielmum Bellaium Langaeum moecaenatum suum, in quo cum alia tum Imperatoris Caroli describitur ab regno Galliae depulsio, ... eiusdem Catoptron et alia quaedam poematia...*, Paris, Pierre Roffet 1537.

[40] Herminjard 4.267.

with the Froben press.[41]   The Du Bellays certainly were instrumental in the appointment of Baïf in 1540 as French ambassador to the conference of German Protestant princes at Haguenau.   However, he played his role so ineffectually that Langey hurried Sleidanus from Strasbourg to Haguenau with secret orders to double for the French ambassador.[42]   Strasbourg was by now a main centre for French intelligence, but its key men, Johannes Sturm, Ulrich Chelius and Sleidanus, all maintained close contacts with Basle.

With the end of Langey's special mission Basle was restored to the domain of the regular French embassy in the Swiss cantons.   One of the king's principal representatives, Antoine Morelet du Museau, was personally fond of Basle and often stayed there between 1545 and 1552.[43]   Like many of his colleagues, he was haunted by threatening manifestations of Swiss impatience because of outstanding pension payments.   Especially after the death of Francis I in 1547, emissaries of his successor sent to re-negotiate the military convention found themselves opposed by a variety of obstacles.   Apart from Swiss greed there was the solidarity of the Protestant cantons with Geneva and the Huguenots in France, as well as the effective counter-action of imperial diplomats, especially among the Catholic cantons.[44]   In the face of determined opposition the French made slow progress.   However, in August 1549 Basle joined the cantons who were signatories to the new agreement, even though her sister cities Berne and Zurich rejected it.[45]   The change came in the wake of a special mission to Basle by Christophe Richer in 1548-49.   Although Richer was a protégé of the chancellor Poyet, a well-known enemy of the Du Bellays, he paid his tribute to Bâlois habits by registering at the university, just as Langey's men had done before him.   In several letters despatched from Basle he informed Henry II of the general circumstances influencing his mission.[46]   Long after his death a literary account of his earlier embassy to the Turks was re-published in the Basle *Historicum opus*.   In 1554 two French diplomats, Charles de Marillac and Bernardin Bochetel, went to Basle to report at close quarters on the imperialist intrigues and to renew there, in the following year a treaty ensuring the neutrality of Franche-Comté and French Burgundy to which the Swiss attached great importance.[47]

The precarious situation of Calvinism in Strasbourg and Montbéliard together with the severe Edict of Châteaubriant in 1551 tended to swell the numbers of Huguenot refugees in Basle.   Their presence, and even more the subsequent outbreak of the religious civil wars in France, added diversification both to the diplomatic involvement of the town government and the productions of its printers. The crown continued to require Swiss regiments, and in 1564 a crucial renewal of the military alliance of 1549 was due.   After some hesitation Basle joined the signatories whereas Zurich and Berne kept aloof.[48]   However, active recruitment remained on the whole restricted to Catholic cantons.   The first religious war led

---

[41] **No. 77, 79** ; cf. below pp. 197ff.

[42] V.-L. Bourrilly, Lazare de Bayf et le Landgrave de Hesse, *BSHPF* 50 (1901), 369-376 ; Jean Sleidan et le Cardinal du Bellay, *ibid*. 225-242.

[43] See above p. 58f.

[44] Rott 1.455ff. and passim.

[45] Rott 1.467.

[46] *Matrikel* 2.60 ; Droz, *Etudiants français;* Rott 1.428, 509.   Cf. **No. 898**.

[47] Rott 1.436, 477ff. ; M. de L'Hospital, *Œuvres complètes*, Paris 1824f., 2.449.

[48] Rott 2.52ff., 158f.

to unprecedented diplomatic activity among the Protestant cantons on the part of Condé and the Huguenots, but only Berne felt a moral obligation to send soldiers towards Lyons, and even these returned in the end without having given proof of their valour.[49]   In subsequent wars they adopted an increasingly strict neutrality ;[50] Basle banned recruitment for the king in 1562, but also closed her territory to a Protestant relief force in 1569.[51]   At least the wealthy Protestant towns might have been expected to float loans in support of the Huguenot war efforts, but after 1563 urgent requests fell on deaf ears, and the initial embezzlement of Protestant aid by the treacherous Antoine de Bourbon cannot serve as an excuse for the continued stinginess of Basle, Berne and Zurich throughout the religious wars.[52]   To some extent the Basle city fathers might have claimed impartiality when in 1567 they joined Strasbourg and Berne in refusing a loan for the crown requested through the intermediation of the Duke of Lorraine.[53]   But only four years later more successful negotiations were conducted in Basle by a French interpreter, Polier, who was a Protestant, had acquired citizenship and had a necklace studded with rubies to pawn.   Zurich and Berne too responded positively to the needs of Charles IX.[54]

The Basle printers by and large came to serve the Huguenot cause quite faithfully, but in the winter 1557-58 a mysterious incident occurred, in which a local press obliged Spanish agents with a supply of rather extraordinary pamphlets.[55] They were designed to instigate a rebellion in favour of Spain among the citizens of Bordeaux, some of whom had already ten years earlier revolted against their king.[56]   On the way to France a consignment of these pamphlets was stopped at Geneva and three men involved in the matter were arrested.   The incident produced

---

[49] R. Feller, *Geschichte Berns*, Berne 1946ff., 2.417 ; *Correspondance de Bèze* 4.109, 112.

[50] *Ibid.* 5.114, 116, 136.   In 1582 Basle, like other Protestant cantons, renewed the mercenary alliance under the condition that her soldiers were not to fight the Huguenots, but her contingent was soon sent home (Rott 2.249ff., 269 ; Dareste 411).   Only in 1587 did the agents of Navarre succeed in recruiting soldiers from Berne, Basle and other Protestant cantons.   They promptly went over to the king, but the miserable outcome of this first arrangement did not preclude its renewal.   After the death of Henry III the Swiss regiments transferred their loyalty to Henry IV.   In the battle of Ivry Swiss troops were fighting on both sides.   Afterwards even the Catholic cantons dropped their opposition to Henry's claim.   Between 1600 and 1602 a new, comprehensive mercenary agreement was reached between the French crown and all cantons except Zurich.   Cf. Rott 2.281, 288f., 301f., 371f., 516ff. ; F. Holzach, *Die Basler in den Hugenottenkriegen* (80. Neujahrsblatt der Ges. des Guten und Gemeinnützigen), Basle 1902, passim.

[51] *Ibid.* 9 ; Rott 2.80.

[52] *Correspondance de Bèze* 3.69f. ; 4.33f., 88f., 100ff., 109 ; Rott 2.8f., 149.   In 1575 Condé, from Basle, negotiated with Berne and received a personal loan of 4000 *écus*. He tried again for a more substantial sum but was politely refused : Rott 2.346.   Cf. Kingdon, *Geneva and the Coming* 118f., and *Geneva and the Consolidation* 175ff., 183ff.

[53] Languet in *Arcana* [I]. 40.

[54] Rott 2.85, 90f. ; F. Holzach, *op. cit.* 10.

[55] For the following episode see J. A. Gautier, *Histoire de Genève* 4 (Geneva 1901), 196-199 ; A. Dufour, Vers latins pour Servet, contre Calvin et contre Genève, *Mém. et doc. Société d'Hist. et d'Archéol. de Genève* 40 (1961), 483-496.   A number of highly interesting documents are assembled in a fascicle of the file : Handel und Gewerbe, JJJ 6, Staatsarchiv Basel-Stadt.   However, the arrangement is very confused.   I hope to publish Grymoult's declaration and some relevant diplomatic letters in vol. 2 of this study.

[56] Cf. *Histoire de Bordeaux*, ed. C. Higounet, Bordeaux 1962ff., 4.304ff.

a flurry of diplomatic correspondence between Geneva, Basle, Berne, Zurich and the French embassy at Soleure. As far as Basle was concerned, it led to the imprisonment of Léger Grymoult and of the Francophone printer Jacobus Parcus together with his son. All were carefully interrogated and Grymoult wrote down a lengthy statement, relating as much of the matter as he knew himself and wanted others to know. In particular, he confirmed that the pamphlets were printed in Basle, but claimed that he did not know by which press. The Basle government accepted his declarations and released its three prisoners—to the dismay of the French embassy where it was felt that the use of torture would have produced more revealing information. The lack of curiosity displayed by the Basle council is indeed astonishing, even if the traditionally friendly relations with the neighbouring Austrian and Spanish Habsburg territories are taken into account. Once again the government proved that it was prepared to expose itself to some diplomatic embarrassment for the sake of Basle's flourishing printing industry.

The Genevan authorities investigated with greater diligence and better success than the Bâlois. One of their prisoners, Jacques Cardon (Chardon, Cherdon), a resident of Lausanne, was also charged with the possession of inflammatory verses, defending the executed Servetus against Calvin and Geneva. Léger Grymoult, well known to be a supporter of Castellio, was once again named as the supplier of the incriminated material. It can be added that one of his colleagues in the press of Froben and Episcopius had the same family name as Cardon's fellow prisoner, François Roussin.[57] In fact, the involvement of some Castellionists in the affair of the anti-French pamphlets seems undeniable. Nor can it be doubted that pecuniary motives pushed them to collaborate with the agents of Philip II. At considerable risk Castellio's friends established their own secret connections between the presses of Basle and some Francophone cities, especially Geneva and Lyons. While these links primarily served to propagate their ideas, there was no good reason why they should not be used for financial profit when the right sort of customers presented themselves.

After the second war of religion the activities of political agents in Basle seem to have multiplied. The numbers of refugees in town increased too, and it is often impossible to say whether a French visitor who matriculated at the university was merely an emigrant or whether he arrived with specific political instructions. To some extent every refugee was an agent willing to serve his cause if the occasion arose. We do know that Condé's special emissaries passed through Basle in 1570,[58] but we cannot tell what Charles de Chateauneuf, Sieur de Mollèges, was doing at Basle after he had matriculated in 1568-69 [59] together with his compatriot from Aix-en-Provence, André Pena. What we do know is that eight years earlier Chateauneuf had organized Provençal support for the conspiracy of Amboise. After the massacre of Saint Bartholomew the situation was indeed intriguing. Amid the princes of the blood and their large suite of Huguenot nobles, the publicist Hubert Languet arrived in Basle [60] to denounce publicly the crown diplomats at Soleure, who for some months were unhappy men indeed. Pomponne de Bellièvre, the

---

[57] Cf. above p. 80, n. 39.

[58] Rott 2.163; cf. 177.

[59] S.v. Castro-Novo: *Matrikel* 2.183 and Droz, *Etudiants français*; cf. *ibid.* Droz's unanswered questions with regard to Antoine Bernard of Paris (*Matrikel* 2.77).

[60] Rott 2.169f.

ambassador, once even thought that his life was in danger.[61] In spite of everything the embassy reacted to the awkward situation with zeal and with skill. The first Frenchman to matriculate in 1572-73 was one of Bellièvre's agents, who supported his master's difficult stand by publishing a justification of the massacre. Pierre Charpentier had earlier gone to Geneva, where for some years he taught law so negligently as to be fired. His task in Basle obviously was to spy on his compatriots.[62] Before long even the sons of Coligny and d'Andelot were approached on behalf of the ambassador and urged to return to France.[63]

Bellièvre's most formidable opponent in 1572-73, however, was François Hotman.[64] The famous Huguenot frequently turned up, and twice resided, in Basle between the mid-1550s and 1590 when he died there embittered and in debt. The ostensible reason for his presence in Basle was a long series of his juridical publications handled by the Episcopius press. Despite this impressive scholarly output, the distinguished law professor was reduced to misery once his political career had drawn to a close. No doubt he was devoted to the study of law, and seriously endeavoured to find in it the historical and logical bases for the reorganization of French society.[65] But his frequent moves and his personal contacts usually served the political ends of his masters much better than his own career as a scholar. As his legal thought proved truly fertile only where it covered political ground, so intelligence work and propaganda revealed his true nature, whereas his academic interests remained more superficial than he himself may have realized. He had a knack for intrigue and personal denigration, and his untiring efforts in that direction awkwardly but effectively complemented his sincere zeal for the Calvinist cause.[66]

As early as 1552 Hotman received from Calvin a letter of introduction to Simon Sulzer, now in Basle.[67] In 1555 he stopped there on his way to a teaching position and political liaison work in Strasbourg. He paused in Basle just long enough to write a letter to Bullinger, accusing Castellio of stupidity and shaking his head at the high esteem in which the latter was held by many Bâlois.[68] In 1558

---

[61] Rott 2.166.

[62] *Matrikel* 2.212 ; Droz, *Etudiants français*. Charpentier's defense of the massacre, in the form of a letter addressed to Franciscus Portus, had been published repeatedly, at times with a rejoinder. Of such anonymous eds. as I have seen, none shows much similarity to Basle productions.

[63] Rott 2.170.

[64] Rott 1.166.

[65] Cf. especially : P. Mesnard, F. Hotman (1524-1590) et le complexe de Tribonian, *BSHPF* 101 (1955), 117-137. V. de Caprariis, *Propaganda e pensiero politico in Francia durante le guerre di religione*, Naples 1959, 225ff.

[66] His correspondence (for the most part still to be published) with the lawyers Bonifacius and Basilius Amerbach and other Bâlois offers no broad reflection of his legal thought. His chief concerns seem of a practical nature : negotiations with his publishers at Basle and the forwarding of his letters to Germany, etc. By contrast, the editors of Calvin's correspondence have published many pieces which emphasize rather strikingly his continuous involvement in more or less secret political negotiations : cf. e.g. *Calvini opera* 17.579f., 672f. ; 18.92, 97ff., 201f., 292ff. ; 19.223, 415f. His secretiveness, selfishness and bluffing at times even angered Calvin and led to an astonishing ' Phillipic ' of J. Sturm against his former friend : *ibid.* 18.231, 481ff., 507ff. ; cf. 19.507f. For Hotman's attacks on J. Sturm concerning the Amboise conspiracy see Naef, *Conjuration d'Amboise*, esp. 385ff. For the impact of Hotman's strict Calvinism at Basle cf. M. Geiger, *Die Basler Kirche und Theologie im Zeitalter der Hochorthodoxie*, Zollikon-Zurich 1952, 34ff.

[67] *Calvini opera* 14.358.

[68] *Ibid.* 15.803.

Hotman's name appeared in the university roll, as a doctoral degree was conferred upon him in a private ceremony,[69] but before long he must have left Basle to plunge into the organization of the Amboise conspiracy. Thereafter he maintained a correspondence with Basle, sending to Bonifacius Amerbach, for instance, his Latin translation of a description of the massacre at Vassy in 1562.[70] There is no evidence that such a description was ever published in Basle, but eleven years later Guarinus printed the first, probably, of several editions of *De furoribus Gallicis*, Hotman's dramatic account of the massacre of Saint Bartholomew based on the experiences of eye witnesses.[71] Between 1578 and 1584 Hotman must have been living in Basle more often than not. He also moved his family there. It was not exactly a happy time for the agent of the king of Navarre. To judge from evidence of misbehaviour in the public records, Hotman's son Daniel must have been a constant embarrass-

---

[69] *Matrikel* 2.113f.

[70] Dareste 34f.

[71] **No. 553.** The typographical material used in this ed. can be found elsewhere in the work of Guarinus. At the same time Hotman was trying hard to persuade Guarinus to print a new ed. of the *Francogallia*. On 13 August, 1575, he wrote from Geneva to Basilius Amerbach : " Eidem [libro] alterum adiungo a Thoma [Guarino] nostro iampridem impressum [i.e. *De furoribus Gallicis*, **No. 553**], sed iam multis locis, ut videre poteris, locupletatum. Peto abs te maiorem in modum itemque a D. Tenantio, pio et erudito viro, ut eidem Thomae secundam commendetis. Ea tamen lege, ut eadem prorsus forma qua *Vita Gasparis* imprimatur. Idem enim utriusque libelli argumentum est." **No. 553** is in 4°; Hotman's *Gasparis Colinii vita*, s.l. 1575, which Guarinus was asked to imitate is in 8°. The BN has a copy (8° Ln²⁷ 4550) of this anonymous work with the following ms. words on the titlepage : " Authore Fr. Hotomano. Ex dono authoris. Domino Tenantio." The book was no doubt printed in Geneva. In the quoted letter (UBB ms. Ki.Ar.18ᵃ, fol. 242) Hotman goes on to say that the Genevan authorities had refused to grant a permit for the desired second edition of *De furoribus Gallicis*. He urged that Guarinus produce it in time for the Frankfurt fair. The printer was also asked to send part of the new copies to his representative in Geneva so that they might be despatched into France together with the matching *Colinii vita*. I have no knowledge of a second ed. *De furoribus Gallicis* printed by Guarinus. Moreover, I cannot decide whether or not a German translation (BN : 4° Lb³³ 312) was printed in Basle. Cf. also **No. 4005.**

Dareste (*op. cit.* 380)—and after him several others—stated that a third ed. of the *Francogallia*, increased by one or even two thirds, was published by Guarinus. If so, I have failed to trace any copy of it. There is, however, no doubt that Hotman pressed the Basle printer to undertake such an ed. His letters to Basilius Amerbach return repeatedly to this subject and offer considerable problems of interpretation. An undated letter (UBB ms. G. II.19, fol. 162) mentions three copies of the *Francogallia*, sent to Basle three weeks ago. This clearly cannot refer to an ed. by Guarinus. However, Hotman writes from Geneva on 15 June, 1575 (*ibid.*, fol. 164), offering to send Amerbach the amplified text and to pay for the cost of a new ed., if the printer " tibi decem coronatos solares committat pro meo honorario." He adds that there is no danger that a rival ed. might be published in Geneva. On 6 July (*ibid.*, fol. 165) Hotman thanks Amerbach for his efforts regarding the *Francogallia* and continues : " Eam tibi mitto, ut eius editionem Guerino nostro commendes ea lege, ut praeter 6 coronatos 20 exemplaria mihi mittat, quae amicis distribuam, et opuscula Plutarchi Gallica ab se impressa mihi mittat." The deal seems perfect, but then, on 13 August (UBB ms. Ki, Ar. 18ᵃ, fol. 242), Hotman writes again from Geneva : " Francogalliam nostram recepi. Et cum Guerino nostro pactus sum, ut ipsius more hic apud nos imprimeretur. Nam spero fore, ut hac ratione magistratus noster de suo consideratissimo timore aliquid remittat." What Hotman received back must have been his manuscript, I think, for in subsequent letters he continues to urge an ed. by Guarinus (G. II.19, fol. 171-173) and still on 29 November 1575 (*ibid.*, fol. 175) he writes : " Ceterum Francogallia nostra honorifice te salutat suumque negotium tibi etiam atque etiam commendat." Cf. R. E. Giesey, When and Why Hotman wrote the *Francogallia*, *BHR* 29 (1967), 581-611.

ment to his parents.[72]   As a staunch Calvinist the father too was increasingly exposed to friction.   The growing measure of his frustration is reflected in his relations with the theologian J. J. Grynaeus.   When Hotman arrived in 1578 he saw in the Basle minister one of the few loyal supporters of the French church, but by 1584 he called Grynaeus his arch enemy and an Ubiquitarian.   In that same year he left for Geneva and on arrival there insisted that his friends should congratulate him on his escape from the Rhenish city.[73]

During his stay at Basle Hotman continued to supply information to his regular employers, William of Hesse and Henry of Navarre.[74]   He also volunteered to assist the physician Gratarolo who reported regularly and confidentially to the Genevan leaders.   In particular Hotman's wrath was unleashed against the printer Perna and his friend, the professor N. Stupanus. In 1580 the two men dared to publish a Latin edition of Machiavelli's *Prince*[75] at a time when the ' Machiavellism ' of Catherine de' Medici and of the *politiques* appeared most heinous to the Huguenot conscience.   There were, as always, many good reasons to condemn Machiavelli's views, and Hotman was by no means the only one to do so at the time.   In his case, however, dissent turned into hatred because he also suspected Stupanus of popish tendencies and sensed in Basle what seemed to him and other Calvinists the poisonous fumes of a general Lutheran-popish plot for the extermination of Calvinism.[76] It was therefore left to Hotman's penchant for intrigue to arrange with Zurich and Geneva for the denunciation of Perna and Stupanus before the Basle authorities. As so often in his life, personal commitment was expressed in rather distasteful ways. Perhaps it should be added in his defence that his duties as a foreign agent did not always permit him to follow the dictates of his heart.   Hotman may have obeyed with somewhat less than enthusiasm when William of Hesse ordered him to offer Erastus a position at Marburg University.[77]   Erastus had by then just returned to Basle from Heidelberg and his widely publicized feud with the Palatine Calvinists. He also happened to be one of Perna's most faithful authors.   The same employer, William of Hesse, assigned to Hotman such duties as acquiring standard theological works at Basle for his newly established library at Cassel, not to mention an errand in quest of preserved plums.[78]

In the fall of 1584 Hotman moved to Geneva.   From there he continued a busy correspondence with Basle, supporting the efforts of Navarrese diplomats among the Protestant cantons.   Between 1585 and 1588, while the Sieur de Clervant was allowed to establish at Basle his headquarters for the recruitment of Swiss and German troops,[79] Hotman had no fewer than three consecutive editions of his famous

---

[72] *Matrikel* 2.262f. ; cf. UBB ms. G. I. 13, fol. 10, 18.

[73] *Hotomanorum epistolae* 96, 179-181 ; cf. 201f.   Two years later Hotman was again writing friendly letters to Grynaeus : UBB ms. G. II. 6, fol. 438ff. and passim.

[74] Rott 2.188, 358 ; *Hotomanorum epistolae* 158f.

[75] Bietenholz, *Ital. Humanismus* 78ff. ; W. Kaegi, *Historische Meditationen*, Basle 1942-1946, I. 121-181 ; *Hotomanorum epistolae* 135f., 139f., 142f.

[76] *Ibid.* 148 : a desperate appeal on behalf of the French Calvinist church in Strasbourg.   It considers itself as threatened in its further existence now that the ' Ubiquitarians ' have triumphed and Sturm has been forced to resign.

[77] *Hotomanorum epistolae* 141f.

[78] *Ibid.* 122, 137f., 161 ; UBB ms. G. II.19, fol. 189, 194 : To Hotman's dismay a carrier left the barrel of plums at Strasbourg and forgot it there for more than half a year.

[79] F. Holzach, *op. cit.* 18ff. ; Rott 2.199ff., 366ff. and passim.

Brutum fulmen published from Basle presses.[80]   This was a reply to the papal bull of excommunication against Navarre and Condé in September 1585, issued in the crucial situation after the death of François, Duke of Alençon, which according to Salic law left Henry of Navarre the heir to the crown.   The League was therefore driven into firm military commitment to Spain and the presentation of the aged Cardinal of Bourbon as successor to the throne.   Hotman's refutation was undertaken with the calm logic and dignity of legal expertise.   Its conclusions were based upon abundant historical evidence and the exact text of the bull.   In subsequent editions lengthy excerpts from both Protestant and Catholic authors were added.

The *Brutum fulmen* was preceded by a *Disputatio de controversia successionis*, both undertaken at the specific request of Navarre's advisers.[81]   These publications, however, ended the period of Hotman's immediate usefulness to Henry.   As Swiss soldiers returned to his camp and military victories enhanced his legal claims, Henry's ambassadors answered Hotman's numerous letters with evasive replies and less and less money.   The old man was no longer needed.   After addressing many imploring letters to J. J. Grynaeus and Basilius Amerbach, he finally returned to Basle in 1589.   But the university offered him only an irregular position which resembled a charity,[82] private students too were getting scarce, and his mounting fever for alchemy could not provide him with a livelihood.   His death in 1590 may have come as a relief to him.   To his memory at least the tribute of a funeral in Basle's cathedral was paid, and when his son, Jean Hotman de Villiers, arrived in Basle late in 1592 [83] he was kindly received.

Hotman's political publications underline the crucial significance of two events in the progress of the Huguenot struggle.   One was the massacre of Saint Bartholomew, the other was the death of Alençon in 1584.   Both events proved decisive in swinging Swiss Protestant sympathies in favour of the Huguenots and of Navarre, and their importance is clearly emphasized by some other publications undertaken by Basle presses.   Even though still in the later 1580s the continued desire for official neutrality led the Protestant cantons to offer their mediation between the crown and the Huguenot leader,[84] public opinion was no longer affected by the official policy of neutrality, nor were the Basle presses.

---

[80] **No. 562-564.**   The typographical material used in all three eds. is identical with that used by P. Perna and his successors.   **No. 562** may confidently be attributed to either Waldkirch or Foillet, who moved in 1586 from Basle to Montbéliard.   The material of **No. 563** and **564** is also used by other printers in Basle and elsewhere, but the similarities between all three eds. are best explained by attributing them to the same press.   Cf. Dareste 411; *Correspondance inédite de Robert Dudley ... et de François et Jean Hotman*, ed. P. J. Blok, Haarlem 1911, 219f.   On the *Brutum fulmen* and other pamphlets mentioned on the following pages cf. also H. Hauser, *Les Sources de l'histoire de France*, II : *XVIe siècle*, Paris 1906ff., 3.299f. and passim.

[81] *Disputatio de controversia successionis*, apud Nicolaum Panningerum, 1585.   The imprint is pseudonymous, but the ed. is better attributed to Frankfurt than to Basle.   *De iure successionis*, [Paris] 1588, is a new version of this treatise.   UBB has a copy of it with Hotman's ms. dedication to Basilius Amerbach.   For Hotman's instructions see P. J. Blok, *op. cit.* 204ff., 219ff.

[82] Dareste 419ff., 430ff.; E. Blocaille, *Etude sur F. Hotman*, Dijon 1902, 53ff.; L. Ehinger, F. Hotmann, *Beiträge zur vaterländ. Geschichte* 14 (Basle 1896), 57ff.

[83] See below p. 212.

[84] Rott 2.274; F. Holzach, *op. cit.* 18f.

It was during the years 1573-75 that Guarinus printed Hotman's *De furoribus Gallicis* and that Hotman urged him to launch a new edition of the *Francogallia*.[85] In the same period Nicolas Barnaud visited Basle.[86] Although skilled in many trades Barnaud is not known to have engaged in intelligence work. But the time of his visit roughly coincided with the publication, probably by the same Guarinus, of the Latin version of the famous *Réveille-matin* under the title *Dialogi ab Eusebio Philadelphio Cosmopolita ... compositi*.[87] This treatise has often been attributed to Barnaud. Its text shows notable affinities with *De furoribus Gallicis*. Moreover the impressions of the texts referred to are both published with the fictitious imprint of Edinburgh. Guarinus is also the likely publisher of the first edition of another and still more important political treatise directed against the alleged Machiavellism of the French court, Languet's *Vindiciae contra tyrannos* (" Edinburgh," 1579), completed and edited, it seems, by Philippe de Mornay, Sieur du Plessis-Marly.[88] Neither Languet nor Mornay have so far been traced to Basle at the time of the first edition, but the noble and eminent Languet was frequently in touch with local circles and their friends abroad. He was an intimate friend of Melanchthon, and in 1555 he travelled to Rome with Melanchthon's letters to Langey, then French

---

[85] See above p. 116 n. 71.

[86] *Matrikel* 2.229 ; *France prot.*[2] ; *DBF*. UBB possesses a few ms. letters by Barnaud, addressed to T. Zwinger and dating from the years 1582-1586 : UBB ms. Fr.Gr.II.8, No. 78, etc.

[87] **No. 80.** The first Latin ed. of the first of the two dialogues contained in the *Réveille-matin* (*Dialogus quo multa exponuntur, quae Lutheranis et Hugonotis Gallis acciderunt*, Oragniae, Adamus de Monte, 1573) has convincingly been attributed to the press of M. Schirat in Heidelberg. The short preface is dated : " Basilaeae [sic], die 7. mensis quinti ab infausto et funesto die proditionis." However, so many French refugees were in Basle after the massacre of Saint Bartholomew that this statement could have been intended to conceal, rather than reveal, the whereabouts of the writer. In the same way a French version of this dialogue was published with the fictitious imprint " Basle " (**No. 4002**). I cannot ascribe with certainty the *Dialogi ab Eusebio ... compositi* (**No. 80**) to Guarinus. The impression is deliberately designed to elude identification, but it shows the characteristics and the neatness of Guarinus' work. Moreover, in another case at about the same time it is safely documented that a production of Schirat's press was continued in another impression produced by Guarinus. Schirat printed several books by the English Calvinist T. Cartwright, among them *The second replie against Maister Whitgiftes second answer*, 1575. The death of the Elector Frederick caused trouble for Calvinists in Heidelberg and towards the end of 1576 Cartwright left for Basle. There Guarinus printed for him *The Rest of the Second Replie against Maister Whitgift*, 1577 : see A. F. Johnson, Books Printed at Heidelberg for Thomas Cartwright, *The Library*, 5th series, 2 (1947-1948), 284-286. The links between Guarinus and Schirat probably originated with the French publisher and book merchant Jehan Mareschal for whom both printed : cf. **No. 478** and E. Droz in *BHR* 23 (1961), 151. I have seen two slightly different German transl. of the *Réveille-matin*, dated 1575 and would rather not ascribe them to Basle. Was Barnaud the author of the *Réveille-matin* ? J. J. Fries in his revised ed. of C. Gesner's *Bibliotheca* (Zurich 1583, 833) alleges his authorship when relating a curious incident said to have occurred on the Basle *Kornmarkt*. But Fries does not deserve much credit ; he is so obviously in the dark about the issues involved.

[88] **No. 632.** The pictorial and ornamental initials used in this ed. make the ascription to Guarinus virtually certain. There are two editions of the *Vindiciae*, dated 1580, which also contain Beza's *De iure magistratuum in subditos* (**No. 633** and **634**). The first one is in every way characteristic of the productions of P. Perna ; the second looks somewhat like a *contrefaçon* of the first, but since all the typographical material used in it was available to Perna, it may also be ascribed to his press.

ambassador there.[89]   In the spring and summer of 1557 he paid an extended visit to Basle, where he obviously met Castellio.   The Savoyard was then under bitter attack, and by recommending him warmly to Melanchthon a few months later, Languet was able to render him a timely service.[90]   Since Languet was also a friend and correspondent of Baudouin, it is not surprising that Calvin came to watch his movements with the utmost suspicion.[91]   Languet often acted as a diplomat in the service of Sweden, Saxony, and other Protestant powers.   In 1579, the year indicated on the title-page of the first *Vindiciae*, Languet is known to have visited Strasbourg.[92] In 1580 two more editions of the *Vindiciae* may have originated from a Basle press.[93]

Great caution is needed in ascribing to specific presses the flood of political pamphlets in support of the French Huguenot party and its diplomatic efforts. Basle's share of it may be much larger than can now be reliably stated.   In 1585 the publication, probably at Basle, of a pamphlet by Philippe de Mornay [94] coincides in time with the appearance of a Basle impression of Hotman's *Brutum fulmen*. Behind such industry on the part of the Basle printers one may safely postulate the efforts of Navarrese diplomats, which reached a peak during the mid-1580s and frequently affected Basle.   It was here that Hotman late in 1584 met Paul Choart de Buzanval.[95]   The Huguenot diplomat had just completed a tour of the Protestant cantons in an effort to woo them to a great alliance to oppose the League which, backed by Spain and the Pope, was busily recruiting mercenaries in the Catholic cantons.   Hotman also maintained relations with Charles de Fresne-Canaye who was despatched to Switzerland in 1588-89—already for the third time— to promote the cause of Navarre.[96]   From Basle, where he spent the last year of his

---

[89] *France prot.* s.v. Languet.   UBB has one short autograph letter by Languet addressed to Basilius Amerbach and dated from Frankfurt, 27 March, 1578, recommending a student to the Bâlois : UBB ms. G.II.20, fol. 206.

[90] See below p. 135.   Contacts between Castellio and Languet still continued in 1559 : Buisson, *Castellion* 2.448.

[91] *Arcana* [3].3, 20 ; *Calvini opera* 17.386.

[92] H. Languet, *Epistolae ... ad Philippum Sydnaeum*, Leyden 1646, 379-383.

[93] **No. 633** and **634.**   In the spring of 1581 the name of Théophile de Banos appears in the university roll (*Matrikel* 2.292).   Banos was a prime disciple of Ramus and, as his master had been, a friend of Languet.   Banos also collaborated with Mornay, and between 1570 and 1578 he ministered to the French church at Frankfurt.   It was from there that Languet wrote in 1577 a letter to Philips van Marnix of St. Aldegonde which was to be remitted by Banos at the first Synod of Dordrecht : E. Droz in *BHR* 19 (1957), 502-504.   Marnix, the distinguished diplomat of William of Orange, had represented his master at the diet of Worms in the spring of 1578.   His address to the princes of the Empire was very likely printed by the same press as the two *Vindiciae* eds. of 1580 (**No. 733** ; cf. Herzog s.v. Marnix).

[94] **No. 761** ; cf. **No. 1** and **372.**   *France prot.* confirms the existence of a German transl. of Mornay's *Traité de l'Eglise*, published by C. Waldkirch in 1589 : " *Bericht von der Kirchen*, transl. J. J. Koler (cf. UBB, Druckerkatalog).   L. Nardin, *Jacques Foillet*, Paris 1906, 37n., mentions two more Basle eds. of works by Mornay in German transl. by F. Castiglione : of *Discours de la vie et de la mort* (1590) and of *Traité de la vérité de la religion chrétienne* (1597).   Neither of them is listed in *France prot.* UBB possesses three original letters by Mornay (1607-1615) ; the earliest is a recommendation for A. Krag, addressed to J. J. Grynaeus : UBB ms. G.II.8, pp. 1008-1111.

[95] P. J. Blok, *op. cit.* 209ff ; cf. *Matrikel* 2.216 and Droz, *Etudiants français*.

[96] *Ibid.* 222f.   A Seigneur de Fresnes-les-Rungis had come to Switzerland as a French envoy in 1550.   A Jacques Canaye, perhaps his grand-son, can be found in the university roll in 1575-76 ; cf. *Matrikel* 2.234 and Droz, *Etudiants français*, Rott 2.205.

life, Hotman continued to plead with the French ambassador at Soleure, Nicolas Brulart, Sieur de Sillery. The latter had already worked for Henry of Navarre while still officially representing Henry III.[97] In 1593-94 the university roll, finally, witnesses the presence in Basle of Charles de Harlay, Sieur de Dolot, younger brother of the more famous Achille de Harlay. Charles had earlier engaged in intelligence work. Now, already in his forties, he was shuttling back and forth to Italy, repeatedly registering at the university of Padua. Whether he really came to study in Basle may seem doubtful. Before long he left again, giving sciatica as the reason.[98]

After the pacification of France Basle no longer played a conspicuous role in the diplomacy of Henry IV. The presses apparently ceased to publish anything directly related to the ends of French propaganda. Some Basle merchants, however, continued to sell supplies to both the French and Spanish armies.[99]

---

[97] P. J. Blok, *op. cit.* 232ff.

[98] *Matrikel* 2.410 and E. Droz in *BHR* 19 (1957), 500-502. Cf. Rott 2.206 : in 1589 Nicolas de Harlay, Sieur de Sancy also spent a day at Basle.

[99] E. Rott, *Henri IV, Les Suisses et la haute Italie*, Paris 1882, 186f.

CHAPTER FIVE

SÉBASTIEN CASTELLIO

Castellio deserves a short chapter to himself, though he might also have been included in any of the preceding ones. From poverty and the humble position of a corrector in Oporinus' press he rose to the modest security of a teaching position in the faculty of arts. His keen probing intellect, although combined with natural modesty and simplicity of taste, caused a noticeable ferment in the religious life of Basle. Of those contemporaries to whom the name of Basle had a special ring, few can have failed to notice his unassuming presence there. He never became a citizen but today his name, together with that of another denizen, Erasmus, is among the very few to stand out in the Reformation era. Of all Gallic responses to the traditional and typical appeal of Basle, his was the most noteworthy, bold and intelligent. Actually he both reinforced and modified that appeal. Amid the vague ideals of post-Erasmian humanism and religious concord he formulated his concrete pleas for reason and tolerance as opposed to dogma.

Born in the Savoyard mountains between Geneva and Lyons, Castellio spent his early adult years (1535-40) at the latter town. The ties between Lyons and Basle were then close and numerous.[1] The humanistic and poetic circles with which he associated had repeatedly come to the attention of the Basle printers, although a fuller acquaintance with works of these poets had to await Castellio's own arrival in the Rhine city.[2] It was probably among such friends that Castellio encountered Calvin's *Institutes* in either the Basle or the Strasbourg edition.[3] In 1540 he joined Calvin in Strasbourg and, a year later, followed him to Geneva.

Their friendship, however, ended in deep personal distrust. When Castellio left Geneva in 1545 his hopes of ministering to the faithful of his own tongue were dead. While commending his service at the school in Geneva, Calvin had expressly advised against his suitability for the pulpit.[4] His vocation, nevertheless, was a sincere one. Theology lay largely at the roots of his disagreement with Calvin. With parts of his Bible translations already in hand, he now substituted the apostolate of letters for his hopes of becoming a minister. Yet in spite of her printing industry, Basle was not his immediate choice of residence. He had no friends there and settled down reluctantly when no positions were available in either the Vaud or

---

[1] See below pp. 218ff.; cf. Buisson, *Castellion* 1.103. In 1536-1537 the *Matrikel* (2.12) seems to indicate the presence at Basle of a relative of Castellio, Mathieu Exautier: cf. Buisson, *Castellion* 2.224f.

[2] See vol. 2.

[3] Cf. Buisson, *Castellion* 1.99 and passim.

[4] *Ibid.* 1.198f.

Neuchâtel.[5]   All that Basle could offer him during the first eight years was indeed the scarce and bitter bread of exile.   He was forced to supplement his meagre income from Oporinus' press with manual labour.   The story of his poverty has become widely known, partly because of the calumnious twists with which it was first told by Calvin.[6]   But poverty could not stop him from spending every free moment bent over his books and writings.

In the spring of 1545 Castellio and his family settled down in Basle, and it is tempting to credit this modest man with exerting considerable influence upon the city's intellectual climate from the beginning.   In August 1545 and October 1546 respectively two Italian emigrants arrived, Celio Secondo Curione and Bernardino Ochino, who had known him before[7] and now became his close friends.   They were among the first Italian Protestant refugees to sign the university roll.[8]   Like Castellio himself, both had then reached a turning point in their lives.   Curione had to blame his own conduct for losing his teaching position at Lausanne, but he weathered the crisis and received a modestly remunerated chair in the Basle faculty of arts years before Castellio became his colleague.[9]   Both were strong-minded individuals; to the hour of Castellio's death they must frequently have shared their thoughts, although it is not easy now to assess to what extent each influenced the other, since they did not need to exchange letters.   Curione was certainly no stranger to the art of humanistic compromise.   Well aware of many heterodox tendencies, he yet retained the outward appearance of a somewhat unmoved, even critical, listener to the thoughts of his more radical brethren among the Italian émigrés.   Yet he doubtless transmitted many of these thoughts to Castellio and participated whole-heartedly in his lifelong struggle for religious freedom.

Castellio's relationship to Ochino is even more interesting.   Both had formerly been attracted to Geneva and personally impressed by Calvin.[10]   Both were now ready to embark on a series of writings that exhibited radical tendencies and cast considerable doubt on their orthodoxy.   In 1545 Ochino no more than passed through Basle, but he was able to arrange for Castellio's co-operation in translating one of his Italian works into Latin.   It was later to be followed by others.[11]   On the whole their lives moved at some distance from one another, but whenever they

[5] Cf. Buisson, *Castellion* 1.230ff.

[6] *Ibid.* 1.248ff.

[7] *Ibid.* 1.226f., 233.

[8] *Matrikel* 2.47 : Ochino's and Curione's names are followed immediately by that of Francesco Stancaro, another Italian who stayed in Basle for some months and knew Castellio (cf. Buisson, *Castellion* 1.281n.).   His Antitrinitarian opinions drove him later to Transylvania and Poland.   A few positions further up in the list we find the name of Franciscus Dryander, the famous translator of the New Testament into Spanish, who later corresponded with Castellio (Buisson, *Castellion* 1.253 ; Steinmann 82ff.).

[9] M. Kutter, *Celio Secondo Curione*, Basle 1955, 86ff., 124ff., 178ff. and passim. Like Castellio Curione was later involved in the David Joris scandal and the preparation of *De haereticis*, but on both occasions his reactions to an official investigation differed unfavourably from those of Castellio : Buisson, *Castellion* 2.8, 154 ; however, cf. also Cantimori, *Ital. Haeretiker* 253ff.   There is a French transl. of Curione's small catechism : *Institution de la religion chrestienne*, s.l. 1561, but it cannot be attributed to a Basle press. Apart from Curione, Castellio knew the Basle professor Martin Borrhaus.

[10] Buisson, *Castellion* 1.224f. and passim ; Cantimori, *Ital. Haeretiker* 112 ; R. H. Bainton, The *Travail of Religious Liberty*, New York 1958, 97ff.

[11] Buisson, *Castellion* 1. 226f. ; 2.368 ; Cantimori, *Ital. Haeretiker* 236f., and below p. 133.

converged the moment was crucial to each. The simplicity and sincerity innate in Castellio's rationalism must have appealed to the former general of the Franciscans. *Vice versa* Ochino's mildly mystical individualism, his insistence on a personal approach to God, suited the pious, moralizing atmosphere of Castellio's home, as it suited the conventicle-like air that pervaded the circle of David Joris.[12] Ochino's masterly use of the vernacular to convey his religious message may have left its mark on Castellio's writings in French. At least in *De haereticis* he drew also close to Ochino's impressive technique of indirect challenge to religious authority.[13] They both developed the fundamental conviction that dogma never mattered and often harmed. Ochino, apparently, was first led to reject the intricacies of the Trinitarian creed but Castellio followed suit in no uncertain manner.[14] In a remarkable, but alas undated, letter to Castellio Ochino advanced the very theme which his friend was to treat so fully in his most rationalistic work, the famous *Ars dubitandi*.[15]

One cannot help doubting whether the ferment of Italian radicalism would ever have affected Basle the way it did without the presence of Castellio there. In the eyes of Calvin, Beza, and the world at large he became the central figure of the ' other ' Basle. To be sure, his scholarly reputation suited the ' official ' Basle well enough, and some of its representatives even viewed his religious leanings with a, fair measure of sympathy, but the only true friend he found among the Swiss, Niklaus Zurkinden,[16] lived in Berne rather than Basle. Among the Basle citizens of good standing who sympathized with Castellio the printer Oporinus deserves to be mentioned first. He never resisted the temptation of a calculated risk. Without him, the number of *Castellioniana* published in their author's lifetime might have been substantially smaller, and the imbalance between Castellio's fame in the sixteenth as against successive centuries even more marked.[17] It was only fair, therefore, that no other printer profited from Castellio's presence in town to the same extent as Oporinus. The printer's own interest in neo-Latin poetry of a Christian tenor was greatly encouraged by Castellio. Apart from his own attempts in this direction, he collected the text of his former fellow-poets at Lyons, of their models and their French followers.[18] In addition he was producing a number of fine editions of Greek classics for Oporinus and other printers. He may have been instrumental in securing for the Basle printers the co-operation of other classical scholars, such as Jean Ribit, who was his friend.[19]

---

[12] Cf. Cantimori, *Ital. Haeretiker* 111ff.

[13] See Bietenholz, *Ital. Humanismus* 30ff. and cf. with *De haereticis, an sint persequendi*.

[14] Buisson, *Castellion* 1.224 ; Cantimori, *Ital. Haeretiker* 115 ; Bainton, *Studies* 167f.

[15] Ochino's letter : Buisson, *Castellion* 1.228f. *De arte dubitandi* has been published in *Per la storia degli eretici italiani...*, testi raccolti da D. Cantimori e E. Feist, Rome 1937, 307-430 ; there is a French translation by C. Baudouin, Geneva 1953.

[16] Buisson, *Castellion* 2.94ff. and passim ; cf. E. Bähler, Nikolaus Zurkinden von Bern, 1506-1588, *Jahrbuch für schweiz. Geschichte* 36 (1911), 215-344 ; 37 (1912), 1*-106*.

[17] Cf. Guggisberg, passim.

[18] Cf. **No. 48, 260a** ; Buisson, *Castellion* 1.284ff. Where Castellio left off, his one time reluctant pupil Karel Utenhove took over ; see below p. 206, and **No. 200**.

[19] Buisson, *Castellion* 1.40, 202f. ; 2.131 and passim. **No. 297, 887ff.** Castellio also obliged the printers by dedicating his *Sibyllina oracula* (**No. 280**) to the well known Basle patron Morelet du Museau. It is a remarkable preface, not only for its attempt to draw the Sibyls historically closer to the Christian tradition but also for the philological

Even before Castellio was able to obtain a permanent teaching position in the university, he was asked to further, with his knowledge and firm moral convictions, the education of Basilius Amerbach, the son of Bonifacius. He also taught Zwinger, the nephew of Oporinus, and Felix Platter, the son of Thomas, the headmaster of the Basle gymnasium. The latter quickly introduced Castellio's *Dialogi sacri* into the curriculum of his school, and he may have employed the Savoyard for some Greek lessons.[20] The influence of such highly reputable men no doubt proved decisive in finally adding Castellio to the regular university teaching staff. Like other professors he continued to lodge and tutor some of the younger students. Although he was fearful of the Gallic temper, French youths frequently appeared among them.[21]

More important, however, than his amiable relations with some good burghers of Basle were his contacts with Francophones who had come to stay temporarily or permanently in the Rhenish town. He may have known and respected François Baudouin even before he had reason to sympathize with him as a fellow victim of the supreme wrath of Geneva. If they did in fact meet during Baudouin's journey from Geneva to Strasbourg and back to Paris in 1545,[22] the name of Georgius Cassander may have been mentioned in their conversation, for we possess a letter from Castellio to the irenic Catholic, dated August 1546.[23] Both men were later in a position to recommend Castellio to Philipp Melanchthon. So also, and more specifically, was Hubert Languet, the close friend of Germany's quiet reformer, who was to spend some time at Basle in 1557.[24] Baudouin and Jean Bauhin were born in the neighbouring cities of Arras and Amiens. The latter was already residing in Basle when Castellio arrived there. In his case there can be no doubt as to the intimate character of his relations with our Savoyard,[25] since on Castellio's death Bauhin became guardian of his children. It was Bauhin who introduced Castellio to the eccentric Guillaume Postel[26] and especially to the circle of David Joris, the Dutch Anabaptist leader, who lived incognito at Basle and maintained contacts with scattered disciples in France.[27] How far Castellio's acquaintance with Joris went it is now impossible to say. It is difficult to imagine what language would have been used in the intimate

---

method it exhibits. Morelet, who no doubt secured the French royal privilege for this edition, is also asked to arrange for the collation of the printed text with another ms. in France. With a succinctness most unusual in sixteenth century prefaces the reader is being told exactly as much as he ought to know about the following text edition. Cf. Buisson, *Castellion* 1.282.

[20] Buisson, *Castellion* 1.247f., 256ff., 2.93f., 413, 422, 425. Another student of the early years was J. J. Grynaeus, son of the late Greek professor Simon Grynaeus and after Castellio's death a loyal defender of his reputation. One of his last students at Basle, Paul Cherler, became Castellio's first biographer: Guggisberg 10ff., 31; cf. Buisson, *Castellion* 2.264., 500. On Bonifacius Amerbach's generosity towards Castellio: Hartmann 6.366ff.

[21] *Ibid.* 2.91f. and passim. The *Matrikel* reveals some additional names of French visitors and students influenced by Castellio, e.g. Jérôme and Jean Des Gouttes, Thomas Lafarge, and Jean Vertunien de Lavau: see above p. 96f.

[22] See below p. 146.

[23] *Illustrium et clarorum virorum epistolae selectiores*, ed. P. Bertius, Leyden 1617, 49; cf. 173f.

[24] Buisson, *Castellion* 2.116f., 448.

[25] See above p. 63.

[26] See below p. 140f.

[27] Droz, *Hendrik van Schor*, passim.

talks between them which F. Buisson has suggested,[28] and the gap created by Castellio's humanistic education and by his rationalism must have been even greater. This does not, however, preclude the possibility that Castellio translated some Dutch text by Joris, or might at least have wished to do so.[29]   Other inferences may be accepted more readily.   Anyone who knew from personal, painful experience what the life of a hunted heretic was like—as Joris did—must have greeted Castellio's historic battle for religious toleration with profound and passionate sympathy.[30] Castellio, on the other hand, given his close friendship with Bauhin, probably knew the secret, if not the true identity, of the strange old man when few other inhabitants of Basle yet did so.   However in the one extant letter which Joris addressed to Castellio there are hints of a certain reserve.[31]   This ties in well with other bits of information about a growing conflict of opinion between Joris and his son-in-law, Niklaus Blesdyck.   Both Bauhin and Castellio remained in friendly correspondence with Blesdyck after the Basle authorities belatedly accepted the truth about Joris and Blesdyck went to the Palatinate to become an orthodox minister.[32]   During the official investigation Castellio was not seriously implicated. He had no qualms in condemning a few incoherent articles allegedly excerpted from Joris' writings.   Not with one syllable did he condemn the Anabaptist himself, and he got away with it.[33]

Joris was well served by the substantial means he had brought to Basle and the liberal use he made of them.   It is not difficult to imagine that Castellio and his cause profited by his generosity.[34]   The same may be assumed for G. B. Bonifacio, Marquis of Oria, who arrived in Basle in 1557.[35]   Castellio's contacts with this highly respected Italian nobleman were close and enduring.   Bonifacio was exactly the kind of stranger any Bâlois would covet as a godfather to his child.   Together with Blesdyck, Bonifacio answered at the baptismal font for the little Bonifacius Castellio.[36] The marquis also befriended many among the most radical of his émigré compatriots and in 1563 he urged Castellio to migrate to Poland where so many of them found shelter.[37]

---

[28] Buisson, *Castellion* 2.136f.; cf. Burckhardt, *Joris* 43f.

[29] Buisson, *Castellion* 2.162; B. Becker in *Autour de Servet et de Castellion* 287f.; Droz, *Hendrik van Schor* 99f.

[30] Joris petitioned the Protestant Swiss cities in favour of Servetus.   However, the identification of Joris with Georg Kleinberg, one of the pseudonyms used in *De haereticis*, is no longer acceptable: cf. Buisson, *Castellion* 2.164 and R. H. Bainton's transl. of *De haereticis: Concerning Heretics*[2], New York 1965, 10f.

[31] Buisson, *Castellion* 2. 162; cf. Bainton, *Joris* 62.

[32] Buisson, *Castellion* 2.455f., 462ff., 417f.; cf. above p. 63.

[33] Buisson, *Castellion* 2.155.

[34] *Ibid.* 2. 14ff.   For the hypothesis of a connection between Joris and Oporinus cf. Steinmann 77f.   One also notes that still in 1562 Blesdyck negotiated, through Bauhin and Castellio, with Oporinus about the printing of a book which, as he says, " expe[c?]-tatur a multis in Belgia." (Buisson, *Castellion* 2.462).

[35] A. Bertini, Giovanni Bernardino Bonifacio, *BZGA* 47 (1948), 19-84; M. Welti, La contribution de Giovanni Bernardino Bonifacio, marquis d'Oria, à l'édition princeps du " De haereticis an sint persequendi ", *Bolletino della Società di Studi Valdesi*, No. 125 (June 1969), 45-49.

[36] Buisson, *Castellion* 2.276f.

[37] See below p. 133.

On an earlier page we noted the temporary presence in Basle of Monsieur de Falais. From that day the French nobleman belonged among the most influential sympathizers of Castellio. On his estate outside the gates of Geneva he lodged Bolsec. When the latter was banished, Falais too moved to the neighbouring Bernese territory. From there he helped organize the Genevan movement of protest against the burning of Servetus, causing, thus, immense embarrassment to his former friend, Calvin. On one of his very few absences from Basle Castellio later visited Strasbourg for alleged contacts with " Schwenckfelders and Falaisians".[38] A typical associate of Falais was Jean Colinet, a teacher at the very school that Castellio had formerly headed, and a faithful propagator of his writings. In 1552, while the publication of Castellio's French Bible was still being delayed, Colinet circulated in Geneva certain copies of its preface. They were obtained through the co-operation of Léger Grymoult who worked as a corrector in a Basle press. A year later on the very eve of Servetus' execution, Colinet passed another manifesto around. It was the epistle dedicatory of Castellio's Latin Bible, addressed to Edward VI. He was censured and soon afterwards relieved of his duties in Geneva. He may then have come to Basle and, afterwards, he can be traced to Lausanne and Neuchâtel. Wherever he went he frequented anti-Calvinist circles.[39] Léger Grymoult, the Basle corrector who had supplied Colinet's ammunition was himself a Castellionist of long standing. Once an Augustinian at La Rochelle, he was convicted of heresy and came to Geneva. There he met Castellio while making a living from private lessons. From 1551 he too lived in Basle. Later he was to be appointed to a teaching position at Montbéliard, another Castellionist stronghold.[40]

Also conveniently close to Geneva was the estate where an aristocratic Italian professor of law, Matteo Gribaldi Mofa, used to spend his summer vacations. A teacher at various Italian and French universities in turn, a frequent visitor to Lyons where some of his writings were printed, he also had close ties with Basle. On his road to Antitrinitarianism, and consequently trouble, he passed through Geneva at the time of the trial of Servetus and he returned there the following summer. On both occasions he protested loudly against the execution of heretics ; in the meantime, however, he had also visited Basle. From there he returned to Italy, taking with him Castellio's former pupil, Basilius Amerbach. Castellio himself knew him ; he referred to him in a letter to Zurkinden and in *Contra libellum Calvini*.[41]

Before we turn, however, to the wider appeal of Castellio's ideas beyond the walls of Basle, we must glance at the principal vehicles of that appeal, his writings published by the Basle presses. Reference has already been made to his contributions

[38] Buisson, *Castellion* 2.30f., 60ff., 270, 425 ; *Calvini opera* 16.260.

[39] *Ibid.* 14.492, 499ff., 585ff. ; Buisson, *Castellion* 1.309n., 341n. ; 2.62f., 130f., 441f., 444. I was unable to discover specific evidence for his presence at Basle (cf. Cantimori, *Ital. Haeretiker* 150). The preface to the French Bible is reprinted, in part, in *Calvini opera* 14.727ff.

[40] Cf. above p. 114 and below p. 245f. ; A. Dufour, Vers latins pour Servet, contre Calvin et contre Genève, *Mémoirs et documents*, Soc. d'hist. et d'archéol. de Genève, 40 (1961), 483-496 ; Buisson, *Castellion* 2.62. Two short unpublished letters (UBB ms.G. II.17, fol. 388f.) show Grymoult as a fellow student of Basilius Amerbach in Padua (1556) as a guest of J. J. Grynaeus and a friend of the Bauhin family. Cf. also *Correspondance de Bèze*, 4.158f.

[41] Buisson, *Castellion* 1.83, 257, 344f. ; 2.41, 390f. ; Cantimori, *Ital. Haeretiker* 194ff. and passim ; Hartmann 6.361f. ; *Correspondance de Bèze* 4.206 and passim ; Baudrier *(Tables)* 144 ; *Matthaei Gribaldi et Basilii Amerbachii epistolae Patavinae*, ed. C. Roth et al., Basle 1922 ; F. Ruffini, *Studi sui Reformatori italiani*, Turin 1955, 43-140 ; **No. 481ff.**

to Oporinus' collections of neo-Latin poetry. The same pious and moral concern inspired Castellio's *Dialogi sacri*, a school book which combined the *Colloquies* tradition of Erasmus and Vives with specifically Protestant concerns, and enjoyed uncommon success in the sixteenth century and well beyond. It had originated during Castellio's headmaster days at Geneva, and was prefaced by a letter to Maturin Cordier, the founding father of the French Protestant school.[42] The *Dialogi sacri* ware published immediately after Castellio's arrival. Before the sequence of Basle editions was broken soon after the author's death eleven reprints had been published, and possibly more.[43] Likewise Castellio's concern for the humanistic school together with his scholarly interests and his desire to serve Oporinus and other printers resulted in numerous editions of Greek classics, partly edited and partly translated by him.

Although his humanistic activities continued, Castellio came to draw a neat distinction between such useful undertakings and his real mission. Reluctantly he consented to assist Oporinus in a weighty edition of Homer which was published in 1561. But in the preface he described that obligation as divine punishment for the immoderate admiration he had twenty-two years earlier bestowed on the pagan poet.[44] In the same way he expressed pious contrition at the sight of his own secular poetry.[45] Already by the time of his move to Basle he felt that the Muses could not be entertained unless they inspired religious elevation.[46] All his efforts were now devoted to his Bible translations. In the sober Word of God he recognized the principal instrument of moral as well as specifically religious instruction. Shortly after his arrival at Basle he offered to the public the first-fruits of his unremitting labours in the form of a new Latin Pentateuch and Psalter. In 1551 the entire Latin Bible was published and after years of difficulties and delays caused by censorship it was followed by Castellio's French translation in 1555. A year earlier a second, revised, edition of the Latin Bible had reached the market. A careful collation of the various editions of his Bibles until the posthumous publications *ultima manu* is still outstanding, but well beyond the scope of this study. A few general points, however, must be noted in order to trace the further progress of Castellionism in Basle as well as the reactions it encountered.

Ever since the remarkable preface of his *Moses Latinus* [47] Castellio never tired of reaffirming his Erasmian belief in the continued progress of biblical scholarship. Perfection, however, was unattainable, he thought, since certain pages were of necessity obscure. He also asserted that the application of the Mosaic Law had always been confined to temporal punishment and rewards, and moreover that it had been abrogated by the coming of Christ. In general he contested the adequacy of a literal and dogmatizing exegesis in favour of a purely rational and moral interpretation.[48] On the basis of these convictions his epistle to Edward VI, prefixed

---

[42] Buisson, *Castellion* 1.158f. and passim.

[43] *Ibid.* 2.341ff. E.g. on p. 344 a ref. to an unidentified ed., Basle 1578 in 16° [?].

[44] *Ibid* 2.88 ; Steinmann 63.

[45] Buisson, *Castellion* 1.26ff.

[46] *Ibid.* 1.270ff. ; **No. 260f**.

[47] *Ibid.* 1.294ff.

[48] Cf. H. Liebing, Die Frage nach einem hermeneutischen Prinzip bei S. Castellio, *Autour de Servet et de Castellion* 206-224. Liebing's careful and penetrating analysis of Castellio's hermeneutics is especially valuable in view of some exaggerated and unten-

to the Latin Bible of 1551, resounded with the first of his passionate pleas for religious toleration.[49]   In his efforts to reconcile precision with common sense he gradually shifted from the elegant style of the first Latin Bible to the down-to-earth tenor of the French translation and the increased concern with accuracy in the revised Latin text.[50]

In a general way Castellio revived the tendencies of Erasmus' biblical philology and exegesis, even to the point of following his trend to moderation from the first edition to the next.   Castellio's formulation, however, was sometimes bolder than that of Erasmus.   Also he may have gone farther in questioning the inspired character of many passages as well as an entire book, the Canticle, and in eroding the distinction between canon and apocrypha, but in view of Erasmus' struggles and triumphs Castellio's efforts appeared respectable to the Bâlois.[51]   Nevertheless, controversy was bound to arise.   After all it had been over his earliest translations from the Bible and over unusual points of his understanding of Scripture that the first disagreements with Calvin occurred.[52]   However, the most heated and vicious attacks against Castellio's Bibles were touched off by his general stand for religious freedom rather than the singularities of his biblical scholarship alone.   Once aroused, controversy was bound to continue, for Castellio's Bibles were read and reprinted down to the French Revolution, although Perna's Latin Bible with Castellio's last revisions was still considered the best edition in the days of Pierre Bayle.[53]   Information ought to be collected on subsequent writers who were accustomed to quote the Bible in Castellio's translation.   One who did so was Mino Celsi, his prominent successor in the struggle for toleration, who also assisted Perna in his re-editions of Castellio's Bible.[54]   Castellio's translation was favoured by Gilbert Cousin, a Catholic canon, and by Pierre Ramus.[55]   If found a warm reception in Arminian Holland, still more so in Erasmian Britain, and even proved acceptable to an occasional Calvinist theologian such as Polanus of Polansdorf.[56]   Most of Polanus' colleagues, however, remained violently opposed and repeated the arguments handed down from the days of Calvin and Beza.   At the turn of the eighteenth century Pierre

---

able statements by other scholars: cf. e.g. Busson 330ff. and A. Renaudet, *Humanisme et Renaissance*, Geneva 1955, 256: " ... Castellion, que la logique du protestantisme conduit au rationalisme en matière d'exégèse comme en matière de dogme, et qui finalement ne trouve plus dans la Bible que l'expression, propre au seul peuple juif, de la loi naturelle, et ne voit en Jésus qu'un philosophe."

[49] Buisson, *Castellion* 1.301ff.

[50] Cf. *ibid.* 1.317ff., 415ff.; J. van Andel, La langue de Castellion dans sa Bible française, *Autour de Servet et de Castellion* 195-205.

[51] Cf. Bainton, *Studies* 150ff.; Buisson, *Castellion* 1.312 and passim.   A similar act of broad-mindedness enabled Postel to publish at the same time his *Protevangelion* at Oporinus' press: see below p. 142.

[52] Buisson, *Castellion* 1.183f., 196ff.

[53] Guggisberg 26.

[54] On Celsi see L. Fimpel, *Mino Celsis Traktat gegen die Ketzertötung*, Basle 1967.   I am presently preparing a critical edition of Celsi's works for the Corpus Reformatorum Italicorum.

[55] See below p. 237 and p. 155, n. 13.   One wonders who may have been using the copy of the Latin New Testament, Basle 1556, with the device of Diane de Poitiers on the binding (*BMC* 18.1276).

[56] Guggisberg 28f., 47, 95ff., 114ff.

Bayle was first induced to examine Castellio's translations when the continuous flood of repetitive criticism aroused his suspicion.[57]

The Basle authorities had to consider carefully how far they could afford to go in condoning Castellio's self-appointed office as a translator of Scripture. The events of 1554-55, in particular, could not fail to alarm the council and its appointed censors. The first outraged protests against the burning of Servetus reverberated throughout the Protestant world, while the leaders of the Swiss and German churches rallied behind Calvin. In Geneva the repercussions coincided with a smouldering power struggle which the government of Berne observed with partisan interest.[58] These facts could not be ignored by the Basle town council, pledged as it was to a policy of neutrality towards conflicting interests among its confederates. The release of Castellio's French Bible was delayed for two years and the revised Latin edition of 1554 was critically examined between printing and publication. The censors insisted on the removal of a long note to *Romans* 9 which refuted the Calvinist doctrine of predestination [59] and was bound to be branded as heretical even within the city walls. With this, however, the censors had done their duty. Rather than having to destroy them, Oporinus was free to circulate the suppressed fascicles among Castellio's friends. One copy found its way into Beza's hands. Even without this the Genevan pastors would no doubt have endeavoured to cut the circulation of Castellio's Bibles and to counteract their effect. The third edition of his Latin Bible in 1556 coincided with the publication of Beza's Latin version of the New Testament, while Castellio's French translation prompted the Genevans to revise their own vernacular version.[60] Beza fitted his New Testament with notes, many of which were critical of Castellio. However the opponent was not mentioned by name and the language remained moderate.[61] But subsequently Calvin and Beza were gripped by hatred and outrage at Castellio's doings. When in 1560 the revised version the *Nouveau Testament* was published in Geneva Castellio was singled out for anathema on the first page of the holiest of books and described as an " *instrument choisi de Satan.*" [62] Similar excesses at long last drew enough attention to his plight that the Basle authorities felt their professor of Greek should be allowed to answer in public. Whereas in 1554 he had been refused permission to publish his answer *Contra libellum Calvini*, he could in 1562 produce an expurgated edition of his *Defensio suarum translationum*,[63] primarily aimed at Beza, and the candid, simple, but none-the-less incendiary, *Conseil à la France désolée*.[64]

---

[57] Guggisberg 146f.

[58] Buisson, *Castellion* 2.60ff.; R. Feller, *Geschichte Berns*, Berne 1946ff., 2.394ff.

[59] Buisson, *Castellion* 2.57ff.

[60] *Ibid.* 2.250ff.

[61] The commentary on *Romans* 9 is still missing in the subsequent Basle eds. of Castellio's Bible (1556 and 1572), whereas Beza in the re-editions of his New Testament no longer hesitated to insert Castellio's name: Buisson, *Castellion* 2.104ff.; *Correspondance de Bèze* 2.168ff., 201f.; Guggisberg 20f.

[62] Buisson, *Castellion* 2.250f.

[63] Suppressed were especially passages which accused Beza—and rightly so—of offering misleading translations in his New Testament so as to bear out the Calvinist doctrine of predestination. The censured passages have been edited by S. van der Woude in *Autour de Servet et de Castellion* 259-279.

[64] There can be no doubt that the *Conseil* was printed at Basle. The typographical material points to the presses of either Oporinus or Parcus who often printed for Oporinus. The continued presence of Castellionism even in Geneva is demonstrated by the fact that

To mention the *Conseil* is to enter the field of that famous battle for religious toleration, touched off by the anonymous publication of *De haereticis, an sint persequendi* by Oporinus in 1554.[65] The story of this book needs no repetition. It is now clear that Castellio was both the central promotor and the final formulator, supported by a circle of friends which included Lelio Sozzini, C. S. Curione, and perhaps others.[66] Servetus, who had just been tried for heresy and burnt together with his books by the magistrate of Geneva, had come to Basle in 1530 in search of a publisher for his *De trinitatis erroribus*. However he had to go on to Haguenau in order to find one.[67] At Basle his passing left no trace over the next sixteen years before Antitrinitarian positions were gradually reasserted by new visitors, Ochino, Lelio Sozzini, to a lesser degree Castellio, and finally Fausto Sozzini.[68] In spite of many accusations from the part of Geneva and Zurich,[69] none of them was officially condemned in Basle for holding the views of Servetus. Castellio, in particular, was too well-known to the Bâlois for them to have mistaken the nature of his protest against the burning of Servetus. He too read the books of the Spaniard but clearly did not react with the shudders of excitement experienced by some of his Italian friends. Even less would he grope in them for a hidden ' message ' as did apparently some of the sectarians of David Joris.[70]

Official Basle loyally backed the action taken against Servetus in Geneva; yet nobody could fail to notice that it also listened sympathetically to Castellio's pleas for toleration. In view of Genevan requests for clarification, only evasiveness could save the face of *antistes* Sulzer and those for whom he spoke.[71] The attitude was illogical, but it did not lack common sense : Servetus had clearly been a heretic and was now dead. There was no point in weakening the authority of a sister church

---

the book was distributed there. The Geneva *Consistoire* conducted a lengthy inquiry which showed that the copies had been smuggled in from Basle. In August 1563, the national synod of the French Protestant church condemned the book in one of its articles : Buisson, *Castellion* 2.225ff.; Chaix, *Recherches* 83. A new ed. by M. F. Valkhoff, Geneva 1967.

[65] Cf. Buisson, *Castellion* 1.358ff. and passim; Lecler, *Tolérance* 1.322ff.; W. Kaegi, *Castellio und die Anfänge der Toleranz*, Basle 1953; a facsimile reproduction of **No. 246**, ed. by S. van der Woude, Geneva 1954; an annotated English transl. by Bainton: see above p. 126 n. 30. The French ed. : *Traicté des hérétiques*, Rouen 1554, was definitely not printed in Basle. Cornell University Library owns a copy of a rare German translation and obligingly supplied me with some sample photographs : *Von Ketzeren. Ob man auch die verfolgen / oder wie man mit jnen handlen solle / des D. Martinj Lutherj unnd Johann Brentij / auch anderer viler der alten und unserer zeyten glerten meinung unnd bericht*, s.l., s.d. It is difficult to indicate the provenance of this edition; Basle may safely be excluded. One might investigate the typographical material used by various printers in Württemberg around 1560. Cf. the introduction of S. van der Woude to *De haereticis*, Geneva 1954, xix. Cf. also Cassander's reference : below p. 152, n. 40.

[66] Bainton, *Studies* 154; Cantimori, *Ital. Haeretiker* 149ff.

[67] R. H. Bainton, *Hunted Heretic*, Boston 1953, passim; J. F. Fulton, *Michael Servetus, Humanist and Martyr*, New York 1953, 51ff.

[68] Cantimori, *Ital. Haeretiker* 31ff., 145ff. and passim; S. Kot in *Autour de Servet et de Castellion* 90ff. and passim.

[69] Cf. the case of the Italian merchant A. M. Besozzi in 1564. Having been convicted of Servetian heresies at Zurich, he moved to Basle where he was soon admitted to citizenship. After two years, however, he moved on to Lyons : Cantimori, *Ital. Haeretiker* 262ff.

[70] Cf. Droz, *Hendrik van Schor* 110ff.

[71] Cf. in particular *Calvini opera* 14. 627, 637, 644f; 15. 44, 74f., 156, 169f., 189f., 209, 298; 16. 148; *Correspondance de Bèze* 3.57; 4.49ff., 184ff., 195ff.

by denying that it had acted in good faith. Castellio, however, was alive within the city walls. His modesty and probity were generally known. There was no point in joining the witch hunt of the Genevans and sharing their responsibility and, perhaps, guilt. Ambiguity seemed less damaging than controversy. The printing industry must have welcomed this calculated indecision of the authorities. It was on the side of Castellio and of tolerance. For once it was committed to a cause and until the end of the century it never faltered.

If the larger part of Castellio's polemical rejoinders to his assailants in Geneva could not be printed at Basle during his lifetime,[72] two other writings did actually appear. Their nature sheds some light on the complexity of Bâlois reaction to the controversial professor of Greek. In 1557 he published a Latin rendering of the famous *Theologia Germanica*,[73] and in 1563 there followed his "translation" into sixteenth century Latin of the *Imitatio Christi*. Mysticism had been deeply rooted in medieval Basle, and this tradition was zealously kept alive through the efforts of many printers. The scope of Castellio's rationalism was wide enough to allow a genuine affection for the mystical tendencies of his Italian friends and of the Anabaptists. The mystic path, to be sure, was not his own, but like his own it led to the core of religion, the true flame of piety freed from the cover of stifling dogma. Both treatises reflect to some degree the attitudes of David Joris, the Dutch Anabaptist who had withdrawn from the battle line to the peace of Basle, who no longer sought the earthly realisation of the realm of God but the illumination of his soul. They also reflect the situation of Basle, a commercial and publishing centre turned Protestant, but always ready to invoke the spells of spiritualism both to save its own consciousness of tradition and its friendly links with Catholic lands and individuals. It was the atmosphere that induced Castellio and Cassander, the irenic Catholic, to seek out one another.

Among the Bâlois Castellio possessed perhaps the clearest mind of his generation, clearly ahead of others in rejecting alchemy [74] or when criticizing dogmatism on account of its lack of logic and conduciveness to atrocity. But perhaps one has insisted too much on these qualities that would make him an Enlightener *avant la lettre*. He felt that the divine inspiration and truth of Scripture were sufficiently proved by the authentic miracles which it related.[75] Outside the specifically Christian tradition he recognized and respected the power of prophecy in the Sibylline oracles.[76] Never published in his lifetime, Castellio's *Ars dubitandi* is often praised

---

[72] Cf. Buisson, *Castellion* 2.372ff.

[73] I cannot offer any evidence that a French translation of the *Theologia Germanica* was published in Basle. Cf. G. Baring, Die französischen Ausgaben der *Theologia Deutsch*, *Theolog. Zeitschrift* 16 (1960), 176-194. Baring suggests that Castellio used, inadvertently, a version of the text which can be traced back to the German Anabaptist Ludwig Hätzer. Without quoting evidence, Cantimori (*Ital. Haeretiker* 108) states that Joris may have drawn Castellio's attention to the *Theologia Germanica*; cf. Bainton, *Joris* 35.

[74] E.g. in the *Conseil à la France désolée*, Geneva 1967, 54 : " ... ne soyés point opiniastres comme les Alcumistes, lesquels aiment mieux dépendre sac et bagues, corps et entendement, et finablement ou mourir en soufflant le charbon, ou aller mourir en l'hospital, que de laisser leur forcenée entreprinse." Castellio's arch-enemies in Basle, Bodenstein, Gratarolo, and Hotman, were all passionate alchemists.

[75] Cf. e.g. S. Castellio, *De l'art de douter*..., Geneva 1953, 54, 79, 143f. and passim.

[76] Cantimori, *Ital. Haeretiker* 107 ; D. Cantimori, Note su alcuni aspetti del misticismo del Castellione e della sua fortuna, and V. L. Saulnier, Castellion, Jean Rouxel, et les Oracles Sibyllins, both in : *Autour de Servet et de Castellion* 225-243.

as the first great work of European rationalism. Has the fact that it opens with a statement of unconcealed eschatological doom been sufficiently considered? It is as a last resort that Castellio offers his *Art* of methodical reasoning. He does so in deep frustration at the absence of inspired prophecy, and the failure of his own appeals to common sense and natural morality in such writings as the *Conseil à la France désolée*.[77] To his friend Niklaus Zurkinden Castellio sent the German text of the *Theologia Germanica* and the gift directed their correspondence towards meditation on death. They also discussed together, sympathetically, some writings of the German mystic Schwenckfeld, who maintained contacts with Ochino.[78]

The insecurity of all things mortal indeed cast a long shadow on Castellio's remaining years at Basle, as well as on his friend Ochino whose last great work, the *Dialogi*, he translated for the Basle printer Perna. Poverty and censorship must have weighed him down, although the Bâlois did their best to leave him untroubled. The first official inquiry into his allegedly heterodox views on predestination was occasioned somewhat accidentally in 1557. It produced a frank, precise statement of his position which was accepted both by the university and the council.[79] A year and a half later the storm over the belated identification of David Joris left him equally unruffled. But Castellio could not fail to realize that his enemies in Geneva would give him no quarter. For some time he considered the possibility of a further migration, and in the summer of 1561 the Marquis of Oria wrote to him from Poland, urging him to come. It was a land without wine, so the friend wrote, but without censors too. His long suppressed writings could here finally see the light of day.[80] But Castellio trusted the Bâlois, and appreciated the security of his position. He stayed, in spite of the censors. In the following year he had the satisfaction of seeing the *Defensio suarum translationum Bibliorum* and his *Conseil à la France désolée* published.

New storms were gathering, however. In 1563 Adam von Bodenstein, a colleague from the university's medical faculty, accused him of heresy, libertinism

---

[77] " Christ le maitre de vérité a prédit (Mat. xxiv, 24) que dans les derniers temps surgiraient en si grand nombre les faux christs et les faux docteurs que les élus eux-mêmes, s'il était possible, se laisseraient séduire. Or, ces derniers temps, ne sont-ils pas proches? Je le crois, si j'en juge, entre autres raisons, par tant d'erreurs et de dissensions graves que je vois se multiplier ... en religion, s'il vous arrive de donner un conseil qui ne reçoive pas l'approbation de ceux à qui vous le donnez, ne vous attendez pas à être aimé : bien plutôt vous serez tenu pour hérétique ... Je veux donner ici des règles par lesquelles chacun puisse, au milieu du flot des dissensions dont l'Eglise est aujourd'hui battue, se tenir debout et posséder une vérité si sûre et si éprouvée qu'il demeure dans la foi et le devoir ... (*De l'art de douter, op. cit.* 27-29).

[78] Buisson, *Castellion* 2. 382-392, 400.

[79] *Ibid.* 2.114ff.

[80] Rather than the incomplete English translation (Bainton, *Studies* 158f.), see the original text: Cantimori, *Ital. Haeretiker* 461f. A year earlier, G. Gratarolo, Castellio's principal enemy at Basle, wrote in one of his regular reports to Calvin that he felt no longer secure in the town and considered emigration to England or Poland! (*Calvini opera* 18.17f.) In fact, neither Gratarolo nor Castellio had reason to expect much danger from the Bâlois and both stayed in the end. In 1562 Zurkinden attempted, rather surprisingly, to have his friend, Castellio, appointed to a chair at the Lausanne academy (Buisson, *Castellion* 2.249f.; *Calvini opera* 19.235 and passim). When the plan failed, J. L'Archier wrote to Castellio: " ... Pour ma part jen feusse este bien joyeux pource que nous feussions veus plus souvent. Mais ayant considere les grandes commoditez quavez a Basle, a scavoir questes en paix, que y avez de grans amys ... je juge que cest vostre grand bien dy demeurer." (*Ibid.* 19.551).

and popery. Bodenstein made it clear that he acted at the inspiration of Beza. Castellio answered firmly and quietly. In spite of the general uproar caused by Ochino's *Dialogi*, which he had translated, he felt it was scarcely necessary to answer Bodenstein's charges in that matter.[81] It is true that Ochino, once driven out of Zurich, was not permitted to stay at Basle and took the road to Poland. Castellio, however, died at Basle in December 1563, before the council had passed judgment on Bodenstein's charges. For weeks to come Beza still expressed fear that the magistrate of Basle might come up with a posthumous vindication of his enemy which would equal his own condemnation.[82] His alarm proved unfounded, but in other ways Basle paid tribute to the quiet greatness of Castellio. The university honoured its former member in the usual manner. He was buried *honestissimo loco* and wealthy Polish students donated a marble slab of classic dignity. Oporinus published a worthy epicedium composed by a promising student just about to receive his baccalaureate, Bauhin's son-in-law, Paul Cherler.[83] Theodor Zwinger honoured him eight years later in his *Theatrum humanae vitae*. He added that pious and well-to-do men had taken it upon themselves to provide the orphans with an education.[84]

Castellio's ultimate hour of triumph at Basle came a decade after his death, when the Huguenot colony was reaching its peak and heading for a confrontation between its Calvinist church and an influential body of dissidents, heavily indebted to Castellio's views.[85] More directly, however, the Castellionist revival was the work of a group of Italians. Pietro Perna, the printer of Ochino's *Dialogi*, republished in 1572-73 no fewer than four editions of Castellio's Bibles: an excellent and beautiful reprint of the entire Latin Bible, furnished with a number of favourable judgments by noted contemporaries;[86] a part of the Latin Old Testament; a cheap pocket edition of the Latin New Testament without apparatus; and a small parallel edition of the same text in Latin and French with a preface by Mino Celsi, who wrote at the same time his own learned defense of religious toleration.[87] These Bibles were followed by a small collection of writings, faithfully preserved by Bauhin and another friend since the death of their author and now published for the first time. In four dialogues the collection summarized the main points of Castellio's anti-Calvinist theology, and among other appendices it offered two of his more outspoken rejoinders to attacks by Calvin. Hidden behind a fictitious imprint was the printer Pietro Perna again; he was consequently afforded an opportunity to contemplate the wisdom of his action during a short imprisonment.[88] The soul of the entire enterprise, however, was the editor, also protected by a pseudonym. He was Fausto Sozzini, nephew of Castellio's friend Lelio. Shortly before Castellio's death Fausto had reached Basle

---

[81] Buisson, *Castellion* 2.257ff.; *Correspondance de Bèze* 4.231f.; 5.163f. Castellio's apology is published in *Calvini opera* 20.190ff.

[82] *Correspondance de Bèze* 5.16n., 18; cf. 5.13, 25; *Calvini opera* 20.241.

[83] *Matrikel* 2.139; Guggisberg 10ff.

[84] Among them was certainly Basilius Amerbach: Buisson, *Castellion* 2.280ff.

[85] See above pp. 99ff.

[86] Guggisberg 26ff.

[87] M. Celsi, *In haereticis coercendis quatenus progredi liceat*, Christlingae [Basle, P. Perna] 1577; cf. above p. 129, n.54.

[88] Buisson, *Castellion* 2.317ff., 372f.; H. R. Guggisberg, Pietro Perna, Fausto Sozzini und die *Dialogi quatuor* Sebastian Castellios, *Studia bibliographica in honorem Herman de La Fontaine Verwey*, ed. S. van Der Woude, Amsterdam 1968, 171-201.

after having spent a year at Lyons. A later statement by this great Antitrinitarian suggests a certain intimacy between the venerable professor and the eager student. While it is certain that Fausto learned a great deal from Castellio's published and unpublished writings, it is by no means improbable that in spite of his youth he was able to show the older man some fresh consequences of the Antitrinitarian position.[89]

Taken as a whole, Castellio's influence in Basle was immense. The classical scholarship exhibited in his translations and editions could be accepted without reserve, except for the Bible and Ochino's *Dialogi* where the issue was complicated by the controversy on toleration and by theological dispute. Clearly he was not an Anabaptist, and his Antitrinitarian views, although constantly alleged by his enemies, remained unpublished or, at any rate, unpublicized. By contrast he was very firm in expressing his opposition to the Calvinist view of predestination, but then the latter was far from sacrosanct in Basle. Castellio normally approached the topic with formulations of admirable simplicity, such as, for instance, the succinct: " *salutis prima causa Deus, exitii homo.*"[90] Daring as such formulas were, they would lend themselves, with some good will, to an orthodox Lutheran interpretation and, therefore, need not shock the Basle *antistes* Sulzer and others with a Lutheran leaning. In November 1557, when Castellio had to defend his stand on predestination before the university and the Basle magistrate, no less a man than Melanchthon wrote him a warm letter of sympathy.[91] The Lutheran leader probably acted at the suggestion of Castellio's friend, Hubert Languet, and no doubt did so *en connaissance de cause*. He wrote from Worms, where he had met Beza during the recent Colloquy. As one recalls it was only in 1556 that Beza had unleashed his personal polemic against Castellio. If Calvin is to be believed, Melanchthon's letter enclosed for good measure a note of greeting from another prominent foe of the Genevans, François Baudouin, whom Melanchthon had met a few days earlier on a visit to the University of Heidelberg.[92] Castellio was still alive at Basle in 1561 when Baudouin arrived there to have Cassander's famous *De officio* printed. The fact of Castellio's relations with these two advocates of church unity is among the most significant, especially since there is no reason to think that either side ever repudiated them completely.[93]

The accusation of popery too in Bodenstein's denunciation of Castellio was not entirely unmotivated. To a simple mind it was easy to link Castellio's insistence on the moral effort demanded of man with the Catholic belief in the efficacy of works. One recalls how even forty years later Antoine Lescaille, that remote disciple of Castellio, was travelling on this road and finally found peace among the faithful of the Catholic church.[94] Whether he would have approved of this or not, Castellio

---

[89] A. Rotondò, Atteggiamenti della vita morale italiana del Cinquecento : la pratica nicodemita, *Rivista storica italiana* 79 (1967), 991-1030, esp. 1003, 1006.

[90] Buisson, *Castellion* 2.192ff. ; cf. 2.115.

[91] *Ibid.* 2.116ff.

[92] *Ibid.* 2.117ff : In his *Responsio altera ad Jo. Calvinum* Baudouin recalled how he and Cassander had met Melanchthon at the Colloquy of Worms. He also mentioned Melanchthon's letter to Castellio and said that it expressed approval of Castellio's stand on predestination and free will. No such statement, however, can be found in Melanchthon's letter. Cf. Duquesne 94f.

[93] Only two letters from Castellio to Cassander have survived (see above p. 125, n. 23), and no direct correspondence between Castellio and Baudouin seems to exist, but contacts obviously continued right to Castellio's death : cf. below p. 152, n. 40, and Buisson, *Castellion* 2.429., 468, 470.

[94] See above p. 102.

to us represents a significant example for that latitudinarian tendency that continued to characterize theology *à la Bâloise* and to direct the policy of most printers. Other examples included men like Postel, who veered between Anabaptism and the Society of Jesus, Blesdyck, who from an Anabaptist became an orthodox pastor, Baudouin, who forsook Calvinism in the hope of realizing his vision of unity on Catholic premisses, and many others. It is impossible, on the other hand, not to associate Castellio with tendencies that were heterodox rather than merely latitudinarian. His friendship with Ochino and the two Sozzinis poses the problem of Castellio's Christology which is, however, not fully answered by a reference to his more or less open rejections of the Trinity. More than any specific theological views he held or did not hold, it was his broad and disarmingly natural rationalism that influenced many contemporaries. In this respect, his presence at Basle attracted and generally stimulated inquisitive spirits rather than presenting a specific message to be taken away. Nothing was farther from his mind than to surround himself with a sect of Castellionists. The fact that Calvin and Beza chose him as a scapegoat for fluctuating trends of opinion that seemed to question, and even threaten, their work tends to give Castellio a prominence in matters with which this unassuming man was not actually much concerned.

The term 'Castellionist'[95] would seem better justified when related to Castellio's untiring battle for religious toleration and freedom from the narrow spirit of discipline that prevailed in Geneva. In this respect his friendships in French-speaking Switzerland, Lyons, Montbéliard, among the refugee groups of Strasbourg, Frankfurt and London, and among Italians and Poles[96] must be credited with considerable influence on the forming of the image of Basle. In this respect too his spirit, and often his very arguments and formulations, lived on in a body of publications subsequently produced by the Basle presses.[97]

---

[95] The term most frequently used in the 16th century seems, in fact, to have been '' Bellianist.''

[96] Buisson, *Castellion* 2.91f., 243ff. and passim.

[97] See vol. 2.

CHAPTER SIX

GUILLAUME POSTEL

At long last we have come to understand Guillaume Postel[1] : one of the most curious and heroic figures of a generation richly endowed with courage and imagination, an eccentric with a sharp, if unbalanced mind, but certainly not mad, a dreamer and idealist who incessantly appealed to reason, a pragmatist who forever read his own ideas into the authors of the past and the events of his day, who respected other peoples' political and religious loyalties as means to his own end.   Above all, he was a humanitarian who believed in the natural goodness of man and expected ultimate salvation for all, who sacrificed his own career and convenience to the good of universal reconciliation.   He may not have spent much time in the town, but Basle clearly played a significant role in his life and thought, and a number of his most important books were published there.   Printing, he thought, would be the lance and sword of Christ's victory.[2]   Towards the end of his life he knew he had ground to praise God for the staunchness of Basle and the friendship of Oporinus, both of which had contributed so much to the dissemination of his writings.[3]

The beginnings of Postel's contacts with Basle remain in the dark.   All we know is that Oporinus in 1543 reprinted his *De magistratibus Atheniensium* from the Paris first edition of 1541.   Oporinus' own press was then in its first year of production ; the printer was, not unnaturally, heavily in debt[4] and eager to obtain

---

[1] See W. J. Bouwsma's remarkable analysis of Postel's thought.

[2] Bouwsma 240, based on a letter of Postel to Plantin.

[3] Letter to T. Zwinger : " ... Laudem vero Deo et Domino Jesu Christo, Regi Judaeorum creatorique mundi do, quod mihi per stabilitatem vestrae civitatis, optimo cive ejus et amico meo bonae memoriae Johanne virente aptissimoque fructificante Oporino res meas curante, dederit, ut bona pars meorum operum hinc, id est a regia civitate vestra, in universum prodiret prostaretque typis et maxime quod opusculum omnium meorum minimum *Protevangelium*, secundo, id est Joh[a]n[nis] Marci Evangelio praefixum, impresserit, quia duce illo scriptulo, velit aut nolit, non solum etiam Maranthizata gens Judaica, sed etiam tota generatione humana assentiente, evincam et falsitatis arguam summa illa mendacia, quae a *Thalmudi* impiis authoribus sunt contra Christum et ejus matrem perpetuo virginem excogitata, ita ut mihi dare poenas per mea scripta cogantur, non quia ego sim velimve, qui nil sum, sed quia Deus est." (F. Secret in *BHR* 26 (1964), 140 ; as in subsequent quotes from Postel, the interpunctuation is my own.)

[4] Steinmann, esp. 30ff.   In his letter to Calvin of 10 November, 1542 (*Calvini Opera* 11.464ff.) the printer describes his difficulties as the direct result of the Qu'ran edition and implores the reformer to secure a loan for him.   One also notes that Oporinus here reprinted an edition that had appeared elsewhere ; whenever possible he avoided this practice.   His calculation proved correct : in 1551 he could publish an enlarged re-ed. of *De magistr. Athen.* and the work was still reprinted in the 17th century.

promising copy. Through his previous activities as university lecturer and editor, he had acquired a wide reputation for Greek scholarship. Postel's topic, then, sounded excellent. In his preface to Guillaume Poyet the author professed to follow the lead of Budé and Baïf. This claim would remind readers not only of a scholarly tradition at Paris, but also of an editorial one at Basle.[5] If Oporinus took the initiative in this enterprise, the reprinting was hardly carried out without the author's consent. Connections between Paris and Basle that might have served as a link between the two men were plentiful. Budé was Postel's friend. One may recall also Pierre Duchâtel, who had been a student at Basle before—like Postel—he journeyed to the East and on return became a royal lecturer. He was the Bishop of Tulle in 1540 when Postel dedicated his *Syriae descriptio* to him.[6] Postel's close friendship with the family Morelet du Museau and the patronage of Cardinal Du Bellay may also date back to this time.[7]

In addition to its fashionable Hellenistic appeal Postel's book spoke a language which must have gone to the heart of Oporinus and helped to foster a lifelong relationship of mutual confidence and sympathy. Postel was an activist: nothing was farther from his mind than antiquarian studies unrelated to the problems of the present. In his view the Athenian constitution prepared the way for a future of continuous political progress which culminated in his own reform proposals.[8] He analysed his topic by way of frequent comparisons with the institutions of other peoples, in particular the Turks. This was an approach which Oporinus understood. He resembled Postel in his taste for action, and his idealism accompanied occasionally by opportunistic ends. He thought little of the conservative circles of Basle, and Postel's obsession with the Turks found a parallel in Oporinus' devotion to Byzantine studies.[9] Moreover, he was just then involved in the publication of the first Latin Qu'ran, an enterprise that brought him much harassment, but also the support of such luminaries as Luther and Melanchthon.[10] In view of this publishing venture Postel shortly thereafter sent Oporinus the manuscript of his *De orbis terrae concordia*, which could not be published in Paris.[11]

This large work, which Postel considered his most important, is primarily an urgent appeal to, and practical manual for, the Christian mission among the Muslim. It contained an exposition of Islam based on quotations from the Qu'ran and a series of rational arguments for the correctness of Christian views which, however, do not show Postel at his best.[12] Above all, Postel here embarked on his crucial endeavour

---

[5] See below pp. 187-201.

[6] F. Secret in *BHR* 23 (1961), 122; on Duchâtel cf. above p. 57.

[7] F. Secret in *BHR* 22 (1960), 554f. and 23 (1961), 545.

[8] Cf. Bouwsma 286ff. In his preface Postel recalled how Plato had proposed to merge the laws and institutions of all times and places into one perfect system. This he felt called upon to achieve.

[9] Cf. F. Husner, Die Editio princeps des " corpus historiae Byzantinae "; Johannes Oporin, Hieronymus Wolf und die Fugger, *Festschrift Karl Schwarber*, Basel 1949, 143-162; F. Secret in *BHR* 23 (1961), 363ff.

[10] Steinmann 20ff.; P. G. Bietenholz, *Pietro Della Valle*, Basle 1962, 33f.

[11] Steinmann 31ff.; Bouwsma 9f. The work was written after Postel had been dismissed from his royal lectureship. It failed to obtain the Sorbonne's *imprimatur* and contained passages bound to embarrass the court, e.g. an indirect attack upon the military alliance of Francis I with the Turks. Only the first book could appear in Paris (1543).

[12] Bouwsma 243ff.; cf. also 233f., 269f.

138

to bring about world concord, both in the religious and political spheres. To this end he produced a long list of essential propositions which, he believed, were common to all faiths.[13] All this he was going to expound further in his subsequent writings, also to be published in Basle.

Basically, Postel presented the idea of world concord with complete confidence in the universal role of the Catholic Church. *De orbis terrae concordia*, as published by Oporinus, was intended to offer Postel's credentials as he set out for Rome and membership in the Society of Jesus. It was also, however, the first document of his patient journey of compromise with Protestant views. To make it acceptable to the Basle publisher, he had to suppress part of the preface and no doubt many passages of his original text, among them an entire book of unflattering comparisons between the Muslim and the Protestants, which he published separately in Paris.[14] Even so, Oporinus felt obliged to add some marginalia which politely took exception to Postel's text. He also announced this step on the book's title page.[15]

At Rome Postel was refused admission to the Jesuit order, but he became a priest and in 1547 he arrived in Venice, where he supported himself as a hospital chaplain and also worked for Vincenzo Valgrisio [16] and other publishers. In the same year Oporinus published, without an imprint, three more works by Postel: *Absconditorum a constitutione mundi clavis*, Πανθενωσία, and *De nativitate Mediatoris ultima*.[17] Among them they show so much scathing criticism of the papacy, the Council of Trent, and Catholic practices that they must occupy a special place in Postel's published works. They might even show him on the path to conversion, if many other statements did not testify to the contrary, especially after the incident at Laon (1566), which he considered as a miraculous and irrefutable proof of the truth of Catholicism. After this he even used his correspondence with Theodor Zwinger to preach the communion of the Roman faith to his Basle friends.[18]

Taken together the publications of 1547 proclaim for the first time his fundamental message to the world. It was based upon the *Zohar*, Joachite writings and innumerable other fruits of his reading, and was delivered in a language clearly marked by eschatology. Its purpose was the *restitutio omnium*—or *concordia mundi* —to which everybody would have to contribute his talent, the Protestants no less

---

[13] Bouwsma 195.

[14] *Alcorani seu legis Mahometi et Evangelistarum concordiae liber*, Paris 1543.

[15] Some examples are quoted in Steinmann 35.

[16] Bouwsma 14; F. Secret in *BHR* 23 (1961), 372f. On Valgrisio see above p. 32.

[17] The three publications, as well as *De orbis terrae concordia*, can be ascribed to Oporinus on the evidence of typographical material used and of cross-references in Postel's texts. That the former three were published together in 1547 is revealed, in particular, by the preface to *De nativitate Mediatoris ultima*; cf. also F. Secret in *BHR* 25 (1963), 217, and 26 (1964), 123.

[18] Cf. F. Secret in BHR 21 (1959), 453f. and 26 (1964) 130ff., e.g. 132, letter to Zwinger: " ... quia Divinitatis, quae ubique est, virtus et animae mundi, quae tota in massa mundi est, substantia sive omnis creatura universoque aequivalens virtus atque substantia in suo summo gradu, et natura humana in suo gradu summo consistens necessario in unum illum panem omnibus mundi potentiis fortiorem coalescant oportet, ut anno Sal. 1566 et creationis 5566 probatus est per 84000 personarum sensibile oculatumque testimonium Laumduni, sicut 1566 annis ante Christus per 84 testium fidem juratam in B. Marci domo in Jerusalem factum et institutum esse a se docuerat, nempe inter 12 Apostolos et 72 discipulos. Cura, mi Zvinghere, ut recta sententia universalis Ecclesiae in te et in tuis amicis vigeat. Saluta Bohinum et, si adhuc vivat, patrem ejus et matrem tuam et, si sunt apud vos, Castalionis haeredes. Vale 21 9bris 1571."

than the Muslim.[19]   For himself he reserved a crucial role, a mediatory function in world history comparable to the several mundane interventions of Christ.   That meant that, although possessed by an Erasmian need for continuity and unity in world history which only the Roman Church could guarantee, he had to embrace the Bâlois Protestants with that holy opportunism sanctioned by Saint Paul and demonstrated by Erasmus.[20]

From Venice Postel again visited the East, but in 1550 he was back in Paris. Since he now enjoyed some measure of patronage by Margareth, the sister of Henry II, the contact with Basle and the publications resulting from it may not have been entirely unprofitable to him.   He came to develop a strong biblicism with a bent to action, reminiscent of Lefèvre d'Etaples and also of Ramon Lull, whom Lefèvre had helped to resuscitate.[21]   This period of his life culminated in the *restitutio*, a mystical experience in early 1552 which put the seal on his Messianic mission.   This singular event took place in the house of Antoine Morelet du Museau, son of the Protestant French diplomat who had lived in Basle, despatched Protestant books to Lefèvre, and finally died in the town.[22]

After all this it is hardly surprising that Postel should have turned to Basle when, a year later, he was forbidden to teach in Paris.   We cannot say whether this was the first time he came or how long he stayed, but we know with whom he associated, and the choice could hardly be more revealing.   Oporinus put him up and showed him much kindness that was later warmly remembered by Postel in spite of his friend's failure to publish many of the manuscripts which he continued to send him.[23]   Postel was also included in Oporinus' friendship with the Zurich pastor Theodor Bibliander.   The latter had edited Oporinus' Qu'ran and became deeply and favourably impressed by Postel's ideas.[24]   Even more important, however, was his friendship with the French-born physician Jean Bauhin, which may date from this visit, and was later extended to Bauhin's sons.[25]   It was partly due to Bauhin that Postel acquired an important insight into Castellio's thought, and no doubt met the man himself, for Castellio was Bauhin's closest friend in Basle and had for some years now been a corrector in Oporinus' press.   No direct acknow-

---

[19] Cf. Bouwsma 277 and passim ; a good formulation of the essential message is found at the end of a long letter to Zwinger : " Iterum vale, et si typis proderit istud voles, sic inscribes : ' De Restitutione omnium Guil. Postelli Rorispergii epistola at TH. Zwingherum, ubi de fine embryonici mundi agitur pro abolenda universi violentia '." *BHR* 26 (1964), 150.

[20] Cf. F. Secret in *BHR* 25 (1963), 216 and 26 (1964), 129 ; Bietenholz, *History and Biography* 86ff.

[21] Bouwsma 33f. 215, 241 and passim.

[22] F. Secret in *BHR* 22 (1960), 553f. ; Bouwsma 17 ; cf. above p. 58f.

[23] See above n. 20, and F. Secret in *BHR* 25 (1963), 216ff. and 26 (1964), 124ff., e.g. 127f. : (Postel to Zwinger) " Nolim esse molestus charissimo amico Oporino aere alieno pergravato, licet 19 thaleros discedens illi reliqui.   Nam magno ibi sumptu me aluit, licet putem mea exemplaria maxime autem *dispunctionum cosmographicarum* libros, qui importunissime hic a me petuntur ubinam excusi, posse apud illum vel haeredes longe majorem impensam compensare posse [sic]."   When Postel left Basle in 1553 for Italy Oporinus recommended him to his Milanese acquaintance, Francesco Ciceri (F. Secret in *BHR* 23 (1961), 549f.).

[24] Steinmann 73f., 78f.

[25] See above p. 63f., and F. Secret in *BHR* 25 (1963), 216, 221, and 26 (1964), 126, 132, 135, 145.

ledgment of his debt to Castellio has come to light, but Postel's constant stress on reason and his tendency to minimize the importance of many dogmas were certainly shared by Castellio and, in both cases, have led to comparisons with the *philosophes* of a subsequent age.[26] Postel also shared with Castellio his interest in Sibylline prophecy [27] as well as Origen's fundamental belief in the eventual redemption of all mankind, though this view was approached less openly by Castellio himself than by his Basle friend and comrade in causes, C. S. Curione.[28]

Postel's association with this circle—Calvin called them ' Servetists '—had yet another consequence. Postel was in Basle when the Genevan authorities tried and executed Servetus. He must have witnessed the shock of his friends. The ensuing controversy between Basle and Geneva caused a continental sensation ; Postel was kept informed even after he left Basle. When Calvin published his *Defensio orthodoxae fidei ... contra ... errores ... Serveti* Postel jumped to the conclusion that he himself had been the target of an attack, although his name was not mentioned. He lost no time in countering this supposed attack in a treatise somewhat misleadingly entitled *Apologia pro Serveto*. At the same time Castellio was working on his *Contra libellum Calvini*. One notes that he too paid special attention to the passage Postel may have had in mind.[29] Postel's search for world harmony produced its own kind of tolerance which differed visibly from the cause of Castellio but gave him plenty of reasons for disliking rigid Calvinism. Here then was another point on which he had discovered kindred spirits in Basle. More than a decade later he could still burst into a blistering attack on Beza when writing to the Bâlois Zwinger.[30]

On another path his acquaintance with Bauhin led Postel into the immediate neighbourhood of the circle of Dutch Anabaptists living quietly and incognito around their leader David Joris in Basle. When the Basle authorities finally caught up with the Joris sect, Bauhin was questioned and some of his papers were impounded. The only extant letter from Postel to Bauhin still lies in the files collected by the prosecution for the posthumous trial of Joris.[31] There are analogies between some tenets of Dutch Anabaptism and Postel's own unbridled prophetism. There is even evidence that Dutch heterodox circles had shown interest in his writings as early as 1549, shortly after he had published the Basle trilogy, but nothing more is known about personal contacts.[32]

---

[26] Bouwsma 193, 212, 298 and above p. 132f.

[27] Bouwsma 207f., 255 and passim ; cf. above p. 132.

[28] Cf. C. S. Curione, *De amplitudine beati regni Dei*, [Poschiavo ?] 1554, and Cantimori, *Ital. Haeretiker* 101f., 175ff. and passim. Erasmus and the Joachite tradition should also be considered in this context.

[29] Bouwsma 23 ; Buisson, *Castellion* 2.37. Cf. F. Secret in *BHR* 23 (1961), 132ff. Calvin was probably thinking of Castellio himself, but his crucial accusation against that unnamed " brother " of Servetus was that he thought the Bible was at times " obscure." Such a ' heresy ' could very well be attributed to Postel too, so that his misinterpretation of Calvin's text, in fact, demonstrates his closeness to Castellio.

[30] F. Secret in *BHR* 26 (1964), 130 : Beza's " Evangelism " here is seen to lead to slaughter and torture.

[31] UBB ms. Jorislade III.G.10.

[32] Bainton, *Studies* 185-198 and *Joris* 64f. ; Bouwsma 20 ; F. Secret in *BHR* 23 (1961), 135f. ; 20 (1958), 63. While he was in Basle Postel kept a sharp eye on potential ' prophets ' : *BHR* 22 (1960), 553 ; but it is unlikely that he knew the true identity of Joris any better than did most Bâlois.

Probably through Oporinus, Postel also knew Wolfgang Wissenburg.[33] A respectable pastor and professor of theology, Wissenburg lacked the gift of original thought. He was easily fascinated by Postel, but he also served as a liaison man between Matthias Flacius Illyricus and Oporinus, the printer of the Magdeburg Centurions. Flacius Illyricus, however, was a sworn enemy of Postel.[34] More noteworthy was Postel's friendship with another respectable Basle professor, Theodor Zwinger, a nephew of Oporinus. Zwinger's tastes were encyclopedic: hardly anybody seemed so radical to him that he was unwilling to engage in a polite correspondence. But if he himself had any sympathy with radical views, it fell regularly short of open support. Zwinger treated Postel's fractured leg during one of his—presumably repeated—short visits to Basle in 1560-61, and was rewarded with two astrological essays composed by his patient.[35] He also continued a friendly correspondence with the ageing pensioner of Saint-Martin-des-Champs at Paris, and after the death of Oporinus he saved his unpublished manuscripts for him.[36]

Between 1551 and 1553 Oporinus accepted the risk of three more Postel publications, among them the important *Protevangelion*.[37] This was the pseudo-gospel of James, an account of the early life of the Virgin and the birth of her Son, which Postel had brought back from the Orient and translated into Latin. His title reflects his assumption that Saint Peter in Rome knew this text when he commissioned Mark in Venice to compose his canonical gospel as a chronological continuation of it. Thus, the authenticity and priceless value of the *Protevangelion* were to Postel beyond doubt. Bibliander, the Zurich theologian to whom Oporinus had referred Postel's Latin translation, was less certain, but sufficiently impressed to edit it. His preface clearly embodies Postel's own introduction. It also is a striking example of the embarrassment which Postel caused to his Swiss friends. Bibliander's preface speaks of him with warm appreciation and does not directly reject his conclusions, but the Swiss theologian preferred to rank the new text somewhere between the canonical writings and the less significant apocrypha. A last Basle edition of Postel was produced by Oporinus in 1561. The uncompromising title of *Cosmographiae disciplinae compendium* permitted the publisher's name to stand in the imprint, but the work was, again, a summary of Postel's central ideas. Nevertheless, it also reflected a change in his political thought which was bound to please his friends in Basle. He was accustomed to credit the French crown and people with a unique historical role in the achievement of cosmic concord, but—temporarily at least—he modified this position in favour of analogous references to the Emperor Ferdinand.[38]

---

[33] Cf. Burckhardt, *Herold* 22ff.; *Steinmann* 30, 69ff.; Bietenholz, *Ital. Humanismus* 155.

[34] Bouwsma 24f.

[35] UBB ms. Fr. Gr. II. 5ᵃ, No. 95f.: two astrological *iudicia* addressed to Zwinger by Postel; there is also another unpublished letter to [Zwinger]: Fr. Gr. II. 14, No. 22 (s.l., 28 Nov., 1560).

[36] F. Secret has reprinted Postel's letters to Zwinger with his commentaries in *BHR* 26 (1964), 120ff. However, like all other writings of Postel, they badly need a definitive, critical edition. Over and above the abstrusities of his thought, Postel wrote with singular carelessness and Castellio and other correctors in Oporinus' press may have had their share of trouble over his manuscripts.

[37] The other two were an enlarged and revised ed. of *De magistratibus Atheniensium* (1551) and a short treatise *De originibus* (1553); on the latter cf. Bouwsma 214. On the *Protevangelion* cf. Bouwsma 36f. and F. Secret in *BHR* 25 (1963), 216f. On the critical reception of this work cf. F. Secret in *BHR* 23 (1961), 358.

[38] See the epistle dedicatory to Ferdinand, and Bouwsma 227f.; cf. 176, 204.

Postel's gratitude for the co-operation of Oporinus was mixed with deep concern. The number of books that gradually left his friend's press was in very small proportion to the number of manuscripts he kept on sending him. However, even Postel himself showed some understanding of Oporinus' dilemma. All his writings were saturated with the most extravagant theological views; Oporinus would have been foolish to consider publication without obtaining a favourable opinion from a reputable Swiss theologian. As a rule, Postel's urgent pleas remained unheard. On one occasion the desperate author set his hopes on Perna and other rivals of Oporinus; [39] on another he tried subterfuge. In 1561 he sent Oporinus a manuscript allegedly composed by a close friend of his. Oporinus consulted Wissenburg, who could tell at once from the handwriting how close that ' friend ' was to Postel. He spoke with warm admiration of the prophet, but advised against publication. The manuscript, he thought, contained pestilential heresies.[40] Among the manuscripts that remained in Basle were Postel's *Apologia pro Serveto*,[41] his Latin translation of the *Zohar* [42] and an *Evangelium aeternum* [43] of which Oporinus printed only some attacks upon the papacy in the empty pages at the end of Πανθενωσία. A number of these Basle manuscripts are now in the Sloane collection in the British Museum.[44] In addition to Postel's disappointment over his own still-born writings came his vehement opposition to a famous text actually published in Basle. The first Hebrew edition of the Talmud was prepared and printed in Basle during the last years of Postel's life. Highly as he valued the Qabbalah, the Talmud had always seemed dangerous to Postel. In his letters to Zwinger he protested vigorously, even viciously, against the planned edition,[45] thereby manifesting that he did not escape from the Antisemitism latent among his contemporaries.

Is it possible, then, to form some conclusions on the contacts which Postel maintained with Basle for close to forty years? It is easy to see what the city meant to him. His visits followed upon a series of rejections and humiliations suffered in Paris and Venice, where he had been pronounced mad by an Inquisitional court, in Ravenna and Rome where he had spent four years in the papal prisons.[46] He arrived in Basle as a prophet filled with new hope, behind him the proverbial rejection by his own people, before him a land of promise. He felt able here to continue his mission in the service of eternal truth, to speak his own Catholic language, even though it was not always acceptable to Roman orthodoxy, and to dress in it a message destined for the Protestant part of that world he so wanted to convert. To allow them to become instruments in his scheme for eternal salvation was the greatest honour he could do the Bâlois. Yet he also had a spirit of ingrained curiosity, always eager for new intellectual experiences. The impulses he received from the Basle of Erasmus, Castellio and David Joris were not of themselves essential to the formulation of his creed, but they added significant nuances and filled him with

---

[39] F. Secret in *BHR* 26 (1964), 128.

[40] *Ibid.* 124 and Steinmann 79.

[41] Cf. Bouwsma 23, 149f.; F. Secret in *BHR* 23 (1961), 133.

[42] F. Secret in *BHR* 22 (1960), 553.

[43] F. Secret in *BHR* 25 (1963), 216f.; Bouwsma 14.

[44] For some references to other mss. sent to Basle see F. Secret in *BHR* 23 (1961) 133, 356; 25 (1963), 212; 26 (1964), 120, 125f.

[45] *Ibid.* 121, 135ff.; cf. 21(1959), 455 and 23 (1961), 358f.; above p. 81.

[46] Bouwsma 22ff.

heartening confidence in the validity of some of his most cherished views which, in fact, they did confirm.

What Postel meant to the Bâlois and their reputation abroad can only be inferred from the whole context of this study.   He enjoyed the fame of a formidable, ultra-profound savant whom many admired and wished to understand more fully. It was true that some prominent Protestants strongly denounced his heresies,[47] but for the most part such voices were lost in the general stir and bewilderment which his message provoked.   He clearly was a Catholic, yet paid enough tribute to typically Protestant views and causes to challenge the finality of the new, confessional, boundaries—a finality which some of the Basle printers opposed for reasons of their own, involving both ideology and prosperity.   Lastly, to contemporary sympathizers in Basle and elsewhere—as, in fact, to modern scholars—Postel's message may have sounded more Erasmian than he himself realised.   He believed in the innate goodness of all men, in the final salvation of all through a Christianity founded in nature and responsive to human progress, but fundamentally opposed to coercion.   To this belief he clung in an atmosphere of eschatological anxiety which Erasmus and many of his Basle disciples also experienced in varying degrees.[48]   Postel, it has been said, " is significant above all as ... a witness to the character and concerns of the sixteenth century." [49]   There can be no doubt that his concerns were shared in Basle and elsewhere.   This fact explains the demand for his publications and it proves that Oporinus was—*inter alia*—a clearsighted businessman.

---

[47] Beza denounced his heresy as " *Melchisedeci genus* " (F. Secret in *BHR* 23 (1961), 128ff.) ; his letters to the heretical Schwenckfeld—he too was a correspondent of Oporinus —aroused Flacius Illyricus (Bouwsma 20, 24 ; Steinmann 80).   By contrast, Florimond de Raemond defended later his orthodoxy (V.L. Saulnier in *BHR* 20 (1958), 63) and Mersenne thought he was mad (F. Secret in *BHR* 21 (1959), 464).

[48] Cf. Bietenholz, *History and Biography* 21f., 26f., 76f. and above p. 133.

[49] Bouwsma 294.

CHAPTER SEVEN

FRANÇOIS BAUDOUIN

In the fall of 1563, Theodore Beza published rejoinders to two books originally published in Basle. One was Castellio's *Defensio suarum translationum Bibliorum*,[1] the other the anonymous *De officio pii ac publicae tranquillitatis vere amantis viri* which Beza had first attributed to François Baudouin though, in fact, he was only the editor.[2] It is with visible relief that Beza's biographer turns from his hero's attacks on Castellio to those on Baudouin : "*Les deux écrits sont de la même encre, mais Baudouin méritait mieux que Castellion la colère et les invectives.*"[3] Did he? When Beza wrote, he knew that Baudouin had just knelt before the Cardinal of Tournon to abjure his reformed faith. He had thus become a renegade to the whole Protestant world. To this day, and in spite of an able vindicator,[4] his reputation remains unjustifiably stained.[5] His contacts with Basle too seem to have ceased almost completely from the time of his conversion. Perhaps he no longer needed the Basle printers now that he could publish his books in Catholic centres. Nevertheless, his apostasy, even though it was leading him towards the mildest form of Erasmian Catholicism, was clearly less acceptable to the Bâlois than were the heretical leanings of Castellio and his Italian friends. There was a limit to the flexible business practices of the Basle printers and the general mood of tolerance in the town.

---

[1] *Responsio ad defensiones ... Castellionis*, Geneva 1563 ; for good measure it was dedicated to the ministers of Basle. See Buisson, *Castellion* 2.255 and *Correspondance de Bèze* 4. 195, Beza to Bullinger : " ... Scripsi his diebus tumultuarie duas responsiones, unam adversus perditissimum Apostatam Balduinum, qui nunc in Flandria Ecclesias a fundamentis eruit, alteram ad Castellionis accusationes. ... Ibi videbis quod monstrum tandiu aluerint Basilienses fratres, quibus hanc ipsam ob causam responsum meum dicavi, ut tandem intelligant quid cum sua ista mollitie proficiant. Nam si haec monstra in nostris visceribus fovere diutius constitutum est, nemo non videt quorsum sit res evasura."

[2] *Ad Francisci Balduini apostatae Ecebolii convicia ... responsio*, [Geneva] 1563. Beza must have had before him an ed. in which *De officio* was reprinted together with Baudouin's *Defensio insontis libelli "De officio pii viri."* Cf. *Correspondance de Bèze* 3.148-150 ; 4.23, 195-197 ; 5.18-20.

[3] Geisendorf 233, 236.

[4] See the excellent biography of Duquesne, passim.

[5] Buisson, *Castellion* 2.18n., speaks of his "malignité ordinaire"; D. R. Kelley, Historia integra : François Baudouin and his Conception of History, *Jour. Hist. of Ideas* 25 (1964), 41, remarks somewhat ironically: "But in spite of this apparent religious 'versatility', Baudouin was following his own line all along ; the trouble was that nobody else could follow it." Even the Jesuit Lecler denies Baudouin more than a passing treatment.

At the age of twenty Baudouin had started his legal career as the secretary of the famous Charles Du Moulin in Paris. No direct links with Basle are recorded from this period of Baudouin's life. One does notice, however, that Oporinus reprinted an early sample of his scholarship in the very year he had opened his press and successfully pursued another Paris scholar, the well-known Guillaume Postel.[6] In 1544 Baudouin was back at his native Arras, attending clandestine Protestant services together with Jean Crespin.[7] In the following year he had to flee. He went to Geneva and thereafter clearly considered himself a Calvinist. He then travelled on to Strasbourg and Paris. On his trips to and from Geneva it would have been difficult for him to avoid passing through Basle. Did he? Did he stop, did he meet anybody? Perhaps Oporinus, who had printed his work, or Castellio who had just arrived from Geneva to take employment with Oporinus? Perhaps Jean Bauhin, a native of Amiens in the neighbourhood of Arras, who had recently immigrated from Belgium? Such speculations cannot so far be substantiated, but they call for further investigation. If it could be established that the friendship between him and Castellio was sealed in the early days of the Savoyard's break with Calvin, amid the difficulties and deep resentment caused by his removal from Geneva, this might modify our view of Baudouin. It might help us to recognize in his future actions the inner logic and coherence that has so often been denied them. The hypothesis of an early encounter with Castellio is particularly intriguing because of Baudouin's subsequent contacts with some of Castellio's acquaintances. As early as August 1546 Castellio was corresponding with Georgius Cassander,[8] destined to be the decisive figure in Baudouin's life. The text of one preserved letter makes it rather likely that others were exchanged between them in this period, which may now be lost. At any rate the contacts between Cassander and Castellio continued; in 1553 Cassander sent two of his young disciples to Castellio.[9] Moreover, when Baudouin returned to Geneva in 1547 he obliged Calvin by translating Monsieur de Falais' *Apology* for his rejection of the Catholic church. Coming from Strasbourg, Falais had just arrived in Basle. Here he received a letter from Baudouin in Geneva.[10] Here he also met Castellio, whose cause he was later to defend so valiantly in the very lion's den of Geneva. In Basle Falais finally found the man best suited to write a preface to the *Apology* which Baudouin was to translate. This was Dryander, a common friend of Cassander and Castellio and the latter's fellow collaborator in the press of Oporinus.[11] Falais himself corresponded with Cassander. He was at that time still the noble convert whom Calvin treated with distinction; soon, however, he would be an embarrassing critic of Calvin and a loyal supporter of Castellio.[12]

Baudouin himself was not to enjoy Calvin's sympathy much longer. From the fall of 1547 we find him at Lyons. His excuse that he was attending a sick brother

---

[6] **No. 92**; cf. above p. 137f.

[7] Duquesne 74.

[8] See above p. 125, n. 23.

[9] Buisson, *Castellion* 2.412.

[10] *Calvini opera* 12.573-575. In the affair between Falais and Valérand Poullain Baudouin seems to have taken the side of Poullain, a native of Lille who was at Strasbourg since 1543 : *ibid.* 12.643f. ; cf. also *Correspondance de Bèze* 2.92, 94 ; above p.60.

[11] See above p. 123, n. 8 ; cf. M. E. Nolte, *Georgius Cassander en zijn oecumenisch streven*, Nimeguen 1951, 149, 151.

[12] See above pp. 59f., 127.

and a dying mother did not spare him some stern admonitions from Calvin. The reformer clearly had set great hopes on the brilliant young lawyer, and now lost patience at his obvious practice of crypto-Protestantism.[13] There may have been other aspects that worried Calvin, although he did not mention them. Baudouin's letters to Calvin touched repeatedly such issues as predestination and the competences of the presbytery. There was no hint of heresy as yet, but perhaps the signs of preoccupation. Did Baudouin meet in Lyons the sort of people who were later to lend their hearty support to Castellio and Morély?[14]

By 1549 Baudouin had moved to Bourges where he was to teach law until 1555. Twenty years earlier Roman Law had been expounded here by Alciato, whose historicising approach Baudouin was now to develop afresh.[15] After Alciato's departure close ties between Bourges and Basle had continued and the capital city of Berry was still a centre of religious Erasmianism. Baudouin continued to practise Nicodemism and his correspondence with Calvin seems to have stopped for about three years.[16] He met a kindred spirit in Pierre Bouquin, a doctor of theology who in 1541 had stopped at Basle for several months, after abandoning the Carmelite convent of Bourges which he had formerly headed. At about the time of Baudouin's own arrival Bouquin returned to Bourges and thanks to the support of Marguerite de Navarre he was given the post of cathedral preacher. He may have met Baudouin while both were wandering in that rugged borderland between Erasmian reform and Protestantism. Together they left Bourges in 1555. Later both taught at Heidelberg, where they were exposed to the influence of Erastus and Ramus; but Bouquin finally died as a member of the Lausanne Academy.[17]

After a temporary reconciliation with Calvin, Baudouin found employment in Strasbourg, where Bouquin was provisionally ministering to the French community. But just as rivalry with his distinguished colleague Douaren had earlier forced Baudouin from Bourges, he now suffered from the intrigues of François Hotman, his former secretary and friend. Calvin and Beza at once threw their support behind Hotman, and rigid Calvinists everywhere were mobilized against Baudouin. Despite the sympathy of Du Moulin and the support of Johannes Sturm, he was compelled to leave, and Hotman inherited his academic position.[18] Baudouin moved on to a chair in Heidelberg and to the denouement of his life, which occurred between 1555 and 1557 rather than at the time of his abjuration in 1563. During these same crucial years he found in Oporinus his principal publisher. No longer on speaking terms with Calvin, he now sought the friendship of Bonifacius Amerbach[19] and

---

[13] Duquesne 79ff.; *Calvini opera* 20.377ff.

[14] *Calvini opera* 12.649 n.; 20.380f. Cf. below pp. 222f.

[15] D. R. Kelley, Historia integra, *op. cit.*, and: Budé and the First Historical School of Law, *American Historical Review* 72 (1966-67), 828.

[16] Duquesne 82ff., 87.

[17] On Bouquin see *France prot.*[2] and Herzog; cf. **No. 180f**.

[18] Mesnard (*Essor* 326ff.) lays the blame correctly on Hotman; cf. *Calvini opera*, especially 16.81ff., 135ff.; 18.483f.; 19.507f. Even Calvin felt uncomfortable in view of Hotman's exaggerations and counselled moderation: *ibid.* 16.172f. Typical of the trend against Baudouin was e.g. Vermigli who had first received him into his house and was later Hotman's host: *ibid.* 15.434, 467n., 687f., 724.; cf. also Naef, *Conjuration d'Amboise* 385ff. and passim.

[19] UBB ms. G.II.15[1], fol. 10-14: three letters to Bonifacius, written in 1555 and 1556. They also contain evidence of some replies sent by Amerbach. On the whole,

Castellio.[20]   Again we do not have specific evidence for his presence at Basle, but in view of the short distance from Strasbourg, and the number of important manuscripts he entrusted to Oporinus, it is unlikely that he would not have gone there at one time or another.

At Heidelberg he still professed a nominal Calvinism, but he had never been a party man and the latitudinarian nature of his views and contacts was fully manifested by the events accompanying the Colloquy of Worms.   If Baudouin condemned Beza's famous compromise formula, cause of so much embarrassment to the Genevans, his motives no doubt were predominantly personal.   Beza, in return, reported pointedly to Calvin how Baudouin and the Catholic Cassander had embraced each other at Worms.[21]   He may have sensed the importance of this encounter and its potential threat to the Calvinist cause.   The Genevans also were aware of Baudouin's repeated meetings with Melanchthon, and their common sympathy for Castellio. An exchange of letters between Baudouin and Cassander in January and February 1558 shows how both had been deeply impressed by Castellio's attack upon the execution of heretics and how each of them pondered the implications in his own field of study.[22]

Baudouin might not have been able to act the way he did act during the Colloquy of Worms if he had not gone through the painful experiences at Strasbourg and the more gratifying contacts with Basle.   The work which he completed at Strasbourg and which Oporinus published for him in 1556 gives ample proof that he had found himself.   The *Constantinus Magnus* clearly is an outstanding achievement.   The work deserves a much more careful analysis than it has so far received, as well as an extensive study of the impact it had upon others.   To Baudouin himself it revealed the full relevance of his continued studies in the historical progress of Roman Law. In particular, the actions taken by Constantine the Great advanced some exemplary solutions for the politico-religious difficulties of the immediate present.   To the

---

Baudouin is desperate to retain the sympathy of the highly respected Basle lawyer in view of the attacks by Hotman and Douaren.   The last letter ends with a postscript: " De *Constantino* nostro, quem tibi probari valde vellem, iudicium etiam tuum expecto, ut secunda editio castiget quod tu tuique similes corrigendum esse censueritis."

[20] Cf. above p. 135 and Buisson, *Castellion* 2.429f.

[21] *Correspondance de Bèze* 2.110f.; 3.148ff.; Buisson, *Castellion* 2.116ff.

[22] In reply to a letter by Baudouin (*Illustrium et clarorum virorum epistolae selectiores*, ed. P. Bertius, Leyden 1617, 67-70), Cassander wrote in part: " ... Cuius, quaeso, hoc exempli est, ut iudicio superintendentis homo deprehensus vi carcerem abripiatur ibique ab eodem in vinculis non tam instituatur quam inquiratur, deinde in potestate magistratus constitutus atque ex lege nexus spiritali quoque excommunicationis gladio feriatur, quo statim carnifici iugulandus tradatur?   Certe tectius agunt inquisitores nostri, qui cum sciant irregularitatem sibi propositam, si opera vel consilio eorum aliquis morte vel corporis mutilatione puniatur, hominem suo iudicio convictum et tandem excommunicationis ultimo supplicio affectum, tandem bracchio seculari permittunt, sed non antequam gravissime obtestati sint, ut si quam forte magistratus secularis poenam in eum decernat, eam ita moderetur, ut neque mors, neque membri mutilatio subsequatur, neque sanguinis effusio.   Hic certe species aliqua aequitatis retinetur, quae in nostris legislatoribus nulla apparet.   Quid de his constituturos fuisse putas Martinum et Ambrosium, qui Ursacii, Ithacii ac aliorum episcoporum communionem fugiebant, quod iis aliquo modo auctoribus Priscillanus exitialis et manifestarius haereticus capitale supplicium Treveris ab Enodio praefecto subiisset?   Miror sane hos non videre quo praeiudicio se suosque passim per varia regna et provincias dispersos gravent, cum huiusmodi leges ferant, cum praeclarum illud, videlicet Genevensium, facinus in Serveto cremando laudibus efferant " (G. Cassander, *Opera ... omnia*, Paris 1616, 1087).

council fathers assembled at Trent, Baudouin recalled the precedents of Nicaea and Constantine's intervention in a way that showed how well he was now prepared for the subsequent encounter with Erastus at Heidelberg. In fact, the Council of Trent promptly listed the work on its Index.[23] With no better success Baudouin encouraged Calvin to read the book in the last letter he was ever to address to the master of Geneva. But Bullinger, at least, praised it highly.[24] The study of the times of Constantine also brought Baudouin face to face with the emperor's desire to restore church unity and with some of his edicts which would soon figure prominently in the toleration controversy.

The discussion on religious toleration was resumed in a book which Baudouin published in the following year, explicitly as a continuation in reverse chronological order of the *Constantinus Magnus*, his commentary on the earlier imperial laws concerning the Christians.[25] Again he displayed that breadth and objectivity of historical knowledge which entitles him to a similar degree of prominence among the sixteenth century historians as he had traditionally enjoyed among the lawyers. The epistle dedicatory addressed to Caspar von Nidbruck points to another consequence of his historical interests as well as to his close co-operation with Oporinus in Basle. Nidbruck, a moderate Protestant and high official of the mildly Catholic Habsburgs of Austria, was one of the outstanding patrons of Oporinus. Without his generous and energetic support the corpus of church-historical sources and surveys, published by Oporinus for the militantly Lutheran Magdeburg Centurions, might have been a far less significant enterprise.[26] As Baudouin himself suggested in his epistle, his own historical researches and those of the Magdeburg group could complement one another. In fact, he was willing to supply them with material, although personally he was now ready for Cassander and the gradual *rapprochement* with the Catholic church. Oporinus himself might well have recruited Baudouin to assist in the gigantic enterprise, for he was asked specifically to look for French collaborators.[27] If the preface thus offered proof of Baudouin's practical capacity for religious toleration, the work itself dealt with the same issue on the level of historic precedents. It did so with a legal and historical circumspection pointing beyond Castellio to the work of Mino Celsi.

Basically Baudouin's field remained Roman Law. Jurisprudence lent a common emphasis to the thematically interlocking works which were published through Oporinus.[28] The assessment of Baudouin's place within the French school of Roman Law is beyond the scope of this study, but it should be noted how closely his approach to law resembled the Erasmian view of church history: in either case historical differentiation led to accepting schools and doctrines as merely relative and sub-

---

[23] Duquesne 89ff. On the changing views of Constantine see W. Kaegi, Vom Nachleben Constantins, *Schweiz. Zs. für Geschichte* 8 (1958), 289-326.

[24] *Calvini opera* 16.120.

[25] *Ad edicta veterum principum Rom. de Christianis, ex commentariis Francisci Balduini...* (No. 81).

[26] Burckhardt, *Herold* 20ff.; Steinmann 69ff.

[27] Steinmann 71; cf. Duquesne 63n., 94.

[28] On the legal works cf. A. Wicquot, *François Balduin d'Arras*, Arras 1890, esp. 119ff. To No. 83 Wicquot (179) adds a reference to a fourth ed., Basle, H. Petri 1559, which omitted the improvements of Oporinus' third ed. I failed to trace a copy of such a reprint by H. Petri.

ordinated to an overruling consensus.[29]   Here also lay the key to Baudouin's personal religious progression.   Cassander, himself a prominent Erasmian, was perfectly right in linking Baudouin's religious position in Paris to the prophetic *prudentia* of the sage of Rotterdam.[30]   The same sense of continuity, as documented in the tradition of Roman Law, led Baudouin to his original concept of *universal* history.   Some of his writings, published at Basle,[31] announce the ideas later formulated more comprehensively in lecture courses at Heidelberg and published in 1561 as *Institution of Universal History*.[32]   The treatise however was not republished in Basle until after Baudouin's death.

The *Institution of Universal History* is dedicated to the Chancellor Michel de L'Hospital: an indication that by 1561 Baudouin was involved in that startling enterprise which brought his collaboration with Cassander to full, if temporary, fruition and exposed the Basle publishers again to the ire of orthodox Calvinists. In the spring and summer he visited Paris and talked to the Queen Mother, Antoine de Bourbon and the Cardinal of Lorraine.   Subsequently he returned to Germany to enlist Cassander's support for the proposed Colloquy of Poissy.[33]   At last there is specific evidence that Baudouin came to Basle once or twice during this period to have Cassander's famous *De officio* printed anonymously.   That Oporinus was once again the printer is made likely by the fact that Baudouin on this occasion lent him the considerable sum of 1200 florins.   Eight years later, after the death of Oporinus, the loan amounted to almost ten per cent of the total debt he had left behind him, and Baudouin applied to his friends in Basle, Basilius Amerbach and Daniel Osiander, in an attempt to recover the money.[34]   Whether he succeeded seems more than doubtful.

Cassander's *De officio*, like the equally Erasmian *Via Regia* of Georg Witzel, was originally written in support of the irenic policies of Ferdinand I and his advisors. After the failure of the Colloquy of Worms in 1557, the emperor no longer set his hopes on direct talks between the exponents of the various confessions, but rather encouraged his spokesmen to take the pen, particularly so in view of the diplomatic tug-of-war concerning the resumption of the Council of Trent.   Baudouin not only overcame the timidity of his modest friend Cassander, who so far had not published

---

[29] For Baudouin as for Erasmus the crucial and everlasting pattern of the true church was laid down in the works of the third and fourth century fathers: Bietenholz, *History and Biography* 35ff.; Duquesne 100; cf. also Baudouin's *De ecclesia et reformatione epistola quaedam*, s.l., s.a. (BN D².3808 No. 8).   The title page of this illuminating pamphlet is missing.   It could have been published anywhere, even in Basle.

[30] G. Cassander, *Opera ... omnia*, Paris 1616, 1155: a letter to J. Hopper, dated June 6, 1563, quotes another letter which Cassander just received from Baudouin: " ... Nunc iterum aliqua in spe sumus informandae alicuius moderationis; partim quia de Concilio vix speratur quicquam, partim quia utraque pars fatigata sit facta aequior..." and adds: " Quod autem scribit F. Balduinus utramque partem fatigatam iam factam aequiorem, in mentem venit Erasmus Roterodamus, qui pro singulari sua in rebus ecclesiasticis prudentia prope mihi vates fuisse videtur."

[31] See the prefaces to the reader of *Ad leges de iure civili Voconiam, etc.*, and *Commentarius de iurisprudentia Muciana* (**No. 82** and **85**).

[32] *De institutione historiae universae et eius cum iurisprudentia coniunctione*, Paris 1561; cf. D. R. Kelley, Historia integra, *op. cit.* and *Correspondance de Bèze* 3, 149f.

[33] Duquesne 63ff.

[34] UBB ms. G.II.15¹, fol. 15-17: two letters of summer 1569; Steinmann 115, but cf. 113 (?).   The typographical arrangement and material of *De officio* (**No. 93**) are compatible with the assumption that it was printed by Oporinus.

his proposals for concord, he also applied them to a new purpose in a different area.[35] In France the Queen Mother and de L'Hospital were about to repeat the experiment of Worms—and its eventual failure—with their own Colloquy of Poissy.[36] The preparations for the synod were well under way when Baudouin left Basle for Paris. With him he took a supply of the little books fresh from the press.

The Erasmian tradition in Basle publishing to which *De officio* belongs and the impact of that tradition upon France will be examined later. It should be noted here, however, that the printing of *De officio* was a landmark. When Basle first entered the Swiss Confederacy she had been bound over to attempt to mediate if serious divisions threatened to disrupt the efficacy of the union.[37] To some degree at least she continued to honour this pledge when the Confederacy was split into confessional camps. In ignoring, and thus condoning, the publication of *De officio*, in spite of the resulting storm of protest,[38] the authorities now seemed to sanction conciliatory efforts on an international level. Soon this attitude was made more explicit. In 1562, while their chief pastor signed the *Confessio Augustana*,[39] they authorized Castellio to publish his *Conseil à la France désolée*. Sympathy with the common goal, but also with Protestant rejection of the Erasmian *via media* as preached by Cassander and Witzel, are clearly discernible in Castellio's treatise. The failure of the Poissy conference, the outbreak of the second religious war and Baudouin's incumbent apostasy, all must have added to Castellio's determination to offer better advice. Nevertheless, Cassander, Baudouin, and Castellio, old friends, read one another's books with fair and serious interest.[40] As Castellio did with his famous simile of the

---

[35] Cf. Lecler, *Tolérance*, esp. 1.259ff.; M. E. Nolte, *Cassander, op. cit.* 22f., 78, 103, 134, 199, 216f.; Duquesne 93f.

[36] Cf. below pp. 204ff.

[37] Wackernagel 2.1.148f.

[38] *Correspondance de Bèze* 3.174-176, 255ff. and passim.

[39] *Calvini opera* 20.24, 26f. and passim. Sulzer had also advocated the participation of Lutherans in the Colloquy of Poissy.

[40] On February 11, 1563, N. Zurkinden addressed to Castellio a long letter about *De officio* and one of Baudouin's rejoinders to Calvin's attack upon the former: both had obviously been given to him by Castellio. " Perlegi Balduini adversus Calvinum defensionem valde acrem et criminosam. Utinam Calvinus in Balduinum non scripsisset, hic non respondisset ! Depingit Calvinum qualem ex parte dudum novi, plus satis irritabilem, implacabilem et, si vis etiam, rigidum ac saevum. Ipse, contra, se prodit non transire ad pontificios, sed currere. ... Deinde cum tantopere eas partes tuetur quae Romanam ecclesiam sequuntur, non video quomodo Cassandri librum nunc, ut ante, probare possit, qui nostris libertatem aliquam suo instinctu Deum colendi impetrare conatur, praesertim quum hanc libertatem, ut licentiosam, alteri parti intollerabilem esse innuat et tacite quantum potest ad eos deficiat quos scimus nunquam serio de vera et solida pietate esse sollicitos. Haec fiunt permittente Domino, ob antesignatorum ecclesiae errores et nostros. Si Calvinus se contineret intra metas officii sui in spiritu humilitatis Christi neque tam temere insultaret omnibus, si ferre posset moderatas bonorum virorum sententias a suis licet dissentientes, non audiret haec a Balduino. Si Balduinus testimonio conscientiae acquiesceret, deficeret a Calvini erroribus ad Christum, non ad errores pontificios et eos homines qui sic sunt moderaturi religionis controversias ut nihil accedat pietati, multum caerimoniis, nihil pauperibus Christi, omnia ipsis [probably a reference to Baudouin's relations with the exceedingly well provided Cardinal of Lorraine]. ... Ego relinquo Calvino suas speculationes argutas, ipsi authori tenebras offundentes de praedestinatione, Balduino suum apparatum caerimoniarum. Compendiosam sequor (utinam assequar !) viam, qua itur in coelum, paucissimis Christi verbis praescriptam : ' dilige Dominum Deum tuum ex toto corde, et proximum ut te ipsum'. ... " (Buisson, *Castellion* 2.406f.) This letter, written by such a close friend of

gold coins in *De haereticis*, Cassander sought to restore unity by distinguishing non-essentials from the essential articles of the faith. Consensus was necessary only on essentials. Catholic and Protestant, however, disagreed not only in what their views of the essentials were; they also differed over the treatment of dissenters. Castellio rejected all coercion, while Cassander was content to counsel the utmost moderation.

By the end of 1563 Oporinus no longer needed to expose himself to embarrassing attacks for publishing Castellio and Baudouin. One died before the year was out; the other had abjured. Basle had no part in the quick sequence of polemical publications brought about by the first edition of *De officio*.[41] Baudouin had acquired new and influential friends among both French and German Catholics and thus may have found it more convenient to resort to the printers of Paris and Cologne. On the other hand it would seem that the Basle printers made no effort to retain the co-operation of Baudouin, and if so they may well have placed themselves at a disadvantage. His relations not only with the Chancellor de L'Hospital, but also with the Queen Mother and the Cardinal of Lorraine,[42] at a time when all were anxious to discuss conciliation and perhaps even meant it, might have profited the presses. Baudouin's advocacy of church unity, with its marked deference for the secular establishment, was in a sense more Erasmian and Bâlois than the radical toleration preached by Castellio. However, the strings had come loose. There is no evidence of an echo in Basle of Baudouin's subsequent missions which led him to the entourage of William of Orange on the eve of his open defiance to Alba as well as to an honourable reputation with the royal houses of France and of Bourbon.[43]

Castellio and of some influentious Bâlois, may be taken as a good reflection of the attitudes prevailing at Basle. Cf. also Jean L'Archier to Castellio, June 25, 1563 : "... P.S. Je vous prie de m'apporter ou envoyer Balduinus contre Cal." (*ibid.* 2.470). Castellio's interest for Baudouin continued to his last day. Sulzer first learned about Baudouin's 'apostasy' from a letter addressed to Castellio which arrived after his death and was opened : *Calvini opera* 20.290). Cassander recorded his impressions in an undated letter to Albada, written late in 1562 or in 1563 : " Libellum Gallice conscriptum [i.e. *Conseil à la France désolée*], quem ad nos misisti, antea videram et legeram. Curavique per Birckmannium nostrum exemplar ad D. Hopperum transmitti, si forte nostra aula ... ad meliora remedia ... adhibenda excitari possit. Auctor huius scripti..., si nescis, est Sebastianus Castalio, cuius eiusdem argumenti epistolae partem ad quendam eruditum virum scriptae ad te mitto, cuius etiam libellus Latine et Germanice extat de haereticis non puniendis sub titulo Ioannis Belli [sic]. Recte is mihi de falsis remediis admonere videtur, eiusque sententiae ipsa etiam experientia suffragatur. Verum illud unum in eo desidero, quod nullam prorsus coercitionem et coactionem, nisi quae verbo doctrinae et adhortationis fiat, adhibendam errantibus putat. Certum enim est mediocrem coercionem nonnullis profuisse...": G. Cassander, *Opera ... omnia*, Paris 1616, 1152 ; cf. 1153, 1162f. and passim.

[41] Cf. *CBN* ; *BMC* and *Correspondance de Bèze* 5.20.

[42] The Cardinal's memorandum on the question of concord drew from Baudouin's *Constantinus Magnus*. Baudouin may also have assisted him in preparing his address to the Synod of Poissy : Evennett, *Lorraine* 266f., 274 ; *Calvini opera* 19.144.

[43] Duquesne 97ff., 102ff. ; A. Wicquot, *op. cit.* 60ff., 78ff.

Chapter Eight

PIERRE RAMUS

It was in the days of the Colloquy of Poissy that Baudouin entered the circle of the Cardinal of Lorraine and that Protestants came to anticipate his eventual return to the Roman church. Another member of the cardinal's clientèle, by contrast, would later date from that same synod his determination to break with Rome. Pierre Ramus became less and less hesitant to assert his sympathy for Calvinism until in 1568 he was openly known to be a Protestant.[1] The royal lecturer in eloquence and philosophy and the head of the Paris College of Presles was by then a European celebrity, albeit a controversial one. At the approach of the second war of religion he left Paris and stopped for some time at the gathering place of the Huguenot army near the German border before heading for Strasbourg and subsequently Basle.[2] There he arrived in the fall of 1568 and stayed with a few interruptions throughout the year of 1569. He may have passed through the city again in 1570 on his return from Germany. It does not appear that he travelled in a diplomatic capacity or represented any interests but his own. Prior to his arrival his personal contacts with Basle had been casual and infrequent.[3] In view of the minor avalanche of his books issued from a local press during his presence in the town there can be little doubt that the printing industry rather than the university induced him to stay.[4]

If he thus spent most of his days at Basle over his manuscripts and galleys, there was still time for talks and debates. Heightened by an ebullient temperament, his consummate eloquence was respected everywhere. He had proven himself a most popular lecturer, and his willingness to listen to others and accept criticism made

---

[1] Waddington 123ff.; Ong, *Ramus* 28.

[2] Kingdon, *Geneva and the Consolidation* 100; *Matrikel* 2.176; A. Bernus, Pierre Ramus à Bâle, *BSHPF* 39 (1890), 508-530.

[3] In December 1550 Ramus wrote a short letter to Johann Herwagen, the son of the Basle printer who had recently been studying at Paris, thanking him for a gift of books and urging him to undertake an ed. of Plato (Waddington 423). Zwinger's study under Ramus and the latter's contacts with Curione will be mentioned shortly. A first, isolated, reprint of a work by Ramus appeared in Basle in 1554: **No. 645**, the *Institutiones dialecticae*. The text was at this time very often republished both in France and in Germany (Ong, *Inventory* 46ff.). Oporinus' ed. of collected *Lucubrationes* on the speeches of Cicero (1553, **No. 676**) contained commentaries by Ramus as well as by his enemy, A. de Gouvea.

[4] No evidence for Ong's repeated assertion that Ramus was lecturing at Basle (e.g. *Ramus* 28) has come to my knowledge; cf. P. Roth, Petrus Ramus et l'université de Bâle, *Mém. et doc. Soc. d'hist. et archéol. de Genève*, 40 (1961), 271-278.

him an excellent partner in debate. At Basle he probably found the theologians more versed in that art, and more eager to practise it than were his somewhat reserved colleagues of older Basle stock who occupied the legal and medical chairs. Published posthumously at Frankfurt, Ramus' *Commentarii de religione Christiana* may have been written in Basle, and certainly reflect his debates with Sulzer and his brother-in-law, Ulrich Koch, who held the chair of New Testament.[5] Ramus was just the man to expose and attack their leaning towards Lutheranism, if only because the conflict was by then studiously buried within the bosom of the Basle church. Besides, he was also enough of a Zwinglian to form a lasting friendship with Bullinger and other pastors of Zurich. His Protestantism may have been sincere enough, but his doctrinal convictions clearly were less profound than his penchant for controversy. When he moved from Basle to Heidelberg, he attended Calvinist services, but he also quarrelled with Erastus. Subsequently, in Geneva, Beza and the Venerable Company objected to his teaching methods and his philosophy. Finally, during the last years of his life he used his prestige and his friendship with Bullinger to support the congregational, anti-Genevan wing of the French Huguenot movement. Beza secured his personal condemnation at the national synod at Nîmes in May, 1572, only three months before Ramus became one of Calvinism's best known martyrs in the massacre of Saint Bartholomew.[6]

The main problems raised by Ramus' stay at Basle, however, are not connected with his theology but rather with his method of dialectic. Basle, it has been claimed, was thereafter a proven centre of Ramism.[7] It has been suggested of young scholars like Jacob Arminius and Jean de Sponde that they left Geneva for Basle because Ramism was outlawed in the first city but flourished in the second.[8] There are two obvious ways in which the correctness of such claims may be checked. First, the personal contacts of Ramus with the scholars of Basle as well as the possible role of his admirers in the university after his death must be investigated. And, secondly, so must the harvest of Ramist and anti-Ramist books produced at Basle. Because of the elusive nature of Ramism, however, and because of personal exchanges of which we have no record, the following conclusions must remain tentative.

There is no reason to suppose that Ramus was charging at an open door when he arrived in Basle, and took quarters with a little-known widow who had formerly lodged Calvin.[9] The Basle professor of rhetoric, C. S. Curione, had earlier propagated the work of Joachim Périon, a bitter adversary of Ramus.[10] It has often been noted

---

[5] A. Bernus, *op. cit.* 511f. and passim.

[6] Kingdon, *Geneva and the Consolidation* 101ff.; cf. 212: Beza even managed to accuse Ramus and his friends of making overtures to the renegade Baudouin and of condoning in the Zurich pastors the same Erastian tenets which Ramus had formerly attacked at Heidelberg. Beza to Bullinger: " Quid quod illum ipsum Balduinum quater Apostatam et capitalem Ecclesiae hostem conati sunt scriptis honorificentissimis literis in suae factionis societatem pellicere ? Nam ne hoc quidem possunt inficiari, quin mendacii rei peragantur. Omitto haec, inqua[m], et illud ipsum urgeo de quo nunc agimus. Erasti dogm[a] Consistorium et excommunicationem semel evertentis sic P. Ramo displicuit, ut quum Heidelbergae esset, libellum etiam adversus eum scripserit, cuius exemplum brevi habiturum me spero. Eius dogmatis si vos istic putant adstipulatores, quo pudore, quaeso, nos apud vos accusant ? " Cf. Cantimori, *Ital. Haeretiker* 256ff.

[7] Ong, *Ramus* 28, 295ff.

[8] See above p. 83 n. 59.

[9] *Basilea* 53.

[10] See below p. 158.

that in 1555 he wrote to Ramus to recommend a Polish student then leaving for Paris, but what has been overlooked is that Curione gave the same student two more letters of introduction, one for Périon, the other for A. Turnèbe, another well-known enemy of Ramus.[11]   Curione died in late 1569; whether by then he was a convert to Ramism must remain more than doubtful.   Since Ramism at Basle is commonly dated from Ramus' own stay there, its active propagation by Curione is effectively ruled out by his death.   There remains, however, the fact that Curione did not like Sulzer and had earlier opposed him in the matter of sacramental doctrine in much the same way as Ramus did now.[12]   Moreover, Curione recommended Ramus with some warmth to Gwalter and Bullinger in Zurich.   This was indeed an important service, and Ramus showed his gratitude by denouncing, in a letter to Gwalter and Lavater, not only Sulzer's Lutheranism, but also the unfair accusation of Servetism levelled against the Basle refugee group.[13]   The issues of method and dialectic, however, do not arise here.

Theodor Zwinger had in his youth attended the lectures of Ramus.   Later he looked back on his study years at Paris with rather mixed feelings.   However, by 1566 he felt that that his subsequent studies in Italy and his own researches over many years had given him an independent mastery of the field of Aristotelian philosophy.   Towards the end of a lengthy preface to his diagrams expounding the *Nicomachean Ethic* he admitted with grumbling honesty his considerable debt to Ramus.[14]   It is a precious testimony to the freshness and stimulating method of his preceptor in Paris, given in full consciousness of the differences between their positions.   The balance and fairness of Zwinger's statement may well reflect his knowledge of the Paris scene where Ramus now had apparently been reconciled to Turnèbe and acquired the friendship of Denis Lambin, another philologian closely allied to

---

[11] UBB ms. G.I. 66, fol. 19-20 ; cf. Ong, *Ramus* 379.

[12] M. Kutter, *Celio Secondo Curione*, Basle 1955, 171ff., 224ff.

[13] Bernus, *op. cit.* 524ff ; cf. *Basilea* 37f. Although Castellio's *New Testament* apparently was the only Bible in Ramus' huge library (Ong, *Ramus* 33) the *Basilea* referred to him in rather ambiguous terms.

[14] T. Zwinger, *Aristotelis ... de moribus ad Nicomachum libri decem tabulis perpetuis ... illustrati*, Basle, J. Oporinus & E. Episcopius, [1566].   Preface : " ... Illud ego non obscure fateor ex praelectionibus simul atque scriptis Talaei, maxime vero Petri Rami, quem praeceptoris loco et colui olim et nunc vero veneror, id boni me consecutum, ut in omnibus omnium scriptis analysin, in privatis commentationibus genesin logicam meditarer, illud mali, ut Aristotelis philosophiam omnem, ceu lernam omnium sophismatum, plus quam vatiniano odio prosequerer et execrarer.   Posteaquam vero et aetas iudicium confirmavit et peregrinationes Italicae studia nostra medica exacuerunt, necessitate quadam Peripatetica illa — non Stoica — ad Peripateticas scholas deductus, tum demum quid distarent aera lupinis deprehendi.   Odium igitur excepit admiratio ; admirationem subsecuta est investigatio.   Rameum tamen illud alta manebat mente repostum, ex Aristotele Aristotelem declarari, praecepta ad usum revocari debere.   Rami itaque monitus, Aristotelis vestigia secutus, reconditos sapientiae methodique Aristotelicae thesauros pro ingenii mei tenuitate pervestigare coepi et eruere in logicis primum, mox in rhetoricis, tandem in physicis, ad extremum in ethicis, eorumque ita sum delectatus, ut sine hac luce neminem quicquam in philosophia laude dignum praestare posse constanter affirmare audeam.   Ramo interim multa debere me fateor qui, quantumvis ironicôs, digitum ad fontem intenderit et quodammodo per regulam falsi, ut loquuntur arithmetici, ad veritatis investigationem nos deduxerit, longe plura vero δαιμονίῳ Aristoteli ... ."   Cf. R. Thommen, *Geschichte der Universität Basel, 1532-1632*, Basle 1889, 242 ; J. Karcher, *Theodor Zwinger und seine Zeitgenossen*, Basle 1956, 11ff.   The methodical use of diagrams had also been impressed upon Zwinger by his teacher in Padua, G. Falloppio : *ibid.* 16f.

Turnèbe.[15]   In the same preface Zwinger mentioned Lambin.   It is a short reference, but its warm tone contrasts noticeably with the elaborate judgment of Ramus. Zwinger was at this moment in personal contact with Lambin whose studies of Aristotle, he felt, were congenial to his own, whereas Ramus' teaching had only been stimulating and provocative.

Nevertheless, Ramus could now be sure of a friendly reception by his former student when he arrived at Basle in 1568.   But in spite of their conversations Zwinger's interests remained encyclopedic.   Even in his immense work of Aristotelian exegesis, philological and factual explanation outweighed methodical analysis. Ramus must have known what he did when in the *Basilea* he only mentioned Zwinger's encyclopedic *Theatrum vitae humanae* and noted his principal devotion to medicine.[16]   As a result of Ramus' visit to Basle one of those affable but sometimes superficial correspondences for which Zwinger had a genius developed.   It is no accident that their letters remain in part unpublished.[17]   While they do attest to a friendly personal exchange and a certain degree of intimacy, any statements pertaining to the Ramist method are exceedingly rare.[18]   A younger colleague of Zwinger, Christian Wurstisen, was at the time of Ramus' visit the Basle professor of mathematics and apparently impressed by the Frenchman's attempts to methodize arithmetic.   It is conceivable that Wurstisen tried to implement Ramus' method in his teaching, but he was hardly more of a mathematician than was Ramus himself and later gained a reputation as a historiographer.

There is no conclusive evidence that any of the above mentioned or, indeed, any of their colleagues in the university down to the end of the century was a Ramist[19] even in the vague sense in which the term was then becoming fashionable in German universities.   By contrast, the man who was to be the chief exponent of Ramism at Basle had at best a very limited and temporary connection with the university. Both in 1568-69 and again later on, J. T. Freigius lived in Basle as an exile, like so many others working for the printers while writing his own books.   Ramus arrived with a letter of introduction to him, and here made an undoubted conquest.   But while Freigius went on to become a recognized speaker for the German Ramists, his career was jeopardized by a series of personal rebuffs.[20]

The major biographical document of Ramus' stay in Basle is his beautiful and impressive oration entitled *Basilea*.   It may have been written after he left Basle[21]

---

[15] Lefranc, *Collège de France* 216 ; Waddington 159f.

[16] *Basilea* 40.

[17] In addition to the letters published by Waddington, 421ff., cf. UBB ms., especially Fr. Gr. II.26, No. 9ff.

[18] Cf. Waddington 426, 437 ; cf. also 193 ; Ong, *Inventory* 379.

[19] Ong, *Inventory* 510ff., lists Polanus as a semi-Ramist (" S "), but Zwinger and Wurstisen as definite Ramists (" R "). Other listings are even more puzzling, e.g. " R " against Eusebius Episcopius. We know very little about this Basle printer (cf. *Matrikel* 2.83). He did publish many books by Ramus ; but if this fact makes him a Ramist, many -isms, and often conflicting ones, could be attributed to most Basle printers. By the same criterion Oporinus would certainly have to be listed as an anti-Ramist rather than an " individual whose works show some Ramist affinities." Why is Peter Ryff (*Matrikel* 2.189) listed as a Ramist ?

[20] See *ADB*.

[21] Ong (*Inventory* 380) states that " Ramus delivered at Basle this eulogy..." There is not the slightest evidence for an oral performance and the structure of the work points to the contrary.   The last sentence in praise of Curione suggests that the latter, like Grynaeus, was dead when Ramus wrote : " Quapropter, quamdiu homines erunt,

and seems to have been published at Lausanne.[22] It was later reprinted in two collections of his works.[23] In substance the *Basilea* presents a string of eulogies, varying in their degree of profusion or compression, offered to many more or less famous men then present at Basle or associated with her in the past. No guiding principle in the selection or omission of names can be discerned in the work,[24] nor does it significantly commit its author to any peculiar views other than the religious heritage of Oecolampadius and the scientific legacy of Paracelsus. Praise of the Basle reformer,[25] of course, equals another attack upon the Lutheran deviations of Sulzer, the present leader of the Basle church. The significance of Paracelsism was probably pointed out to him by Adam von Bodenstein, its current propagandist in Basle publishing. What has been called the " Paracelsian revival " through the Basle presses coincides with the flood of Ramist publications. To praise Paracelsus as a luminary of their university would now no longer antagonize the Bâlois as it no doubt would have done three decades earlier. Moreover, Ramus may well have respected Paracelsus as a kindred spirit. He too had been fiercely defiant of classical authority and obsessed with infinite curiosity. He too had tried to reform the programme of academic instruction.[26]

Turning to dialectic, Ramus found nothing much to say about significant representatives of that art in the annals of Basle university. He did, however, strongly urge its application to the study of the classics rather than the teaching of abstract precepts, although he realized that the Aristotelian tradition of the university would at best allow for a compromise.[27] This message aligned one fundamental aspect of Ramism with the humanistic tradition of Basle,[28] but it also forecast quite soberly the future direction of Ramist publishing in Basle, where the *Dialectic*, "this most important of all Ramus' works" was never to enjoy a prominent place.[29] Ramus could be certain that this cautious statement would be well received

qui latine loquentur aut intelligent, tamdiu humanitatis grata erga Grynaeum et Caelium memoria exstabit.'' Curione died on November 24, 1569. Cf. *Basilea* 20 (H. Fleig's introduction).

[22] The first edition is quite untypical of Basle products ; cf. Ong, *Inventory* 381f.

[23] **No. 650f.**

[24] *Basilea* 15 ff. (H. Fleig's introduction).

[25] *Basilea* 49ff., e.g. : '' Oecolampadii constantia et sua sibi similis aequalitas, immutabilis perpetuo permansit. Maxima vero omnium et gravissima concertatio de coena Domini fuit : ut ad veritatem perduceret, quam confessio Basiliensis, Oecolampadio mortuo (ne quis hypocrita perverteret) senatus mandato germanice edita, sanxit atque approbavit.''

[26] Bietenholz, *Ital. Humanismus* 137, 159.

[27] *Basilea* 41f., especially : '' Sed tu [Hospiniane], tuique professionis huius collegae caeteri partibus infinitis ampliorem laudem consequemini, si dialecticum ut artificium, sic artificii usum in Virgilio et Homero, in Cicerone et Demosthene iuventuti proponatis et quotidianae imitationis exemplo et opere informetis. Partiamini tempora professionis logicae : minimam temporis partem logicae praeceptis, maximam usui, meo consilio, tribuetis. Sin vobis Aristotelis iudicium atque exemplum luculentius est, professionis partem philosophiae et praeceptis, partem eloquentiae et exemplis assignabitis ; ut tamen memineritis, usum artis, non artem usus finem esse. Nec interea leges academiae vereamini. Academia enim pro ista culpa (qua pro logica mortua in libris vivam in ipso opere logico proque plumbea auream feceritis) praemium coronamque decernet vobisque authoribus Rodolphos Agricolas Basileam adductos liberali gratoque animo accipiet.''

[28] Cf. Ong, *Ramus* 41ff., 190ff., 298ff.

[29] Ong, *Inventory* 178 ; Ong's table (*Ramus* 296) demonstrates well the modest role of the four Basle editions of Ramus' *Dialectic* in the general dissemination of this work which down to 1650 ran through 224 editions, including adaptations.

in Basle, and he must have known it was not necessarily so in the case of his proper message. What the *Basilea* does make clear is that Ramus was pleased with his stay in Basle and that he considered the peaceful city and its typographical resources might prove even more useful to him at some future date.[30]

If the Basle printers had taken little notice of Ramus' own work before he came to live in the town, they had not failed to take advantage of the controversies which he stirred up. The writings of the great conservative of Aristotelianism in Paris, Joachim Périon, had been printed here during the 1540s and 1550s with a measure of persistence equal to the later flood of Ramist publications. In particular, his bitter *Orations in defense of Aristotle against P. Ramus* appeared in two editions (1549 and 1553).[31] Basle produced an outstanding series of editions of Aristotle.[32] Zwinger, for one, expounded Aristotle's works to his students as zealously as he edited and annotated them for the printers. Any accusation of being Aristotle's detractor, therefore, was bound to weigh heavily at Basle, and Périon was joined in such accusation by Sebastian Fox Morcillo, another author favoured by Basle printers.[33] It is true that neither was being published there by the mid-sixties, and that Zwinger, in his preface to the diagrams of Aristotle's *Ethic*, defended Ramus, saying that he wanted only to bring out the true meaning of Aristotle's philosophy. Was it then a turning point? The assumption is hardly warranted, for at the same time Zwinger published Lambin's Latin translation of the *Ethic* which the author had newly revised for Zwinger's edition.[34] It is true that in his preface and commentary Lambin was persistently and justifiably critical of Périon's preceding translation of the same text, but their disagreements mostly concerned the correct rendering of numerous passages. In addition to Lambin's translation Zwinger's volume also included his own presentation of the Greek text together with his copious commentary in the traditional style of humanistic scholarship. Zwinger's study in diagrams of the *Ethic*, therefore, was a complementary exercise, undertaken to prove his own versatility as well as to pay yet further tribute to Aristotle rather than Ramus.

Moreover, the printer Oporinus who had formerly published most of the Basle editions of Périon and Fox Morcillo produced in 1564 a book by Jacob Schegk, Ramus' most formidable critic in Germany.[35] In view of the severe and explicit attacks contained in this work, it is hardly a coincidence that Ramus got involved in an epistolary controversy with Schegk as soon as he had arrived at Basle, and that

---

[30] It is impossible to overlook the solicitude of his praise for Basilius Amerbach and the Spanish millionaire Marco Perez, the two most likely sources of patronage in Basle; cf. *Basilea* 33, 46, 53ff. Both are mentioned with similar distinction in Ramus' letters to Zwinger. In 1569 Ramus had offered his services to the school of Strasbourg, but he was turned down; cf. Waddington 195f.

[31] **No. 804f.** Cf. below p. 179 and Ong, *Inventory* 495f. and *Ramus* 214f.

[32] Cf. Bietenholz, *Ital. Humanismus* 129f.

[33] Cf. S. Fox Morcillo, *De usu et exercitatione dialecticae*, Basle, J. Oporinus, 1556, 10f. and passim.

[34] **No. 626f.**; cf. below p. 203.

[35] J. Schegk, *De demonstratione libri XV*, Basle, J. Oporinus and brothers Episcopius, 1564 (reproducing in extenso the privilege granted to Oporinus by the French King specifically for this ed.); the attacks on Ramus: 9f., 142. There are two earlier Basle eds. of Aristotelian commentaries by Schegk, both in large folio like *De demonstratione*, and for the most part original: *In octo Physicorum ... commentarii*, J. Herwagen, 1546, and *In reliquos Naturalium ... commentarii*, ibid. 1550.

he felt obliged to publish his defences there, together with at least some of Schegk's very serious charges.[36]

As will be seen shortly, Schegk himself did not lack critics and, once again, Basle's printers were quick to lend them their facilities. First, however, a look at Basle's role in the dissemination of Ramus' own writings is now in order. During his presence in the town the dialectical works, core of the Ramist method, and his most outspoken polemics against Aristotle remained significantly in the background. Emphasis was laid instead on the outer fringes of his educational reform where the mathematical works and his commentaries on Cicero may be placed. Noticeable also is the interest in his ideas on rhetoric and in his qualified acceptance of Ciceronian imitation. It was only years after his death that, at the prompting of Freigius, Ramus' most controversial works gained a modest foothold in the Basle presses. At this time, however, they must be seen against the background of the general controversy which was then splitting German universities into Ramist and anti-Ramist camps. These later publications, therefore, cannot primarily be evaluated as part of the cultural exchange between Basle and France.

In 1569 no fewer than three publications demonstrated how Ramus applied his method to mathematics.[37] For two years prior to his departure from Paris he had been involved in a bitter feud with Pierre Charpentier, the royal lecturer in mathematics since 1566 and a familiar figure in the Paris opposition to Ramus. In the university, as in Ramus' publications, the issue was essentially how mathematics should be taught. Ramus advocated, for instance, reliance on Euclid rather than John of Sacrobosco.[38] His ideas seem to have interested the Bâlois. Wurstisen translated his *Arithmetica* into German, while a copy of the Latin edition preserves Ramus' handwritten dedication to Basilius Amerbach.[39] But like Ramus and Charpentier, the Bâlois, including Wurstisen, were hardly expert mathematicians. The Greek *editio princeps* of Euclid had earlier been undertaken here by a philologian while, in 1569, Oswald Schreckenfuchs published his important commentaries on Sacrobosco.[40] In 1572 Ramus' publisher Episcopius launched an edition of

---

[36] Ong, *Inventory* 374ff. and *Ramus* 258f. and passim; **No. 649**. Among those whom Ramus failed to remember in the *Basilea* was Karel Utenhove, the younger, whose name figured in the university roll immediately above his own (*Matrikel* 2.176). And yet Utenhove published in the same year at Basle a collection of epigrams, including three in praise of Ramus (**No. 200**, [part 3], 91f.). Was Ramus simply unaware of this publication or was he unhappy about the fact that only his Ciceronian eloquence aroused Utenhove's admiration? Utenhove was a close friend of Turnèbe and also of Oporinus. His sharp criticism of Paracelsus and the alchemists may also have displeased Ramus. And what about the epigrams in praise of Beza and Sulzer which the intrepid poet managed to unite on opposite pages (**No. 200**, [part 3], 102f.)?

[37] **No. 635, 637, 655.** Ong *(Inventory* 169, No. 214) also lists an ed. of *Arithemetica*, Basle 1567, but he has not found a copy of it.

[38] Ong, *Inventory* 500ff. and *Ramus* 33; cf. 220ff.

[39] UBB: K.c. IV.4 (Amerbach's copy). The reasons for Wurstisen's appreciation of Ramus can be gathered from his preface: " ... Dann ob schon ein jeder one Zweifel nach seinem Vermögen gethon und derhalben von seinem Lob der Gebür nach nichts soll entzogen werden, so darff ich doch frey herauss sagen, das die satten und rechten Gründ, ja das grundtlich Fürgeben zuo diser herrlichen Kunst nottwendig bey einem jedem Guldenschreiber, dem sonst seine Tag im philosophischen Kampffplatz die schuoch (wie man zuo reden pflegt) wenig seind bestaubet worden, und seinen Bücheren sich jergendt nicht finden lasse. Daher kompt es, das bey vilen weyt mehr blosser Exemplen dann kunstlicher Lehren, in gewüsse und steiffe Reglen verfasset, gesehen werden. ..."

[40] **No. 916;** cf. Bietenholz, *Ital. Humanismus* 66, 153ff.

Alhazen's *Optic*, for which Ramus had supplied both the encouragement and the manuscripts,[41] but before the year was out Charpentier himself arrived at Basle in the wake of the massacre which had been fatal to his adversary, Ramus.[42]

One major original edition of a work by Ramus was issued at Basle during his visit. It was the *Scholae in liberales artes*, collected lecture texts on grammar, rhetoric, dialectic, physics, and metaphysics.[43] Once again the preface, addressed in part to Johannes Sturm, shows that Ramus' overriding concern was the practice of advanced teaching. His basic search for method asserted itself with a breadth well beyond the technicalities of pure dialectic. The same didactic purpose was served by a reprint of his *Grammar*, a school text which merely superficially rearranged the usual material although the preface made a pretence of revolution. Further compressed and dressed in the form of a catechistic dialogue the same material was also offered in the *Rudimenta grammatica Latinae*.[44] Finally, the series of the 1569 publications was completed by the fullest edition of Ramus' *Dialectic* to appear in his lifetime [45] and by the apologetic correspondence with Schegk, already mentioned.

A second phase of Basle publications of works by Ramus falls in the years 1573 to 1576 and includes chiefly a number of re-editions undertaken by Freigius. While the *Dialectic* continued to run through three more unchanged editions, Freigius went back to the first major sources of controversy in his master's life. The famous *Institutiones dialecticae* and *Aristotelicae animadversiones*, both published originally in 1543, were launched afresh to open a new and more militant chapter in Ramist publishing. In his preface addressed to Eusebius Episcopius, Freigius entreated the printer to become the chosen instrument of a Ramist palingenesis.[46] A year earlier Freigius edited a couple of minor writings in which Ramus chose the text of Caesar as the object of his urge to methodize, thus subjecting it to a philologico-historical inquiry. While the *Liber de moribus veterum Gallorum* was based on ethical terms derived from Plato, *De Caesaris militia* approached its subject rather from the technical and historical angle.[47] Both were well suited to the outlook of Basle, as was Freigius' re-edition in 1573 of the *Ciceronianus* composed by Ramus, a treatise on education and the place reserved therein to imitation, all featured in a biographical study. Not only Ramus' title, but also his rejection of unrestrained Ciceronianism, were reminiscent of the famous dialogue of Erasmus. Freigius supplemented Ramus' text with a dichotomized chart of Cicero's life.[48] Only in a

---

[41] *Opticae thesaurus Alhazeni Arabis*, ed. by. F. Risner who acknowledges Ramus' help in a preface addressed to Catherine de' Medici. Reisner, Ramus' *famulus*, was repeatedly sent to Basle (*Matrikel* 2.181). It was most probably with reference to the delays incurred in producing this ed. that Ramus complained : " Sunt enim typographi vestri graviter ignavi " (Waddington 436 ; cf. 425f. ; Ong, *Inventory* 401ff.).

[42] Cf. above p. 115.

[43] Ong, *Inventory* 431ff.

[44] *Ibid.* 310ff., 323ff.

[45] *Ibid.* 181, 190f.

[46] " ... ut quod olim Bogardus, hodie Wechelus Ramo fuerunt et sunt, idem tu illi esse velis et eum hac tua typographica palingenesia in vitam revoces. Vale et me ama." Cf. Ong, *Ramus* 23f., 172ff.

[47] Cf. Ong, *Repertory* 303ff., 307f. and *Ramus* 30.

[48] Ong, *Ramus* 30f., 274 and *Repertory* 296ff. Ong lists an edition of the *Ciceronianus*, Basle 1557, but has not seen a copy of it. His No. 489 and 490 presumably describe copies of the same impression (Basle 1573), bound in a slightly different order.

160

second Basle edition of 1577 was the *Ciceronianus* accompanied by the *Brutinae quaestiones*, an essay dating from Ramus' early years and pointedly critical of Cicero.[49] Nothing, perhaps, is more typical of Freigius' concessions to the general preferences of Basle publishers than that his largest collection of Ramus texts was published under the *pars pro toto* title of *Praelectiones in Ciceronis octo consulares*. The volume contained a whole series of partly descriptive, partly polemical, and partly methodo-analytical commentaries on works by Cicero. It also included some other texts, especially rhetorical ones, and among them the *Basilea*, as well as Freigius' biography of Ramus which is still valuable in spite of its eulogizing tendency.[50] If the purely logico-theoretical approach was excluded from this collection, that is not to say that it was uncontroversial. Rather there were certain aspects of the Ramist controversy that fitted the general framework of Basle culture better than others.

Freigius' collection contained, for instance, Ramus' commentary on Cicero's treatise *De fato*. It suggested that the issues of free will and predestination should be tackled with dialectical tools rather than theological ones, and that this had been done successfully by scholastics teaching in the medieval faculties of arts.[51] Only when the implications of specific issues such as this can be fully investigated will the true dimension of Ramism in Basle ever be known. Ciceronian themes also dominated Freigius' first edition of Talon's collected works which, nine years later, was superseded by an even more complete one.[52] Omer Talon had until his death in 1562 been Ramus' lieutenant in Paris. In some of their works they had co-operated so closely that it is hard to sort out individual contributions. Specifically this is the case with the *Rhetoric* of which the Bâlois published three editions under Talon's name.[53] To Freigius' own mind abstract dialectic probably was more fascinating than the general tendency of his presentation of the Ramist legacy in Basle editions would lead one to think. His personal concern was exhibited in his *P. Rami professio regia* of 1576 which presented the contents of Ramus' *Scholae in liberales artes* in a series of dichotomized diagrams.[54]

To sum up, one may say that the reception of Ramist literature was subjected to the peculiar philologico-rhetorical emphasis of Basle. One should add, however, that even so it was far from committing the Basle publishers unilaterally to the Ramist

---

[49] **No. 639.** Ong (*Inventory* 440f.) lists two more Basle eds., 1574 and 1576, of which he has not found any copies.

[50] **No. 650** and **651.** Freigius' *vita* of Ramus in the 1580 ed., pp. 3-46. Interesting are, for instance, the remarks on Ramus' great *temperantia* illustrated both with his total abstinence from the use of wine and with his restraint in answering his critics. According to Freigius, Ramus refrained from polemical exchanges with Gouvea, Garland, Périon, and even Melanchthon; only Schegk's attack compelled him to answer. Freigius' essay provided much material for Ramus' next biographer, T. de Banos, who also visited Basle; cf. above p. 120, n. 93.

[51] Ong, *Inventory* 151f., 289ff. This treatise especially irritated A. Turnèbe.

[52] **No. 961-963**; cf. Ong, *Inventory* 484ff.

[53] **No. 964-966**; cf. Ong, *Inventory* 82ff. On Talon see Ong, *Ramus* 270ff.; Michaud. Orations in praise of the royal station, allegedly delivered by five pupils of Talon were reprinted at Basle in 1578 in conjunction with a treatise by Freigius and other material: **No. 624f.**; cf. Ong, *Inventory* 481f.

[54] **No. 659**; cf. Ong, *Inventory* 403f. For Freigius' dichotomization of a series of other topics, including the plague see J. T. Freigius, *Paedagogus*, Basle, Seb. Henricpetri, 1582 (Ong, *Inventory* 407). Notice also Freigius' application of Ramist method to jurisprudence in *Partitiones iuris utriusque*, Basle, Seb. Henricpetri, 1581 (**No. 573**), and *De logica iureconsultorum*, ibid. 1582 (Ong, *Inventory* 205).

camp. Jacob Schegk, whose attacks Ramus felt impelled to answer during his visit to Basle, was a Basle author, published in part by the same Oporinus who had earlier printed many books by Périon and Fox Morcillo. The subsequent masters of the *officina Oporiniana* continued this anti-Ramist tradition with three editions of Georg Liebler's *Epitome* of Aristotle's natural philosophy, in part devoted to " the detection of the errors of Peter Ramus," in 1573, 1575 and 1586.[55] Liebler, a Tübingen professor, repeated in a pedestrian manner the charges made by his friend and colleague Schegk, whose biography he was later to write.[56] Nothing new was added to this controversy when the Dane Anders Krag arrived in Basle to publish three Ramist studies of his own, among them an explicit reply to Liebler.[57] Even before Liebler and Krag entered the contest, an Italian teaching at Heidelberg, Simone Simoni, had published in Basle a book of *Antischegkiana*. On this occasion Simoni took issue with Schegk over Aristotelianism and the method of dialectic, but in the background of their lengthy feud Calvinist objections to the Lutheran Ubiquitarians of Württemberg loomed largely. As it happened, two noted critics of Ramus, Beza and Erastus, sided in this quarrel with Simoni against a third anti-Ramist, Schegk.[58] This fact may indicate how easily the individual Pierre Ramus was lost sight of in the general maze of philosophical and theological polemic.

The later stages of Ramist publishing in Basle reflect primarily the controversies of philosophical schools at German universities. Typical among them was a camp claiming common dependence upon Melanchthon and Ramus. In Basle this tendency was represented by three or more editions of Johann Bilsten's *Syntagma Philippo-Rameum artium liberalium*, published between 1588 and 1607. Bilsten studied at intervals in Basle and was promoted to the theological doctorate by A. Polanus of Polansdorf.[59] Polanus, a Silesian, taught theology at Basle from 1596 to his death in 1610. His attitude serves as a further demonstration of the integrating and conciliatory nature of Basle Ramism. From his first student year at Tübingen, 1583-84, Polanus was an outspoken Calvinist, so much so that Jacob Schegk himself gave him the friendly advice that he had better continue his studies at Basle, where by that time Sulzer was blending the prevailing Evangelical tradition with his personal leaning to Lutheranism. Polanus was to remain a Calvinist, but otherwise did not escape the influence of the Basle atmosphere. He was later to defend the record of Castellio, and he also became acquainted with Ramist logic, as he recalled, through Zwinger and Jacob Arminius. Ramist ideas must have reached him well integrated in a comprehensive and syncretistic system which he adapted to his own logical and methodical approach to exegesis and dogmatics. Only in 1605, after several previous editions of his *Logicae libri duo* did he rename

---

[55] **No. 664-666.** Two earlier Basle eds. of this work (Oporinus, 1561 and 1566) do not refer to Ramus.

[56] *De vita et morte J. Schegkii*, Tübingen 1587. Liebler's son, Joseph, received in Basle his degree of MD in 1593 (*Matrikel* 2.408).

[57] **No. 661-663.** For Krag cf. **No. 621** and *ADB*.

[58] S. Simoni, *Antischegkianorum liber unus*, Basle 1570 and again, " correctus et auctus ", Basle 1571; cf. Bietenholz, *Ital. Humanismus* 134f.; R. Wesel-Roth, *Thomas Erastus*, Lahr 1954, 39.

[59] J. Bilstenius, *Syntagma Philippo-Rameaum artium liberalium*, Basle, C. Waldkirch, 1588, 1596, and 1607; cf. Ong, *Inventory* 406ff. *Ibid.* also a reference to an additional Basle ed., 1589, but Ong has not found a copy of it. For Bilsten see *Matrikel* 2.360 and Staehelin, *Polanus* 71.

a revised version of the work *Synatagma logicum Aristotelico-Ramaeum ad usum imprimis theologicum accommodatum.*[60]

It may then be concluded that the presence of Ramism in Basle is undeniable, but that neither the book output nor university teaching support the assumption that Basle became a Ramist centre *par excellence*. To understand what Ramism in Basle failed to be, one might compare it with the legacy of Castellio. The latter felt free to develop in Basle his original and controversial views in almost every direction. He found a noticeable measure of general approval, or at least official protection. His ideas formed a seminal and easily discernible current in the general culture of Basle. Ramus, by contrast, cannot be credited with a similar active and enlivening function. His personal influence was minimal. From the beginning his thought was either flatly rejected or subjected to selective adaptation and in the process came to lose its original identity.

---

[60] Published by C. Waldkirch; cf. Ong, *Inventory* 237 and Staehelin, *Polanus*, especially 13ff., 65, 93. See also above p. 129.

PART THREE

THE FOCAL CONTACTS
IN FRANCE

Chapter One

THE BÂLOIS IN PARIS

The principal ways by which the Basle book reached the French public have been indicated; but beyond this, its subsequent dissemination and the resulting association of specific interests and attitudes with the name of Basle present a process which largely eludes investigation. We can, however, indicate the contacts between Basle and some prominent circles in France, and we may infer to what degree these circles were focal for the wider diffusion of the Basle image.

From the early decades of the sixteenth century, France and the Swiss Confederacy were allied powers. After the treaties of 1516 and 1521 distinguished citizens and civil servants of Basle received their share of the subsidies which the French king distributed annually among his loyal allies of Switzerland, and along with her sister cantons Basle nominated regularly two students to receive royal scholarships for support in a French university. Most royal scholars went to Paris, but they were neither the first nor the only Basle students to do so. Around the venerable Sorbonne and the *Ecu de Bâle* in the rue Saint-Jacques there normally lived a whole group of expatriates, mostly young people, having very close ties with Basle.

The man who best represents the early connections between the Sorbonne and Basle's printing industry is Johannes Heynlin, called *de Lapide* after his birthplace, Stein near Pforzheim.[1] In 1455 Heynlin received his M.A. degree in Paris and proceeded to read theology while at the same time taking charge of some arts courses in the College of Burgundy. By 1462 he was a bachelor of theology and thus a member of the Sorbonne. In 1464 he agreed to join the young University of Basle, where he held a chair of philosophy. However, in 1467, prior to the earliest evidence for printing activities in Basle, he returned to Paris.[2] He was rector of the university for 1469, and in 1472 he obtained his doctorate in theology. Two years later he was again in Basle but now he did not figure among the university professors. In 1478-79 he was in Tübingen, but after some more travels he returned to Basle. He joined the chapter and was the cathedral preacher from December 1484 to August 1487, but for the last decade of his life, the restless man settled down as a monk in the Basle Carthusian monastery. He died in 1496 and the Basle library still owns many of the rare books and manuscripts which he left to his monastery.

---

[1] Cf. M. Hossfeld, Johannes Heynlin aus Stein, *BZGA* 6 (1907), 309-356; 7 (1908), 235-431; Wackernagel 2.2.598ff.; Hartmann 1.22n.

[2] Heynlin may have been accompanied to Paris by Johann Ulrich Surgant who in 1470 took his *licentia* in Paris. Surgant was later to enjoy some degree of prominence among the clergy of Basle and the university whose rector he was four times; cf. Hartmann 1.166n.

Heynlin was a curious character. Restless and enterprising, he never faltered in his strict adherence to the *via antiqua* of scholastic Realism. In Paris he was instrumental in the foundation and operation of the first printing press; into the strictly Nominalistic curriculum of Basle he introduced Realism; and in Tübingen he helped to found the university. Yet his personal predilection seems to have narrowed gradually from a broad interest in Christian education touched by humanistic ideals [3] to a pious devotion steeped in theology. In 1470 the establishment of a private press on the premises of the Sorbonne resulted from the co-operation of Heynlin with Guillaume Fichet,[4] another former rector of the university, now its librarian and one of its luminaries. The contributions of the two men, however, were hardly equal. From the adoption of a roundish ' Antiqua ' type inspired by the ones used in Rome by Sweynheim and Pannartz, to the selection of copy among ancient classics and the works of modern Italian humanists, the orientation of the Sorbonne press mirrored the tastes of Fichet, who had recently been to Italy and was to die in Rome. He too professed Thomistic Realism, but his chief objective was the introduction of the new *bonae litterae*. While Fichet directed the press towards these ends, and also raised the funds necessary for its operation, Heynlin's responsibilities were apparently more practical. He took charge of editing and proof reading after he had temporarily left Paris, conceivably to recruit printers, among them Michael Friburger, who had been his contemporary in the University of Basle, and Martin Krantz, who was perhaps his compatriot.[5]

There is good reason to assume that Johann Amerbach,[6] a Franconian, also lived in Paris when the Sorbonne press was in the planning stage. After studying under Heynlin he seems to have received his M. A. in Paris not later than 1464. Subsequently he may have accompanied his teacher to the University of Basle (1464-67) and afterwards back to Paris. However, his name cannot be directly associated with the Sorbonne press, and Amerbach may owe to Italy his acquaintance with typography. From 1478 Amerbach was printing in Basle, and Heynlin acted as an influential adviser to his younger printer friend, especially during the last decade of his life, which was spent in the Carthusian monastery. Amerbach occasionally reprinted treatises on orthography which had formerly appeared in the Sorbonne press.[7] However, among his new editions those which bear the marks of Heynlin's co-operation are of a more ambitious and predominantly theological character. From Heynlin's prefaces we know that he persistently urged Amerbach to publish

---

[3] Cf. Renaudet, *Préréforme* 93n. on Heynlin's contacts with J. Reuchlin. In Paris Reuchlin studied grammar with Heynlin and in 1474 he may have followed his master to Basle.

[4] Renaudet, *Préréforme* 83ff. and passim.

[5] J. Monfrin, Les lectures de G. Fichet et de J. Heynlin, *BHR* 17 (1955), 7-23, 145-153, esp. 147; A. Claudin, *The First Paris Press*, London 1898; Harrisse 3f.; Febvre-Martin 114, 267f.; S. H. Steinberg, *Fivehundred Years of Printing*, London 1955, 33f.; Haebler 171ff.; F. Stock, *Die ersten deutschen Buchdrucker in Paris*, Freiburg i.Br. 1940, 36ff. Robert Gaguin too took a warm interest in the press. His taste for *bonae litterae* ancillary to Thomism resembled that of Fichet. Gaguin may have induced Josse Bade to come to Paris and later in his life he showed much kindness to the young monk Erasmus: Febvre-Martin 224; Allen 1.146n. Barthélemy Buyer saw the Sorbonne press at work before installing in his house at Lyons a printer, Leroy, who had arrived from Basle: Febvre-Martin 178; cf. above p. 25f.

[6] Hartmann 1. xixff.

[7] Cf. **No. 518ff.**

the salutary writings of Augustine, Ambrose, Jerome, and Gregory, that he warmly welcomed the edition of Cassiodorus' *Commentary on the Psalms*, and that he recommend the reprint of Trithemius' *De scriptoribus ecclesiasticis* when Amerbach asked for his opinion.[8] The chronicler of the Carthusian monastery also bears witness to Heynlin's helping hand in Amerbach's editions of the Bible.[9] Heynlin's preface to Cassiodorus explicitly defended this Christian author for his humble and uncultivated style, which lacked the frills of secular eloquence and rhetorical splendour.[10] Written in his Carthusian seclusion, the words may indicate a certain disenchantment with the texts of Valla, Barzizza and others formerly published by the Sorbonne press. But by and large the Sorbonne press as well as that of Amerbach responded to the same demands for humanistic education as ancillary to the study of divinity.

In his faith in the *via antiqua* Johann Amerbach proved as adamant as Heynlin himself. When he sent his sons to study in Paris, he was disturbed to learn that Realism had become unfashionable among the *magistri*.[11] Nevertheless, in the light of the general preference for scholastic works Amerbach's editions of some church fathers were as remarkable as his collection of Petrarch's writings.[12] Many of these enterprises no doubt reflected Amerbach's own taste for the weighty folio volumes as well as the requirements of his foremost customer, Anton Koberger.[13] Yet we may take Heynlin's word for it that he persistently encouraged Amerbach's Bibles and editions of the fathers. In the case of the great edition of St. Augustine their joint endeavours were well known even to their old friends in Paris.[14] Allowing for the obvious differences, one may still say that on a smaller scale Heynlin was to Johann Amerbach what Erasmus was to be to Amerbach's successor, Johann Froben.

Throughout the first half of the sixteenth century a steady trickle of Bâlois teachers and students can be traced to the *Quartier Latin*. Their presence indicates the frequency of ties between the Seine and the Rhine, but beyond this only a few Bâlois enjoyed a special degree of consideration in Paris. Among them was Ludwig Ber.[15] He began his studies in the early 1490s and continued to learn and teach in Paris until 1513, two years after he had stood first in the examination for the Sorbonne doctorate in theology. Then he returned to his native region. Being wealthy, he swiftly joined the ecclesiastical and academic establishment, and had no need to exhibit his learning in publications.[16]

---

[8] Hartmann 1.22f., 31ff., 40f.

[9] M. Hossfeld, *op. cit.* 7.284.

[10] Hartmann 1.22f.: "...sunt tamen plurimi, quos loquendi modus, quo sermone contexitur, horrore concutit ex eo, quod sine fuco saecularis eloquentiae ac splendore artis rhetoricae humili et inculto dicendi genera videatur incedere...".

[11] Hartmann 1.120f., 139f.

[12] F. Luchsinger, *Der Basler Buchdruck als Vermittler italienischen Geistes*, Basle 1953, 115ff.

[13] Hase, *Die Koberger*, lxxviiif., xci: Koberger urges Amerbach to proceed slowly with a new ed. of the *Postilla Hugonis* since he has large unsold stocks of the earlier ed. Instead Amerbach should consider an ed. of St. Ambrose, who seems to be in demand. Koberger also urges the completion of the Collected Works of St. Augustine and offers to buy the entire ed., or half of it. Cf. **No. 527, 578ff.**

[14] Hartmann 1.47f.

[15] Cf. Hartmann 1.134; Allen 2.381; Wackernagel 3.147f.

[16] Only towards the end of his life he published **No. 135**.

In Paris he proved himself a good customer of the Basle printers. As a *Magister Sorboniensis* he was a central and respected figure in the circle of Bâlois in Paris. Some of his younger compatriots boarded with him. However, Johann Amerbach was warned not to trust his sons to his tuition ; according to Amerbach's informant Ber was neither eager to impart lessons nor so close to Scotism as Amerbach might have desired.[17]

Ber was, in fact, in friendly contact with Lefèvre d'Etaples, though Erasmus, much later, was probably dramatizing Ber's position in having him turn to the Gospel after many years spent in scholastic squabbles.[18] Ber was definitely not a humanist. Later on in Basle he represented the solid prestige of Parisian theology and, a respected friend of Johannes Eck,[19] he proved himself an unrelenting enemy of the reformers. Erasmus gladly relied on him for the explanation of some subtle theological matters when drafting his *Diatribe* against Luther.[20] Ber also examined Erasmus' bold proposals for reform in *De esu carnium*, and to the dismay of his former Sorbonne *confrère*, Noël Béda, he found no fault with them.[21] Again in a typically Bâlois way Ber disapproved of Erasmus' harshness in the *Apologia* against Lefèvre d'Etaples [22] as later on he advocated moderation in his friend's dealings with other opponents in both the Catholic and Protestant camps.[23] Ber's attitude towards reform was neatly epitomized when on a trip to Rome in 1535 he became associated with Paul III's famous overture to the aged Erasmus : by the offer of preferment and even hints of a cardinal's hat, Paul hoped to gain Erasmus' attendance at his projected Council.[24]

In the final balance Erasmus' faithful friendship with the theologian Ber may remain somewhat astonishing.[25] Less surprising, on the other hand, was Erasmus' respect for a Bâlois doctor who once cured him in the French capital. In 1500 he wrote to his friend Jacob Batt reporting his recovery from a severe attack of fever :

Had that fever assailed me again, your Erasmus would have been done for, my dear Batt. However, we have good reason to hope, trusting in Saint Geneviève, whose ready help we experienced more than once, but chiefly because we happened to find a doctor, Guillaume Cop, not only a true authority in his field, but also a faithful friend and, what is rarest, a cultivator of the Muses, as you can see from his extemporized letter which I enclose.[26]

---

[17] Hartmann 1. 125f., 139, 232 ; cf. 1.188.

[18] Allen 2.244 ; cf. Hartmann 1.289f.

[19] When addressing a letter of protest to Erasmus, Eck could refer to Ber as a " communis amicus noster " : Allen 9.53f.

[20] Allen 5.399ff.

[21] Allen 5.46n. ; 6.104.

[22] Allen 3.158 (Erasmus to Ber, 6 December, 1517) : " Video te Fabro vehementer aequum esse, qui me dicas indulsisse bili " ; cf. 159ff. ; Hartmann 1.289f.

[23] Cf. Allen 7.297n. ; 10.110.

[24] Allen 11.138, 140ff., 212ff., 217.

[25] Allen 2.326 shows how firmly Erasmus trusted Ber as a devoted friend. However, he also had some consideration for Ber's wealth ; cf. 5.405. In exchange, Ber's reaction to Erasmus' death in letters to Bonifacius Amerbach sounds somewhat dry : Hartmann 4.418-21.

[26] Allen 1.286 ; on Cop see also J.-C. Margolin, Le " Chant alpestre " d'Erasme, *BHR* 27 (1965), 49-54 ; Hartmann 1.199 ; Wackernagel 3.200f.

On another occasion Erasmus entertained his readers with Cop's joke of having baffled all the learned physicians on his dinner table with a sprig of simple parsley and having then called the kitchen-maid to tell them what it was.[27]

Cop went to Paris in the late 1490s, and first served in the university as a physician to the German nation. Under both Louis XII and Francis I he was a court physician. Once a pupil of a disciple of Reuchlin, he now studied Greek in Paris under Lascaris, Erasmus, and Aleander. Until his death in 1532 he enjoyed considerable prestige as a scholar as well as doctor. Both Erasmus and Aleander dedicated works to him. Lefèvre d'Etaples believed that he had cured him of insomnia. In 1517 Francis I relied on Cop's influence with Erasmus when he tried to attract the great scholar to Paris.[28] Cop proved himself an intrepid defender of the cause of Christian humanism, and more than once counted on his prestige at court to weather the suspicions of theological circles. In 1514 he spoke firmly to Louis XII in defence of Reuchlin, who had been condemned by the Sorbonne.[29] In fact, much of Cop's boldness and some of the causes which it served seem to have been passed on to his offspring. His son Nicolas, who was rector of the University of Paris for 1533, gave that famous inaugural address which had been inspired by Calvin, a friend of the family. The stir caused by this speech compelled the younger Cop at once to seek shelter first in Basle,[30] and then in Geneva. Nicolas' brother Michel became a pastor in Geneva. But Michel's son, Luc, in his turn escaped from Geneva where he had been condemned for reading Rabelais and seducing a servant girl. In 1570 he was enrolled at the University of Basle.[31]

The evolution in the object of family enthusiasm from Reuchlin to Calvin and Rabelais was hardly compatible with the tastes prevailing in Basle. In spite of his continued residence in Paris for nearly forty years, it was the grandfather Guillaume who preserved the closest ties with his native city. A member of the royal household and a friend of the leading humanists, he was also a patron of the Basle publishers, probably the most influential one they had in Paris. Guillaume visited Basle from time to time.[32] He maintained friendly contacts with the Amerbach family and took an interest in Bruno and Basilius when they were studying in Paris. However, he was a busy man, and when the older Amerbach asked him to have some Paris manuscripts traced and copied for the Basle edition of St. Augustine, Cop's assistance, though willingly tendered, was not the most valuable.[33] Many of his Latin translations of Galen and Hippocrates can be found in Basle editions, but all were reprinted from originals published in Paris. He was frequently in touch with the

---

[27] Allen 2.56 : the story is perhaps too good to be believed, but it shows that Erasmus wished to honour Cop even when joking at the expense of the medical profession at large.

[28] Allen 2.449 ; cf. Lefranc, *Collège de France* 46ff.

[29] Herminjard 1.16n. ; A year after the *Placards* affair Jean Cop, a son of Guillaume, chose a university audience to which to deliver his panegyric *De restitutis a Christianissimo Francorum rege Francisco litteris*. " L'Université dut subir sans murmurer cette manifestation si désagréable pour elle : malicieuse revanche imaginée sans doute par les humanistes parisiens " (Lefranc, *Collège de France* 149). Jean too had contacts with Basle. Sphyractes received from him a gift copy of his *De fructibus libri IV* (Paris, Wechel, 1535) and passed it on to Bonifacius Amerbach (Hartmann 4.396).

[30] Herminjard 3.130 ; Mann 164f ; cf. above p. 95.

[31] Droz, *Etudiants français* ; *Matrikel* 2.194.

[32] Hartmann 1.188, 197 ; 3.301 ; Allen 2.22.

[33] Hartmann 1.220f ; 224, 232.

Ecu de Bâle, and Resch paid him a long visit shortly before his death.[34]   The respect which the Bâlois showed for Cop was appropriate.   His presence in Paris provided the strongest link between the Christian humanist circles of the two cities prior to the *Placards* affair.   Besides he had become the friend of Erasmus at a time when no other Bâlois seems to have been aware of the rising star of Rotterdam.

In the year 1501, when Johann Amerbach sent his two older sons to the University of Paris, Basle was admitted to the Swiss Confederacy.   In the days of the Franco-Helvetic alliance and the broadening curriculum of humanities offered in Paris, Amerbach's example was often followed in Basle.   None of these later arrivals, however, were to spend a substantial period of their lives in France, as did Heynlin, Ber and Cop.   A number of the Bâlois students in France represented the second and third generations of well-known printer families.   Polycarp Cratander,[35] Niklaus Episcopius the younger, and Johann Herwagen the younger[36] studied in Paris. Caspar Petri went on a royal scholarship to Montpellier.[37] Caspar Herwagen graduated from Poitiers.[38]   Bonifacius Amerbach read law in Avignon and took his doctoral degree there.   Hieronymus Gemusaeus, the son-in-law of Andreas Cratander, was in Avignon and received his medical doctorate in 1533 from French occupied Turin.[39]

Paris also attracted some of the scholars who were known to collaborate with the Basle publishers.   Beatus Rhenanus, the scholarly collaborator of the Froben press, was in Paris between 1503 and 1507.[40]   He studied under Lefèvre d'Etaples in the College of Cardinal Lemoine, and worked as a corrector in the press of Henri Estienne.   Beatus Rhenanus later became one of the closest friends of Erasmus, but no evidence has survived of any contacts between them during the two lengthy visits which Erasmus paid to Paris between 1504 and 1506.[41]   In 1517, only a year after the conclusion of the Perpetual Peace between the French Crown and the Swiss Cantons, Heinrich Glareanus obtained from the King a special grant of 150 pounds.[42]   Glareanus had recently been Rhenanus' colleague in the Froben press. He now moved to Paris, taking with him a group of youths who had been lodging with him in Basle and studying under his supervision.   They included such hopefuls as Aegidius Tschudi together with two brothers.   Glareanus was warmly received by Lefèvre d'Etaples, but he was dismayed by the general indifference to Greek studies.[43]   The mentality which Glareanus awakened in his protégés is well demonstrated by a letter of Valentin Tschudi, who was reading for the Paris *magisterium*.

---

[34] Hartmann 4.136.

[35] Hartmann 4.91, 251f. ; after his father sold the Basle press in 1536 both Cratanders became book merchants.

[36] Hartmann 5.212 ; 6.276f. and passim.   Herwagen seems to have known Ramus ; Episcopius became later his faithful publisher : cf. above p. 153 ,n. 3.   In 1529 Erasmus was alarmed at the mere suggestion that his godson Erasmius Froben might be sent to Paris : Allen 8.297, 302.

[37] Hartmann 5.374ff. ; 6.xxxixff., 19f. and passim ; *Matrikel* 2.16.

[38] *Matrikel* 2.43.

[39] Hartmann 3.236 ; 6.xxvi, 9f.

[40] Hartmann 1.441f. ; Allen 2.60n. ; Wackernagel 3.144ff.

[41] *B.Rh.B.* 3f., 592f.   Only one letter from Rhenanus' days in Paris is known : *B.Rh.B.* 576.

[42] Hartmann 2.20 and passim ; Allen 2.279f. and passim ; Lefranc, *Collège de France* 57ff.

[43] Allen 3.36f.

He unleashed his sarcastic humour at the expense of the Paris theologians who seemed to him as puerile as their students and looked like school boys if compared to their colleagues in Vienna or Basle.[44] When in 1519 the plague ravaged Paris, Glareanus' group moved to Marly. So did Budé, who received them all.[45] Budé was the most influential of Glareanus' contacts in Paris. He recommended the Swiss as royal poet in succession to Andrelini, but the resulting arrangement was not very satisfactory.[46] Nor was Glareanus acceptable, despite Erasmus' glowing recommendations, to fill the important place left vacant by Erasmus' own polite rejection of Francis I's overtures.[47]

Glareanus returned to Basle in 1522, and again joined a group of scholars assembled around the presses of Froben and the study of Erasmus. Another member of this same group was Ludwig Carinus (Kiel), a native of Lucerne, who had received his B. A. from Basle. He studied in Paris in 1517 and a year later was permitted to contribute a laudatory letter to the edition of Erasmus' *Colloquies* which Estienne printed for Conrad Resch.[48] In the course of his strange roving life he returned to Paris in 1533-34, where he lodged with the printer Vascosan, cultivated Johannes Sturm and defended the poet Nicolas Bourbon, who was then under accusation of heresy.[49]

Among the numerous Bâlois students in Paris one finds some future professors of the University of Basle. Johann Sphyractes (Jeuchdenhammer) was a royal scholar from 1530 to 1533. In 1537 the Basle Council had a hard time winning him back for the local university after he had passed an examination in Bourges.[50] Bernhard Brand, son of a Basle burgomaster and later the son-in-law of the printer Johann Herwagen, financed his studies in Paris with a grant from the Erasmus bequest and also a royal scholarship. In 1546, after five years spent on preparations, he was only just ready to begin his law course in Poitiers. Yet two years later he returned to Basle to take a chair of law. It is hard to imagine that he had much success in his academic endeavours, but at least he showed some loyalty to France ; in 1552 he left his chair and family, enrolled in a Swiss regiment, and served Henry II against Charles V. After his return he sat on the town council and served in the administration of Basle's territories.[51] Johann Ulrich Iselin, a nephew of Ludwig Ber and later the son-in-law of Bonifacius Amerbach, taught and practised law with greater stability and distinction, though essentially he must have been dull. Ber, his uncle, had helped to finance his studies in Paris from 1536 to 1540, when he moved on to Poitiers and Valence.[52] His son Johann Lucas studied at Paris in

[44] Herminjard 1.38ff. ; Lefranc, *Collège de France* 60ff.

[45] Budé, *Opera* 1.282 ; Hartmann 2.207.

[46] Allen 3.280 ; cf. Hartmann 2.203.

[47] Allen 2.456f. ; Lefranc, *Collège de France* 54f. On a curious Swiss friend of Glareanus who, as an ex-student, established a gathering place for his compatriots in the Red Lantern district of Paris see Hartmann 6.422f.

[48] Hartmann 2.122n. ; Allen 3.496f. ; cf. **No. 3003.**

[49] Buisson, *Castellion* 1.81 ; 2.148f.

[50] Hartmann 4.10ff. and passim ; Staatsarchiv Basel-Stadt, Missiven B.1.551 ; 2.31 recto ; *Matrikel* 2.15.

[51] Hartmann 5.276 ; 6.274, 362 and passim ; *Matrikel* 2.37.   For Brand's companion J. W. Heptenring cf. Hartmann 5.449 ; 6.133f.

[52] Hartmann 5.15f., 92 ; 6.23f., 130ff. : After his return to Basle he sent a friend in Valence a new portrait of Erasmus published by the Froben press.

1571-72 and brought Guillaume Postel letters from Theodor Zwinger.[53] The latter —nephew of Iselin's step-father Oporinus—had twenty years earlier been taught in Paris by Pierre Ramus.

Without continuing the enumeration of Basle students in France, it may safely be assumed that throughout the sixteenth century the interest of French humanist circles for Basle was paralleled by a broad experience of French culture among the ranks of Basle's educated bourgeois. While it does not seem that royal scholarships were offered, or filled, very regularly during the decades of the religious wars, the young Bâlois were again applying for them in the early seventeenth century and continued to do so until well into the eighteenth.[54]

---

[53] F. Secret in *BHR* 26 (1964), 131ff.; *Matrikel* 2.164. Cf. also Hartmann 6.92f. for Veit Ardüser, a native of the Grisons, who went to Paris in 1525 and stayed for almost a decade before he came to Basle as professor of mathematics.

[54] Staatsarchiv Basel-Stadt, Fremde Staaten, Frankreich A 4, " Nominationen zum französischen Stipendium " (1554-1738).

CHAPTER TWO

THE UNIVERSITY OF PARIS

The *Quartier Latin* with its various colleges clustering around the venerable Sorbonne was the destination of most Bâlois who went to Paris. It was in the same *Quartier Latin* that Basle's books were offered for sale. In turn one might have expected to find the French friends of Basle gathered for the most part in the colleges, but this was hardly the case. Relatively few of the French authors who represented the capital in the books produced in Basle were typical exponents of the university.

Despite a Heynlin and a Ber, none of their French contemporaries in the Sorbonne had a major stake in the publications of Basle. In the early decades of printing prior to 1520 a huge number of works by the great *magistri Parisienses* emerged from the presses of Basle, but most of them represented the glorious past of theology in Paris from Thomas Aquinas to Gerson. These classics of scholasticism were in constant demand among the German universities, but the recent *magistri* of the Sorbonne had so little use for them that they were printed less frequently in Paris than almost anywhere else.[1]

Of the Nominalists who had dominated the teaching in Paris throughout the fifteenth century no significant trace is to be found in our bibliography. Their Realist rivals fared little better despite the favour in which they were held by Johann Amerbach and some of his advisors. Above all, the writings of recent Sorbonists more or less closely associated with one or the other school which were actually reprinted in Basle might well have figured even in the libraries of humanistic scholars who disliked the old school methods. Johann Wessel of Gansfort had come to champion first the Scotist and subsequently the Nominalist cause. Consequently he left Paris during a short ascendancy of Realism. In 1474 he passed through Basle, where he may have met Reuchlin [2] but failed to attract the attention of the printers. A selection of his theological writings was not reprinted in Basle until almost fifty years later and by that time it presented Wessel as a forerunner of the Reformation rather than a Nominalist.[3]

The Paris Realists found a little more favour with the Basle printers. The master of Scotism in the 1480s, Brulefer, appears twice among the authors of J. Wolff. In particular, Wolff printed his commentary on Saint Bonaventura for the first time.

---

[1] Renaudet, *Préréforme* 99ff., 105.

[2] *Ibid.* 83, 93.

[3] **No. 1042f.** The origin of these eds. has been connected with the presence in Basle of Hinne Rode. In addition to the contents of the preceding eds., the Basle *Farrago* offers a letter by Luther : O. Clemen in *Zeitschrift für Kirchengeschichte* 18 (1898), 346-372.

The work, however, was written during Brulefer's years in Metz and Mainz rather than in Paris, although his first contacts with Basle certainly dated back to his teaching in the Sorbonne. The unnamed Franciscan addressed in the preface to the commentary may be Franz Wiler, who had sat at Brulefer's feet in Paris and still recalled him with veneration while living now in the Basle convent of his order. Since Wiler's opinion was greatly respected by Johann Amerbach, it seems reasonable to assume that Wolff too may have acted on his advice. By the time the Basle editions of his works appeared, Brulefer was dead. His biographer presented him to posterity as an uncompromising advocate of reform and an ascetic model of Franciscan observantism.[4] These qualities may have impressed the Bâlois as much as his learning. Brulefer was succeeded as Paris' leading authority on Scotism by Pierre Tateret, who continued to profess the traditional tenets with increasing pedantry. His commentaries on Aristotle opposed the more humanistic ones of Lefèvre d'Etaples, his colleague in the College of Cardinal Lemoine.[5] Impressed by Wiler's stern condemnation of Nominalism, Johann Amerbach considered at one point trusting Tateret with the tuition of his sons. He also thought of Lefèvre, but finally consented to a Nominalist training in the Colleges of Sainte-Barbe and Lisieux.[6] In the presses of Basle at least Tateret's Scotist commentaries on Aristotle obtained a modest triumph over those of Lefèvre d'Etaples. The former alone were to be reprinted by Johann Froben. Froben's associate, Lachner, kept a close watch on the prevailing trends in German universities, and in Wittenberg, for instance, Tateret's commentaries were used as text books until the days of Melanchthon.[7]

In view of Basle's indifference to contemporary Sorbonists, one may recall the scornful remarks of an Erasmus, a Glareanus, or a Valentin Tschudi, but they were all preceded by a letter which Jean Raulin, until then himself a college man, addressed to the Guardian of the Basle Franciscans. Raulin, who had only a few days before exchanged his position in the College of Navarre for a noviciate in the Abbey of Cluny, denounced the fatal worldliness of the schools. A year later, in 1498, Raulin addressed the general chapter of Cluny and his text was first printed in Basle.[8] Its ascetic demand for monastic reform recalls the new spirit which had eventually reached the University of Paris with Standonck's take-over of the College of Montaigu. When introducing to Paris the ideals of *Devotio moderna* Standonck was assisted by Johan Mombaer, whose famous *Rosetum* was likewise reprinted in Basle.[9]

After 1520 the Sorbonne no longer appears in Basle books except as the target of bitter criticism. Between 1521 and 1523 the condemnation of Luther by the theological faculty caused two Basle printers to publish some pointed answers in Latin and German, part of which included for better focus the text of the faculty's *Determinatio*.[10] More immediate and complex, if only a little less hostile, relations

---

[4] Hartmann 1.151ff.; Renaudet, *Préréforme* 95, 370, 405.

[5] *Ibid.* 95f., 247f.

[6] Hartmann 1.139 and passim; Renaudet, *Préréforme* 404ff.

[7] *Wetzer-Welte's Kirchenlexikon*², Freiburg i.Br. 1882ff., s.v. Tartaret. For Lachner's business policy cf. Grimm 1371. I could not locate a copy of Tateret's *Praelecta in universam Aristotelis philosophiam*, Basle 1508, mentioned by Panzer.

[8] Renaudet, *Préréforme* 234f., 370; **No. 886**, in 1499 it was reprinted in Paris.

[9] Renaudet, *Préréforme* 219ff.

[10] **No. 375-377**; cf. M. Luther, *Werke* 8, Weimar 1889, 255ff.; Imbart, *Origines* 3.175.

with the Sorbonne resulted from Erasmus' clashes with individual Paris theologians as well as the faculty at large. His chief critics were Noël Béda and Pierre Cousturier called Sutor. Erasmus characterized the latter as hot-tempered and craving to establish a reputation. If he called Béda by comparison equally insane but much more stupid,[11] the implication is that this second opponent worried him the most. In fact Béda was more intelligent and more persistent in his attacks. Both Paris theologians were certainly intemperate in their criticisms of Erasmus, and narrow-minded in their defence of orthodoxy, yet significantly both belonged to the group of reformers inspired by monastic and ascetic ideals, whose appeals to the Paris theological establishment evoked, as we have seen, a positive response among the Basle printers prior to Erasmus' arrival. Cousturier was a pure-bred Sorbonist turned Carthusian; of Béda Erasmus stated correctly that he was not a monk but " *ex medio quodam genere, quod Standoncus quidam instituit* ".[12] Béda was, in fact, Standonck's successor as director of the Montaigu College and—outwardly at least —he developed a similar inclination toward austere discipline, although his overriding taste for academic politics betrayed the ideals of *Devotio moderna* and ruined the college.[13] Béda was perhaps less prone than Cousturier to lump Erasmus and Luther together : he associated the Dutch scholar primarily with Lefèvre d'Etaples, but did not therefore judge him less severely.[14] Béda complacently advised Erasmus to read Gerson and accused him of following Origen rather blindly. In his defence Erasmus argued at some length the transitory merits of successive theological approaches and mildly suggested that perhaps a future age might be right in finding some fault even with a Tateret or a Sutor.[15] Most of all Béda took Erasmus to task for his neglect of Saint Augustine. In so doing, Béda based his arguments on numerous and precise references to Augustine's works which he used in Amerbach's edition

---

[11] Allen 7.17 ; cf. **No. 113ff.**, and Allen 6.130ff ; 9.161ff. and passim.

[12] Allen 7.17.

[13] Renaudet, *Préréforme* 359, 456ff., 575f., 655 ; Allen 6.65ff. ; 7.343f. : Henri Botteus, a canonist from the Lyonnais, recalls his days in the Montaigu College under Béda's direction : " Ubi primum legi tuis literis nomen Bedae, statim subiit recordatio Collegii Montisacuti, exhorruique ne praeceptor plagosus iterum ferula me feriret. Hunc alias bonum virum arbitratus sum, donec leviculo illo dicterio Iesus, ' Beta Luteciae sapit ' in tantam maledicentiam prorupit, ut apertius ementitam sactimoniam atque latens sub gibbo illo suo virus evulgare non potuisset." Cf. Allen 9.480ff.

[14] The controversy between Béda and Erasmus started in 1524 when Resch applied for a privilege to republish in Paris Erasmus' *Paraphrase on Luke*. On examining the book, Béda found numerous errors (Allen 6.66f.) and an epistolary altercation between the Basle humanist and the Paris theologian began. It first retained the polite form of friendly admonitions between two fellow priests and fellow theologians (Allen 6.81f., 88), but with the publication of their polemical tracts (cf. Allen 6.258f.) unconcealed bitterness prevailed. Although in a direct reply to Béda Erasmus could still emphasize the common ground between them, in letters to others he wrote in a different key. Béda was instrumental in bringing about the banishment of Lefèvre d'Etaples. But after Lefèvre's return to favour with the king, and encouraged by the evidence of bitter animosity against Béda from within his own circles (Allen 7.166), Erasmus too engaged in bold attacks. Relying on Francis' often demonstrated sympathy and on his good friends at court, he wrote repeatedly to the *Parlement* of Paris, the king and even the Sorbonne, and was on the whole successful (Allen 6. 357ff., 7.233ff.). For Béda's association of Erasmus with Lefèvre rather than with Luther cf. e.g. Allen 6.298ff ; for the general context cf. Imbart, *Origines* 3.212.

[15] Allen 6. 81, 85, 89f., 101f.

of 1506.[16] Béda's attacks must have influenced Erasmus' decision to undertake personally a great edition of Augustine for Froben, a task which heightened his appreciation of the church father, but also led to much frustration and uncertainty.[17] Under Béda's attacks Erasmus continued to rely on the support of the Paris court and humanist circles. It was hardly a coincidence that Béda chose the moment of the greatest stir caused by Erasmus' alleged slight of Budé in the *Ciceronianus* (published in March 1528) to approach the university at large (23 June, 1528).[18] He was now able to secure an edict condemning the writings of Erasmus. Yet even so Erasmus was careful not to treat Béda as the official spokesman of the university : rather he appealed for help from friends and moderates in the faculty. He wrote to the Sorbonist Nicolas Leclerc, an old friend of Ber, and had Ber write to him as well, but failed to divert Leclerc from his vigorous support of Béda.[19] Erasmus had more success with another Sorbonne doctor, Gervasius Wain of Memmingen, who had published a book with Conrad Resch [20] and was a former pupil of Ber. In May 1527 Wain had visited Erasmus and Ber in Basle, and the humanist took great comfort from their conversations.[21] Back in Paris, Wain continued to prove himself a true friend and a valuable source of information about the steps taken by Béda.[22] Erasmus' sometime *famulus* in Basle, Philippe Montanus, and François Dubois could also be relied upon. Both were distinguished representatives of the humanities in the university and had contacts with the humanists around Budé, though they could hardly be called members of that circle.[23]

The theological faculty, however, could not much longer be silenced. In 1531 they published their own *Determinatio* against Erasmus, and in the following year they seized his books in the Paris book shops.[24] In spite of this Basle printers remained fully committed to the Erasmian party as they had been throughout the dispute. The Froben press published his rejoinders to Béda and Sutor as well as to the faculty's *Determinatio*.[25] Of the Paris professors involved in the issue only Erasmus' friends, Montanus and Dubois, appear among the authors printed in Basle.

In other respects relations between the Basle presses and the University of Paris focused, not on the Sorbonne, but on the corporation specifically created to offer a humanistic alternative to the academic curriculum dominated by theology : the *Collège de France*, as it later came to be called. The Bâlois Guillaume Cop [26] and his

---

[16] Allen 6.82n.

[17] Bietenholz, *History and Biography* 77ff. ; cf. Erasmus' admission of his pains over Augustine in a letter to Germain de Brie : " Nunc totus Augustinus sex praelis acceleratur, scriptor et obscurae subtilitatis et parum amoenae prolixitatis " (Allen 7.261, cf. 492f.). Erasmus also tried—unsuccessfully—to obtain a royal French privilege for the Froben edition of Augustine (Allen 7.502, 8.391).

[18] Allen 7.460n.

[19] Allen 7.473f., 502f., 522 ; 11.34.

[20] **No. 3009.**

[21] Allen 7.74.

[22] Allen 7.189ff., 242f., 263, 444f. Cf. in this context the two letters by Gerard Morrhe, a friend of the Erasmian Jacob Omphalius : Allen 8. 423ff. ; 9.480ff.

[23] Allen 7.520ff. ; 6.151f. ; 11.364 ; cf. below pp. 197, 203.

[24] Allen 7.233f. ; 9.357 ; 10.302 ; Febvre-Martin 457ff.

[25] **No. 113ff., 365f., 421ff.**

[26] Cf. above pp. 170ff.

son Jean both took an active interest in the new creation. Erasmus was enthusiastic, and as usual Basle humanists and printers followed his example. Of all Paris professors ever printed in Basle the majority were royal lecturers. Their names range from the earliest holders of that title, which Francis I first bestowed in 1530, to those teaching in the days of the massacre of Saint Bartholomew; then the line breaks off. Among the Basle authors were the Hellenists J. Toussain, A. Turnèbe, J. Dorat, and D. Lambin. Vatable represented Hebrew, Postel Oriental languages, B. Latomus Latin eloquence, P. Ramus Greek and Latin philosophy. O. Finé held a royal lectureship in mathematics, J. Dubois and J. Goupyl in medicine.[27] Only at the end of his life, in 1546, did Francis I give his group of lecturers the status of a proper corporation, and even so his work fell short of creating an institution. The royal professors still went about their tasks individually.[28] In the programme of Basle publishing, too, they—and for that matter some other authors who happened to be Paris professors—do not represent an institution, either the university or any of its separate colleges. Such royal professors as Postel and Ramus have attracted our attention because of their significant visits to Basle, but it is clear that the Bâlois did not consider them primarily as representatives of Paris University. The same is true of a mathematician like Finé and a physician like Goupyl, who manifestly belonged to humanist circles by virtue both of their friends and of their scholarly work. By contrast, the major representatives of humanism inside the university prior to the establishment of royal chairs, Fichet and Gaguin, were never printed in Basle, although the friends of Erasmus cannot have been unaware of their work. At least the Basle printers took ample advantage of the remarkable crop of Greek scholarship harvested in Paris. Among these scholars Joachim Périon, a Benedictine and an outstanding exponent of traditional Aristotelian dialectic, remained obviously indebted to the conservative climate of the university;[29] and the great innovator whom he opposed so zealously, Pierre Ramus, was a typical school man too, in the sense that he was never so happy and brilliant as when he could address a large audience of enthusiastic students. The Basle printers terminated in the early 1550s their remarkable series of reprints offering most of Aristotle's works translated and commented by Périon, but just at that time Bernard Bertrand and René Perdrier arrived from Paris to have Oporinus publish their translations of Greek poets.[30] The impressive Paris tradition of Greek patristic studies too was occasionally reflected by a Basle publication. For instance in 1554 Philippe Montanus gave to Herwagen his final edition of Theophylactus in Latin. In his will Erasmus had left the sum of 150 crowns to the Paris professor. Montanus continued to be as faithful an advocate of Erasmian reform as ever there was in the colleges of Paris. He also showed kindness to some Basle students whom Amerbach had recommended to him.[31] Fifteen years later Ramus visited Basle and was at once adopted by the printers, whereas his colleague A. Turnèbe proved less popular. Only after another decade were his monumental *Adversaria* republished in Basle through the efforts of Jean de Sponde.

---

[27] Lefranc, *Collège de France* 381ff. and passim; cf. A. Lefranc, Les commencements du Collège de France, *Mélanges d'histoire offerts à Henri Pirenne*, Brussels 1926, 1.291-306.

[28] Lefranc, *Collège de France* 109ff., 161ff.

[29] Cf. Michaud and above p. 158, below p. 203f.

[30] Cf. below p. 204.

[31] Hartmann 4.417f., 440, 467f.; 5.32, 43, 276, 405; 6.172, 274f., 287; **No. 750f.**

In spite of such individual contacts, there never was an identifiable group of scholars within the university that would have shown a special affinity with the aims of Basle humanists. In their search for suitable copy Basle publishers naturally were drawn toward some more illustrious circles which had an identity and an international reputation of their own, although they did not lack close contacts with and even regular status in the university. Jacques Lefèvre d'Etaples, for instance, though he taught for some time in the College of Cardinal Lemoine, embodied by and large intellectual ambitions of a sweep uncommon in the narrow streets of the *Quartier Latin*.

Chapter Three

LEFÈVRE D'ETAPLES AND HIS CIRCLE

On 3-4 May, 1516, Conrad Pellican, later Guardian of the Basle Franciscan convent, and a collaborator of Froben, stopped in Paris on his way to the general chapter of his order. Pellican had already read most of Lefèvre's works; now he was to meet him personally in the Minorite monastery. He was kindly greeted and taken to the Church for a private chat, in the course of which Lefèvre asked about Beatus Rhenanus, and Bruno and Basilius Amerbach. Leaving the monastery, Pellican passed the *Ecu de Bâle* in the rue Saint-Jacques and noticed there some barrels newly arrived from Basle which contained Erasmus' recently published New Testament.[1] As if the meeting with Lefèvre and the display at the *Ecu* exhausted the relevance of Paris from the Bâlois point of view, Pellican did not bother to relate any other incidents of his short visit to the French capital. And none, indeed, could have had more significance in the present context. The path by which Lefèvre was led to study the writings of Erasmus and Luther, and to reflect their influence in his own later works, must often have passed through the *Ecu de Bâle*. Lefèvre used Erasmus' New Testament which, as Pellican had observed, was on sale at the *Ecu* only two months after its publication.[2] Nine years later Lefèvre's own *Nouveau Testament* was reprinted in Basle at the expense of Wattenschnee for distribution in France.[3] Yet when he had to escape from Paris in the same year, Lefèvre took shelter in Strasbourg rather than in Erasmian Basle.[4] There he met his former pupil and colleague in the College of Cardinal Lemoine, Guillaume Farel, who had

---

[1] *Das Chronikon des Konrad Pellikan*, ed. B. Riggenbach, Basle 1877, 53. On Pellican cf. Hartmann 1.177: he resided for long periods in Basle and worked for several printers before and after his accession to the Protestant party. He taught Ludwig Ber Hebrew.

[2] Cf. Allen 2.183n., 229n.; Renaudet, *Humanisme et Renaissance* 211ff.

[3] See above p. 35.

[4] A remark in one of Erasmus' letters suggested to Allen that Lefèvre visited Basle during his stay in Strasbourg: " Faber Stapulensis hac iter faciens consternavit animum meum, nuncians Budaeum ... fato functum esse: quem rumorem esse vanum ... coniicio ..." (Allen 6.345f.). Allen's interpretation of *hac* seems doubtful. Even if Basle is meant, it does not necessarily follow that the two men met. Cf. Allen 7.66: " Faber hinc ... revocatus est in Galliam ", clearly not a reference to Basle. From an equally laconic remark Allen concluded that Erasmus solicited his Roman friends to speak up for the exiled Lefèvre. Allen 6.234f., from J. M. Giberti in Rome: " Ego vero hic tam ero tuus tuorumque quam fui semper, agamque sedulo quoad potero ut Iacobus Fabri, si admonitus ab eius procuratoribus fuero, intelligat suam quidem virtutem maxime, tuam vero commendationem non minus sibi profuisse." I am rather inclined to think that Giberti promised his assistance mostly of his own initiative. Aware of their former friendship, he had plenty of reason to associate Lefèvre closely with Erasmus

recently been expelled from Basle. Lefèvre's translation of the Old Testament, and finally his complete Bible, which in 1528 and 1530 could no longer be published in France, appeared in Antwerp, not Basle. As it was, Lefèvre's ideas formed the most influential current to reach the Rhine in the early sixteenth century from the neighbouring realm in the West, but Basle humanists never fully acknowledged this debt, and perhaps Lefèvre did not give them much chance to do so. Personal contacts, nevertheless, were frequent. Lefèvre was sought out by Cop and Ber, by Beatus Rhenanus, Michael Hummelberg, the Amerbach sons, Conrad Pellican, Glareanus, Hieronymus Gebwiler, Melchior Volmar, and Wilhelm Nesen, all of them residents in, or visitors to Paris, who at some time had close ties with the Basle presses; in turn a Farel, an A. de Coct, a M. Bentin, among the French circle of Basle openly exhibited their admiration for Lefèvre.

The depth of Lefèvre's influence upon Basle humanism and publishing is not easy to fathom. His own vital experience of Christian humanism led the young Paris Aristotelian through his acquaintance with the Platonic Academy of Florence to the work of the Christian fathers. Lefèvre's name ought to figure prominently in the great Basle editions of Plato and Plotinus, of Ficino, Pico and Dionysius the Areopagite.[5] It ought to be found in Erasmus' edition of Basil the Great, prefaced by one of the most platonizing texts ever to flow from his pen,[6] and also in the Froben edition of Origen published in the year of Erasmus' death and crowning the decades of his loving study of the controversial Greek father.[7] The names of Lefèvre and Beatus Rhenanus ought to accompany every one of the impressive succession of Basle publications devoted to the concept of human dignity.[8] Yet the Basle publishers of Renaissance *Platonica* could often rely on earlier publications by their rivals in Strasbourg rather than draw on the direct inspiration of Lefèvre's Paris circle or even the Italian centres of Platonic humanism.[9]

---

since both were now under attack by Béda and others. Throughout the time of Lefèvre's presence in Strasbourg Erasmus' attitude to him can hardly be described in other terms than indifference. For several years he had barely mentioned Lefèvre in his letters. Apart from Allen 6.345f., referred to above, Erasmus noted Lefèvre's arrival in Strasbourg only once and in words that are decidedly less than friendly : " Faber Stapulensis Gallia profugus agit Argentorati, sed mutato nomine, quemadmodum comicus ille senex Athenis Chremes erat, in Lemno Stilpho " (Allen 6. 281). Hereafter, only Lefèvre's rehabilitation is again mentioned, now in somewhat more amicable terms : " Iacobus Faber, qui metu profugerat, non ob aliud nisi quod verterat Evangelia Gallice, revocatus est in aulam " (Allen 6.351). At the same time Erasmus dared again to write to his own friends in Paris. Two more references to Lefèvre in the year after his return to Paris stated that the king trusted Lefèvre and that he could now speak for himself (Allen 6.362 ; 7.66 ; cf. 9.10. Subsequently there even was a short letter to Lefèvre himself, suggesting some form of collaboration in the translation of Chrysostom, but it brought no results (Allen 6.479).

[5] Only the preface to N. Cusanus, *Opera*, Basle 1565, quotes at length from the *elogium* on Cusa by the " gravissimus testis et incorruptissimus iudex Faber Stapul." Cf. E. F. Rice, jr., The Humanist Idea of Christian Antiquity, *Studies in the Renaissance* 9 (1962), 126-160 ; Bietenholz, *Ital. Humanismus* 115ff.

[6] Allen 9.435ff. The Basle ed. was preceded by a Paris collection produced in 1520 by Josse Bade, which can be associated with Lefèvre's circle, and by *Basilii oratio de invidia*, Strasbourg, Schürer, 1508 : E. F. Rice, *op. cit.* 129f., 151f.

[7] Cf. E. F. Rice, *op. cit.* passim ; Bietenholz, *History and Biography* 41-44 ; D. P. Walker, Origène en France, *Courants religieux et humanisme* ... (Colloque de Strasbourg), Paris 1959, 109ff.

[8] Bietenholz, *Ital. Humanismus* 121ff.

[9] *Ibid.* 124.

Alsace was the native province of one of the most understanding pupils of Lefèvre, Beatus Rhenanus. It was in Strasbourg in 1512 that a great edition of Gregory of Nyssa appeared. It contained two translations and a preface by Lefèvre,[10] but more significantly an epistle dedicatory to Lefèvre by Beatus Rhenanus and another by Johannes Cono, both dated from Basle. Cono celebrated Lefèvre as another Daedalus, the expert " *faber* " restoring the fabric of Aristotelian philosophy as well as the Platonism which inspired the Christian father Gregory of Nyssa.[11] Beatus Rhenanus, in turn, used his epistle to Lefèvre to formulate his own praise of human dignity modelled after Nemesius of Emesa's *De natura hominis*, a text which he had assigned to Gregory and included in the edition. In doing so he also evoked the name of Nicolaus Cusanus, and reserved for Reuchlin the supreme epithet of " *totius Europae decus* ".[12] The Lefèvre here addressed was indeed the friend of Reuchlin from his days at Paris; like him he had sat at Pico's feet and admired him above any other philosopher. It was the Lefèvre who appreciated, perhaps even republished, Ficino's *De triplici vita*. Beatus Rhenanus bought his copy of this treatise in Paris while working under Lefèvre in the College of Cardinal Lemoine. It then reappeared in Strasbourg, and several times in Basle.[13] Already while both Beatus Rhenanus and Erasmus were living in Paris, Lefèvre was busy preparing patristic editions, and more such publications emerged from his circle in the years before Beatus and Erasmus strode along the same path.[14] Most remarkably, the programme of Christian humanism was announced in this circle with formulations that closely resembled the ones Erasmus was to use shortly thereafter.[15]

A clever enemy like Noël Béda denounced Lefèvre and Erasmus as " *humanistae theologizantes* ", arrogantly pretending to " drink from the rivers which flow close to the very sources of divine wisdom," [16] and stated explicitly the ideals they held in common. Yet in Basle Erasmus was destined to eclipse Lefèvre whose ways and methods came gradually to diverge from his own. As we have seen earlier, Erasmus' final move to Basle was partly motivated by his alarm at the undertakings of Froben and his associates in Basle and Paris, who were publishing some of his texts in a way

---

[10] *B.Rh.B.* 37f.

[11] *B.Rh.B.* 45ff. The importance of this remarkable text has been well noted by E. F. Rice. On Cono see Hartmann 1.411n. and Wackernagel 3.145, who wrongly attributes Beatus Rhenanus' interest in Plato to Cono's influence over against the Aristotelianism of Lefèvre.

[12] *B.Rh.B.* 41ff.; cf. E. F. Rice, *op. cit.* 137ff., who shows that in his praise of human dignity Nemesius was indebted to Origen's *Commentary on Genesis*. Lefèvre and his circle liked the ed. of Beatus Rhenanus and Cono. It was reprinted by Josse Bade in 1513: *ibid.* 148f.

[13] Renaudet, *Préréforme* 149f., 423, Bietenholz, *Ital. Humanismus* 117, 156.

[14] Cf. E. F. Rice, *op. cit.* 142ff.

[15] Cf. E. F. Rice, *op. cit.* passim with Bietenholz, *History and Biography* 35ff.

[16] Quoted by D. P. Walker, *op. cit.* 110f., from Béda's *Annotationes* against Lefèvre and Erasmus (praefatio): " Bibant insuper de fluminibus, quae ab ipso divinae sapientiae fonte propius emanant, non a distantibus et per longa iam intervalla ab ipsa origine degenerantibus rivulis: id est qui veterum doctorum scripta, Origenis, Tertuliani, Cypriani, Basilii, Hilarii, Chrysostomi, Ambrosii, Hieronymi, et consimilium prae manibus habeant, non autem scholasticorum... Ita suis se verbis iactitant humanistae." Béda goes on to explain that the patristic writings contained obscure and equivocal points which were exploited by the ancient and medieval heretics; whereas the scholastics removed such obstacles and defeated the heretics.

and at a time which he deemed unsuitable.[17]   On·e Erasmus was settled in Basle, Froben was faced with inevitable alternatives.   Erasmus could offer a steady flow of his own writings and his great patristic text editions; but he would not tolerate his printer continuing to publish *Lutheriana*.   Froben accepted the necessity of choosing his priorities, and Lefèvre was another victim.   In spite of the continued association of Beatus Rhenanus with his press, Froben was never to publish a single work by Lefèvre.

After the publication of Erasmus' New Testament in 1516 and the subsequent appearance of Luther's first treatises, Lefèvre tended to abandon his earlier devotion to philosophy in favour of the Bible.   Even his patristic studies gave way to the search for a pure Evangelism directly derived from the Gospel.   This new emphasis coincided somewhat inexplicably with a broadening historical interest in church tradition.   In the course of this development Lefèvre forfeited a possible place of honour in the Basle publishing programme.   He was never directly associated with the great Basle editions of the fathers that marked Erasmus' presence in the city or in the neighbouring Freiburg.[18]   Moreover, the rivalry in Basle publishing during the 1520s between an Erasmian and Lutheran orientation left a deplorably small niche for Lefèvre's own type of Evangelism.

In 1519 Lefèvre wrote a generous and warm-hearted letter to Beatus Rhenanus. It remains the last one of which we know and it shows the author on the verge of internal transition.   The earlier Lefèvre is reflected by the promise to inquire of the Bishop of Meaux about a Latin manuscript translation of Philo of Alexandria, and if possible to make it available for copying to Conrad Resch or Wilhelm Nesen. The new Lefèvre announces himself with greetings to Luther, "*si aliquando tibi occurret.*"[19]   Despite the warm tone of this letter Lefèvre now grew visibly aloof from his old friends in Basle.   On his part, Beatus Rhenanus in his mounting patriotism and enthusiasm for German history allowed the ties with his former friends in Paris to slacken.   The Basle printers, moreover, could not fail to notice that Lefèvre did not and never really wanted to belong to the group of Paris humanists around Budé whose connections offered the dazzling prospects of court patronage. His association with the circles of Meaux and the Queen of Navarre did not compensate for the freely spending Poncher, Grolier, and Francis I who stood behind Budé and his influential friends.   The Meaux group was further discredited in the eyes of many Bâlois by Farel's tumultuous clamour in their town.[20]   Even Ber,

---

[17] See above p. 38f.

[18] An isolated request by Erasmus for collaboration in translating the works of Chrysostom was prompted by a report on the projects of Lefèvre's circle.   These projects do not seem to have materialized and Erasmus remained without an answer (Allen 6.479).

[19] *B.Rh.B.* 151f.

[20] The close relationship between Farel and Lefèvre was well known in Basel: cf. Lefèvre's letter to Farel (Herminjard 1.219ff.) with greetings to Oecolampadius, Pellican, and Hugwald.   It answered several letters by Farel, the last one of which had just been handed over to him by Conrad Resch.   It also acknowledged receipt of some books, among them Bugenhagen's *In librum Psalmorum interpretatio* (Basle, A. Petri, 1524) which was a gift from Hugwald.   It continued: " Accepi etiam illam acrem subsannationem, quae si in manus multorum venerit, vehementer motura est bilem et nobis etiam inconsciis conflatura invidiam, quasi quippiam tale promoverimus.   Utinam scriptor comoediae pepercisset aliquorum nominibus, quorum mallem resipiscentiam quam nomini eorum inuri notam.''   If one accepts Herminjard's plausible suggestion that the passage refers to one of Farel's own anonymous pamphlets (see above p. 92), Erasmus would probably have been among those who were, to Lefèvre's regret, mentioned by name.

who at first defended Lefèvre valiantly against Erasmus' *Apologia*,[21] was bound to fall silent in the days when the Meaux and the Basle reformers were visibly connected through the presence of Farel and his friends in the Rhine town. It is true that due to their presence Oecolampadius and other outspoken Protestants for a short time maintained epistolary contacts with the Meaux circle[22] while Cratander, the printer of numerous *Lutheriana*, also published a new edition of Lefèvre's Gospel commentaries and the first edition of his commentary on the Catholic letters. But even if Wattenschnee's 'export' edition of the *Nouveau Testament* is added, the crop seems poor when measured against the capacity of the Basle presses, the importance of Lefèvre's work and its compatibility with many ideals of Basle.

In the years of the Protestant break the more radical supporters of change in Basle may have found Lefèvre's Evangelism too unemotional, too un-German, and in several ways too Erasmian. Yet sincere friendship between Lefèvre and Erasmus had perhaps not really outlasted the latter's days in Paris. After a crisis culminating in Erasmus' bitter *Apologia ad J. Fabrum* of 1517[23] the two men settled down to a state of aloofness and friendly, but tragic, disagreement over details which seemed all the more significant to themselves as their common outlook in many areas remained very obvious and was noted by friend and foe alike.[24] To both, Lefèvre and Erasmus, Valla's philology had had the significance of a revelation. Both were impressed by the humanism and allegorizing exegesis of the Alexandrine fathers and of Origen. Yet Erasmus' courage in attributing to the earthly Christ the shortcomings of human nature seemed unjustifiable to Lefèvre, whereas Lefèvre's own boldness in discarding the literal text of the Vulgate seemed shocking to Erasmus.[25] Sensing a certain incompatibility of their characters, each feared the other's alleged excesses in the cause for which they both stood. Erasmus' personal attitude was underlined by the fact that Froben reprinted his friend's *Apologia* against Lefèvre but never one of the latter's own writings.

Basle's responses to Lefèvre's endeavours in church history were sporadic. The casual reappearance of his edition of the letters of the martyrs Saint Ignatius

---

[21] See above p. 170, n. 22.

[22] Herminjard 1.220 and esp. 1.274ff.; cf. E. Staehelin, *Oekolampads Beziehungen zu den Romanen*, Basle 1917, 20ff. On the Meaux circle see Imbart, *Origines* 3.109ff. and passim.

[23] In a letter by Josse Bade of August 1515 Lefèvre still appears together with Cop as the most obvious friend of Erasmus in Paris (Allen 2.125), but Erasmus' own letters from the same period express growing uneasiness: Allen 2.57f., 112, 324; 3.5f., 19f., etc. For the harsh tone of some passages in the *Apologia* see e.g. Erasmus, *LB* 9.43DE.

[24] In the *Apologia* Erasmus himself made the point: " En, inquient [the critics], egregios correctores quibus auctoribus oporteat novari tot seculis comprobabtam editionem [Sacrae scripturae]? Qui fidemus illis, si inter ipsos non convenit? Ita fiet, ut fabula mundi simus et in … aulis, in tonstrinis, in essedis et in navibus Erasmi Fabrique nomen obambulet. Tot exalantis laboribus hoc praemii denique feremus ! " (Erasmus, *LB* 9. 58E). Even Francis I once confounded the names of Lefèvre and Erasmus: Allen 5.217. A good example for the continued esteem for Erasmus in Lefèvre's own circle offers Jean Angelus (Lange). On 1 January, 1524 he despatched from Meaux two letters, one to Erasmus, the other to Farel, for both of whom he showed sincere admiration, although he regretted Erasmus' unduly severe criticism of Lefèvre: Allen 5.375ff.; Herminjard 1.178ff.

[25] Erasmus, *LB* 9.33C and passim; cf. Mann 24ff.; Renaudet, *Humanisme et Renaissance* 210ff. Cf. Bietenholz, *History and Biography* 88f.; J.-C. Margolin, Erasme et la Nature, *Canadian Journal of History* 3 (1968), No. 1, 25f. and passim.

and Saint Polycarp [26] recalls his earliest patristic studies, while his later hagiological interests prompted an equally casual request for the legends of local martyrs, which Glareanus in Paris transmitted to Zwingli in Zurich.[27]   Only Lefèvre's revival of John of Damascus found a somewhat more lasting echo in Basle due to the Basle editions of his translation of the Greek text.   However, the significance which Lefèvre had seen in this text was lost on its way through successive Basle editions. To Lefèvre the eighth century Byzantine monk had offered a purer and more specifically Evangelical alternative to the dogmatics of Peter Lombard; [28] to the Basle editors it was merely an addition to their encyclopedia of patristic publications.

Like master, like disciples.   The occasional contact between Basle and other members of the Fabrist circle in Paris and later in Meaux and Nérac failed to produce a sizeable crop of Basle books.   Among the patrons Bishop Briçonnet was hardly even mentioned in Erasmus' letters.[29]   Margaret, Queen of Navarre, never thought highly of Erasmus and showed no interest in Basle.   She failed to respond to the two flattering letters Erasmus had addressed to her, and she had no apparent use for the French translation of his *Modus confitendi* which Chansonnette had dedicated to her.[30]

Of the disciples and collaborators of Lefèvre, the name of Charles de Bouelles appears only in passing in the pages of some Basle reprint.[31]   Jodocus Clichtoveus, at least, could not entirely be passed over in the limited reception given to the work of the Fabrists.   This first, and for a time most faithful, disciple of Lefèvre, who participated in his philosophical no less than in his theological studies was close to Beatus Rhenanus while the Rhenish humanist lived in Paris, and co-operated with him after his return to Alsace and Basle.[32]   In the days of the controversy over Reuchlin, Clichtoveus was still on the side of the reformers; however, from 1521 onwards his solid grounding in theology and his position in the Sorbonne caused him to turn resolutely against Wittenberg as well as Basle and to join the growing chorus of Erasmus' critics in Paris.[33]

[26] **No. 688.** Erasmus' dislike for the letters of St. Ignatius is well documented by an isolated reference as late as 1530 in a letter to John Choler : '' Demiror quid te delectet in Epistolis Ignatii.   Si mihi essent, lubens tibi copiam facerem.   Nunc neminem audivi qui illas habeat '' (Allen 8.456).

[27] Herminjard 1.41.

[28] Cf. Renaudet, *Préréforme* 497f., and *Humanisme et Renaissance* 209f.

[29] Allen 5.380n.; 6.85, 95, 479; 9.10.

[30] **No. 241**; Allen 6.174ff.; 7.118. Cf. Mann, 79ff.; Herminjard 1.218.

[31] Cf. below : Index.

[32] Cf. Renaudet, *Préréforme* 507 on their collaboration in editing Ficino's *De religione Christiana*, 1510; *B.Rh.B.* 52f. : Beatus Rhenanus' epistle dedicatory to Clichtoveus in the Gregory of Nyssa ed., Strasbourg 1512; cf. *B.Rh.B.* 576.

[33] **No. 312ff.**; Allen 9.160; Renaudet, *Préréforme* 649f., 703.

Chapter Four

BUDÉ AND PARIS HUMANISM UNDER
THE PATRONAGE OF FRANCIS Ist AND HIS COURT

Between Lefèvre d'Etaples and Guillaume Budé there was no declared rivalry and some of their followers succeeded for a long time in maintaining friendly ties with both. Yet when in 1521 Budé's letters became the first of his publications to be reprinted in Basle, Lefèvre's was not among the names of correspondents listed on the back of the title page. The contents of the volume confirmed what by then the Basle humanists certainly knew: Budé had emerged as the head of a separate circle more splendid and more cosmopolitan than Lefèvre's. In their own approach to the Budé circle Basle humanists and printers overstressed, if anything, the difference in outlook between the two outstanding humanists of Paris. The religious bent of their editions of Lefèvre was in marked contrast to the almost exclusively philological orientation of those originating with the Budé circle. In reality Budé and Lefèvre were both led from different positions within the humanist movement toward a confrontation with the ideals of religious reform. Yet while there were Protestant publishers in Basle who lent their presses to Lefèvre's Evangelism, there was none to produce a separate edition of Budé's *De transitu Hellenismi ad Christianismum*, although this work contained the fundamental expression of his religious beliefs and breathed an Evangelical Catholicism often reminiscent of Erasmus if not even dependent upon him.

Although he never gave them one of his manuscripts to print, the Bâlois showed more consideration for Budé than they had ever done for Lefèvre. They honoured him by publishing the only, still not superseded, edition of his Collected Works. They thus classed him with Cusanus, Erasmus, Vives, and the lights of Italian humanism, a tribute no other Frenchman was to share with him, and which fairly reflected the reputation he enjoyed throughout the continent. Budé's lack of organization, especially in the earlier works, and the obscurity of his style surcharged with learned oddities, were noted by his contemporaries but proved more palatable to them than to modern scholars. Consequently a fair evaluation and a synthesis of Budé's thought have yet to be made.[1] Until they are available his tortured correspondence with Erasmus is difficult to analyse. However, since this correspondence is the

---

[1] In addition to the studies of Delaruelle and Bohatec see D. R. Kelley, Budé and the First Historical School of Law, *American Historical Review* 72 (1966-67), 807-834; Allen 2.227f. Useful new insights, especially into the relations between Budé and Erasmus, are also offered by M.-M. de la Garanderie in the introduction and notes of her recent translation: *La correspondance d'Erasme et de Guillaume Budé*, Paris 1967.

key to all contacts between Basle and the Budé circle, the following conclusions may be offered tentatively.

There is some evidence that the Bâlois were aware of Budé even before Erasmus came to settle among them. It was not until 1516 that he and Budé exchanged the first letters, opening a regular correspondence which ended twelve years later in mutual distrust. When it began Erasmus' *New Testament* was in Budé's hand and his star had already risen above that of the author of *De asse*.[2] A year earlier, however, in 1515, Bonifacius Amerbach, then a student of Zasius in Freiburg, placed an urgent order for a copy of *De asse* through Froben.[3] Amerbach's interest in Budé continued, and in 1519 he acted as a clearing agent for the correspondence between Budé on the one side, and Zasius, Alciato, and Chansonnette on the other. He showed himself angered—unduly perhaps—by Longueil's preference for Budé over Erasmus and by Budé's criticisms of Zasius and Alciato. Yet he could not even induce his lawyer friends to express publicly their doubts about Budé's qualifications for legal scholarship, and this may have inclined him to moderate his own position, for the time being at least.[4] In Avignon, through the services of Jean Vaugris, he received a copy of the Basle edition of Budé's letters, and in May 1522 he reported to his brother how during the court's residence in Lyons he had met Budé, been invited to dinner, and treated *mira humanitate*.[5] In November 1526 Beatus Rhenanus eargerly requested a copy of Budé's second series of *Annotationes* to the Pandect. Such ardour was lost on Amerbach, who merely replied with some petty criticism of Budé's new work.[6] Writing to Amerbach, Alciato too listed his objections to it and again questioned Budé's knowledge of legal matters. This, however, was said confidentially. In his further correspondence with Amerbach, Alciato remained respectful of Budé, whom he credited with a favourable influence on his career in France.[7]

In view of the persistent misgivings of Amerbach and Erasmus, it was fortunate for Basle that Claude Chansonnette developed a more satisfactory relationship with Budé. In 1520 the bilingual Chansonnette was made a town clerk in Basle, an appointment occasioned by a round of mutual political overtures following a period of strain and suspense between France and the Swiss Cantons. Basle too had responded to the anti-French agitation of Cardinal Schiner and proved extremely sensitive to French menaces against the neighbouring city of Montbéliard.[8] In a

---

[2] Allen 2.229; cf. 2.125; Delaruelle, *Une amitié d'humanistes* 321ff.

[3] Hartmann 2.37.

[4] Hartmann 2. 179-197, 285; 3.1, 371f. E.g. Bonifacius Amerbach to Zasius (September 1519): " Nescio, quas simultates cum Erasmo exerceat homo Gallus nimirum superbus et Pompei quiddam non parem ferentis pre se ferens. Ad extremum tamen manus dabit; tanto enim huic in iure antecellens es, quanto in theologia Erasmus. O ter felicem Germaniam, cunctis nationibus par, ne dicam superior!" (Hartmann 2.186). In a letter to Glareanus in Paris Amerbach showed more restraint: " Budeus in omnibus disciplinis apud Gallos primus, in legali prudentia Zasius nulli secundus " (Hartmann 2.204). Zasius himself expressed anxiety lest his controversy with Budé should be publicized through some letters appearing in print (cf. Hartmann 2.211).

[5] Hartmann 2. 277, 378.

[6] Hartmann 3.210, 215; Amerbach continued to be critical of Budé: Hartmann 3.371f.

[7] Hartmann 3.287f., 408, 475; 5.3.

[8] Wackernagel 3.8, 123f., 304; *B.Rh.B.* 144; cf. Amerbach's feelings in the same year as quoted in n.4. Cf. above p. 105.

remarkable letter of 25 October, 1518, to Vadianus Budé had gone out of his way to remind his Swiss humanist friends of the traditional character of the Franco-Helvetian alliance and to assure them of his continued personal sympathy in the case of renewed warfare between their nations.[9] Narrowly predating the turning point in political relations, the correspondence between Budé and Chansonnette began in 1519.[10] Basically it reflected their common interest in Roman Law, but since both held public office the prominence accorded to Chansonnette in Budé's collected letters may have added a political touch to the decision of a Basle printer to reprint the collection in 1521. From such glimpses as the Bâlois could cast on Budé's personal activities they may have been inclined to overrate his political influence.[11] Moreover he repeatedly transmitted King Francis' invitations to Erasmus, and answered the latter's evasions with gentle but sustained pressure. This must have added to the impression of the Basle humanists and publishers that the patronage of the French king and his *grands seigneurs* was best secured through the friendship of Budé and his circle. In view of the preceding polite exchanges between Budé and Chansonnette it seems improbable that they did not meet when in 1523 Chansonnette was in Paris and saw the king, who gave him a personal invitation for Erasmus.[12]

Budé's personal kindness was also extended to other members of the Basle circle. Glareanus often visited him while in Paris, and with his whole boarding school was entertained in Budé's country house at the village of Marly, where they had escaped from the plague-ridden capital. Budé also endeavoured to secure for Glareanus the succession to Andrelini's chair of poetry.[13] Upon the recommendation of Bonifacius Amerbach, Budé repeatedly received the Basle student Johann Sphyractes in 1531-32. Passing lightly over some less pleasant aspects of his relations with the Bâlois, Budé charmed his visitor with a well informed conversation on the notable scholars of Germany, and even showed him the manuscript of *De philologia* and *De studio litterarum* which was published shortly thereafter and reprinted in Basle almost at once. Through the lips of Sphyractes Amerbach returned Budé's compliments, for a change.[14]

Budé's attentions to the Bâlois, however, were soon overshadowed by his relations with Erasmus. From the outset each watched the products of the other's scholarly activity with a somewhat uneasy interest. Aware of the more widely established fame of Erasmus, Budé was anxious to see his own works approved and recommended

[9] Budé, *Opera* 1.263 : " ... velim ita tibi persuadeas periucundas mihi literas tuas eo nomine fuisse, usqueadeo ut luculento quodam loco et conspicuo nomen tuum in numeris meis ascripturus sim. Et enim hoc libens hilarisque fecerim, ut Vadiani capite Glarianique complectendis de nomine universo Helvetiaco ipse benemerear, quo cum ipso nunc Francia nostra foedere coniuncta est non novo sed vetere, etsi aliquandiu deterrimi cuiuspiam daemonis invidia interrupto. Neque vero, si temporarium hoc foedus esse quispiam male ominator aut contendat aut suspicari se dictitet, in causam tamen ego publicam animo tam obnixo incumbere mihi persuaserim, ut si — quod ominari nolim — rursu bella exoriantur, me vivo, inter nostros et Helvetios, ego quoque hostem me protinus doctorum hominum profitear et eis bellum indicam una cum republica.''

[10] Cf. Delaruelle, *Répertoire* 67ff., 108 ; Allen 5.440.

[11] Cf. e.g. Hartmann 2.378 ; 3.321 ; Allen 5.217.

[12] Allen 5.306f.

[13] See above p. 173.

[14] Hartmann 4.11f., 35, 116, 136.

by him, but Erasmus continued to reply ambiguously. He noted Budé's arrogance though it was primarily directed against others and he constantly feared an attack upon his toilsomely acquired reputation. However, as late as 1524 he was still toying with the idea of settling in Paris [15] and he had no reason to doubt the sincerity of Budé in promoting the project.

They had been exchanging letters since 1516, and their friendship had already passed through difficult moments before Erasmus moved to Basle. His *Apologia* against Lefèvre, in particular, had offended the national pride of Budé and his friends.[16] Without any obvious reason, the latent tension exploded by October 1518 with Budé's dramatic threat of rupture. Erasmus however, narrowly avoided the break by a saving display of common sense,[17] but the reconciliation remained superficial. In the days of the contested imperial election and thereafter both humanists were likely to be seen by their followers as the champions of a national cause. A letter from Longueil of March 1519 achieved notoriety not only for its comparison of their respective styles, but also for the pointed question of why Francis I should ever have preferred the German Erasmus to Budé, who was his peer in every respect and a Frenchman besides.[18] Patriotic sentiment persisted on both sides throughout the years Erasmus spent in Basle. It was expressed in the reactions of Bonifacius Amerbach, who was after all not a blind nationalist. It was prominent in the controversy over a supposed slight to Budé contained in Erasmus' *Ciceronianus*. It was unfortunate, for it tended to cloud the fact that the highest achievements of both scholars were complementary rather than competitive. In the last analysis, the textual criticism of Erasmus was directed to the understanding of an author's personality and thought. He surpassed Budé in literary skill and in the clear expression of his fundamental beliefs. But he could not match Budé's antiquarian diligence, his familiarity with the materials rather than personalities of antiquity, and his knowledge of the Greek language. For all his suspicions, Erasmus was aware of these differences. He genuinely admired a work such as *De asse* and tried persistently to appease Budé's jealousy by encouraging him to attempt a complete lexicon of the Greek language. No doubt he hoped that such an undertaking might leave Budé with an achievement of his own, an achievement in a field where he had no rivals, and where Erasmus could heartily join in the chorus of acclaim. Erasmus realized, however, that his proposal put a high demand on Budé's modesty.[19] Only a careful investigation of Erasmus' own works could show whether he underrated Budé's powers to develop a personal philosophy, or whether he learned more from the Frenchman than he wished to acknowledge. Perhaps to counteract the agitating comparisons between Budé and himself, he momentarily envisaged composing in

---

[15] Cf. Delaruelle, *Une amitié d'humanistes* 322ff.; Allen 5.137f., 217, 470f.

[16] Cf. Delaruelle, *Une amitié d'humanistes* 332f.

[17] Allen 3.434ff., 448ff.

[18] Allen 3.473ff. : " Nam quod ad eruditionem pertinet, non video qua in re Budaeus Erasmo cedat, sive humaniores sive Christiano dignas homine literas aestimare libeat. ... Illud tantum miror, quod ab initio dicebam : cur Princeps vester in tanta Budaei probitate, doctrina, eloquentia, Germanum Gallo, exterum civi, ignotum familiari praetuleri." Large sections, but not the most partisan passages, of this letter were reprinted by L. Le Roy in a biography of Budé (see Budé, *Opera* I). On the reactions of Bonifacius Amerbach and his friends to Longueil's letter cf. Hartmann 2.179-183 ; 4.11.

[19] See below p. 191, n. 24.

Plutarchian fashion the parallel lives of Budé and Thomas More.[20] If carried out the project could only have meant sincere tribute to both humanist-courtiers. But Erasmus dropped the idea, and his relations with Budé remained uneasy. Their direct correspondence ended in the year before Erasmus moved from Basle to Freiburg. In a letter to Germain de Brie Erasmus had formally apologized for any offense caused by the publication of his *Ciceronianus*. The letter was published without delay both in Basle and Paris, but Budé remained unreconciled.[21] Yet there were comparable elements in the further progress of both scholars. Each devoted his last work to the final formulation of his religious beliefs. It is here that the question of their mutual interdependence becomes most interesting. However, the Basle printers showed no regard for the old Budé who desired to be more than a philologian.

The Basle publishers reprinted some of Budé's works in an order of priorities strongly reminiscent of the attention paid to them in the correspondence of Amerbach, Erasmus, and their friends. Since Budé never co-operated with them they were free to select whatever texts they preferred for their unauthorized reprints. From an early date Budé and his circle had formed a high opinion of the accomplishments of Basle printers.[22] Early in 1520 Nicolas Bérauld, a special friend of Basle within the entourage of Budé, apparently pleaded with the master to give Froben some copy—perhaps a revised edition of his first series of *Annotationes* on the Pandect. But Budé declined and expressed on the next occasion his full satisfaction with Josse Bade who had recently acquired an adequate supply of Greek type from Germany. Until the death of Bade all first editions of Budé's works were printed by him.[23]

In 1521 Cratander reprinted Budé's collected letters. The volume tended to highlight personal relations among the Paris humanists and with their friends abroad, including Switzerland. Carefully selected by their author for their style and for the prestige of the addressees, these letters rarely reflected Budé's deeper thoughts or the scholarly projects of his circle. Significantly no further works by Budé were published in Basle during the following nine years.

In 1530 Budé's earlier works were all bypassed for the immediate reproduction of his new *Commentaria linguae Graecae*, offering a long series of reasoned interpretations of Greek vocables. As early as 1521 Erasmus had encouraged Budé to undertake such a work [24] and he continued to show the warmest interest in its progress.[25] However when the published book finally reached him he realized that the work was not, as he would have wished, a well-organized alphabetical lexicon

---

[20] Allen 4.579 : " Interim illa cogitatio subiit animum meum, ut vos duos [i.e. Budé and More] ceu duces quosdam eximios in hoc laudis genere componam, veluti si quis Camillum committat cum Scipione Africano." Cf. Bietenholz, *History and Biography* 93.

[21] Allen 7.434ff., 483ff., 493f. ; Hartmann 3.366.

[22] See above p. 39f., and Budé, *Opera* 1.261.

[23] Delaruelle, *Répertoire* 102ff. ; only *De transitu* was published by R. Estienne. Bade died in 1534-35. Cf. Allen 3.286.

[24] Allen 4.579f. : " Video qua in re plurimum adiumenti possis adferre Graecanicis studiis, nimirum si copiosissimo Lexico nobis non tantum recenseas vocabula, verumetiam idiomata et Graeci sermonis tropos non quibuslibet notos et obvios explices. Est quidem, fateor, hoc argumentum humilius et infra tuam dignitatem ; sed arbitror esse boni viri publicae utilitatis gratia semet aliquo usque demittere ; quod a sapiente suo exigit Plato." Cf. Allen's n. to this passage.

[25] Allen 6.477f. ; 7.501, 541.

with concise entries, and he therefore stated some reservations.[26]   But Bonifacius Amerbach praised the book [27] and Simon Grynaeus, Basle's professor of Greek, contributed a laudatory epigram to the title page of Bebel's reprint.   During the last stages of its preparation, Budé's work caused some fearful apprehensions on the part of Erasmus and some frantic activity on that of Amerbach.   From a hint of Gervase Wain [28] both expected that Budé might use the occasion to retaliate for the gaffe contained in Erasmus' *Ciceronianus*.   This fear proved unfounded, but the Basle reprint was undertaken for purely commercial reasons and obviously appeared against the wishes of Erasmus and Amerbach.   Though he refrained from public protest, Budé too reacted angrily to the pirated edition, which had been contrived in the *Ecu de Bâle* of Paris.[29]   The *Commentarii linguae Graecae* offered an auspicious introduction to Budé's Greek scholarship.   The book was followed in Basle by a number of text editions and later even lexica to which he had contributed more or less prominently.   But Budé himself was not satisfied by merely exercising his authoritative knowledge of Greek.   In 1533 he published two dialogues which contained a concise statement of his humanistic and philological ideals and hopes. *De philologia* and *De studio literarum* appeared together and were swiftly reprinted by one of the lesser Basle presses, exactly like the previous *Commentarii linguae Graecae*.   Although nothing is known on this occasion of the involvement of the *Ecu* book merchants, the participation of Resch and Wattenschnee may be surmised from the similarity of the two cases.   The same firm also had an interest in a third Budé reprint to be published from Basle in the following year, the *Annotationes* on the Pandect.

The *Annotationes* were Budé's earliest work, but since their first appearance they had been increased by a second part, and now formed by far the most voluminous of his publications.   The learned lawyers who befriended Amerbach and Erasmus were not always satisfied with Budé, but they showed little resentment against the outsider who had entered a field until now reserved to the professors of law.   They were themselves too strongly opposed to the traditional approach of the glossators not to welcome Budé's contention that philological rather than legal training would provide the accurate understanding of the Pandect which was badly needed.[30]   The work was not designed to serve lawyers alone, but rather enlarged upon the views of *De philologia*, which had just preceded it in Basle.   In its efforts to restore the original wording and to reveal the correct meaning of each passage, it followed the philological and historical criticism of Valla and Erasmus.[31]   In the pursuit of his historical method Budé often compared ancient institutions with those of modern France.   In the course of such arguments Bâlois readers had to brace themselves for outbursts of Budé's patriotism.   On the other hand they might feel compensated by his severe censure of the French ruling class and especially the prelates.   No doubt they appreciated some hearty expressions of Budé's Evangelism.[32]

---

[26] Allen 8.341 : " Budaeus emisit librum De phrasibus linguae Graecae, adprime doctum ; diligentior tamen in congerendo quam acutior in digerendo, mea quidem sententia."

[27] Hartmann 3.498.

[28] Allen 7.445.

[29] See above p. 42.

[30] Cf. Delaruelle, *G. Budé* 103, 127-130.

[31] Cf. Kelley, *op. cit.* esp. 818ff.

[32] Cf. Delaruelle, *G. Budé* 117ff. ; Bohatec 90f.

It is surprising that no edition of *De asse* was added to this group of Basle reprints. This investigation of the ancient monetary system with its wealth of antiquarian detail was greatly admired by contemporaries. The theme was new and proved highly seminal; the many digressions repeated more persistently the social and religious criticisms formerly contained in the *Annotationes* on the Pandect.[33] Some of Budé's basic calculations were wrong and it seems that Simon Grynaeus unearthed an old document which was at variance with Budé's conclusions,[34] but the work would have fitted admirably into the Basle publishing programme. A treatise with the same title *De asse* by Glareanus was only one of several Basle productions visibly influenced by Budé's studies.[35] The Basle publishers also produced two pamphlets with comparative monetary tables. Both were simple and practical. They could only serve in the class room or perhaps in business, but even the Frobens were not ashamed to market theirs as a *Breviarium* of Budé's great work. It is easier to understand why Budé's last major work, *De transitu Hellenismi in Christianismum*, failed to attract the Basle printers. In part it was an avowal of Catholic faith, and this aspect was eagerly noted in the Protestant camp.[36] But it also seemed to oppose the profound conviction of Erasmus and the Italian humanists that neither the form nor the spirit of classical antiquity were in themselves inconsistent with true Christianity as demonstrated by the church fathers.[37]

The Basle edition of Budé's Collected Works (1556-57) excluded *De l'institution du prince*, a treatise composed in French for King Francis I's personal enlightenment, but the *Forensia* were included, although only after some hesitation.[38] At the

---

[33] Cf. Delaruelle, *G. Budé* 158-198.

[34] Sphyractes to Bonifacius Amerbach, from Paris, 1531 : " D. Grynaeus haud magnam iniit gratiam apud Budaeum cum charta illa pervetusta de multiplicatione assis et partium eius " (Hartmann 4.11).

[35] H. Loriti Glareanus, *Liber de asse et partibus eius*, Basle, M. Isengrin, 1550. In his preface the author points out how many scholars had been puzzled by, and tried to solve, the problems tackled in his study : " Nemo tamen, ut verum fatear, hac in re conferendus est Budaeo, gravissimi styli et magni iudicii viro, qui quae semel in manum sumpsit solide docet, tum quae nescit ingenue se nescire fatetur — secus, hercle, quam quidam alii omni aetate facere solent. Eum nos secuti a longe, perpetuo nihilominus in ipsum coniectis oculis, schemata duntaxat alicientes quibus ipsius liber caret. Ni enim typi adsint, res ita impedita est divisionum sylva, vocabulorum turba, denique ingenti opinionum multiplicitate, ut lector non facile ... sese expediat... Nec caruit Budaeus eo nomine reprehensoribus, inter quos et D. Erasmus Rot. fuit, praeceptor noster." He goes on to recall the frequent visits he had paid to Budé at Paris and the kindness the latter had showed to him and his students. " Porro post Budaeum fuit et D. Erasmus sedulus eius negocii exhortator, antequam ipsum noscerem Budaeum, quippe qui primus quinque De asse Budaei libros illos, praelecta eius prima non absque summis tum viri, tum operis laudibus praefatione, mihi ostendit." For another work written in response to Budé's see below p. 198, n. 66.

[36] Cf. Bohatec 102 ; Melanchthon to J. Camerarius : " Budaei *Transitum Hellenismi an Christianismum* et Sadoleti commentarios in Romanos vidisse te spero ; sane tragice invehitur uterque ad nostros " (*Corpus Ref.* 2.936f.). Only months before the publication of *De transitu* Conrad Gesner had reported to Bullinger : " Budaeus quoque, non est quod dubitem, noster est totus " (Herminjard 3.239). Such illusions were now destroyed.

[37] Cf. Bohatec 55, 104f. Bohatec, on the other hand, draws attention to a number of passages (e.g. 39, 45ff., 53, 80, 83) which suggest that Budé was inspired by a specific text of Erasmus.

[38] A short prefatory note by N. Episcopius the younger defended the decision to include the work in the *Opera omnia*. Rather illogically this note also appears in another ed. in 8⁰, published in the same year. The publisher obviously believed that he could

author's death the work had lacked the finishing touches, but the Basel publishers finally copied the Paris edition arranged by one of Budé's disciples. It aimed at nothing less than a thorough reform of the habitual lawyers' Latin with its many concessions to post-classical usage. It was a large accumulation of notes and therefore altered the balance of Budé's life work in favour of his philologico-juridical efforts. However, the fruits of his Greek scholarship still occupied the larger space. The Basle edition also offered a remarkable epistle dedicatory which C. S. Curione addressed to Johann Fichard. Enlisting the conciliatory spirit of Basle, Curione pronounced the balanced judgment on Budé of a later generation. Fichard was said to be worthy of this dedication since he was a lawyer, a humanist, and above all an Erasmian. The comparison between Budé and Erasmus was so important to Curione that he returned to it repeatedly. Admitting that their rivalry caused some grief to Erasmus, Curione still insisted that it should be viewed as an honest contest to surpass one another in scholarly excellence.[39] The deplorable obscurity of Budé's style called for lengthy treatment in which Curione endeavoured to understand its causes and its aims. Curione, who himself wrote in a neat Ciceronian style may have failed to do justice to Budé's deeper thoughts. In reviewing the various works, he reserved his highest praise for Budé's letters, and this judgment was hardly exceptional. At least he drew attention to the moralizing and Evangelical digressions of *De asse*. Turning to *De transitu*, Curione mildly suggested that Budé considered Greek philosophy as the humble but indispensable handmaid of true Christian learning.[40] As a whole Curione's evaluation supplemented and on some points rectified the views expressed in Le Roy's life of Budé which followed it in the Basle edition.

As late as 1535 Erasmus wrote of his sincere admiration for Budé and of his faith in their friendship even though certain people had tried to obscure it.[41] Direct correspondence between them had ceased, but polite contacts continued. This was largely the work of Germain de Brie, the man most commonly associated with Budé in correspondence with the Bâlois and at the same time the most faithful friend Erasmus had in Paris. As a young student in Italy, he had met Erasmus in Venice.

---

sell an economically priced separate ed. of the work. In his efforts to keep the price down, he even omitted the substantial alphabetical index which may be found in the folio ed. Today it is not easy to accept that any one should have been willing to use Budé's work without its index.

[39] Budaeus " ... acutus est in dictis et interdum, quod Erasmus agnovit et sensit, amarus, insidiosus, contortus, violentus, et tum maxime cum cessisse ac sese recipere videtur. ... Huiusmodi certamen inter Budaeum Erasmumque extitit et tale quidem quale Romanis cum Latinis et Pyrrho, non quale cum Celtiberis et Cimbris : non uter esset, sed uter gloria et eruditione superaret, quod quidem certamen ingenuis et generosis animis incidere plerumque solet.''

[40] " ... succedunt totidem libri *De transitu Hellenismi ad Christianismum*, quibus nihil in eo genere gravius, augustiusve. In quibus quid aliud docet quam ab humana sapientia, quam sibi potissimum veteres illi Graeci vendicarunt, ad divinam et coelestem — quam vetustissima Dei oracula Christique, qui Dei est sapientia veraque coelestis Minerva, sanctissima placita — transeundum et ascendendum ? Non quidem ut illa abiiciatur tanquam inutilis et indecora, sed ut se huius administram et ancillam agnoscat, utpote cuius munus sit haec inferiora illustrare et quasi lucina in hac rerum humanarum nocte ignorantiaque dominatum habere...''

[41] Allen 11.215 ; cf. 4.275 : recommended by Erasmus in the most fervent terms, Vives presented himself to Budé in 1520. In a remarkable, very open conversation Budé spoke to him about his relation to Erasmus and showed him " literas ad se a furiis quibusdam ... scriptas, qui dividere vestros animos et ex unico duos facere moliebantur...''

On his return to France his humanistic interests naturally drew him into Budé's circle. A degree of intimacy with the master developed, but whereas Budé mostly preferred a scholarly privacy to the duties and rewards of court life, Brie made the opposite decision. He rose to wealth and respect, being a canon of Notre Dame and serving Francis I as an almoner. There were moments when Budé sent him a friendly admonition for his elaborately set lenten table or for his unpatriotic lamentations at the king's threat to tax the rich clergy.[42]

Through two decades Germain de Brie's correspondence with Erasmus continued with remarkable steadiness. In 1518 Brie and Thomas More fell out over the soldierly virtues of their respective nations. Erasmus did his best to appease them and eventually succeeded in ending the childish quarrel.[43] Thereafter Germain de Brie never missed an opportunity to do Erasmus a similar service. Remarkably free from personal ambition, he was well suited to help in weathering the crises which erupted over the publication of *Ciceronianus* and the *Commentaria linguae Graecae*.[44] Constantly encouraged by Erasmus, Brie translated several writings of Chrysostom. Some of these were published by Froben. Brie did not complain about the Froben firm when it would seem that he had good reason to do so,[45] but in the end even Erasmus was contributing to a Chrysostom edition designed to supersede that of Froben. It was published in 1536 by Chevallon in Paris, and Germain de Brie was one of its editors. Erasmus' death prompted him to compose a spontaneous obituary for his great friend, which he inserted in a letter to Langey. It impressed Bonifacius Amerbach and Beatus Rhenanus sufficiently to warrant publication in the *Catalogi duo* of Erasmus' works.[46] Brie declared that Erasmus had no peer as a writer and few only as a scholar. Coming from a close friend of Budé, the words seemed worth retaining.

Nicolas Bérauld, who was about the same age as Budé and Erasmus, was a sincere admirer of both and was, besides, a close friend of Germain de Brie and Berquin.[47] He too had gone to Italy in his youth. Back in France, he continued to acknowledge his debt to the challenge of Italian humanism by editing works by Lorenzo Valla, Baptista Mantuanus, Politian and others, as well as Lucretius and the elder Pliny.[48] As a humanist and as a scholar he enjoyed the patronage of Etienne Poncher, Cardinal Odet de Coligny, and Francis I, who made him royal

---

[42] Delaruelle, *Répertoire* 110ff., 156f. On de Brie see Allen 1.447f.; *DBF*; Bourrilly, *Langey* 114.

[43] See especially Allen 3.42f.; 4.128f., 580.

[44] See above pp. 190ff. and also Allen 8.392.

[45] See in particular Allen 6.375ff., 381f.; 8.390f., 470; 9.3ff., 30ff., and **No. 184ff**.

[46] *Catalogi duo operum Des. Erasmi Roterodami ab ipso conscripti*, Froben 1537. The ed. also offered some epitaphs by G. de Brie. Brie's letter is reprinted in Erasmus, *LB* I among the introductory pieces. For the decision to publish it see Hartmann 4.454f., 468; 5.18.

[47] On Bérauld see L. Delaruelle, Etudes sur l'humanisme français: Nicole Bérault, *Le Musée Belge* 13 (1909), 253-312; Allen 3.503f.; *DBF*; Renaudet, *Préréforme* 661. In 1515 or 1516 he married the widow of Jean Barbier and for some time carried on his press and bookstore. Still in 1526 Berquin could use the store as a *poste restante* address. He wrote to Erasmus: " Apud scutum Basiliense aut apud Beraldum sciet tabellarius ubinam fuero : quanquam Beraldus nunc plurimum abest ab urbe " (Allen 6.317).

[48] Renaudet, *Préréforme* 661; the Lucretius ed. was dedicated to François Deloynes, a close relative and confident of Budé who also corresponded with Erasmus (Allen 2.405n.); cf. Busson 29f. and passim.

historiographer in succession to Paolo Emili. He also boarded students both in his native Orléans and in Paris, where he taught Greek in the university. Like Budé, he often collaborated with Josse Bade. In 1512 Bade dedicated his edition of Politian to him and to Berquin,[49] who had probably been Bérauld's student. In view of his friendship with Berquin, Jean de Pins and Dolet, and also of his services to the Coligny family over a number of years it is not easy to ascertain Bérauld's Catholic orthodoxy.[50] In 1506 he received Erasmus in his house at Orléans. It is clear that his admiration for him was rewarded by lasting trust, even though their correspondence would seem to have been casual.[51]

Erasmus apart, Bérauld knew other affiliates of the Basle humanist circle. Among his pupils were Melchior Volmar and A. Morelet du Museau, among his friends Wilhelm Nesen.[52] To another pupil, the Bâlois Anton Chrysorianus he dedicated a re-edition of Valla's *Elegantiae* (Séléstat 1522).[53] After entering the service of the Cardinal Jean de Lorraine, Chansonnette was in touch with Bérauld.[54] Simon Grynaeus questioned Morelet du Museau about the life and faith of his former teacher , and as a result wrote directly to Bérauld, offering his friendship.[55] However, it was soon realized in Basle that Bérauld preferred to align himself with humanist rather than Evangelical circles. In Budé's collection of Latin letters, which was highly thought of in Basle, the very first pages recommended Bérauld to Richard Pace in England as a " *hominem mihi familiarem et Erasmi tui aliquando hospitem.*" [56] Bonifacius Amerbach placed Bérauld in the same environment. On one occasion he shared liberally in Amerbach's misgivings about Budé,[57] and French humanism in general. Again it was as a humanist that Bérauld once appeared among the Basle authors. In 1518 Froben reprinted his Paris edition of Politian's *Rusticus* provided as it was with rather trivial commentaries.

To Bérauld, his older friend, Louis Berquin may initially have owed his admiration for Erasmus. When he came to Paris he must have found that similar feelings were common among the men who sat in the *Parlement* or held court and municipal offices. Some, like Berquin himself or Morelet du Museau, were members of the lesser nobility. Others, like Louis Ruzé, were chiefly friends of Budé. Antoine Papillon, like Berquin, was inclined towards the Reformation.[58] All maintained contacts among the humanist circles and many were known in Basle. None outdid Berquin in devotion to Erasmus ; however, what he gleaned from the writings of Erasmus seemed rather like the message of Luther. Writing to Erasmus in 1519, Bérauld described Berquin as " *tui nominis studiosissimum,*" but the earliest extant correspondence between the master and his young admirer dates from 1525 and

---

[49] Renaudet, *Préréforme* 598.

[50] Delaruelle's arguments to this effect are unconvincing.

[51] Cf. Allen 11.268f.

[52] On Nesen see Allen 2.65n. ; 4.172n. ; Hartmann 2.8 ; cf. Allen 3.618 ; 4.3.

[53] Delaruelle, N. Bérault, *op. cit.* 303.

[54] Hartmann 3.369.

[55] Herminjard 3.194ff. (with erroneous dates ?) ; cf. Delaruelle, N. Bérault, *op. cit.* 281f.

[56] Budé, *Opera* 1.243.

[57] Hartmann 3.371. In 1516 Bérauld prepared a Paris ed. of Guillaume d'Auvergne, an author formerly published in Basle ; cf. Renaudet, *Préréforme* 658, and **No. 490f**.

[58] On Morelet du Museau see above p. 58f., on Papillon p. 40. On Ruzé see Allen 2.402 ; 3.506ff.

coincided with the first serious attacks upon the Evangelicals of Paris.[59]   Berquin's impetuosity embarrassed Erasmus considerably, but when his young friend was in serious trouble he recommended him, in letters that were far from timid, to the protection of Francis I and his sister.   Berquin was saved on one occasion, but refused to learn his lesson.   When he was executed Erasmus was deeply moved and somewhat confused.   Finally, however, he preferred to think that Berquin had died as an orthodox martyr and victim of the Sorbonne conspiracy against Christian humanism.[60]

It seems that Berquin's contact with Basle was limited to his correspondence with Erasmus.   Similarly other members of the Paris humanist circles, and often friends of Budé, may be mentioned here because their names occur in the enormous correspondence of Erasmus, and his influence may be surmised when some of their writings were reprinted in Basle.   Jacques Toussain, for example, figures in our bibliography—much as he did in real life—as the faithful disciple of Budé, to whom he owed his appointment as a royal professor of Greek.   In the storm over *Ciceronianus* Erasmus feared Toussain's pen more than any other, and was not easily persuaded by Germain de Brie that Toussain would keep the peace.[61]   On a visit to Paris, the printer N. Episcopius called on Toussain with a recommendation from Erasmus.[62]   Like Toussain, François Dubois may be listed here along with the Belgians Christophe de Longueil and Bartholomaeus Latomus, and with two early promoters of humanistic studies in Paris, Fausto Andrelini and Janus Lascaris, both brought in from Italy.[63]   Guillaume Cop has already been mentioned: there were other royal physicians to Francis I like him, such as Johannes Guinterius of Andernach and Jean Ruel, whose names appear in the Basle editions of Greek medical science.[64]

The contacts between the Basle printers and Lazare de Baïf [65] deserve a somewhat fuller treatment.   In his aspirations for scholarly fame and its earthly rewards Baïf modelled himself after Budé, but he cannot be seen merely as a member of Budé's circle.   Although a protégé of Cardinal Jean de Lorraine and subsequently a French ambassador and master of requests, Baïf remained, first and last, an independent humanist.   He was inspired by Budé's philologico-antiquarian method, but he adapted it to establish a reputation of his own.   Erasmus showed an unusually

---

[59] Allen 3.505 ; 6.150f.   On Berquin see Mann 113ff.

[60] Cf. Allen 6.362f. ; 7.118, 472, 523ff. ; 8.164, 210ff., 255 ; 9.10.

[61] Allen 7.540 ; 8.81, 470ff ; 9.34ff., 105.   On Toussain see Allen 3.281n. ; Lefranc, *Collège de France* 173ff. ; Delaruelle, *Répertoire* 33f.   He also seems to have corresponded with Glareanus : cf. Allen 9.184.

[62] Allen 6.345ff.

[63] On Latomus cf. Allen 5.1f. and Hartmann 2.84.   He studied in Basle and Freiburg where, like Bonifacius Amerbach, he belonged to the circle of Zasius.   From 1531 to 1541 he taught in Paris.   Budé promoted his appointment to one of the first royal lectureships and apparently remained his good friend (cf. Allen 11.215).   In 1535 Latomus stated in a letter to Erasmus that they had known one another for twenty years (Allen 11.145ff.).   Erasmus answered with a lively, informal letter which shows clear marks of personal trust (Allen 11.214ff.).

[64] On Guinterius see Hirsch s.v. Winther ; Erasmus states that Guinterius wrote to him from Paris (Allen 10.314).   Hieronymus Gemusaeus later complained to Amerbach that he had been unfairly critized by Guinterius (Hartmann 5.417).   For Ruel see Hirsch, and Allen 2.125f., 489.

[65] Cf. Allen 7.341f. and *DBF*.

high regard for Baïf's treatises. This may have been prompted to some degree by his uneasy relations with Budé and by the inadvertent desire to promote a rival to Budé's fame.

Erasmus' interest in Baïf is first documented in 1524, when Haio Herman, a young Dutchman, wrote about him as a fellow student in Padua. Replying to Herman, Erasmus was visibly pleased by the prospect of Baïf's producing a treatise on ancient clothing comparable to Budé's study of ancient coinage. Baïf had ventured to correct Erasmus' Latin translation in the *Adages* of the names of two Greek garments. Erasmus expressed his appreciation, and made appropriate changes in his 1526 re-edition of the *Adages*.[66] In the same year the first edition of Baïf's *De re vestiaria* was published in Basle. The manuscript had probably passed through the hands of Erasmus. In the case of a subsequent treatise, *De vasculis*, we know that it was sent to him and that he personally revised the text for Froben's press.[67] It was published there in 1531 together with a revised edition of *De re vestiaria*.

Beginning in 1528, parts of the correspondence between Baïf and Erasmus are preserved. Baïf had meanwhile entered the service of Jean de Lorraine, and Erasmus rejoiced at the suggestion that henceforward they would share the patronage of the influential cardinal.[68] At the same time he hastened to repeat his praise of Baïf's *De re vestiaria* in his *Ciceronianus*.[69] The publication of this work caused a major controversy over pretended slights to Budé and Longueil. Baïf, however, was conveniently dispensed from taking sides by his appointment to the French embassy in Venice. Erasmus regarded this mission as a well deserved " *otium cum dignitate.*" He may have been correct. In any event Baïf's diplomatic talents could not match his scholarly knowledge and his genial hospitality to a number of independent-minded French students and scholars.[70] The subsequent fiasco of Baïf's diplomatic career in the Haguenau conference of 1540 does not seem to have found an echo in Basle, although it was well advertised in Calvinist circles.[71]

From Venice Baïf maintained his contacts with Erasmus as well as with Sadoleto in Carpentras through the commercial network of the Vaugris family and its extension to Parmentier's *Ecu de Bâle* at Lyons.[72] To his earlier antiquarian studies he now added the most successful one, an essay on ancient ships, presented in the form of a commentary on a law in the Pandect. The subject befitted the leisure hours of an ambassador to the *Serenissima*. The beautiful first edition of *De re navali* (1536) with illustrations by Geoffroy Tory was produced by Robert Estienne and protected by a privilege from the *Parlement* of Paris. But the Froben firm almost immediately launched a reprint, undoubtedly with the agreement of Baïf, who improved his text

---

[66] Allen 5.514f. : " Lazarum Bayfum gaudeo vehementer hoc praestitisse in vestibus quod Budaeus in Asse. Cum primis exosculor hominis candorem cum exquisita coniunctum eruditione, quod in litteratos rarissimum est. ... Mutabo tamen hunc locum, ubi librum Lazari videro : quod equidem opto ut quam primum fiat."

[67] Allen 9.178f. ; as the preceding work it was dedicated to Cardinal Jean de Lorraine.

[68] Allen 7.342f.

[69] Erasmus, *LB* 1. 1012 A.

[70] Allen 9.122 ; cf. 9.414 ; Busson 75ff.

[71] See above p. 112 ; cf. V.-L. Bourrilly, Lazare de Bayf et le Landgrave de Hesse, *BSHPF* 50 (1901), 369-376.

[72] Benoît Vaugris carried letters and manuscripts between Venice and Erasmus' house in Freiburg (Allen 9.179) ; for Parmentier see above p. 42.

by some few revisions. Although Tory's plates were carefully re-cut, the Froben edition did not quite equal the beauty of Estienne's product. Even so it sold well and could be reprinted after four years in spite of a cheaper unillustrated edition which also issued from Basle.[73] Friendly relations with Erasmus continued after Baïf's return to Paris. The sincerity of Erasmus' esteem for him is revealed by a pointed remark addressed to L. Vives, advising him to enhance his fame by producing, for a change, a *useful* work like Baïf's treatises.[74] Baïf also supplied Simon Grynaeus with a manuscript needed for Froben's first Greek edition of Euclid which was published in 1533.[75]

Behind the active humanists stood the patrons. Their names figure prominently in the correspondence of Erasmus with Budé and his circle: Francis I, Guillaume Petit, the king's influential confessor, Etienne Poncher, the powerful Bishop of Paris, Jean Grolier, the financial expert and lavish book collector, and finally Jean de Lorraine and François de Tournon, the cardinals representing two of the great houses of the realm. Some Paris humanists willingly conveyed messages between their ecclesiastical patrons and the great scholar of Basle: Gervasius Wain wrote to him on behalf of the Cardinal of Lorraine, Pierre Duchâtel provided contact with the Cardinal de Tournon.[76]

Poncher, Petit, Tournon and Francis I eagerly schemed to bring Erasmus to Paris. With whom the idea originated is now hard to say. Petit had the deepest understanding of his learning, while the others respected his unique reputation. Beyond their unsuccessful wooing of Erasmus they showed little interest in Basle humanism. At Budé's request Poncher received Glareanus with kindness.[77] Royal support was obtained for him, but not enough to keep him in Paris for long. Despite the fervent recommendation of Erasmus the young Swiss could not obtain regular, prestigious employment. Yet no other member of the Basle humanist circle received comparable personal encouragement in Paris. The annual royal scholarships were given and taken as a fringe benefit in a political pact, not as proof of personal favour at the French court. Chansonnette was admitted to the king's presence, and given a letter for Erasmus with a postscript in Francis' own hand, but not the job he was probably seeking. Erasmus' intercession could not secure a royal privilege when the Froben press launched his enormous edition of Saint Augustine, nor could a royal privilege be obtained after Erasmus' death for the edition of his Collected Works.[78] Only in the second half of the century, after the death of Francis I, did royal privileges appear more frequently in Basle editions.

---

[73] **No. 77.** All four treatises reproduced in the Froben ed. were already contained in that of Estienne. For evidence that this second ed. of *De re navali* was revised cf. e.g. pp. 30 and 120 with pp. 24 and 135 of the Estienne ed. On the illustrations see A. Bernard, *Geoffroy Tory*, Paris 1865, 269f. The popularity of Baïf's three treatsises contained in **No. 77** is well documented by the existence of abridgments made by Charles Estienne and designed to meet didactic rather than scholarly needs. They were published in Lyons (1536) and Paris (1537).

[74] Allen 7.471.

[75] Allen 7.341n.; cf. 6.245n.

[76] Cf. Allen 7.190; 8.276 and passim.

[77] Allen 3.174, 280; on Erasmus' relations to Poncher cf. Allen 2.454ff., 4.73f. (the latter is a formal letter to Poncher which Erasmus gave to Bérauld for publication in one of his publications.) Pocher's grandson, Jean Cherpont, son of a pastor in the region of Neuchâtel, studied at Basle in 1575: cf. Droz, *Etudiants français*.

[78] Allen 7.502; 8.391; Hartmann 5.124.

There is no indication that the Bâlois had a specific and clear view of Francis I. Erasmus, though flattered by the king's continued admiration and always tempted by his offers, felt and frankly expressed superior loyalty to the emperor, his own lord of Burgundy. A similar loyalty to the Empire was latent in the anti-French patriotism of his Bâlois friends. The preface of Erasmus' paraphrase of Saint Mark,[79] addressed to Francis I, is a major document of his political thought. It focuses on Christian conscience and liberty faced with the realities of peace and war. Only his concessions to French Gallicanism, however, have a direct bearing on France, and here he may have mistaken the king's position for anti-clericalism. From 1526 onward he continued to see in Francis the protector of the French Evangelicals.[80] Only the consequences of the *Placards* affair seem to have exposed him to doubts about the king's influence or intentions. At the time of Langey's mission and the dedication to Francis I of Calvin's *Institutes*, many Bâlois may have shared Erasmus' view albeit perhaps with less assurance.

A somewhat different relationship developed between the Bâlois and Jean Grolier, the bibliophile to whom books perhaps meant as much as their authors. Grolier was the treasurer of Milan during the French occupation of the duchy (1515-21). In 1518 Erasmus honoured him with a formal letter, following a suggestion made by the north-Italian book merchant Francesco Giulio Calvo, who did business with Basle and other printing centres of the north, including Paris.[81] To judge from the impetuosity of Calvo's request,[82] Grolier must have been a good customer. While he seems to have appreciated Italian books above all others, a considerable number of Basle books too were deemed worthy of his prize collection.[83] In 1519 Beatus Rhenanus dedicated to him an edition of Maximus Tyrius then published by Froben. Rhenanus' passionate defence of Christian Platonism may have pleased Grolier and was rewarded by an elaborately phrased reply.[84]

With the death of Erasmus in 1536 contacts between Basle and the humanist circle around Budé and Francis I dwindled. Berquin, Poncher and Josse Bade, the printer of this circle, were already dead; Germain de Brie died in 1538 and Budé in 1540. Francis I, Bérauld, Toussain, and Baïf survived Erasmus for roughly a decade; Grolier lived much longer. But the flux of personal letters was exhausted, and with the exception of Baïf's slightly revised *De re navali* in 1537, and after another twenty years Budé's *Opera omnia*, no original or otherwise remarkable publications continued the earlier trend.

During the last years of Erasmus' life, controversy over his work had risen to a peak in Paris. He had given his personal support and collaboration to Chevallon's editions of Jerome (1533) and Chrysostom (1536), and unauthorized reprints of his

---

[79] Allen 5.352ff.; cf. 2.476f.; 5.365f.

[80] E.g. Allen 6.360ff; 7.469; 8.95; 9.225f.; 11.34, 79, 221.

[81] Allen 3.297ff. Grolier's son in the Roman curia seems to have inherited the father's interest in Erasmus (cf. Allen 11.137n.). On Calvo, his relations to Froben and his services to the Protestant cause see Allen 2.558; 11.186; Hartmann 2.284; *B.Rh.B.* 94, 167f.

[82] Allen 4.34.

[83] A British Museum Catalogue: *Bookbindings from the Library of Jean Grolier, A Loan Exhibition*, London 1965, lists 21 Basle productions out of a total of 138 exhibits, the largest single group from outside Italy. The Basle books were published between 1520 and 1557; almost half of them were *Frobeniana*.

[84] *B.Rh.B.* 133ff., 139f.

own writings [85] continued despite the suppressive measures taken by the Sorbonne. But, on the other hand, Paris emerged as the obvious publishing centre of polemical attacks upon him. Béda and Cousturier, the old foes, were now succeeded by a Carvajal, a Virues, an Alberto Pio, a J. C. Scaliger. Campester even published a perfidiously corrupted version of the *Colloquies* [86] in Paris. Erasmus alone was the centre of such preoccupation. After his death attention was no longer focused upon Basle.

---

[85] Cf. Allen 9.4n., 93 ; 10.123, 144f.

[86] Cf. e.g. Allen 9.226 ; 10.1, 17, 181 ; R. Wiriath, Les rapports de Josse Bade Ascenius avec Erasme et Lefebvre d'Etaples, *BHR* 11 (1949), 66-71.

CHAPTER FIVE

THE PARIS OPPONENTS
OF RELIGIOUS STRIFE IN THE SECOND HALF
OF THE SIXTEENTH CENTURY

When Erasmus died his personal position amid the opposing confessional camps was clear and adequately expressed in his many works, but the implications were subtle and in the heat of religious battles few people could grasp them. Similar complexities mark the religious thought of his contemporary, Guillaume Budé who waited until the last years of his life before he attempted to clarify his stand. Even Budé's king, Francis I proved equally hesitant, although less differentiating, in his religious policy. In the two decades following the death of Erasmus, coinciding with the Council of Trent, it became less and less possible to remain uncommitted or to maintain an individually balanced profession of faith. The head-on clash of religious parties in the French wars, finally, seemed designed to stamp out every remnant of indecisiveness. Yet so thoroughly did the wars achieve their destructive purpose that new, more conciliatory, attitudes were bound to spring from the ashes. The arguments of the French *politiques* evidence varying degrees of Erasmian inspiration. More often than not Erasmian ideals were subordinated to nationalist sentiment and political and economic considerations alien to the humanist of Rotterdam. But it was a Francophone in Basle, Castellio, who modified and re-interpreted some crucial concerns of Erasmus. His achievement was among the most original and significant of the century, but the modifications were serious. Towards the turn of the century a more authentic Erasmianism was revived by an irenic circle at Paris. While failing to reach their immediate goals, these men were highly instrumental in passing the Erasmian tradition on to Jean Leclerc and the European Enlightenment.

Meanwhile, when Erasmus died Basle no longer radiated fresh beams of sparkling inspiration, although it still harboured a tradition. The intellectual initiative, and in part the commercial one too, passed to the Francophone Italian expatriates, but local professors and printers continued as the faithful custodians of their huge inheritance. Thanks to them Basle remained the European centre of Erasmianism to which most sympathetic foreigners sooner or later would turn. If the developments analysed in this chapter thus bear witness to a fundamental change from the first half of the century to the second, a certain continuity in the relations described in the preceding chapters should not be overlooked. The scholars of Paris continued to sing the praises of their benefactors in epistles dedicatory and other suitable occasions. Such a display of prominent names still impressed the Basle printers. They continued to publish some of their works and for major enterprises they eagerly sought French royal privileges.[1] The Paris Aristotelian Joachim Périon dedicated most of his works to Cardinal Jean Du Bellay. Many of them were published in Basle during the 1540s and early 1550s, as were at other times works by Baïf, Des Masures, Foës, Ramus and others, which carried epistles dedicatory and epigrams addressed to various members of the house of Lorraine.[2] Irrespective of the tides of his political fortunes, Cardinal François de Tournon, too, continued to patronize many humanists.[3] Several of them became Basle authors : Lazare Baïf, Pierre Belon, Nicolas Bourbon, Symphorien Champier, Denis Lambin, Jacques Peletier, and marginally even M.-A. Muret. However, no personal ties developed now resembling those with Sadoleto or the patrons of the Budé circle. Together with Tournon, his master, the humanist Denis Lambin passed through Basle in 1552, and the occasion proved as uneventful as their subsequent passage through Calvin's Geneva.[4]

In the period of Henry II and the Council of Trent the scholarly slant of Basle publishing continued to promote an atmosphere of confessional neutrality. The Catholic humanists of the French capital still could count on the presses of Basle. That quite a few actually did send their manuscripts was chiefly to the credit of Oporinus, by far the most scholarly of all Basle printers. Year after year between 1542 and 1567 he launched his critical editions of classical authors as well as the works of contemporary philologians and historians. He was personally devoted to the publication of Greek works but at the same time was open-minded enough to welcome such unusual authors as a Guillaume Postel. Like Postel, and perhaps more deliberately, other Paris authors welcomed co-operation with a Protestant publisher, thus demonstrating the compatibility of scholarly endeavour and pious concern in spite of the separation of churches. Philippe Montanus in the College of Tournai borrowed from Amerbach a manuscript of Theophylactus which had formerly been used by Erasmus. Since he made use of the Basle codex to improve his Latin translation of the Byzantine bishop, it seemed fitting that he should offer his second, revised edition of Theophylactus to a Basle press. When it appeared in 1554 it repeated the elegant and elaborate preface of the first edition. This text was origin-ally composed at the time of the opening of the Council of Trent. It combined a clear rejection of Protestantism with powerful attacks upon the corrupted power structure of the Catholic church in a tone reminiscent of Erasmus' *Praise of Folly*. No wonder that the title page of the Basle edition drew attention to this preface " *in qua de operis utilitate agitur et aliis quibusdam non parum ad rectam ecclesiae restitutionem pertinentibus.*" [5]

In the same year of 1554 Joachim Périon wrote from Paris to Oporinus. In true Erasmian fashion he strove to ignore the gulf between the confessions. He apologized for his silence over the last two years and emphasized that he felt no hatred for those who had divorced themselves from the Catholic church. In particu-lar he expressed confidence that Oporinus would always abide by the holy faith he had imbibed with his mother's milk. Finally, he listed the editions of Oporinus which he had been able to purchase for the library of his master from the shop of

---

[1] See above p. 53f.

[2] E.g. **No. 75, 374, 441f., 638**.

[3] François, *F. de Tournon* 491ff.

[4] *Ibid*. 286n. and passim.

[5] **No. 750** ; cf. Bietenholz, *Erasmus und der Basler Buchhandel in Frankreich*, 301f.

Jacques Dupuys, among them Postel's *Protevangelion* and the Qu'ran, but regretted that Castellio's Bible was not available.[6]

Périon's confidence in Oporinus is understandable in view of such enterprises as two translations of Greek authors by Gentian Hervet which the Bâlois had published in 1548-49. Once again it is the epistles dedicatory of the two books which are relevant to our study. Both are addressed to Cardinal Marcello Cervini, with whom the French author was attending the Council of Trent. One of them, faithfully reprinted at Basle from a Venice edition of the preceding year, took issue with the fraud and impostures of the heretics, which had always been confounded in the past and would be confounded again with the help of Christ.[7] Ten years passed, and in spite of his well-known attitudes the original edition of another text translated by Hervet was published in Basle. By that time Hervet had entered the priesthood. A protégé of the Cardinal of Lorraine, he figured a few years later among the Catholic theologians attending the Colloquy of Poissy, and subsequently helped to place Catholic polemics in France on a higher intellectual plane.[8] The clue to his continued relations with Basle no doubt lay in the past. Hervet's beginnings were solidly Erasmian. In 1526 the young French humanist was in England, employed as a tutor by the Pole family, and there produced an English translation of Erasmus' *De immensa misericordia Dei*.[9] Still in the 1560s Theodor Zwinger established friendly contacts with Denis Lambin, the client of the Cardinal de Tournon.

Other Paris scholars may have turned to Basle inspired by the French Evangelical tradition rather than by Catholic Erasmianism, but the concrete results of their approaches were still editions of Greek scholarship undertaken by Oporinus. Bernard Bertrand had, like Beza, been a student of Oronce Finé. In 1553-54 he matriculated at Basle together with his friend René Perdrier, who was later to fight on the side of Henry IV. Both arrived together from Paris and seem to have remained in Basle for a few years, publishing there the results of their studies.[10]

Around the time of the Colloquy of Poissy the contacts between Paris and Basle entered a new phase of special promise. As formerly in the days of Budé, personal links united the Basle printers with friends in the immediate vicinity of those who ruled France. In some memorable Basle editions, directly motivated by events in

---

[6] UBB ms. Fr. Gr. II. 19², fol. 283f.; cf. Steinmann 65f. This is Périon's only letter preserved in Basle. Apart from **No. 868** and **922**, he also bought copies of **No. 335** and **786**.

[7] **No. 516.**

[8] Cf. Michaud; Kingdon, *Geneva and the Consolidation* 84f.

[9] J. K. McConica, *English Humanists and Reformation Politics*, Oxford 1965, 66ff. and passim.

[10] *Matrikel* 2.82. Bertrand was in Zurich during October 1557 and there met with Bullinger and Lelio Sozzini; in January 1558 he met at Strasbourg with François Hotman: *Hotomanorum epistolae* 15-17. His dedication of Dionysius Periegetes (**No. 152**) to Jean Dodieu, " regius consiliarius apud Lugdunenses " is dated from Basle, 1556. In the preface of the same book he refers to Oronce Finé as his preceptor. The epistle dedicatory to the King of Denmark in Betrand's Lycophron (**No. 153**) is dated from Strasbourg, 1558. For Perdrier see *France prot.* His ed. of Orpheus is dedicated to Jacques d'Albon, Sieur de Saint-André, "provinciae Lugdunensis praefectus", and dated from Basle, Cal. Oct., 1554. There is as yet no trace of Perdrier's subsequent quarrels with Saint-André. The UBB copy of this book, B.C. VI. 77 (5), was given by Perdrier to Bonifacius Amerbach. Betrand contributed a preface to Perdrier's Orpheus as well as some verses to Perdrier's Coluthus Thebanus (**No. 802f.**).

Paris, concern for religious peace and equanimity was no longer expressed as a minor corollary to philological scholarship, but rather represented the fundamental message of the book concerned. Three publications, in particular, formed Basle's contribution, or reaction, to the historical events of 1561-62, and the initiative for each rested mostly with Francophones. F. Baudouin's edition of *De officio pii ac publicae tranquillitatis vere amantis viri* by G. Cassander and Castellio's *Conseil à la France désolée* were discussed on preceding pages. Here it is enough to recall the differences in their approach to the common goal of religious toleration. Passing through Basle on his way to Paris and Poissy, Baudouin evidently hoped for the success of the colloquy, for some progress in formulating a broadly acceptable creed, or perhaps other ways of reasserting the common ground between the confessional camps. Castellio, by contrast, writing after the colloquy had failed, certainly did not entertain any illusions about the chances of a *rapprochement*. All the more he urged mutual respect for freedom of conscience and the avoidance of bloodshed.

A kind of synthesis between these two approaches was reached in a third work, not published until 1563, though its planning may have begun in the days of energetic optimism preceding the Colloquy of Poissy. The only French translation of Erasmus' complete paraphrases to the New Testament [11] was a major undertaking since only the paraphrase of the canonical letters could be copied from an earlier translation previously published at Lyons. In accomplishing the huge work the Froben firm no doubt relied on some of the several Francophones it employed at that time, among them Castellio's friend, the well educated corrector Léger Grymoult. Awareness of the new political course in Paris, and indeed the spirit in which the translation was undertaken, are reflected by the epistle dedicatory. Reminiscent of Erasmus' own dedication to Francis I of the original paraphrase on Saint Mark, with its pleas for freedom of conscience, the new epistle was addressed to Charles IX, a boy of thirteen who had just recently been declared of age. It was signed by " the translators, his humble subjects " and was obviously destined for the French market. The translators may have been inspired by Castellio's French Bible ; at least the preface betrays their familiarity with his writings over and above their general commitment to Protestantism. Essentially, however, their approach resembled more closely that of Baudouin and Cassander as they urged the young king, and in fact those who ruled France in his name, to remedy the religious strife by encouraging his subjects to heed the voice of Erasmus.

It is obvious that these Basle publications were issued in response to specific policies usually associated with the Queen Mother, Catherine de ' Medici, her chancellor, Michel de L'Hospital and, to a lesser degree, the Cardinal of Lorraine. Their appearance documents a solid grasp of the French scene on the part of the Basle publishers. If they tended to stress the moral responsibilities created by the religious conflict, perhaps to the point of somewhat neglecting political realities, they only followed the example set by Michel de L'Hospital. Since he was personally inspired by the ideals of Erasmus [12] the three Basle publications represent a response to French Erasmianism. Above all they reflect, perhaps not direct communication with some principal actors in Paris, but an unmistakable affinity of aims enhanced by the existence of friends in common.

---

[11] **No. 424.** For the text of the epistle dedicatory and a fuller analysis of this ed. see Bietenholz, *Erasmus und der Basler Buchhandel in Frankreich* 305ff., 318ff.

[12] A. Buisson, *Michel de L'Hospital*, Paris 1950, 66ff. and passim ; Lecler, *Tolérance* 2.36ff. For the Zurich response to the Colloquy of Poissy cf. Bouvier 279ff.

One of these was Jean Morel of Embrun.[13] Once the confidential secretary of Langey at Basle, he now lived at Paris as the master of a brilliant and open house frequented by many members of the Ronsard circle. Joachim Du Bellay, in particular, was a regular guest under its hospitable roof. Many of his verses were addressed to Morel, and after the poet's death Morel collected his works and saw to it that they were published. Michel de L'Hospital, himself a respected poet both in Latin and French, was Morel's neighbour and his close friend. Literary tastes were an important, but clearly not the only bond between the two men. Morel had introduced his friend at court. He had officiated as the *maréchal des logis* of Catherine de' Medici while she was still the *Dauphine*. Now that power rested in her hands she chose L'Hospital as her chancellor and influential advisor. No evidence has come to light of direct relations between Morel and the Bâlois after he had settled in Paris, but his Erasmian inclinations were evidenced by the careful humanistic education of his three daughters, who grew up amid the intoxicating flattery of scholars and poets. In 1556 Morel found them a promising young tutor in the person of the younger Karel Utenhove, recently arrived from Basle. After the restrictions endured in Basle under such a master as Castellio,[14] the liberal and aristocratic atmosphere of Morel's home must have been a revelation to Utenhove. When he left Paris he remained in close touch with Morel. In 1568 he was in Basle and published there a volume of Latin poems by L'Hospital, Joachim Du Bellay, and other members of their literary circle, containing also many epigrams of his own not only in praise of Morel and his daughters and their friends in Paris, but also of Hubert Languet and Georgius Cassander.[15] Twenty years later Utenhove still showed fidelity to the ideals of his French and Bâlois friends when attempting to collect the unpublished letters of Erasmus.[16]

After the death of Morel and L'Hospital the memory of this circle was revived in Basle when Pierre Gaultier-Chabot arrived to publish, or re-publish, his voluminous commentaries on Horace gathered over decades of single-minded devotion to that one author. After studying under Ramus and Talon, Gaultier-Chabot had discovered his Horace in the congenial atmosphere of L'Hospital's country home at Vignay while tutoring the chancellor's grandsons. To his former pupils, the brothers Hurault-de L'Hospital, he dedicated an analytic exposition of Horace which was republished at Basle in 1589.[17] Two years earlier the same Basle press reprinted a curious little book, again no doubt at the instigation of Gaultier-Chabot. It contained an essay on the controversial pronunciation of the Greek language, and was published in the names of the Hurault brothers, though it should perhaps be credited to Gaultier's pen as much as to the exercises of his pupils. Catherine's

---

[13] A. Buisson, *op. cit.* 24f., 77 ; H. Chamard, *Joachim Du Bellay*, Lille 1900, 389ff. 489f. and passim ; cf. above pp. 108ff.

[14] Buisson, *Castellion* 2.89f., 277n. W. Janssen, *Charles Utenhove, sa vie et son œuvre (1536-1600)*, Diss. Nijmegen, Maastricht 1939, 19ff. and passim.

[15] **No. 200** ; see vol. 2 of this study.

[16] Among several ms. letters by Utenhove in the UBB there is an appeal in verse to send him any unpublished letters of Erasmus. It is dated from Düsseldorf, 10 April, 1587, and addressed to " Eusebio Episcopio et Aurelio Frobenio reliquisque typographis Basiliensibus omnibus et singulis, Basileam Rauracorum vel Francofordiam : Fr. Gr. II. 26, No. 518.

[17] **No. 454**, published with a royal privilege for ten years. The epistle dedicatory is dated from Paris, 1581, but there is an additional preface to the second edition, dated from Strasbourg, 1588.

great chancellor had died in disgrace fourteen years earlier, but the Basle title page still perpetuated his fame and claimed his personal interest in the pronunciation controversy : " *ad clarissimum virum D. Michaelem Hospitalium Franciae cancellarium ipsius olim disceptatorem, ut aliarum controversiarum verissimum ac sapientissimum iudicem.*" [18]

From time to time the Bâlois reprinted a French work dedicated to either Catherine de' Medici or L'Hospital.[19] However, only some publications falling in the years of 1561-62 may be noted here since all evidence for contacts between Basle and France at that time seems valuable. In 1561 the Froben firm republished two legal studies by André Tiraqueau, a famous councillor in the *Parlement* of Paris who had recently died. At the same time this press issued another volume with unpublished material edited by a son of the late jurist. A friend of Tiraqueau, L'Hospital had contributed some verse to one of the two volumes now republished at Basle.[20] While the legal topics of the three publications, predominantly marriage and inheritance, do not appear to be relevant to the political situation of 1561, one observes an affinity with another original Basle publication, Etienne de Malescot's *De nuptiis liber paradoxicus* (1572) which also pays tribute to Michel de l'Hospital.[21] Tiraqueau's books were followed in 1562 by the *Epitomes oeconomicae artis iuris civilis libri duo ad Michaelem Hospitalem* by Jacobus Concenatius, a collection of legal *loci communes* since Moses, designed to prove that jurisprudence was the " true philosophy." Like in Malescot's work L'Hospital here is envisaged as the reformer of the French judicial system rather than the Erasmian convener of the Colloquy of Poissy. But that Concenatius whose other legal works appeared in Lyons should address to the chancellor an epistle dedicatory dated from Basle at the beginning of May 1562, and moreover that a royal privilege for this book was obtained from Paris, adds to the evidence of direct links between Basle and the French capital at the time when Baudouin visited Basle and Erasmus' *Paraphrases* were being translated into French.[22] In no small degree it was the ideals of the Erasmian Basle that were tested at the Colloquy of Poissy, and failed to work.

This is not to overlook the measure in which the colloquy was meant to serve the national and purely political aspirations of the French court. It was held during a national assembly of the French clergy convened in open opposition to the Council of Trent. It resulted from the Gallican tradition endorsed by the Cardinal of Lorraine no less than by the chancellor and his lawyer friends at court.[23] It

---

[18] **No. 583**, the preface is dated from Vignay, 1578, and mentions Gaultier-Chabot.

[19] Dedicated to L'Hospital : **No. 319, 320, 1016** ; to Catherine : **No. 655**.

[20] **No. 1006** ; cf. J. Brejon, *André Tiraqueau, 1488-1558*, Paris 1937.

[21] **No. 711**, the compliment for L'Hospital in a long epistle dedicatory adressed to Frederick of the Palatinate and the Vidame of Chartres, dated from Paris, 1570 ; cf. **No. 4017**.

[22] **No. 320.** UBB : N.L. IV.11 (2) contains a complete copy of the work ; glued to the inner cover is a single title page with the date of 1552. No doubt such title pages with the misprinted date were removed in the press as soon as the error was discovered. The privilege, in French, is printed in extenso and dated from Saint Germain, 14 June, 1561. I cannot identify Concenatius, but see Baudrier 5.240 and 9.230 with indications that he was in contact with Gribaldi. While Concenatius is not listed, *Matrikel* 2.126f. registers for 1560-1561 two matriculants from Paris : Claude Paulmier, an *avocat*, subsequently sentenced for heresy, and Bertrandus Parvus.

[23] The chancellor opened the colloquy with a speech in which he compared the king with Constantine the Great presiding over the Council of Nicaea : Baudouin's *Constantinus*

followed in the wake of an assembly of the Estates General, but the fact that it followed shows that religion was considered the key to the political and economic problems of the crown. Subsequent *politiques* were to think differently. Herein lies, in fact, the Erasmian quality of L'Hospital's policy, that he placed crucial emphasis on the unity of all Frenchmen in the spirit of Christ rather than in loyalty to the crown alone, and that he thought it within the power of scholarly, well-intentioned representatives from both sides to overcome religious dissension. In Basle, likewise, churchmen, professors and printers all seemed agreed in their abhorrence of religious strife and in their faith that scholarly learning always contained the seeds of true Christianity. It was as scholars that Catholic authors like Montanus, Postel, Périon, Lambin, and even a Hervet, were admissible along with a Castellio and his radical Italian friends, while polemicists without the saving grace of scholarship were ignored, at least until the last quarter of the century. Erasmus understood history as essentially a perpetual contest between those who through the ages disseminated classical learning, like the Christian fathers in their time, and those who devoted their energies to selfish fanaticism, like the early Christian martyrs.[24] Similarly, all further co-operation between Basle printing and the French capital depended on a positive and scholarly response to Erasmus' ideal of *philosophia Christi*.

While willing to support the political and legal ideology behind the Huguenot war effort, the Basle printers largely failed to promote the work of Calvinist theologians. Attention has been given in an earlier chapter to the Basle publications of such well known Paris lawyers as Charles Du Moulin and especially François Hotman;[25] apparently there was no corresponding interest in the Huguenot ministers of the French capital. Although a French Calvinist church had been established in Basle in 1572, it was not until the turn of the century that the minister Jacques Couet travelled back and forth between Basle and Paris, and another twenty-five years elapsed before some writings of his Paris confrères Pierre Du Moulin and Charles Drelincourt would be issued from Basle in German translation.[26] At least the Catholic theologians fared no better than the Calvinists, nor did the Basle presses collaborate with the handful of Protestant radicals in the French capital.

Traces of an interest in the Antitrinitarianism of Servetus and the Anabaptism of David Joris can be discovered in Paris as well as in Lyons. The radicals of Lyons will be dealt with subsequently;[27] they maintained contacts with the Bauhin family and, especially, with Castellio. By and large they soldiered on in the Calvinist cause although, of course, they failed to please the generals. The contacts between Basle and some radicals in Paris were different. They deserve a passing glance here since their limitations tend to underline the pre-eminence of the Erasmian and intellectual ties. Some French translations of Jorist pamphlets have come to light, a specimen of a circular letter to the faithful in France, and scraps of some letters from the time of the posthumous trial of Joris. The latter were written by a son of

---

Magnus had served its purpose; cf. Lecler, *Tolérance* 2.52 and passim; Evennett, *Lorraine* 283ff. and passim.

[24] Bietenholz, *History and Biography* 37f. and passim.

[25] See above pp. 61f., 115ff.

[26] See above p. 98f. and **No. 390ff., 403ff.** Cf. **No. 698**: one part of Jean de L'Espine's *Excellens Discours* appeared at Basle in German translation (1598) merely because its Frankfurt publishers had just opened a press there.

[27] See below pp. 222ff.

Joris who called himself Jörg von Brügge and addressed to Mathias Rousillon, a surgeon at Paris.[28] In so far as this material was published, the printing was not done in Basle. In addition, Joris' secretary at Basle, Hendrik van Schor, a native of Limburg, should be mentioned. As early as 1541 he had been hired in Paris, apparently because of his capacity to translate from Dutch into French. He left Basle after the post-mortem trial of his master, and settled in the Catholic part of Alsace. There he transcribed Servetus' *Christianismi restitutio* from a printed copy which belonged to the second husband of the widow of Monsieur de Falais. Schor's manuscript was in turn copied by a French visitor whose apograph is preserved in Paris, as may be the case with the printed copy Schor had used.

These details confirm the existence of scattered Jorists within the French boundaries. Beyond this they emphasize the isolation and the sectarian character of the Jorist circle in Basle. Apparently Schor had no access to, or no use for, Servetus' treatise when he lived in Basle, even though it was available to Castellio's friends, Curione and the Basle minister Martin Borrhaus, and was probably read by Castellio himself.[29] Similarly one is inclined to envisage the scattered Jorists of the French capital as isolated sectarians rather than non-conformist Calvinists like Castellio and many of his scholar friends who seem to have ignored them.

A much better documented tradition runs from L'Hospital's circle to another one gathered some forty years later around such men as J.-A. de Thou and Jean Hotman de Villiers. Only then perhaps did relations between Basle and Paris regain some of the significance they had lost with the death of Erasmus. Of several figures who stood somewhere between L'Hospital and the later circle, Estienne Pasquier may be mentioned first. The contacts between Basle and the celebrated councillor of the *Parlement* of Paris are well documented. While they continued for more than a decade they focused, once again, on the year of 1561. However, Pasquier's place in the history of toleration differs markedly from that of L'Hospital. Apart from his regular correspondence with two Francophone Protestants closely connected with Basle, Pasquier's letters reveal his links with Pierre Pithou, Turnèbe, Cujas, J.-A. de Thou, Ramus, and many others. While never inclined to think lightly of his own commitment to Catholicism, nor of its rejection by others, Pasquier basically felt and acted like other French *politiques*.

In 1561 an *Exhortation aux Princes et Seigneurs du Conseil Privé du Roy, pour obvier aux séditions qui semblent nous menacer pour le faict de la Religion* was published. Coinciding with the various assemblies held in that year, it was widely read, several times reprinted, and translated into Latin and German.[30] The question of whether or not Pasquier was its author has given rise lately to considerable debate. In what follows the attribution has been retained in view of its age and solidity and of Pasquier's acknowledged ability to present his views on the religious conflict in somewhat contradictory terms. In Basle too the text aroused attention. Castellio twice mentioned it approvingly in his *Conseil à la France désolée* of 1562. Fifteen years later his disciple Mino Celsi quoted it extensively.[31]

---

[28] Droz, *Hendrik van Schor* 101ff. and passim for what follows.

[29] *Ibid.* 113f.; Buisson, *Castellion* 2.478; S. Kot in *Autour de Servet et de Castellion* 90f.

[30] See D. Thickett, *Bibliographie des œuvres d'Estienne Pasquier*, Geneva 1956, No. 50ff. None of the French editions I have seen can be attributed to Basle, but No. 53 looks very much like other anonymous productions of Wechel in Frankfurt. E. M. Beame, The Limits of Toleration in Sixteenth-century France, *Studies in the Renaissance* 13 (1966), 250-265, gives a summary of the controversy over Pasquier's authorship.

[31] Buisson, *Castellion* 2.234, 237ff., 312.

The Latin translation was made without delay and perhaps in Basle. At least it is reasonably certain that it was published there. To judge from the typographical material employed Oporinus may have been the printer.[32] To the Swiss the *Exhortatio* paid the flattering, but unjustified, compliment that they permitted two different forms of religion in every village.[33] If Pasquier designed his manifesto for distribution by Protestant publishers both in France and abroad,[34] this might account for the liberal slant of the *Exhortatio* which finds few parallels in Pasquier's other statements of this period. It would also seem typical that in Basle the *Exhortatio* appealed to Castellio, who, unlike the more conservative Erasmians, showed no special affinity with the Paris circle of L'Hospital. The *Exhortatio* rejected the idea of a National Council as advocated by the chancellor. In its emphasis on national sentiment, history, and the economy it departed from the Erasmian tradition and heralded the views of the *politiques*. Likewise outspoken laicism was reflected by the absence of biblical references and by attacks on pope and clergy.[35]

The *Exhortatio* will have to be re-examined in conjunction with other Basle publications concerning the debate on toleration. What is relevant in this context, however, is Pasquier himself, regardless of whether he was the author of the *Exhortatio*. Here was a conservative Paris lawyer, inclined to blame the divisions and the bloodshed in his country upon the government's concessions to the Huguenots. Yet at the same time he carried on an elaborate exchange of letters with a Protestant compatriot in the Rhine city, always eager to learn "*ce que l'on dit à Basle*"[36] about any event, and aiming to maintain judicial objectivity in his own summaries of events at home. His chief Protestant correspondent was the Vermandois noble Christophe de Fonsomme, who registered at Basle University in 1553.[37] Fonsomme also visited Rome and Paris, but seems to have lived in Basle off and on until well into the 1560s. Nothing is known about his activities. We are hardly better informed about Pasquier's other Protestant correspondent in exile, Claude de Kerquefinen. There is nothing to prove that he lived in Basle, but his French translations of treatises by P. M. Vermigli[38] and Juan Valdès seem to link him with the Italian émigré circle in the Rhine town. In particular the *Cent-et-dix consydérations divines de Jan de Val d'Esso*, translated from C. S. Curione's Basle edition

---

[32] **No. 792.** UBB owns a copy, N.u.VI.1 (12), which shows on the titlepage the words "D Castalionis", written by a librarian, probably in the 17th century. In her *Bibliographie, op. cit.* D. Thickett reproduces the titlepage of a famous copy in the library of Troyes, identifying Pasquier as the author and Castellio as the translator. There is no basis for the reference to Castellio, except perhaps the desire to add weight to a further remark, added by the same hand: "Liber prohibitus." The style of the translation is unlike Castellio's. The attribution of the *Exhortatio* to the press of Oporinus is based on a comparison with some of the printer's acknowledged productions dating from the same years, especially with **No. 737.**

[33] *Exhortatio* 44.

[34] Cf. above p. 209, n. 30.

[35] D. Thickett, Estienne Pasquier and His Part in the Struggle for Tolerance, *Propagande religieuse* 377-402, esp. 386ff.; Lecler, *Tolérance* 2.43ff.

[36] E. Pasquier, *Lettres historiques pour les années 1556-1594,* ed. by D. Thickett, Geneva 1966, 42; cf. 22. See also E. Pasquier, *Les lettres*, Paris 1619.

[37] *Matrikel* 2.78 and Droz, *Etudiants français*.

[38] *Dialogue des deux natures de Christ*, Lyons 1565; no copy is known at present. Cf. S. F. Baridon, *Claude de Kerquefinen, italianisant et hérétique*, Geneva 1954, 16 and passim for what follows.

of Valdès' work, deserve attention. The first French edition, published in 1563 at Lyons, though undoubtedly Protestant in its inspiration, had a mild, moralizing emphasis which could be interpreted as gesture of religious reconciliation comparable to the spirit of Erasmus' *Paraphrases* and other Basle publications in French or Latin dating from the period of the Colloquy of Poissy. Kerquefinen himself saw fit to publish a new edition of his translation as late as 1601, well after his return to the Catholic church.

The noble exiles with whom Pasquier corresponded had little in common with the frugal Castellio. In the absence of more specific evidence of his possible interest in Castellio, it is hardly significant that Pasquier knew enough of his French Bible to drop a critical remark about the style of its translation ;[39] it was the fashionable thing to do. However, one must also remember that Pasquier was a very cautious man. Finally, Pasquier's friendship with the younger Pierre Pithou was well established long before Pithou's conversion to Catholicism and his entry into the service of Henry IV. The presence of the Pithou brothers at Basle, and their scholarly activity there, have been referred to in another context. Pierre Pithou, one recalls, associated and afterwards corresponded with Basilius Amerbach and Theodor Zwinger, representatives of the open-minded but not very outspoken academe, the same sort of people Michel de Montaigne met on his visit to Basle some fifteen years later.[40]

So far, all this adds up to a rather vague impression of mutual respect between the Basle humanists and the Paris circles of *politiques* and lawyers. As they saw it, Basle was the place in which to trade informed opinions in a gentlemanlike manner, and to publish scholarly works. It was a good place to have friends in, and even to retire to in an emergency, but it was no longer the source of profound inspiration it still had been, to some extent, in 1561. Erasmianism seemed to work in Basle, but beyond its theoretic validity it offered no practical remedies for the French dilemma. Castellionism was even more lost on these men. The visit of another famed professor from Paris, Pierre Ramus, coinciding with the sojourn in Basle of Pierre Pithou and his brothers, tends to confirm this conclusion, and the arrival of François Hotman ten years later does not contradict it.

The little we know about the two short visits paid to Basle by Jacques-Auguste de Thou would seem to conform to this pattern. In 1579, the year after he had accepted a position in the *Parlement* of Paris, J.-A. de Thou visited Lorraine and, following the path of conciliar tradition, pushed as far as Constance and Basle. He met Basilius Amerbach for whom he had an introduction by François Pithou. In Amerbach's house he inspected various objects which had once been the property of Erasmus. Afterwards Felix Platter showed him his collection of natural science, including a live marmot, and Theodor Zwinger took him to the press of Pietro Perna.[41] He found the printer admirably active in spite of his advanced age. The man thus honoured by J.-A. de Thou's visit was the publisher of many historical works to which in that same year the famous *Artis historicae penus* was added. Nobody probably told the guest that Perna had recently been in prison after the clandestine publication of Castellio's *Dialogi quatuor*.[42] Ten years later J.-A. de Thou passed

---

[39] Buisson, *Castellion* 1.318n. ; 2.289 ; Guggisberg 40.

[40] See above pp. 72f., 84f.

[41] J.-A. de Thou, De vita sua 33f., in vol. 7 of *Historiae*, London 1733.

[42] See above p. 134f. : **No. 169, 248.**

once more through Basle and attended a lecture or two by J. J. Grynaeus who commented on the *Commentaria* of Sleidanus and added many details about the courts of Germany.[43]

This second visit preceded by three years the arrival of Jean Hotman de Villiers with whom J.-A. de Thou was later to co-operate in Paris on a number of important projects. However, unlike his future friend, Hotman did not come to Basle merely as a distinguished tourist. It was here that Hotman, the Huguenot, began to find fault with the Genevan ecclesiology, and discovered instead the potential merits of a Gallican Council in order to restore the universal brotherhood of Frenchmen in accordance with the oldest and purest dogmatic liturgical traditions. This position would later enable Hotman to collaborate closely with de Thou, a Catholic and a Gallican, when the idea of a National Council was aired again in attempts to prevent the king from promulgating the decrees of Trent.[44]

The oldest son of François Hotman was not a total stranger when he arrived in Basle towards the end of 1592, primarily to settle his father's estate. He had corresponded with family friends in the Rhine town, and he seems to have lived there briefly towards the end of his adolescence, after François had moved to Basle in 1578.[45] In the following year he began his apprenticeship as a courtier and diplomat, moving first to England and later, as Leicester's secretary, to the Netherlands. From the years he spent there dates his friendship with a fellow Huguenot who had become chaplain to William of Orange, the Erasmian Pierre Loyseleur de Villiers. By the time of Henry IV's succession to the French throne Hotman had transferred to the service of the Bourbon king. However, when he arrived in Basle his status was still modest and his purse depleted, and his sense of personal inferiority must have further accentuated the difference between his appearance and the lordly deportment of such visitors as J.-A. de Thou. The settlement of the paternal estate brought new disappointment. Perhaps this tended to lower his consideration for the old friends of his father;[46] at any rate it did not discourage him from seeking the acquaintance of men of a rather different hue. Zwinger and Amerbach were dead, but a nephew of Pierre Pithou, Pierre Nevelet de Dosches, who was living at Basle in the days of the older Hotman, was still there when the younger arrived. After his return to France he was to recall the town of his exile with nostalgic love, and to acknowledge the inspiration he had received from Jean's company, yet he remained a rather timid supporter of his friend's irenic ideals.[47] Likewise another

---

[43] J.-A. de Thou, De vita sua, *op. cit.* 108f. This second visit was apparently quite short since it gave the author no opportunity to correct his mistaken impression that his old friend Basilius Amerbach had died in the meantime. Amerbach only died on 25 June, 1591.

[44] Vivanti 228ff., 292ff., 325ff. On Hotman and his stay in Basle cf. also F. Schickler, Hotman de Villiers et son temps, *BSHPF* 17 (1868), 97-111, 145-161, 401-413, 513-533.

[45] Vivanti 191f. UBB ms. G. II.19, fol. 250ff. contains some letters to Basilius Amerbach, written by the young Jean in the name of his father, 1575. For their subsequent correspondence see *Hotomanorum epistolae.*

[46] *Hotomanorum epistolae* 351ff., 358ff. It may be recalled that the trustee of the estate, Jacques Battier, was an important opponent of Lescaille in the French congregation: cf. above pp. 88, 100n.

[47] Schickler, *op. cit.* 108; Vivanti 219ff., 331ff., and 289f. where Nevelet's letter to Hotman from September 1598 is quoted: " Où trouveray-je desormais à qui me plaindre de mes ennuis cuisans ? aux discours et aux consolations de qui chercheray-je allegement ? O Basle, Basle ! et vous dites que je n'ay eu raison de lui offrir ces vers que me dites avoir veu [I am not aware of any other expression of such discontent with Basle from the part

212

friend, the Zurich minister Johann Wilhelm Stucki, shared and even to a certain extent inspired Hotman's irenic commitment but tended later to take the more firmly anti-Catholic line of Philippe de Mornay.[48]

Hotman's own irenic programme was given its first comprehensive expression in his *Avis et dessein nouveau sur le fait de la religion pour estre proposé au prochain Concile national ... de l'Eglise Gallicane* which he wrote, and apparently published, in 1592 or 1593,[49] that is to say, at the time of his stay at Basle. In his efforts to render the Protestant position more flexible Hotman here adopted some of the anti-presbyterian views of Morély and Ramus. In particular his emphasis on Christian liberty and the rights of the individual lay member of the congregation resembles the views of Lescaille and Aubery in a very obvious way. One recalls that the quarrel between Lescaille and the Huguenot ministers kept smouldering throughout the time of Hotman's presence at Basle.[50] One notices, moreover, that during these same months another former pacifist and friend of Hotman, Nicolas Séguier, brought up in Paris but now the minister of Payerne in the Vaud, felt obliged to remind Hotman rather sharply of the depth of the gulf dividing Protestantism and Catholicism, and of the fact that heresy remained heresy.[51] Basle may have implanted in Hotman's thought the message of Morély and that of Castellio, but the remarkable fact is that all radical tendencies merely helped to foster his Erasmian concern for concord and peaceful reconciliation and to intensify his search for a universal Gallican religion based upon the tenets of early Christianity.

Finally another compatriot and friend of Hotman must be mentioned here, Denis Godefroy of Paris, a former student of Baudouin and a relative, not only of J.-A. de Thou, but also of Couet and the Basle headmaster Daniel Toussain. Godefroy lived in Basle from 1589 to 1591, when he was called to Strasbourg to teach the Pandect. In a letter to J.-J. Grynaeus he regretted his past involvement in a religious controversy, obviously that about Lescaille, and pledged his future silence in an attempt to help restore the peace.[52] Godefroy put Hotman in touch with the Strasbourg historian Philipp Glaser,[53] and since he continued to correspond with J.-A. de Thou he may have provided the subsequent contacts between his Paris friends and the Strasbourg publisher Lazarus Zetzner.

The valiant efforts of Hotman and his friends ultimately failed to change the course of French policy and religious history in their lifetime, but they produced an

---

of Hotman de Villiers], aïant en son sejour tiré plus de contentement et plus appris en vostre douce et docte compagnie, que je n'ai faict depuis les quatre ans de mon retour. Je diroi volontiers ce qu'un bon vieillard dict en Tacite : redde mihi exilium meum.'' On Nevelet's poem *Basilea*, Frankfurt 1597, and his debt to Ramus' oration by the same title see vol. 2 of this study.

[48] Vivanti 180ff., 196f., 330.

[49] Vivanti 225ff., esp. 228f. In Hotman's published check-list of *Irenica* (see below p. 215) the date of publication, it would seem, is given as 1592. No printed copy of this text has come to light so far.

[50] See above p. 100.

[51] Vivanti 210ff., 222ff., 244f. ; Schickler, *op. cit.* 513ff.

[52] D.-C. Godefroy-Ménilglaise, *Les savants Godefroy*, Paris 1873, 21-63. Denis' daughter Renée, born at Basle in 1590, married a grandson of Joachim Camerarius. Joachim corresponded with Hotman and especially with Jacques Bongars, a Huguenot diplomat who showed a degree of sympathy for Hotman's ideals : Vivanti 95, 134f., 219n., 222 ; for Bongars cf. *Matrikel* 2.338 and Droz, *Etudiants français*.

[53] *Hotomanorum epistolae* 372 and passim ; Vivanti 218f.

important literature which carried their ideals on to posterity. Since Paris was to be the centre of this circle, she came to account for most of its publications, but prior to this development, the significance of Hotman's stay in Basle was underlined by some products of the local presses. Not all of them presented the irenic message ; those of Godefroy were philological and antiquarian.[54] Assisted by Nevelet de Dosches, Jean Hotman began to arrange the papers of his late father, but only one legal treatise found among them was printed at Basle, by Jacques Foillet. It was headed by Jean's plaintive preface about the troubles of France and mankind.[55] The great collection of François' works appeared eight years later in Geneva, but excluded his polemical treatises, among them the *Brutum fulmen*. A new reprint of this treatise was published in 1603 and may tentatively be attributed to Basle. Since in May 1606 Jean Hotman noted that he had effected four editions of it since the death of his father, the reprint of 1603 may have been among them.[56]

Two publications of the year 1591 were instrumental in establishing the atmosphere in which Hotman's visit to Basle was to take place. A paraphrase of Isaiah I, in both Latin and French verse, by L.-F. Le Duchat forcefully expressed the feelings of a typical *politique* at the murder of Henry III, alternating between scornful grief and pleas for reconciliation. This pamphlet was very much the style of Nevelet de Dosches and, by the way, its author was a native of Troyes like the Pithous and Nevelet himself.[57] In the same year the irenic *Dialogus de statu turbulento ecclesiae huius seculi* [58] was published, a short treatise of uncommon interest which focused on religious rather than political means to solve the French troubles, and at one point quoted the *Iurisconsultus* or François Hotman. In the present context it can only be mentioned that the *Dialogus* was probably printed by one of the two successors of Pietro Perna, Waldkirch or Foillet, like Jean Hotman's own later publications. A copy of the *Dialogus* figured afterwards in Hotman's famous library of *Irenica*, as did also the exchange of letters between Andreas Dudith and Beza arguing for and against religious toleration which was reprinted in Basle,[59] probably by Waldkirch in the year of Hotman's presence, 1593. It had formerly been published first by Perna and then by Waldkirch in the appendix of Mino Celsi's treatise against the

---

[54] **No. 474f.** The first publication in Basle (1594) of some legal *Praelectiones* by Cujas may also have been connected with the presence of Nevelet and Hotman (**No. 369**). The great teacher of J.-A. de Thou and many outstanding French lawyers, the friend of L'Hospital and Pasquier, had died in 1590. In the following year a Basle press reprinted his biography written by J.-P. Masson (**No. 736**) ; cf. Vivanti 221, 297f.

[55] **No. 551f.**

[56] **No. 565** ; F. Schickler, *op. cit.* 109. The ed., s.l. 1604, does not look like a Basle production.

[57] **No. 683** : cf. Vivanti 220f. For Le Duchat see *France prot.*

[58] **No. 378.** Cf. Vivanti 183ff. ; it is hoped to supply the text and an analysis of the *Dialogus* in vol. 2 of this study.

[59] **No. 160.** Hotman's check list of *Irenica* (see next page) indicates Basle as the place of publication for this anonymous edition and also lists the *Dialogus*. The typographical material used in **No. 160** points to the Perna-Waldkirch press from which other books by Dudith had been published. For the controversy between Beza and Dudith see : P. Costil, *André Dudith, 1533-1589*, Paris 1935, 345, 421f. and passim ; Cantimori, *Ital. Haeretiker* 470f. and passim ; Vivanti 214. Dudith had contacts in Basle : UBB possesses a ms. letter to Curione, dated from Paris, 3 November, 1556 (G.I. 66, fol. 95f.) and two letters to J. J. Grynaeus from the last decade of his life (G.II. 4, No. 114f.). However, in 1593 Dudith was dead and it seems logical to expect that the printing of **No. 160** was undertaken at the request of Hotman and his friends.

execution of heretics. Jean Hotman's interest in this publication thus shows again how Basle brought him face to face with the tradition of Castellio.

Jean Hotman's movements after he left Basle at the end of 1593 have not so far been established very clearly. Like many of his friends he had to accept his share of roving missions in the diplomatic service of Henry IV. Yet before the end of the century a circle of friends had formed around Hotman and J.-A. de Thou, most of them highly mobile, but all bound to meet one another from time to time in Paris. Some were Catholics, others Huguenots, and the individual measure of their support for the irenic ideals of J.-A. de Thou and, especially, Hotman varied a good deal, but all served Henry IV loyally, and all accepted, indeed helped to shape, the framework of his policy, although they certainly did not agree in all details. Among them were many families and individuals who had at one time or another more or less important connections in Basle, like the Pithous, the Huraults, the Harlays, the Canayes de Fresne, P. Nevelet de Dosches, N. Brulart de Sillery, Jacques Bongars, and others.[60]

An inherent affinity with the Erasmian heritage of Basle found its truest and most congenial expression in the idealism and tenacity with which Hotman and J.-A. de Thou continued to urge the need for religious reconciliation. For once a moderate Huguenot had met with an equally moderate Catholic, and the co-operation which resulted from their fellowship was characterized by a supreme degree of impartiality. As editors they matched texts of Catholic and Protestant inspiration, measure for measure, with a neatness and deliberation that far surpassed any comparable tendency among the Basle publishers. Yet the very extent to which they relied on the presses to communicate their irenic message owed something to the inspiration of Basle. Thus many of their reprints originated with Hotman's famous collection of *Irenica*, parts of which are now preserved in the library of the *Société de l'histoire du protestantisme français* at Paris. Nothing can better epitomize the issues and the contacts sketched in this chapter, as well as many cognate ones which would not find room here, than a brief reference to Hotman's reprint of Cassander's *De officio*, anonymously published in 1607 and supplemented in the appendix by a check list of "*Doctorum aliquot ac piorum virorum libri et epistolae ex quibus videri potest, quam non sit difficilis controversiarum in religione conciliatio, si controvertendi studium vitetur.*"[61]

The very first title is remarkable. It presents some Protestant opinions on the conditions for religious concord prepared in 1534 at the request of Langey, in the course of a diplomatic mission which had focused rather heavily on Basle. After more than sixty years these opinions by Melanchthon, Bucer and other German theologians did not escape Hotman's zealous investigations and were now published in the same year as Cassander's *De officio*, and by the same unnamed press located no doubt in Paris.[62] Thus the Catholic Cassander was carefully associated with Protestant advocates of religious peace. Taken together the two little books formed a moving manifesto of good will, even though a probing reader would look in vain for significant areas of agreement. Among the sixty-two titles included in

---

[60] Cf. Vivanti 129, 180, 219n., 296, 305, 355ff. and passim. See also above pp. 73, 121 and **No. 2083**, a Basle thesis dedicated to Bongars.

[61] Cf. Vivanti 204ff., 369ff.

[62] See *BNC* 21.1128: *Sententiae Philippi Melanthonis...*, 1607. Already during his stay at Basle Hotman collected eagerly the writings of Melanchthon and Bucer: Vivanti 222.

the check list many others too were likely to convey a tinge of Basle's culture to the French public. Hotman's correspondent Joachim Camerarius was represented by a Basle reprint of 1595,[63] conceivably undertaken at the request of the Paris apostle of peace and his friends in the Rhine town. Martin Bucer, Langey's reluctant ally in Strasbourg, and a shining example to Hotman's own friends there, appeared with his *Scripta Anglicana*, published in 1577 by Pietro Perna.[64] A. Dudith's epistolary controversy with Beza was first published by the same press in the same year, but appeared in the check list in the anonymous Basle edition of 1593, launched at the time of Hotman's own presence in the Rhine town. A London edition of Thomas Erastus recalled a Basle professor who ranked more prominently than Dudith, although on different grounds, among the adversaries of Beza.[65] So did Jean de Serres, another friend of the Bâlois circle, who was entered in Hotman's list immediately after Pierre Loyseleur de Villiers.[66] An unpublished treatise by Nicolas Séguier and another manuscript from the library of Pierre Pithou remind us of Hotman's personal contacts as well as the attraction of Basle for many of his friends.

The Catholic advocates of religious peace were fairly represented on Hotman's list, beginning with Erasmus, of course. His *De sarcienda ecclesiae concordia* was entered with the Paris edition of Chrétien Wechel, the successor to Conrad Resch in the *Ecu de Bâle*.[67] In fact the entire check list conveys the typical message of French Erasmianism; already the short preface defends the advocates of concord against both confessional fanatics and sceptical *politiques*, and calls for renewed talks between the moderates capable of scholarly detachment, talks in which the government would play an ancillary role only.[68] After this opening it is not surprising that the writings of Witzel and Baudouin made their appearance on Hotman's list, and that the largest space assigned to any one author was reserved for Cassander. These entries also make it clear that the publication formed part of a deliberate and sustained campaign. Cassander's *De articulis inter Catholicos et Protestantes controversis consultatio*, for example, was listed in two editions of 1594, one published at

---

[63] *BMC* 53.598 : *De dissidio religionis nostrorum temporum et collatione veteris et novae liturgiae*. Once again it seems reasonable to think that this ed. was undertaken at the request of Hotman and his friends.

[64] *BMC* 28.1008. For the role of J. Sturm, both in the original negotiations between Langey and Bucer, and in the publication of this work see V.L. Bourrilly in *BSHPF* 49 (1900), 363f., 479ff.; M. E. Welti, *Der Basler Buchdruck und Britannien*, Basle 1964, 178f., 238ff.

[65] " Theses de excommunicatione, in quibus de synedrii ecclesiastici auctoritate disputatur " : obviously the famous *Explicatio*, Pesclavii [London], 1589, to which Beza replied a year later; cf. above pp. 68ff.

[66] P. Loyseleur, *Theses de libero arbitrio*, The Hague 1587; J. de Serres, *De fide Catholica apparatus*, Paris 1597 (rather than 1596 as indicated in the check list) and 1607 : *BNC* 171.98 and *BMC* 219.425. Especially the latter ed., for which Hotman may bear his share of responsibility, infuriated the Huguenot ministers : *France prot.* s.v. Serres.

[67] *BNC* 47.831, published in 1533, immediately after the Basle editio princeps.

[68] " LECTORI S. Quia vacabant paginae reliquae, visum est libros indicare qui de pace ecclesiae scripti sunt : editi, non editi, quorum quidem copia facta nobis est ab amicis. ... Boni omnes probabunt consilium, laudabunt conatum in re tanti momenti tot et tam illustrium virorum utriusque partis, quos certe vel impudentiae vel imprudentiae insimulare, quasi rem aggressi sint Deo non gratam vel plane desperatam, scelus est. ... In primis Dei gloriam et dilectionem proximi ponamus ob oculos. Partium studium vitemus. Privati commodi spem omnem abiiciamus. Consulamus in commune. Nulli praeterquam docti et moderati ad hoc colloquium adhibeantur. Accedat legitima summi magistratus auctoritas. Quis tandem de exitu dubitabit ? "

Cologne, the other at Strasbourg, and both probably inspired by Hotman and his friends. Moreover, a new edition of that same *Consultatio*, which Cassander had never dared to publish, was promised to the public on the back of the title page to this 1607 edition of *De officio*. It did, in fact, appear in 1608, published by Lazarus Zetzner in Strasbourg.[69] The check list also promised a collection of Cassander's religious " *opuscula* ". This pledge was fulfilled in 1616 on a much larger scale with the Paris edition of his *Opera omnia*, accomplished chiefly through the efforts of de Thou, Hotman, and their Dutch friends Hugo Grotius and Daniel Heinsius.[70] It symbolized the ways in which the Erasmian message was passed from the sixteenth century to the seventeenth.

[69] *BNC* 24.629f. Unfortunately I failed to trace a copy of the ed., Strasbourg 1594. Was it too the work of Zetzner? Cf. above p. 77.

In 1576 a ms. of the *Consultatio* was in the hands of B. Vulcanius, the friend of Jean de Serres, then working at Basle for the Froben firm. Vulcanius, who had lived in Cassander's house as a youth, considered publishing the ms. at Basle, but was apparently not encouraged to do so by his theological advisers. The ed. princeps appeared a year later in Cologne: *Correspondance de B. Vulcanius* 200f.; cf. 270ff., 276.

[70] Vivanti 406ff.

Chapter Six

LYONS AND THE RHONE VALLEY

Of all the letters, manuscripts, and printed books *en route* between the Rhine and southern France only a few did not pass from one hand to another once they had reached Lyons. Indeed, for a considerable number Lyons was the point of origin or the final destination. The commercial ties between that cosmopolitan city with its regular fairs and Basle have been noted more than once in the first chapter of this book. A brief summary will serve to recall their singular intensity. It will also pose a puzzling problem; for the two intellectual microcosms at either end of this commercial artery would seem less closely interrelated than might perhaps have been presumed.

Down to the close of the fifteenth century quite a number of printers had migrated from Basle to Lyons and beyond. With the turn of the century the Lyons fairs entered the most significant phase of their development. It was usually from Lyons that Hans Koberger settled the transactions which connected the international book trade of his cousin with the Basle presses of Johann Amerbach and others and channelled the Basle book production into the south of Europe. Subsequently, in the days of the *Ecu de Bâle* the book trade between Basle and the Rhone valley lay, thanks to Wattenschnee, primarily in Bâlois hands. Only under the management of Parmentier did the Lyons *Ecu* gradually integrate with the local industry. The evidence for technical skill acquired from Basle in the early days of printing at Lyons would finally come to include some of Holbein's masterpieces in the field of book illustration. The co-operation between the two typographical centres was further encouraged by the progress of the Reformation at Lyons, and not immediately disrupted when from 1536 onwards with the arrival of the Cardinal of Tournon a sharp reaction set in.[1] During the 1540s and 1550s a slow decline in the exchange of copy as well as printed books for sale must be attributed to economic as well as ideological reasons. The trend was not reversed in the days of Protestant ascendancy at Lyons during the first war of religion.

Parmentier owned a house in Basle until 1543; Resch and the Frellon brothers of Lyons were described as business partners in the same year. Oporinus' collaboration with the Lyons firm of Barthélemy Vincent continued, very actively it would seem, even after the Protestant domination of Lyons was over, and only ended when the Basle publisher sold his business in 1567. Earlier he apprenticed his ne'er-do-well stepson to Gryphius in Lyons, the aggressive rival of the Bâlois printers in many ways, and in return Barthélemy Vincent's son, Antoine, was living in Oporinus'

---

[1] Buisson, *Castellion* 1.91ff. and passim; François, *F. de Tournon* 133ff. and passim.

house by 1564. During the 1550s, finally, Guarinus and Parcus seem to have divided their activities between Lyons and Basle.[2]

There is clear evidence for the continuation of individual links between Basle and Lyons well beyond the first war of religion, but on the whole the commercial exchange seems never to have recovered from the slump suffered in this crisis. Already by the middle of the century the Lyons book industry had grown to a size which made it difficult for Basle to compete in a market where the demand for Latin books was sharply declining.[3] During the second half of the century the importance of the Lyons fairs was dwindling and there is some indication that during the 1560s the local presses were no longer working to capacity. Originally brought about by fiscal measures, the general decline was accentuated by religious troubles and a growing tendency to xenophobia.[4] Although other factors may have contributed, hard times alone would sufficiently account for the growing unpopularity at Lyons of the compatriots of both Luther and Catherine de' Medici. After 1550 the bulk of Basle's book trade with France was shifting to the Frankfurt fairs, but a decade later only one merchant from Lyons, Clément Baudin, is listed recurrently as a customer in the accounts of the Froben-Episcopius firm, and his purchases were modest.[5]

Thus from the outset of the religious wars economic developments were unfavourable to a fertile exchange of ideas between Basle and southern France. In fact, the intellectual contacts may at no time have reached the level of the commercial transactions. The evidence for the exchange of personnel and copy between the printing centres is not paralleled, if we turn to the matriculation roll of Basle University. In the entire course of the sixteenth century only five students indicated Lyons as their domicile.[6] With the exception of the Protestant stronghold of Nîmes, other towns in the lower Rhone region were no better represented than Lyons.[7] The young Bâlois, however, reciprocated with more enthusiasm. Bonifacius Amerbach received his doctorate in law from Avignon in 1525. Twenty years later his contacts with the papal city were strengthened through the letters of a young Savoyard, Mamertus Bramet, who went there after several years of study at Basle.[8] The Basle theologian J. J. Grasser was teaching at Nîmes between 1604 and 1607, and wrote a short study on the archeological sites of that region. After his return to Basle he translated a number of books from the French, and also befriended

---

[2] Cf. above pp. 74ff.; Steinmann 108.

[3] See D. T. Pottinger, *The French Book Trade in the Ancien Régime*, Cambridge, Mass. 1958, 18. Using a sample of 600 authors, Pottinger establishes a drop in Latin language printing from 63% in 1530-1539 to 35% in 1540-1549. The share was 38% in 1550-1559 and then dropped below 30%.

[4] M. Brésard, *Les foires de Lyon aux XVe et XVIe siècles*, Paris 1914, 79ff.

[5] *Rechnungsbuch*, passim; cf. above p. 36, n. 74 and pp. 48ff., below **No. 551f.**

[6] *Matrikel* 1, 2, indices s.v. Lyon. These figures are suitable for comparison only; many entries do not indicate a home town.

[7] *Matrikel* 2 (1532-1601) indexes 8 names s.v. Nîmes, 2 each s.v. Montpellier and Languedoc, 1 each s.v. Arles and Marseille. There are no entries for Avignon, Carpentras and Provence. By comparison there are 8 entries for Toulouse, 4 for Bordeaux, 3 for Béarn, 15 for Dauphiné, 5 more for Grenoble, 13 for Dijon and many more for other localities in Burgundy.

[8] Hartmann 6.1 and passim; *Matrikel* 2.27f.

Francophone students.[9]   While Grasser taught at Nîmes, another young Bâlois, Johannes Steck, was studying theology there; he went on to teach at Die in the Dauphiné before obtaining a doctorate in law from Montpellier and becoming a professor in Lausanne and Geneva.[10]   During the 1540s a Basle student, the Rhetian Antonius Stuppa, and the famous Theodor Zwinger were working for Lyons presses. Both were obviously earning money to begin, or continue, their studies at French universities.[11]   Among these universities Montpellier, with its Mediterranean climate and prestigious medical school, continued to attract Bâlois students in respectable numbers.   Best known among them were the brothers Felix and Thomas (II) Platter,[12] who have offered lively accounts of their travels and studies.   Their presence in Montpellier during the mid-1550s and the mid-1590s, respectively, seems to mark the two peaks of its popularity with the young Bâlois, partly because their accounts provide the best source of information about their compatriots. However, there is little doubt that the French wars of religion affected the trend adversely.   Although the visits of well-to-do Bâlois students continued until well into the seventeenth century, they tended to be much shorter as the *Bildungsreise* gradually replaced a prolonged period of study in any one foreign university.[13]

The fact that Lyons had no university may in part explain why the intellectual links with Basle weakened as soon as the commercial interchange began to decline. If one tries to compare the progress of humanism in Basle and Lyons it would seem that the affinities were strongest during the formative phase prior to and around the turn of the sixteenth century.   The beginnings of humanistic learning and printing in both cities point to Italy as well as the Paris of Lefèvre d'Etaples. Didactic manuals for moral and literary instruction were in high demand.   In 1493 two richly illustrated editions of Terence were prepared concurrently by Josse Bade for a Lyons press and by Sebastian Brant for a printer in Basle.   Soon there was to be more significant proof of the identical tastes of these two men.   During his years at Lyons (1492-1498) the humanist and printer Josse Bade became acquainted with Brant's *Ship of Fools* and, in turn, contributed to its incomparable success in France. The various editions of this work offer the best evidence for the similarity of aims manifested by the presses of Basle and Lyons.   The German text (1494) and a

---

[9] *Matrikel* 2.434; V. Vetter, *Baslerische Italienreisen vom ausgehenden Mittelalter bis in das 17. Jahrhundert*, Basle 1952, 165ff.; **No. 479**.   Grasser also translated **No. 791** and **833** and contributed verses to the theses of two Francophone students (**No. 2061** and **2089**).   A number of ms. letters addressed to his former teacher J. J. Grynaeus deal with the topography of southern France, the Jesuits and the persecution of Protestants: UBB ms. G. 11.5, pp. 130-147.

[10] *Matrikel* 2.447.

[11] For Zwinger see above pp. 70f., 174; for Stuppa, who visited Sadoleto in Carpentras see Hartmann 5.434f. and passim; *Matrikel* 2.67.

[12] *Matrikel* 2.73, 383; cf. 2.78 for Gilbert Catalan from Montpellier who lived at Basle with Felix's father while Felix stayed in Montpellier with Gilbert's.   The Catalan family continued its connection with Basle for over sixty years: *Matrikel* 3.80.

[13] For Basle students at Montpellier see *Matrikel* 2.4 (J. H. Muntzinger); 2.11 (M. Bäris of Mulhouse, recipient of an Erasmus scholarship and correspondent of Bonifacius Amerbach; cf. Hartmann 5.338 and passim); 2.28 (J. H. Ryhiner: M. D. in Montpellier, married a French girl and died in French military service); 2.38 (J. Brombach); 2.46f. (I. Keller and J. J. Huggelin); 2.61 (J. F. Ryhiner); 2.67 (T. Ber); 2.68 (S. O. Hugwaldt); 2.89 (J. Bauhin jun.); 2.212f. (G. Bauhin); 2.326 (J. H. Cherler); 2.407 (J. F. Werdenberg and J. J. Huber); 2.414 (J. J. Müller); 3.65 (J. J. a Brunn); 3.80 (J. J. Hoffmann and E. Ryhiner); 3.131 (M. Harscher); 3.211 (J. C. Bauhin); 3.235 (F. Platter jun.); cf. also V. Vetter, *Baslerische Italienreisen, op. cit.*, esp. 98ff.

Latin version (1497) were first printed in Basle with the addition of a French translation published in Paris (1498), all three rather varied in text and intent. Publishers in Lyons wasted no time in launching their own reprint of the Latin edition (1498) and also a new prose version in French by the Lyonnais Jehan Drouyn (1499). To these Bade added his own imitation of the original *Ship* in Latin verse, characterized by a more distinctly humanist outlook. Bade's text, in turn, was twice reprinted in Basle (1507 and 1508).[14] In the meantime, however, yet another Lyonnais, the physician Symphorien Champier, had entered the lists with two *Nefs* of his own. They were not reprinted in Basle, but in several other ways Champier's record is peculiarly suited to recall the intellectual compatibility of the early humanist circles in Lyons and Basle. Lefèvre's commentaries on Aristotle, Cicero's *Somnium Scipionis*, and Ficino's *De vita libri tres* figure prominently among his sources of inspiration and attest to aspirations with which the contemporary Bâlois humanists were equally familiar.[15] Champier's interests, including his studies in medicine and magic, forecast the presence in Lyons of Agrippa of Nettesheim, who was in touch with Parmentier and through him with the Froben circle in Basle, although an attempt to have Froben publish some of Agrippa's writings was apparently unsuccessful.[16] Prior to the Paracelsian revival of the 1560s Basle was hardly ready for occultism, but some of Champier's more conventional writings were, in fact, published there during the second quarter of the sixteenth century.[17] Among them was his encyclopedic essay on the *artes* [18] which acknowledged its Platonic inspiration. Since it was an original publication it indicates the existence of personal links between Champier and Basle of which we have no direct record.

From the early 1520s both the character of Basle humanism and its reception in France were profoundly affected by the presence of Erasmus in the Rhine town. In spite of the impressive series of his works published at Lyons [19] our evidence for personal responses to the thought of the Dutch humanist remains somewhat scarce and rather mixed. Rabelais' passionate enthusiasm for him was offset by the lively attacks of Etienne Dolet and Bonaventure Des Périers. It is hardly a mere coincidence that while at Lyons Dolet rallied to the defence of Longueil and his Ciceronianism *à l'italienne*, whereas his feelings towards Erasmus changed considerably during his last years at Paris. This change is reflected in the contradictory spirit of statements in the first and second volumes of his *Commentaria linguae Latinae*. Bonifacius Amerbach eagerly noted this change for the better at the very time when an epitome of Dolet's work was being reprinted in Basle.[20] A few years earlier,

---

[14] J. Lefebvre, passim; J. B. Wadsworth, *Lyons 1473-1503*, Cambridge, Mass. 1962, 98ff.

[15] *Ibid.* 73ff.; Renaudet, *Préréforme* 669ff. and passim.

[16] J. Orsier, *Henri Cornélis Agrippa*, Paris 1911, 83f.; cf. Allen 9.350ff.

[17] **No. 232ff.**; Champier's short biography of Arnaldus of Villanova was reprinted in the 1585 ed. of the latter's works: **No. 54**.

[18] **No. 233**; ... *libri VII de dialectica, rhetorica, geometria, arithmetica, astronomia, musica, philosophia naturali, medicina et theologia; et de legibus et republica eaque parte philosophiae quae de moribus tractat. Atque haec omnia sunt tractata ex Aristotelis et Platonis sententia.*

[19] Cf. Baudrier (*Tables*) 128.

[20] **No. 387ff.**; Hartmann 5.57f., 112f.; cf. 6.20f., 298f. For Dolet's connections with the printing industry and Protestant circles see Febvre-Martin 230ff.; C. A. Meyer in *BHR* 17 (1955), 405-414; *Calvini opera* 11.357; Allen 11.248f. and passim; M. B. Kline, *Rabelais and the Age of Printing*, Geneva 1963, 18f.

in 1531, Nicolas Mallarius had visited Erasmus in Freiburg, but the few letters exchanged between the two and Mallarius' patron, the abbot Antoine d'Albon, who later became the Primate of Lyons, offer no evidence for the existence in the Rhone town of enthusiastic circles of Erasmians comparable to those of Franche-Comté.[21]

The Catholic hierarchy of Lyons and southern France could hardly be expected to take a major interest in Basle. Sadoleto's attentions, although modest, were still exceptional. But, as we shall see, he was an outsider, hardly representative of the native ecclesiastical circles. If the Catholics were aloof, it does not follow that the Lyons Calvinists were particularly anxious to retain links with Basle. Ever since the inauspicious visits of such southerners as François Lambert and Guillaume Farel relations between Basle and the reformers of southern France had remained rather lukewarm.[22] At the coming of the religious wars Basle reacted unenthusiastically, to say the least, to Lyonnais requests for financial aid. Apparently not a single work of Pierre Viret, that devoted Swiss church leader in the *Midi* during much of the 1560s, was ever published in Basle. Innocent Gentillet, a native of Vienne, was dead forty years before his *Anti-Machiavel* was reprinted in Basle. By that time the work had become a classic, but its wisdom and moderation should have appealed to the mood of Basle right from the beginning.[23] By and large it was left to the one unorthodox and ostracized Calvinist, Sébastien Castellio, to establish important links between Basle and the Protestantism of Lyons.

During his early years in Lyons Castellio had to be content with a modest existence of near-anonymity on the fringes of a brilliant literary society, no doubt even further removed from the prestigious centre than he was later to be among the unassuming bourgeoisie of Basle. It may in no small part be due to Castellio that, in addition to the name of Nicolas Bourbon, those of some less distinguished members of the Lyons literary circles—Ducher, Girinet, Raynier, not to mention Beaulieu—appeared in the Basle editions of poetry.[24] On the other hand it may indicate the limitations of his social contacts in Lyons that the more illustrious names of Clément Marot, the Scève brothers, and even Barthélemy Aneau are not to be found in Basle publications.

Once he had settled in Basle, Castellio's work and his ideas began to filter back to Lyons, but, as happened elsewhere, it was mostly the outsiders whom they affected. Throughout the Rhone region, the men most likely to maintain direct contacts with Basle were usually strangers and many were religiously suspect. Apart from the Spaniard Servetus, a remarkable number of Italian names come to mind. The presence of Italians in southern France, of course, is a fact well noted throughout the Renaissance, but in contacts with Basle such humanist theologians as Sadoleto and Sante Pagnini, such lawyers as Alciato and Matteo Gribaldi, such physicians as Fenotti and the Argentieri family, early patrons of Castellio,[25] play a role beyond all proportion to the basic presence of Italians in southern France. Moreover those among them to stand out are not the assimilated Italians like Grolier, the Argentieris or Pagnini, but the temporary expatriates like Alciato, Gribaldi, and Sadoleto. During the mid-1560s Beza was profoundly alarmed by " Castellionist "

---

[21] Allen 9.88ff., 111ff., 224ff., 242ff.

[22] See e.g. Wernle, *Calvin und Basel* 32, 50ff., 83ff., 91ff. ; cf. above pp. 90ff.

[23] Cf. above p. 60f.

[24] Cf. above p. 124. In the case of highly popular works in French it is understandable that the Basle printers should have shied away from overwhelming competition.

[25] Buisson, *Castellion* 1.33f. and passim ; Baudrier 5.174 ; 8.243 and passim.

aberrations among the Protestant Italians of Lyons. The matter will be taken up later on, but it may be noted here that these troubles occurred at a time of economic decline, growing xenophobia and heightened Catholic pressure.

Castellio's following in Lyons was, however, not restricted to foreigners. In the spring of 1553 the brothers Jean and Jérôme Des Gouttes registered in the University of Basle. Jean knew Castellio from his days in the Lyons literary circle, and his visit to Basle may at least in part have been a tribute to an old friend. In the fall the brothers returned home and passed through Geneva just in time to see Servetus' stake aflame.[26] What views they took back with them from Basle may be inferred from a letter which the faithful Paris minister François Morel sent to Calvin in June 1558. Morel announced the arrival from Lyons of one Des Gouttes who had applied for admission to his congregation; no doubt, to stir up trouble, Morel thought, for the man was a Castellionist and a Servetist. Of course he was turned down.[27] There is also a letter to Castellio's friend Jean Bauhin written by a Laurent Montdesir, presumably from Lyons. Montdesir refers to his good friend and brother Jérôme Des Gouttes, and recommends himself to Castellio's prayers.[28] There is a similar letter from Thomas Lafarge who had matriculated at Basle in 1558-59. Now, after his return to Lyons, he remembered with gratitude his visits to the homes of Castellio, Bauhin, and the ex-Jorist Niklaus Blesdyck.[29] Both documents give a vivid impression of that faithful circle of Lyons disciples who turned to their master in Basle for inspiration and comfort in much the same way as Calvinists all over France addressed themselves to the master of Geneva. They read Castellio's writings eagerly and even planned a Lyons edition of the *Theologia Germanica*, that common bond between Castellio and the spirit of Jorist Anabaptism.[30]

In this context the most precious, though inadequately explored, evidence is the presence at Lyons of the younger Jean Bauhin. In 1561 he left Basle in the company of the son of the Jorist Peter of Mechlin who was headed for Lyons. Ironically they were expected to meet Beza, also *en route*, at Soleure and to hand him a letter from Gratarolo, Castellio's past accuser in Basle.[31] In 1562 Bauhin obtained

---

[26] *Matrikel* 2.79; Droz, *Etudiants français*; Buisson, *Castellion* 1.32, 38; 2.91; Baudrier 8.113, 118 and passim.

[27] *Calvini opera* 17.569f.

[28] Buisson, *Castellion* 2.472ff.

[29] *Ibid*. 2.457f.; *Matrikel* 2.117.

[30] Buisson, *Castellion* 2.382f.; cf. 2.402 for highly significant report by N. Zurkinden on a conversation with a Lyons merchant or agent (20 January, 1562): " ... incidi in quendam Lugduno venientem negotii causa ad nos, hominem non indoctum. Percunctatus quomodo succederet evangelii doctrina in Gallia, audio : ' satis feliciter nisi essent inter fratres quosdam dissidia subindeque Satan suos mitteret qui Dei ministros calumniis redderent suspectos, quos inter Basilea unum aleret qui non ita pridem (si recte intellexi) ipse clam Lugduni latuerit ut suum ibi venenum spargeret.' Nominare neminem voluit, sed puto nomen alibi edidisse, nam haud ita multo post rumor auditur te aliquid turbasse Lugduni habereque ibi sectatores detestabilium mysteriorum quae David Georgii ... ingenium plane referrent." Buisson (*Castellion* 2.342, 366) only lists a Lyons ed. of the *Theologia Germanica* in 1665. Apart from this his bibliography records two Lyons eds. of Castellio's *Dialogi sacri*, 1549 and 1550. The recent *Catalogue of Books Printed on the Continent ... in Cambridge Libraries* lists a Lyons ed. of the *Theologia*, 1580.

[31] *Correspondance de Bèze* 3.125f. In the same year the young Fausto Sozzini arrived in Lyons from Italy, still practising Nicodemism. Subsequently, at Basle he was in close touch with the Italian merchant N. Camulio who had important affairs in Lyons. Cf. A. Rotondò, Atteggiamenti della vita morale italiana del Cinquecento: la pratica nicodemita, *Rivista storica italiana* 79 (1967), 991-1030, esp. 1000ff. See above p. 134f.

his doctorate in medicine from Montpellier or Valence. In 1565 he too was at Lyons, now in the company of his own father. On this occasion events proved to what degree both shared the views of Castellio and consequently the suspicions of orthodox Calvinists. The younger Jean Bauhin seems to have remained at Lyons for up to three years, occupying the position of a plague doctor—hardly a popular one with the native medical profession. In this capacity he composed a short treatise, *De auxiliis adversus pestem*.[32] When he desired to marry a local girl, both he and his father had a number of revealing interviews with the Lyons consistory. As Castellio himself had done, they tried to evade some touchy questions by invoking their adherence to the Basle confession. But the ministers insisted that they must take a clear stand on some Castellionist ' heresies ' and, in particular, endorse the Calvinist dogma of predestination. The case dragged on, with consultations between the Lyons ministers and their counterparts in Geneva and Zurich, but in the end a mutually acceptable solution seems to have been found. Bauhin not only married his girl; in 1568 he was even hired by the council of Geneva as the successor of Simone Simoni. For two years he attended their plague patients, thus once again following in the footsteps of Castellio.[33]

The suspicions of the Lyons consistory in this affair may well have been heightened by a scandal which dated back to 1562. In that year Jean Morély, recently removed from Geneva, turned up in Lyons there to publish his rebellious *Traicté de la discipline chrestienne*.[34] Indeed it would seem characteristic of that small segment of radical Protestantism at Lyons that Castellio's pleas for freedom of conscience, Jorist spiritualism, and Morély's political dissent seemed to form a closely knit menace to the local church authorities, whereas they remained more or less separate issues at Basle. By the end of the decade Pierre Ramus, by then the champion of Morély's anti-presbyterianism and the friend of some Basle humanists, would use the theological quarrel which had meanwhile erupted at Lyons to pinpoint the authoritarian self-righteousness of Beza. Beza, in turn, would accuse Ramus of complicity in the dogmatic heresies disseminated among the Italians of Lyons. On the face of it, however, the specific dogmatic issues which Ludovico Alamanni in 1566 raised against Beza bear little affinity with Castellio's thought and the socio-ecclesiastical teachings of Morély and Ramus.[35] Though the dogmatic issues were different, however, Alamanni's basic act of rebellion against the authoritative views endorsed by the presbytery very closely resembles the subsequent revolt in Switzerland of such Castellionists as Aubery and Lescaille. In view of the creeping turmoil among the Italian Protestant community in Lyons—that *altera Corinthus*, as Beza called the Rhone city—it is not surprising that Zanchi in 1564 refused to become its minister.[36] The position would hardly have been calculated to soothe the nerves of the eminent Calvinist theologian after the troubles he had just experienced in Strasbourg.

---

[32] Published at Montbéliard in 1597 ; cf. F. Hasler, Johannes Bauhin d.J. (1541-1613), *Gesnerus* 20 (1963), 7 and passim.

[33] *Ibid.* 6ff. : J. Barnaud, *Pierre Viret*, Saint-Amans 1911, 626ff. ; L. Gautier, La Médecine à Genève jusqu'à la fin du XVIIIe siècle, *Mém. et doc. Société d'Hist. et d'Archéol. de Genève*, 30 (1906), 32ff.

[34] Cf. above p. 68f.

[35] H. Meylan, Bèze et les Italiens de Lyon (1566), *BHR* 14 (1952), 235-249 ; Cantimori, *Ital. Haeretiker* 257ff.

[36] *Correspondance de Bèze* 5.53.

To turn from Lyons to Avignon and Carpentras means to enter a more staid sphere of the relations between Basle and the Rhone region, but still one dominated by contacts with Italian expatriates. Bonifacius Amerbach's student years in Avignon, like the presence of the *Ecu de Bâle* at Lyons, were among the crucial factors in shaping the nature and extent of ties between Basle and southern France. With one interruption Amerbach remained in the papal city from 1520 to 1524. He returned there briefly in 1525 to acquire his doctoral degree of Law. He was already thirty at the time and treated with distinction by everybody he encountered. What made him go to Avignon in the first place was the fact that Andrea Alciato was teaching there. Bonifacius' brother Bruno had known the celebrated jurist in Italy, and visited him again at Avignon.[37] At about the same time Bonifacius announced in a letter to his former teacher Zasius that he no longer planned to complete his training in Italy but intended to work under Alciato.[38] Very shortly thereafter he began to serve as a regular agent in the exchange of letters, messages, and publications between Alciato on the one hand and Zasius, Erasmus and Chansonnette on the other.[39] This service grew naturally out of his own correspondence with the famous Italian, a correspondence that continued faithfully to Alciato's death in 1550. However, the interest of these letters is not as great as their frequency might indicate. Amerbach's confidence in his teacher is undoubted. He did occasionally mention his religious dilemma in the reformed Basle as well as related personal problems. Alciato, however, tended to be less personal, and by and large their communications remained somewhat superficial. As a result it has not given historians much assistance in ascertaining in what ways Amerbach was indebted to the influence of his great teacher, especially since in the course of his own career he tended to revindicate the medieval Glossarists.[40] This means that in the present context important questions must go unanswered. Alciato's impact upon legal scholarship in France both during his teaching years at Avignon (1518-1522 and 1527-1529) and the even more important ones at Bourges (1529-1533) has often been emphasized. When publishing a considerable number of original legal studies by Baudouin, Hotman and others, the Basle presses helped to reveal the effects of Alciato's teaching, which established in France the primacy of theoretical over practical law, and especially the historical approach. The latter applied the methods of literary humanism to discern in Roman Law the rational principles of society both during classical antiquity and all subsequent cultures worthy of that name.[41] Yet none of the famous French lawyers such as Baudouin, Hotman, Du Moulin or Cujas owed his contacts with Basle, even indirectly, to Alciato. Moreover, just as Amerbach's debt to Alciato is not conclusively revealed by their correspondence, so Alciato's appreciation of the Erasmian humanism of Basle remains a matter of conjecture. However, whatever the degree of inspiration Alciato and the humanists of Basle owed one another, the local printers soon learned how well the Italian's books sold. The major interest of Alciato's correspondence with Basle lies here: there is hardly another case in which the complicated negotiations between the Basle printers and a most exacting sixteenth century author in great demand are so well documented.

---

[37] Hartmann 2.92n., 177f., 205f.

[38] *Ibid.* 2.162.

[39] *Ibid.* 2.178, 202f. and passim; Allen 4.611ff, 485f. and passim.

[40] Cf. G. Kisch, *Bonifacius Amerbach, Gedenkrede*, Basle 1962, esp. 15ff., 21ff.; M. P. Gilmore, *Humanists and Jurists*, Cambridge, Mass. 1963, 146ff., esp. 157f.

[41] Cf. G. Kisch, *Erasmus und die Jurisprudenz seiner Zeit*, Basle 1960, 304ff.

While the technical detail of these transactions does not make for summarization some incidents do emerge which shed some light on the progress of Alciato's career as well as the practices of Basle printers. The first involved Erasmus and the north-Italian book merchant and publisher Francesco Giulio Calvo, a friend of Alciato and a frequent visitor to Basle, especially in the years around 1520.[42] Calvo probably acquainted the Bâlois with the early legal work of Alciato as he supplied the latter with early samples of Germany's Reformation literature. Alciato savoured the *genre*, at least initially. Some time before 1520 Calvo brought Erasmus the manuscript of Alciato's polemical declamation *Contra vitam monasticam*. However, from 1521 onwards the author, now a professor in papal Avignon, remembered that youthful extravaganza with growing alarm, especially when the Basle presses showed increasing eagerness to publish any text by him they could obtain. Repeated approaches to Erasmus only netted the fact that he had misplaced the manuscript. His reply to the last one in 1531 made it clear that he no longer remembered—or wished to remember—the text entrusted to him.[43]

If the case of *Contra vitam monasticam* suggests a change of opinion in the course of Alciato's relations with Basle, there were other changes caused by the growth of his reputation in France rather than by ideological implications. Alciato demanded of his writings a high degree of perfection but since he was usually pressed by other work he found it hard to put the finishing touches to his text. In spite of this Bonifacius Amerbach during his first months at Avignon managed to secure for Basle printers a copy of Alciato's *Paradoxa* and other legal treatises formerly published in Italy which the author had freshly corrected and somewhat enlarged.[44] Alciato might then have been willing to pass more work on to them,[45] but Cratander was remarkably slow in producing that first book in spite of repeated pleas from Amerbach, Chansonnette, and the author himself.[46] Once it had appeared, however, it was reprinted at Lyons without delay. The same fate later met some other Basle editions of important works by Alciato.[47] Moreover, as his fame was growing, most of his first editions went to Gryphius and other rivals of the Basle presses despite the continued representations of Amerbach and the high esteem which Alciato had for the accuracy and format of Basle books. In another context one case has been reported [48] where abundant evidence suggests that the Lyonnais were simply faster and smarter. The Bâlois did realize that like other celebrated jurists, and unlike most sixteenth century authors, Alciato expected payment for his manuscripts,[49]

---

[42] Cf. Hartmann 2.284n. ; Allen 2.558n. ; 9.186n.

[43] Hartmann 2.284f. ; 3.542 ; 4.31 ; Allen 4.485f. A good illustration of the changing attitudes in Avignon is provided in a letter which Alciato addressed to Amerbach in 1522. He describes a conversation with the Papal Legate. The latter refers to a pamphlet in favour of priest marriage which he attributes to Erasmus of Rotterdam : " Statim libellum exhibet, paulisper lego. Roterodami esse opus nego : ' Aliter longe catuli olent.' Ait ille. Rursus pernego hominemque in sententiam meam traho. Ubi perlegi, ' non adeo ' inquam ' sacerdotibus conducit hic liber ' ...", and he ends with a joke (Hartmann 2.362).

[44] **No. 18** ; cf. Hartmann 2.289.

[45] Hartmann 2.413.

[46] *Ibid.* 2.246f., 280ff., 328, 338, 386f., 403f., 408, 420f., 434 ; 3.6f., 103, 130.

[47] So e.g. **No. 20** and **21**.

[48] See above p. 42f. For Amerbach's continued pleas and frustrations see also Hartmann 2.504 ; 3.7, 101, 130f., 210.

[49] E.g. Hartmann 3.317, 346. For the fees of other legal authors such as Zasius, Chansonnette, and the less well known Bellone cf. Hartmann 2.39ff ; 5.407f., 410f.

but what they could offer apparently did not usually induce him to reverse his priorities in their favour. However, in 1530 Froben's gift of a copy of his huge edition of St. Augustine, prepared by Erasmus, embarrassed him sufficiently that he offered payment since he could not promise publishable copy in return.[50]

This generous gift actually came in the wake of two embarrassing incidents, the first of which concerned Alciato's antiquarian essay *De ponderibus et mensuris*. The author was persuaded to send his own manuscript to Basle when he learned that the Bâlois had obtained an unauthorized copy and he wished to prevent the appearance of an inadequate text. No sooner had he done so than he was offered a highly desirable position at Bourges. He then implored Amerbach to stop the publication of *De ponderibus et mensuris* since he feared it might upset the influential Budé and jeopardize his career in France.[51] He had also sent a polemical rejoinder to the attacks of two French lawyers, written under the name of one of his own pupils. Since one of the antagonists was a Bourges professor, he regretted his action almost immediately, but in this case Froben had acted too promptly to be stopped.[52]

Subsequent Basle editions of some of his writings were less controversial and finally opened the way for the first edition of his Collected Works, to be published by Isengrin in four folio volumes during the years immediately preceding Alciato's death (1546-1550). As for previous publications, the *Opera omnia* were discussed at great length and in detail in the correspondence between the Bâlois and the discriminating author.[53] Twice reprinted in Basle, they may perhaps deserve a place second only to the Collected Works of Erasmus and Budé in the history of Basle books with an impact in France. Yet, as mentioned before, the impact of Alciato's work did not demonstrably intensify the contacts between the French jurists and Basle. As for Basle humanists, spontaneous reactions to Alciato's work were equally rare. A favourable echo, however, is noticeable in the case of *De formula Romani imperii* and his edition of the *Notitia dignitatum*, works, that is, of broad antiquarian or even political interest.[54] Some Basle students followed Amerbach's example and attended Alciato's courses in Avignon, Bourges and various Italian universities. His critical opinion of Budé, though for the most part carefully concealed, may have added to Amerbach's hostile disposition vis-à-vis the famous scholar in Paris. On the other hand Alciato tried, and failed, to obstruct the Basle edition of the works of the Italian humanist Francesco Florido [55] who was soon thereafter called to Paris by Francis I. The friendly contact, however, which Alciato maintained from Avignon with Sadoleto may have confirmed the favourable opinion the Bâlois had formed of the Bishop of Carpentras. Much of this remains

---

[50] Hartmann 3.502, 523, 541 ; 4.2f., 18f.

[51] *Ibid.* 3.346, 350f., 378, 408, 412 and passim ; cf. P. E. Viard, *André Alciat*, Paris 1926, 66ff.

[52] **No. 15** ; Hartmann 3.371, 402f., 412.

[53] The project was envisaged as early as 1531 : cf. Hartmann 4.41, 51, 54, 112 and passim to 6.176, 225, 520ff.

[54] **No. 16** and **17** ; cf. Burckhardt, *Herold* 154, 197ff. ; Bietenholz, *Ital. Humanismus* 106ff., 112.

[55] **No. 440.** Alciato informed Amerbach that Gryphius had turned down the project because of Florido's attacks on Zasius and himself. Florido's defense of Erasmus against Dolet may have been more to the taste of the Bâlois : Hartmann 5.267ff. ; cf. 6.287f.

within the domain of conjecture; at least it is a fact that wherever Alciato went he remained an important customer of the Basle book trade. In his correspondence with Amerbach over thirty years generous space is reserved for references to, and orders for, new Basle editions. Basle books may not have had a more faithful collector in southern France. His expert knowledge of the market is demonstrated by his complaint about the dearness of Basle editions in Lyons [56] and, consequently, his preference for consignments sent directly to him from Basle.

The correspondence of Bonifacius Amerbach shows that his friendship with Alciato was not the only one he had contracted during his years at Avignon. In general these letters leave an impression of educated and civilized bourgeois, bent on continuing the humanistic tradition in both cities, but otherwise not eager to express and share original ideas. Until his death in 1538 Jean Montaigne remained a faithful correspondent of Amerbach, though hardly a profound one. In the 1530s he was rated as the most prominent member of Avignon's legal profession, and after his death Bonifacius urged a common friend to publish in Lyons the legal commentaries on which Montaigne had been working for many years.[57] Like Alciato, Montaigne was a devoted reader of Erasmus. His commitment to Christian humanist ideals was further emphasized by his friendship with the Dominican Sante Pagnini.[58] Following the death of his patron, Leo X, this distinguished Orientalist and Bible scholar lived in Avignon for three years before moving on to Lyons. Amerbach apparently did not know him well, but he was aware of Pagnini's scholarly achievements. He encouraged Parmentier in Lyons to promote a new edition of Pagnini's Greek grammar just published at Avignon. To the booksellers of Basle he recommended another work by the Dominican, but was told that there was no market there for a book so poorly printed. He also offered to the Basle presses a new manuscript by Pagnini, but seems to have met with little enthusiasm, especially when he inquired about a possible fee for the author.[59]

After Montaigne's death Hieronymus Lopis remained Amerbach's only regular correspondent in Avignon; he was a physician and possibly a converted Jew. His letters, to a degree more lively and more Erasmian in outlook than others Bonifacius received from Avignon, show him in close contact with Amerbach's jurist friends and also with the Bishop of Carpentras.[60] Sadoleto may have relied on his professional advice; Bonifacius too solicited his opinion in the case of a mentally and physically afflicted Basle girl.[61] Despite, or probably because of, his professional competence, Sadoleto suddenly advised him to forsake practical medicine for the higher flight of Greek studies and Peripatetic philosophy, thus thrusting the poor doctor into a considerable dilemma, since he was no longer young and balked at the thought of cramming Greek vocables.[62] In view of his frequent visits to Carpentras his letters served the Bâlois as a welcome supplement to the rare messages received directly from Sadoleto.

---

[56] E.g. Hartmann 4.137, 150f.

[57] Montaigne obviously did not enjoy an international reputation so that Amerbach would not envisage publication at Basle; in fact it did not even materialize in Lyons: Hartmann 2.394f.; 4.245; 5.98f., 120f., 156.

[58] Hartmann 2.518f.; 3.91.

[59] *Ibid.* 2.505f., 512; 3.8, 21f.; cf. **No. 1023**.

[60] *Ibid.* 2.510ff., 217f., 508; 5.431 and passim.

[61] *Ibid.* 3.108ff., 149ff.

[62] *Ibid.* 4.15, 36, 69, 124.

Jacopo Sadoleto was forty-five when he first visited his self-governing diocese of Carpentras, but then he spent the greater part of his remaining years there. He lost few opportunities of expressing how much he preferred the quiet peace of his modest residence to the expensive and feverish life of Rome where he was called occasionally by his curial duties.[63] It was at Carpentras that most of his works were written, among them three of the four pieces subsequently published in Basle. From Carpentras he maintained frequent contacts with Alciato and other fellow-Italians in Avignon. It was natural that Amerbach, when he was studying in Avignon, should seize the opportunity of introducing himself to the prelate.[64] While serving as a papal secretary to Leo X Sadoleto had been rated as the sincerest friend Erasmus had at the Roman curia.[65] After Erasmus had left Basle for Freiburg, his correspondence with Sadoleto continued through the intermediation of Amerbach, and their mutual appreciation was further demonstrated by the manuscripts which they submitted to one another's judgment. On one such occasion Erasmus feared that Sadoleto might have been offended by the candour of his remarks, but the doubts evaporated before long.[66] After the death of Erasmus, Amerbach and Sadoleto continued to exchange occasional letters and greetings as long as the bishop resided in Carpentras. Yet the locale of southern France had little direct influence on the nature of Sadoleto's contacts with Basle. Essentially they appear as an extension of Erasmus' ties with the Roman curia. In return for book gifts in his own name and that of Erasmus, Amerbach felt free to ask the prelate for curial favours ranging from a special permission for his sister to visit the parental tomb in Basle's Carthusian monastery (1526) to a papal privilege for Froben's edition of the Collected Works of Erasmus (1538).[67] This second request, however, failed to produce the desired effect.

It is curious that the Basle printers waited until after the Reformation of their city before they published, rather casually, a few of Sadoleto's writings. Their choice of texts, however, was characteristic. The message contained in them was that of Christian humanism, Italian style; the fact that the author was a high Catholic prelate added a special flavour, of which many Protestant Bâlois remained appreciative. It also opened sales opportunities. Sadoleto's dialogue on liberal education, though an original outline for a model curriculum, was written in 1530 shortly after the publication of Erasmus' treatises on education, and was later published at Basle in conjunction with Erasmus' *De civilitate morum puerilium* and other Italian essays on education.[68] Sadoleto's oration in favour of a crusade against the Turk, though dedicated to Louis XII of France, was Italian in outlook and not uncritical of French political aspirations in Italy. Apart from this its approach was similar to that of Erasmus' *Querela pacis*. Both aspects would account equally for the warm approval which Bonifacius Amerbach gave to Sadoleto's treatise.[69] In like

---

[63] Douglas, *Sadoleto* 32ff., 198f. and passim.

[64] Hartmann 2.441-445, 461.

[65] Cf. Douglas, *Sadoleto* 17, 21, 73ff.; Allen 5.572; 7.509f. and passim.

[66] Cf. Douglas, *Sadoleto* 223f. Douglas is puzzled by the fact that as far as we know no letters were exchanged between Erasmus and Sadoleto after October 1534, but a natural explanation might lie in Erasmus' failing health. Cf. Allen 11.126f., 259.

[67] Hartmann 3. 164, 363; cf. 2.522f.

[68] **No. 919-921**; Douglas, *Sadoleto* 75f.; Bietenholz, *Ital. Humanismus* 58f.

[69] **No. 917**; Douglas, *Sadoleto* 10f.; Hartmann 2.443.

manner *De laudibus philosophiae*, which encompassed Sadoleto's thought on the themes of contemplative life and the dignity of man, was republished at Basle, in line with the extensive reception of Italian humanist literature. This treatise presents Sadoleto as the Christian philosopher to whom Erasmus had addressed his platonizing epistle dedicatory to the works of Saint Basil.[70] It also projects the pastor of Carpentras who was to hire Florentius Volusenus to head the local school; in fact the contacts between this Scottish humanist philosopher and Basle coincide with his years in Carpentras and Lyons and his relations to Sadoleto.[71] *De laudibus philosophiae* also gave expression to Sadoleto's attachment to the Ciceronianism of his friend Bembo, just as his *Commentary on Psalm 93* recalled the pious reforming tendencies of his friend Contarini.[72] The Basle re-editions of these two works thus might demonstrate Sadoleto's suspension between two sets of ideals based on common ground but developing in different directions. It is perhaps typical that the Psalm commentary was his first work to reach the Basle publishers. It was reprinted in 1530 from Gryphius' first edition, which had just appeared in Lyons. A copy of the Basle edition was sent to Sadoleto by Amerbach as proof of Bâlois detachment in the midst of Germany's Reformation fever.[73]

Apart from this commentary, however, Basle failed to respond positively to Sadoleto's theological efforts and even his writings designed to further religious conciliation. Erasmus received the manuscript of his commentary on Romans; asked for his comments, the Dutch humanist sounded a warning note even before the Sorbonne had a chance to censure the work. Amerbach had meant to support the bishop's efforts by presenting him with a copy of Melanchthon's recent exposition of Romans,[74] but when Sadoleto's commentary was available, Amerbach did not propose its publication in Basle. Likewise only the faintest echo from Basle greeted Sadoleto's efforts to enter into dialogue with some exponents of Protestantism. His approaches to Melanchthon, Sturm, and to the German nation at large fell in the years 1537-39, thus following closely in the wake of Langey's mission to Germany which had taken a similar direction.[75] But unlike Langey's activities, Sadoleto's action did not bear upon Basle. In his letter to the citizens of Geneva, published in 1539, he presented the irenic message with the touch of the controversialist. The letter marks one of the few occasions when Sadoleto was significantly collaborating with French ecclesiastical circles, the Cardinal of Tournon and Pierre de La Baume, the Bishop of Geneva.[76] Once again there is no echo from Basle, although it does appear that in a general way Sadoleto was considered to be Rome's sincerest advocate

---

[70] **No. 918** ; Douglas, *Sadoleto* 77ff. ; Bietenholz, *Ital. Humanismus* 116f.

[71] Cf. Douglas, *Sadoleto* 65f. and passim. Volusenus was subsequently in Lyons where he met Conrad Gesner in 1540 and, perhaps, Castellio : Buisson, *Castellion* 1.35f. A. Péricaud, *Erasme dans ses rapports avec Lyon*, Lyons 1843, 16, credits Volusenus with a visit to Erasmus and the University of Basle, on what evidence is not clear. Cf. **No. 260a** and **1044**. The latter reference was given to me by Mr. Dominic Baker-Smith who is preparing a monograph on Volusenus.

[72] Douglas, *Sadoleto* 61, 73.

[73] **No. 923** ; Hartmann 3.515, 536.

[74] Douglas, *Sadoleto* 80ff. ; Hartmann 4.230f. and passim.

[75] Cf. Douglas, *Sadoleto* 117ff., 131ff. For Sadoleto's relations with the Du Bellays in these years see J. Sadoleto, *Opera*, Verona 1737, 1.91ff., 125f., 246f. Cf. above p. 107f.

[76] Douglas, *Sadoleto* 144.

of reform, peace and unity.[77] Given the importance which many Bâlois attached
to the search for church unity, and the desire of many printers to retain Catholic
authors in their lists, it may seem surprising that Basle publishers did not lavish
more attention on Sadoleto. He appears to have had everything to recommend
him for one of those editions of Collected Works in which the Bâlois excelled. Yet
this honour went twice to Cardinal Bembo [78] who avoided religious topics but
seemed otherwise less suited to receive it than Sadoleto, to whom it was denied.
The Bishop of Carpentras lacked a strong advocate in Basle in that decade after
the death of Erasmus, when the printing industry seemed disorientated and singularly dependent upon impulses received from abroad. Nor could energetic impulses
be expected on the part of Sadoleto, who had no passion for action and seemed
frequently out of touch with his times and environment.

Sadoleto was not an exception: a certain atmosphere of detachment charac-
terizes the entire intellectual exchange between southern France and Basle and
contrasts markedly with the lively and spontaneous relations which linked the
Rhine town with the modest humanist movement of Franche-Comté.

------

[77] Cf. Hartmann 5.41 ; similar views were expressed by J. B. Herold who encouraged
G. Cousin to promote religious reconciliation in Burgundy the same way as Sadoleto
was doing in Italy and Calvin in France : Burckhardt, *Herold* 132, 140. Writing to
Calvin, Myconius commented on an unconfirmed rumor about Sadoleto's participation
in the persecution of Provençal Protestants : " Non id exspectaram ab homine humano " :
Calvini opera 12.363.

[78] Cf. Bietenholz, *Ital. Humanismus* 67.

CHAPTER SEVEN

BURGUNDY AND GILBERT COUSIN

A certain affinity with Basle, and an attraction to her, was experienced in all regions of Burgundy, but most intensely so in the Franche-Comté. This Spanish territory was completely Francophone, but under the weight of political developments, both past and present, it was sufficiently alienated from the adjacent French provinces to make room for a special relationship with the Swiss and Basle in particular. The political and commercial ties between the Comté and the Swiss cantons were sufficiently strong to ensure some degree of neutrality for all Burgundy during the Habsburg-Valois wars—at the specific request of the Swiss.[1] In spite of Basle's eventual secession from the Catholic faith the Comtois were inclined to consider her as the foremost friendly metropolis in their neighbourhood, in cultural matters no less than economic ones. Trade was brisk, and in the sixteenth century the University of Dole, older but more restricted than that of Basle, possessed a law school of comparable reputation. However, Basle remained popular with students from all parts of Burgundy throughout the century and after.[2] In the eyes of history-conscious Gauls Basle had always been the frontier town between their own hemisphere and the Teutonic lands: " *per intermedium Rhenum veterem Galliae Germaniaeque terminum,*" as Pierre Ramus put it in the opening sentences of his *Basilea.*[3] Her bishop, and for a long time her master, had since the early Middle Ages been a diocesan of the Burgundian Archbishop of Besançon. Erasmus most appropriately paid his respects to the Bishop of Basle, now residing in Porrentruy, when he travelled to Besançon for a short holiday in the spring of 1524.[4]

In the context of this study Erasmus' correspondence, once again, supplies the basis from which to begin a survey of the personal contacts between Burgundy and the Rhine city. The idea of that holiday in 1524 had sprung from his correspondence with friends in Burgundy. In Porrentruy the parish priest Theobaldus Bietricius was his special friend.[5] In Bietricius' company he set out for Besançon where other friends and admirers waited eagerly to receive him, in particular the official Léonard de Gruyère, the treasurer François Bonvalot and the archdeacon Ferry Carondelet.[6]

---

[1] L. Febvre, *Histoire de Franche-Comté* [9], Paris 1932, 155f.;

[2] Cf. above p. 219, n. 6f. Some comparable figures for Burgundian matriculants are (*Matrikel* 2): Autun: 4; Beaune: 3; Besançon: 3; Bourgogne: 7; Dijon: 13; Dôle: 0; Mâcon: 2; Nozeroy: 7; Salins: 1; Vesoul: 3.

[3] *Basilea* 24.

[4] Cf. Allen 6.167.

[5] Allen 5.341f. and passim.

[6] Allen 5.254n., 615f., 617n. and passim.

The trip on horseback as well as the lavish hospitality of his friends and the city council somewhat strained his frail health, but the visit was an obvious success. It led on the side of Erasmus to intensified correspondence and the occasional dedication of a work to one of his Burgundian friends.[7] On the side of the ecclesiastical dignitaries it established the habit of supplying Erasmus with the light Burgundian wine which he firmly believed was vital to him.[8] As a result he often thought of moving to Besançon. When he left Basle for Freiburg, Besançon too had received serious consideration. Subsequently, in 1531, he solicited, and received, a formal invitation from the town council, and still in the last year of his life he wondered about the feasibility of a transfer to Besançon.[9]

Back in 1524 Erasmus, if he is to be believed, was merely planning a spring holiday when visiting Burgundy.[10] However, in choosing that destination he probably had something more in mind than merely pleasure and recreation. During the year of 1524 his involvement in the Reformation controversy was intensified and publicized. At the same time it was bound to appear more ambiguous than ever, especially in France. In Basle he published his *De libero arbitrio diatribe* against Luther and faced the violent opposition of Farel and his Francophone friends, but in Paris some of his earlier writings were circulated in French translation and served to heighten the suspicions of the Sorbonne.[11] The political situation also added to the complexity of his personal position. Budé was still urging him to join the French court,[12] but in Italy the Franco-Spanish war was gathering momentum. 1525 brought Francis I's defeat at Pavia, the exile of Lefèvre d'Etaples, and for Erasmus the necessity of publishing his first apologia against a Sorbonist.[13] With these developments in mind one understands his consideration for the high clergy of the Franche-Comté. Wealthy and generous, liberal-minded and solidly Catholic, subjects of Charles V, and yet exponents of the Francophone culture which he admired, these men could indeed be expected to provide an environment calculated to harmonize the conflicts within him and about him. At the very least, they could be expected to offer precious support against the attacks from the Sorbonne.

If thes pring excursion to Burgundy was designed to demonstrate his orthodoxy in the eyes of French-speaking Catholics, it did not, however, fully achieve this end. True, the mass for the cult of Loretto which Erasmus had dedicated to Bietricius some months before his trip to Burgundy found favour with the Archbishop of Besançon,[14] but his spontaneous reaction to an amusing situation [15] served to crystal-

---

[7] Allen 5.341f.; 7.406ff.

[8] Allen 6.411f.; 8.124f., 127; 11.237, 294f. and passim.

[9] Allen 11.258, 295ff.

[10] Allen 5.442n.

[11] **No. 241** and Mann 131ff.

[12] Allen 5.440ff.

[13] Against Cousturier: **No. 365**.

[14] In the course of Erasmus' visit to Besançon the archbishop granted forty days remission of penance to any one within his diocese who should make use of it: Allen 5.341n.

[15] In Erasmus' words: " De beatis visceribus Mariae virginis sic res habet. Procurator Archidiaconi vocarat nos ad prandium. Sedimus usque ad horam tertiam. Id erat molestissimum, qui vix unquam sedeam ultra dimidium horae. Actae sunt gratiae prolixae et ex variis fragmentis consarcinatae, ' Kyrie eleeyson ', ' Pater noster ', ' De profundis ' aliisque multis, qui fortassis alio tempore dicerentur tempestivius. Ubi iam putabam finem, texi caput et coepi salutare convivas. Hic puer addidit praeter expecta-

lize the latent animosity of some canons and the repercussions spread as far as the Sorbonne. In 1531 Erasmus could still blame it on the hostility of the chapter that he had preferred Freiburg to Besançon.[16]

Erasmus' trip to Burgundy reveals the climate in which the further cultural exchanges between Basle and Burgundy were to take place. The ecclesiastical establishment of Besançon, the circles of the *Parlement* and University in Dole, all provide textbook examples of Erasmianism among a prestige-conscious bourgeois élite.[17] In the face of such widespread, if perhaps shallow, enthusiasm the fanatic opposition was subdued for the time being, although, kept alive as always in the monasteries, it would subsequently force the liberals to give battle. The intellectual atmosphere closely resembled that of another Habsburg town with a cathedral chapter and a modest university, Freiburg, and except for its printing industry Basle might have fallen into the same category. Basle printers, merchants and books passed regularly through Burgundy on their way to and from Lyons,[18] and, above all, the presses attracted the continued attention of the Erasmian circles in Franche-Comté. If the death of Erasmus seemed to terminate some of the most valuable contacts the Basle printers had had in Paris, the collaboration of Burgundians, by contrast, intensified appreciably during the middle decades of the century, although it reflected the topical concerns and social amenities of the region rather than scholarly excellence. Most of it was due to one central figure, the typical bourgeois Erasmian of his generation as well as one of the most assiduous contributors to Basle publishing, Gilbert Cousin.[19]

The product of a middle class family and the local University of Dole, Gilbert reached Freiburg towards the end of 1530. The Habsburg university town might have been a logical choice for any young Comtois eager to complete his education in Germany, but Cousin had particular ambitions and was speedily received into the house of Erasmus. At a time when the old humanist was considering permanent settlement in Besançon, what better *famulus* could he have desired than this young man with an impeccable script and family connections among the higher clergy of the Comté?[20] The move to Besançon, of course, was never undertaken, but Cousin stayed with Erasmus long enough to accompany him back to Basle in 1535, where he acquired many personal friends among the humanists and printers. In the same year he published his first essay, the Οἰκέτης *sive de officio famulorum*.[21] He desired to present himself to the world as the great man's secretary and companion, as throughout his life he would continually employ his modest resources to recreate

---

tionem ' Et beata viscera '. Hic ego ridens ' Hoc ' inquam ' deerat '..." : Allen 6.288 ; cf. 6.166ff. ; 7.336.

[16] Allen 9.89, 307f.

[17] Febvre, *Cousin* 109ff.

[18] See above pp. 36, n. 75, 218f.

[19] Apart from Febvre, *Cousin*, see Allen 9.42ff. and P.-A. Pidoux, *Un humaniste comtois, Gilbert Cousin, 1506-1572*, Lons-le-Saunier 1910 (also published in *Mémoires de la Société d'émulation du Jura* 1910) ; P.-A. Pidoux, *Bibliographie historique des œuvres de Gilbert Cousin*, Besançon 1912 (also published in *Le Bibliographe moderne* 15 (1911), 132-171) Pidoux lists many Basle editions which do not figure in the bibliography attached to this study. In many cases Pidoux himself has never seen a copy ; in the case of an *Opuscula quaedam*, Basle 1535, he refers to a copy in UBB. There is no evidence that UBB ever owned such a copy.

[20] On Louis de Vers : Allen 10.331n. and P.-A. Pidoux, *Cousin, op. cit.* 26 and passim.

[21] **No. 347** ; cf. Febvre, *Cousin* 102.

234

and disseminate the spiritual and intellectual atmosphere he had encountered in Erasmus' house.

He finally left the master to return to his native Nozeroy when relatives effected his nomination to a canonry in the collegiate chapter. The time had come for him to take holy orders, but unfortunately his return to Franche-Comté was closely followed by the first serious outbreak of counter-reformatory agitation,[22] and Cousin's religious views happened to be debatable. Suspicion of heresy was to cast a long shadow on his otherwise peaceful and comfortable existence. Cousin was soon accused of professing and propagating " *la religion de Bâle.*" [23] He did so, but no more than Erasmus himself had done. Like Erasmus he loathed superstitions and abuses ; like him he tended to question the value of celibacy, monastic life, and many ceremonies of medieval origin ; like him he savoured anti-Roman satire, and refused to break with worthy and scholarly friends for want of Catholic faith. His letter of June 1554 to a friend, the Italo-Bâlois C. S. Curione, may serve as an example.[24] He mentioned his delight at reading the anti-Roman polemic of Girolamo Massari, another Italian refugee at Basle.[25] Yet in that same letter to a radical Protestant he listed lengthy proposals for liturgical reform designed to restore the Catholic mass to its ancient dignity. His " *religion de Bâle* " combined respect for Catholic tradition, Erasmus' *philosophia Christi* and humanistic scholarship with abhorrence of fanaticism and ignorance. In the long run it was enough to warrant an investigation on explicit orders from Rome, and to jail, or detain, the old canon for the better part of five years between 1567 and his death in 1572. Those who knew him, however, the archbishop and his curials, as well as the lawyers of the *Parlement* at Dole remained convinced of his harmlessness. Treated as well as the circumstances permitted, he managed from time to time to despatch a letter to his friends in Basle, who hastened to intervene in his favour.[26]

The unhappy circumstances of his last years were not entirely unprecedented in Cousin's life, but in spite of some harassment and the resulting anguish his previous career for more than thirty years had remained surprisingly unimpeded and singularly active. His ecclesiastical duties were light, enabling him to devote his time and energy to a private school which soon enjoyed a high reputation. The cultured families of the Comté, both bourgeois and noble, entrusted their sons to him. Other pupils came from French Burgundy and, of course, from Basle. So did Immanuel,

---

[22] Cf. Febvre, *Cousin* 127ff. ; cf. Cousin's letter to Bonifacius Amerbach from March 1538 : " De persecutione, quam Erasmi observatores passi sunt et quidam adhuc patiuntur, non satis tutum est scribere. Et edictum illud quod scis de libris non legendis saepe repetitur " (Hartmann 5.97).

[23] See e.g. Febvre, *Cousin* 138n. Febvre and Pidoux present opposing views of Cousin's faith ; e.g. his letter to Bonifacius Amerbach of 19 October, 1533, gave raise to grotesque interpretations. Erasmus wrote : " Optarim aliquem germanice peritum, et utcumque latine, qui posset Gylberto succedere. Modo ne sit huius regionis. Gustasse simul sat est." (Allen 10.306 ; Hartmann 4.243). Following an 18th century ed., Febvre and Pidoux read " *religionis* " for " *regionis* ", one concluded that to Erasmus Cousin's views were too Protestant, the other that they were too Catholic : Febvre, *Cousin* 103 ; P.-A. Pidoux, *Cousin, op. cit.* 71f.

[24] Published in part by Febvre and now completely in Bietenholz, *Erasmus und der Basler Buchhandel in Frankreich* 315ff. Cousin's proposals for liturgical reform also reflect the attitudes of Erasmus : cf. e.g. J.-C. Margolin, *Recherches érasmiennes*, Geneva 1969, 87.

[25] Cf. G. Busino in *BHR* 20 (1958), 517 ; Cantimori, *Ital. Haeretiker* 198 and S. Kot in *Autour de Servet et de Castellion* 90.

[26] Bietenholz, *Erasmus und der Basler Buchhandel in Frankreich* 303f. ; cf. Bouvier 535f.

the son of the Basle publicist J. B. Herold, who had himself earlier spent a happy week under Cousin's roof. In prefaces to works dedicated to Cousin, the grateful father took pains to acknowledge his debt to the teacher of his son, all the more so since, the Protestant Bâlois background notwithstanding, the school of Nozeroy seemed an ideal stepping stone to future employment in the household of some Comtois prelate.[27] Cousin also received the sons of the printer H. Petri [28] and his friend Sigismund Gelenius. Even Bonifacius Amerbach thought for some time of sending Basilius to him, though in the end the youngster remained in the care of Castellio.[29]

Leaving aside the probability of some short visits to Basle,[30] a frequent exchange of letters permitted Cousin to keep in touch with his friends and fellow Erasmians there and elsewhere. The letters were often carried by relatives, former pupils and other Burgundians setting out for the University of Basle and sometimes eager to be recommended to the consideration of Amerbach for a grant from the Erasmus fund.[31] Cousin's correspondents in Basle were respected citizens, the minister Johannes Gast, Amerbach, Theodor Zwinger who wanted him as god-father for one of his children, the printer Heinrich Petri. Even Curione, the professor, fitted the pattern at least outwardly. Cousin's contacts, however, reached beyond Basle, to Gwalter and Bullinger in Zurich, to Gian Angelo Oddone in Strasbourg, to his compatriot Jean Matal, who studied in Bologna and became an associate of Georgius Cassander, to mention only a few of his correspondents.[32] Philippus Montanus, who had lived briefly in Erasmus' household prior to Cousin's arrival and his own appointment to a teaching position in the College of Tournai in Paris, collaborated with Cousin to some extent in editing the *Expositio fidelis de morte D. Thomae Mori.* They were also associated in a recommendation which Erasmus sent to François Bonvalot on behalf of both.[33]

Cousin's correspondence with the Bâlois reveals his character as clearly as it expresses his recurrent thoughts. He spoke his mind freely; still, during the time of his detention he referred to his enemies with a curious mixture of blunt language and secretiveness. He dreaded the intentions of the Cardinals of Granvelle and Lorraine, and mentioned the Council of Trent and the Colloquy of Poissy with an equal lack of enthusiasm.[34] Such organized attempts to restore Christian unity

---

[27] Burckhardt, *Herold*, 132f., 229n.

[28] Still in 1564 the old printer chose his preface to an ed. of Sallust to assure Cousin of his friendship and his gratitude : Febvre, *Cousin* 146f.

[29] *Ibid.* 117f.

[30] **No. 362** is dated from Augustae Rauricae, " ipsis Nonis Iulii ", 1557. This is, of course, a reference to Basle, and not Augst, as assumed by Febvre. On the other hand, there is a mysterious sentence in a letter to Theodor Zwinger, dated from Nozeroy, " 7. Cal. Decemb., 1561 ", which sounds as if Cousin had not yet met Zwinger personally : " Et quoniam de Basiliensi concilio non dubius est sermo, reservetur spes nostri congressus ad id tempus, quo praeter caeteras causas non erit ultima mei istuc accessus, ut talem virum coram salutem atque amplectar." *Opera* (**No. 332**) 3.207.

[31] Cf. Allen 8.126f. ; Hartmann 5.98, 104 ; 6.45, 166, 500f.

[32] *Opera* (**No. 332**) 1.306ff. ; 315f. ; P.-A. Pidoux, *Cousin, op. cit.*, passim. For Matal (Metellus) see Jöcher ; for Cousin's correspondence with Bullinger see Bouvier 346ff.

[33] Cf. **No. 748** ; Allen 10.332 ; 11.368ff. ; Herminjard 3.197. Montanus and Cousin were also corresponding directly : Allen 11.297.

[34] Cf. the passages quoted by Hartmann 6.500 ; Febvre, *Cousin* 123 ; and Bietenholz, *Erasmus und der Basler Buchhandel in Frankreich*, 304f., n. 31.

could not stand up to his extreme Erasmianism, which let him simply ignore the existence of confessional divisions in all of his personal relations. To comfort himself during one of his earlier tribulations, when the religious section of his own library had been sent away to a safe place, he gladly borrowed from a friend Castellio's Latin version of the Bible together with Erasmus' paraphrase of St. Matthew.[35]

One may wonder, however, on what grounds the Bâlois really sympathized with their friend in Nozeroy. They clearly revered him as an educator, and they pitied his misfortunes; but was this enough? In retrospect Cousin's Nozeroy seems hopelessly remote, not only from the Rome and Trent or the Geneva of his contemporaries, but also from the Carpentras of a Sadoleto, the Paris of a L'Hospital and the neighbouring Montbéliard of a Toussain, not to mention the Basle of a Castellio. These men can all be associated with specific, if different, causes and while the staid humanists and printers of Basle hardly adopted them on their own initiative, they supported many of them willingly and indiscriminately, if and when approached. Cousin, by contrast, had no message for the world. Not even the propagation of Erasmian ideals could convincingly be named as an ideological basis for his relation to the Bâlois. In fact no such basis was needed, since the natural ties between neighbouring lands and personal acquaintances proved sufficiently strong to produce a common outlook in many matters. The true nature of the exchanges between Comtois humanists and Basle is well demonstrated in Cousin's own writings published in the Rhine town.

References to Erasmus are numerous in Cousin's published works, while in his letters, as in those of Bonifacius Amerbach, the spontaneous recurrence of Erasmian diction may be noted. Similarly some of the topics he treated confirm the continuity of Erasmian impulses, but Cousin's treatment itself is characteristically void of interest. Even though he had very little to say about them, he eagerly tackled Lucian and Origen, the problems of literal and allegorical exegesis, and the periodization of history according to spiritual ages.[36] As we have seen, Erasmianism added an exciting, and tragic, keynote to Cousin's life, but only in the documents pertaining to his trial and in his unpublished letters can it be discovered, whereas his learned publications belabour the obvious. What an awkward agglomeration are his Collected Works—*opera multifarii argumenti*, as the Basle publishers appropriately entitled them—printed in 1562 on 864 folio pages! In leafing through them one is puzzled to recall that with the exception of Budé no other Francophone author was deemed worthy in Basle of such a collection. The haphazard selection and arrangement of the material and the absence of any general preface or epistle dedicatory emphasize the unpremeditated nature of the project. Clearly no qualified editor had been engaged and consultation with the author himself had at best been sporadic. Rather, the volume amounted to a candid gesture of friendship and gratitude, made at a moment when new inquisitorial persecutions in the Franche-

---

[35] UBB ms. Ki.Ar.18ᵃ, fol. 158f., Cousin to Bonifacius Amerbach, Nozeroy, 2 December, 1554: " Hoc ocii quod datur non sacris studiis, neque tamen moerori, sed prophanis damus, siquidem in hac Babylone bonis libris uti non licet. Est mihi quam ab amico quopiam nactus sum, Er[asmi] nostri Paraphrasis in Evangelium Matthei. Nactus sum praeterea contextum sacrorum voluminum ex Castel[lionis] versione : haec, cum legere libet, lego ; reliqui siquidem libri nostri absunt, ne a Caesareo fisco appellentur." (Contextum sacrorum voluminum : perhaps the text without the compromising title page and preface ?) ; cf. Febvre, *Cousin* 127, 134f.

[36] See **No. 341, 346, 351, 358f.**

Comté [37] were likely to aggravate the danger for Cousin. Adam Henricpetri, a former pupil, now assisted his father, the printer, in this enterprise.

The contents nevertheless remain disappointing. A sequence of prayers reflects neatly, but without distinction, Cousin's Erasmian religion, whereas a small collection of letters derives its significance mostly from the fact that compromising texts were carefully excluded.[38] While the reprinting of Cousin's topographical essays seems appropriate, many of the newly published writings could hardly have been of much use outside his own classroom and might have been offered more profitably in the form of an inexpensive school text. What is one to think, for instance, of the lengthy excerpts copied from Seneca and Cicero, or the uninspired commentary on *Romans*? Likewise, of Cousin's many separate writings published at Basle, quite a number await evaluation in terms of social, rather than intellectual, history. They serve to exhibit a multiplicity of epigrams and letters written by the canon of Nozeroy and his humanist friends in Burgundy and Basle with the purpose of advancing one another and of eulogizing influential members of the great families of the Comté. To secure the goodwill of these families, leagued by marriage and with a secure footing at court and in the church, was no doubt the primary concern of the bourgeois humanists as well as of the co-operating printers. From the days of Erasmus the Bâlois had retained the highest respect for the aristocracy of the Comté, who seemed to govern the world from their important positions in the immediate entourage of Charles V.[39] The names which occur most persistently in Cousin's compositions, or those of his friends which he edited, often belong to the successors of the influential Burgundian prelates and officials who had been friends of Erasmus. In addition to the profoundly bourgeois consideration for rank, the importance of the Comté for Basle's southwestern trade may best explain why her publishers lent themselves so willingly to the laborious glorification of the families de La Baume, Bonvalot, de Rye, de Poupet, de Chalon and even Perrenot de Granvelle.[40] Only Cousin's personal troubles in the years following the death of Charles V made them realize that the traditional assumptions on which their relations with the Comté were based had lost their validity.

Illustrious patrons apart, Cousin's publications reveal the names of a great many of his friends and fellow humanists in Burgundy—so many, indeed, that the scrutiny of this material, fascinating in its own way, must be left to the specialists of regional history.[41] In a collection of epigrams, for instance, which Cousin published at Basle in 1557 [42] one encounters, among many others, some contributions by Hugues Babet,[43] Laurent Privé,[44] and many verses addressed to Claude Frontin, whose nephew Anatole

---

[37] Cf. Febvre, *Cousin* 135.

[38] Cf., however, *Opera* (**No. 332**) 1.416 : a note written by Cousin in 1556-57 and certainly not intended for publication, containing an emphatic plea for cautious selection in the reprinting of his works.

[39] L. Febvre, *Hist. de Franche-Comté, op. cit.* 168ff.

[40] Cf. e.g. **No. 337, 355f., 361, 622, 709,** and epistles dedicatory in **No. 120f., 124, 346, 354, 357, 710.** The great Basle ed. of Ficino's *Opera,* 1561, contains an epistle dedicatory by Adam Henricpetri to Guillaume de Poupet, containing a ref. to Cousin.

[41] Very useful biographical notes on Cousin's friends, including the ones mentioned in this chapter, on the University of Dôle, etc. may be found in E. Monot's ed. of G. Cousin's *Descriptio Burgundiae: La Franche-Comté au milieu du XVIe siècle,* Lons-le-Saunier 1907.

[42] **No. 362.**

[43] See Michaud. J. J. Boissard was Babet's nephew and heir to his library.

[44] He also contributed a hymn on St. Nicholas to **No. 806.**

had recently advanced from Cousin's school at Nozeroy to the University of Basle and was to publish there a series of diagrams on rhetoric.[45]

In his assiduous attention to personal visits, student exchanges and occasional publications, then, lies Cousin's real contribution as far as it comes within the scope of this study. His religious views, his personal tastes, his intellectual orientation and literary expression, all had been formed in the years spent under the roof of Erasmus. As far as they lay within his grasp he faithfully adopted the thoughts of his master, and he retained them under increasingly adverse circumstances. Apparently unaware of the diverging tendencies of Erasmianism in Basle and of the resulting tensions, he must have taught his friends in Burgundy to see in the Rhenish town a haven for liberal piety, civilized wit and polite manners. In return for the stimulation he found in books sent to him from Basle, he offered his friends there the encouraging example of his own existence and his friendship in defiance of confessional frontiers. However this example was discredited by the fate he suffered during his last years, and after his death the Franche-Comté was no longer treated with special consideration in the Basle publishing programme. Unlike Paris and Lyons, Burgundy offered no intellectual challenge and few of Cousin's many publications seem to have encouraged the Basle printers to look for more copy dealing with the same topics. However, Cousin himself may have suggested a reprint of Guillaume Paradin's *De antiquo statu Burgundiae*.[46] Probably published by Oporinus, it presented a French counterpart to Cousin's own *Descriptio Burgundiae* with its unmistakable Comtois emphasis, also issued from the press of Oporinus. Only three years after Cousin's death Nicolas Vignier, a physician and for the time being a Protestant refugee, resumed in Basle analogous historical studies with the publication of his annals of medieval Burgundy.[47]

Cousin's severe, if unpublished, criticism of certain practices and institutions of the Catholic church found a curious continuation in the publications of Guillaume Pasquelin, who until his death in 1632 taught theology in Beaune, his native town. Was he a sort of seventeenth century Cousin? The Basle minister J. J. Grasser, who translated his *Protocatastasis* into German,[48] may have thought so. Pasquelin had returned from Rome when denied admission to the final vows of the Jesuit order from which he had received his entire education. For a time vengeance became his very *raison d'être*. Grasser may have been pleased to find such fierce attacks upon the Jesuits in the text of a devout Catholic priest. Nevertheless, it is hard to imagine

---

[45] **No. 449**, with a preface by C. S. Curione and Frontin's epistle dedicatory addressed to the brothers de La Baume. On both Frontins see Michaud ; *France prot.*[2]; and *Matrikel* 2.103, 615 where Anatole's place of birth is erroneously given as Stadtamhof (Palatinate) instead of La Rivière near Pontarlier. Adam Henricpetri, Cousin's former student, dedicated to Claude Frontin an ed. of Aulus Gellius, published by the family press in 1565. Anatole may have returned from Basle as a Huguenot and died among the victims of the night of Saint Bartholomew. If so, the case seems unprecedented among Cousin's close personal friends in the Franche-Comté. However, Nozeroy would not so soon be rid of heretics : in 1608 one Claudius Brocardus alias Justinus received a scholarship in the University of Basle after having shed his cowl : *Matrikel* 3.76.

[46] **No. 786.** Paradin's patriotic outbursts against Charles V are particularly noticeable in another historical essay, belatedly reprinted in Basle : **No. 787.** On Paradin, who died in 1590 as the dean of the chapter of Beaujeu, see Michaud ; J. Descroix, *Les épigrammes latins de Guillaume Paradin*, Lyons 1936, 112 and passim.

[47] **No. 1024.** Cf. Michaud ; *France Prot.*

[48] **No. 791.** On Pasquelin see S. Gautheret-Comboulot, *Les auteurs beaunois du XVIe au XIXe siècle*[2], Beaune 1893, 185-223.

that orthodox Calvinists found the book much to their taste and the Basle printer judged it wise to withhold his name. In fact, Pasquelin demanded nothing more than reforms within the Society and he seems to have been reconciled to it before his death.

Next to Cousin's Nozeroy, the city of Dole played a prominent role in the exchanges between Basle and the Comté. Many students went back and forth between the two university towns, and the rivalry between their law schools was highlighted in 1532 by Dole's timely, if ultimately unsuccessful, attempt to attract Bonifacius Amerbach, whose pay at Basle was niggardly and who was harassed for his refusal to attend the reformed communion service. His decision to stay in Basle may have been influenced by the very unattractive picture of Dole painted for him by Erasmus.[49]

The university had more luck in retaining from 1541 for five years the experienced Italian law teacher Niccolò Bellone. He was brought to the Comté by Nicolas Perrenot de Granvelle, to whom he remained closely attached while at the same time establishing friendly contacts with many local humanists, Cousin among them. In 1546 he abandoned his teaching career in favour of more prominent missions in the service of Charles V. Bellone had formerly been Alciato's colleague in the University of Pavia and he remained committed to Alciato's conception of jurisprudence.[50] Both in choosing Basle presses for the publication of his legal treatises and in maintaining a regular correspondence with Bonifacius Amerbach he again followed the example of Alciato. However, he was even more careful than the latter to avoid in his letters to Amerbach any kind of ideological topic. Most of their correspondence concerned Bellone's publications in Basle, which the author attempted to make as profitable to himself as possible,[51] and the financial provisions for his nephew who was studying at the Rhine town.[52] The special atmosphere of Dole and her university is well demonstrated by the fact that a Spaniard, Antonius Lullus, was Bellone's colleague, teaching initially rhetoric and subsequently theology while rising to the position of vicar general of the diocese of Besançon. Lullus was a good friend of Bellone and Cousin, at least as long as the latter's orthodoxy was not officially questioned, but his publications in Basle mostly dealt with the teaching of rhetoric.[53]

Of all representatives of Dole among the Basle authors, the least known is the most interesting, especially with respect to the progress of French Erasmianism. Jean Morisot, born at Dole and a physician there until his death some time after 1551, was not given to letter writing, nor was he inclined to subject himself to the exigencies

---

[49] Burckhardt, *Amerbach* 96ff.; Hartmann 4.111, 114 and passim. Still in 1545 Amerbach considered accepting Bellone's invitation to spend a holiday at Dole: Hartmann 6.165.

[50] Hartmann 5.402n. and passim; *Dizionario biografico degli Italiani*, Rome 1960ff. (with vague references to several Basle editions, including Bellone's *Opera*, 1549, none of which I have seen).

[51] From Hartmann 5.410 we learn that Oporinus published an earlier ed. of Bellone's *Supputationes* (**No. 123**) in 1542 (according to Gesner; I failed to trace a copy of it). Bellone received 30 copies free, but requested an additional 70 copies for sale among his students at the rate charged to book merchants. Nothing to this effect had been stated in the original agreement, and Oporinus refused. Cf. also Hartmann 5.426, 470f.

[52] Paolo Emilio Bellone: *Matrikel* 2.41; Hartmann 6.28f. and passim.

[53] **No. 708ff.**; cf. Michaud; Hartmann 5.411; 6.xxxvi. Cousin dedicated to him **No. 341.**

of a public career. But he was an esteemed friend of Lullus and Cousin,[54] and to judge from the few *opuscula* that were published among the many that he wrote,[55] his was the most original mind of the whole circle of native Comtois humanists. His own bilingual edition of Hippocrates' *Aphorismi* gave him an opportunity to take such authorities as Theodore Gaza and Niccolò Leoniceno to task. Oporinus, who printed the little book, also undertook the publication of Morisot's translation into Greek of Cicero's *Paradoxa*. The same press finally issued the most noteworthy of his books, a collection of *Colloquia*, composed for the linguistic training and moral benefit of his son.[56]

In this work Morisot makes no effort to hide his dependence upon Erasmus. Many of his dialogues are frank imitations of some of the best known colloquies of the latter. The message too is an often much simplified repetition of the typically Erasmian concerns: analogous figures are introduced by both authors to express abhorrence of national pride, war and soldiers, of a father sacrificing his daughter to a rich syphilitic, or of vice-addicted and lazy priests. On the positive side Morisot expresses Erasmian confidence in the purifying, humanizing power of the Gospel, although perhaps with greater concessions to Stoicism and with a pessimism not typical of his great model. For the most part he seems unable to think of any remedies for the specific vices he exposes, a fact which somewhat discredits his claim to a pedagogical intention. By contrast, his literary talent asserts itself freely. Compared with Erasmus, his style is far less subtle and elegant, the settings are less skilful, and the art of characterization less developed; yet little insights reveal the power of observation acquired by the medical practitioner: there is a doctor at the sickbed of a dying patient, mechanically dispensing his stock of bland encouragements to all present; there is a little girl intuitively frightened by the birth of a brother, because he might come to resemble her father who neglects her for his business. Repeated touches of immorality defy the decorum carefully observed by Erasmus: there is, for instance, the husband who has to enter a church to discover his wife's adultery with a priest; there is a frank report of the highly natural contacts between adolescent boys and girls. In view of such concessions to sensual reality, combined with his general dependence upon Erasmus, it is indeed remarkable that in his preface Morisot should dare to criticize the Erasmian *Colloquies* for their paganizing Lucianism and their tendency to sacrifice the pedagogical end to personal vindictiveness.

In the final analysis, Morisot's *Colloquia* lend vivacious and graceful expression to the epigonic Erasmianism of the Comté. He represents a group of bourgeois humanists held together by ideals well worth living for, although perhaps not dying for, as many of them were to discover at the time of Cousin's trial. Their scholarly and literary production, as far as it was published at Basle, cannot have made an impact on posterity, but everyday life affords many opportunities unfathomed by historians to influence future generations.

---

[54] Cf. Michaud. He contributed epigrams to two of Lullus' Basle publications: **No. 708f.**

[55] A list of his writings is appended to **No. 758**. It is reprinted in Simler's re-edition of Gesner's *Bibliotheca*, but no published books are indicated apart from those listed in our bibliography. In an undated letter from Morisot to Oporinus (UBB ms. Fr. Gr. II.4 No. 225) the printer is urged to finally publish a new work by Morisot to be dedicated to the Archbishop of Besançon, Claude de La Baume, as well as an enlarged re-edition of the *Colloquia*.

[56] **No. 758.**

CONCLUSION

It seems advisable to stop the present investigation of personal exchanges between Bâlois and Francophones well short of a complete survey which would require another series of chapters and produce a maze of additional information without, however, significantly modifying the general conclusions to be drawn from this first part of the proposed study.

Of the Francophones personally in touch with Basle, or simply authors of books reprinted there, many have gone unmentioned. The relations between Basle and Geneva require a treatment of their own and will receive it before long.[1] Without this study the further investigation of personal exchanges among the various communities of Huguenot exiles, both at Basle and elsewhere, seems premature. Other Francophones might have been grouped according to their towns of birth or domicile. Bordeaux affords a good example.[2] Her many humanists and lawyers were served by an efficient local book commerce. Her religious life was enriched by the presence of numerous Erasmians, Evangelicals and Huguenots. Learning flourished in the College of Guyenne ; the work of its many scholars was represented in Basle printing by the names of A. de Gouvea, Elie Vinet, Maturin Cordier, Robert Breton, G. Buchanan, N. de Grouchy, and M.-A. Muret ; the *Parlement* of Bordeaux by Arnoul Le Ferron. The poet E. de Beaulieu lived at Bordeaux for some time. Likewise Bourges might have been examined, with her university popular among Bâlois students and her *Ecu de Bâle*,[3] or Troyes, which was the home of a number of distinguished visitors to Basle and of students attending her university.[4] None of these local circles, however, seems to call for a particular characterization of their attitudes towards Basle humanism and of their publications reflecting the progress of French Erasmianism in the way this has been attempted for Paris and Lyons on preceding pages. On the other hand the contacts of individuals with the Rhine city normally developed along patterns already investigated.

In like manner a broad description of the exchanges between Basle and some neighbouring towns which were wholly or predominantly Francophone, in particular Metz and Montbéliard, would essentially repeat the tale of Franche-Comté : neighbourhood naturally produces an intensive intercourse not dependent upon, or neces-

---

[1] Mr. U. Plath is presently finalizing his Basle dissertation on Calvin and Basle after 1552.

[2] For the following cf. *Histoire de Bordeaux*, ed. C. Higounet, Bordeaux 1962ff., 4.186ff.

[3] Cf. our references to Alciato, Baudouin, Bouquin, Brand, F. Platter and Sphyractes. For contacts between Erasmus and Alciato as well as some of his students at Bourges see Allen 9.23f., 61ff., 103, 231ff.

[4] Cf. our references to the Pithou brothers and *Matrikel* 2.617, where the names of some other students from Troyes are listed.

sarily conducive to, intellectual curiosity. As in the case of the Franche-Comté the biographical information pertinent to this study, if assembled with any measure of completeness, would be copious indeed. A glance at the matriculation roll of Basle University shows that students from these adjacent regions always outnumbered the visitors from the heartland of France, and that this disproportion grew as the numbers of the latter were falling off towards the end of the sixteenth century.[5] The case of Metz must do as the sole example of the kind of ties that united Basle with other towns in Lorraine, in the Vaud and in Savoy. Metz was dominated by a ruling class of commercial and capitalistic orientation, rarely given to intellectual pursuits,[6] not even when economic recession hit them during the first half of the sixteenth century. However, during the seminal phase of the Reformation there developed religious connections to the Rhine town [7] which proved enduring in the course of the many vicissitudes befalling Messin Protestantism over the next fifty years.

Claude Chansonnette [8] who was the outstanding son of Metz in his generation is also suited to symbolize the relations between the two cities. Well capable of holding his own among the foremost legal scholars of the day, the friend of Zasius, Amerbach, Alciato and Budé, he nevertheless preferred the practical duties of a jurisconsultant and administrator in the service of princely and urban governments. As a result he consented to a series of moves, leading from the Basle of Erasmus back to Metz and on to Vic-sur-Seille and Ensisheim, and obliging him to put up with intellectual provincialism freshly accentuated by every new transfer. The common attraction of his successive employments was no doubt the subtle diplomacy needed by those managing the affairs of the town republics of Basle and Metz, of the bishopric of Metz which belonged to the Cardinal of Lorraine, and of the Habsburg dependency of Upper Alsace. Moving thus up and down through the border region separating France from the German lands, Chansonnette was an Erasmian only in the sense of showing conciliatory inclinations and irenic convictions. He was little touched by scholarly and religious litigations of the day, although the militant Protestants in Metz came to count him among their opponents. By contrast, Jean-Jacques Boissard, the only typical representative of the liberal arts at Metz, who visited Basle and published there a collection of poems and epigrams,[9] was a Protestant. A native of the Franche-Comté, he proved more enterprising and mobile than Gilbert Cousin and his friends, whom he otherwise closely resembled in his literary and topographico-antiquarian interests as well as in his acceptance of educational duties. After much travelling he settled at Metz as preceptor in the house of a local Huguenot nobleman, Claude-Antoine de Vienne. To the latter was also dedicated a curious treatise on fossils discovered in the region and thought to prove the existence of human giants in prehistoric times. Its author was a Huguenot minister at Metz,

---

[5] For the names of students coming from Metz, Lorraine and Montbéliard see *Matrikel* 2.602, 604f.

[6] Cf. G. Zeller, *La Réunion de Metz à la France*, Strasbourg 1926, 1.192 and passim ; also G. Zeller, Marchands-Capitalistes de Metz et de Lorraine au XVIe siècle, *Eventail de l'histoire vivante* (Hommage à Lucien Febvre), Paris 1953, 2.273-281.

[7] Viénot, *Montbéliard* 1.40ff. ; G. Zeller, *La Réunion, op. cit.* 1.187ff.

[8] Cf. above p. 188f. and Hartmann 2.289n. and passim ; Allen 3.349n. ; J. Schneider, Claude Chansonnette ... au service de la maison de Lorraine, *Eventail, op. cit.* 2.231-239.

[9] **No. 170** ; contains also various contributions by the Messin Jacques Pasquier. On Boissard cf. *France prot.*[2]; *Matrikel* 2.220 ; Droz, *Etudiants français*.

Jean Chassanion, who published it in 1580 at Basle, where he seems to have withdrawn at a time of heightened pressure upon the Messin Protestant community, perhaps on the advice of Boissard.[10]   Next to the reformed party it was, as elsewhere in Francophone territory, the medical profession of Metz that showed a special consideration for Basle.   In addition to Jacques Pasquier, the Messin student of medicine who was a familiar figure to the Basle printers,[11] his compatriot Jacques Saint-Aubin [12] also graduated from Basle University.   He was later appointed a municipal physician in his home town, and from there he corresponded frequently with Theodor Zwinger,[13] urging the Bâlois professor, not always successfully, to interest the Basle publishers in the various medical works of Anuce Foës,[14] Saint-Aubin's senior colleague at Metz.

On the face of it, the intercourse between Basle and Montbéliard too seems to conform to the general pattern of good-neighbourly relations investigated in the case of Franche-Comté.   Our examination of them should therefore be brief.   To have saved it for the last may seem arbitrary, yet perhaps no better example could be found of the various influences spreading from Basle into French-speaking countries and, eventually, reaching back to her presses, although in the case of modest Montbéliard no revelations can be expected from the productions of her men of letters.

In the first half of the sixteenth century the County of Montbéliard was not adversely affected by the political misfortunes besetting her counts, the Dukes of Württemberg, in their German territories.   On the contrary, Montbéliard may have profited somewhat from the fact that Duke Ulrich was forced to establish his court there from 1519 to 1526, although the peaceful little country was in no danger of a sudden exposure to the limelight of economic and cultural development.   By contrast, Montbéliard was quickly and profoundly affected by the Reformation and the major controversies springing from it.   Her reformer, Pierre Toussain, had been gained to the Gospel and prepared for his mission mostly during his stays at Metz, Basle and Paris.[15]   Under his leadership a highly successful Protestant church was organized throughout the County of Montbéliard.   Although a formal ban on Catholicism was wisely avoided, the country could be said to stand behind its reformer.   But only for a time, for the Lutheranism of the dynasty and its German pastors in Württemberg was bound to clash, sooner or later, with the Calvinistic bent of Toussain and his Francophone ministers in Montbéliard.   The tensions grew, years before Montbéliard's sister church at Basle was to be exposed to a comparable dilemma when her *antistes* Sulzer tended to prefer the Lutheran doctrines to those of Zurich and Geneva.   However, Toussain rose to the occasion.   Not for nothing

---

[10] **No. 243** ; the author's preface is dated from Basle, s.a. Boissard contributed some Latin verses to this ed.   On Chassanion see *France prot.*[2]   A predecessor of Chassanion, Jean Garnier, had come to Metz from Strasbourg.   His short catechism was written for the French church at Strasbourg : **No. 453** ; cf. Bouvier 337 ; *France prot.*[2].

[11] Cf. above p. 72.

[12] *Matrikel* 2.239 ; Droz, *Etudiants français; France prot.; Correspondance politique adressée au magistrat de Strasbourg par ses agents à Metz*, ed. E. de Bouteiller & E. Hepp, Paris 1882, 397ff. ; *Correspondance de B. Vulcanius* 217f.

[13] UBB ms. Fr. Gr. II.26, No. 234ff. ; Fr. Gr. II.4, No. 262ff. ; Fr. Gr. II.23, No. 420ff.

[14] **No. 441f.**   On Foës cf. Michaud and Hirsch.   Some letters by him to Theodor Zwinger are in UBB ms.   Fr. Gr. II.4, No. 101ff.

[15] Viénot, *Montbéliard* 1.4ff., 39ff. and passim, also for what follows ; *Guillaume Farel, 1489-1565*, Neuchâtel-Paris 1930, 131ff.

244

had he learned, during his earlier stay at Basle, to divide his admiration loyally between Erasmus and Oecolampadius and to retain the goodwill of both.[16] Now, in 1545, his sense of moderation as well as his subtle diplomacy impressed Duke Ulrich and paved the way for compromise between the conflicting tendencies within the church of Montbéliard. From his renewed exile at Basle he was summoned to meet the duke personally. In essence the fourteen articles agreed upon by them protected Toussain's church from interference by the Lutherans at Montbéliard, while at the same time ensuring its full submission to the duke and his court theologians at Tübingen.[17] The resulting situation did not lack analogies with that of the Basle church. The *antistes* Myconius too had struggled in vain to escape substantial control of his ministers by the magistrate and its faithful servant, the university. Moreover he supported against the Zurich theologians Bucer's conciliatory attitude in the Eucharistic controversy. No wonder that he followed Toussain's moves with sympathetic interest.[18]

Soon thereafter Montbéliard was exposed to the consequences of Charles V's victory at Mühlberg. In view of the threatening attitude of François Bonvalot, the administrator of the neighbouring Archdiocese of Besançon, the county's very existence was imperilled and resistance to the *Interim* of Charles V could not continue indefinitely. From 1548 to 1552 Mass and *Prêche* competed openly throughout the county.[19] It was, however, after the final suppression of Catholicism that the most fascinating chapter in Montbéliard's religious history opened. Pierre Toussain obtained ducal recognition for his moderately Calvinistic liturgy of the church of Montbéliard, a French translation of which was published a few years later at Basle,[20] while the Huguenot and Lutheran factions soon resumed their customary litigations. But suddenly there appeared among them a group of ministers openly committed to the tradition of Castellio. They had arrived one by one, mostly by way of Basle, and at first went about their duties in the unassuming manner of their master. No doubt they had been encouraged to come, or stay, by Toussain's own defection from the Geneva camp over the burning of Servetus.[21] All had close contacts with the Basle presses. Jacques Gette, who had been serving in Toussain's church from the beginning, publicly maintained in 1554 that it was difficult to prove Anabaptists and Antitrinitarians wrong, and that heretics should not be punished by the secular arm. The following year he published in Basle his collection of *Bucolica Christiana*.[22] In it he warmly applauded Luther and Melanchthon, but failed to mention Calvin. The Genevans were hardly wrong in branding him a Castellionist, even though he may never have known the Savoyard personally and intimately, as had his colleague Léger Grymoult during the decade of his employment with Basle presses.[23] While both Gette and Grymoult ministered to parishes in the

---

[16] Cf. above p. 93f.

[17] Viénot, *Montbéliard* 1.130ff.

[18] M. Geiger, *Die Basler Kirche und Theologie im Zeitalter der Hochorthodoxie*, Zollikon-Zurich 1952, 10f.; R. Thommen, *Geschichte der Universität Basel, 1532-1632*, Basle 1889, 104f.; Wernle, *Calvin* 46.

[19] Viénot, *Montbéliard* 1. 141ff.

[20] *Ibid.* 1.194 ; **No. 1012**.

[21] Viénot, *Montbéliard* 1. 196ff.

[22] *Ibid.* 1.71, 197ff.; **No. 465**.

[23] Cf. above p. 127 and Viénot, *Montbéliard* 1.278, 302.

County of Montbéliard, the actual leadership of this group fell to Jean L'Archier, another admirer and correspondent of long standing of Castellio, who since 1563 had directed the church of Héricourt, a small Württemberg territory in the neighbourhood of the County of Montbéliard, and who published in 1567 with Oporinus a huge *Dictionarium theologicum*. It was L'Archier who introduced at Héricourt in 1564 a pro-Lutheran church ordinance, issued in 1559 but not so far implemented at Montbéliard. This text was now translated into French by Grymoult, revised by L'Archier himself and finally published at Basle in 1568.[24] The Castellionists had thus joined forces with the Lutheran opposition against Toussain. In 1571 their names, along with that of the minister Ogier Barthol who had formerly worked with Grymoult in the Froben press at Basle, were all found among the signatures on a document that provoked the retirement of Pierre Toussain and the banishment of his resolutely Calvinist nephew, Daniel.[25] The document was the concord formula of 1536, signed by Luther, Melanchthon, Bucer and others. Whether Jean Bauhin the younger had any connection with this group of Castellionist ministers remains to be investigated. Along with other prominent officials the highly respected court physician put his signature to a new document which reaffirmed and finalized the decision of 1571 and had subsequently to be signed by all ministers.[26]

We need not follow the ecclesiastical history of Montbéliard beyond this extraordinary moment when a group of Castellionists helped to ensure the victory of a moderate Lutheranism over a Calvinism rendered more militant than in past decades by the arrival of Daniel Toussain. The conflict continued to smoulder, and the subsequent developments offer plenty of drama, but little originality.[27] Moreover, the principal facts which may tie the perplexing story of Montbéliard to the general conclusions to be derived from this volume have been presented.

Montbéliard received a number of men who represented all, or nearly all, aspects of Basle's influence among the French-speaking community. Her reformer Pierre Toussain arrived from Basle as the friend of Oecolampadius and Farel, but also as the promising scholar whom Erasmus had treated with consideration. Although himself not quite an Erasmian, he relied on commonsense and his personal knack for compromise to build a Protestant church that retained flexibility, dignity, and even basic unity despite all doctrinal and political pressures, thus adding a religious parallel to the geographical contiguity of Montbéliard and Basle. Moreover, although himself not a Castellionist, Toussain's spontaneous protest against the burning of Servetus resembled the reaction of the Basle emigré circle in its motives as well as consequences. Later on a group of admirers of Castellio contributed to Toussain's downfall and the introduction of a Lutheranism which they may have expected to be more latitudinarian than it really was. Apart from ministers, the duke's physician and the duke's printer at Montbéliard had been trained at Basle and recruited from there. Jean Bauhin not only inherited his father's record of religious independence, as shown by his open clash with a Calvinist presbytery of Lyons, he was also a distinguished naturalist and author, and founded at Montbéliard

[24] Viénot, *Montbéliard* 1.270ff., 288ff. ; **No. 487**. Cf. above p. 133, n. 80. A short letter to Jean Bauhin senior at Basle, written from Héricourt on 7 October, 1565, shows that the two men knew one another quite well : UBB ms. G². I. 23f., No. 9.

[25] Viénot, *Montbéliard* 1.311f. ; 2.236f. ; cf. above p. 80.

[26] *Ibid.* 2.304.

[27] Cf. H. Hermelink, *Geschichte der evangelischen Kirche in Württemberg*, Stuttgart and Tübingen 1949, 117f. and passim ; Geisendorf 351ff.

an exemplary botanical garden.[28] Jacques Foillet, the printer, brought from Basle part of Perna's equipment and used it to re-launch some of Perna's controversial authors, including Machiavelli and Paracelsus.[29] So many of Basle's distinctive traditions were passed on Montbéliard, and yet the results seem disappointing, or, at least, were not enduring. Quiet resignation and pastoral routine followed the various periods of turbulence in the church of Montbéliard. Bauhin and Foillet found no successors. One vital difference may explain why Montbéliard never became a sort of minor Basle and why her intellectual life, though perhaps more inclined to adventure than that of Gilbert Cousin's Franche-Comté, lacked the Erasmian tinge of the latter. Humanistic scholarship in the fields of philology, literature and history seems to have been poorly represented in the Württemberg town.[30] Exercised in all its broadness, which for the historian often involves tedious repetition, humanism, nevertheless had contributed immeasurably to Basle's traditional equilibrium based upon the Erasmian *philosophia Christi* and *bonae litterae*, the ideal of a balanced exercise of Christian virtues and rational diligence, applied both to the arts and natural sciences. Foillet at Montbéliard never printed the classics ; by contrast Basle publishing could live up to its mission and reputation as long as the classics, in their original languages rather than vernacular translations, remained the staple diet not only in the class room but of educated men throughout their lives. It was this broad consensus on humanistic values which kept the presses alive, and with them the cosmopolitan flair about Basle, which attracted men of such different minds as Castellio, Périon, Ramus and Hotman de Villiers, which even induced little known refugees from various walks of life to seek relief from their miseries by composing a book of epigrams or a commentary on Cicero's *Moralia*.

The Bâlois themselves paid a heavy price for achieving this cosmopolitan consensus. Originality seemed largely banned from their own ranks. The Amerbachs, Zwingers, Grynaei were all epigones characterized by intellectual vagueness, by a sense of indecision. They were all Erasmians, but a truly exceptional figure, another Erasmus, might have been unthinkable among them. Instead they developed a collective capacity for tolerance, a preference for passive approval over the exigencies of opposition. The radical views of Castellio and his Italian friends, the Paracelsian legacy, Ramism and many other currents were accommodated within certain limits, whereas in the days of Erasmus a Paracelsus, a Farel, a Calvin had been turned away or at least discouraged from staying.

Despite the passive attitude of individuals it was a positive feat, the collective achievement of an educated bourgeois class, resulting in the creation of a liberal climate at home and a corresponding Bâlois image abroad, which in an age of multiplying mental barriers proved more widely acceptable than perhaps any other. It was a collective achievement, by a group of unexceptional intellectuals and printers, supported by a host of sympathizers abroad. Hence it had to be investigated by

---

[28] Viénot, *Montbéliard* 1.353f. and above p. 63.

[29] See above p. 77f.

[30] Cf., however, the not very inspired historical works of the schoolmaster Richard Dinoth : **No. 379-383**. On Dinoth and his visit to Basle cf. *France prot.*[2] ; my short note in *Moreana* No. 13 (1967), 59-62 ; *Matrikel* 2.208, 417 : Dinoth's son Antoine studied at Basle. A more distinguished son of Montbéliard was the philosopher Nicolaus Taurellus, 1547-1606. He was a student and for a short time a professor at Basle, but spent the rest of his life in Germany. It does not seem that he was of Francophone descent : see *Matrikel* 2.162, and P. Petersen, *Geschichte der aristotelischen Philosophie im protestantischen Deutschland*, Leipzig 1921, 219ff. against *France prot.*

the somewhat cumbersome methods applied in this study.   Moreover, it created an image that somehow defies definition.   Of those who came to Basle, or sent their manuscripts to be printed, many differed from one another in almost every conceivable respect.   Yet all had set their hopes on the liberal city, and felt an affinity with her.   They knew her to be Protestant, but by no means rigidly opposed to Catholicism, even less to individual Catholics.   Perhaps they liked to think of her as rather anti-Calvinist, or rather anti-Lutheran.   Whether they approached her in search of Paracelsus or Ramus, of Plato or Aristotle, and above all of Erasmus, they were unlikely to be too disappointed.   Rather they were encouraged to contribute their own emphases to Bâlois culture, and to enhance its image without compromising their own identities.

In this sense then, and in this sense only, sixteenth century Basle may have presented the French-speaking community with a true alternative to Geneva, setting freedom and flexibility, or sheer indecision, against rigour and discipline, a tradition which invited modifications against the authoritative faith and will of a great leader, complexity against single-mindedness, impulsive inspiration and intellectual curiosity against obedience and solid achievement.   The Erasmian heritage of Basle, although perhaps undefinable, is vividly reflected in the casual impressions and recollections of travelling gentlemen such as J.-A. de Thou and M. de Montaigne.[31]   Books were its true record, and for the most part books only published at Basle rather than written there.   Its impact upon the French mind is illustrated by such men as Lefèvre d'Etaples, Cousin, Périon and Hotman de Villiers, who loved Basle books and eagerly read them, including some which in the view of the censors at Rome or Geneva [32] they ought never to have wished to read.

It seems appropriate to reserve the remaining pages of this book for a bibliography, but the reader should perhaps be reminded of the limitations imposed by the specific nature of its topic.   To do justice to the versatility of the Basle printers as well as to their priorities, the Latin translation of Machiavelli's *Prince* ought to be weighed against the first edition of Calvin's *Institutes* and against Castellio's *De haereticis, an sint persequendi*, the Magdeburg *Centuriae* against Baudouin's *Constantinus Magnus* and Sleidanus' *Commentarii*, the presence in the Basle publishing programme of Petrarca's *Canzoniere* against the absence of Ronsard and Rabelais. To the Collected Works of Budé and Alciato, those of Erasmus, Pico, Plato and many others ougth to be added, and the presence of a collective critical apparatus in many a classics edition ought to be noted where only the names of Francophone commentators appear in the bibliography.

---

[31] Cf. above p. 72f.

[32] Cf. above pp. 58, 91, 203f., 215f., 237.

PART FOUR

SHORT TITLE BIBLIOGRAPHY

SHORT TITLE BIBLIOGRAPHY

1. Books published at Basle, 1470-1650: Francophone Authors, Editors, Translators and Contributors; Subjects Related to France

This bibliography is based on the holdings of the Universitätsbibliothek in Basle, the Bibliothèque Nationale in Paris, and the British Museum in London. In addition to the printed catalogues of the Bibliothèque Nationale and the British Museum, the unpublished *Druckerkatalog* in the Basle Library was used to trace relevant books. A few entries were checked in libraries other than the three mentioned above. Some books not seen by the author were listed on the evidence of specific references in reliable and specialized bibliographies. A systematic search in other libraries, in general bibliographies, and in sales catalogues would have yielded additional entries, but the work would have required a whole team of researchers, not to mention the problems resulting from the inclusion of information which can no longer be verified. The author believes that the limits he has imposed on his investigation are reasonable and that apart from unidentified anonymous material only a few original editions and probably less than twenty per cent of all reprints have escaped his attention. Besides the pleasure derived from poking one's nose into so many early printed books, the author at least could avoid repeating some errors of others even though he may have added some mistakes of his own. Whenever a book can be found in one or more of the three libraries systematically researched, no mention has been made of this fact. In all other cases a source of information is indicated. The same has been done for all incunables and in other cases where the abbreviated form of entry would not easily permit identification.

For every book listed the bibliography attempts to indicate primarily the contribution of Francophones and others who lived in France for a considerable and significant portion of their lives. While only short contributions, such as introductory epigrams or appendices of no more than a couple of pages were ignored, care was taken to avoid the duplication of entries except for some major collections including several authors. The entries were arranged alphabetically according to the name of the most important Francophone contributor and include, where applicable, references to shorter contributions by other Francophones. To obtain the full record of references to any one individual, the reader therefore must consult the alphabetical index at the end of this volume. This inconvenience seemed justifiable, since multiple entries for one and the same book would have given a false, inflated impression of the total output of the Basle presses. Translations into French are listed under the author's name if no Francophone translator could be identified. Basle books on topics, or with fictitious imprints, relating to France are also listed under the name of the author; only where the author is not known will the entry be found under the first word of the title.

Books published anonymously or with a fictitious imprint were included in the bibliography only if this examiner felt confident that the title should be assigned to Basle. Question marks are placed against all such listings unless contemporary records seem to confirm the attribution beyond reasonable doubt. This means that question marks were added to every assignation based on typographical evidence only. No title was included if its printing at Basle was deemed a mere possibility. The author is not aware of any techniques for the identification of typographical material or paper that could with complete confidence be applied to the numerous products of Basle printers in the sixteenth century. Some presses had a considerable capacity and commensurate resources of typographical material. Most would lend one another equipment, or even do some printing iɪ a fellow master were hard pressed to meet the deadline of an approaching fair. All in all, decorated initials, fleurons, and similar adornments remain the safest elements on which to base an identification. Comparison of such material was used a great deal in the preparation of this study. However, in the absence of any comprehensive check lists of initial alphabets and other typographical equipment used by various Basle presses in the sixteenth century, it would be tedious to detail for the reader proofs for the correctness of a specific attribution. Any such attempt would subvert the purposes of a comprehensive check list, but an effort at greater explicitness has been made in the footnotes of the preceding chapters. The method applied in this study often yielded reasonably conclusive results in the case of Latin and French language printing. Yet the author must confess his difficulties in recognizing unidentified Basle books printed in German. Therefore many anonymous German translations from the French may be missing from this bibliography.

For the purposes of this study much depended on distinguishing original Basle publications and mere reprints. Original editions document the existence of direct or indirect contacts between the printer and the author or editor. They often represent an initiative taken by the latter. Reprints copied from earlier editions, on the other hand, normally represent the initiative of the publisher, and reflect his belief that he can market the reprinted title. Obviously to print a new work from the manuscript is one thing ; to copy the recent edition of a text is quite another, even if a few misprints are corrected or perhaps a few words added to an alphabetical index. However between these two situations there is room for endless gradations of major and minor original contributions : printed and manuscript copies of a text might be collated for a new edition ; the Greek original might be added to a formerly published Latin translation ; a new edition might be revised by the author, or improved by others through the addition of a critical commentary, and so on. There is no end to this kind of differentiation, but in the present check list relatively clear cases only could be registered. An " O " was placed against a title if it was thought that the text, or substantial portions of it, had been printed directly from manuscript. An " R " was placed against items thought to be reprinted from a previous edition without significant changes. As usual square brackets have been used for the identification of unnamed contributors and publishers ; round brackets indicate some types of supplementary information.

1. **Abrégé**

   Abrege d'un discours faict avec sa Saincteté par aucuns de ses confidents...,
   trouvé entre les papiers de l'advocat David
   [Basle ?], 1585
   UBB : N.u. VI.20 (3) ; cf. No. 761

2. **ACONCIO, Jacopo**

   O *Les ruzes de Satan* [transl. of Stratagemata Satanae]
   Basle, P. Perna, 1565

3. **ADO, St., Abp. of Vienne**

   R *Breviarium chronicorum*
   Basle, P. Perna, 1568

4. **AGRIPPA of Nettesheim, Heinrich Cornelius**

   R De duplici coronatione Caroli V. : in
   S. Schard, ed., *Historicum opus*
   Basle, Offic. Henricpetrina, 1574

5. **AILLY, Pierre d' (Petrus ab Alliaco)**

   R *De emendatione ecclesiae libellus*
   [Basle ?, c. 1536-1552]

6. —

   O — : *De reformatione ecclesiae*, also :
   De squaloribus curiae Romanae
   Basle, N. Brylinger, 1551

7. —

   R In septem psalmos poenitentiales meditatio, in XXX. psalmum medi-
   tatio, in XLI. psalmum meditatio : in
   J. B. Herold, ed., *Orthodoxographa*
   Basle, H. Petri, 1555

8. —

   R — : in
   J. J. Grynaeus, ed., *Monumenta S. Patrum orthodoxographa*
   Basle, Offic. Henricpetrina, 1569

9. **ALAIN de Lille (Alanus ab Insulis)**

   R *Alanus de maximis theologie* [i.e. Theologiae regulae]
   Basle, J. Amerbach, c. 1492]
   GKW No. 510

10. —

    O *Anticlaudiani ... libri IX*
    Basle, H. Petri, 1536

11. **ALCIATO, Andrea**

    Omnia ... opera
    Basle, M. Isengrin, 1546-1551
    (The title pages are dated 1550 or 1551,
    the colophon of vol. 2 is 1546)

12. —

    R —   ibid., 1557-1558
    DGK

13. —

    R   —   Basle, T. Guarinus, 1571

14. —

    R   — : *Opera omnia*

                          ibid., 1582

15. [—]

    O   Aurelius Albucius, *Andreae Alciati ... in Stellam et Longovallium ... defensio*

                          Basle, H. Froben, 1529

16. —

    O   *De formula Romani imperii libellus*, contains also :
    O   Landolfo Colonna (Radulphus Carnotensis), De translatione imperii libellus

                          Basle, J. Oporinus, 1559

17. —

    R   Libellus de magistratibus, civilibusque ac militaribus officiis : in *Notitia* [*dignitatum*]

                          Basle, H. Froben & N. Episcopius, 1552

18. —

    Paradoxa and other works
    (Ex secunda authoris recognitione)

                          Basle, A. Cratander, 1523
                          DGK

19. —

    — (Ex novissima autoris recognitione)

                          ibid., 1531

20. —

    O   Παρέργων *iuris libri III*

                          Basle, J. Herwagen & J. E. Froben, 1538

21. —

    O   *Parergon iuris libri X*

                          Basle, 1543
                          DGK

22. —

    Responsa [Complementary vol. to *Opera* published the same year]
                          Basle, T. Guarinus, 1582

23. —, transl.

    Galenus, De ponderibus et mensuris : in
    Galenus, *De compositione medicamentorum* (Greek & Latin)
                          Basle, A. Cratander, 1530

24. —, introd. & comment.

    R ? De Plautinorum carminum ratione ; de Plautinis vocabulis lexicon : in Plautus, *Opera*, also in this ed. :
    R   A. Turnèbe, Variae lectiones in Plautum ;
        J. C. Scaliger, De comoediae origine ; de versibus comicis
                          Basle, Offic. Herwagiana per Eus. Episcopium, 1568

25. —, —
    O   *Selecta epigrammata Graeca* (Greek and Latin ; other transl. by M. Bentin, J. Sleidanus
                 Basle, J. Bebel, 1529

26. —, introd. & comment.
    R   Praefatio ad Galeacium Viscomitem ; annotationes in Tacitum : in Tacitus, *Opera*
                 Basle, J. Froben, 1519

27. —, —
    R   —
                 Basle, Offic. Frobeniana, 1533

28. —, —
    R   —
                 ibid., 1544

29. —, —
    R   [Praefatio only under the title :] Encomium historiae : appended to *Opus historiarum*
                 Basle, B. Westheimer, 1541

30. **ALCUINUS (Albinus)**
    R   Confessio sive de doctrina Dei, and other short selections : in J. J. Grynaeus, ed., *Monumenta S. Patrum orthodoxographa*
                 Basle, Offic. Henricpetrina, 1569

31. —
    O   *In Ecclesiasten commentaria*
                 Basle, Offic. Bebeliana, 1531

32. —
    R   In Genesim quaestiones : in Μιχροπρεσβυτιχόν (contains also :
    R   Ratramnus of Corbie, Bertrami presbyteri De corpore et sanguine Domini)
                 Basle, H. Petri, 1550

33. —
    R   — and other opuscula, also Ratramnus : in J. B. Herold ed., *Orthodoxographa*
                 ibid., 1555

34. —
        Tres libri de fide trinitatis : in *Homiliarius doctorum*
                 Basle, N. Kessler, 1506

35. **(ALEXANDER of Hales)**
    O   P. Keschinger, *Clavis theologie* (a concordance to the *Summa* of A. of H.)
                 ibid., 1502

36. **ALEXANDER of Villedieu (Villa Dei)**
    R   *Doctrinale* (complete work or parts thereof)
                 [Basle, B. Richel ?, 1475 ?]
                 GKW No. 939

255

37. —
    R —
    Basle, [J. Amerbach], 1486
    GKW No. 995

38. —
    R —
    Basle, N. Kessler, 1486
    GKW No. 998

39. —
    R —
    ibid., 1489
    GKW No. 1014

40. —
    R —
    ibid., 1494
    GKW No. 1120

41. —
    R —
    [Basle, M. Furter, c. 1495-1496]
    GKW No. 971

42. —
    R —
    Basle, M. Furter, 1496-1497
    GKW No. 1077, 1111, 1204

43. —
    R —
    Basle, J. Wolff, 1498
    GKW No. 1079, 1112, 1207

44. —
    R —
    ibid., 1499
    GKW No. 1081, 1116

45. **AMADEUS, St., Bp. of Lausanne**
    O   *De Maria virginea matre homiliae octo*
    Basle, A. Petri, 1517

46. **AMYOT, Jacques,** transl.
    R ? Plutarchus, *Les œuvres morales et meslees*
    Basle, T. Guarinus, 1574

47. **ANDRELINI, Fausto**
    R   Disticha, Aegloga : in
    [L. Bigi], *Pictorii sacra et satyrica epigrammata*
    Basle, J. Froben, 1518

48. —
    R   Ecloges XII : in
    J. Oporinus, ed., *En habes, lector, bucolicorum autores* (with shorter
    contributions by J. Arnolet, S. Châteillon, G. Cousin (Nucillanus),
    G. Ducher, P. Girinet, J. Raenerius, J. Sturm (Synesius)
    Basle, J. Oporinus, 1546

49. [— ?]

    O   *Iulius, dialogus*

                [Basle ?, c. 1517-1518]
                Cf. *Erasmi opuscula*, ed. W. K. Ferguson,
                55ff., also for the following eds.

50. [— ?]

    R   —

                [Basle ?, c. 1520]

51. [— ?]

    R   — : in
        Pasquillorum tomi duo

                Eleutheropoli [Basle, J. Oporinus], 1544

52. (— ?)

        Oratio ad Christum Opt. Max. pro Iulio secundo (an imitation of No. 49)
        In Germania tandem iam sapiente
        [Basle, V. Curio ? or A. Cratander ?,
        c. 1522]

53. **APOLLONIUS, Laevinus**

    O   Von der Frantzosen Schiffarth in die Landtschafft Florida (transl. from
        De navigatione Gallorum) : in
        N. Höniger, ed., *Dritte Theil der newen Welt*
                Basle, Seb. Henricpetri, 1583

54. **ARNALDUS of Villanova**

    R   *Opera omnia*

                Basle, C. Waldkirch, 1585

55. —

    R   De conferentibus et nocentibus membris... corporis : in
        Georg Pictorius, *Medicinae tam simplices quam compositae*
                Basle, H. Petri 1560

56. —

    R   De sanitate conservanda regimen : in
        Georg Pictorius, *Sanitatis tuendae methodus*
                ibid., 1561

57. —

        Regulae universales curationis morborum (better known as Parabolae
        or Aphorismi medicationis, the commentary to each *regula* being
        abridged and ed. by G. Pictorius)
                ibid., 1565

58. —

        G. Gratarolo ed., *Verae alchemiae... doctrina* (contains several small
        treatises ascribed to A. of V. as well as one ascribed to Jean of
        Roquetaillade)
                Basle, [P. Perna,] 1561

59. (—)

        Adam of Bodenstein, *Isagoge in ... Arnoldi de Villa Nova rosarium
        chymicum*
                Basle, Gabriel Ringysen, 1559

60. **[ARNAULD, Antoine]**

L'antiespagnol oder ausführliche Erklerunge (transl. from the French)
Ausserhalb von Madrill durch Giovan
Spinardum in Basilisco [Basle ?, S. Apia-
rius ?], 1590
DGK

61. **ARNOLET, Jean (Arnolletus)**

R   Fides, spes, charitas and other poems : in
Poematia aliquot insignia illustrium poetarum recentiorum (contains
O?   also : Claude Budin, Faustina)
Basle, R. Winter, 1544

62. **AUBERT, Jacques**

R   De signis morborum : in
W. Fabricius Hildanus, ed., *Cheirurgia militaris* (an individual title page
gives the name of Aubert's work as Σημειωτική and the year of publ.
as 1632)
Basle, J. J. Genath, 1634

63. —

O   *Progymnasmata in Ioan. Fernelii ... librum de abditis rerum naturalium
et medicamentorum causis*
Basle, Seb. Henricpetri, 1579

64. **AUBERY, Claude,** transl. & introd.

O   Theodorus II Ducas Lascaris, *De communicatione naturali*
Basle, Offic. Episcopiana, 1571

65. **AUSONIUS D. Magnus Burdigalensis**

Varia opuscula
Basle, V. Curio, 1523

66. **AVITUS, St., Abp. of Vienne**

R   *De origine mundi*, etc.
Basle, 1545

67. —

R   —: in G. Fabricius ed., *Poetarum veterum ecclesiasticorum opera*
Basle, J. Oporinus, 1564

68. **BADE, Josse**

R   *Navis stultifera*
Basle, N. Lamparter 1406 [erron. for 1506]

69. —

R   —
ibid., 1507

70. —

ed. with commentaries, summaries, appendices etc.
R   A. Dati, *Elegantiae* (other comment. by J. Clichtoveus)
Basle, A. Petri, 1520

71. —, comment.

R   Juvencus, Evangelica historia : in
J. Gast, ed., *Opera poetarum Christianorum*
Basle, B. Westheimer, 1545

72. —, introd. & comment.
   R Persius, Satyrae : in
    I. Iuvenalis et A. Persii Flacci Satyrae
        Basle, H. Froben & N. Episcopius, 1551

73. —, ed.
   R Glareani chronologia [based on Livy, chiefly] in seriem redacta : in
    H. Loriti Glareanus, *In omneis ... Titi Livii ... decadas annotationes*
        Basle, M. Isengrin, 1540

74. —, —
   R — : in Livius, *Opera*
        Basle, J. Herwagen, 1555

75. **BAÏF, Lazare de**
   O *Annotationum in L. Vestis ff. de auro et argento leg. seu de re vestiaria liber*
        Basle, J. Bebel, 1526

76. —
    — (revised) : *Opus de re vestimentaria*, followed by :
   O *De vasculorum materiis ac varietate tractatus*
        Basle, H. Froben, J. Herwagen, N. Episcopius, 1531

77. —
    Annotationes in legem II de captivis ... in quibus tractatur de re navali, followed by :
   R *De re vestiaria, de vasculorum materiis*
        Basle, H. Froben & N. Episcopius, 1537

78. —
   R —
        ibid., 1541

79. —
   R *De re navali*
        Basle, B. Lasius & T. Platter, 1537

80. **[BARNAUD, Nicolas ?]**
   O *Dialogi ab Eusebio Philadelpho Cosmopolita ... compositi*
        Edimburgi, ex typographia Iacobi Iamaei,
        [Basle ?, T. Guarinus ?,] 1574

81. **BAUDOUIN, François**
   O *Ad edicta veterum principum Romanorum de Christianis*
        Basle, J. Oporinus, [1557]

82. —
   O *Ad leges de iure civili Voconiam...*
        ibid., 1559

83. —
   O *Commentarii de legibus XII Tabularum*, tertia sed plane nova editio
        ibid., 1557

84. —
   O *Commentarii de pignoribus et hypothecis*, and other essays
        ibid. [1556-1558 ?]

85. —

    O   *Commentarius de iurisprudentia Muciana*
                  ibid., 1558

86. —

    O   *Constantinus Magnus*
                  ibid., 1556

87. —

    R   De institutione historiae universae : in
        J. Bodin, *Methodus historica*
                  Basle, P. Perna, 1576

88. —

    R   — : in Johann Wolf, ed., *Artis historicae penus*
                  ibid., 1579

89. —

    O   *Iuris civilis catechesis*
                  Basle, J. Oporinus [1557 ?]

90. —

    O   *Iustinianus sive de iure novo*
                  ibid., 1560

91. —

    O   *Notae ad lib. I & II Digestorum*
                  ibid. [1557 ?]

92. —, ed., transl. & comment.

    R   Justinianus, Leges de re rustica etc. : in
    O   Antonius Garro, *In titulum Pomponii De origine iuris... commentaria*
        (ed. by Gilbert Cousin)
                  ibid., 1543

93. [—, ed.]

    O   Georgius Cassander, *De officio pii ac publicae tranquillitatis vere amantis viri*
                  [Basle, J. Oporinus ?, 1561]

94. **BAUHIN, Gaspard**

    Anatomes ... liber primus (Iterata ed., priore [i.e. No. 100] longe auctior)
                  Basle, Seb. Henricpetri, 1591

95. —

    O   *Anatomes ... liber secundus*
                  ibid. 1592

96. —

    R   — : liber primus (ed. tertia) ; liber secundus (ed. altera ; mostly identical set of types)
                  ibid. 1597

97. —

    O   *Catalogus plantarum circa Basileam nascentium*
                  Basle, J. J. Genath, 1622

98. —

    R —
                  ibid., 1622

99. —

    O   *De corporis humani fabrica libri* IIII
                  Basle, Seb. Henricpetri, 1590

100. —

    O   *De corporis humani partibus externis tractatus*
                  Basle, Offic. Episcopiana, 1588

101. —

    O   *De lapidis Bezaar ... natura*
                  Basle, C. Waldkirch, 1613

102. —

    — (priore ed. auctior)
                  Basle, L. König, 1624 (in some copies the
                  date on the title page is 1625)

103. —

    Institutiones anatomicae (hac editione quarta auctae)
                  Basle, J. Schröter, 1609

104. —

    — (5th ed.)
                  ibid., 1615
                  DGK

105. —

    O   Introductio pulsuum synopsin continens: in
    R   J. Struthius, *Ars sphygmica*
                  Basle, L. König, 1602

106. —

    O   Φυτοπίναξ *seu enumeratio plantarum*
                  Basle, Seb. Henricpetri, 1596

107. —

    O   Πίναξ *theatri botanici*
                  Basle, L. König, 1623

108. —, ed.

    R   Guglielmo Varignana, *Secreta medicinae*
                  Basle, Seb. Henricpetri, 1597

109. **BAUHIN, Jean II**

    De plantis a divis sanctisve nomen habentibus
    (ed. by Gaspard Bauhin)
                  Basle, C. Waldkirch, 1591
                  UBB: copy missing since 1915

110. **BEAULIEU, Eustorg de**

    O   *Le souverain blason d'honneur à la louange du tresdigne corps de Iesus*
       Christ
                  [Basle], J. Parcus, [c. 1547-1550]
                  Zentralbibliothek, Zurich: Z VI 263(6)

111. —
    O *L'espinglier des filles*
                        Basle, 1548

112. —
    — ; a few changes and additions
                        ibid., 1550

113. **(BÉDA, Noël)**
    O Erasmus of Rotterdam, *Prologus ... in supputationem calumniorum Natalis Bedae,*
    O *Responsiunculae ad propositiones Bedae,*
    O *Appendix de antapologia Petri Sutoris et scriptis Iodoci Clichtovei, Elenchus erratorum in censuris Bedae*
                        Basle, J. Froben, 1526

114. **(—)**
    O Erasmus of Rotterdam, *Supputationes errorum in censuris Natalis Bedae,*
    R followed by the various pieces contained in the preceding No. 113
                        ibid., 1527

115. **(—)**
    R —: in
    Erasmus of Rotterdam, *Opera omnia*
                        Basle, J. Froben & N. Episcopius, 1540

116. **(—)**
    R Responsiunculae : in
    Erasmus of Rotterdam, *Responsio ad epistolam ... Alberti Pii*
                        Basle, J. Froben, 1529

117. **BELLEPERCHE, Pierre de (P. de Bella Pertica, etc)**
    R *Quaestiones et decisiones aureae ... super quolibet titulo iuris Caesarei*
                        Basle, L. König, 1607

118. **BELLEVUE, Armand de (A. de Bello Visu, etc.)**
    R *De declaratione difficlium terminorum tam theologiae quam philosophiae ac logicae*
                        Basle, M. Wenssler, 1491
                        GKW No. 2501

119. —
    R —
                        ibid., 1491
                        GKW No. 2502

120. **BELLONE, Niccolò**
    O *Consiliorum volumen*
                        Basle, M. Isengrin, 1544

121. —
    O *Repetitiones et tractatus*
                        Basle, J. Oporinus, 1544

122. —
    O *Super utraque parte Institutionum lucubrationes*
                        Basle, M. Isengrin, 1544

123. —

   Supputationum iuris libri quatuor (revised by the author)
   ibid., 1544

124. —, ed.

   O   Cristofero Porzio (Portius), *Super tres priores Institutionum divi Iusti-*
   niani libro commentaria (pref. by Guillaume de Saint-Mauris of Dole)
   Basle, M. Isengrin, 1547 (some copies
   with the date of 1548 on the title page)

125. **[BELLOY, Pierre de]**

   R   E.D.L.I.C., *Apologie catholique contre ... les Liguez*
   [Basle ?, T. Guarinus ?,] 1585
   BN : 8⁰ Lb³⁴ 240A

126. (—)

   O   E.D.L.I.C., *Apologia catholica* (transl. from the French)
   [Basle ?, C. Waldkirch ?,] CIↃ IↃ XVIC
   [1585-1586]

127. **[BENTIN, Michel]**, ed.

   Cicero, *Opera*

   Basle, A. Cratander, 1528

128. [—, —]

   C. Claudianus, *Omnia ... opera*
   Basle, J. Bebel, 1534

129. —, ed. & introd.

   O   Q. Horatius Flaccus, *Opera*

   Basle, V. Curio, 1527

130. [—, ed. in part]

   Lexicon Graecum

   ibid., 1525

131. —, comment.

   O   M. Terentius Varro, S. Pompeius Festus, Nonius Marcellus : appended
   to : N. Perotti, *Cornucopia*

   ibid., 1526

132. —, —

   R   —

   ibid., 1532

133. —, —

   R   —

   ibid., 1536

134. —, —

   R   M. Terentius Varro, *De lingua Latina...*, *de analogia*
   Basle, B. Westheimer, 1536

135. **BER, Ludwig**

   O   *Pro salutari hominis ad felicem mortem praeparatione*
   Basle, J. Oporinus, 1549

136. —

    R —

          ibid., 1551

137. **BÉRAULD, Nicolas (Béraud, Bérault, Beraldus),** ed. & comment.

    R A. Poliziano, *Sylva cuius titulus est Rusticus*

          Basle, J. Froben, 1518

138. **BERCHORIUS, Petrus (Berthorius, Bercheur, Bercuire)**

    R *Morale reductorium super totam Bibliam*

          Basle, A. Petri, 1515, for T. Berlear of Cologne

139. —

    R —

          ibid., 1517, for A. Koberger of Nuremberg

140. **BERNARDUS, St., of Clairvaux**

    Opera ... omnia

          Basle, J. Herwagen, 1552

141. —

    R —

          Basle, heirs of J. Herwagen, 1566

142. — (ascribed to)

    R *Epistola de gubernatione rei familiaris*

          [Basle, M. Flach, c. 1475]

          GKW No. 3966

143. —

    R Ex epistola CXC ... de Petri Abailhardi haeresi : in

    O L. Lucius, *De satisfactione Christi ... disceptatio,* and *Synopsis Antisociniana*

          Basle, Offic. Henricpetrina, 1628

144. —

    R *Opus ... epistolarum*

          Basle, [N. Kessler], 1494

          GKW No. 3926

145. —

    R *Opus sermonum*

          Basle, N. Kessler, 1495

          GKW No. 3944

146. — (ascribed to)

    R *Liber meditationum*

          [Basle, J. Amerbach,] 1492

          GKW No. 4032

147. — (ascribed to)

    O *Sant Bernarts Rosenkrantz* (transl. of Sertum)

          [ibid., 1497]

          cf. Hartmann 1.71n.

148. —

    O *Speculum de honestate vitae*

          [Basle, M. Flach, c. 1472-1474]

          GKW No. 4071

149. **BÉROALD, Matthieu (Brouard)**
R *Chronologia*
Basle, T. Guarinus, 1577

150. **BERTIN, Georges**
O *De consultationibus medicorum*
Basle, C. Waldkirch, 1586

151. **—**
O *Medicina*
ibid., 1587

152. **BERTRAND, Bernard,** transl. & introd.
Dionysius [Periegetes] Alexandrinus, *De situ orbis* (Greek & Latin),
together with :
O Latin transl. of the commentary by Eustathius Thessalonicensis
Basle, J. Oporinus, 1556

153. **—, —**
O Lycophron, *Cassandra*, with commentary by Isaac Tzetzes (Latin)
ibid., 1558

154. **BÈZE, Théodore de**
O *Brevis et utilis zographia Ioannis Cochleae*
[Basle], 1549

155. **—**
R Eximia tractatio de consolandis iis qui circa praedestinationem ten-
tantur (e secunda responsione ad acta colloquii Mompelgart.) : in
R William Perkins, *Armilla aurea*
Basle, C. Waldkirch, 1596

156. **—**
R —
ibid., 1599

157. **—**
*Gründlicher Gegenbericht auff die zu Tübingen aussgegangenen Schrifften
des Mümpelgartischen Gesprächs* (transl. of Ad acta colloquii Montisbel-
gardensis)
ibid., 1588
F. Gardy, *Bibliogr. de Bèze*, Geneva 1960,
No. 369

158. **(—)**
O A. Dudith, Epistolam ... ad Theodorum Bezam : appended to
O Mino Celsi, *In haereticis coercendis quatenus progredi liceat*
Christlingae [Basle, P. Perna], 1577

159. **—**
Epistola ... ad Andream Dudithium (together with Dudith's letter
which it answers) : appended to
Mino Celsi, *De haereticis capitali supplicio non afficiendis*
[Basle ?, C. Waldkirch ?], 1584

160. **(—)**
R A. Dudith, *Epistola ... ad Theodorum Bezam*
[Basle ?, C. Waldkirch ?], 1593

161. —
    R   *Poemata, ... nunc denuo recusa*
                  Lugduni [Basle], mark of T. Guarinus,
                  [c. 1580]

162. [—, ed.]
    R   Responsio illustriss. viri D. Castilonaei ... de morte ducis Guisiani : in
       S. Schard, ed., *Historicum opus*
                  Basle, Offic. Henricpetrina, 1574

163. —, transl. & comment.
    R   *Novum Testamentum* (Greek and Latin)
                  [Basle, J. Oporinus & Zurich, C.
                  Froschauer]
       published with different title pages :
       a) Basileae, impensis Nicolai Barbirii et Thomae Courteau, MDLIX
       b) —, MDLX
       c) Tiguri, MDLIX

164. **BIGOT, Guillaume**
    O   *Catoptron*
                  Basle, T. Platter & B. Lasius, mark of
                  R. Winter, 1536

165. **BLETZ, Zacharias,** transl.
       In disem Biechly wirt heyter anzeigt ... wie vil Ertzbistum, Bistum,
       Hertzogthum, Grafschafften in der edlen Cron zuo Franckrych erfunden
       [transl. from the French]
                  Basle, Lux Schauber, 1536

166. **BOAISTUAU, Pierre**
    R   *Theatrum mundi* (German transl.)
                  Basle, Jacob Trew for Hans Conrad, 1607

167. **BODIN, Jean**
    O   *De magorum daemonomania* (transl. from the French by François
       Du Jon ?)
                  Basle, T. Guarinus, 1581

168. —
    R   *Methodus historica*
                  Basle, P. Perna, 1576

169. —
    R   —: in
       J. Wolf ed., *Artis historicae penus*
                ibid., 1579

170. **BOISSARD, Jean Jacques**
    O   *Poemata*
                  Basle, [T. Guarinus], 1574

171. **BONADE, François**
    R? *Divi Pauli Apostoli ... epistolae divinae ad Orphicam lyram traductae*
                  Basle, B. Westheimer, 1537

172. —

     R   —: in
     (*Evangelica carmina*)
                      [Basle], B. Westheimer, [ca. 1538-40]
                      Cf. No. 301

173. **BONAVENTURA, St.**

     Compendium sacre theologie pauperis
                      Basle, J. Wolff, 1501

174. — (ascribed to)

     O   *Psalterium beatae virginis Mariae*
                      [Basle, M. Flach, c. 1474]
                      GKW No. 4798

175. — (ascribed to)

     R   *Sermones aurei ... de tempore et de sanctis*
                      Basle, J. Wolff, 1502

176. —

     O   *Speculum Mariae* and other treatises by, or ascribed to, St. Bonaventura, St. Bernardus of Clairvaux and St. Thomas Aquinas in German transl.
                      Basle, M. Furter, one piece dated 1507

177. —

     O   *Ein schon, nützlich Büchlin dreyen Stetten der heiligen Cristenheit* (partly identical with the preceding collection, partly other treatises)
                      ibid., one piece dated 1507

178. **(BONIFACIUS of Ceva)**

     O   [*Kaspar Schatzger*], *Apologia status fratrum ordinis minorum de observantia ... adversus Bonifacium provinciae Franciae ministrum*
                      [Basle, J. Froben, 1516]

179. **[BOUCHER, Jean]**

     Fuchschwentzer Spiegel (a transl. of the epistle dedicatory prefixed to the French transl. of T. Walsingham's biography of Peter Gaverston)
                      Basle, S. (II) Apiarius, 1588
                      Cf. *BMC ST Germany*, s.v. Walsingham

180. **BOUQUIN, Pierre (Boquinus)**

     O   *Examen libri quem D. Tilemannus Heshusius nuper scripsit*
                      Basle, J. Oporinus, 1561
                      Steinmann, p. 100

181. [—]

     O   *Theses, quae veram de Coena Domini sententiam ... continent*
                      [Basle ?, J. Oporinus ?], 1560
                      BN : D². 3892 (1)

182. **BOURBON, Nicolas (Borbonius)**

     Nugae, Ferraria (enlarged and revised)
                      Basle, A. Cratander, 1533

183. —

     R   *Nugae* (enlarged and revised)
                      Basle, heirs of A. Cratander, 1540

184. **BRIE, Germain de (Brixius),** transl.

   R St. Johannes Chrysostomus, De sacerdotio : in
     Lucubrationes (Latin)
          Basle, J. Froben, 1528

185. —, —

   R — and Contra gentiles : in
     St. Johannes Chrysostomus, *Opera* (Latin)
          Basle, J. Froben, J. Herwagen & N. Epis-
          copius, 1530

186. —, —

   R —
          Basle, J. Herwagen, 1539

187. —, —

   R —
          Basle, H. Froben & N. Episcopius, 1547

188. —, —

   R —
          Basle, J. (II) Herwagen, 1557

189. **BRISSOT, Pierre**

   R *Apologetica disceptatio, qua docetur per quae loca sanguis mitti debeat*
     Basle, T. Wolff, 1529

190. **BRIZARD, Nicolas (Brissard)**

   R *Pugna syllogismorum*
          Basle, J. Parcus, 1554

191. **BRODEAU, Jean**

   O *Annotationes in Oppiani ..., Quinti Calabri ..., Coluthi Thebani ...*
     [libros]
          Basle, J. Herwagen, 1552

192. —

   O *In omnia Xenophontis opera ... annotationes*
          Basle, N. Brylinger, 1559

193. —

   O *Miscellaneorum libri sex*
          Basle, J. Oporinus, [1555 ?]

194. —, comment.

   O Annotationes : in
     Euripides, (Works, Greek & Latin)
          ibid., 1562

195. —, —

   O [Maximus Planudes, ed.,] *Epigrammata Graeca*
          Basle, H. Froben & N. Episcopius, 1549

196. **BRULEFER, Stephanus (Etienne Pillet)**

   R *Formalitatum textus unacum ... commento*
          Basle, J. Wolff, 1501

197. —

  R —

        ibid., 1507

198. —

  Reportata ... in ... Sancti Bonaventure ... Sententiarum libros
      Basle, J. Wolff, 1501

199. —

  R —

        ibid., 1507

200. **BUCHANAN, George**

  Franciscanus et fratres, quibus accessere varia eiusdem et aliorum poemata
  ed. by Karel Utenhove ; contains also : Euripides, *Medea* and *Alcestis*
  in Lat. transl. by G. Buchanan, and poems and epigrams by A. Turnèbe,
  M. de L'Hospital, J. Dorat, K. Utenhove, and Joachim Du Bellay.
      Basle, T. Guarinus, [1568]

201. —

  R Quatuor Psalmi ... heroico carmine redditi :
   Flores poetici elegantiores ... in usum auditorum quintae classis gymnasii
   Basiliensis
      Basle, Seb. Henricpetri, 1619

202. **BUDÉ, Guillaume**

  Opera omnia (fol.)
      Basle, N. Episcopius, 1557
  The various parts were also published separately with individual title-
  pages :
  R *Annotationes in Pandectas*
      ibid., 1557
  R *Commentarii linguae Graecae*
      ibid., 1556
  R *De asse*
      ibid., 1556
  R *Forensia*
      ibid., 1557
  R *Lucubrationes variae*, contains also :
  R Louis Le Roy, G. Budaei ... vita
      ibid., 1557

203. —

  R *Annotationes in ... Pandectarum libros* (revised and enlarged)
      Basle, T. Wolff, 1534 (in Part II : opera
      et expensis Conradi Resch)

204. —

  Breviarium de asse (a short summary)
      [Basle], J. Froben, [1518 ?]

205. —

  —, similar text
      Basle, J. Parcus, 1546

206. —

    —

      ibid., 1563

207. —

    R   *Commentarii linguae Graecae*
                          Basle, J. Bebel, 1530

208. —

    R   *De studio literarum* ... and ... *de philologia*
                          Basle, J. Walder, 1533

209. —

    R   *Epistolae*

                          Basle, A. Cratander, 1521

210. —

    R   *Forensia* (8°)

                          Basle, N. Episcopius, 1557

211. — (unspecified contribution)

        Dictionarium Graecolatinum ... *illustratum et emendatum per*
        G. Budaeum, I. Tusanum and some others
                          Basle, Offic. Henricpetrina, 1565

212. —

         —

                          ibid., 1572

213. —

         —

                          ibid., 1577

214. —

    —, similar ed.
                          Basle, Seb. Henricpetri, 1584

215. (—)

        Demosthenes, *Opera* (Greek & Latin), with annotations collected by
        J. Ruberus and J. Oporinus " ex Budaei praesertim commentariis ".
                          Basle, J. Herwagen, 1532

216. —, transl.

    R   Philo Iudaeus, De mundo : in
        Philonis ... *libri* (Latin)
                          Basle, A. Petri, 1527

217. —, —

    R   Aristoteles & Philo Iudaeus, *De mundo* (Greek & Latin)
                          Basle, J. Walder, 1533

218. —, —

    R   Aristoteles, De mundo : in
        J. J. Beurer, *Prooemium Peripateticum*
                          Basle, Seb. Henricpetri, 1587

219. —, transl. in part

    R   Plutarchus, *Opuscula*

                          Basle, A. Cratander, 1530

220. —, —

    R   — : *Opera moralia*

                          Basle, M. Isengrin, 1541

221. —, —
    R   —, similar ed.
                     ibid., 1554

222. —, transl.
    R   Plutarchus, *De placitis philosophiae* (Greek & Latin)
                     Basle, J. Herwagen, 1531

223. **CAESARIUS St., Abp. of Arles**
    O   *Homiliae XL* (ed. by G. Cousin)
                     Basle, H. Petri, 1558

224. —
    R   —: in
       J. J. Grynaeus, ed., *Monumenta S. Patrum Orthodoxographa*
                     Basle, Offic. Henricpetrina, 1569

225. **CALVIN, Jean**
    O   *Catechismus sive Christianae religionis institutio*
                     Basle, R. Winter, 1538
                     A. Erichson, *Bibliogr. Calvin.*, Berlin 1900

226. —
    O   *Catechismus oder Fragstucken* (German transl.)
                     " Getruckt zuo Basel, by Jacob Kündig
                     [= Parcus] durch Jacob Derbilly ", 1556

227. —
    O   *Christianae religionis institutio*
                     Basle, T. Platter & B. Lasius, 1536

228. —
    O   *Epistolae duae de rebus hoc saeculo cognitu apprime necessariis*
                     ibid., 1537

229. [—], ed. & annot.
    O   Paul III, Pope, *Admonitio paterna Pauli III* ... cum scholiis [by
       J. Calvin]
       [Basle], 1545

230. **(CAPPEL, Louis, the younger)**
    O   J. Buxtorf, the younger, *Tractatus de punctorum vocalium* ... *Veteris
       Testamenti* ... *oppositus Arcano punctationis revelato Ludovici Cappelli*
                     Basle, Martin Wagner for the heirs of
                     L. König, 1648

231. (—)
    O   J. Buxtorf, the younger, *Vindiciae exercitationis suae in historiam
       institutionis S. S. Coenae Dominicae: adversus Animadversiones Ludovici
       Cappelli*
                     Basle, heirs of L. König, 1646

CASTELLIO : see CHÂTEILLON

232. **CHAMPIER, Symphorien (Campegius)**
    R   Ἰατρικὴ πρᾶξις ... *de omnibus morborum generibus,* ... *de omnibus
       febrium generibus*
                     Basle, H. Petri, 1547

233. —

    O   *Libri VII de dialectica...*

                ibid. 1537

234. —, ed. & comment.

    O ? Galenus, *Historiales campi* ; also :
        S. Champier, *Clysteriorum camporum secundum Galeni mentem libellus*
        and *De phlebotomia*

                Basle, A. Cratander & J. Bebel, 1532

235. **CHANSONNETTE, Claude (Cantiuncula)**

    O   *De officio iudicis*

                Basle, M. Isengrin, 1543

236. —

    O   *Oratio apologetica in patrocinium iuris civilis; de ratione studii legalis*
       paraenesis

                Basle, A. Cratander, 1522

237. —

    R   De ratione studii legalis paraenesis : in
       Jacob Spiegel, *Lexicon iuris civilis*

                Basle, J. Herwagen, 1549

238. —

    R   — : in Gregorius Haloander, ed., *Iuris civilis pandectarum seu digestorum*
       libri

                Basle, T. Guarinus, 1570

239. —

    O   *Topica*

                Basle, A. Cratander, 1520

240. —

    R   — : *Topica legalia*

                Basle, H. Curio, 1545

241. —, transl.

    O   Erasmus of Rotterdam, *Maniere de se confesser* (transl. of Modus
       confitendi)

                Basle, 1524
                Bibl. Mazarine : 2250(5)

242. —, —

    O   Thomas More, *Von der wunderbarlichen Innsel Utopia* (transl. of Utopia,
       book II)

                Basle, J. Bebel, 1524

243. **CHASSANION, Jean (Cassanio)**

    O   *De gigantibus eorumque reliquiis*

                Basle, [T. Guarinus ?,] 1580

244. **CHÂTEILLON, Sébastien (Castalio, Castellio)**

    O   *Conseil à la France désolée*

                [Basle, J. Oporinus ?], 1562

245. —

    O   *Defensio suarum translationum Bibliorum*

                Basle, J. Oporinus, 1562

246. [—]

    O   Martinus Bellius, ed., *De haereticis, an sint persequendi*
                             Magdeburg, Georg Rausch [Basle, J. Oporinus ?], 1554

247. [—]

       — (identical set of types, a few changes)
                             ibid., 1554
                             Buisson, *Castellion* 2.363

248. —

    O   *Dialogi IIII de praedestinatione, de electione, de libero, arbitrio, de fide, eiusdem opuscula quaedam*
                             Aresdorffij, per Theophil. Philadelph. [Basle, P. Perna,] 1578

249. —

    R   *Dialogi de sacris literis excerpti*
                             Basle, Erasmus Xylotectus [= Zimmermann], 1545

250. —

    O   *Dialogorum sacrorum libri IV*
                             Basle, R. Winter, 1545
                             Buisson, *Castellion* 2.341

251. —

       —, revised and enlarged
                             Basle, J. Oporinus, 1547
                             Buisson, *Castellion* 2.342

252. —

    R   —
                             ibid., 1548
                             Buisson, *Castellion* 2.342

253. —

    R   —
                             ibid., 1551

254. —

    R   —
                             ibid., 1555
                             Buisson, *Castellion* 2.342

255. —

    R   —
                             ibid., 1557

256. —

    R   —
                             ibid., 1559
                             Buisson, *Castellion* 2.343

257. —

    R   —
                             ibid., 1562
                             Buisson, *Castellion* 2.343

258. —
    R —
               Basle, 1562
               Buisson, *Castellion* 2.343

259. —
    R —
               Basle, J. Oporinus, 1565

260. —
    O *Ionas Propheta* (in Latin verse) and Πρόδρομος ... *id est vita Ioannis Baptistae* (in Greek verse)
               Basle, J. Oporinus, 1545

260a. —
    O Odae in Psalmos XL, and other paraphrases in verse : in *Pii, graves atque elegantes poetae aliquot* ; contains also :
    R F. Wilson, De vera animi tranquillitate ode una
               Basle, J. Oporinus, [1547-1550]

261. —, transl. & annot.
    O *Biblia*
               Basle, J. Parcus for J. Oporinus, 1551

262. —, —
        —, revised and supplemented by selections from Josephus, books 11-18
               Basle, J. Oporinus, 1554

263. —, —
    R —
               ibid., 1556

264. —, —
        — (ex S. Castalionis postrema recognitione)
               Basle, P. Perna, 1573

265. —, —
    O *La Bible, nouvellement translatée*
               Basle, for J. Herwagen, 1555

266. —, —
        Testamentum novum
               Basle, J. Oporinus, 1551

267. —, —
    R —
               ibid., 1553

268. —, —
        —, with notes
               Basle, L. Lucius, 1556

269. —, transl.
        — (without notes), " ex postrema ... castigatione "
               Basle, P. Perna, 1572

270. —, —
    R —, (Latin and French)
               ibid., 1572

271. —, transl. & annot.
    O   (The Pentateuch) : *Moses Latinus*
             Basle, J. Oporinus, 1546

272. —, —
    O   *Psalterium reliquaque Sacrarum Literarum carmina et precationes*
             ibid., 1547

273. —, —
    R   —
             ibid., 1554

274. —, —
       — (types of preceding ed. except for first two leaves)
             ibid., date on title page : 1556

275. —, —
    R   — : *Davidis ... Psalterium, Salomonis Proverbia, Ecclesiastes, Sapientia,*
       omnia ex ... postrema castigatione
             Basle, P. Perna, [c. 1572-73]

276. —, —
    R   *Salomonis Proverbia, Ecclesiastes, Sapientia*
             Basle, J. Oporinus, 1556
             Buisson, *Castellion* 2.356

277. [—], transl.
    O   Joannes Chrysostomus (ascribed to), *De patientia et consumatione huius*
       saeculi ... sermo, Ioanne Theophilo interprete : appended to M. A. Fla-
       minio, *In Psalmos aliquot paraphrasis*
             Basle, [R. Winter?, 1540?]

278. —, transl. & ed.
    O   Josephus, *Mosis institutio reipublicae Graecolatina*, ex Iosepho in gra-
       tiam puerorum decerpta
             Basle, [J. Oporinus?, 1546]

279. [—], transl.
    O   B. Ochino, *Dialogi XXX* (Latin transl. from the Italian)
             Basle, P. Perna, 1563

280. —, transl. & annot.
    O   *Sibyllina oracula*
             Basle, J. Oporinus, 1546

281. —, —
    R   — (transl. & preface) in :
       Sibyllina oracula (Greek & Latin)
             ibid., 1555

282. —, transl.
    R   — (transl. only) in :
       J. B. Herold, ed. *Orthodoxographa*
             Basle, H. Petri, 1555

283. —, —
    R   — (transl. only) in :
       J. J. Grynaeus, ed., *Monumenta S. Patrum orthodoxographa*
             Basle, Offic. Henricpetrina, 1569

284. [—], —
    O   *Theologia Germanica*, Libellus aureus ... ex Germanico translatus, Ioanne Theophilo interprete
           Basle, J. Oporinus, 1557

285. —, paraphrases
    O   Thomas a Kempis, *De imitando Christo*
           Basle, [J. Oporinus], 1563

286. —, —
    R   —
           Basle, 1576

287. —, —
    R   —
           Basle, 1606

288. —, ed. & partly transl.
    Diodorus Siculus, *Bibliothecae historicae libri XV*
           Basle, H. Petri, 1559

289. —, —
    R   —
           Basle, Offic. Henricpetrina, 1578

290. —, ed.
    Herodotus, *Historiae libri IX* and *Libellus de vita Homeri* (Latin)
           Basle, H. Curio for H. Petri, 1559

291. —, —
    R   —
           Basle, Offic. Henricpetrina, 1573

292. —, —
    Homerus, *Opera* (Greek & Latin)
           Basle, N. Brylinger for J. Oporinus, 1561

293. —, —
    —, revised, " tertia ed."
           Basle, heirs of N. Brylinger, 1567

294. —, —
    —, similar ed.
           Basle, Offic. Brylingeriana, 1582

295. —, —
    Thucydides, [*Historia*] (Latin)
           Basle, for H. Petri and Maternus Collinus, 1564

296. —, —
    Xenophon, *Opera* (Greek)
           Basle, M. Isengrin, [1548 ?]

297. —
    — (Latin) among the translators :
    Jean Ribit, J. L. Strebaeus, S. Châteillon
           ibid. 1551

298. —

    R —

           ibid., 1553

299. **CHAUMETTE, Antoine (Chalmeteus)**

    R *Enchiridion chirurgicum* ... ; *morbi venerei curandi methodus*

           Basle, J. J. Genath, 1620 (some copies with the date of 1621 on the title page)

300. —

    — (identical set of types) bound into :
    W. Fabricius Hildanus, ed., *Cheirurgia militaris*
           ibid. 1634

301. **CHAUSSÉ, Jean (Calceator)**

    R De passione domini nostri Jesu Christi : in
      (*Evangelica carmina*)

           [Basle], B. Westheimer, [c. 1538-40 ?]
           BN : Yc 9028 (incomplete, title page missing)

302. **CLAMANGES, Nicolas de (N. de Clemangiis)**

    O ? *De lapsu et reparatione iusticiae* and other treatises
           [Basle ?, A. Cratander ?, 1519 ?]

303. **CLEMENS V., Pope (Bertrand de Got)**

    R *Constitutiones*

           Basle, M. Wenssler, 1476
           GKW No. 7087

304. —

    R — (another ed. dated from the same day)
           ibid., 1476
           GKW No. 7088

305. —

    R —

           ibid., 1478
           GKW No. 7092

306. —

    R —

           ibid., 1478
           GKW No. 7093

307. —

    R *Constitutiones* and *Decretales extravagantes*
           ibid., 1486
           GKW No. 7104

308. —

    R *Constitutiones*

           [Basle, N. Kessler, c. 1490]
           GKW No. 7105

309. —

    R —

           Basle, J. Froben, 1494
           GKW No. 4890

310. —
    R   —, new ed.
               Basle, J. Amerbach & J. Froben, 1500
               GKW No. 4905

311. —
    R   —
               Basle, J. Amerbach, J. Petri & J. Froben,
               1511

312. **CLICHTOVEUS, Jodocus**
    R   *Elucidatorium ecclesiasticum*
               Basle, J. Froben, 1517

313. —
    R   —
               ibid., 1519

314. —
    R   In Evangelium Ioannis liber quintus [—octavus] adiectus explanationi
       Cyrilli (a substitute for the missing four books in Cyril's commen-
       tary) : in
       St. Cyrillus, *In Evangelium Iohannis commentaria*
               Basle, A. Cratander, 1524

315. (—)
    O   Erasmus of Rotterdam, *Dilutio eorum quae scripsit Iodocus Clithoveus*
       adversus Declamationem suasoriam matrimonii
               Basle, Offic. Frobeniana, [January] 1532

316. (—)
    — (new impression)
               ibid., September 1532

317. **COMMYNES, Philippe de**
    R   *Historiae ... a Ioan. Sleidano Latinitate donatae*
               Basle, Seb. Henricpetri, 1574

318. —
    R   —
               ibid., 1599

319. **CONAN, François (Connanus)**
    Commentariorum iuris civilis libri X (ed. by F. Hotman)
               Basle, N. (II) Episcopius, 1557

320. **CONCENATIUS, Jacobus**
    O   *Epitomes oeconomicae artis iuris civilis libri duo ad Michaelem Hos-*
       pitalem
               ibid., 1562

321. —, ed.
    Bartolo di Sassoferrato, *In ius universum civile commentaria*
               Basle, Offic. Frobeniana, 1562

322. **COP, Wilhelm (Kopp, Copus)**, transl.
    R   Galenus, De locis affectis (and smaller treatises) : in
       Opera
               Basle, A. Cratander, 1529

323. —, transl. in part
        A. de Laguna, ed., *Epitome Galeni ... operum*
                Basle, 1571

324. —, transl.
    R Hippocrates, De ratione victus in morbis acutis ; praesagia : in
       Opera (Latin)
                Basle, A. Cratander, 1526

325. —, —
    R — : in
       Hippocrates, *Aphorismi* and other works
                Basle, H. Petri, 1543

326. **CORDIER, Maturin**
    O ? *De Latini sermonis varietate*
                Basle, B. Westheimer & N. Brylinger,
                1537

327. **(CORNELIUS of Mechlin)**
    Sebastian Austrius of Ruffach, *De infantium sive puerorum morborum ... dignotione* (based on a French (?) work by C. of M., dedicated to Philip I, King of Castile)
                Basle, B. Westheimer, 1540

328. **COUET, Jacques**
    Apologia de iustificatione
                [Basle ?], 1594

329. —
    O *Christliche und dieser Zeit notwendige Antwort* (transl. by Frédéric Châteillon of Response chrestienne et très-necessaire)
                Basle, for Claude de Marne & Jean Aubry,
                1599

330. —
    O *La conference faicte à Nancy*
                Basle, 1600

331. —
    O *Traicte servant a l'eclaircissement de la doctrine de la predestination*
                Basle, J. Schroeter, 1599

332. **COUSIN, Gilbert (Cognatus)**
    Opera
                Basle, H. Petri, 1562

333. —
    Adagiorum συλλογή ; Nova adagiorum appendix : in
    Erasmus, *Adagiorum chiliades* (with minor appendices by others including Charles de Bouelles and A. Turnèbe)
                Basle, Offic. Episcopiana, 1574

334. —
    O *Aliquot epistolae*
                Basle, 1566
                Zentralbibliothek Zurich : Z XXVI 443(2)

335. —

    O   *Brevis ac dilucida Burgundiae superioris ... descriptio ..., item brevis admodum totius Galliae descriptio*
                               Basle, J. Oporinus, 1552

336. —

    O   *Collectanea ex M. T. Ciceronis De oratore, item partium oratoriae facultatis distributiones*
                               Basle, R. Winter, [1544]
                               Bibl. Mazarine : 20414

337. —

    O   *Consolatoria* (with pieces by H. Babet, R. Breton, L. Pellatanus)
                               Basle, J. Parcus, [1546 ?]

338. —

        De iis qui Romae ius dicebant olim ... libellus (and other legal essays)
                               Basle, H. Petri, 1562

339. —

    O   *De legali studio ... epistolae* (in part formerly published as letter dedicatory to No. 92)
                               Basle, 1560

340. —

        De sylva narrationum ... surculi et frutices aliquot
                               Basle, [c. 1560]

341. —

    O   *De usu seu fine legis et Evangelii ex D. Pauli sententia* συνόψις
                               Basle, J. Parcus, 1558

342. —

    O   Enarratinunculae ... in aliquot ... Pontani dialogos : in G. G. Pontano, *Opera*
                               Basle, Offic. Henricpetrina, 1556

343. —

    O   *In concordiae commendationem ... oratio*
                               [Basle, R. Winter ?, c. 1536-40]

344. —

        In Philomelam [Ovidio falso attributam] commentarius : in Ovidius, *Opera*
                               Basle, Offic. Henricpetrina, 1568

345. —

    R   *Narrationum sylva*
                                 ibid, 1567

346. —

    R   *Observationes in allegorias Origenis;*
    R   *De tropice et figurate dictis in Divina Scriptura*
                                 Basle, J. Parcus, 1556

347. —

    R ? Οἰκέτης *sive de officio famulorum*
                                 Basle, H. Froben & N. Episcopius, 1535

348. —

    O *Quaedam opuscula, ... accessit ... C. Nucillani* [i.e. G. Cousin]
    oratio adversus rhetoricen

                      Basle, J. Oporinus, 1547

349. —

    O *Syntaxeos et prosodiae Latinae tabulae*

                      Basle, R. Winter, 1544
                      Zentralbibliothek Zurich : Z XXVI 443 (5)

350. —

    Τιμήτης *seu de censoria virgula* and other small works : appended to
    Natale Conti, *De terminis rhetoricis*

                      Basle, H. Petri, 1560

351. —

    O *Utrum ex his quae tropice et figurate in Divina Scriptura dicuntur possit*
    aliquid efficaciter probari ?; epigrammata ... in laudem D. Erasmi

                      Basle, [J. Parcus, c. 1545]

352. —, ed., introd. & annot.

    (O) Aegidius Delphus, *Divi Pauli apostoli scripta Romanis epistola ...*
    carmine deliaco expressa

                      Basle, J. Oporinus, [1550-1555]
                      Bibl. Mazarine : 23570

353. —, ed.

    O *Effigies D. Erasmis Rotterodami... et Gilberti Cognati*

                      Basle, J. Oporinus, 1553

354. —, —

    O *Epistolae laconicae* (contains among others, letters by F. Andrelini and
    G. Cousin as well as J. Sturm's scholastic selection of Cicero's letters)

                      ibid., 1554

355. —, —

    O *Epitaphia ... in funere ... Philiberti à Rye*

                      Augustae Rauracorum [Basle], Ioannes
                      Nucerianus, 1556

356. —, —

    O S. Gelenius, *Consolatiuncula ad D. Gilbertum Cognatum Nozerenum in*
    obitu ... Guilhelmi a Balma (followed by similar pieces by Robert
    Breton, G. Cousin, Claude Frontin and others)

                      [Basle, J. Parcus, 1546 ?]
                      BN : C. 2577

357. —, —

    Georgius of Trebizond, *In locum illum Evangelii ...* and other small
    works ; contains also :
    G. Cousin, Iuxta sensum allegoricum apud Origenem observata, and
    other small works by Cousin and A. Lebrixa ; also Pierre Gilles of Albi,
    In quinquaginta Sacrae scripturae locos annotationes

                      Basle, R. Winter, 1543

358. —, introd. & annot.

    Lucianus, *Opera* (Greek & Latin)

                      Basle, H. Petri, 1563

359. —, —

—, similar ed.

Basle, Seb. Henricpetri, 1602

360. —, ed.

Martinus, St. Bp. of Dumio (later Abp. of Braga), *Formula honestae vitae*, adiecta sunt Theologorum Sorbonae ex orthodoxis autoribus collectanea adversus Ciceronianos

Basle, R. Winter, 1545

361. —, —

Domingo Melguiz, *Philiberti a Chalon ... rerum gestarum commentariolus* (and other texts by S. Champier, G. Cousin, L. Pellatanus, N. Perrenot de Granvelle)

Basle, B. Westheimer, [c. 1545]

362. —, ed. & contrib.

Poematia aliquot insignia recentium poetarum

Basle, 1557

363. —, ed.

Sallustius, *Opera omnia* (with commentaries by Josse Bade and many others)

Basle, H. Petri, 1564

364. —, —

Suidas, *De Iesu Christi sacerdotio* (Greek & Latin)

[Basle], 1541

365. **(COUSTURIER, Pierre) (Petrus Sutor)**

O   Erasmus of Rotterdam, *Adversus Petri Sutoris ... debacchationem apologia*

Basle, J. Froben, 1525

366. **(—)**

R   —, : in
Opera omnia

Basle, J. Froben & N. Episcopius, 1540

367. **[CRESPIN, Jean]**

R   *Maertyrbuch* (selections from Le livre des martyrs in German transl.)

Basle, publ. by L. Koenig, 1597

368. **CROY, François de**

O   *Heydnisch Bapsthumb* (first part of Les trois conformitez in German transl.)

[Basle], 1607

369. **CUJAS, Jacques**

O   *Praelectiones in tit. D[igestorum] De diversis regulis iuris antiqui*

Basle, C. Waldkirch, 1594

370. **—**

R   Matthias Wesenbeck, *In Pandectas ... commentarii ... quibus de novo ad singulos titulos praefata sunt paratitla Sebastiani Brandii et Iac. Cujacii*

Basle, E. & heirs of N. (II) Episcopius, 1589-1590

371. **[DARIOT, Claude]**

O ? *Vereinigung der galenischen und paracelsischen Artzney-Kunst* (transl. from the French)

Basle, publ. by L. Koenig, 1623

372. **Déclaration**

Declaration des causes qui ont meu Monseigneur le Cardinal de Bourbon ... de s'armer

[Basle ?], 1585
UBB : N.u.VI.20(1) ; cf. No. 761

373. **DENYSE, Nicolas (de Nyse, Denisse, Niseus, etc.)**

R *Gemma predicantium*

Basle, J. Wolff, 1508

374. **DES MASURES, Louis (Masurius)**

Poemata (revised and enlarged)

Basle, T. Guarinus, 1574

375. **Determinatio**

R *Determinatio theologice facultatis Parisiensis super doctrina Lutheriana hactenus per eam visa*

Basle, N. Lamparter, 1521

376. **(—)**

R *Confutatio determinationis doctorum Parrhisiensium contra M. L.*

Basle, 1523

377. **—**

R *Eyn Urteyl der Theologen zuo Pariss über die Lere Doctor Luthers; Ein gegen Urteyl Doctor Luthers; Schützrede Philippi Melanchthon*

[Basle ?, A. Petri ?], 1522
UBB : F.M.[1]. X.18 (14)

378. **Dialogus**

O *Dialogus de statu turbulento ecclesiae huius seculi*

Ex specula Halcyonia [Basle ? or Montbéliard ?, C. Waldkirch or J. Foillet ?], 1591

379. **DINOTH, Richard**

O *Adversaria historica*

Basle, P. Perna, 1581

380. **—**

O *De bello civili Belgico libri VI*

Basle, C. Waldkirch, 1586

381. **—**

O *De bello civili Gallico ... libri VI*

Basle, P. Perna, 1582

382. **—**

O *De rebus et factis memorabilibus loci communes historici*

ibid., 1580

383. **—**

O *Sententiae historicorum*

ibid., 1580

283

384. **Discours**

Discours véritable des horribles meurtres et massacres commis ... par les
troupes du duc de Savoye ... sur les pauvres paysans du baillage de Gex
Langres, Jean Le Court [Basle ?,
C. Waldkirch ?], 1590
UBB : E.f.II.44 (24)

385. **Discours**

Discours. Warhafftige Erzehlung wie Heinricus 3. ... erstochen worden
Erstlich gedruckt zu Basel, in Verlegung
Petri Cesaree, anno 1589

386. **Discursus**

Discursus de rebus Gallicis
Ex specula Halcyonia [Basle ?,
C. Waldkirch ?], 1589
UBB : C.E.III.24 (4)

387. **DOLET, Etienne**

R   Commentariorum linguae Latinae ... epitome duplex (contains only the
first part)
Basle, [B. Westheimer ? or R. Winter ?],
1537

388. —

R   Tomus secundus commentariorum de Latina lingua ... in epitomen
redactus
Basle, B. Westheimer, 1539

389. —

R   Tomi primi epitome commentariorum linguae Latinae
Basle, B. Westheimer & R. Winter, 1540

390. **DRELINCOURT, Charles, the older**

O   Gebätt und christliche Gedancken (transl. of 4th ed. of Traité sur la pré-
pration à la Cène)
Basle, J. J. Genath, 1633

391. —

R   —
ibid., 1643

392. —

O   Kurtzer Begriff der streitigen Puncten (transl. of 4th ed. of Abrégé des
controverses)
Basle, publ. by J. J. Genath, 1628

393. **[DU BELLAY, Guillaume, sieur de Langey ?]**

O ?   Exemplum responsionis Christianissimi Galliarum Regis ad protestatio-
nem, qua Caesarea Maiestas Romae in eum invecta est
[Basle ?, J. Oporinus, T. Platter,
B. Lasius & R. Winter ?], 1536

394. **DUBOIS, François of Amiens (Sylvius)**

R   Lucubrationes in M. Tullii Ciceronis orationes, 2 parts, containing commentaries by Dubois, B. Latomus, J. Tislinus, J. Sturm and others ;
in the 2nd part a letter dedicatory by Jean Morel
Basle, T. Platter & B. Lasius, 1536-1537

395. **DUBOIS, Jacques (Sylvius)**
     R   *Commentarius in Claudii Galeni duos libros de differentiis febrium*
                       Basle, [for Jacques Derbilly], 1556

396. —
     R   *De mensibus mulierum et hominis generatione* (ed. by Alexandre Arnaud)
                       Basle, [for] Jacques Derbilly, 1556

397. —
     R   —: in
        H. K. Wolf, ed., *Gynaeciorum hoc est de mulierum... affectibus ... libri*
                       Basle, T. Guarinus, 1566

398. —
     R   —: in
        G. Bauhin, ed., *Gynaecia*
                       Basle, C. Waldkirch, 1586

399. —
     R   *In Hippocratis et Galeni physiologiae partem anatomicam isagoge* (ed. by
        Alexandre Arnaud)
                       Basle, [for] Jacques Derbilly, 1556

400. —
     O   *Ordo et ordinis ratio in legendis Hippocratis et Galeni libris*
                       Basle, [B. Westheimer ?, 1535-1540]

401. **DU MOULIN, Charles (Molinaeus)**
        Commentarius ad edictum Henrici Secundi ... contra parvas datas
                       Basle, J. Parcus [for M. Isengrin ?], 1552

402. —
     R   Oratio habita in inclyta Tubingensi academia : in
        Matthias Flacius Illyricus, *Refutatio invectivae Bruni contra Centurias*
                       Basle, J. Oporinus, 1566

403. **DU MOULIN, Pierre (Molinaeus)**
     O   *Anatomey oder Zerlegung der Mess* (2 parts, transl. of Anatomie de la
        messe and Deuxième partie de l'anatomie...)
                       Basle, J. J. Genath, 1642

404. —
     O   *Capuciner* (German transl. of Le Capucin)
                       ibid., 1642

405. —
     O   *Erfüllung der Propheceyungen von den letsten Zeiten ... wider die*
        Eynwürfe Roberti Bellarmini und Fr. N. Coeffeteau (transl. of Accom-
        plissement des prophéties)
                       ibid., 1630

406. —
     R   *Glaubens-Schildt* (transl. of Bouclier de la foy)
                       ibid., 1628

407. —
        Kampffplatz der Kindern Gottes (transl. of Du combat chrestien)
                       ibid., 1623

408. **DU PUY, François (de Puteo, Puteanus)**
      O   Tertia compilatio statutorum : in
          Statuta ordinis Cartusiensis
                              Basle, J. Amerbach for the Carthusian
                              convent Johannesberg near Freiburg i.
                              Br., 1510

409. —
      O   *Vita beati Brunonis*
                              Basle, [J. Froben, 1515 ?]

410. **DU QUESNOY, Eustache (Quercetanus, Duchesne)**
      O   *Acroamaton in librum Hippocratis de natura hominis commentarius . . .*
          and . . . *in Cl. Galeni libros tres de temperamentis scholia*
                              Basle, J. Oporinus, 1549

411. **DURANDUS, Gulielmus (Durand, Durantes)**
      R   *Racionale divinorum officiorum*
                              [Basle, M. Wenssler, not after 1476]
                              GKW No. 9110

412. —
      R   —
                              [Basle, B. Ruppel & M. Wenssler, not
                              after 1477]
                              GKW No. 9111

413. —
      R   — : *Rationale . . .*
                              Basle, N. Kessler, 1488
                              GKW No. 9134

414. —
      R   *Speculum iuris*
                              Basle, H. Froben & N. Episcopius, 1563

415. —
      R   —, revised
                              Basle, Ambrosius & Aurelius Froben, 1574

416. **(DU VOISIN, Martin)**
      O   J. J. Grynaeus, *Ein christliche Predigt . . . von Verehrung der H. Jung-*
          frawen Marie (delivered at a memorial service for the Protestant
          martyr M. Du Voisin)
                              Basle, J. J. Genath, 1608

417. **EMILI, Paolo (Aemylius, Paul-Emile)**
          Historiae . . . de rebus gestis Francorum; also :
          Arnoul Le Ferron, De rebus gestis Gallorum ; Jean Du Tillet,Chronicon
                              Basle, Sixtus Henricpetri, 1569

418. —
          —, brought up to date
                              Basle, Seb. Henricpetri, 1601

419. —
      O   *Frantzösischer und anderer Nationen . . . Historien;* also :
      O   Arnoul Le Ferron, Eigentliche Beschreibung frantzösischer . . . His-
          torien (transl. from No. 417)
                              ibid., 1572
                              DGK

420. —
—; brought up to date (mostly identical set of types ?)
ibid., 1574

421. **ERASMUS of Rotterdam**
O   *Declarationes ... ad censuras ... facultatis theologiae Parisiensis*
Basle, H. Froben & N. Episcopius,
[January] 1532

422. —
R   — (a new impression)
ibid., September 1532
Allen 9.397n.

423. —
R   —, in :
Opera omnia
ibid., 1540

424. —
O   *Les paraphrases ... nouvellement translatées de Latin en Françoys*
Basle, Ambrosius & Aurelius Froben,1563

425. **ESTIENNE, Henri (II)**
In Chiliades Erasmi animadversiones : in
Erasmus of Rotterdam, *Adagiorum Chiliades*
Basle, Offic. Episcopiana, 1574

426. —
O   *Principum monitrix musa ...; Cavete vobis principes* (two poems
together with other works and) : *Libellus ... de Aristotelicae ethices
differentia ab historica et poetica*
Basle, 1590

427. **EUCHERIUS, St., Bp. of Lyons**
R   Epistola paraenetica ad Valerianum : in
Opuscula quaedam moralia
Basle, J. Froben, 1520

428. —
R   *Formularum intelligentiae spiritualis liber* and other opuscula
Basle, A. Cratander, 1530

429. —
O   *Lucubrationes*
Basle, H. Froben & N. Episcopius, 1531

430. **FABRY, Marie**
O   *Trewhertziger Wegweiser zuo einem christenlichen, gottseligen Leben und
Absterben* (transl. by the author from the revised French original)
Basle, Martin Wagner, 1626

431. **FAREL, Guillaume**
O   *Gulielmus Farellus Christianis lectoribus* (broadsheet listing 13 theses
for a public disputation)
Basle, 1524
ABR 1.95

432. (—)

    O   *Mandat von einem ersamen Rat der Stat Basel* (pamphlet permitting Farel to proceed with his disputation)

                    Basle, 1524
                    ABR 1.95ff; 6.413

433. **FAUSTUS, St., Bp. of Riez**

    O   *De gratia Dei et humanae mentis libero arbitrio; ... de fide versus Arianos*

                    Basle, Johann Faber, 1528

434. —

    R   —: in

    J. B. Herold, ed., *Orthodoxographa*

                    Basle, H. Petri, 1555

435. —

    R   —: in

    J. J. Grynaeus, ed., *Monumenta S. Patrum orthodoxographa*

                    Basle, Offic. Henricpetrina, 1569

436. **FENOTTI, Giovanni Antonio (Fenotius, Fenot)**

    O   *Alexipharmacum*; preface by J. A. Sarasin

                    Basle, [1576]

437. **FINÉ, Oronce, ed.**

    Gregor Reisch, *Margarita philosophica*; among the appendices:

    R   J. Lefèvre d'Etaples, Introductio in arithmeticam ... Boethii et Iordani; J. Clichtoveus, Ars supputandi; epitome of Introductio geometriae by Charles de Bouelles

                    Basle, H. Petri for C. Resch, 1535

438. —

    R   —

                    Basle, Seb. Henricpetri, 1583

439. (—)

    R   Pedro Nuñez, De erratis Orontii Finaei: in *Opera*

                    ibid. 1592

440. **FLORIDO, Francesco (F. Floridus Sabinus)**

    In M. A. Plauti aliorumque ... scriptorum calumniatores apologia (and collected works)

                    Basle, 1540

441. **FOËS, Anuce**

    O   *Pharmacopeia*

                    Basle, T. Guarinus, 1561

442. —, transl., ed. & comment.

    O   Hippocrates, *Liber secundus de morbis vulgaribus*

                    Basle, J. Parcus for M. Isengrin's widow, 1560

443. **FOULLON, Abel**

    O   *De holometri fabrica et usu* (transl. from the Italian or French)

                    Basle, P. Perna, 1577

444. **FOUQUELIN, Antoine (Foquelinus),** comment.
    R *In Auli Flacci Persii satyras sex quatuor praestantium virorum commentaria;* (among them Fouquelin's)
    ibid., [1578]

445. —
    — (identical set of types) : in
    Persius, *Satyrae*
    ibid. 1582

446. **[FRANCKE, Christian]**
    O *Epistola Pauli Albutii ad Iesuitas*
    Lutetiae Parisiorum, per Gotthardum
    Vilarmum
    [Basle ?, P. Perna ?], 1573
    BM : 860.k.11 (1)

447. **FRANCUS, Hieronymus**
    O *In regulas iuris ... commentarii*
    Basle, J. Oporinus, [1558-1559]

448. **Französische Historie**
    O *Frantzösische Historÿ allerlaÿ Religion und Wälthändlen, so sich under
    Konig Henrico II., Francisco II. unnd Carolo IX. ... zugetragen*
    (transl. from Res in Gallia ob religionem gestae)
    [Basle, for H. Petri & P. Perna ?], 1574

449. **FRONTIN, Anatole**
    O Tabellae oratoriae inventionis : in
    Natale Conti, *De terminis rhetoricis*
    Basle, [H. Petri, 1560]

450. **GALLOT, Nicolas (N. Galottus Catalaunensis),** ed. & comment.
    O Demosthenes, *Olynthiacae tres* (Greek & Latin)
    Basle, J. Oporinus, 1560

451. **GARLAND, John (J. de Garlandia)**
    O *Compendium alchimiae;* with other material ascribed to Garland and
    a commentary by Arnaldus of Villanova
    Basle, [P. Perna ?], 1560

452. —
    R Compendium alchimiae ; De mineralibus : in
    Lorenzo Ventura, *De ratione conficiendi lapidis*
    Basle, [P. Perna], 1571

453. **GARNIER, Jean**
    O *Briefve et claire confession de la foy chrestienne ...* faicte et declairee
    l'an 1549
    [Basle], J. Parcus, [1549 ?]
    Zentralbibliothek Zurich : Z C 260 (3)

454. **GAULTIER-CHABOT, Pierre (Gualterius Chabotius)**
    In Q. Horatii Flacci poema expositio analytica; 2nd ed., revised
    Basle, L. Osten, 1589

455. —
    O *Praelectiones ... quibus Q. Horatii Flacci ... poemata ... explicantur*
    ibid., 1587

456. —
                    —, similar title (identical set of types)
                                        ibid., 1591

457. —, ed., introd. & comment.
        O   Horatius, *Opera omnia;* with a biography of Gaultier by J. J. Boissard
                                        Coloniae Munatianae [i.e. Basle],
                                        L. König, 1615

458. **GENTILLET, Innocent**
        O   *Examen, das ist Ergründunge und Widerlegunge des Tridentinischen
             Conciliums* (transl. of Examen Concilii Tridentini)
                                        Basle, Huldrych Frölich, 1587

459. [—]
        R   *Regentenkunst oder Fürstenspiegel* (transl. of Commentariorum de regno
             ... libri III)
                                        [Basle ?], " Erstlich gedruckt zu Strass-
                                        burg bey Johann Carolo. Jtzo aber in
                                        Ludwig Königs selig. Erben Buchladen
                                        zu finden ", 1646

460. **GERSON, Jean**
        R   *Opera*
                                        Basle, N. Kessler, 1489
                                        BMC 15th c. 3.767

461. —
                    —; larger collection
                                        Basle, A. Petri, 1517 [?]-1518

462. [—]
                    Alphabetum divini amoris
                                        [Basle, J. Amerbach, c. 1490]
                                        BMC 15th c. 3.753

463. —
                    Donatus moralisatus
                                        [Basle, M. Flach, c. 1475-1577]
                                        BMC 15th c. 3.740

464. —
        R   *Sermo de passione Domini*
                                        Basle, [M. Furter], 1515
                                        BMC

465. **GETTE, Jacques (Gète, Geteus Boloniensis)**
        O   *Bucolica Christiana*
                                        Basle, J. Parcus, 1555

466. **GEUFFROY, Antoine**
        O   *Aulae Turcicae ... descriptio* (transl. from the French)
                                        Basle, Seb. Henricpetri, 1573

467. —
                    —, ; rearranged with additional texts
                                        ibid., 1577

468. —
        O   *Hoffhaltung des türckhischen Keisers* (mostly a transl. of No. 466)
                                        ibid., [1573]

290

469. —
      — (mostly a transl. of No. 467)
          ibid., 1596

470. **GILLES de Corbeil (Aegidius Corboliensis)**
      R   *Carmina de urinarum iudiciis*
          Basle, T. Wolff, 1529

471. **GILLES, Nicole (N. Aegidius)**
      O   *Frantzoesische Chronica* (transl. from the French)
          Basle, heirs of N. Brylinger, 1572

472. **GILLES, Pierre (Gyllius, etc.), ed.**
      O   *Lexicon Graecolatinum*
          Basle, V. Curio, 1532

473. **GILLEY, Jean de**
      O   *In laudem Hannibalis ... commentariolus*
          Basle, J. Parcus for J. Oporinus, 1550

474. **GODEFROY, Denis (Gothofredus)**
      O   *Antiquae historiae ex XXVII authoribus contextae libri VI*
          Basle, C. Waldkirch, 1590

475. —
      O   *In L. Annaei Senecae opera coniecturarum ... libri V*
          Basle, E. Episcopius, 1590

476. **[GOHORY, Jacques], ed. & comment.**
      R   *Theophrasti Paracelsi philosophiae et medicinae ... compendium ...,*
      auctore Leone Suavio I.G.P.; also contains
      O   appendices critical of the editor
          Basle, P. Perna, 1568

477. **[GOULART, Simon]**
      O   *Expositio verissima iuxta et succincta de rebus nuper bello gestis inter*
          Allobrogum regulum et Helveticas regis Galliarum auxiliares copias
          Augustae Rauracorum [Basle ?], 1589

478. **(GRANGIER, Bonaventure)**
          Georg Caspius, *Ad indoctam ... Grangerii ... admonitionem de cau-*
          tionibus in sanguinis missione adhibendis brevis responsio, qua Leonar.
          Botalli ... libellus de curatione per sanguinis missionem defenditur
          Basle, [T. Guarinus for ?] Jehan Mareschal,
          1579 (some copies with the date of 1580
          on the title page)

479. **GRASSER, Johann Jakob**
      R   De Nemausensibus antiquitatibus dissertatio; appended to:
          Poemata
          Coloniae Munatianae [i.e. Basle]
          J. Schröter, 1614 (some copies with the
          date of 1615 on the title page)

480. **GREGORIUS, St., Bp. of Tours**
          Historia Francorum
          Basle, P. Perna, 1568

481. **GRIBALDl Mofa, Matteo**

   O *Communium opinionum in iure loci communes; Regulae causarum criminalium*

   Basle, E. Episcopius, 1567

482. —

   O Epistola : in
   C.S. Curione, ed., *Francisci Spierae ... historia* (another contribution by J. Calvin)

   [Basle, 1549-1550]

483. —

   —; identical set of types, one addition

   Basle, 1550

484. —

   — (German transl.) : *Ein Epistel oder Sentbrieff*

   [Basle ?], 1549

485. —

   R — : Historia von Francisco Spiera : in
   N. Sobaeus, *Von der Beständigkeit im Glauben*

   Basle, publ. by J. J. Genath, 1631

486. —

   O Recentiorum iurisconsultorum catalogus : in
   Johannes Lorichius, *Iureconsulti*

   Basle, J. Oporinus, 1545

487. **[GRYMOULT, Léger], (Grimaldus),** transl.

   O *Ordonnance ecclesiastique des comté, terres et seigneuries de Montbeliart et Richeville*

   Basle, Johann Lucas Iselin & Basilius Immanuel Herold, 1568

488. **GUIDO de Monte Rocherio**

   Manipulus curatorum

   [Basle, M. Flach, c. 1475]
   BMC 15th c. 3.742

489. —

   R —

   [Basle ?, c. 1485]
   BM : IA. 38005

490. **GUILLAUME d'Auvergne, Bp. of Paris**

   R *Rhetorica divina*

   [Basle ?, J. Amerbach ?, c. 1490]
   BM : IB.37440

491. —

   — and other treatises

   [Basle, J. Froben, 1491-1492]
   BMC 15th c. 3.790

492. **[GUILLAUME de Conches]**

    O   Philosophia mundi : *Philosophicarum et astronomicarum institutionum Gulielmi Hirsgauensis ... libri tres*
            Basle, H. Petri, 1531
            For this and the following No. cf.
            M. Grabmann, *Hs. Forschungen und Mitteilungen zum Schrifttum des W. von Conches*, 1935

493. **[—]**

    — ; attributed to Bede : in
    Beda Venerabilis, *Opera*
            Basle, J. (II) Herwagen, 1563

494. **GUILLAUME, Bp. of Tyrus**

    O   *Belli sacri historia*, ed. by Philibert Poissenot [or rather J. B. Herold]
            Basle, N. Brylinger & J. Oporinus, 1549

495. **—**

    R   — : *Historia belli sacri*, revised
            Basle, N. Brylinger, 1564

496. **(—)**

    O   J. B. Herold, *De bello sacro continuatae historiae libri IV commentariis ... Guilhelmi Tyrensis ... additi* ; with additional shorter texts said to be ed. by P. Poissenot
            Basle, [N. Brylinger & J. Oporinus], 1549

497. **(—)**

    R   —
            Basle, N. Brylinger, 1560

498. **GUINTERIUS, Johannes**

    Anatomicarum institutionum ex Galeni sententia libri IV (revised and enlarged)
            Basle, R. Winter, 1539

499. **—**

    O ? *De medicina veteri et nova ... commentarii duo*
            Basle, Offic. Henricpetrina, 1571

500. **—**

    R   De victus et medicinae ratione ... pestilentiae tempore observanda commentarius : in
    M. Ficino, *De vita libri tres*
            Basle, A. Cratander, 1549

501. **—, ed. transl. & annot.**

    R   *Alexandri Tralliani medici libri duodecim*, Greek and Latin, with Castigationes by Jacques Goupyl
            Basle, H. Petri, 1556

502. **—, ed. & partly transl.**

    O   *Cl. Galeni aliquot libelli*
            Basle, H. Froben & J. Herwagen, 1529

503. **—, transl.**

    O   Galenus, *De anatomicis administrationibus* and other works
            Basle, A. Cratander, 1531

504. —, —
    R   Galenus, *De compositione medicamentorum* κατὰ γένη
                  ibid., 1530

505. —, —

       Galenus, In Hippocratis librum de natura hominis commentarii and
       smaller treatises : in
       Opera (Latin), also contains : De spirandi difficultate and shorter texts
       transl. by Jean Vasseau
                  ibid., 1536

506. —, —
    (R) Galenus, *Medicorum schola* ... *sive medicus* (Greek & Latin)
                  Basle, T. Platter & B. Lasius, 1537

507. —, transl. in part
    R   Galenus, *Omnia* ... *opera* (Latin), other transl. by G. Cop and J.Vasseau
                  Basle, H. Froben & N. Episcopius, 1542

508. —, —
    R —, similar ed., same translators
                  ibid., 1561-1562

509. —, ed.
    R   Oribasius, *Commentaria in aphorismos Hippocratis*
                  Basle, A. Cratander, 1535

510. **HARCHIES, Josse de (Harchius)**
    O   *De causis haeresis proque eius exilio et concordia*
                  Basle, [P. Perna ?], 1573

511. —
    O   *De Eucharistiae mysterio, dignitate et usu*
                  Vormatiae, apud Davidem Cephalaeum
                  [Basle ?, P. Perna ?, 1573 ?]

512. —
    O   *Enchiridion medicum*
                  Basle, P. Perna, 1573

513. —
    O   *Orthodoxorum patrum* ... *fides de Eucharistia*
                  [Basle ?, P. Perna ?, 1576 ?]

514. **HERVET, Gentian,** transl.
    O   Alexander of Aphrodisias, *Quaestiones* ... *naturales, de anima, morales*
                  Basle, J. Oporinus, 1548

515. —, —
    R   Clemens Alexandrinus, *Omnia* ... *opera*
                  Basle, T. Guarinus, 1561

516. —, —
       Theodoretus of Cyrus, *Eranistes* and other treatises
                  Basle, J. Parcus for J. Oporinus, 1549

517. —, —
    O   Theodorus Metochites, *In Aristotelis Physicorum* ... *libros octo et
       Parva* ... *naturalia paraphrasis*
                  Basle, N. Brylinger, 1559

518. **[HEYNLIN, Johannes] (J. a Lapide)**
    R   Compendiosus dialogus de arte punctuandi : in
    Guarino da Verona, *Ars diphtongandi*
    > Basle, [J. Amerbach], 1478
    > *BMC 15th c.* 3.745

519. **[—]**
    R   —
    > ibid., 1480
    > *BNC*

520. **[—]**
    R   —
    > ibid., 1481
    > *BMC 15th c.* 3.746

521. **[—]**
    R   —
    > ibid. 1482
    > *BMC 15th c.* 3.747

522. **[—]**
    R   —
    > Basle, [N. Kessler ?], 1486
    > UBB

523. **[—]**
    R   —
    > [ibid. ?], 1487
    > *BNC*

524. **—**
    O   *Resolutorium dubiorum circa celebrationem missarum occurrentium*
    > Basle, J. Froben, 1492
    > *BMC 15th c.* 3.790

525. **—**
    R   —
    > [Basle ?, J. Wolff ?, c. 1497]
    > *BMC 15th c.* 3.777

526. **—, ed., comment. & append.**
    O   *Libri artis logicae Porphyrii et Aristotelis;* contains also :
    J. Heynlin, De propositionibus exponibilibus, de arte solvendi impor-
    tunas sophistarum argumentationes ; Gilbert de la Porrée, Liber sex
    principiorum
    > Basle, J. Amerbach, [1495]
    > *BMC 15th c.* 3.756f.

527. **—, ed. & introd.**
    St. Ambrosius, *Opera*
    > Basle, J. Amerbach, 1492
    > *GKW No.* 1599

528. **[—], ed.**
    R   Gaspare Barzizza, *Epistolae*
    > Basle, M. Wenssler & Friedrich Biel
    > [1472-1474]
    > *GKW No.* 3676

529. [—], —
      R —

           [Basle, M. Flach, c. 1474]
           GKW No. 3677

530. [—], —
      R —

           [Basle, M. Furter, 1495-1499]
           GKW No. 3787

531. —, introd.
      O   Cassiodorus, *In Psalterium expositio*
           Basle, J. Amerbach, 1491
           GKW No. 6163

532. —, —
      R   Johannes Trithemius, *De scriptoribus ecclesiasticis*
           ibid., 1494
           BMC 15th c. 3.755

533. **HILARIUS, St., Bp. of Poitiers**
         Lucubrationes

           Basle, J. Froben, 1523

534. —
         —

           Basle, H. Froben & N. Episcopius, 1535

535. —
         —, enlarged & revised

           ibid., 1550

536. —
      R —

           Basle, E. & heirs of N. (II) Episcopius,
           1570

537. —
      R   De patris et filii unitate (mostly selections of De Trinitate, book 9) : in
         J. Sichard, ed., *Antidotum contra . . . haereses*
           Basle, H. Petri, 1528

538. **HOLLIER, Blaise**
      O   *In Hippocratis iusiurandum commentarius*
           Basle, J. Oporinus, [1558 ?]

539. —
      O   *Morborum curandorum brevis institutio*
           Basle, N. Brylinger, 1556

540. —, comment.
         Hippocrates, *De natura hominis* (Greek & Latin) ; Hollier's comment.
         revised and enlarged
           Basle, J. Oporinus, 1562

541. **[HONORIUS of Autun] (H. Augustodunensis)**
      R   *Elucidarius dialogicus theologie*
           Basle, 1508

542. —

    O *Libri septem*; including Guillaume de Conches, De philosophia mundi, here attributed to Honorius

                Basle, heirs of A. Cratander, 1544

543. **HOTMAN, François**

    O *Commentarius in quatuor libros Institutionum iuris civilis*

                Basle, J. (II) Herwagen, 1560

544. —

    —; revised by author

                Basle, E. Episcopius, 1569

545. —

    O *Commentarius in tit. Cod. De usufructu*

                Basle, E. & heirs of N. (II) Episcopius, 1575

546. —

    O *Commentarius in TT. Digestor. et Codic. de pignoribus et hypothecis*

                ibid., 1576

547. —

    O *Commentarius verborum iuris;* appended:
N. de Grouchy, Epitome de comitiis Romanorum

                Basle, N. (II) Episcopius, 1558

548. —

    —; improved, with additions: *Novus commentarius de verbis iuris*

                ibid. 1563

549. —

    O *Commentationum iuris civilis lib. XXII ad tit. Dig.* [et Decretal.] *De usuris etc.*

                Basle, E. & heirs of N. (II) Episcopius, 1576

550. —

    De actionibus novus commentarius

                Basle, J. Herwagen, 1559

551. —

    O *De castis incestisve nuptiis: de spuriis et legitimatione* (ed. & prefaced by Jean Hotman de Villiers)

                Basle, J. Foillet, 1594

552. —

    —, identical set of types

                [ibid. for] J. Lertout, Lyons, 1594

553. [—]

    O *De furoribus Gallicis*

                Edimburgi [Basle, T. Guarinus], 1573
                UBB: F.O.VII.15 (10)
                BN: 4° Lb[33] 311

554. —

    O *De legibus populi Romani liber*

                Basle, N. (II) Episcopius, 1557

555. —

    O De undecimestri partu et de sui haeredis appellatione (ex Observationum libris nondum evulgatis) : in
Johann Wilhelm Neonobellus, *Vacantiae vindemiales*
               Basle, P. Perna, 1579

556. —

    O *Disputatio de aureo Iustinianico*
               Basle, E. & heirs of N. (II) Episcopius,
               1584

557. —

    O *In tit. Cod. De iudiciis commentarius*
               ibid. 1576

558. —

    O *Iurisconsultus*
               Basle, J. (II) Herwagen, 1559

559. —

    Legum Romanorum index
               Basle, N. (II) Episcopius, 1558

560. —

    O *Partitiones iuris civilis elementariae*
               ibid., 1560

561. —

    — ; revised and enlarged
               ibid., 1561

562. [—]

    P. Sixti V. fulmen brutum in Henricum sereniss. regem Navarrae (the text of the Papal bull with the imprint : Rome, heirs of A. Bladius, 1585) ; 8°, 184 pp.
               [Basle ?, C. Waldkirch ? or J. Foillet ?
               1585-86]
               UBB : M.o.VI.5 (4)

563. [—]

    —, ... *item Alciati, Cuiacii et Hotomani coniecturas* (partly identical set of types) ; 8°, 217 pp.
               [ibid. ?, 1585-88 ?]
               BN : Lb[34] 280

564. [—]

    — ; 8°, 231 pp.
               [ibid. ?, 1585-88 ?]
               BN : Lb[34] 280C

565. [—]

    — ; with additional appendices
               [ibid. ?], 1603
               UBB : F.P.IV².5 (1)

566. —

    O *Observationum liber primus*
               Basle, N. (II) Episcopius, 1560

567. —
  R —
                          Basle, E. & heirs of N. (II) Episcopius,
                          1571

568. —
  O *Observationum liber secundus*
                          Basle, N. (II) Episcopius, 1561

569. —
  O *Observationum liber III.*
                          Basle, E. & heirs of N. (II) Episcopius,
                          1574

570. —
  O *Observationum liber IIII.*
                          ibid., 1575

571. —
  O *Observationum liber quinctus*
                          ibid., 1577

572. —, introd. & annot.
        Caesar, *Commentarii* (contains also commentaries by others and the
        index of R. Marlianus)
                          Basle, L. Osten, 1591

573. (—)
        J. T. Freigius, *Partitiones iuris utriusque* ... ; partitiones feudales ex
        clariss. I.C. Udalrici Zasii et Francisci Hotomanni commentariis
        deductae
                          Basle, Seb. Henricpetri, 1581

574. **HUCBALDUS of Saint-Amand**
        R *Aegloga de calvis*
                          Basle, Nicolaus Lamparter, 1519

575. —
        R —
                          Basle, J. Parcus, 1546

576. —
        R — in :
        Acrostichia (contains also an acrostic fragment of Castellio's transl. of
        Sibyllina oracula, No. 280)
                          ibid., 1552

577. **HUGUES de Saint-Cher (Hugo de S. Caro)**
        R *Postilla super Evangelia*
                          Basle, B. Richel, 1482
                          BMC 15th c. 3.738

578. —, comment.
        O *Biblia* (with Hugues' Postilla)
                          [Basle, J. Amerbach and J. Petri for
                          A. Koberger, 1498-1502]
                          BMC 15th c. 3.759

579. —, comment.

R   —

ibid., 1504

580. (—)

O   *Repertorium apostillarum utriusque Testamenti domini Hugonis*
Cardinalis
[Basle, J. Amerbach, 1504]

581. **HUGUES de Saint-Victor**

De studio orandi ; de tribus dietis : in
[Thomas a Kempis], *Hortulus rosarum*
Basle, Johann Bergmann von Olpe, 1499
BMC 15th c. 3.797

582. —

Didascalicon : in W. Brack, *Vocabularius rerum*
[Basle, Peter Kollicker], 1483
BMC 15th c. 3.762

583. **HURAULT de L'Hospital, brothers**

Philopappus Huralthospitaliorum fratrum seu apologeticum pro veteri
ac germana linguae Graecae pronunciatione ... ad ... D. Michaelem
Hospitalium [ed. by P. Gaultier-Chabot ?] ; 2nd ed., enlarged
Basle, L. Osten, 1587

584. **IRENAEUS, St., Bp. of Lyons**

O   *Opus eruditissimum* [adversus haereses]
Basle, J. Froben, 1526

585. —

R   —, revised
Basle, H. Froben & N. Episcopius, 1528

586. —

R   —

ibid., 1534

587. —

R   —

ibid., 1560

588. —

R   —, revised
Basle, E. & heirs of N. (II) Episcopius,
1571

589. **JACOTIUS, Desiderius (Vadoperanus)**

R   De philosophorum doctrina libellus ex Cicerone : in
J. T. Freigius, *Ciceronianus*
Basle, Seb. Henricpetri, 1579

590. —

R   — : in
Hieronymus Wolf, *Tabula compendiosa de origine ... veterum philo-*
sophorum
Basle, Offic. Herwagiana per E. Episcopium, 1580

591. —
    R   — : in
    J. T. Freigius, *Ciceronianus*
        Basle, Seb. Henricpetri, 1596

592. **JEAN de Roquetaillade (Rupescissa)**
    O   *De consideratione quintae essentiae;* with other related texts by Arnaldus de Villanova and others
        Basle, [P. Perna, 1561?]

593. —
    R   —
        Basle, C. Waldkirch, 1597

594. —
    — and other treatises under the name of Jean de R. as well as a letter attributed to Arnaldus de Villanova : in
    G. Gratarolo, ed., *Alchemiae, quam vocant ...*
        Basle, P. Perna, 1572

595. **JOHANNES XXII, Pope (Jacques d'Euse), ed.**
    R   *Extravagantes viginti*
        Basle, J. Amerbach, J. Petri & J. Froben, 1511

596. **JOHANNES Cassianus**
    O   *De institutis coenobiorum; de origine, causis et remediis vitiorum; de collationibus patrum*
        Basle, [J. Amerbach], 1485
        GKW No. 6160

597. —
    R   —, similar ed.
        Basle, J. Amerbach, 1497
        GKW No. 6162

598. —
    R   — and De incarnatione Christi : in
    Johannes Damascenus, *Opera* (Greek & Latin)
        Basle, H. Petri, 1559

599. —
    R   —
        Basle, Offic. Henricpetrina, 1575

600. —
    O   *De incarnatione Domini libri VII*
        Basle, A. Cratander, 1534

601. **JOHANNES, Abbot of Nivelles**
    Concordantia Bibliae et Canonum
        Basle, N. Kessler, 1487
        BMC 15th c. 3.765

602. —
    R   —
        Basle, [M. Furter?], 1489
        BMC 15th c. 3.787

JOHANNES

603. —
  R —

       [Basle, N. Kessler, 1490 ?]
       BMC 15th c. 3.773

604. **JOHANNES of Paris**
  R De potestate regia et papali : in
    S. Schard, ed., *De iurisdictione, autoritate et praeeminentia imperiali,*
    contains also :
  R Landolfo Colonna, De translatione imperii
       Basle, J. Oporinus, 1566

605. **JOHANNES of Segovia**
    Concordantia partium sive dictionum indeclinabilium totius Bibliae : in
    Concordantiae maiores
       Basle, J. Petri & J. Froben, 1496
       BMC 15th c. 3.791

606. —
  R —

       Basle, J. Amerbach, J. Petri & J. Froben,
       1506

607. —
  R —

       Basle, J. Froben, 1516

608. —
  R —

       ibid., 1521

609. —
  R —

       ibid., 1523

610. —
  R —

       ibid., 1525

611. —
  R —

       Basle, H. Froben, J. Herwagen & N. Epi-
       scopius, 1531

612. —
  R —

       Basle, J. Herwagen, 1543

613. —
  R —

       ibid., 1549

614. —
  R —

       ibid., 1553

615. —
  R —

       Basle, J. (II) Herwagen, 1561

616. JOUBERT, Laurent
O *Gantz nutzlicher ... Bericht von rechtem ordenlichen Gebrauch der Artzney* (Erreurs populaires, book I, transl. from the French or Latin text)
Basle, for L. König, 1602

617. (—)
O T. Erastus, Disputatio de febribus, in qua tria ... paradoxa D. Laurentii Iuberti ... excutiuntur: appended to: *Disputatio de putredine*
Basle, L. Osten sumptibus Oporinianorum, 1580

618. (—)
R Simone Simoni, *Examen sententiae a Brunone Seidelio latae de iis quae Laurentius Iubertus ... in suis Paradoxis disputavit* (probably published together with S. Simoni, Synopsis brevissima)
[Basle, P. Perna, 1580?]

619. JULYOT, Ferry
O *Elegies de la belle fille lamentant sa virginité perdue*
[Basle?, J. Parcus] aux despens d'Antoine Ludin ... de Bezanson, 1557

620. Königliche ... Zeitung
O *Konigliche Navarrische Zeitung oder Beschreibung der dreyen vortrefflichen ... Schlachten ... vor Diepen ..., vor Meulon ..., vor Dreux* (transl. from the French)
Basle, publ. by Hans Storck, 1590
UBB: E.A. IX. 51 (No. 18)

621. KRAG, Anders (Kragius)
O *Laurea Apollinea Monspeliensis*
Basle, Seb. Henricpetri, [1586]

622. LA BAUME, Jean de (Baulme, a Balma Peranus)
O *Primitiae quaedam* [ed. by Gilbert Cousin]
Basle, J. Parcus, 1558
BN: C.2577

623. LA FRAMBOISIÈRE, Nicolas-Abraham de (Frambesarius)
R *Canones cheirurgici*: in
W. Fabricius Hildanus, ed., *Cheirurgia militaris*
Basle, J. J. Genath, 1634

624. LA LOUPE, Vincent de (Lupanus)
R Commentarii de magistratibus Francorum: in
O J. T. Freigius, *Quaestiones oeconomicae et politicae*; contains also:
R Quinque orationes de laude regiae dignitatis a quinque discipulis Audomari Talaei habitae Parisiis ... 1548
R Cicero, Epistola ad Quintum fratrem ... de provincia recte administranda et in eandem Franc. Hotomani commentarius
Basle, Seb. Henricpetri, 1578

625. —
R —
ibid., 1591 [perhaps misprint for 1581?]

626. **LAMBIN, Denis,** transl. & comment.
    (R) Aristoteles, *De moribus ad Nicomachum* (Greek & Latin)
                      Basle, J. Oporinus & E. Episcopius, 1566

627. —, —
    —, identical set of types ; with prefaces by D. Lambin and M. A. Muret
                    ibid., 1566

628. —, —
    (R) — : *Ethicorum Nicomachiorum ... libri decem* (Greek & Latin) ; among the appendices :
    O Theophrastus, Morum characteres, transl. & comment. by Claude Aubery
                    Basle, E. Episcopius, 1582

629. —, transl.
    R Aristoteles, *Politicorum libri octo* (Greek & Latin) ;
    O appendix : Pythagoreorum fragmenta politica, ed. & transl. after Stobaeus by Jean de Sponde
                    ibid., 1582

630. **LANFRANC, Abp. of Canterbury**
    O De sacramento Eucharistiae : in
    Philastrius, Bp. of Brescia, *Haeresewn catalogus*
                  [Basle, J. Froben ?, 1528-1529]

631. —
    R — : in
    Μικροπρεσβυτικόν
                  Basle, H. Petri, 1550

632. **[LANGUET, Hubert]**
    O Stephanus Iunius Brutus Celta, *Vindiciae contra tyrannos* ; completed & ed. by Philippe de Mornay, sieur du Plessis-Marly
            Edimburgi [Basle ?, T. Guarinus ?], 1579
            BN : 8⁰ *E.2135 & 8⁰ *E.3867

633. **[—]**
    R —, appendix :
    [Théodore de Bèze], De iure magistratuum in subditos ; 303 pp.
            [Basle ?, P. Perna ? or J. Foillet ?], 1580
            UBB : N.a.IV.13a
            BN : 8⁰ *E.1418

634. **[—]**
    R — ; 326 pp.
            [ibid. ?], 1580
            BN : 8⁰ *E.2136 & 8⁰ *E.2325 (2)

635. **LA RAMÉE, Pierre de (Ramus)**
    O *Arithmeticae libri duo; geometriae septem et viginti*
            Basle, E. & heirs of N. (II) Episcopius, 1569

636. —
    R —
                  ibid., 1580

637. —

    O   *Ein sehr nutzliche unnd kunstreiche Arithmetick* (transl. of Arithmeticae libri duo)

                    Basle, S. Apiarius, 1569

638. —

    R   *Ciceronianus*

                    Basle, P. Perna, 1573

639. —

    R   —, with *Brutinae quaestiones* and some letters

                    ibid., 1577

640. —

       Dialectica, Audomari Talaei praelectionibus illustrata

                    Basle, E. & heirs of N. (II) Episcopius, 1569

641. —

    R   —

                    ibid., 1572

642. —

    R   —

                    ibid., 1577
                    Ong, *Inventory* No. 259

643. —

    R   —

                    ibid., 1585

644. —

    R   *Grammaticae libri IV*

                    ibid, 1569

645. —

    R   *Institutionum dialecticarum libri tres* ... A. Talaei praelectionibus illustrati

                    Basle, N. Episcopius, 1554
                    Ong, *Inventory* No. 16

646. —

    R   —, similar title, and *Aristotelicae animadversiones*

                    Basle, Seb. Henricpetri, 1575

647. —

    R   *Liber de milita C. Iulii Caesaris*

                    ibid., [1574 ?]

648. —

    R   *Liber de moribus veterum Gallorum*

                    ibid., [1574 ?]

649. —

    O   *P. Rami et I. Schecii epistolae*

                    Basle, E. & heirs of N. (II) Episcopius, 1569
                    cf. M. Härtwig in *Zentr. blatt f. Bibl. wesen*, 58 (1941), 131 ; Ong, *Inventory* No. 620

650. —

Praelectiones in Ciceronis orationes octo consulares and other texts,
prefaced by J. T. Freigius, Petri Rami vita ; appendix :
Robert Breton, De optimo statu reipublicae
Basle, P. Perna, 1575

651. —

R   —; similar, slightly larger ed.
ibid., 1580

652. —

R   Rudimenta grammaticae Latinae
Basle, E. & heirs of N. (II) Episcopius,
1569

653. —

O   Scholae in liberales artes
ibid., 1569

654. —

R   —

ibid., 1578
Ong, Inventory No. 696

655. —

O   Scholarum mathematicarum libri unus et triginta
ibid., 1569

656. (—)

O   Johann Bilsten, Syntagma Philippo-Rameum artium liberalium
Basle, C. Waldkirch, 1588

657. (—)

R   —

ibid., 1596

658. (—)

R   —

ibid., 1607

659. (—)

O   J. T. Freigius, P. Rami professio regia
Basle, Seb. Henricpetri, 1576

660. (—)

O   J. T. Freigius, Quaestiones geometricae et stereometricae in Euclidis et
Rami στοιχείωσιν
ibid., 1583

661. (—)

O   Anders Krag, Aristotelica et Ramea
ibid., [1583]

662. (—)

O   Anders Krag, Rameae scholae et defensio Petri Rami contra Georgii
Liebleri calumnias
ibid., 1582

663. (—)

O   Anders Krag, Q. Horatii Flacci ars poetica ad P. Rami dialecticam et
rhetoricam resoluta
ibid., [1583 ?]

664. (—)

    O   Georg Liebler, *Epitome philosophiae naturalis ex Aristotelis ... libris ... excerpta, ... quae etiam Scholarum Petri Rami ... errores passim detegit*

                Basle, Offic. Oporiniana, 1573

665. (—)

    R —

                ibid., 1575

666. (—)

    R —

                Basle, Offic. Oporiniana (Hieronymus Gemusaeus & Balthasar Han), 1586

667. (—)

    O   A. Polanus a Polansdorf, *Syntagma logicum Aristotelico-Ramaeum ad usum imprimis theologicum accomodatum*

                Basle, C. Waldkirch, 1605

                Ong, *Inventory* No. 378

668. (—)

    —, enlarged

                ibid., 1611

669. (—)

    R   G. A. Scribonius, *Triumphus logicae Rameae*

                Basle, Offic. Pernea [= C. Waldkirch], 1587

                Ong, *Inventory* No. 297

670. **L'ARCHIER, Jean (L'Archer, Arquerius)**

    O   *Dictionarium theologicum*

                Basle, B. Franck for J. Oporinus, 1567

671. **LA ROCHE, Nicolas de**

    R   De morbis mulierum : in

       H. K. Wolf, ed., *Gynaeciorum hoc est de mulierum affectibus ... libri*

                Basle, T. Guarinus, 1566

672. —

    R   — : in

       G. Bauhin, ed., *Gynaecia*

                Basle, C. Waldkirch, 1586

673. **LASCARIS, Janus**

       De Romanorum militia (excerpts from Polybius, transl. by J. Lascaris) ; *Epigrammata*

                Basle, B. Lasius & T. Platter, 1537

674. **LATOMUS, Bartholomaeus (Le Masson)**

       Actio memorabilis Francisci ab Siccingen : in

       S. Schard, ed., *Historicum opus*

                Basle, Offic. Henricpetrina, 1574

675. —

    R   Oratio ... de laudibus eloquentiae : in
         In omnes M. Tullii Ciceronis orationes ... lucubrationes (contains many
         commentaries by B. L. and François Dubois, and some by J. Tislinus,
         J. Sturm, etc.
                                       Basle, R. Winter, 1539

676. —

    R   —, similar ed. enlarged with commentaries by P. de La Ramée, Josse
         Bade, A. de Gouvea, etc.
                                         Basle, J. Oporinus, 1553

677. **LATOMUS, Jacobus (Masson), the older**

    R   *De confessione secreta;*
    O   J. Oecolampadius, *Elleboron pro eodem Iacobo Latomo*
                                       Basle, A. Cratander, [1525]

678. —

    R   De trium linguarum et studii theologici ratione dialogus : appended to
    R   Erasmus of Rotterdam, *Apologia refellens suspiciones quorundam dic-*
         tantium dialogum D. Iacobi Latomi ... conscriptum fuisse adversus
         ipsum
                                       Basle, J. Froben, 1519

679. **LATOMUS, Jacobus (Masson), the younger**

    O ? *Psalmi Davidici triginta ... in carmen conversi*
                                    Basle, J. Oporinus, [c. 1555]

680. **LA TOUR-LANDRY, Geoffroy de**

    O   *Der Ritter vom Turm von den Exempelu* [sic] *der Gotsforcht und Erberkeit*
         (transl. from the French)
                                      Basle, M. Furter, 1493
                                       cf. R. Kautzsch, *Studien zur deut. Kunst-*
                                       geschichte, Heft 44, Strasbourg 1903

681. —

    R   —: *Der Spiegel der Tugenden*
                                          ibid., 1513

682. **LE COQ, Pascal (P. Gallus)**

    O   *Bibliotheca medica*
                                       Basle, C. Waldkirch, 1590

683. **LE DUCHAT, Louis-François (Ducatius Sanctaventinus)**

    O   *Iehovae opt. max. oraculum ... ex Isaiae cap. I.* (paraphrases in Latin
         & French verse)
                                        Basle, L. Osten, 1591

684. **LEFÈVRE d'Etaples, Jacques (Faber Stapulensis)**

    O   *Commentarii in epistolas Catholicas*
                                       Basle, A. Cratander, 1527

685. —

    R   *Commentarii initiatorii in quatuor Evangelia*
                                        ibid., 1523

686. —, introd.

    R   Aristoteles, *De anima* (Greek)
                                       Basle, T. Platter, 1538

687. —, transl.
> R   Bible (NT) : *Les choses contenues en ceste partie du Nouveau Testament*
>> Basle, [T. Wolff ? for C. Wattenschnee],
>> 1525

688. —, introd. & ed.
> R   St. Ignatius of Antioch, *Epistolae* ; St. Polycarpius, *Epistola* (Latin)
>> Basle, A. Petri, 1520

689. —, transl. in part
> R   St. Johannes Damascenus, *Opera* (Latin)
>> Basle, H. Petri, 1539

690. —, —
> R   — (Greek & Latin) ; other texts transl. by J. Périon ; also commentaries by J. Clichtoveus
>> ibid., 1548

691. —, —
> R   —
>> ibid., 1559

692. —, —
> R   —
>> Offic. Henricpetrina, 1575

693. (—)
> R   Erasmus of Rotterdam, *Apologia ad Iacobum Fabrum Stapulensem*
>> Basle, J. Froben, 1518

694. (—)
> R   — : in
> Erasmus of Rotterdam, *Apologiae omnes* ; also contains the apology against J. Latomus (cf. No. 678)
>> ibid., 1521-1522

695. (—)
> R   — : in
> Erasmus of Rotterdam, *Opera omnia* ; also contains the apology against J. Latomus
>> Basle, J. Froben & N. Episcopius, 1540

696. **(LESCAILLE, Antoine)**
> O   *Des Herren Burgermeisters unnd Rhats der Statt Basel kurtzer glaubwirdiger Bericht von unruhigen Handlungen in Religionssachen ihres aussgewichenen gewesenen Burgers Antonii Lescallaei*
>> Basle, 1595

697. (—)
> O   *Brieve declaration et veritable de Messeigneurs le Bourgmaistre et Consei de la ville de Basle...* (French transl. of the preceding text)
>> [Basle ?], 1595

698. **L'ESPINE, Jean de**
> O   *Noch ausserlessnere edlere und guldnere Bücher drey* (transl. of Excellens discours, books 8-10)
>> Basle, for Claude de Marne & Jean Aubry, 1598

699. **LE VOYER, Jean (Visorius)**

    R   *Ingeniosa ... dialecticae methodus, item compendiosa librorum Rodolphi Agricolae de inventione dialectica epitome*

                    Basle, [c. 1535]

700. **L'ISLE, Susanne de,** transl.

    O   *Relation veritable de la naissance des controverses en matiere de religion ... composée par un théologien et pasteur evangelique* (transl. of Eygentlicher Bericht vom Ursprung der Streytigkeiten)

                    Basle, G. Decker, 1649

701. **LÖHR, Johann Conrad,** transl.

    O   *Heylsamer Raht, gegeben den Wallonischen Kyrchen in der Pfaltz* (transl. from a French text)

                    Basle, J. J. Genath, 1629

702. **LONGUEIL, Christophe de**

    R   *Epistolarum libri IV*

                    Basle, J. Walder, 1533

703. —

    R —

                    ibid., 1540

704. —

    R —

                    Basle, N. Episcopius, 1558

705. —

    R —

                    ibid., 1562 (date in colophon : 1563)

706. —

    R —

                    Basle, E. & heirs of N. (II) Episcopius, 1570

707. —

    R —

                    ibid., 1580

708. **LULLUS, Antonius**

    O   *De oratione libri septem*

                    Basle, J. Oporinus, 1558

709. —

    O   *Progymnasmata rhetorica ad Franciscum Baumensem*
        ibid., [1554 ?]

710. —, ed., annot. & introd.

    (O) Basilius Magnus, *De grammatica exercitatione* (Greek)
        ibid., 1553

711. **MALESCOT, Etienne de**

    O   *De nuptiis liber paradoxicus*

                    Basle, T. Guarinus, 1572

712. **MARBODUS, Bp. of Rennes**

    R   (De gemmis) : *Dactylotheca*

                    Basle, H. Petri, 1555

713. **MARCELLUS (Empiricus, Burdigalensis)**

    O *De medicamentis*

                    Basle, H. Froben & N. Episcopius, 1536

714. **MARESCHAL, Samuel**

    O *Porta musices: das ist Eynführung zu der edlen Kunst Musica*

                    Basle, Seb. Henricpetri, [1589]

715. —, ed.

    A. Lobwasser, transl., *Der gantz Psalter ... auss der frantzösischen Composition ... in teutsche Reymen ... gebracht*

                    Basle, for L. König, 1606

716. —, —

    O *Melodiae suaves ... collectae in usum ... gymnasii*

                    Basle, L. König, 1622

717. —, —

    O *Psalmen Davids, Kirchen Gesänge und geistliche Lieder ... mit vier Stimmen ... gesetzet*

                    Basle, for L. König, 1606

718. **MARIUS VICTOR, Claudius**

    Genesis : in

    G. Fabricius ed., *Poetarum veterum ecclesiasticorum opera* (contains other poetical works of ancient Gaul by Hilarius of Poitiers, Prosper of Aquitaine, Drepanius Florus, Paulinus, Claudianus Mamertus, etc.

                    Basle, J. Oporinus, 1564

719. **MARLIANUS, Raymundus**

    R Index : in Julius Caesar, *Commentaria*

                    Basle, T. Wolff, 1521

720. —

    R —

                    ibid., 1528

721. —

    R —

                    Basle, J. Herwagen, 1535

722. —

    R —

                    Basle, N. Brylinger, 1539

723. —

    R —

                    ibid., 1544

724. —

    R —

                    ibid., 1548

725. —

    R —

                    ibid., 1561

726. —

    R —

                    Basle, heirs of N. Brylinger, 1566

727. —

    R —

                    Basle, Offic. Brylingeriana, 1581

728. (MARLORAT, Augustin)

    O   I. L. Feguernekinus, *Enchiridion locorum communium theologicorum* ... *ex Aug. Marlorati Thesauro* ... *conflatum*

                Basle, C. Waldkirch, 1586

729. (—)

    R —, editio secunda

                Basle, [C. Waldkirch, 1589]

730. (—)

    R —, ed. tertia

                Basle, [C. Waldkirch, 1595]

731. (—)

    R —, ed. quinta

                Basle, [C. Waldkirch, 1604 ?]

732. (—)

    —, ed. by Paul Toussain

                Basle, L. König, 1628

733. MARNIX, Philips van, heer van St. Aldegonde

    Oratio pro serenissimo archiduce Austriae Matthia et ordinibus Belgicis ... *Wormatiano conventu habita*

                [Basle ?, P. Perna ?, 1578 ?]

734. —

    R *Via veritatis divinae regulis quindecim* ... *exposita*, 3rd ed. (transl. from the Flemish)

                Basle, J. J. Genath, 1624

735. MARSILIUS of Inghen

    O *Commentum novum in primum et quartum tractatus Petri Hispani cum commento Parvorum logicalium Marsilii*

                Basle, N. Kessler, 1487

                BMC 15th c. : 3.765

736. MASSON, Jean Papire

    Iacobi Cuiacii ... *vita*

                Basle, C. Waldkirch, 1591

737. MATTHIEU de Vendôme (Matthaeus Vindocinensis)

    Genius sive DD. Thobiae patris et filii sacrosancta historia

                Basle, J. Oporinus, 1563

738. MEYRONNES, François de (Maronis, de Mayronis)

    R *Sermones de sanctis* (and other texts)

                Basle, J. Wolff, 1498

                BMC 15th c. 3.777

739. —

    R *Super primo libro Sententiarum*

                Basle, N. Kessler, 1489

                BMC 15th c. 3.768

740. —

    R *Theologicae veritates* (a commentary to each chapter) : in St. Augustinus, *De trinitate* & *De civitate Dei* (contains also commentaries by T. Valois)

                Basle, A. Petri, 1515

741. **MILIEU, Christophe de (Mylaeus)**

    R   *De scribenda universitatis rerum historia*

                          Basle, J. Oporinus, 1551

742. —

    R   — : in

    in Johann Wolf, ed., *Artis historicae penus*

                          Basle, P. Perna, 1579

743. **MIZAULD, Antoine (Mizaldus)**

    O   *Artztgarten; Artztbüchlin* (transl. of Alexikepus seu auxiliaris hortus; Artificiosa methodus)

                          ibid., 1575 ; 1574

744. —

    — ; (partly identical set of types)

                          ibid., 1577

745. —

    R   —

                          Basle, L. König, 1616

746. —

    O   *Neunhundert gedechtnusswürdige Geheimnuss ... von mancherley Kreutern, Metallen, Thieren* (transl. of Memorabilium ... centuriae IX)

                          Basle, P. Perna, 1575

747. **[MOMBAER, Johan] (Mauburnus, Jean de Bruxelles)**

    R   *Rosetum exercitiorum spiritualium*

                          Basle, J. Wolff, 1404 [1504]

748. **[MONTANUS, Philippus ?]**

    O   *Expositio fidelis de morte D. Thomae Mori* [ed. by G. Cousin ?]

                          [Basle ?], 1535

749. [— ?]

    R   — : in

    T. More, *Lucubrationes*

                          Basle, N. (II) Episcopius, 1563

750. —, ed. & introd.

    O   Theophylactus, *In quatuor Evangelia* [and other Biblical texts] *enarrationes*

                          Basle, J. Herwagen, 1554

751. —, —

    R   —

                          Basle, heirs of J. (II) Herwagen, 1570
                          BMC

752. **(MONTEUX, Sébastien de) (Montuus)**

    Leonhard Fuchs, *Paradoxorum medicinae libri tres* ..., *obiter denique hic Sebastiano Montuo medico Rivoriensi respondetur, eiusque annotatiunculae velut omnium frigidissimae prorsus exploduntur*

                          Basle, J. Bebel, 1535

753. **(MOREL, Guillaume)**

    Hieronymus Wolf, *Tabula compendiosa de origine ... veterum philosophorum a G. Morellio Tiliano collecta* (Morel's Tabula and Wolf's commentary thereof)

                          Basle, Offic. Herwagiana per E. Episcopium, 1580

754. **MOREL, Pierre**
Methodus praescribendi formulas remediorum (revised)
Basle, J. J. Genath, 1630

755. **MORILLON, Guy**
In Heroidas epistolas argumenta : in
Ovidius, *Amatoria*
Basle, H. Petri, 1548

756. —
R —: in
Ovidius, *Opera*
Basle, J. Herwagen, 1549

757. —
R —: in
Ovidius, *Amatoria*
Basle, H. Petri, 1560

758. **MORISOT, Jean**
O *Colloquiorum libri quatuor: Libellus de parechemate*
Basle, J. Oporinus, [1549-1550]

759. —, ed., transl. & comment.
O Cicero, *Paradoxa* (Latin text and Greek transl. by J. M. ; in the appendix some notes by B. Latomus)
ibid., 1547

760. —, ed. & transl.
O Hippocrates, *Aphorismi* (Greek & Latin)
ibid., 1547

761. **[MORNAY, Philippe, sieur du Plessis-Marly ?]**
Advertissement sur l'intention et but de Messieurs de Guise en la prise des armes
[Basle ?], 1585
UBB : N.u.VI.20(2)

762. **MÜNSTER, Sebastian**
O *La cosmographie universelle* (transl. from the German & Latin)
Basle, for H. Petri, 1552

763. —
R —
ibid., 1556
BN : Rés. G. 664

764. —
R —, mostly reset ; a few additions
ibid., 1556
BN : Rés. G. 70

765. —
R —
ibid., 1560

766. —
R —; a few additions
ibid., 1565

767. —

    R —

        ibid., 1568
        K. H. Burmeister, *S. Münster Bibliogr.*,
        Wiesbaden 1964, 82f.

768. **MURET, Marc-Antoine,** preface & comment.

    R   Horatius, *Opera* (with other commentaries by Josse Bade and Gilbert
        Cousin)
        Basle, S. Henricpetri, 1580

769. **Neue Zeitung**

    Neuwe Zeitung allerley Sachen ... allenthalben in Franckreich unnd
    Teutschland (August 1575-April 1576)
        Basle, [S. Apiarius?], 1576

770. —

    Newe Zeyttung in Gesangs weiss von der Statt Genff
        Basle, S. Apiarius, 1590

771. **Neue Zeitungen**

    Newe Zeitungen auss Franckreich. Erklärung und Protestation Hein-
    richen von Monmorancy ... von wegen des Kriegs so er ... wider den
    König ... führt
        Basle, S. Apiarius, 1575

772. **NICOLAI, Gilbertus (Nicolas)**

    O   *Lucerna beate Marie virginis*
        [Basle, c. 1512-1515]
        UBB: F.P.VIII^2.4(2)

773. —

    O   *Questio super regulam sancti Francisci ad litteram*
        [Basle, A. Petri?, 1514?]
        UBB: F.G.IX^2.24(II)

774. **NICOLAUS of Lyra,** comment.

    Opus totius Biblie cum glosa ordinaria et expositione Lyre
        Basle, J. Petri & J. Froben, 1498
        BMC 15th c. 3.791f.

775. —, —

    R —

        Basle, J. Froben for himself, J. Amerbach
        & J. Petri, 1501-1502

776. —, —

    R   —: *Textus Biblie*

        Basle, J. Petri & J. Froben, 1506-1508

777. **OLIVER, Pedro Juan (Olivarius)**

    O   *De prophetia*

        Basle, J. Oporinus, 1543

778. —

    O   *In M. T. Ciceronis De somnio Scipionis ... scholia; In Ciceronis*
    moralem philosophiam
        Basle, R. Winter, 1538

779. —, ed., introd. & annot.
  R Pomponius Mela, *De situ orbis libri tres*
      [Basle, c. 1536-1537]

780. —, —
  R — : in
      C. Iulius Solinus & Pomponius Mela, [*Opera*]
      Basle, M. Isengrin, 1543

781. **OLIVETAN, Robert,** transl.
  R *Le Nouveau Testament ... translaté de Grec en Francoys*
      [Basle], 1539
      BM : C.36 d.8

782. **OMPHALIUS, Jacob**
  O *De officio et potestate principis in republica ... libri duo*
      Basle, J. Oporinus, 1550

783. —
  O *De usurpatione legum ... libri octo*
      ibid., 1550

784. **ORVAUX, Nicolas d' (N. de Orbellis)**
  R *Summulae philosophiae rationalis; Cursus librorum philosophiae natu-*
      ralis [Aristotelis] (with separate title page)
      Basle, M. Furter, 1494
      BMC 15th c. 3.782f.
      BN : Rés. R.839

785. —
  R —

      Basle, [M. Furter], 1503

786. **PARADIN, Guillaume**
      De antiquo statu Burgundiae (contains also D. Melguiz, Philiberti a
      Chalon rerum gestarum commentariolus, and shorter texts by S. Cham-
      pier, G. Cousin, L. Pellatanus, N. Perrenot de Grandvelle)
      Basle, [J. Oporinus ?, c. 1547-50]

787. —
  R De motibus Galliae anno 1558 : in
      S. Schard, ed., *Historicum opus* (also Perrenot's text as in No. 786)
      Basle, Offic. Henricpetrina, 1574

788. **PARCUS, Jacobus (Kündig, Estauge, Qadier, Cadier),** transl.
  O S. Münster, *La declaration de l'instrument ... pour cognoistre le cours*
      du ciel (transl. by Jacques Estauge from the German and Latin text)
      Basle, Jacques Estauge for Jehan Mares-
      chal, 1554

789. **PARÉ, Ambroise**
  R De hominis generatione liber : in
      G. Bauhin, ed., *Gynaecia*, contains also :
  R Jean Le Bon, Therapia puerperarum
      Basle, C. Waldkirch, 1586

790. **PASCHASIUS, Radbertus, St., Abbot of Corbie**
  O *Commentaria in lamentationibus Jeremie*
      Basle, J. Wolff, 1502

791. **[PASQUELIN, Guillaume]**
    O   Theophilus Eugenius, *Zwo merckliche* ... *Missiven* (transl. of Proto-catastasis)
               [Basle], 1615

792. **[PASQUIER, Etienne]**
    O   *Ad regis Galliae consiliarios exhortatio* (transl. from the French)
               [Basle ?, J. Oporinus ?], 1561

793. **PELETIER, Jacques (Peletarius)**
    O   *Commentarii tres:* de dimensione circuli, de contactu linearum ..., de constitutione horoscopi
               Basle, J. Oporinus, 1563

794. —
    O   *De peste compendium* (preface by Bernard Bertrand)
               ibid., [1563 ?]

795. **PENOT, Bernard Georges**
       Tractatus varii de vera preparatione et usu medicamentorum chymicorum (4th ed., enlarged by a treatise De lapide philosophorum)
               Basle, L. König, 1616

796. **PERAULT, Guillaume (Peraldus, Petra Alta, etc.)**
       Summa de vitiis; summa de virtutibus
               [Basle, M. Wenssler, 1473-1475]
               BMC 15th c. 3.722

797. —
       —
               [Basle, B. Ruppel, 1474 ?]
               BMC 15th c. 3.715

798. —
    R —
               Basle, J. Amerbach, 1497
               BMC 15th c. 3.758

799. **PERAULT, Raymond, ed.**
    O   *Legenda beatissime virginis Katherine*
               Basle, J. Wolff for the editor, 1504

800. —, —
    O   *Sermo ad laudem Dei beate Ursule*
               [Basle, M. Furter for the editor, 1504 ?]
               UBB : **א** C.IV.2(6)

801. —, —
    R —
               [ibid., 1504 ?]
               UBB : F.P. VII 16 (10)

802. **PERDRIER, René, transl.**
    O   Coluthus Thebanus, *Helenae raptus*, with annot. by Bernard Bertrand, and
    O   Tryphiodorus, *De Ilii expugnatione*
               Basle, J. Oporinus, 1555

803. —, —
    O   *Orphei* ... *opera*
               ibid., 1555

804. **PÉRION, Joachim**

    R   *De dialectica libri III; Orationes duae pro Aristotele ... in Petrum Ramum*

                Basle, J. Oporinus, 1549

805. —

    R —

                ibid., 1554

806. —

    (R) De rebus gestis vitisque Apostolorum : in
         Wolfgang Lazius, ed., *Hoc opere continentur* (further : Sulpicius Severus, Divi Martini vita, and other appendices ed. by G. Cousin, Pierre Gilles, etc.)

                ibid., 1552

807. —

    R   *In omnes T. Livii conciones ... annotationes* (with the text of Livy)

                Basle, R. Winter, 1545

808. —, transl. & introd.

    (R) Aristoteles, *Opera omnia Latina*, with many transl. and prefaces by J. P. and others by N. de Grouchy, J. Lefèvre d'Etaples, A. Chamaillard, etc.

                Basle, J. (II) Herwagen, 1563

809. —, transl.

    R ? Aristoteles, *Ad Nicomachum filium de moribus*

                Basle, J. Oporinus, 1540
                DGK

810. —, transl., comment. & introd.

    R   —: *De moribus*, with   BM : 1471 f. 16
    R   Périon's commentary in a separate vol. : *De optimo genere interpretandi*, and   BN : R.25537
    R   *Ex Platonis Timaeo particula Ciceronis De universitate respondens*
                UBB : D.F.VI.16(6)
                Basle, R. Winter, 1542

811. —, transl. & introd.

    R   —, revised : *Ethicorum ... libri* (without the commentary)
                Basle, B. Westheimer, 1545

812. —, —

    R   —: *Ad Nicomachum*

                Basle, J. Oporinus, 1552
                DGK

813. —, —

    —: *Ethicorum ... libri*, revised by N. de Grouchy
                ibid., 1555
                DGK

814. —, transl. & annot.

    R   Aristoteles, *De animo libri tres*
                ibid., 1553
                DGK

815. —, —
    R   Aristoteles, *De coelo libri quatuor*
                    ibid., 1553
                    DGK

816. —, —
    R   Aristoteles, *De dialectica libri tres*
                    Basle, R. Winter, 1545

817. —, transl., annot. & introd.
    R   Aristoteles, *De natura* [Physics] ... *inserto ... orationis, qua* ...
        Strebaei calumniis respondit, compendio
                    Basle, J. Oporinus, 1552

818. —, —
    R   Aristoteles, *De ortu et interitu libri duo*
                    ibid., 1553

819. —, —
    R   Aristoteles, *De republica ... libri octo*
                    Basle, for J. Oporinus, 1544

820. —, —
    R   —
                    Basle, J. Oporinus, 1549
                    DGK

821. —, —
    R   Aristoteles, *Libelli qui Parva naturalia vulgo appellantur*
                    ibid., 1553
                    DGK

822. —, —
        Aristoteles, *Meteorologicorum libri quatuor*
                    ibid., 1553
                    DGK

823. —, —
    O   Aristoteles, *Topicorum libri octo* ..., *item de reprehensionibus* [Elenchi]
                    ibid., 1543

824. —, —
    R   — : *De arte inveniendi*
                    Basle, for J. Oporinus, 1544

825. —, —
    R   — (enlarged) : *Organum universum una cum Porphyrii eisagoge*
                    Basle, J. Oporinus, 1554
                    DGK

826. —, —
    R   — ; some transl. by N. de Grouchy
                    ibid., 1559
                    DGK

827. —, —
    R   —
                    Basle, [Offic. ?] Oporin[iana], 1585
                    DGK

828. —, —
    R   Plato (attributed to), *Axiochus* (Greek & Latin)
                    Basle, J. Oporinus, 1543

829. —, —
    O   Porphyrius, *Institutiones* ;
    O   Aristoteles, *Categoriae* & *De interpretatione*
                    Basle, R. Winter, 1542

830. (—)
    O   C.S. Curione, *Epitome dialecticae Ioachimi Perionii ... tyronibus ...
        accomodata*
                    Basle, J. Oporinus, 1549

831. (—)
    R   —
                    ibid., 1551

832. **PERRELLE, Jean,** ed. & transl.
    R   Theodorus Gaza, *De mensibus Atticis* (Greek & Latin) ; and other
        opuscula
                    Basle, T. Platter & B. Lasius, 1536

833. **[PERRIN, Jean Paul]**
    O   *Waldenser Chronick* (transl. from the French)
                    Basle, Martin Wagner, 1623

834. **PETRUS Comestor (Manducator, Pierre le Mangeur)**
    R   *Scholastica historia*
                    Basle, [J. Amerbach ?], 1486
                    BMC 15th c. 3.749

835. **PETRUS Lombardus, Bp. of Paris**
    R   *Liber sententiarum*
                    [Basle, B. Richel, c. 1482]
                    BMC 15th c. 3.739

835a. —
    R   —
                    [Basle], 1484
                    BMC 15th c. 3.761

836. —
    R   —
                    Basle, N. Kessler, 1486
                    BMC 15th c. 3.763

837. —
    R   —
                    ibid., 1487
                    BMC 15th c. 3.764

838. —
    R   —, cum ... titulis questionum S. Thome articulisque Parisien. et in
        quibus magister communiter non tenetur
                    ibid., 1488
                    BMC 15th c. 3.766f.

839. —
    R   —
                    ibid., 1489
                    BMC 15th c. 3.768f.

840. —
    R   —
                    [ibid., 1490 ?]
                    BM : IB 37498

841. —

    R   — ; similar ed.

                  ibid., *1492*
                  BMC 15th c. 3.770

842. —

    R   — ; similar ed.

                  ibid., *1498*
                  BMC 15th c. 3.772f.

843. —

    R   —

                  ibid., *1502*

844. —

    R   —

                  ibid., *1507*

845. —

    R   — ; similar ed.

                  Basle, A. Petri, *1513*

846. —

    R   —

                  Basle, A. Petri for L. Hornken, *1516*

847. —

    *Von dem hochwirdigen Sacrament under beder Gestalt: aus dem vierden
    Buoch Sententiarum*

                  [Basle ?, A. Cratander ?, *1522* ?]

848. **PETRUS Pictaviensis (P. of Poitiers), Chancellor of the Church of Paris**

    O   *Genealogia et chronologia Sanctorum patrum*

                  Basle, L. Osten, *1592*

849. **PHILANDRIER, Guillaume (G. Philander Castilloneus), annot.**

    R   Quintilianus, *Oratorianum institutionum libri XII*

                  Basle, R. Winter, *1541*

850. —

    R   —

                  ibid., *1543*

851. —

    R   —

                  Basle, N. Brylinger, *1548*

852. —

    R   —

                  ibid., *1561*

853. **PITHOU, [François], ed.**

    O   *Imp. Iustiniani Novellae constitutiones* (Latin) ex bibliotheca Petri
        Pithoei

                  Basle, P. Perna, *1576*

854. **PITHOU, Pierre, the younger**

    R   *Adversariorum subsecivorum libri duo* (revised)

                  ibid., *1574*

855. —, introd. & annot.

> *Mosaycarum et Romanarum legum collatio*... ex bibliotheca P. Pithoei
>> Basle, T. Guarinus, 1579

856. —, ed. & introd.

> Otto of Freising, *Chronicon; De gestis Friderici* (and other texts concerning Frederick I)
>> Basle, P. Perna, 1569

857. —, —

> Paulus Diaconus & Landolfus Sagax, *Historia miscella*
>> ibid., 1569

858. (—)

> O   Aethicus, *Cosmographia* ; Antoninus Augustus, *Itinerarium* ex bibliotheca P. Pithoei (contains also : Rutilius Claud. Numatianus Gallus, Itinerarium ; Libellus provinciarum Galliae ... ex bibliotheca Tigurina)
>> Basle, T. Guarinus, 1575

859. **[PLAIX, César de]**

> O   *Anti-Cotton* (German transl. of the French text)
>> [Basle ?], 1610
>> UBB : א .E.VI.14(2)

860. **POSTEL, Guillaume**

> O   *Absconditorum a constitutione mundi clavis*
>> [Basle, J. Oporinus, 1547]

861. —

> O   *Cosmographicae disciplinae compendium*
>> Basle, J. Oporinus,1561

862. —

> R   *De magistratibus Atheniensium liber*
>> ibid., 1543

863. —

> —; revised and enlarged
>> Basle, [J. Oporinus], 1551

864. —

> O   *De nativitate Mediatoris ultima*
>> [Basle, J. Oporinus, 1547]

865. —

> O   *De orbis terrae concordia*
>> [Basle, J. Oporinus, 1544 ?]

866. —

> O   *De originibus seu de varia ... incognita ... historia ... totius Orientis*
>> Basle, J. Oporinus, [1553]

867. [—]

> O   Elias Pandocheus, Πανθενωσία : *compositio omnium dissidiorum*
>> [Basle, J. Oporinus, 1547]

868. [—], transl. & introd.
      O   Jacobus, Apostle, *Protevangelion*
                Basle, J. Oporinus, 1552

869. [—], transl.
      R   —: in
          J. B. Herold, ed., *Orthodoxographa*
                Basle, H. Petri, 1555

870. [—], —
      R   —: in
          J. J. Grynaeus, ed., *Monumenta S. Patrum orthodoxographa*
                Basle, Offic. Henricpetrina, 1569

871. **PROSPER of Aquitaine**
      R   Adversus colluctatorem [i.e. Joh. Cassianum] de libero arbitrio: in
          J. Sichard, ed., *Antidotum contra diversas ... haereses*
                Basle, H. Petri, 1528

872. —
      R   —: in
          J. B. Herold, ed., *Haereseologia*
                ibid., 1556

873. —
      R   Chronicon: appended to
          J. Sichard, ed., *Chronicon* (Eusebius, Hieronymus and continuators)
                ibid., 1529

874. —
      R   —
                ibid., 1536

875. —
      R   —
                ibid., [1549]

876. —
      R   —
                Basle, Offic. Henricpetrina, 1579

877. —
      R   Chronicon: in
          Eusebius, *Opera omnia*
                Basle, H. Petri, 1542

878. —
          — (Prosper: set of types identical with No. 875)
                ibid., 1549

879. —
      R   —
                ibid., 1559

880. —
          — (identical set of types)
                Basle, Offic. Henricpetrina, 1570

881. —
          — (Prosper: set of types identical with No. 876)
                ibid., 1579

882. —
          De libero arbitrio divorum Prosperi, Augustini et Ambrosii opuscula
                Basle, T. Wolff, 1524

883. —
    R Responsiones ad obiectiones Gallorum calumniantium : in
       St. Fulgentius, *Opera theologica*
       Basle, Seb. Henricpetri, 1621

884. **QUINTIN, Jean (J. Quintinus Haeduus)**
    R [Melitae insulae descriptio] : in
       Opus historiarum
       Basle, B. Westheimer, 1541

885. **RAENERIUS, Johannes (Raynier), comment.**
       L. Valla, *Elegantiarum libri sex*
       ibid., 1543

RAMUS see LA RAMÉE

886. **RAULIN, Jean**
    O *Collacio habita in publico conventu Cluniacensium ordinis*
       [Basle], J. Bergmann von Olpe, 1498
       BMC 15th c. 3.796

887. **RIBIT, Jean**
    O *Disputatio an Iudas proditor Coenae Dominicae interfuerit*
       Basle, [1555 ?]

888. —, ed.
       Lucianus, *Opera* (Greek)
       Basle, M. Isengrin, 1545

889. —, —
    R —
       ibid., 1555

890. —, transl.
    O Xenophon, Pori, Hipparchicus, Symposium : in
       Opera omnia (Greek & Latin), also contains S. Châteillon's transl. of
       De Athen. republica
       Basle, N. Brylinger, 1545

891. —, —
       — (Latin only), Châteillon's transl. of De Athen. republica replaced by
       one made by Ribit
       Basle, M. Isengrin, 1545

892. **RICCIO, Michele (Ritius, Riz)**
    R *De regibus Francorum*, etc.
       Basle, J. Froben, 1517

893. —
    R —
       Basle, H. Froben & N. Episcopius, 1534
       (in the colophon : 1535)

894. —
    R De regibus Ungariae : in
       A. Bonfini, *Rerum Ungaricarum decades*
       Basle, R. Winter, 1543

895. —
    R —
       Basle, Offic. Oporiniana, 1568

896. **RICHARD de Saint-Victor**
    O   *De arca mystica*
          [Basle, J. Amerbach, 1494]
          BMC 15th c. 3.756

897. —
    R   *De duodecim patriarchis*
          [ibid.], 1494
          BMC 15th c. 3.755f.

898. **RICHER, Christophe**
    R   De rebus Turcarum : in
       S. Schard, ed., *Historicum opus*
          Basle, Offic. Henricpetrina, 1574

899. **RIOLAN, Jean (the older)**
    R   *Morborum curandorum ratio generalis et particularis*
          Basle, L. König, 1629

900. —
    R   *Universae medicinae compendia*
          Basle, C. Waldkirch for L. König, 1601

901. —
    — (revised) : *Artis medicinalis theoreticae et practicae ... systema*
          Basle, L. König, 1629

902. **ROBERT d'Envermeuil (Euremodio, Eudemodio),** comment.
    R   Dionysius Cato, *Disticha moralia*
          Basle, [J. Amerbach], 1486
          GKW No. 6284

903. —
    R   —
          Basle, N. Kessler, 1486
          GKW Nº 6285

904. —
    R   —
          ibid., 1488
          GKW No. 6288

905. **ROBERT de Saint-Rémy (Robertus Monachus)**
    O   *Historia de itinere contra Turcos*
          [Basle ?, J. Schilling ?, 1472 ?]
          BMC ST Germany

906. —
    O   — : *Bellum Christianorum principum, praecipue Gallorum, contra Saracenos*
          Basle, H. Petri, 1533

907. **ROUSSET, François**
    O   Ὑστεροτομοτοκυα [sic] (Latin transl. by G. Bauhin) in :
       G. Bauhin, ed., *Gynaecia*
          Basle, C. Waldkirch, 1586

908. —
    R   Ὑστεροτομοτοκία, also contains :
       Jean Albosius, Lithopaedium, and other appendices by G. Bauhin
       & Simon Provancherius
          ibid., 1588

909. —
    R   —: *Foetus vivi ex matre viva ... caesura* (with appendices by G. Bauhin).
                ibid., 1591

910. **RUEL, Jean (Ruellius, de la Ruelle)**
    R   *De natura stirpium*
                Basle, H. Froben & N. Episcopius, 1537

911. —
    R   —
                ibid., 1543

912. —, transl.
    R   J. Actuarius, *De medicamentorum compositione* (Latin)
                Basle, R. Winter, 1540

913. —, —
    R   Dioscorides, *De medica materia libri sex*
                Basle, M. Isengrin, 1539

914. —, ed.
    R   Scribonius Largus, *De compositione medicamentorum liber* (Appendix:
       Polybius, De salubri victus ratione, transl. by J. Guinterius)
                Basle, A. Cratander, 1529

915. (—)
    O   *Veterinariae medicinae libri duo, a Ioanne Ruellio ... olim quidem*
       Latinitate donati (Greek only)
                Basle, J. Walder, 1537

916. **SACROBOSCO, Johannes de (John Holywood)**
    R   De sphaera mundi: in
    O   E. O. Schreckenfuchs, *Commentaria in sphaeram Ioannis de Sacrobusto*
                Basle, Offic. Henricpetrina, 1569

917. **SADOLETO, Jacopo**
    R   *De bello Turcis inferendo oratio*
                Basle, T. Platter, 1538

918. —
    R   *De laudibus philosophiae*
                Basle, N. Brylinger, 1541

919. —
    R   *De pueris recte ac liberaliter instituendis*
                Basle, T. Platter, 1538

920. —
    R   —: in:
       De ratione studii ... opuscula diversorum
                Basle, [B. Lasius], 1541
                BMC

921. —
    R   —: in
       De disciplina puerorum ... libelli aliquot doctorum virorum
                Berne, S. Apiarius for J. Oporinus, Basle,
                1556

922. —
    R   De regno Ungariae ... homilia: in
       Machumetis Sarracenorum principis vita et doctrina
                [Basle, J. Oporinus, 1543]

923. —
    R   *In psalmum XCIII. interpretatio*
        Basle, Offic. Frobeniana, 1530

924. **SALONIUS, St., Bp. of Geneva**
    R   In Parabolas Salomonis ... explicatio; In Ecclesiastem explicatio: in Μικροπρεσβυτικόν; also contains: St. Martialis, Bp. of Limoges, Epistolae duae
        Basle, H. Petri, 1550

925. —
    R   —: in
    J. B. Herold, ed., *Orthodoxographa*
        ibid., 1555

926. —
    R   —: in
    J. J. Grynaeus, ed., *Monumenta S. Patrum orthodoxographa*; also contains St. Avitus, Abp. of Vienne, Homelia de festo rogationum
        Basle, Offic. Henricpetrina, 1569

927. **SALVIANUS**
    O   *De vero iudicio et providentia Dei*
        Basle, Offic. Frobeniana, 1530

928. [—]
    Timothei ad ecclesiam Catholicam libri IV: in
    J. Sichard, ed., *Antidotum contra diversas ... haereses*
        Basle, H. Petri, 1528

929. [—]
    R   —: in
    J. B. Herold, ed., *Haereseologia*
        ibid., 1556

930. **SCAPULA, Johannes (Espaulaz)**
    O   *Lexicon Graecolatinum*
        Basle, Offic. Herwagiana per E. Episcopium, 1580

931. —
    —, revised
        ibid., 1589

932. —
    —, new ed.
        Basle, Seb. Henricpetri, 1600

933. —
    R   —
        ibid., 1605

934. —
    R   —
        ibid., 1615

935. —
    R   —
        ibid., 1620

936. —
    R   —
        Basle, Offic. Henricpetrina, 1628

937. **SENARCLENS, Claude de** (attributed to)
    O *Historia vera de morte sancti viri Ioannis Diazii Hispani*
        [Basle, J. Oporinus], 1546

938. **SEYSSEL, Claude de**
    O *Speculum feudorum*

        Basle, T. Guarinus, 1566

939. **SIDONIUS Apollinaris**
      [Epistolae; Panegyricae]

      [Basle], H. Petri, [c. 1530 ?]
      UBB : B.b.III.1 (severely mutilated copy)

940. —
    R *Lucubrationes*

        Basle, H. Petri, 1542

941. —
    R —

        Basle, Seb. Henricpetri, 1597

942. **SLEIDANUS, Johannes (Philippson)**
    R *De statu religionis et reipublicae, Carolo Quinto Caesare, commentarii*
        Basle, N. Brylinger, 1556

943. —
    —, mostly identical set of types; with a continuation
        ibid., 1562

944. —
    O *Warhafftige Beschreibung geistlicher unnd welttlicher Sachen* (transl. of
    De statu)
        ibid., 1556

945. —
    R —

        ibid., 1557

946. —
    O *Beschreibung der vier Monarcheyen* (transl. of De quatuor summis
    imperiis)
        ibid., 1557

947. —
    Historia expeditionis ab Henrico rege Francorum in Germaniam
    susceptae : in
    S. Schard, ed., *Historicum opus*
        Basle, Offic. Henricpetrina, 1574

948. **SPONDE, Jean de (Spondanus),** ed., transl. & annot.
    O Aristoteles, *Organum* (Greek & Latin)
        Basle, Offic. Oporiniana, 1583

949. —, ed. & comment.
    O Homerus, *Opera* (Greek & Latin)
        Basle, Offic. Herwagiana per E. Episco-
        pium, 1583

950. —, —
    R —

        Basle, Seb. Henricpetri, 1606

951. **STREBAEUS, Jacobus Ludovicus (d'Estrebay)**
    R   *De verborum electione et collocatione oratoria*
                    Basle, R. Winter, 1539

952. —, introd. & comment.
    (R) *En habes, lector, in omnes de arte rhetorica M. Tul. Ciceronis libros doctissimorum virorum commentaria;* also contains :
    R   commentaries by J. Le Voyer, B. Latomus and C. de Longueil
                    Basle, R. Winter & T. Platter, 1541

953. **STURM, Johannes**
    O   Vita Beati Rhenani : in
        Beatus Rhenanus, *Rerum Germanicarum libri tres*
                    Basle, H. Froben & N. Episcopius, 1551

954. —, ed.
    Galenus, *Opera iam recens versa;* contains also De ratione victus, transl. by J. Guinterius
                    Basle, A. Cratander, 1531

955. —, introd.
    O   Conrad Heresbach, *Psalmorum Davidicorum ... explicatio*
                    Basle, P. Perna, 1578

956. (—)
    O   Michael Toxites, *Commentarii ... in libros quatuor rhetoricorum ad C. Herennium ex scholis Ioannis Sturmii*
                    Basle, J. Oporinus, 1556

957. (—)
    R   —
                    ibid., 1564

958. (—)
    R   —
                    Basle, Offic. Oporiniana, 1568

959. **SULPICIUS Severus**
    O   *Sacrae historiae ... libri II*
                    Basle, J. Oporinus, [1556?]

960. —
    R   —, and Vita S. Martini : in
        J. J. Grynaeus, ed., *Monumenta S. Patrum orthodoxographa*
                    Basle, Offic. Henricpetrina, 1569

961. **TALON, Omer (Audomarus Talaeus)**
    R   *Opera*
                    Basle, P. Perna, 1575

962. —
    R   — (same set of types ?)
                    ibid., 1576

963. —
    R   — ; a larger collection
                    Basle, C. Waldkirch, 1584

964. —
    R   *Rhetoricae libri duo P. Rami praelectionibus illustrati*
                    Basle, E. & heirs of N. (II) Episcopius, 1569

965. —
R —
ibid., 1573

966. —
R —
Basle, C. Waldkirch, 1589
Ong, *Inventory* No. 107

967. **TARANTA, Valescus de (Balescon de Tarante)**
R *Tractatus de epidemia et peste*
[Basle, M. Flach, c. 1475]
BMC 15th c. 3.741

968. **TATERET, Pierre (Tartaretus)**
R *Commentarii in Isagogas Porphyrii et libros logicorum Aristotelis*
Basle, J. Froben, [1514]

969. —
R *Commentarii in libros philosophie naturalis et metaphysice Aristotelis;*
In Aristotelis sex ethicos libros questiones
ibid., 1514

970. —
R *Expositio in summulas Petri Hispani*
ibid., [1514]

971. **TEXTOR, Johannes Ravisius (Tissier, Tixier de Ravisy)**
R *Dialogi; Epigrammata*
Basle, L. König, 1615

972. —
R *Epistolae*
Basle, L. Osten, 1590

973. —
R —
Basle, L. König, 1640

974. —
R *Epithetorum opus*
Basle, N. Brylinger, 1558

975. —
R —, 4th ed.
ibid., 1565

976. —
R —, similar ed.
Basle, heirs of N. Brylinger, 1571

977. —
R —
ibid., 1573

978. —
R —, similar ed.
ibid., 1581

979. —
R —
Basle, L. Osten, 1592

980. —
    R   —, similar ed.
                    Basle, A. Cellarius, 1598

981. —
    R   —, similar ed.
                    ibid., 1602

982. —
    R   —, revised and enlarged
                    Basle, C. Waldkirch, 1612

983. —
    R   —
                    Basle, L. König, 1635

984. —
       Epitome ... epithetorum
                    Basle, B. Westheimer & N. Brylinger,
                    [c. 1540 ?]

985. —
       —, enlarged : *Epithetorum ... epitome*
                    Basle, B. Westheimer, 1541

986. —
    R *Officina*
                    ibid., 1538

987. —
    R   —, new ed.
                    Basle, N. Brylinger, 1552

988. —
    R   —
                    ibid., 1562

989. —
    R   —
                    Basle, heirs of N. Brylinger, 1566

990. —
    R   —
                    Basle, Officina Brylingeriana, 1581

991. —
    R   — : *Theatrum poeticum et historicum sive officina*
                    Basle, L. Osten, 1592

992. —
    R   —
                    Basle, A. Cellarius, 1600

993. **THIERRY, Jean, of Beauvais (Johannes Theodericus)**
       R *Annotationes in Laurentii Vallae de Latinae linguae elegantia libros*
                    Basle, B. Lasius, 1541

994. **THIERRY, Jean, of Langres**
       R *Ioan. Bertachini Firmani I.U.D. ... Repertorium olim quidem Io. Thierry Lingonensis ... opera locupletatum ...*
                    Basle, Ambrosius & Aurelius Froben, 1573

995. **THOMAS Aquinas, St.**
       R *Catena aurea*
                    [Basle, M. Wenssler], 1476
                    BMC 15th c. 3.723

996. —, in part erroneously ascribed to

    R   *Commentaria in omnes epistolas beati Pauli*
                  Basle, M. Furter for W. Lachner, 1495
                  BMC 15th c. 3.783

997. —

        Summa de articulis fidei

                  [Basle, M. Flach, 1472-1474]
                  BMC 15th c. 3.741

998. —

        —

                  [Basle, M. Wenssler, c. 1473-1474]
                  BMC 15th c. 3.720

999. —

        Summa theologica, parts 1-3

                  Basle, [M. Wenssler], 1485
                  BMC 15th c. 3.729

1000. —

    R   —, part 2.2

                  [Basle, B. Ruppel, not after 1474]
                  BMC 15th c. 3.715

1001. —

    O   —, part 3

                  [Basle, M. Wenssler, c. 1472-1473 ?]
                  BMC 15th c. 3.720

1002. (—)

    O   [Annibaldo Annibaldi], *Sancti Thome ... scripta ad Hannibaldum episcopum super quatuor libros Sententiarum*
                  Basle, N. Kessler, 1492
                  BMC 15th c. 3.770

1003. (—)

    Petrus de Bergamo, *Tabula operum Thomae Aquinatis*
                  Basle, B. Richel, 1478
                  BMC 15th c. 3.738

1004. (—)

    R   —

                  Basle, N. Kessler, 1495
                  BMC 15th c. 3.771

1005. **TIRAQUEAU, André (Tiraquellus)**

    R   *Commentarii de nobilitate et iure primigeniorum*
                  Basle, H. Froben & N. Episcopius, 1561
                  Cf. J. Brejon, *A. Tiraqueau*, Paris 1937, 388f.

1006. —

    R   *Ex commentariis in Pictonum consuetudines sectio de legibus connubialibus et iure maritali*
                  ibid., 1561

1007. —

    O   *Tractatus de privilegiis piae causae; De praescriptionibus tractatus;* ed. by André Tiraqueau, the son
                  ibid., 1561

1008. **TOUSSAIN, Daniel, the nephew (Tossanus)**
Exemplar epistolae datae ad Cunradium Vorstium : appended to
L. Lucius, *De causa meritoria*
Basle, J. J. Genath, 1630

1009. **TOUSSAIN, Jacques (Tusanus)**
R *Annotata in G. Budaei epistolas priores*
Basle, A. Cratander, 1528

1010. **TOUSSAIN, Paul (Tossanus)**
Dictionum Hebraicarum ... syllabus geminus
Basle, 1615

1011. —, ed. & comment.
R *Biblia* (German version by M. Luther)
Basle, heirs of L. König, 1644

1012. **[TOUSSAIN, Pierre] (Tossanus)**
O *L'ordre qu'on tient en l'eglise de Montbeliard en instruisant les enfants et administrant les saints sacremens, avec la forme du mariage et des prieres*
Basle, Jacques Estauge [i.e. Parcus], 1559
Viénot, *Montbéliard*, illustrations opposite 1.175f.

1013. **Translation**
Translation usz hispanischer Sprach zuo Frantzösisch gemacht, so durch den Vice Rey in Neapols Fraw Margareten, Hertzogin inn Burgundi zuo geschriben (7 Oct. 1522) (transl. from the French)
[Basle, P. Gengenbach ?, 1522 ?]
UBB : Hist. Conv. XIV, No. 18 & 18bis

1014. **TREMELLIO, Emmanuele, ed.**
O M. Bucer, *Libellus ... de vi et usu sacri ministerii*
Basle, P. Perna, 1562

1015. —, —
O M. Bucer, *Praelectiones ... in epistolam divi Pauli ad Ephesios*
ibid., 1562

1016. **TURNÈBE, Adrien (Turnebus)**
R *Adversaria;* with
O Observationes by Jean de Sponde
Basle, T. Guarinus, 1581

1017. —, ed.
R Aristoteles, *De moribus ad Nicomachum libri* X (Greek & Latin)
Basle, L. Lucius, 1556

1018. —, —
R —

Basle, P. Queck for J. Oporinus, 1567
DGK

1019. —, —
R —

Basle, Offic. Oporiniana, 1573

1020. —, —
R —

ibid., 1586

1021. —, —
R —
ibid., 1592
DGK

1022. —, —
R —
ibid., 1612
DGK

1023. **VATABLE, François, ed.**
R *Biblia* (F. Vatable and S. Pagnini mentioned among the doctissimi
interpretes)
Basel, T. Guarinus, 1564

1024. **VIGNIER, Nicolas**
O *Rerum Burgundionum chronicon*
ibid., 1575

1025. **VILLEGAGNON, Nicolas Durand de**
R Caroli V. Imp. expeditio in Africam : in
L. Chalcondyles, *De origine et rebus Turcorum*
Basle, J. Oporinus, 1556

1026. —
R —: in
S. Schard, ed., *Historicum opus*
Basle, Offic. Henricpetrina, 1574

1027. **VINCENT de Beauvais (Vincentius Bellovacensis)**
R *De alchimia et rebus metallicis* (selected chapters of book 8 of Speculum
naturale) : in
Lorenzo Ventura, *De ratione conficiendi lapidis philosophici*
Basle, [P. Perna ?], 1571

1028. —
(Opuscula)
Basle, J. Amerbach, 1481
BMC 15th c. 3.746

1029. **VINCENTIUS Lirinensis (Vincent de Lérins)**
(R) (Commonitorium) : in
J. Sichard, ed., *Antidotum contra diversas* ... *haereses* (contains also
short selections from Faustus, Bp. of Riez)
Basle, H. Petri, 1528

1030. —
(R) —, incl. Faustus : in
J. B. Herold, ed., *Haereseologia*
ibid., 1556

1031. **VINCIOLO, Federigo di**
R *Les singuliers et nouveaux pourtraicts* ... *pour toutes sortes d'ouvrages
de lingerie*
Basle, L. König, 1599

1032. **VINET, Elie,** comment.

(O?) Eutropius, *Historiae Romanae breviarium*

Basle, J. Oporinus, 1561-1559 (misprint for 1561?)

1033. —, transl. & introd.

(R) Theognis Megariensis, *Sententiae* (Greek & Latin, without Vinet's Scholiae promised on the title page)

ibid., 1550

1034. —, transl., introd. & annot.

(R) — (with Scholiae)

ibid., 1561

1035. —, transl. & introd.

R — (without Scholiae)

Basle, [for J. Oporinus?]; printed in Frankfurt by L. Lucius, 1563

1036. —, transl., introd. & annot.

R — (with Scholiae)

Basle, Offic. Oporiniana, 1572

1037. —, —

R —

ibid., 1576

1038. **[VIREL, Matthieu] (Virellus, Virelle)**

O *Regulae generales et perpetuae de rebus ad calendarium spectantibus*

Basle, T. Guarinus, 1579

1039. **VOLMAR, Melchior,** ed. & introd.

Demetrius Chalcondyles, *Erotemata sive institutiones grammaticae studiosis, vel magno Budaeo teste, accomodatissimae* (Greek)

Basle, [J. Oporinus], 1546

1040. **VORILLON, Guillaume (Vorilongus)**

R *Quattuor librorum Sententiarum compendium*

Basle, A. Petri, 1510

1041. **Wahrhaftige ... Geschichte**

Warhafftige und eygentliche Geschicht, aus was Ursachen der Hertzog von Guisen die Statt Parys eyn bekommen

Basle, S. (II) Apiarius, [1588]

1042. **WESSEL Gansfort, Jan**

R? *Farrago rerum theologicarum*

Basle, A. Petri, 1522

1043. —

R —

ibid., 1523

1044. **WILSON, Florent (Volusenus)**

R *Commentatio quaedam theologica*

Basle, V. Curio, 1544
BN : Rés. D. 78948

1045. **ZIELY, Wilhelm (Zyely), transl.**

      O   *In disem Buoch werden ... gefunden zwo wunderbarlicher Hystorien*
         (transl. of L'Histoire d'Olivier et d'Artus and L'Histoire de Valentin
         et d'Orson)

                                        ibid., 1521 [1522]

1046. **[—], —**

      R   *Von Valentino und Orso*

                                      Basle, Jacob Treu, 1605

Addenda

1047. **CLAUDIANUS Mamertus**

      O   *De Statu animae libri tres*

                                    Basle, A Petri for L. Hornken &
                                    G. Hittorp, 1520

1048. **—**

      R   —: in
         J. B. Herold, ed., *Orthodoxographa*

                                    Basle, H. Petri, 1555

1049. **—**

      R   —: in
         J. J. Grynaeus, ed., *Monumenta S. Patrum orthodoxographa*

                                Basle, Offic. Henricpetrina, 1569

2. Theses of French-Speaking Students and Academic Addresses Related to France, to 1650

The printed theses of French-speaking students in the University of Basle, and similar materials related to France or to Francophones, offer an appreciable amount of biographical information since many of them contain dedications to parents or patrons, epigrams by fellow students, and references to teachers. Also the topics treated in the theses may to some degree reflect the disputant's special interests within his professional field. However, these publications cannot, of course, be considered original contributions to scholarship. They normally comprise just a few pages; some are mere broadsheets listing the topics for the oral disputation to be held in public—topics which may have been selected by the student himself or by his professor. The circulation too was very limited. In most cases the only copies known to exist belong to the Universitätsbibliothek in Basle and are registered in the special *Dissertationenkatalog* of that library. In view of the nature of this material it would have been misleading to include it in the preceding general bibliography, but listed separately it may prove helpful to others as it proved useful in the preparation of this study. Only the printed programmes for collective disputations have been excluded from the following list since they do not offer relevant information on individual candidates. References to the Basle *Matrikel* and E. Droz's survey of French students in Basle have been added to the names of all students listed in these works and not otherwise mentioned in the present volume.

While those registered in the following list were mostly *bona fide* students and even took a degree from Basle—one recalls that the same may not be said about the *Matrikel*—it would be incorrect to assume that the list includes the names of most Francophone graduates. Theses were rarely printed prior to 1570. Even afterwards it would appear that the requirement of publication, and perhaps the means of individual students to have their theses printed, differed greatly from faculty to faculty. Although among Francophone students medical students were, in fact, the most numerous, their representation in this list is quite disproportionate. The number of Francophone students in theology increased considerably towards the end of the sixteenth century, but the majority of them did not seek a degree from Basle. Besides, the average theological candidate was certainly poorer than his contemporary aspiring to the lucrative careers open to doctors and lawyers.

2001. **(AILLY, Pierre d')**

'Ανασκευή *opinionis a Petro de Aliaco ... de coena Dominica olim repetitae*. President: J. J. Grynaeus; respondent: J. Buxtorf
Basle, Offic. Oporiniana, 1588

2002 **ALLARD, Louis, of Uzès**

Assertiones medicae περὶ τῆς τοῦ ἀνθρώπου γενέσεως
Basle, J. Schroeter, 1599
Matrikel 2.460

337

ALLARD

2003. —
> *Theses medicae miscellaneae*
>> ibid., 1599

2004. **AMIET, Pierre Armand, of Grandson**
> *Theses medicae ... de ephialte*
>> Basle, G. Decker, 1646
>> *Matrikel* 3.398

2005. **AUBERY, Claude**
> *Theses medicae*
>> Basle, 1574

2006. **AUGIER, Robert**
> *Theses physiologicae de animae facultatibus*
>> Basle, L. Osten, 1583

2007. —
> *Theses de methodo generali ... curandarum febrium*
>> ibid., 1583

2008. **BAUCINET, Guillaume**
> *Theses de epilepsia*
>> ibid., 1584
>> *Matrikel* 2.261

2009. —
> *Theses de febre hectica*
>> ibid. 1584

2010. **BAUHIN, Gaspard**
> *Theses de corporis humani constitutione*
>> Basle, L. Osten, 1577

2011. —
> 'Αποθεραπεία ἰατρική, *quam medicae laureae causa ... subibit*
>> Basle, A. Froben, 1581

2012. —
> *Disputatio ... prandium an coena frugalior esse debeat.* Respondents:
> H. Michael and J. Steinbach
>> Basle, Offic. Oporiniana, 1584

2013. —
> *Menstrua diatribe Ianuario debita.* Respondent: J. Haun
>> Basle, L. Osten, 1587

2014. —
> *Praeludia anatomica.* Respondent: P. Höchstetter
>> Basle, [C. Waldkirch], 1601

2015. —
> *Disputatio secunda de partibus humani corporis.* Respondent:
> P. Höchstetter
>> Basle, C. Waldkirch, 1602

2016. —
> *Disputatio tertia de ossium natura.* Respondent: J. H. Froelich
>> ibid., 1604

338

2017. —
        De homine oratio
                Basle, J. J. Genath, 1614

2018. (—)
        Michael Meier, *Melos Apollini Rauraco, i.e. Casparo Bauhino ... promotori suo observandissimo ... cantatum*
                Basle, C. Waldkirch, 1596

2019. (—)
        Emanuel Stupanus, *Parentalia ... Caspari Bauhini* (oratio de vita et obitu Caspari Bauhini)
                Basle, J. Schroeter, 1625

2020. **BAUHIN, Jean I**
        Theses ... de lienis natura. Respondent : Bernhard von Kilchen
                Basle, L. Osten, 1580

2021. **BAUHIN, Jean II**
        Conclusiones [medicae]
                [Basle, c. 1558 ?]

2022. —
        Conclusiones [medicae]
                Basle, 1571

2023. **BEAUFORT, Jean de, of Sedan**
        Theses ... de angina
                Basle, J. Schroeter, 1606
                Matrikel 3.60

2024. **BELLENÉ, Jean Nicolas, of Porrentruy**
        Conclusiones [iuridicae]
                Basle, J. Schroeter, 1600
                Matrikel 2.488

2025. **BERMOND, Gaspard, of Antibes**
        De pactis positiones quaedam (for LL. D.)
                Basle, L. Osten, 1586
                Matrikel 2.341

2026. **BERTIN, Jean, of Joinville (Haute-Marne)**
        Theses medicae de epilepsia
                Basle, C. Waldkirch, [1587]
                Matrikel 2.352 ; Droz, *Etudiants français*

2027. **BÈZE, Théodore de**
        Epistola de origine animae (Genevae, Cal. April. 1571) : appended to *Theologicum de spiritus qui in homine est ortu theorema.* Respondent : H. Jeckelmann
                Basle, [1586]

2028. **BLANDIN, Pierre, of Geneva**
        Exercitatio physico-medica de concoctionum trium constitutione naturali
                Basle, J. Schroeter, 1612
                Matrikel 3.125

2029. —
        Disquisitio medica de calculo renum
                Basle, J. J. Genath, 1613

2030. **(BODIN, Jean)**
>   *Fasciculus paradoxorum ... ex Ioannis Bodini ... libris de Republica collectus.* Respondent: Joachim Cluten, candidate for M. A. and LL. D.
>   Basle, J. J. Genath, 1613

2031. **BOUCARD, Antoine**
>   *De functionibus animae disputatio menstrua*
>   Basle, 1587

2032. **—**
>   *Theses ... de catarrho*
>   Basle, Offic. Episcopiana, 1588

2033. **—**
>   *Theses ... de febre syncopali et paradoxa*
>   [Basle], 1589

2034. **—**
>   'Αγώνισμα ἰατρικόν ... *de venenis*
>   Basle, L. Osten, 1590

2035. **BULET, Guillaume, of Yverdon**
>   *Themata et paradoxa philosophiatrica*
>   Basle, J. Schroeter, 1610
>   *Matrikel* 3.64

2036. **CARRAY, Jules Frédéric, of Montbéliard**
>   *Disputatio de iure pugnae*
>   Basle, J. J. Genath, 1609
>   *Matrikel* 3.105

2037. **CARRÉ, Moïse, of Sedan**
>   *Medicae quaestiones miscellaneae*
>   Basle, J. Schroeter, [1608]
>   *Matrikel* 3.92

2038. **CHABREY, Dominique, of Geneva**
>   *Disputatio ... de febre ephemera*
>   Basle, J. J. Genath, 1633
>   *Matrikel* 3.354

2039. **CHAIGNEAU, Pierre, of Saint-Maixent (Deux-Sèvres)**
>   *Generalis arthridis, podagrae* ... γνῶσις τε καὶ θεραπεία
>   ibid., 1630
>   *Matrikel* 3.259

2040. **CHÂTEILLON, Frédéric (Castellio)**
>   *Ternarii gemelli* (theological disputation)
>   Basle, L. Osten, 1587

2041. **CLIVE, Jean de, of Paris**
>   *Carmen gratulatorium in honorem D. Bernhardi Mülleri Holsati*
>   Basle, J. J. Genath, 1616
>   *Matrikel* 3.173

2042. **COLLADON, Esaïe**
>   *Disputatio medica.* President: G. Bauhin
>   Basle, L. Osten, 1587

340

2043. —
> *Theses medicae de purgatione*
>> Basle, Offic. Oporiniana, 1587

2044. **COLLADON, Théodore**
> *Theses medicae*
>> [Basle, 1590]

2045. —
> *Theses medicae de tussi*
>> Basle, L. Osten, 1590

2046. **CORANTIUS, Louis (Corault, Courant)**
> *Theses theologicae de resipiscentia*
>> Basle, C. Waldkirch, 1600
>> *Matrikel* 2.473

2047. **CORNE, Jacques, of Beaune**
> *Miscellanea ... iuris controversi*
>> ibid., 1598
>> *Matrikel* 2.459

2048. —
> *Controversiae medicae*
>> ibid., 1598

2049. **COUET, Jacques, junior**
> *De methodis theses*
>> Basle, J. Schroeter, 1598
>> *Matrikel* 2.446

2050. **DE PREZ, Pierre, of Thonon**
> *Theses [iuridicae] de substitutionibus*
>> Basle, Offic. Oporiniana, 1587
>> *Matrikel* 2.334

2051. **DES CONFINS, Jean Pierre, of Geneva**
> *Disputatio iuridica de fructibus et eorum perceptione*
>> Basle, J. J. Genath, 1624
>> *Matrikel* 3.221

2052. **DES MARETS, Philippe, of Saumur**
> *Disputatio medica de variolis*
>> ibid., 1624
>> *Matrikel* 3.250

2053. **D'HANUS, Jean, of Badonviller (Meurthe-et-Moselle)**
> *Disputatio politica de subditis*
>> ibid., 1628
>> *Matrikel* 3.297

2054. **DORIVAL, Matthieu Florent, of Verdun**
> *De ventriculi imbecillitatis diagnosi*
>> ibid., 1622
>> *Matrikel* 3.242

2055. **DUFOUR, Denis, of Geneva**
> *Aprilis medicus menstruo agone ... D. Furnio Genevensi insigniendus.*
> President : G. Bauhin
>> Basle, Offic. Oporiniana, 1587
>> *Matrikel* 2.348

2056. **DURAND, Joseph, of Grenoble**
> *Theses theologicae de Antichristo*
>> Basle, C. Waldkirch, 1601
>> *Matrikel* 2.503 ; Droz, *Etudiants français*

2057. **DU VERNOY, Daniel, of Montbéliard**
> *Positiones ... physiologicas de temperamentis*
>> Basle, J. Schroeter, 1600
>> *Matrikel* 2.475 ; Droz, *Etudiants français*

2058. **DU VERNOY, David, of Montbéliard**
> *Decades tres positionum [iuridicarum]*
>> ibid., 1603
>> *Matrikel* 2.417 ; Droz, *Etudiants français*

2059. **FLORIETUS, Josias, of Beaune**
> Θεωρήματα haec medica
>> ibid., 1624
>> *Matrikel* 3.263

2060. —
> *Disputatio ... de mola matricis*
>> Basle, J. J. Genath, 1627

2061. **GAVIRAT, Timothée, of Geneva**
> *Conclusiones de sedibus partium animae*
>> Basle, 1603
>> *Matrikel* 2.435

2062. —
> *Ex officina Aesculapii ... theses medicae*
>> Basle, J. Schroeter, 1606

2063. **GEORGES, Paul (Georgius), of Laon**
> *Disputatio inauguralis de hepatitide*
>> Basle, G. Decker, 1648
>> *Matrikel* 3.448

2064. **GIRARD des Bergeries, Jean Jacques, of Lausanne**
> *Quaestiones philosophicae miscellaneae*
>> Basle, J. J. Genath, 1632
>> *Matrikel* 3.328

2065. (—)
> *Gratulatoria ... carmina* (on his graduation)
>> ibid., 1633

2066. **GRAS, Henri**
> Ἔνδοξα παράδοξα *philosophica-medica miscellanea*
>> ibid., 1615
>> *Matrikel* 3.150

2067. **GYMNOSIUS, Jean, of Saint-Ambroix (Gard)**
>> *Theses medicae* περὶ τοῦ ἐμφύτου θερμοῦ
>>> Basle, C. Waldkirch, 1597
>>> *Matrikel* 2.441

2068. **—**
>> *Theses medicae miscellaneae*
>>> ibid., 1598

2069. **HARSY, Alexandre de, of Lyons**
>> *Disputatio physica de principiis internis generationis*
>>> G. Decker, 1647
>>> *Matrikel* 3.440

2070. **JACOBUS, François, of Autun**
>> *Theses medicae de temperamentis*
>>> Basle, 1584
>>> *Matrikel* 2.287

2071. **JORDAN, François, of Granges (Vaud)**
>> *Theses theologicae de bonis operibus*
>>> Basle, J. J. Genath, 1625
>>> *Matrikel* 3.200

2072. **LAMAND, Jean, of Aucelon (Drôme)**
>> *Theses medicae de natura amoris et amantium amentium cura*
>>> ibid., 1614
>>> *Matrikel* 3.150

2073. **LAMY, Jean, of Caën**
>> *Theses medicae de febre quotidiana intermittente*
>>> ibid., 1617
>>> *Matrikel* 3.186

2074. **LA RIVE, Jean de, of Geneva**
>> *Axiomata controversa ex praecipuis iuris Caesarei et Pontificii materiis deprompta*
>>> Basle, C. Waldkirch, 1594
>>> *Matrikel* 2.417

2075. **LE COQ, Pascal**
>> *Conclusiones aliquot psychologicae de sensibus*
>>> Basle, Offic. Oporiniana, 1589

2076. **—**
>> *Theoria pathologica de dolore*
>>> ibid., 1590

2077. **LE JAY, Samuel, of France**
>> *De dysenteria theses*
>>> ibid., 1586
>>> Not in *Matrikel*

2078. **LE VASSEUR du Vaugosse, Gilles, of Rouen**
>> *Suprema laurea medica* (Disputation for M. D.)
>>> Basle, J. Schroeter, 1612
>>> *Matrikel* 3.140

343

2079. **LORIS, Daniel, of Montbéliard**
Assertiones et controversiae de hecticae febris definitione
Basle, J. J. Genath, 1617
Matrikel 3.187

2080. **MAHUET, Samuel, of Lausanne**
Disputatio iuridica de auctoritate tutoris
ibid., 1624
Matrikel 3.253

2081. **MAILLARD, Jean, of Châteauroux (Indre)**
Utrum in angina sit tendenda laryngotomia
ibid., 1623
Matrikel 3.259

2082. **MAISTRE, Paul, of Tonnerre (Yonne)**
These medicae de febrium continuarum diagnosi
Basle, L. Osten 1590
Matrikel 2.384

2083. **MASSONIUS, Timothaeus, Fontanus Aurelianensis**
De convulsione disputatio medica
Basle, Offic. Oporiniana, 1589
Matrikel 2.369

2084. **MEYSONNIER, Pierre, of Auvergne**
De apoplexia positiones
ibid., 1582
Matrikel 2.299

2085. **MONTMOLLIN, Georges de, of Neuchâtel**
Dissertatio politica de magistratu in genere
Basle, G. Decker, 1645
Matrikel 3.413

2086. **MORELOT, Marc, of Fontenay (Vosges)**
Theses [medicae] de temperamentis
Basle, L. Osten, 1581
Matrikel 2.286 ; Droz, *Etudiants français*

2087. **OFFREDI, Paul, of Geneva**
Quaestiones medicae
Basle, J. Foillet, 1603
Matrikel 2.496

2088. **PANISSOD, Isaac, of Geneva**
Progymnasmata de morbis haereditariis
Basle, L. Osten, 1591
Matrikel 2.388

2089. **PASCAL, Pierre, of Geneva**
Disputatio medica ... de febre vulgo ardente dicta
Basle, J. J. Genath, 1626
Matrikel 3.165

2090. **PASQUIER, Jacques**
Assertiones de arthritide
Basle, D. & L. Osten, 1575

2091. (—)

> Theobald Müller, *Dialogus gratulatorius in solemnitatem doctoralem* ...
> *Iac. Pascharii Lotharingi*
>
> [Basle, 1575]

2092. **PELTRE, Jacques, of Metz**

> *Theses inaugurales de* ἀνορεξία
>
> Basle, G. Decker, 1647
> *Matrikel* 3.440

2093. **PERRENON, Pierre, of Montbéliard**

> *Positiones de legitima quae liberis debetur auctoritate*
>
> Basle, C. Waldkirch, 1594
> *Matrikel* 2.421

2094. **PETRA, Jacques de, of Lausanne**

> *Theses philosophicae*
>
> Basle, J. J. Genath, 1631
> *Matrikel* 3.335

2095. (—)

> *Carmina gratulatoria in laudem et honorem* ... *Jacobi de Petra*
>
> Basle, J. Schroeter, [1631]

2096. **PISO, Samuel, of Metz**

> *Theorema de filiorum Dei spirituali ablutione*
>
> Basle, Offic. Oporiniana, 1589
> *Matrikel* 2.376

2097. —

> *Quaestio rectene fecerint Lutherus et Calvinus, quod ecclesiis per Germa-*
> *niam et Galliam auctores fuerunt*
>
> ibid., 1590

2098. —

> *Quaestiones controversae de Scriptura Sacra*
>
> ibid., 1590

2099. —

> *Problemata sacra tria de verbo Dei scripto*
>
> ibid., 1591

2100. **PISTORIUS, Jean, of Nîmes**

> *Pentas miscellanea* (theses for M. D.)
>
> J. Schroeter, 1605
> *Matrikel* 3.61

2101. **ROSSEL, François, of Porrentruy**

> *De iure publico disceptationis defensio*
>
> Basle, Jean Exertier, 1605
> *Matrikel* 3.47

2102. **SAINT-AUBIN, Jacques**

> *Conclusiones* [*medicae*]
>
> Basle, D. & L. Osten, 1576

2103. **SARASIN, Jean, of Geneva**
>> *Disputatio ... medica de apoplexia*
>>> Basle, J. J. Genath, 1633
>>> *Matrikel* 3.315

2104. **SERREIUS, Jean, of Badonviller (Meurthe-et-Moselle)**
>> *Theses medicae de paralysi*
>>> Basle, C. Waldkirch, 1604
>>> *Matrikel* 3.45

2105. **STAPEDIUS, Frédéric, of Lyons**
>> *Theses [medicae] ... de temperamentis*
>>> ibid., 1596
>>> *Matrikel* 2.428

2106. **SUPERVILLE, Jean de, of Béarn**
>> *Disputatio medica.*   President : G. Bauhin
>>> Basle, Offic. Oporiniana, 1587
>>> *Matrikel* 2.351

2107. **—**
>> *Theses ... medicae de venae sectione*
>>> ibid., 1587

2108. **TAVERNIER, Nicolas, of Mortain (Manche)**
>> *Theses iatricae de lapide, calculo ...*
>>> Basle, J. Schroeter, 1608
>>> *Matrikel* 3.89

2109. **TOUSSAIN, Daniel**
>> *Ioannis Buxtorfii ... vitae et mors*
>>> Basle, L. König, 1630

2110. **—**
>> Χαριστήρια *supremo exercituum principi Deo Opt. Max. reddita* (delivered in the presence of the rector and H. van Brederode)
>>> Basle, J. J. Genath, [1631]

2111. **—**
>> *Oratio panegyrica in mortem ... J. J. Frey*
>>> Basle, G. Decker, 1636

2112. **—**
>> *Johanni Zwingero ... oda votiva*
>>> ibid., 1648

2113. **—**
>> *Panegyricus ... Friderico Spanhemio dictus*
>>> ibid., 1649

2114. **TOUSSAIN, Paul,**
>> *De unico et aeterno Dei foedere theses*
>>> Basle, J. Schroeter, 1599

2115. **VIRIOT, Théodore, of Châlons-sur-Marne**
>> *Quaestiones medicae*
>>> ibid., 1602
>>> *Matrikel* 2.503

3. Books Printed at Paris for Conrad Resch, the Librarian à l'Ecu de Bâle, 1516-1526

The following check list was assembled in an attempt to better understand the activities of Conrad Resch. Enough of his publications, and quite remarkable ones, have been identified by several scholars. Taken together, they permit certain conclusions as to his policy and his character (see above pp .33 ff.). By contrast, the books known to have been published for Michel Parmentier in Lyons are not so numerous and far less revealing, as can be seen from the information gathered by Baudrier. Very few books published at Basle record in their imprints the involvement of any merchant of the *Ecu* group, and Wattenschnee's partnership in Paris editions would seem to have been equally sporadic. I believe the following list of Resch's books to be reasonably complete and accurate. If this is the case, much of the credit should be given to the manuscript notes gathered by P. Renouard which have been made available to me through the kindness of Madame Veyrin-Forrer of the Bibliothèque Nationale at Paris.

3001. **LOKERT, Georges**, ed.
> *Questiones et decisiones physicales*
>> Paris, J. Bade for himself and C. Resch, 1516
>> *BNC*

3002. —   —
>> ibid., 1518
>> *BNC;* Johnson, *Basle Ornaments* 356

3003. **ERASMUS of Rotterdam**
> *Familiarium Colloquiorum formulae*
>> Paris, H. Estienne for C. Resch, 1518 [1519]
>> Allen 3.464n., 496n., *Bibl. Erasmiana*

3004. **BECICHEMUS, Marinus**
> *In C. Plinium praelectio*
>> Paris, P. Vidoue for C. Resch, 1519
>> *BMC;* Renouard, " ms."

3005. **BRIE, Germain de**
> *Antimorus*
>> Paris, P. Vidoue for C. Resch, [1519]
>> *BMC;* Koegler, *Wechselbeziehungen* 184 ; Johnson, *Basle Ornaments* 356

3006. **HUTTEN, Ulrich von**
> *De guaiaci medicina*
>> [Paris], P. Vidoue for C. Resch, 1519
>> *BNC;* Renouard, " ms."

347

3007. **LATOMUS, Jacobus, the older**

> *De trium linguarum ratione dialogus*
>> Paris, H. Estienne for C. Resch, 1519
>> Renouard, " ms."

3008. **NESEN, Wilhelm [and/or ERASMUS of Rotterdam]**

> Dialogus sane quam festivus bilinguium ac trilinguium
>> [Paris, J. Bade] for C. Resch, [1519]
>> Allen 4.171f.

3009. **WAIN, Gervasius**

> *Tractatus noticiarum*
>> Paris, Nicolas des Prez for C. Resch, 1519
>> E. Armstrong in *BHR* 23 (1961), 342;
>> BN : Rés. R. 678 (1) ; Renouard, " ms."

3010. **ASCONIUS Pedianus, Quintus**

> *In orationes M. Tullii Ciceronis enarrationes*
>> Paris, P. Vidoue for C. Resch, 1520
>> *BNC;* Koegler, *Wechselbeziehungen* 185ff. ;
>> Johnson, *Basle Ornaments* 357

3011. **LEE, Edward**

> *Apologia contra quorundam calumnias; Annotationes in annotationes Novi Testamenti Erasmi*
>> Paris, Gilles de Gourmont for C. Resch, [1520]
>> *BMC;* Johnson, *Basle Ornaments* 356;
>> Allen 4.108

3012. **PIGHIUS, Albert**

> *De aequinoctiorum solsticiorumque inventione*
>> [Paris, P. Vidoue for C. Resch, 1520?]
>> *BMC; BNC;* Johnson, *Basle Ornaments* 356f.

3013. **Probatissimorum**

> *Probatissimorum ecclesiae doctorum sententiae*
>> [Paris, P. Vidoue for C. Resch, c. 1520?]
>> Johnson, *Basle Ornaments* 356

3014. **Quare Papae**

> *Quare Pape ac discipulorum eius libri a M. Luthero combusti sint*
>> [Paris, for C. Resch, c. 1520]
>> *ibid.* 356

3015. **BIEL, Gabriel**

> *Supplementum in octo et viginti distinctiones ultimas quarti Magistri Senten.*
>> [Paris, J. Bade] for C. Resch, 1521
>> *ibid.* 357 ; *BNC*

3016. **CRASTONUS, Johannes,** ed.

> *Dictionarium Graecum*
>> Paris, P. Vidoue for C. Resch, J. Petit & T. Kerver, 1521
>> Koegler, *Wechselbeziehungen* 188 ;
>> Johnson, *Basle Ornaments* 357

3017. **ECK, Johannes**

De primatu Petri adversus Ludderum

Paris, P. Vidoue for C. Resch & T. Kerver,
1521
BNC ; Johnson, *Basle Ornaments* 357

3018. **HORAPOLLO**

Hieroglyphica

[Paris], P. Vidoue for C. Resch, 1521
BMC ; *BNC* ; Renouard, " ms."

3019. **LOPEZ Zúñiga, Jaime**

Annotationes ... contra D. Erasmum

Paris, P. Vidoue for C. Resch, 1522
BNC ; Renouard, " ms."

3020. **OECOLAMPADIUS, Johannes**

Graecae literaturae diagmata

ibid., 1522
Renouard, " ms."

3021. **ORIGENES**

Operum tomi duo

[Paris], J. Petit, J. Bade & C. Resch, 1522
BMC ; Renouard, " ms."

3022. **Breviarium**

Breviarium canonicorum reguliarium ordinis sancti Augustini
[Paris, for C. Resch, c. 1523]
BN ; Rés. B. 5023 ; Renouard, " ms."

3023. **ERASMUS of Rotterdam**

*Ad Christopherum episcopum Basiliensem epistola apologetica de inter-
dicto esu carnium; Apologia contra Lopem Stunicam*

Paris, P. Vidoue for C. Resch, 1523
Johnson, *Basle Ornaments* 358 ;
Renouard, " ms."

3024 (?)—

Familiarium colloquiorum formulae

Paris, for C. Resch, 1523
Renouard, " ms."

3025. —

In epistolas apostolicas paraphrases

Paris, P. Vidoue for C. Resch, 1523
Renouard, " ms." ; *Bibl. Erasmiana*

3026. —

Paraphrases ... in omnes epistolas Pauli

ibid., 1523
BNC ; Koegler, *Wechselbeziehungen* 229

3027. —

Paraphrasis in Evangelium Matthei

ibid., 1523
Renouard, " ms." ; L. Delisle, *Chantilly*,
Paris 1905, No. 701

349

ERASMUS

3028. —
Paraphrasis in Evangelium secundum Ioannem
ibid., 1523
Johnson, *Basle Ornaments* 358

3029. —
Precatio Dominica
ibid., 1523
BNC ; Renouard, " ms."

3030. **AURELIUS, Johannes Valerius**
Declamatio ad Nic. Beraldum
ibid., 1524
Wackernagel, "Aktensammlung"

3031. **BETSBRUGIUS, Aegidius**
Doctum et elegans opusculum de usura centesima, etc.
Paris, P. Vidoue for C. Resch, 1524
BNC ; Koegler, *Wechselbeziehungen* 190

3032. **FISHER, John, St. & VELENUS, Ulricus (Pseud. ?)**
Convulsio calumniarum U. Veleni, quibus Petrus nunquam Romae fuisse
cavillatur, per Joannem Roffensem, with the text of the work commented
upon
Paris, for C. Resch, [1525 ?]
BNC ; *BMC* ; Johnson, *Basle Ornaments*
358

3033. **GAIUS, ed.**
Institutiones

Paris, P. Vidoue for C. Resch, 1525
Renouard, " ms."

3034. **MAFFEI, Raffaele**
Commentariorum urbanorum ... octo et triginta libri
Paris, J. Bade for himself, J. Petit,
C. Chevallon & C. Resch, 1526
BMC ; Koegler, *Wechselbeziehungen* 188

4. Books by Francophone Authors Published under the Fictitious Imprint of Basle

Gathered in the process of surveying the genuine Basle productions, the following list of fictitious imprints does not pretend to completeness. Rather it presents a first step towards a field of study which requires systematic investigation of a highly specialized nature.

4001. **Articles**

Articles contenans la requeste presentee au Roy par les deputez des Eglises du païs de Languedoc

A Basle par Pierre De Roy, 1574 [not Basle ?]
BM : 3900 a. 1

4002. **[BARNAUD, Nicolas ?]**

Dialogue auquel sont traitees plusieurs choses avenues aux Lutheriens et Huguenots de la France

Imprimé à Basle, 1573 [not Basel ?]
BM : 701 a. 29

4003. **BURIN, Pierre**

Response a une epistre commenceant Seigneur Eluide

A Basle, par Martin Cousin, [La Rochelle, Veuve Berton], 1574
BM : 285 a. 32 (10) ; Droz, *Veuve Berton* 15f.

4004. **—**

—, another ed.

ibid., [fictitious imprint], 1574
BM : 1080 c. 9 (2) ; Droz, *Veuve Berton* 15

4005. **[HOTMAN, François]**

Ernest Varamond de Frise, *Discours simple et veritable des rages exer-cées par la France* (French version of : De furoribus Gallicis)

Imprimé à Basle par Pieter Vallemand, 1573 [not Basle ?]

4006. **LA NOUE, François de**

Discours politiques et militaires

A Basle, de l'imprimerie de François Forest [Geneva ?], 1587
BN : R.6332, *E.830
Printer's mark : Heitz-Bernoulli No. 215 ; cf. Bremme 163

4007. —

     —

     ibid., 1587
     BN : *E.2915 [1]

4008. —

     —

     A Basle [Geneva ?], 1590
     BN : *E.2919

4009. —

     — (dernière édition)

     Basle, F. Le Fleuron, 1591 [fictitious imprint]
     BMC

4010. —

     —

     Basle, F. Forest, 1597 [fictitious imprint]
     BMC

4011. **LA POPELINIÈRE, Lancelot Voisin, sieur de**

     La vraye et entiere histoire des troubles
     A Basle, par Pierre Davantes
     [not Basle], 1572
     Cf. E. Droz in *BHR* 23 (1961), 144ff. ;
     Bremme 245f.

4012. —

     —

     A Basle, par Barthelemy Germain
     [not Basle], 1579
     Geneva, Bibl. publ. et univ. : Gg. 228 [2]

4013. **LA PRIMAUDAYE, Pierre de**

     *Academie Francoise . . . , troisieme edition reveue, corrigee, augmentee et
     cotee par l'autheur*
     A Basle, par Philemon de Hus, [an un-
     authorized reprint made in Geneva ?],
     1587
     UBB : K.f.III 9/10 ; Bremme 181

4014. **La somme de l'Ecriture Sainte**

     La summe de lescripture saincte et lordinaire des Chrestiens
     Basle, T. Volff [Alençon, Simon du Bois],
     1523
     BMC ST Germany 124

4015. **L'ESPINE, Jean de**

     Excellens discours . . . touchant le repos et contentement de l'esprit
     A Basle [La Rochelle ?], 1587
     BN : D² 4107

---

[1] Not available when I was in Paris. Cf. also two eds. " Iouxte la forme et exemplaire imprimee à Basle ", 1588, BN. : *E.2916 & *E2918 [not Basle ?]

[2] E. Droz, in *BHR* 23 (1961), 144, lists this ed. " en 1578 (avec retirage en 1579)." I have not seen a copy with the earlier date.

4016. —

—

A Basle, 1588 [*Contrefaçon* of the preceding ed.]
BN : R.41743

4017. **MALESCOT, Etienne de**

Iuris divini ac verae theologiae ... catechesis
Basileae, apud Iacobum Parcum, 1567
[Fictitious imprint ? Frankfurt ?,
A. Wechel ?] [1]
BN : D² 9167

4018. **MURET, Marc-Antoine**

Orationes XXIII; Interpretatio quincti libri Ethicorum Aristotelis
(311 pp. 8º)
Basileae [fictitious imprint ?, Cologne ?],
1577. In the author's possession

4019. **PARCUS, Jacobus,** ed.

Les Dixains Catholiques tirez d'aucuns lieux communs de la Sainte Escriture, & consolans les fideles
A Basle, par Bernardin Vvilmach, 1561
[Fictitious imprint ?]
A. Cartier in *Mélanges E. Picot*, Paris
1913, 1.307

4020. **Remonstrance**

Remonstrance aux seigneurs Gentilshommes et aultres faisans profession de la Religion reformée en France
A Basle, par Pieter Vuallemand
[La Rochelle, Veuve Berton], 1574
BM : 285 a. 32 (5) ; Droz, *Veuve Berton* 12f.

4021. **RONSARD, Pierre de**

Les amours de P. de Ronsard Vaudomois, nouvellement augmentées par luy. Avec les continuations desdits Amours
A Basle, par Augustin Godinet [Rouen,
Nicolas Le Roux], 1557
BN : Rés. p.Ye 1254
Cf. S. de Ricci, *Cat. ed. Ronsard*, London
1927, No. 19

4022. **SUREAU du Rosier, Hugues**

Confession et Recognoissance
A Basle, par Martin Cousin [La Rochelle,
Veuve Berton], 1574
BN : 8ºLd¹⁷⁶ 33 ; Droz, *Veuve Berton* 13f.

---

[1] To the same publisher may be attributed two anonymously printed texts contained in BN : D² 3893 : *Diallacticon, cest a dire reconciliatoire ...* translaté de Latin en Français par un docte et sainct personnage, avocat d'Auxerre, et reveu par Maistre Estienne Malescot... [a transl. of John Poynet, *Diallacticon*] and : Annibal d'Auvergne [E. de Malescot ?], *Censure des erreurs de M. Charles Du Moulin*, 1566.

ALPHABETICAL INDEX

GUILLAUME de Conches, No. 492f., 542
— Bp. of Typhus, No. 494ff.
GUINTERIUS, Johannes, 197, No. 498ff.,
914, 954
GUISE, Charles de, Cardinal of Lorraine,
150ff,. 153, 205, 207, 236
— François de Lorraine, Duke of,
No. 162
— Henri de Lorraine, Duke of,
No. 1041
— Jean de, Cardinal of Lorraine,
82n., 86, 93, 197ff., 243
— de, family, No. 761
GUTMANN, Theophil (pseud.?), 101n.
GWALTER, Rudolf, 155, 236
GYMNOSIUS, Jean, No. 2067f.
GYRART, Robert, 80

HALLER, Berthold, 91
HALOANDER, Gregor, No. 238
HARCHIES, Josse de, 66f., 70, No. 510ff.
HARLAY, Achille de, 121
— Charles de, 121
— Nicolas de, 121n.
— de, family, 215
HARSY, Alexandre de, No. 2069
HÄTZER, Ludwig, 132n.
HEINSIUS, Daniel, 217
HENRICPETRI, Adam, 238f.
HENRY II, King of France, 106, 112, 140,
173, 203, No. 401, 448, 947
— III, King of France, 60, 113n.,
121, 214, No. 385
— IV, King of France (H. III, King
of Navarre), 51, 66, 69, 82f., 99,
113n., 118, 120f., 204, 211f., 215,
No. 562, 620
HERESBACH, Conrad, No. 955
HERMAN, Haio, 198
HERODOTUS, No. 290f.
HEROLD, Immanuel, 235f.
— Johannes Basilius, 231n., 236,
No. 7, 33, 282, 434, 494ff., 869,
872, 925, 929, 1030, 1048
HERVET, Gentian, 204, 208, No. 514ff.
HERWAGEN, Johann (I), 153n., 158n.,
173, 179
— Johann (II), 172
HESSE, William IV, Landgrave of, 117
HEYNLIN, Johannes, 81, 167ff., 172, 175,
No. 518ff.
HILARY, St., Bp. of Poitiers, 183n.,
No. 533ff., 718
HIPPOCRATES, 70n., 171, No. 324f., 399f.,
410, 442, 505, 509, 538, 540, 760
HITTORP, Gottfried, 27n., No. 1047
HOLBEIN, Hans (II), 40f., 218
HOLLIER, Blaise, 72, No. 538ff.
HOMER, 83f., 128, 157n., No. 290ff., 949f.
HONORIUS of Autun, No. 541f.
HORACE, 206, No. 129, 454ff., 663, 768
HORAPOLLO, No. 3018

HORNKEN, Ludwig, 27n., No. 846, 1047
HOTMAN, Daniel, 116
— François, 54n., 62n., 68, 72, 97ff.,
115ff., 119ff., 132n., 147, 208, 211f.,
225, No. 319, 543ff., 624f., 4005
— Jean, sieur de Villiers, 100, 108n.,
118, 209, 212ff., 247f., No. 551f.
HUCBALDUS of Saint-Amand, 75,
No. 574ff.
HUGUES de Saint-Cher, No. 577ff.
— de Saint-Victor, No. 581f.
HUGUETAN, Jean Antoine, 87
HUGWALD, Ulrich, 184n.
HUMMELBERG, Michael, 182
HURAULT de L'Hospital, brothers, 206f.,
215, No. 583
HÜRUS, Paul, 26
HUS, Philemon de (pseud.?), No. 4013
HUSS, Martin & Mathis, 28f.
HUTTEN, Ulrich von, 38, No. 3006

IGNATIUS, St., of Antioch, 186n., No. 688
IRENAEUS, St., Bp. of Lyons, No. 584ff.
ISELIN, Johann Lucas & Johann Ulrich,
173f.
ISENGRIN, Michael, 76, 82n., 193n., 227
ISORNE (Ysoret?), Joann, 80

JACOBUS, François, No. 2070
JACOTIUS, Desiderius, No. 589ff.
JEAN de Roquetaillade, No. 58, 592ff.
JEANNE d'Albret, Queen of Navarre, 82
JEROME, St., 39n., 169, 183n., 200
JOBIN, Bernhard, 77
JOHANNES Cassianus, No. 596ff., 871
— Abbot of Nivelles, No. 601ff.
— of Paris, No. 604
— Sabaudus, 80
— of Segovia, No. 605ff.
JOHN XXII, Pope, No. 595
— Chrysostom, St., 182n., 183n.,
184n., 195, 200, No. 185ff., 277
— of Damascus, St., 186, No. 598ff.,
689ff.
JORDAN, François, No. 2071
JÖRG von Brügge, 209
JORIS, David, 63, 96, 123n., 124ff., 131ff.,
141, 143, 208f., 223n.
JOSEPHUS, Flavius, No. 262f., 278
JOUBERT, Laurent, No. 616ff.
JUD, Leo 95n.
JULIUS II, Pope, No. 49ff.
JULYOT, Ferry, 75n., No. 619
JUSTINIAN I, Emperor, 85n., No. 90, 92,
556, 853
JUVENAL, No. 72
JUVENCUS, No. 71

KERQUEFINEN, Claude de, 210f.
KERVER, Thielman (I), No. 3017
— family, 35
KESCHINGER, Peter, No. 35
KESSLER, Niklaus, 27

LÜTZELBURGER, Hans, 41
LYCOPHRON, 204n., No. 153
Lyons, 25f., 28f., 31ff., 48f., 76f., 82,
    86f., 96, 122, 124, 136, 218ff.

MACHIAVELLI, Niccolò, 61, 78, 99, 247f.
MAFFEI, Raffaele, No. 3034
MAHUET, Samuel, No. 2080
MAILLARD, Jean, No. 2081
MAISTRE, Paul, No. 2082
MALESCOT, Etienne de, 67n., 207, No. 711,
    4017
MALLARIUS, Nicolas, 222
MARBODUS, Bp. of Rennes, No. 712
MARCELLUS (Empiricus, Burdigalensis)
    No. 713
MARCORELLUS, Jacobus, 80
MARESCHAL, Jehan, 79, No. 478, 788
  — Samuel, 62, No. 714ff.
MARGUERITE d'Angoulême, Queen of
    Navarre, 59, 147, 184, 186
  — de Valois (d'Angoulême), 140
MARILLAC, Charles de, 112
MARIUS VICTOR, Claudius, No. 718
MARLIANUS, Raymundus, No. 572, 719ff.
MARLORAT, Augustin, No. 728ff.
MARNE, Claude de, 78f., No. 329, 698
  — Jean de, 79
MARNIX, Philips, van St. Aldegonde
    No. 733f.
MAROT, Clément, 222
MARSILIUS of Inghen, No. 735
MARTIAL, St., Bp. of Limoges, No. 924ff.
MARTINUS, St., Bp. of Dumio, No. 360
MASSARI, Girolamo, 235
MASSON, Jean Papire, 34n., 214n., No. 736
MASSONIUS, Timotheaus, No. 2083
MATAL (Metellus), Jean, 236
MATTHIEU de Vendôme, No. 737
MAXIMUS Tyrius, 200
MEDER, Hieremias, 49
MELANCHTHON, Philipp, 59, 72, 93, 108,
    111, 119f., 125, 135, 138, 148,
    161n., 162, 176, 193n., 215, 230,
    245f., No. 377, 656ff.
MELGUIZ, Domingo, No. 361, 786
MERSENNE, Marin, 144n.
METOCHITES, Theodorus, No. 517
METTLINGER, Peter, 26
Metz, 99, 176, 242ff.
MEYRONNES, François de, No. 738ff.
MEYSONNIER, Pierre, No. 2084
MILIEU, Christophe de, No. 741
MIZAULD, Antoine, No. 743ff.
MOMBAER, Johan, 176, No. 747
MONTAIGNE, Jean, 91, 228
  — Michel de, 72f., 211, 248
MONTANUS, Philippus, 178f., 203, 208,
    236, No. 748ff.
Montbéliard, 49, 70, 94, 136, 188, 237,
    242ff., No. 155ff., 1012

MONTDESIR, Laurent, 223
MONTEUX, Sébastien, No. 752
MONTMOLLIN, Georges de, No. 2085
MONTMORENCY, Henri (I), Duke of,
    No. 771
Montpellier, 76n., 172, 220, 224, No. 621
MORE, Thomas, 191, 195, 236, No. 242,
    748f., 3005
MOREL, François, 223
  — Guillaume, 54n., 87n., No. 753
  — Jean, of Embrun, 95, 108ff., 206,
    No. 394
  — Pierre, No. 754
MORELET du Museau, Antoine, 34, 58f.,
    61, 106, 110ff., 124n., 125n., 196
  — Claude, 58
  — Jean, 58, 106
    family, 138, 140
MORELOT, Marc, No. 2086
MORÉLY, Jean, sieur de Villiers, 68f., 99f.,
    147, 213, 224
MORILLON, Guy, No. 755ff.
MORISOT, Jean, 240f., No. 758ff.
MORNAY, Philippe de, 119f., 213,
    No. 632ff., 761
MOROT, Pierre, 48ff.
MORRHE, Gerard, 178n.
MÜNSTER, Sebastian, 54n., No. 762ff.,
    788
MURET, Marc Antoine, 203, 242, No. 627,
    768, 4018
MYCONIUS, Oswald, 94, 107f., 111, 231n.,
    245

NARDI, Giovanni Leone, 76
NEMESIUS, Bp. of Emesa, 183
NEONOBELLUS, Johann Wilhelm, No. 555
NESEN, Wilhelm, 182, 184, 196, No. 3008
NEUDIN, Richard, 48f.
NEVELET de Dosches, Pierre, 212, 214f.
NICOLAI, Gilbertus, No. 772f.
NICOLAS of Lyra, No. 774ff.
NIDBRUCK, Caspar von, 149
Nîmes, 219f.
NIVELLE, Sébastien, 48f.
NONIUS, Marcellus, No. 131ff.
NORMANDIE, Laurent de, 37
NUCILLANUS, C. (pseud.), No. 348
NUÑEZ, Pedro, No. 439

OCHINO, Bernardino, 123f., 131, 133ff.,
    No. 279
ODDONE, Gian Angelo, 236
OECOLAMPADIUS, Johannes, 58, 82, 92f.,
    157, 184n., 185, 245f., No. 677,
    3020
OFFREDI, Paul, No. 2087
OLIVER, Pedro Juan, No. 777ff.
OLIVETAN, Robert, No. 781
OMPHALIUS, Jacob, 178n., No. 782

OPORINUS, Johannes, 36n., 45, 50f., 57n., 75f., 79n., 85ff., 96ff., 108n., 110f., 122ff., 126n., 128, 130f., 134, 137ff., 142ff., 146, 148ff., 152f., 155n., 156n., 158f., 162, 174, 179, 203f., 210, 218, 239n. 240n., 246, No. 48, 215
OPPIAN, No. 191
ORANGE, William (I), Prince of, 120n., 152, 212
ORIBASIUS, No. 509
ORIGEN, 141, 177, 182f., 185, 237, No. 346, 357, 302
ORPHEUS, 204n., No. 803
ORVAUX, Nicolas d', No. 784f.
OSIANDER, Andreas, 78
— Daniel, 150
OSTEN, Leonhard, 54n., 77, 81n.
OVID, No. 344, 755ff.,

PACE, Richard, 196
PAGNINI, Sante, 77, 222, 228, No. 1023
PANDOCHEUS, Elias (pseud.), No. 867
PANISSOD, Isaac, No. 2088
PAPILLON, Antoine, 40, 196
PARACELSUS, Theophrastus, of Hohenheim, 70f., 78, 157, 159n., 247f., No. 476
PARADIN, Guillaume, 239, No. 786f.
PARCUS, Jacobus (I), 74ff., 78, 114, 130n., 219, No. 788, 4017, 4019
— Jacobus (II), 75n.. 76
— Johannes, 75n., 80
PARÉ, Ambroise, No. 789
PARIN, Frantz, 81n.
Paris, 26f., 29, 33ff., 48ff., 99, 167ff., 175ff., 181ff., 187ff., 202ff., No. 1041
PARMENTIER, Michel, 30n., 32ff., 38, 42f., 198, 218, 221, 228, 347
PARVUS, Bertrandus, 207n.
PASCAL, Pierre, No. 2089
PASCHASIUS, Radbertus, No. 790
PASQUELIN, Guillaume, 239f., No. 791
PASQUIER, Etienne, 209ff., 214n., No. 792
— Jacques, 72, 86, 243n., 244, No. 2090f.
PATRIZI, Francesco, 78
PAUL III, Pope, 170, No. 229
PAULMIER, Claude, 207n.
PAULUS Diaconus, No. 857
PELETIER, Jacques, 86, 203, No. 793f.
PELLATANUS, Ludovicus, No. 337, 361, 786
PELLICAN, Conrad, 29n., 181f., 184n.
PELTRE, Jacques, No. 2092
PENA, André, 114
PENOT, Bernard Georges, No. 795
PERAIN, Iehan, 74n.
PERAULT, Guillaume, No. 796ff.
— Raymond, Cardinal, 57, No. 799ff.
PERDRIER, René, 179, 204, No. 802f.

PEREZ, Marco, 158n.
PÉRION, Joachim, 154f., 158, 161n., 162, 179, 203, 208, 247f., No. 690ff., 804ff.
PERNA, Pietro, 54n., 66f., 69, 71n., 77f., 85, 117ff., 129, 133f., 143, 211, 214, 216, 247
PEROTTI, Niccolò, No. 131ff.
PERRELLE, Jean, No. 832
PERRENON, Pierre, No. 2093
PERRENOT de Granvelle, Antoine, Cardinal, 236
— Nicolas, 240, No. 361, 786f.
— family, 238
PERRIN, Jean Paul, No. 833
PERRUCEL de La Rivière, François, 96f.
PERSIUS, No. 72, 444f.
PETER of Mechlin, 223
PETIT, Guillaume, 199
— Jean, 39f., No. 3016, 3034
— Oudin, 49n.
PETRA, Jacques, No. 2094f.
PETRARCH, 169
PETRI, Caspar, 172
— Heinrich, 50, 236
PETRUS de Bergamo, No. 1003f.
— Comestor, No. 834
— Lombardus, 186, No. 835ff., 3015
— Pictaviensis, No. 848
PHILANDRIER, Guillaume, No. 849ff.
PHILASTRIUS, Bp. of Brescia, No. 630
PHILIP II, King of Spain, 114
PHILO of Alexandria, 184
— Iudaeus, 54n., No. 216f.
PICO della Mirandola, Giovanni, 64, 182f., 248
PICTORIUS, Georg, No. 55ff.
PIGHIUS, Albert, No. 3012
PINETON de Chambrun, Pierre, 73n.
PINS, Jean de, 196
PIO, Alberto, 201, No. 116
PISO, Samuel, No. 2096ff.
PISTORIUS, Jean, No. 2100
PITHOU, François, 84n., 85, 98, 211, No. 853
— Pierre (I), 84
— Pierre (II), 84f., 98, 209, 211f., 216, No. 853ff.
— family, 215, 242n.
PLAIX, César de, No. 859
PLANTIN, Christophe, 137n.
PLANUDES, Maximus, No. 195
PLATO, 45, 138n., 153n., 160, 182f., 191n., 221n., 248, No. 810, 828
PLATTER, Felix, 34, 61, 64, 72n., 125, 211, 220, 242n.
— Thomas, 31n., 33, 57n., 110, 125, 220
PLAUTUS, No. 24, 440
PLINY, 195, No. 3004
PLOTINUS, 182
PLUTARCH, 53n., 77, No. 46, 219ff.

366

367

ACHEVÉ D'IMPRIMER
SUR LES PRESSES DE
L'IMPRIMERIE DU « JOURNAL DE GENÈVE »
EN DÉCEMBRE 1970
POUR LE COMPTE DES ÉDITIONS DROZ S.A.